ARTHURIAN STUDIES XXII

THE LEGENDS OF KING ARTHUR IN ART

ARTHURIAN STUDIES

ISSN 0261–9814

THE LEGENDS OF KING ARTHUR IN ART

Muriel Whitaker

D. S. BREWER

First published 1990 by D. S. Brewer, Cambridge

D. S. Brewer is an imprint of Boydell & Brewer Ltd
PO Box 9, Woodbridge, Suffolk IP12 3DF
and of Boydell & Brewer Inc.
PO Box 41026, Rochester, NY 14604, USA

ISBN 0 85991 306 6

British Library Cataloguing in Publication Data
Whitaker, Muriel
    The legends of King Arthur in art. – (Arthurian studies,
    ISSN 0261–9814 ; 22).
    1. Visual arts. Special subjects. Arthur, King
    I. Title II. Series
    704.947
    ISBN 0–85991–306–6

    Library of Congress Cataloging-in-Publication Data
Whitaker, Muriel A.
    The legends of King Arthur in art / Muriel Whitaker.
        p.   cm.   – (Arthurian studies, ISSN 0261–9814 : 22)
    Includes bibliographical references (p.
    ISBN 0–85991–306–6 (alk. paper)
    1. Arthurian romances – Illustrations. 2. Art – Themes, motives.
    I. Title. II. Series.
    N8215.W47 1990
    704.9'47–dc20   90–32262

This publication is printed on acid-free paper

Printed in Great Britain by
Southampton Book Company Ltd, Southampton, Hants

To A. C. W.

'than was love trouthe and faythefulness'

Malory's *Morte Darthur*, XVII, 25

Contents

Acknowledgements

The Legends of King Arthur in Art is the culmination of more than twenty years' research on Arthurian literature and art. The quest could not have been completed without the assistance of many 'helpful agents' along the way. Curators of art and keepers of manuscripts in the museums, art galleries and libraries of nine countries generously shared their treasures and their expert knowledge. Among many, I would like to thank particularly John Charles, Bruce Peel Special Collections Library, University of Alberta, Edmonton; Peter Cormack, William Morris Gallery, London; Evelyn Wong Lannon, Boston Public Library, Boston, U.S.A.; P.W.G. Lawson, Cartwright Hall, Bradford; Glenise Matheson, John Rylands Library, University of Manchester, Manchester; Jennifer Melville, City of Aberdeen Art Gallery and Museums, Aberdeen; David Scrase and Paul Woudhuysen, the Fitzwilliam Museum, Cambridge, England; Jan Speirs, Guildhall Art Gallery, London; Clive Wainwright, Victoria and Albert Museum, London; Christopher Wood, Christopher Wood Gallery, London and last but not least, Ana Spada, Museo Civico, Bolzano, Italy who effected my entrance through Runkelstein's chained gates, though the castle was closed for repairs, and Marianne Weissensteiner who guided me up the mountainside and sat knitting in the courtyard while I did my research.

Research for a book of this nature involving art in various media produced in ten countries over a period of nine centuries is an expensive undertaking, since one wishes to examine at first hand as many books and artifacts as possible. For financial assistance I am grateful to the Canada Council; its award of a leave fellowship in 1976–77 enabled me to begin my study of Arthurian manuscripts. Grants from the Social Sciences and Humanities Research Council of Canada in 1984 enabled me to attend the congress of the International Arthurian Society in Rennes, France (where my presentation of a paper, 'Illustrating Malory's *Morte Darthur*', led to a book contract) and in 1986 enabled me to see some German Arthurian art. I have received generous assistance from the University of Alberta, Edmonton, Canada in the form of travel grants, research grants, and grants towards the expense of acquiring photographs. The award of a University of Alberta McCalla Research Professorship (1988–89) gave me a year free from teaching and administrative duties so that I could turn my research into a book. I have benefited greatly from the university's programme of support for graduate students which has provided a succession of graduate research assistants. Though they are too numerous to mention individually, I remember them with affection and gratitude.

Finally, I thank my friend Professor Jetske Sybesma, Department of Art and Design, University of Alberta, who not only read my manuscript but unfailingly gave me the benefit of her wisdom, knowledge and encouragement. Now, in the words of William Caxton's Preface to Malory's *Morte Darthur*, I suggest that 'for to passe the tyme thys book shal be plesaunte to rede in, but for to gyve faith and byleve that al is trewe that is conteyned herin, ye be at your lyberté.'

CHAPTER ONE

Images of Arthurian Romance

Arthur of Britain is a mysterious figure whose origins[1] lie in the Celtic fringe, a region of lost wars and lost gods. Was he a culture hero who cleared the land of monsters? A god whose flashing sword mimicked the sun's rays? A cavalry leader who briefly rallied the Britons against the invading Saxons? Was he Riothamus who took a British army to Gaul in 469–70, was briefly noted by Sidonius, then vanished? Although there is no irrefutable evidence of Arthur's historicity, post-Roman Celtic tradition gives tantalising glimpses of a character bearing that name. In *Gododdin*, a battle poem written in 603, a hero is likened to Arthur because he killed enough enemies to glut the ravens. The *Annals of Wales* (*Annales Cambriae*,[2] ca. 960), which incorporated material from earlier chronicles, records for the year 518 the British victory of Badon, when Arthur carried the cross of Christ on his shoulder (or shield); the entry for 539 mentions the battle of Camlann in which Arthur and Medreut fell. The *Historia Brittonum*, (ca. 800) compiled by a Welsh monk Nennius, attributes to the hero twelve victories over the Saxons, provides him with an epaulette depicting the Virgin Mary and credits him with single-handedly killing nine hundred and sixty Saxons at Badon.

That fantastic legends were already becoming attached to the character is clear as well from two of Nennius' *Mirabilia*. Carn Cabal in the Welsh county of Breconshire is topped by a stone imprinted with the foot of Arthur's dog; the stone, if removed, magically returns to the cairn. At the source of the river Gamber is the tomb of Arthur's son Anir; the mound never stays the same size but varies in length from six to fifteen feet. The *Mabinogion*[3] tale 'Culhwch and Olwen' shows

---

[1] On theories of origin see Leslie Alcock, *Arthur's Britain* (London, 1971); Geoffrey Ashe, *The Discovery of King Arthur* (New York, 1985); Richard Barber, *King Arthur, Hero and Legend* (Woodbridge, 1986); E.K. Chambers, *Arthur of Britain: the story of King Arthur in history and legend* (London, 1927); R.G. Collingwood and J.N.L. Myres, *Roman Britain and the English Settlements* (London and New York, 1937); Kenneth H. Jackson, 'The Arthur of History' and 'Arthur in Early Welsh Verse' in *Arthurian Literature in the Middle Ages*, ed. Roger Sherman Loomis (Oxford, 1959); John Morris, *The Age of Arthur* (New York, 1973).
[2] On the *Historia Brittonum*, *Annales Cambriae* and other chronicles see R.H. Fletcher, *The Arthurian Material in the Chronicles*, 2nd. ed. (New York, 1966).
[3] Patrick K. Ford, trans., *The Mabinogi and Other Medieval Welsh Tales* (Berkeley, Los Angeles and London, 1977); Gwyn Jones and Thomas Jones, trans., *Mabinogion* (London, 1949).

Arthur romping about Cornwall in pursuit of the magical boar Twrch Trwyth and with his men accomplishing the various tasks that will enable Culhwch to marry the giant's daughter. The 'Arthur's court' formula as a device for bringing together heroes from unrelated sagas also appears in the Welsh triads[4] which may be ancient mnemonic aids for the bardic schools. Another view of this Jason-like leader comes in *Preiddeu Annwfn*, *The Spoils of Annwfn* (ca. 900), which recounts a journey to an Otherworld castle, 'the glassy fortress', from which only seven return. Quite a different view of the character is presented in two saints' lives, *Vita Paterni* and *Vita Gildae* (eleventh and twelfth centuries) which for the first time describe him as a king but classify him as *rex rebellis et tirannus*, one who is guilty of greed, lust, cruelty, arrogance and pride. This Dark Age hero who possessed both historical and mythic attributes had no place in Arthurian art until modern history and archaeology provided him with an imaginable context.

The most familiar persona, that of British king and continental conqueror, *christianissimus rex*, was created by a twelfth century cleric, Geoffrey of Monmouth.[5] His *Historia Regum Britanniae* (ca. 1136) is a secular history of the British race beginning soon after the Fall of Troy and ending with the death of Cadwallader in 689 A.D. In this largely imaginary roll call of British kings, Arthur's is the climactic biography. Geoffrey ensures the hero's dynastic respectability by providing him with an eponymous ancestor, Brutus,[6] whose Trojan blood validates his descendant's claim to the Roman imperium. From his father, Uther Pendragon, he inherits his dragon insignia, iconographically derived from the Romans' dragon ensign. Through Uther, as well, he becomes associated with the mysteriously powerful magician and prophet, Merlin, whose *Prophetiae* and *Vita* were also Geoffrey's creation.[7] Geoffrey credits him with erecting Stonehenge on Salisbury Plain, solving the puzzle of Vortigern's tumbling tower, and effecting the conception of Arthur by changing the love-lorn King Uther into the form of Ygerna's husband, the Duke of Cornwall. Like Arthur, Merlin sustains the interest of artists

[4]   Rachel Bromwich, 'Celtic Elements in Arthurian Romance: a General Survey' in *The Legend of Arthur in the Middle Ages*, ed. P.B. Grout, R.A. Lodge, C.E. Pickford and E.K.C. Varty (Cambridge, Eng., 1983); see also Mrs. Bromwich's *Trioedd Ynys Prydein: The Welsh Triads* (Cardiff, 1961).

[5]   Geoffrey of Monmouth, *Historia Regum Britanniae*, ed. Acton Griscom (London, 1929); ed. N. Wright (Woodbridge and Dover, N.H., 1985); *History of the Kings of Britain*, trans. Lewis Thorpe (London, 1966). Useful criticism includes E.K. Chambers, *op. cit.*; John J. Parry and Robert A. Caldwell, 'Geoffrey of Monmouth', *Arthurian Literature in the Middle Ages*, pp. 72–93; Robert Hanning, *The Vision of History in Early Britain from Gildas to Geoffrey of Monmouth* (New York and London, 1966); J.S.P. Tatlock, *The Legendary History of Britain* (Berkeley, 1950).

[6]   On Trojan genealogy see T.D. Kendrick, *British Antiquity* (London, 1970 [1950]); George Gordon, 'The Trojans in Britain', *Essays of the English Association*, IX (1924), 9–30; Margaret R. Scherer, *The Legends of Troy in Art and Literature* (New York, 1963).

[7]   *Vita Merlini*, ed. and trans. J.J. Parry (Urbana, 1925) and ed. Basil Clarke (Cardiff, 1973). Critical references include Parry and Caldwell, 'Geoffrey of Monmouth', *Arthurian Literature in the Middle Ages*, pp. 89–93 and Nikolai Tolstoy, *The Quest for Merlin* (London, 1985). On the 'Prophetiae Merlini' see Parry and Caldwell, *op. cit.*, pp. 75–79.

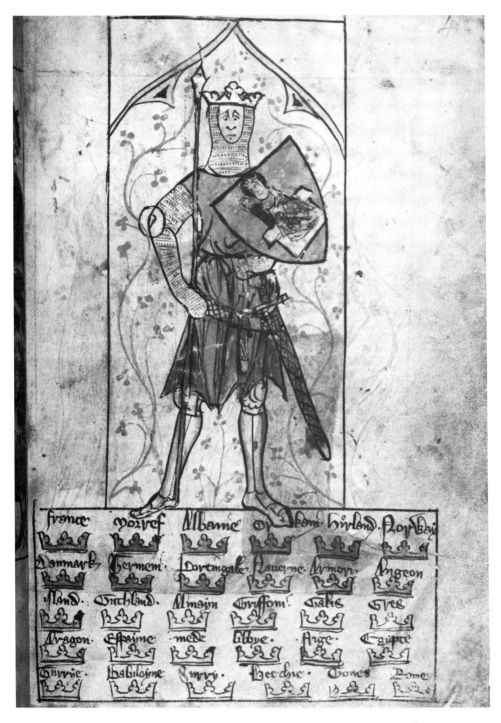

1. Arthur and his Kingdoms. Peter Langtoft's Chronicle of England, BL Royal 20 A II f. 4

for centuries. Perhaps he himself symbolises the artist, whose insight provides him with power but whose sensitivity brings about his doom.

In the *Historia Regum Britanniae* Geoffrey provides several representations of Arthur which affect his depiction in art. When Archbishop Dubricius crowns him, he is a youth of fifteen who, despite his age and inexperience, embodies the regal attributes of courage, generosity, and determination to harry his enemies. Preparing to attack the Saxons in Somerset, he dons a golden helmet with a crest carved in the shape of a dragon. He girds on his sword Caliburn (i.e. Excalibur),[8] forged in the Isle of Avalon, and holds in his hand his long spear Ron. His shield Pridwen bears the painted figure of the Virgin Mary.[9] The illustrator of London, British Library MS Royal 20 A II, Peter Langtoft's romance historiography (ca. 1307), clearly has the Galfridian description in mind when he draws a confident young warrior firmly clasping shield and spear, girded with his sword, his feet bestriding the crowns of thirty conquered countries.

When Geoffrey's king has unified Britain and conquered Gaul, he publicly demonstrates his sovereignty by a Pentecostal crown-wearing ceremony[10] at Caerleon, a Roman city of material splendour. As Geoffrey describes it (IX, 14), the scene includes golden-roofed palaces, great churches, a river flowing on one side and meadows and wooded groves flanking the other side. This combination of landscape elements appears frequently in illuminated manuscripts. After a religious procession and service which feature such iconographic details as four golden swords (victory and justice), four white doves (purity and peace), and the crowns and regalia denoting sovereignty, the king entertains the male guests at a banquet with sumptuous service.[11] Kay, the Seneschal, robed in ermine, and Bedevere, the Cup-bearer, are assisted by a thousand noblemen bearing food and drink. Though illustrators cannot equal the scale of the verbal description, the *topos* of royal feast has remained a standard motif in the Arthurian repertoire until the present. As late as the fifteenth century, illuminations and wall paintings show Arthur entertaining men only, as in Paris, Bibliothèque Nationale MS fr. 363, f. 1, *Guiron le Courtois* (ca. 1470), and in a wall-painting at Schloss Runkelstein in the Italian Tyrol. Not only through the pageantry of the feast but also through references to courteous manners, fashionable female dress, heraldic blazons and ritualistic jousting the writer creates an impression of a sophisticated society.

The most important original episode in the *Historia* is the account of Arthur's

---

[8]   Robert de Boron (d. 1212) was responsible for the idea that Excalibur was fixed in a stone.

[9]   See Helmut Nickel, 'About Arms and Armor in The Age of Arthur', *Avalon to Camelot*, I, 1 (1983), 19–21. Nickel notes that the armour which Geoffrey attributes to Arthur 'corresponds in all details to the actual armor found in the Sutton Hoo ship burial'.

[10] Martin Biddle cites historical examples of such ceremonies in 'Seasonal Festivals and Residence: Winchester, Westminster and Gloucester in the Tenth to Twelfth Centuries' in R. Allen Brown ed., *Proceedings of the Battle Conference 1985*, Anglo-Norman Studies VIII (Woodbridge, 1986), pp. 51–72.

[11] Geoffrey says that it was a Trojan custom for the women to dine apart from the men. In fact, it seems to have been an Anglo-Saxon practice.

Roman wars which culminate in the defeat of Emperor Lucius. This event is preceded and foreshadowed by a mythic tale of giant killing (X, 3),[12] a part of the archetypal hero pattern which demonstrates the protagonist's social responsibilities. (The dragon-slaying, which is an important motif in *Tristan* art, serves a similar purpose). The giant of Mont Saint Michel, a cannibalistic murderer, a ravisher of women, with his monstrous eye, bloody face and weighty club, is contrasted to the smaller, lither Arthur, whose sword brings his opponent crashing to earth. Emile Mâle[13] points out that the grotesque, whether encountered in gargoyles, portals or the margins of illuminated manuscripts, expresses the medieval artist's delight in the fanciful and the eccentric. Not surprisingly, Arthur's encounter with the giant has inspired the same extravagance of monstrosity that was applied also to representations of devils.

Fighting and defeating the Emperor Lucius, Arthur is the British version of the Homeric hero whose *topos*, as described by E.R. Curtius,[14] includes battle-lore, manliness in the field and in the council of war, and proficiency in the use of a particular weapon. As well, he is a model of medieval kingship as embodied in Henry I, Henry II and Frederick Barbarossa. The latter two, says Norman F. Cantor,

> exhibited a rare combination of qualities which made them appear almost superhuman figures to contemporaries: longevity, boundless ambition, extraordinary organizing skills and greatness in the battlefield. . . . they were handsome and proficient in courtly gestures, which some members of the nobility now found attractive without being in any way softened by courtly ideals.[15]

Topologically, the Roman War establishes Arthur as a conqueror of international stature, one who can take his place with Hector, Caesar, Alexander, Joshua, David, Judas Maccabeus, Charlemagne and Godfrey of Bologne to make up the roster of *les neuf preux*. Iconographically, the battles in the *Historia* justify what often amounts to a superfluity of martial scenes – combat on horse and on foot with lances, swords, and battleaxes; serried ranks advancing towards the centre or single champions risking all in one encounter; mêlées and routes that crowd the pictorial space. Banners, standards, couched lances, brandished swords, cloven helmets, severed limbs, bleeding bodies, and broken weapons are the images of chivalric combat in text and illustration.

Finally, in the *Historia*'s Arthurian section Geoffrey deals with a subject which

---

[12] R.H. Fletcher, *op. cit.* pp. 90–91 asserts that the story goes back to very remote mythical antiquity; Arthur has replaced Kei and Beduer who are the principals in a similar version recounted in the *Mabinogion* tale, 'Kulhwch and Olwen'.

[13] Emile Mâle, *L'art religieux du XIIIe siécle en France* (Paris, 1898); The Gothic Image: Religious Art in France of the Thirteenth Century, trans. Dora Nussey (New York, Evanston and London, 1958 [1913]), pp. 59–63.

[14] E.R. Curtius, *European Literature and the Latin Middle Ages*, trans. Willard R. Trask (New York and Evanston, 1963 [1953]), p. 172.

[15] Norman F. Cantor, *Medieval History: The Life and Death of a Civilization* (New York, 1963), p. 460.

did not arouse much artistic interest in the middle ages but had an enormous vogue in the nineteenth century; namely, the 'passing of Arthur'. Geoffrey designates the king's nephew Mordred as the enemy who brings about Arthur's downfall. The last battle ends when Mordred is killed and the mortally wounded Arthur is carried to the Isle of Avalon so that his wounds can be healed. The nature of this Otherworldly *locus amoenus*[16] Geoffrey describes in his *Vita Merlini* (ca. 1150). The speaker is the bard Taliesin:

> The island of Apples, which men call the Fortunate Isle, is so named because it produces all things of itself. The fields there have no need of farmers to plough them, and Nature alone provides all cultivation. Grain and grapes are produced without tending, and apple trees grow in the woods from the close-clipped grass. The earth of its own accord brings forth not merely grass but all things in superabundance. . . . Thither after the battle of Camlan we took the wounded Arthur. . . . With the Prince we arrived there, and Morgan received us with becoming honour. In her own chamber she placed the king on a golden bed, with her own noble hand uncovered the wound, and gazed at it long. At last she said that health could return to him if he were to stay with her for a long time and wished to make use of her healing art. Rejoicing, therefore, we committed the king to her, and returning gave our sails to the favouring winds.[17]

Many of the visual elements in the description reappear more than seven centuries later in Edward Burne-Jones' last great painting, 'The Sleep of King Arthur in Avalon' (1881–98). Geoffrey does not mention directly the possibility of the hero's eventual return but his allusion to Avalon implies knowledge of a myth that was current among the Welsh, Cornish, and Britons in the early twelfth century.[18] An alternative ending was provided by the discovery of 'Arthur's tomb' at Glastonbury in 1191, a revelation possibly staged by the monks on orders from Henry II.[19] This 'fact' found favour with French romancers who had no desire to perpetuate a British myth of eternal return.[20]

[16] On this *topos* see Curtius, *op. cit.*, pp. 192–200.
[17] *Arthurian Literature in the Middle Ages*, pp. 92–93.
[18] On Avalon and the 'Breton hope' see E.K. Chambers, *op. cit.* pp. 121–3; R.H. Fletcher, *op. cit.* pp. 100–2; R.S. Loomis, 'The Legend of Arthur's Survival', *Arthurian Literature in the Middle Ages*, pp. 64–71; H.R. Patch, *The Otherworld According to Descriptions in Medieval Literature* (New York, 1970 [1950]), pp. 284–7; L.A. Paton, *Studies in the Fairy Mythology of Arthurian Romance* (Boston, 1903; rptd. New York, 1959), pp. 25–48.
[19] See C.A. Ralegh Radford, 'Glastonbury Abbey' in *The Quest for Arthur's Britain*, ed. Geoffrey Ashe (London, 1968); J.A. Robinson, *Two Glastonbury Legends: King Arthur and St. Joseph of Arimathea* (Cambridge, Eng., 1926); John Scott, *The Early History of Glastonbury* (Woodbridge, 1981); R.F. Treharne, *The Glastonbury Legends* (London, 1967); John Withrington, 'The Arthurian Epitaph in Malory's "Morte Darthur" ', *Arthurian Literature* vii, ed. Richard Barber (Cambridge, Eng., 1987), pp. 103–144. See also the 'eye witness' account of the tomb's discovery written by Giraldus Cambrensis, *De Principis Instructione* viii, pp. 126–9 (ca. 1194).
[20] On Arthur's varying reputation see Rosemary Morris, *The Character of King Arthur in*

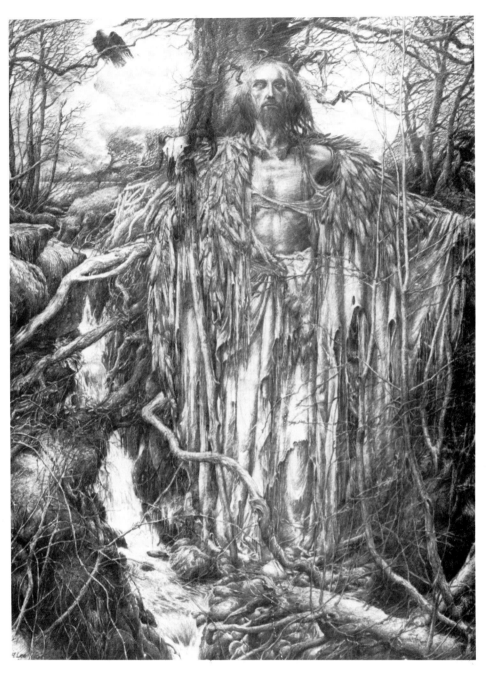

2. Alan Lee's Merlin

In addition to creating the accepted biography of Arthur, Geoffrey provided the basic list of characters, a group that retained their association with the king through the succeeding centuries: Merlin, the magician and seer; Guenevere, the adulterous wife who ended her life by becoming a nun; Kay, the Seneschal; Bedevere, the Cup-bearer; Mordred, the treasonous nephew and nemesis. The king was depicted as a noble, hospitable, and martially active suzerain, an expression of British nationalism. Subsequently, French romancers often treated him as a *roi fainéant*, a 'banal maître de ceremonies'. In Chrétien's *Lancelot* he is degraded 'to the level of a coward and a poltroon', in Frappier's phrase. In *Perlesvaus* his sloth has undermined the Round Table and enervated the whole kingdom while in Robert de Boron's *Mort d'Arthur* his continental expedition is a minor episode motivated by a desire to assist Lancelot in expelling a usurper. In the *Prose Lancelot* he is so weak that he cannot protect his vassal Ban nor avenge his death. However, this literary denigration seems to have had no influence on the pictorial tradition which perpetuates the persona as Geoffrey created it.

The *Historia*'s popularity, substantiated by the survival of more than two hundred manuscripts, was soon apparent. As early as 1139, an Anglo-Norman historian, Henry of Huntingdon, found a copy at the Norman abbey in Bec. An Anglo-Norman poet in the North of England, Geoffrey Gaimer, turned the work into a metrical chronicle before 1150, though no copy of the *Estorie des Bretons* has survived. More long-lived was the adaptation by a Norman poet, Wace, a copy of whose *Roman de Brut* (1158) was presented to Eleanor of Aquitaine, wife of Henry II and mother of Marie de Champagne. This more romantic version in octosyllabic couplets contributed a number of images that went into the artists' storehouse. Wace is the creator of the Round Table, an artifact made by a Cornish carpenter after a fight about precedence at the Christmas feast. Thereafter, when the fair fellowship dined, their chairs were equally high, their service equally generous, and none ranked before or after his comrade. About fifty years later when Layamon wrote the first Middle English *Brut*, he gave the table hyperbolic dimensions – it could seat sixteen hundred men and yet be carried about wherever Arthur went. Despite the qualifying adjective and the pragmatic explanation of origins, the miniaturists generally give the table a rectangular shape. It is also Wace who presents the Breton forest of Broceliande as a marvellous place with a magical storm-producing fountain, though he admits in the *Roman de Rou* that his excursion to view the wonders for himself was unsuccessful. Subsequently, in literature and art the site is associated with the fateful love of Merlin for Vivien and with the adventures of Yvain. The place evokes the fairy-tale atmosphere which for Erich Auerbach is 'the true element of the courtly romance'.[21] Wace is the first to focus on ships and sea voyages, subjects favoured by the miniaturists who illustrate the adventures of Arthur and Tristan, not to mention those of

---

Medieval Literature (Cambridge, Eng., 1982). Re Arthur in French Literature see P. Rickard, *Britain in Medieval French Literature* (Cambridge, Eng., 1956).

[21] On the characteristics of French courtly romance see Erich Auerbach's discussion of Chrétien de Troyes' *Yvain*, 'The Knight Sets Forth', *Mimesis, the Representation of Reality in Western Literature*, trans. Willard R. Trask (Princeton, 1953), pp. 123–142.

peregrinating Grail knights. Wace may also be responsible for enhancing the pageantic aspects of courtly life.

A second, though less tangible, medium for transmitting the 'Matter of Britain' was oral diffusion. It was through the agency of minstrels, R.S. Loomis and others suggest, that Irish, Welsh and Breton motifs and story patterns reached court poets like Marie de France and Chrétien de Troyes.[22] The Celtic materials included the kidnapping of Arthur's queen by the lord of an Otherworld castle, the mortal hero's sojourn with a fairy mistress, and the richly evocative Tristan legends. Originally an independent hero who seems to have had an historical original, the Pictish prince Drust mac Seirb, Tristan is attached to the Arthurian cycle by the device of making him a knight of the Round Table.[23] The archetype which Joseph Bédier reconstructed early in this century from the *Tristans* of Thomas (ca. 1160), Eilhart von Oberge (ca. 1170), Béroul (ca. 1190), Gottfried von Strassburg (ca. 1210), and the Old French Prose *Tristan* includes the story of the hero's parents, Rivalen and Blanchefleur; the *enfances* of the hero; the combat with Morholt; the voyages to Ireland, Cornwall and Brittany; the dragon slaying; the magic love potion which Tristan and Iseult share; the love triangle; the substitute bride; the tryst beneath the tree; the lover as hunter and harper; the cave idyll; the trial by ordeal; the hero's madness; Tristan's marriage to Iseult of the White Hands; and the black or white sails with which the poetic versions conclude. From the prose *Tristan* comes the story that King Mark spears the hero in the back as he sits harping to his lady Iseult. *Tristan* is the single most important source of imagery in the decorative arts, providing subjects for manuscript illuminations, stained glass, murals, ivory boxes, mirror backs, embroideries, drawings, paintings, cups and clothing.

The crucial *conjointure* of chivalry, courtesy and Celtic magic which constitutes the essence of Arthurian romance was the achievement of Chrétien de Troyes (fl. 1160–1191) who wrote under the patronage of Marie de Champagne and Philippe of Flanders.[24] Chrétien's literary world differs markedly from that of the legendary history. Arthur is no longer the major protagonist; rather he is the static centre

[22] R.S. Loomis, 'The Oral Diffusion of the Arthurian Legend', *Arthurian Literature in the Middle Ages*, pp. 52–63; A.C.L. Brown, *The Origin of the Grail Legend* (New York, 1943); Jean Marx, *La Légende Arthurienne et Le Graal* (Paris, 1952).

[23] Helaine Newstead, 'The Origin and Growth of the Tristan Legend', *Arthurian Literature in the Middle Ages*, pp. 122–133; Gertrude Schoepperle, *Tristan and Isolt* (Frankfurt, London, 1913; rptd. New York, 1959).

[24] M. Roques, *Les Romans de Chrétien de Troyes édités d'après la copie de Guiot* (*Bibliothèque Nationale, MS fr. 794*) (Paris, 1952). English translations include W. Wistar Comfort, *Arthurian Romances by Chrétien de Troyes* (London, 1914); Deborah Webster Rogers, *Lancelot The Knight of the Cart* (New York, 1984); Ruth Harwood Cline, *Yvain or The Knight With the Lion* (Athens, Georgia, 1975); William W. Kibler, ed. and trans., *Chrétien de Troyes, The Knight With the Lion, or Yvain (Le Chevalier au Lion)* (New York and London, 1985); Nigel Bryant, *Perceval, The Story of the Grail* (Cambridge and Totawa, N.J., 1982). For a recent bibliography see Jean Frappier, *Chrétien de Troyes, The Man and His Work*, trans. Raymond J. Cormier (Athens, Ohio, 1982), pp. 191–223. See also L.T. Topsfield, *Chrétien de Troyes; a Study of the Arthurian Romances* (Cambridge, Eng., 1981).

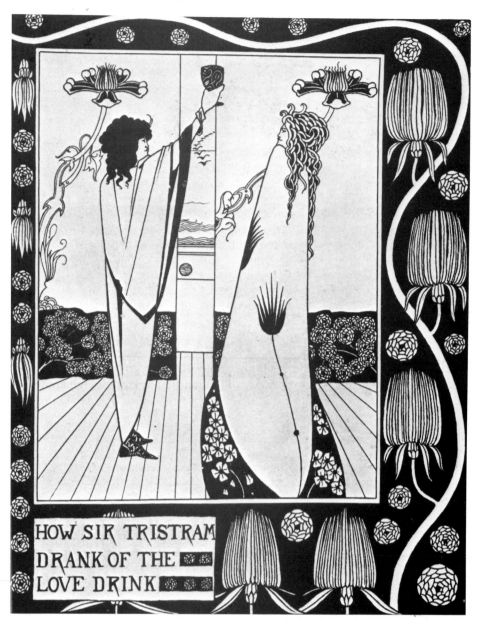

HOW SIR TRISTRAM
DRANK OF THE
LOVE DRINK

3. Aubrey Beardsley's Tristram and La Beale Isoud, Malory's *Morte Darthur* (London: Dent, 1893)

of a court from which individual knights ride out to seek adventure in distant forests and castles and to which they return for recognition of their prowess. Their inspiration is not political (a desire to conquer territories) and feudal (an obligation to serve their overlords and protect their vassals) but amatory and self-serving, based on a sense of individual worth that would justify the lady's bestowal of favours. Although it contains elements of real twelfth century France, Chrétien's terrain is a secondary world of the imagination containing a mythic aristocracy that barely recognizes any class but its own. The seat of romance society is the castle, an image that denotes a privileged class separated from the rest of society by its occupying a different kind of space. In his essay on Chrétien's *Yvain*, Erich Auerbach describes the castle's features:

> The setting is fixed and isolating, as distinct from the mores of other strata of society, as is that of the *chanson de geste*, but it is much more refined and elegant. Women play an important part in it; the mannerly ease and comfort of the social life of a cultured class have been attained.

Here are cultivated the manners and mores implied by the term *courtoisie*. It includes, according to Henri Dupin's study of Old French romances,[25] an antithesis between *courtois* and *vilain*, that is, the ideal of social exclusiveness; the performance of certain ritual gestures associated with hospitality; the moral qualities of loyalty, faith, generosity and compassion; an atmosphere of joy; an observance of *mesure*; and the experience of that particular kind of love known as *amour courtois*.[26] The chief responsibilities of the castle's lord or lady are to provide the knight-errant with hospitality, entertainment, reward, and opportunities for chivalric adventure.

The castle's necessary complement and antithesis is the perilous forest which exists to test the hero's skill in arms as well as his virtue. The hero carries into the forest courage, endurance, a desire for truth and honour, loyalty, abhorrence of evil, and a determination, in the words of Sir Thomas Malory, 'allwayes to do ladyes, damesels and jantilwomen and wydowes socour: strengthe hem in hir ryghtes'. Gervase Mathew suggests that 'the perpetual sense of the forest, the absence of horizon' encourages the practice of 'a simple individualistic code of ethics in which honour and dishonour had the sharp contrasts of heraldic colours'.[27] Like the castle, the forest is an enclosed world with its own kind of

---

[25] Henri Dupin, *La Courtoisie au Moyen Age (d'après les textes du XIIe et du XIIIe siècle)* (Paris, 1906).

[26] The vast critical literature includes Jean Frappier, *Amour Courtois et Table Ronde* (Geneva, 1973); J.M. Ferrante and G.D. Economou eds., *In Pursuit of Perfection: Courtly Love in Medieval Literature*; Alexander J. Denomy, 'Courtly Love and Courtliness', *Speculum* 27 (1953), 44–63; C.S. Lewis, *The Allegory of Love, A Study in Medieval Tradition* (New York, 1958 [1936]); Moshé Lazar, *Amour courtois et 'fin' amors' dans la littérature du XIIe siècle* (Paris, 1964).

[27] Gervase Mathew, 'Ideals of Knighthood in Late-Fourteenth-Century England', *Studies in Medieval History Presented to Frederick Maurice Powicke*, ed. R.W. Hunt, W.A. Pantin, R.W. Southern (Oxford, 1948), p. 362.

consistency and with 'a quality of strangeness and wonder in the Expression derived from the Image'.[28] Its power depends not on a particular botanical make-up but on its suggestion of limitless, uncultivated space, hidden menaces, and the kind of density that allows for the sudden appearance of white stags, lions, giants, dwarfs, distressed maidens, black knights, fées, and Loathly Ladies. What particularly separates this setting from that of the castle (and from the world of our own experience) is not only the opportunity it affords for questing and jousting but also its atmosphere of wonder and terror.

Chrétien's *Erec* (ca. 1170) is, so far as we know, the first Arthurian romance to offer this milieu as a context for exploring the sometimes conflicting demands of *armes* and *amours*. Initially the hero's prowess wins him reputation and a beautiful wife, Enide, but his absorption in marital bliss deprives him of 'worship'. A return to the perilous forest accompanied by his wife, on whom he has imposed a vow of silence, leads eventually to renewed honour and trust. The 'Joy of the Court' (the phrase specifying not only Erec's supreme adventure in a supernatural garden but also the pervasive emotion of courtly life) is evoked partly by material goods, hyperbolic in quantity and splendour.

After winning the kiss of the White Stag for Enide in conformity with an adventure-producing 'custom' of King Arthur's court, the hero demonstrates his courtesy, generosity, kindness, and wealth by sending the lady's impoverished father five sleek mules loaded with scarlet clothing, gold and silver plate, furs (both squirrel and sable), purple material (an expensive colour), and silks. The valuable clothing which Guenevere gives Erec's maiden includes an iridescent mantle embroidered with varicoloured crosses and lined with ermine; two sables with jewel-tipped golden tassels; an ermine-lined tunic banded at the neck with beaten gold in which are set indigo, green, blue and amber jewels; and five yards of ribbons made of silk thread and gold. Even more opulent and ornate is Erec's coronation robe which Chrétien describes meticulously. The luxurious furnishings include beds with white sheets and soft pillows, a Limoge rug portraying a leopard, a silver couch covered with a gold embroidered cloth, and two thrones made entirely of gold and white ivory, one carved with leopards and the other with dragons. No doubt such objects existed in the Middle Ages but they were so far beyond ordinary experience that they must be regarded as among the attractions of romance's wish-fulfilling dream world. Since they are isolatable, author and artist can introduce them singly or in various combinations to suggest a courtly ethos.

As well as depicting forests filled with adventure-producing images and castles evoking the pleasures of idealised courtly life, Chrétien provides ceremonial set pieces which because of their static nature, limited range and conventionality can be readily adapted to the graphic medium; e.g. weddings, coronations, feasts, and tournaments. The tournament's chief purposes were the demonstration of prowess in a social setting, the establishment of a knightly hierarchy, and the attainment of a reward that could be both a valuable artifact and a lady's love. The

---

[28] J.R.R. Tolkien, 'On Fairy-Stories', *Tree and Leaf* (London, 1964), pp. 44–5.

tournament at Tenebroc exhibits the amatory, heraldic and chivalric elements so often repeated in subsequent literature and art:

> La ot tante vermoille ansaigne,
> et tante guinple et tante manche,
> et tante bloe, et tante blanche,
> qui par amors furent donees;
> tant i ot lances aportees
> d'azur et de sinople taintes,
> d'or et d'argent en i ot maintes,
> maintes en i ot d'autre afeire,
> mainte bandee, et tante veire;
> iluec vit an le jor lacier
> maint hiaume, de fer et d'acier;
> tant vert, tant giaune, tant vermoil,
> reluire contre le soloil;
> tant blazon, et taunt hauberc blanc,
> tante espee a senestre flanc,
> tanz boens escuz fres et noviax,
> d'azur et de sinople biax,
> et tant d'argent a bocles d'or;
> tant boen cheval, baucent et sor,
> fauves, et blans, et noirs et bais,
> tuit s'antre vienent a eslais.   (ll. 2084–2104)

(Many an ensign of red, blue, and white, many a veil and many a sleeve were bestowed as tokens of love. Many a lance was carried there, flying the colours argent and green, or gold and azure blue. There were many, too, with different devices, some with stripes and some with dots. That day one saw laced on many a helmet of gold or steel, some green, some yellow, and others red, all glowing in the sun; so many scutcheons and white hauberks; so many swords girt on the left side; so many good shields, fresh and new, some resplendent in silver and green, others of azure with buckles of gold; so many good steeds marked with white or sorrel, tawny, white, black and bay: all gather hastily. Trans. W.W. Comfort).

This richly pictorial passage with its emphasis on bright colours, shining metals, and knightly accoutrements that create a glamorous aura precedes the rituals of jousting and tourneying. The formulaic descriptions hardly vary from one century to the next. First comes the mêlée as mounted knights charge with lances advanced, then the sword fights as the unhorsed combatants continue the battle on foot, then the focus on the particular knights (in this case Erec and Gawain) whose achievements are to be glorified. Broken lances, riddled shields, ripped hauberks, split helmets, foaming horses, empty saddles, and bodies prone on the ground evoke the violence and excitement of the scene. Chrétien's *Erec* was adapted in German by Hartmann von Aue at the end of the twelfth century; there was also an Old Norse version. But the form of the story that influenced artists was a thirteenth century Welsh romance, *Gereint Son of Erbin*. Translated into English by Lady Charlotte Guest (*Mabinogion*, 1849), it was the source of Tennyson's idylls, 'The Marriage of Geraint' (1859) and 'Geraint and Enide' (1870).

Chrétien's *Yvain* or *Le Chevalier au Lion* like *Erec* examines the conflict between domestic love and chivalric obligation. Having defeated Esclados the Red, his adversary at Broceliande's magic fountain, the hero takes the dead knight's place as Laudine's husband and the spring's (i.e. the kingdom's) defender. However, Gawain lures him away to win fame by exhibiting his prowess abroad. Having forgotten the promise that he would return within a year, Yvain must undergo privation, madness, and altruistic service against evil knights, a giant and two devils before he can be reconciled to his wife.

Like *Erec*, *Yvain* is set in an enclosed world that alternates between castle and forest but an increased use of supernatural elements creates a more powerful atmosphere of wonder and terror. The approach to the fountain, as Calogrenant describes it, is impeded by a thick forest full of briars and thorns, wild bulls and a giant herdsman. Like the giant of St Michael's Mount, he is defined by attributes of grotesque horror:

> Uns vileins qui resanbloit Mor,
> leiz et hideus a desmesure,
> einsi tres leide criature
> qu'an ne porroit dire de boche,
> assis s'estoit sor une coche,
> une grant maçue en sa main.   (ll. 288–293)

> (A peasant who resembled a Moor, ugly and hideous in the
> extreme – such an ugly creature that he cannot be described in
> words – was seated on a stump, with a great club in his hand.)

The poet goes on to describe the monster, seventeen feet tall, with a huge head, hairy ears the size of an elephant's, flat face, owl-like eyes, cat's nose, wolf's jowls, boar's teeth, chin reaching his heart, twisted spine, humped back, and so on. The animal images, emphasizing the creature's bestiality, may be read allegorically. On the level of story, however, the *vilain*'s function is to discourage the fainthearted while egging on the hero with his story of the storm-producing spring. It is noon (like midnight a favourable time for supernatural meetings) when Yvain reaches a *locus amoenus* of extraordinary qualities that can only be described in superlatives:

> Bien sai de l'arbre, c'est la fins,
> que cë estoit li plus biax pins

qui onques sor terre creüst . . . .
A l'arbre vi le bacin pandre,
del plus fin or qui fust a vandre
encor onques en nule foire
De la fontainne, pöez croire,
qu'ele boloit com iaue chaude
Li perrons ert d'une esmeraude
perciee ausi com une boz,
et s'a .iiii. rubiz desoz,
plus flanboianz et plus vermauz
que n'est au matin li solauz,
qant il apert en oriant.   (ll. 413–429)

(I know for a fact that the tree was the most beautiful pine that
ever grew upon the earth. . . . From the tree I saw the basin
hanging, made of purest gold that was ever sold at any fair. As
for the spring, you can be assured that it was boiling like hot
water. The stone was of emerald pierced through like a cask,
and it sat upon four rubies, brighter and redder than the morning sun when it first appears in the east. Trans. W.W. Kibler).

In this romance, the spring is the centre about which the forest adventures re-
volve. In the graphic arts, this kind of place with a fountain, a tree, and a challenging basin often functions as a meeting place for knights-errant, damsels and
antagonists.

Esclados' castle is clearly derived from the Otherworld castles of Early Irish
Literature. Its perilous passage is an entrance with a knife-sharp portcullis that
crashes down to mangle intruders. The beautiful ladies, Laudine and Lunete, the
one an object of love, the other an agent of plot, resemble Fand and Liban, the fées
who entice Cuchulinn to the Otherworld where Fand's love is a reward for the
hero's successful combat. The sudden storm signals transition from natural to
supernatural while the singing birds initiate Yvain's bespelling. The castle's splendour – painted walls, golden nails, silk hangings, tapestries and red cushions –
along with its isolated position outside the world which Arthur's court knows are
analogous to the Tuatha Dé Danaan's suddenly encountered dwellings.

Another vivid and detachable image in this unrealistic kingdom of adventure
is the lion which Yvain rescues from a serpent. (Curtius tells us that lions in
Northern forests are remnants of classical rhetoric).[29] Friendly and faithful as a
dog, the beast is the hero's companion and defender. Furthermore, it provides the
knight with a new identity so that he can approach Laudine. In its German form,
Hartmann von Aue's Iwein (1203), this romance inspired medieval mural programmes, two of which have survived.

In the development of Arthurian imagery, Lancelot or Le Chevalier de la Charrette

---

[29] Curtius, op. cit. p. 184.

is vitally important. It is the oldest extant literary work to present Lancelot as a paramount hero and as the lover of Queen Guenevere. In the prologue Chrétien tells us that it was Marie, the Countess of Champagne, who suggested the *matière* (subject matter) and the *sens* (interpretation). The matière centres on the adventures which Lancelot must undergo to rescue the kidnapped queen from Meleagant, son of King Baudemagus. The *sens* requires an explication of *amour courtois*, that revolutionary twelfth-century phenomenon which elevated women, at least in literature, and humbled men.[30] Secret, adulterous, noble and ennobling, it compels the lover to prove his devotion through physical and mental suffering while it allows the lady to define chivalric virtue and to grant – or withhold – its rewards. In W.T.H. Jackson's opinion, Chrétien's *Lancelot* pushed the Arthurian ethos 'to its logical conclusion: a knight whose love service is the finest imaginable, yet who is the total slave of the lady he serves, a lady whose real desire seems to be to prove her dominance whatever the consequences'.[31]

Artists take a less censorious view, often departing from their literary sources, whether French or English, to glorify the lovers. Episodes that lend themselves to pictorial representation include the 'knight of the cart' motif when the horseless hero rides like a criminal in order to reach his lady; the passage of the sword bridge which, along with the water bridge, provides the only access to the castle in the land of Gore (either hell or the Celtic Otherworld); Gawain's adventures in the Perilous Bed (repeated more elaborately in *Perceval*); the lovemaking in Guenevere's bedroom after Lancelot has broken through the window bars; and the battle between Lancelot and Meleagant. These scenes are frequently illustrated by the miniaturists decorating Prose *Lancelot* manuscripts.

Chrétien's final romance, *Perceval* or *Le Conte du Graal*, is a new departure in two important respects. Its central character is a *dümmlingkind*, a boy whose mother has brought him up in a remote Welsh forest to preserve him from all knowledge of the chivalric world which killed her husband and older sons. As blood will out, Perceval cannot evade his knightly destiny. The theme of the romance is the education of the hero. What distinguishes this motivation from the more limited educating of Erec and Yvain is that Perceval's development is not only social and moral; it is also spiritual. The origins of the Grail Legends may lie in ancient fertility myths which related the productivity of a land and its people to the health of its ruler. Celtic mythology added an Otherworld castle, magical artifacts and various motifs identified by R.S. Loomis, A.C.L. Brown, Jean Marx and others. The Christian iconography associated with the Last Supper and the Crucifixion is another component; a bleeding lance and the Grail itself which in *Perceval* is a dish, in Wolfram von Eschenbach's *Parzival* (ca. 1200) a stone and in *La Quête del Saint Graal* (1215–1230) the chalice of the Last Supper.

---

[30] It is ironical that at the same time as poets were investing them with great power, married women were actually losing power socially and economically. See Georges Duby, *The Knight, The Lady and The Priest; The Making of Modern Marriage in Medieval France*, trans. Barbara Bray (London, 1984).

[31] *Lancelot*, trans. Deborah Webster Rogers, Introduction xxiii.

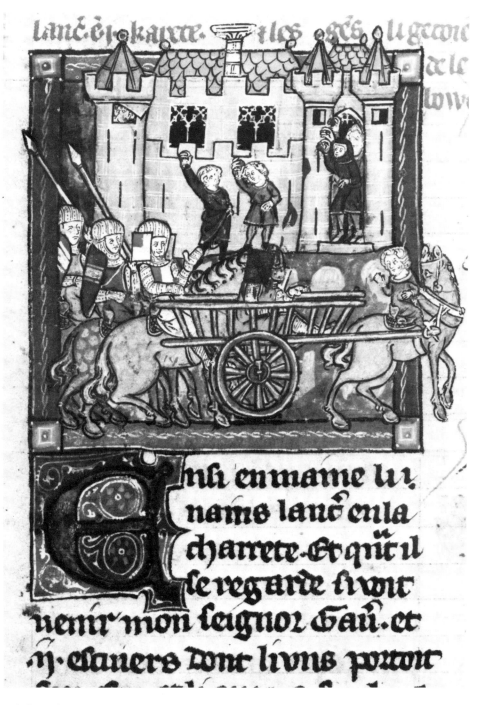

4. Lancelot rides in a cart to rescue Guenevere. BL Add. 10293, f. 183 (*Vulgate Prose Lancelot*)

Chrétien presents an intriguing cast with the kind of identifying characteristics which are useful to the artist: the naive boy in his rustic clothing; the Red Knight who arrogantly steals Arthur's cup; the delectable Blancheflor, her hair like pure gold, her forehead like carved ivory, her face a finer blend of red and white than heraldry could achieve; the Fisher King whose wound can only be healed and joy restored when a hero mends the broken sword and asks the right question; his ascetic father whose only sustenance is a communion wafer served in the the Grail; the hermit in his forest cell; Gawain surviving the Perilous Bed and warding off assailants with a chessboard and Excalibur; the Loathly Lady with her prophecies of doom.

The most powerful images are those of the Grail procession which takes place not in a church but in a castle hall, a scene that establishes a common pictorial formula, the Grail's appearance to a group of feasters. Chrétien's verse is visually evocative as it harmoniously combines images of courtly grace and religious mystery. The procession begins with a boy holding a white lance from the tip of which blood drips to run down his hand. Two more boys follow holding golden candlesticks inlaid with black enamel; in each candelabrum burn ten candles. The aesthetics of light and symbol reach a climax when a beautiful girl appears:

> Quant ele fu laiens entree
> Atot le graal qu'ele tint,
> Une si grans clartez i vint
> Qu'ausi perdirent les chandoiles
> Lor clarté come les estoiles
> Font quant solaus lieve ou la lune,
> Aprés celi en revint une
> Qui tint un tailleoir d'argent.
> Li graaus, qui aloit devant,
> De fin or esmeré estoit,
> Prescieuses pierres avoit
> El graal de maintes manieres,
> Des plus riches et des plus chieres
> Qui en mer ne en terre soient;
> Totes autres pierres passoient
> Celes del graal sanz dotance.   (ll. 3224–3239)

(When she entered holding the Grail, so brilliant a light appeared that the candles lost their brightness like the stars or the moon when the sun rises. After her came another girl, holding a silver trencher. The Grail, which went ahead, was made of fine, pure gold; and in it were set precious stones of many kinds, the richest and most precious in the earth or the sea: those in the Grail surpassed all other jewels without a doubt. Trans. Nigel Bryant).

An evangelisation myth is the device that explains the Grail's presence in England (Logres). Robert de Boron's *Joseph* (1191–1202) describes how the rich Jew of Arimathea acquires the chalice of the Last Supper, establishes the table of the Grail, where only the pure can feast, and effects the vessel's transference to the Vale of Avalon (Glastonbury). This legendary history is expanded in *Estoire del Saint Graal* (1215–1230). The final step in the development of Arthurian source materials is the creation of a new Grail hero, a type of Christ. As the son of secular chivalry's best knight, Lancelot, and the Grail maiden, Elaine, Galahad combines his father's prowess with a virtue immune to sexual temptation. Though the authors of the French *Vulgate Prose Cycle* (1215–1230), probably Cistercians, gave him the attributes of a mystical fighting monk, this hero and his definitive blazon – the red cross on a white ground also attributed to the risen Christ – becomes a universal image of purity, aid and self-sacrifice.

The voluminous thirteenth century prose romances – e.g. the *Vulgate Cycle* (*Estoire del Saint Graal, Merlin, Lancelot, Quête del Saint Graal,* and *Mort Artu*),[32] *Tristan,* and *Suite du Merlin* – proliferate characters and events to satisfy an apparently insatiable taste for romantic literature. In the fifteenth-century, an Englishman, Sir Thomas Malory, combined Geoffrey's pseudo-history, as derived from the fourteenth-century alliterative poem *Morte Arthure* and John Hardyng's *Chronicle* (ca. 1436), with the Vulgate stories of *la chevalerie terrienne* and *la chevalerie célestienne*. His *Morte Darthur* (1470) is the most important source for post-medieval Arthurian art. Its influence on the Victorians was described by Georgiana Burne-Jones as deriving from 'its strength and beauty, its mystical religion and noble chivalry of action, the world of lost history and romance in the names of people and places –'.[33]

The *Morte* provided models of virtuous behaviour appropriate to imperialistic rulers and industrial societies. In illustrated juvenile editions it influenced generations of young readers.

Since the nineteenth century the distinction between literature and art has generally been based on G.E. Lessing's observation that the former exists in time while the latter exists in space. The artist who creates a free standing sculpture, a painting, or a scene carved on an ivory mirror back reduces story to one moment in time. What the two modes share is a common use of metaphor (image) and organization based, says Northrop Frye, on the principle of recurrence 'which is called rhythm when it is temporal and pattern when it is spatial'.[34] The Arthurian artist sometimes helps the viewer identify the subject by providing rubrics under miniatures, scrolls containing the characters' names above figures in a mural, or as William Morris did in his stained glass panels for Harden Grange, narrative summaries at the bottom of each scene. These devices create a certain amount of temporal impetus. Nevertheless, the artist must rely on the spectator's knowledge

[32] *The Vulgate Version of the Arthurian Romances,* ed. H. Oskar Sommer, 8 vols. (Washington, 1908–1916).
[33] Georgiana Burne-Jones, *Memorials of Edward Burne-Jones,* 2 vols. (London, 1904), I, p. 117.
[34] Northrop Frye, *Fables of Identity* (New York, 1963), p. 14.

of the literary sources. Such an image as that of a horse's rear end emerging from a portcullised gate, as in the Chester Cathedral misericord, must be a complete mystery except to the few observers who can connect it with *Yvain*. Sir Galahad and St George share the identifying white shield with a red cross; only the presence or absence of a dragon enables us to determine the figure's name. As E.H. Gombrich puts it in *Art and Illusion: A Study in the Psychology of Pictorial Representation*, 'The figure in space can be conceived only when we have learned to see it as a sign referring to an outer, imagined reality'.

Another element that commonly relates literature to art is style. Since the artist's schema depends on the cultural tradition in which he or she has been trained, the same subject, generally speaking, is portrayed differently in different periods. What gives Arthurian art an unusual degree of uniformity is the fact that it is predominantly Gothic in style. The literature developed almost contemporaneously with the great cathedrals of Northern France and shared the view of reality which they expressed; i.e. the duality of concrete fact and conceptual form. As the principles of medieval aesthetic theory carried on into the Renaissance and surfaced again in the nineteenth century's Gothic Revival, the image in most Arthurian art bears a weight of idea that is not subject to a wide range of interpretation. The fundamental principles of Gothic style combine Neo-Platonic idealism, Aristotelian materiality and Christian didacticism. Beauty depends on proportion, light (including colour), allegory and symbolism, the means by which the material form adumbrates God's invisible and perfect beauty. It is not possible to explore here the various philosophical approaches which medieval scholars explicated. Edgar de Bruyne, summarising the influence of Johannes Scotus Erigena, indicates some of the associations that the word 'beauty' would have had:

> La beauté . . . c'est l'éternel dans les choses: nous appelons belle, toute forme qui nous révèle l'éternité. Mais la beauté c'est aussi la puissance, c'est l'ordre de l'intelligence, c'est la matérialisation du bonheur, c'est la perfection, c'est le symbole de cet équilibre qu'on appelle la vertu, c'est le sourire, c'est le souffle de la vie, c'est ce qui est un, ce qui est vrai, ce qui est bon. Quel que soit le point de départ, le point d'arrivée est l'Ineffable et la route qui les sépare passe par toutes les Idées suprêmes.[35]

If, as Wylie Sypher proposes, all the arts in certain periods are dominated by the techniques of one art, in the Middle Ages architecture was the controlling medium, until the end of the period, when painting became dominant.[36] In *The Rise of Romance*, Eugène Vinaver finds that the literary technique of *entrelacement* which accounts for the 'ornamental complexity' of Arthurian romance parallels the architect's grouping of separate forms (e.g. columns) so that they create a

---

[35] Edgar de Bruyne, *Etudes d'Esthétique Médiévale*, 3 vols. (Genève, 1975), I, pp. 355–6.
[36] Wylie Sypher, *Four Stages of Renaissance Style* (Garden City, 1955), pp. 30–31.

unity.[37] Jean Frappier also asserts that patterns of recurrence adopted from archi-tectural models characterise romance;[38] Chrétien's schema utilises tripartite com-position that combines parallelism with variation, as did cathedral architects when they constructed a facade. Another aspect of proportion relevant to Arthu-rian literature and art concerns the enlargement of heroic figures and the diminu-tion of the supporting cast. Just as the statues of the apostles on Reims Cathedral's north transept are 'grand and massive, wrapped in circulating draperies, individ-ualized works of art of great power and beauty . . . ready to present themselves to the eye from every direction'[39] so Arthur, Yvain, Gawain, Lancelot and Perceval dominate their spaces, whether literary, graphic or plastic. Another analogy be-tween architecture and art is seen in the miniaturists' use of Gothic arches and colonnettes to frame and compartmentalize their scenes.

The most important element in thirteenth century aesthetics was the mystique of light, an expression of the divine that could be conveyed in art by means of metals, marble, precious stones and bright colours. When Abbot Suger (1081–1151) rebuilt the Abbey Church at Saint-Denis, creating what is regarded as the first example of Gothic architecture,[41] he had the walls painted with gold and precious colours, the doors cast in bronze and gilded, a refulgent mosaic created in the tympanum, and the sarcophagi painted with gold. The golden altar frontal contained a wealth of jewels and the altar itself was furnished with splendid artifacts. Suger justified the expenditure and display by emphasising the tran-scendental function that works of art served:

> Thus, when – out of my delight in the beauty of the house of God – the loveliness of the many-colored gems has called me away from eternal cares, and worthy meditation has induced me to reflect, trans-ferring that which is material to that which is immaterial, on the diver-sity of the sacred virtues: then it seems to me that I see myself dwelling, as it were, in some strange region of the universe which neither exists entirely in the slime of the earth nor entirely in the purity of Heaven; and that, by the grace of God, I can be transported from this inferior to that higher world in an anagogical manner.[42]

The beauty of such fine Arthurian manuscripts as New York, Pierpont Morgan Library MS 805; London, British Library MS Royal 14 E III; and Paris, Bibliothèque Nationale MS Fr. 95 (all thirteenth century works) largely depends on the burn-ished gold backgrounds and bright colour harmonics dominated by the blues and

---

[37] Eugène Vinaver, The Rise of Romance (Oxford, 1971), chapter V.
[38] Jean Frappier, Chrétien de Troyes, p. 170.
[39] George Henderson, Gothic (Harmondsworth, 1967).
[40] de Bruyne, III, Bk. IV, ch. 1.
[41] See Henry Foçillon, The Art of the West in the Middle Ages, trans. Donald King, ed. Jean Bony, Vol. II: Gothic Art (London and New York, 1963).
[42] 'De administratione' in Abbot Suger on the Abbey Church of St. Denis and its Art Treasures, 2nd ed., ed. and trans. Erwin Panofsky (Princeton, 1979 [1946]), pp. 62–5.

reds of stained glass windows. The luminosity of silver effects the Burleigh Nef's splendour. Even when, as George Henderson thinks, late medieval Gothic style becomes 'shatteringly superficial'[43] as in a tree-shaped salt cellar with an enamel brook around its base where the spying King Mark is reflected, the art objects retain a beauty grounded in the aesthetics of light.

The influential Victorian critic John Ruskin reiterated the medieval belief that beauty equals God and that light, being the least material of visible things, 'the furthest withdrawn from the earth-prison house', best suggests God's nature.[44] An aesthetic based on brilliant colour characterised the Pre-Raphaelite painters whose technique of applying pure colour over a white ground strove for medieval luminosity. Their first cooperative effort, the Oxford Union Murals, in which Dante Gabriel Rossetti, William Morris, Arthur Hughes and Val Prinsep *inter alia* were involved, reminded observers of medieval illuminations and stained glass, so brilliant was the colouring.

In addition to considerations of form and light, medieval literature and art were affected by the belief, originating in Biblical exegesis, that every story had an underlying metaphysical meaning, allegorical, tropological or anagogical.[45] The multi-level perception affects secular as well as religious works. The heroes of romance move through a 'paysage moralisé' where they act in harmony with or in opposition to 'the scenic tapestry'. The nature of the response is determined by such readable signs as drops of blood on fresh snow (*Parzival*), a lady being dragged away by a black knight (*La Quête del Saint Graal*), the reflection of King Mark's head in a forest pool (*Tristan*). The artist, lacking the author's narrative impulse, focuses on allegorical images and the kind of setting that implies quest or combat. An armed knight riding in a forest is a central figure because he represents both progress and battle (which Angus Fletcher calls allegory's two symbolic actions). Ideas are realized in images with metaphysical implications. *La Quête del Saint Graal* and Edmund Spenser's *Faerie Queene*, both of them consciously allegorical throughout, read on one level like ordinary romances but there are always hermits and other educative figures to explain an adventure's moral and spiritual meaning. Even when the intention is not specifically allegorical, the nature of chivalry determines that a conflict between good and evil is one of the 'givens'. Lacking interpreters, the artist relies on the observer's knowledge of text and familiarity with conventional symbolism.

In the Middle Ages a symbol was a visible figure which represented invisible beauty.[46] Though its meaning might vary with context (its religious significance differing from its secular connotation), a common code, not necessarily related to

[43] *op. cit.* p. 141.
[44] *The Works of John Ruskin*, ed. E.T. Cook and A. Wedderburn, 39 vols. (London, 1903–12), iv, p. 81.
[45] On the allegorical mode see Angus Fletcher, *Allegory: The Theory of a Symbolic Mode* (Ithaca, 1964); Rosemond Tuve, *Allegorical Imagery: Some Medieval Books and Their Posterity* (Princeton, 1966).
[46] On Medieval and Renaissance symbolism see de Bruyne, *op. cit.*; E.H. Gombrich, *Symbolic Images, Studies in the Art of the Renaissance* (London, 1972); Emile Mâle, *op. cit.*; Erwin

reality, constrained the artist's representation. By the fourteenth century symbols were often disguised as real things logically integrated into a work of art. Erwin Panofsky remarks of the Early Netherlandish painters that the more they rejoiced in the visible world, the more they felt the need to saturate all its elements with meaning. The Neo-Platonic attitude which attributed a specific virtue to an image continued to influence the way in which figures were seen. Several centuries later Victorians like A.W.N. Pugin, William Burges, William Holman Hunt and Dante Gabriel Rossetti determinedly used medieval symbols in their architecture and art.

As an explication of symbolism will be one of the concerns in subsequent chapters, it is necessary at this point only to indicate some of the important classifications. Number symbolism derives not only from a medieval regard for proportion but also from an ancient belief that certain numbers have occult powers.[47] The number of The Nine Worthies – three classical heroes, three Jews and three Christians – alludes to the Trinity. The twelve successful Grail heroes who feast with King Pelles suggest Christ and his disciples at the Last Supper. Malory's description of the cavalcade which accompanies Queen Guenevere when Lancelot escorts her back to Arthur plays on the idea of ten as a symbol of perfection and twelve as the combination of material things (four) and spiritual things (three). Colour symbolism is particularly useful since it can indicate hierarchic, tropological and emotive values.[48] For example, gold signifies divinity, sovereignty, wealth and magnanimity; white virtue; black vice; blue fidelity; green amorous passion; grey and brown sadness; yellow hostility. Heraldry developed its own symbolic language based on colour and form. Arms and armour, among the most significant chivalric images, derive their meaning from St Paul's letter to the Ephesians (6, 11–17). The belt represents truth, the coat of mail integrity, the shoes the gospel of peace, the shield faith, the helmet salvation, and the sword the word of God. When the Lady of the Lake acquaints Lancelot with the meaning of his equipment, her interpretation is influenced by the historical context (feudalism and the Crusades). The hauberk represents the knight's duty to defend the Church; the helmet is a watch tower to see and ward off miscreants; the sword is two-edged because a knight must defend both the Church and the people; the sword's point indicates that everyone should obey the knight.

One of the most highly valued symbols in literature and art was the beautiful woman for she represented the beauty of the universe, and hence eternal truth.[49] The Neo-Platonic basis of Medieval and Renaissance art required that the beautiful woman also be good, though it was recognised that devils might take a

---

Panofsky, *Early Netherlandish Painting, its Origins and Character*, 2 vols. (New York and London, 1971, [1952]); Rosemond Tuve, *op. cit.*

[47] See V.F. Hopper, *Medieval Number Symbolism* (New York, 1938).

[48] See de Bruyne, I, p. 298; J. Huizinga, *The Waning of the Middle Ages: A Study of The Forms of Life, Thought and Art in France and the Netherlands in the XIVth and XVth Centuries* (New York, 1954), pp. 119–20, 270–73; Frederic de Portal, *Des Couleurs Symboliques dans l'Antiquité, le Moyen Age et Les Temps Modernes* (Paris, 1857).

[49] de Bruyne, Vol. I, Bk. II, ch. 5; Vol. II, Bk. III, ch. 3.

beautiful form in order to tempt man to sin. In the nineteenth century, the Romantics' discovery of the *femme fatàle*, 'an archetype which united in itself all forms of seduction, all vices, and all delights',[50] gave the beautiful woman an alternative meaning which artists like D.G. Rossetti, J.M. Waterhouse, Edward Burne-Jones, Frederich Sandys, and Aubrey Beardsley sometimes exploited.

One of the most remarkable aspects of Arthurian art is that its range of images remained so limited and consistent through more than eight centuries. Castles and forests, kings and queens, knights and ladies, horses and ships, arms and armour comprise the Arthurian world and with surprisingly few exceptions the material is treated idealistically. Eric Gill has commented that the work of the twentieth century artist, David Jones, combines his two enthusiasms, 'that of a man who is enamoured of the spiritual world and at the same time as much enamoured of the material body in which he must clothe his vision'.[51] Gill may have put his finger on the reason for the Arthurian legends' persistent appeal to artists.

---

[50] Mario Praz, *The Romantic Agony*, trans. Angus Davidson (London, 1933), pp. 209–10.
[51] Eric Gill, *Last Essays* (London, 1942), p. 150.

CHAPTER TWO

'Pluiseurs belles ystores':
Illuminated Arthurian Manuscripts to 1340

Legends about King Arthur and his knights were already circulating widely by the end of the twelfth century, through oral transmission and portable manuscripts. In the *Otia Imperialia* (ca. 1211) Gervase of Tilbury recorded a curious story that he had heard while visiting Sicily around 1190: when the Bishop of Catania's groom followed a horse into Mount Etna, he found King Arthur lying on a palace bed. Between 1174 and 1179 Alanus de Insulis asserted in his *Prophetia Anglicana Merlini Ambrosii Britanni* that Arthur was as well known in Asia as in Britain, according to pilgrims returning from the Holy Land: 'Egypt speaks of him, and the Bosphorus is not silent. Rome, the queen of cities, sings of his deeds, and his wars are not unknown to her former rival Carthage'.[1] Is this claim due to hyperbole, to Geoffrey's characterisation of Arthur as inheritor of the Roman empire, or to authentic reporting? Arthurian manuscripts were also circulating. Ulrich von Zatzikhoven's *Lanzelet* (1194–1205) was based, said its Swiss author, on a romance brought to Austria by one Hugh de Moreville, a hostage who stood surety for the captured Richard I. Hugh evidently eased his imprisonment by reading French manuscripts, as Sir Thomas Malory did more than three hundred years later.

When we think of medieval book manufacturing – the word means 'made by hand' – we imagine a solitary, anonymous monk seated at a desk with a quill pen in one hand and a penknife in the other. He would be responsible for cleaning, stretching and cutting the parchment, pricking and ruling the lines, copying the text and providing the decoration. By the twelfth century he aspired to recognition. In an Anglo-Norman commentary on *Isaiah* written about 1100 (Oxford, Bodleian 717, f. 287ᵛ) the illuminator not only shows himself at work but also identifies himself as Hugo the painter, adding, 'Imago pictoris et illuminatoris huius operis'. A twelfth century German manuscript (*Sigmaringen*, Hohenzollern Library 9, f. 244) depicts a monk seated on a stool, his habit girded up and his feet enclosed in warm boots. Four pots of paint are set on a pedestal table while a second table holds his penknife and bowl. Grasping in his left hand a ruler and a

---

[1] Alanus de Insulis, *Prophetia Anglicana* (Frankfurt, 1608) p. 26 quoted by R.S. Loomis and L.H. Loomis, *Arthurian Legends in Medieval Art* (London, 1938), p. 8; hereafter referred to as ALMA.

dish of paint, he uses the brush in his right hand to finish a historiated initial R within which he and his workplace are enclosed. His name, so he tells us, is Brother Rufillus.[2] This kind of witty individuality was possible when the scribe or illuminator produced books for his own monastic community.

In the twelfth century new genres of vernacular literature and greater literacy increased the demands for books that could be used outside the monastery. Book production shifted from monks to lay craftsmen who might be travelling artisans or members of city workshops.[3] Paris was the natural centre for lay ateliers, being the site of a culture-conscious court and a large university.[4] The work of manu-script production was now divided among a number of specialists – parchmen-ters, ink-makers, scribes, rubricators, illuminators, bookbinders – all classified as 'manual artificers', along with bakers and metal workers.[5] The Paris tax list for 1292 indicates that at least one of the inkmakers was a woman and one of the scribes was called Denise.[6]

The monastery was not entirely closed to secular works. In 1372 a Cistercian monk from Amelungsborn in Germany, Jan von Brunswik (whose self-portrait appears on the last page), copied the Arthurian romance *Wigalois* (Leiden, Bibl. Ryks-Universiteit 537), illustrating it with forty-seven brilliantly coloured mini-atures. Romances and secular chronicles containing Arthurian material were found in monastic libraries.[7] As early as 1248 Glastonbury Abbey had four roman-ces and in 1315 Guy de Beauchamp bequeathed romances to Bordsley Abbey including a *Lancelot*, a *Joseph of Aramathea* and a '*Seint Grael*', a *Brut* and a *Mort Artu*. By the fourteenth and fifteenth centuries monks may have been copying and selling manuscripts to raise money. That arch-Protestant Roger Ascham, tutor of Henry VIII's son, when complaining about the evil effects of chivalric literature

---

[2]   See Andrew Martindale, 'The Changing Status of the Craftsman' in Joan Evans, ed., *The Flowering of the Middle Ages* (London, 1966), pp. 281–314. The miniatures are reproduced pp. 296 and 303.

[3]   A page in Florus' *Commentary on Saint Paul's Epistles*, Paris, Bibliothèque Nationale, Latin 11575 f. 1, reproduced in J.J.G. Alexander, *The Decorated Letter* (London, 1978), plate 24, shows a transitional stage where lay professionals were doing some of the work in monastic scriptoria. The semicircle, part of the initial P, holds a portrait of the monk-scribe who signs himself Johannes Monoculus – one-eyed John – and indicates that he wrote the manuscript in 1163–64. On the initial's stem a roundel contains the illuminator, dressed in the blue robe and red cloak of a layman.

[4]   See Robert Branner, *Manuscript Painting in Paris during the reign of Saint Louis: A Study of Styles* (Berkeley, Los Angeles and London, 1977).

[5]   Andrew Martindale, *The Rise of the Artist in the Middle Ages and Early Renaissance* (New York, 1972), p. 12 cites Jean de Jandun's *Tractus* in praise of Paris (1323) to establish the artist's social position.

[6]   Margaret Alison Stones, *The Illustration of the French Prose Lancelot in Flanders, Belgium and Paris 1250–1340*, 2 vols., unpublished doctoral dissertation presented to The University of London, 1970, p. 50. This chapter is greatly indebted to Dr Stones' research.

[7]   See M.R. James, *Lists of Manuscripts formerly in Peterborough Abbey Library* (Oxford, 1926); N.R. Ker, *Medieval Libraries of Great Britain: A List of Surviving Books*, 2nd ed. (London, 1964); Ernest A. Savage, *Old English Libraries: the Making, Collecting and Use of Books During the Middle Ages* (Detroit, 1968 [1912]).

like Malory's *Morte Darthur* asserted, 'These bokes (as I have heard say) were made the moste parte in Abbayes and Monasteries a very lickely and fit fruite of suche an ydle and blynde kinde of lyvyne'.[8]

Nevertheless, from the thirteenth century book production and book owner-ship were predominantly in the hands of the laity. The five great secular subjects which engaged the ateliers, in addition to religious books, were the legends of Troy, the *Chanson de Roland*, the romances of King Alexander, the *Roman de la Rose*, and the Arthurian material.[9] The monk had had to start from scratch, as it were, scraping the hair from an animal skin, making his own ink, grinding his colours, and polishing the golden backgrounds with the tooth of a boar, bear or beaver.[10] The master of an atelier could buy his parchment pages, ink and gold leaf though the painter might still get his own natural colours. *Il Libro dell' Arte*, a craftsman's handbook which Cennino d'Andrea Cennini wrote about 1400, vividly describes the operation of a medieval workshop. At one point Cennino tells of ac-companying his father to a little valley, a very wild steep place where a scrape of the shovel revealed seams of ocher, dark and light sinoper, blue and white and black, the lines showing up in the earth like wrinkles on a human face:

> I picked out the 'wrinkle' of this color with a penknife; and I do assure
> you that I never tried a handsomer, more perfect ocher color. It did not
> come out so light as giallorino; a little darker; but for hair, and for
> costumes, as I shall teach you later, I never found a better color than
> this.[11]

Not all colours could be acquired so easily. Precious lapis lazuli used for pin-nacled roofs and royal robes could be found only in Afghanistan.

So far as layout was concerned craftsmen did not distinguish between religious

---

[8] Roger Ascham, 'Toxophilus' in *English Works*, ed. W.W. Wright (Cambridge, 1970 [1904]), p. xv.
[9] Iconographical studies of the non-Arthurian secular works include R. Lejeune and J. Stiennon, *La Légende de Roland dans l'art du moyen âge* (Brussels, 1966); D.J.A. Ross, *Alexander Historiatus*, Warburg Institute Surveys, I (London, 1963) and *Illustrated Medieval Alexander-Books in Germany and the Netherlands* (London, 1971); Hugo Buchthal, *Historia Troiana: Studies in the History of Mediaeval Secular Illustration* (London and Leiden, 1971); M.R. Scherer, *The Legends of Troy in Art and Literature* (New York and London, 1964) and F. Saxl, *The Troy Romance in French and Italian Art* (London, 1951); A. Kuhn, *Die Illustration des Rosenromans* (Freiburg and Breisgau, 1911) and J.V. Fleming, *The Roman de la Rose: A Study in Allegory and Iconography* (Princeton, 1969). See also M. Alison Stones, 'Secular Manuscript Illumination in France' in Christopher Kleinhenz, *Medieval Manuscripts and Textual Criticism*, North Carolina Studies in the Romance Languages and Literatures 4 (Chapel Hill, N.C., 1976), pp. 83–102, and 'Notes on Three Illuminated Alexander Manuscripts' in *The Medieval Alexander Legend and Romance Epic: Essays in Honour of David J.A. Ross*, ed. Peter Noble, et al. (New York and London, 1982), pp. 193–241.
[10] See Theophilus, 'An Essay upon Various Arts' in E.S. Holt, *A Documentary History of Art, vol. 1, The Middle Ages and Renaissance* (Princeton, 1957), p. 3.
[11] Daniel V. Thompson, Jr. trans., *The Craftsman's Handbook, 'Il Libro dell' Arte' Cennino d'Andrea Cennini* (New York, 1960 [1933]), p. 27.

and secular works; the patterns of the former were transmitted to the latter. One of the most important embellishments for bibles and psalters was the decorated letter which indicated a division in the text. Its depictions of combat, feasting, hunting, of enthroned kings and admonitory prophets became romance models. Fifty-seven historiated initials decorate what may be the earliest illustrated *Prose Lancelot*[12] manuscript, Rennes 255 (ca. 1220), consisting of an *Estoire*, *Merlin* and *Lancelot*. Alison Stones associates it with a workshop which operated in Paris in the second or third decades of the thirteenth century and specialised in psalters and moralized bibles.[13] Some subjects have been taken directly from religious sources; e.g. *Estoire*, f. 1, initial C showing Christ's appearance to a hermit; *Merlin*, f. 101, initial M showing the Harrowing of Hell; and *Estoire*, f. 9, initial A with the Annunciation. The commonest initial is O which occurs forty-four times. The frame of circle set in square doubly isolates illustration from text and emphasises its iconic quality. Through reference to the text the subject of an initial showing an armed knight on horseback (f. 197) may be identified narratively as 'Lancelot, damsel, and squire (left) ride along and meet a man who tells them that the Queen is at Camelot'.[14] The image also has a symbolic meaning independent of a specific textual passage; it represents knight-errantry with its attendant associations of forest adventure, service of ladies, and the acquisition of what Malory calls 'worship' – honour and fame.

The roundel is a controlling shape into which figures must be fitted. The result can be a sense of frantic movement and temporal progression as when the stag that Lancelot or Arthur is hunting runs up the oval on the right side (cf. Oxford, Bodleian, Rawlinson Q.b.6, f. 28[v] and London, British Library, Additional 38117, f. 193[v]). The artist of Douai, Bibliothèque Municipale, 880, a late twelfth century manuscript of Geoffrey of Monmouth's *Historia Regum Britanniae*, uses the historicated initial, f. 66[v], narratively and emotively. While King Arthur fits comfortably into the O, only the tip of his sword protruding, the Giant of Mont Saint Michel is cramped into too small a space, his feet and his huge club hanging outside the frame. The narrative requires that Arthur decapitate his enemy, an impossible act

---

[12] Manuscripts of *Lancelot Cycle* texts are listed in B. Woledge, *Bibliographie des romans et contes en prose française* (Paris and Geneva, 1954), Supplément (Geneva, 1975). For the complete text see H. Oskar Sommer, ed., *The Vulgate Version of the Arthurian Romances*, 8 vols. (Washington, 1908–1916) and Alexandre Micha, ed., *Lancelot: roman en prose du XIIIe siècle*, 7 vols. (Geneva, 1978–80). Editions of individual texts include Elspeth Kennedy, ed., *Lancelot de Lac, the non-cyclic Old French Prose Romance*, 2 vols. (Oxford, 1980); Albert Pauphilet, ed., *La Queste del Saint Graal* (Paris, 1949); Jean Frappier, ed., *La Mort le Roi Artu* (Geneva, 1954); M.D. Legge, *Le Roman de Balain* (Manchester, 1942); H. Oskar Sommer, ed., *Le Roman de Merlin or The Early History of King Arthur* (London, 1894). Modern translations include Alexandre Micha, ed. and trans., *Lancelot, Roman du XIIIe siècle*, 2 vols. (Paris, 1983); P.M. Matarasso, trans., *The Quest of the Holy Grail* (Harmondsworth, 1969); James Cable, trans., *The Death of King Arthur* (Harmondsworth, 1971).
[13] 'The Earliest Illustrated Prose Lancelot Manuscript', in *Reading Medieval Studies*, III (1977), 3–44. Appendix C lists all thirteenth century Prose *Lancelot* manuscripts, indicating those that have illustrations. Footnote 2 lists all available editions of the *Vulgate Cycle* to 1977.
[14] Sommer III, 201; reference Stones, Appendix B.

as long as the giant is standing. By taking advantage of the roundel, the illuminator shows the characters' relative sizes, effects the climactic action, and invites the spectator to laugh at the giant's ridiculous position.

Like the roundel, the quatrefoil is a shape paralleled in the stained glass of Gothic cathedrals such as Bourges, Chartres and Châlons-sur-Marne.[15] Splendid examples occur in Paris, Bibliothèque Nationale, fr. 2186, *Roman de la Poire* ca. 1260, a North French manuscript with two of the earliest illustrations of famous Arthurian lovers – Cligès and Fénice (f. 3ᵛ) and Tristan and Ysolt (f. 5ᵛ).[16] Rather than being part of the text, the two golden quatrefoils devoted to each pair are set in the centre of a heavily framed page against a chequered background. In f. 3ᵛ smaller quatrefoils, two with stylised eagles, are inset, following a pattern found in thirteenth century stained glass windows and in *bibles moralisées*. The predominant deep blue and red of the lovers' costumes as they sit together on a bench and the jade green bed where Fénice lies insensible are also analogous to glass designs. In f. 5ᵛ Tristan and Ysolt, too, are seated above on a bench. Below they sleep upright in the grotto, separated by a sword, while a mounted King Mark prepares to leave his glove in the aperture which allows a thick golden ray from a sun drawn outside the quatrefoil to fall on the Queen's face. The blue horse, ruby cave, green trees and orange gown reproduce the glass-maker's colours. Perhaps not accidentally Ysolt's costume exactly duplicates the Goddess Fortuna's (f. 2ᵛ). The painted folios in fr. 2186 illustrate the new style of manuscript painting established by the end of the twelfth century. As Erwin Panofsky describes it:

> Instead of breezy, frameless pen drawings we have opaquely pigmented miniatures surrounded by a strong, flat border whose function is to delimit the working area, and not to frame a 'view'. The figures are reduced in number but enlarged in scale, more substantial in appearance and more composed in behaviour.[17]

An effect of spatial depth is replaced by 'inexorable' linearity as figures are pushed to the front of the plane by the *fonds d'or* and the painted backgrounds patterned with rinceaux, tessellation and diapering.

A common layout in Arthurian manuscripts before 1340 is one which places a framed square or rectangular miniature at intervals in one or two columns of text. A group of manuscripts produced in Northern France and Flanders in the late thirteenth and early fourteenth century – Bonn, Universitätsbibl., 526, *Lancelot Cycle*, 1286; London, British Library, Additional 10292–4, *Lancelot Cycle* and Royal 14E III, *Estoire, Queste, Mort Artu*, ca. 1316–30; and Manchester, John Rylands University Library, fr. 1, 2, *Vulgate Cycle*, ca. 1315–25, – features miniatures one

---

[15] Elisabeth von Witzleben's *French Stained Glass* (London, 1968) provides bases for establishing the inter-relationship of manuscript illuminations and stained glass.
[16] Loomis, ALMA, pp. 89–90 and fig. 202, 203. He notes the similarity between the decorative plan and that of a French Bible Moralisée ca. 1260.
[17] Erwin Panofsky, *Early Netherlandish Painting*, I, pp. 13–14. See also Eric Millar, *The Parisian Miniaturist Honoré* (London, 1959).

column wide framed with blue and red bands squared at the corners and decorated with white 'twisted thread' motifs. A stylish Parisian manuscript, Paris,
Bibliothèque Nationale, fr. 95, *Estoire* and *Merlin*, and New Haven, Yale University
Library, 229, *Agravain, Queste, Mort Artu*, ca. 1300–20, with two columns of text,
often presents double miniatures, one scene placed above the other. The illustrator
of the splendid manuscript New York, Pierpont Morgan Library, 805, *Lancelot
Proper*, ca. 1315, creates a more spectacular effect by extending the thirty-nine
large miniatures across three columns of text.[18] They are usually divided in two, a
gold leaf background appearing in one half and a chequered background in rose
or deep blue in the other. Two temporally consecutive scenes are paired except for
crucially dramatic episodes which are permitted to occupy the full width; e.g.
Lancelot's cart-ride to King Baudemagus' castle (f. 158), his raising of the tomb lid
(f. 161ᵛ) and the crossing of the sword bridge (f. 166). The generous layout found
in the Morgan *Lancelot* had been anticipated as early as 1274, the date of Paris,
Bibliothèque Nationale, fr. 342, *Lancelot, Queste, Mort Artu* where ninety-five *fond
d'or* miniatures run across two columns of text. Occasionally, as in f. 150, the
miniature is two-tiered. In addition to the heavy borders with their floral patterning, another kind of enclosure is provided by setting the figures between a castle
or monastery on one side and a forest on the other.

German ateliers like that of Meister Hesse in Strassburg favoured full page
illuminations with three or four panels in tiers, a format popular in Carolingian
Bibles. Munich, Bayerische Staatsbibl., cgm 19, Wolfram von Eschenbach's *Parzival, Titurel, Tagelieder*, ca. 1230, and cgm 51, Gottfried von Strassburg's *Tristan*, use
this arrangement. The result is a sense of narrative continuity, a comic strip effect.
However, the arrangement causes a decisive separation of illustration and text.

A distinguishing feature of Gothic manuscripts is the outer border which not
only frames text, decorated initials, and miniatures but is integrated with them
through leafy arabesques and pinnacles rising from the picture frame.[19] Parisian
workshops used stylised ivy and sycamore leaves; Northern French ateliers developed the rounded trefoil with golden balls. The foliation growing along the
margin might be used on the bottom of the page as the ground line for independent scenes. In BL Royal 20 D IV, *Lancelot*, ca. 1300, for example, a second
series of illustrations appears as bas-de-page scenes painted on the natural parchment background. A tension develops between the miniature – serious, controlled, conventional – and the marginalia which are realistic or fantastic,
free-wheeling, comic, satiric and even vulgar. A common stance is the 'world

---

[18] There are also one hundred and thirty-six historiated initials. Richard Barber, *King
Arthur, Hero and Legend* (Woodbridge, 1986) reproduces fifteen miniatures in colour, plates
I–XV. Chapter VII of Loomis is devoted to French Manuscripts, 1256–1340, pp. 89–102.
[19] Lilian M.C. Randall, *Images in the Margins of Gothic Manuscripts* (Berkeley and Los
Angeles, 1966) includes the following Arthurian MSS: Yale and BN fr. 95; Rylands fr. 1, 2; BL
Royal 20 D iv; BL 10292–4; Paris, Arsenal 5218; Oxford, Bodleian Ashmole 828, BN fr. 776
and Vienna, Osterreichische Nationalbibliothek Codex 2542. See also Lucia N. Valentine,
Ornament in Medieval MSS; A Glossary (London, 1965).

upside down' where rabbits and apes[20] replace men. In BL 20 D IV f. 260 a monkey with a whip makes a man, tied by a long rope, do tricks. The illustrator of BN fr. 95 reveals a lively imagination by showing a woman being removed in a wheelbarrow, a shrew in a gold dress and snood, with a three-thonged whip in one hand and reins in the other riding a bearded man (Aristotle and Phyllis), an archer aiming his crossbow at a bird perching on the tip of a decorative vine, gowned centaurs jousting with lances and shields, and a one-horned man, attacked from the rear by a centaur-archer and from the front by a stork pecking at his eye. Birds are an obvious image in the leafy margins but they must share the space, as in Rylands, fr. 2, f. 212, with passionate lovers, a nun suckling an ape, archers, and an ape in cloak and peaked cap pruning a trefoil leaf from a dangling border branch.

In the monastic scriptorium where the scribe created the illustrations, a knowledge of what the words said informed the visual conception. But the workshop's division of labour meant that several scribes, rubricators, painters of capitals and borders, and miniaturists would be involved in producing a particular manuscript.[21] Timothy A. Shonk's study of the Auchinleck Manuscript (ca. 1330), an English anthology of religious and secular materials that shows a preference for romance, concluded that six independent scribes under the supervision of one major scribe were involved.[22] The scribes showed their awareness of planned decoration by designating the positions of the rubricator's paraphs, the large capitals, and the miniatures. The master attempted to provide a bridge between text and decoration by drawing sketches and writing directions, as in Add. 10292–4, Morgan 805, and Bonn 526. The master of Rylands fr. 1, 2, directed the artist to paint the hero's shield white when depicting the mad Lancelot of f. 172^{v}.[23]

To speed production workshops used model or pattern books.[24] Many models originally devised for religious works could be adapted to Arthurian romance. The Last Supper served for King Arthur's feast, a fact that accounts for the Round Table's depiction in rectangular form.[25] Arthur and Guenevere replaced Christ and John at the centre of the table facing the viewer while Judas, who convention-

[20] On the iconography of apes see H.W. Janson, *Apes and Ape Lore in the Middle Ages and Renaissance*, Studies of the Warburg Institute, vol. 20 (London, 1952).

[21] Paris, Ars. 5218, *Quest del Saint Graal*, Tournai, 1351, is exceptional in having been written, illuminated and bound by one man, Pierart dou Tielt, as indicated in a colophon.

[22] Timothy A. Shonk, 'A Study of the Auchinleck Manuscript: Bookmen and Bookmaking in the Early Fourteenth Century', *Speculum*, 60/1 (1985), 71–91.

[23] C.E. Pickford, 'An Arthurian Manuscript in the John Rylands Library', *Bulletin of the John Rylands Library*, XXXI (1948), 318–344.

[24] On medieval model books see R. Scheller, *A Survey of Medieval Model Books* (Haarlem, 1963); *The Guttingen Model Book*, a facsimile edition and translation of a fifteenth century illuminator's manual, edited with commentary by Hellmut Lehmann-Haupt (Columbia, Miss., 1972); M. Alison Stones, 'Sacred and Profane Art: Secular and Liturgical Book-Illumination in the Thirteenth Century' in *The Epic in Medieval Society: Aesthetic and Moral Values*, ed. Harald Scholler (Tübingen, 1977), pp. 100–112.

[25] For a discussion of Round Table iconography see Emmanuèle Baumgartner, 'La couronne et le cercle: Arthur et la Table Ronde dans les manuscrits du Lancelot-Graal', *Texte et Image*, *Actes du Colloque international de Chantilly* (Paris, 1984), 191–200. BN fr. 343, an Italian

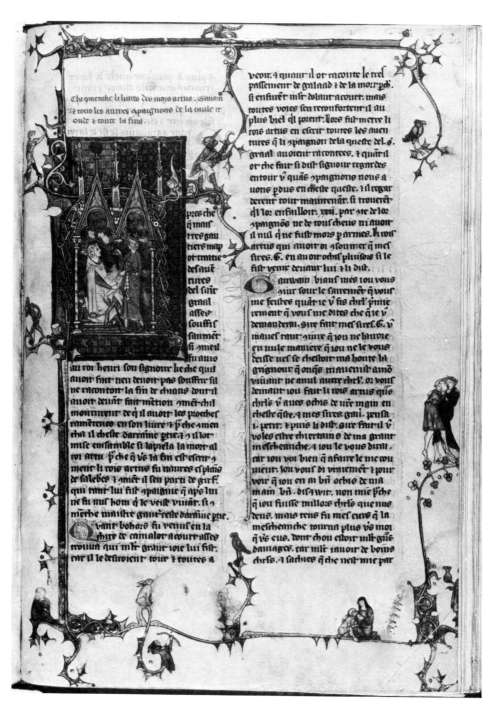

5. Manuscript page decorated in early Gothic style. Rylands fr. 2, f. 212 (*Vulgate Prose Cycle*)

ally appeared on the opposite side of the table facing towards Christ, became a server, a messenger or an importunate maiden asking a boon. The ruler's position could be adjusted to provide for story developments; for example, in BL Add. 38117, f. 84, Arthur and Guenevere sit at the end of the table left of centre to leave room for a wounded knight and his squire who enter on horseback. In Rylands fr. 1, 2, fol. 182ᵛ, the king and queen have a separate table on a dais with an arch above; the illuminator, lacking the technique for depicting a realistic castle hall where tables were set at right angles to the dais, places the guests further back on the picture plane with a different border.

That the Marriage at Cana might provide a feast model is suggested by comparing BL Royal 2 B. vii, f. 168ᵛ, *Queen Mary's Psalter*, English, ca. 1310–20, and BL Royal 14 E III, f. 89. In the religious scene a crowned woman and aureoled man, Mary and Christ, sit at the centre of a rectangular table, each flanked by a guest. In the secular scene Arthur and Guenevere, both crowned, replace Mary and Christ. Each table with its draped white cloth holds a wine flagon, roast fowl, fish, knives and trenchers. A kneeling figure in the foreground of Royal 2 B vii offering a goblet is paralleled in the Arthurian scene by a kneeling servant offering a basin and towel. Each has a musician playing a rebec and each is enclosed in a Gothic architectural frame.[26]

The iconographical source for Arthur's fight with the Giant of Mont Saint Michel was David's victory over Goliath. Since the Bible describes Goliath wearing armour, medieval artists depicted him as a large knight with the latest contemporary equipment (e.g. BN lat. 1023 f. 7).[27] Arthurian illustrators slavishly followed this model (cf. Brussels, Bibl. Royale, 9243, f. 49; BL Add. 10292, f. 205ᵛ; London, Lambeth Palace Library, 6, f. 62) except for the artist of BL Egerton 3028, *Chronique d'Angleterre*, ca. 1350. He is evidently familiar with Wace's text for he has carefully drawn the spitted hog broiling over the fire and the slavering giant with matted hair and beard and grotesque facial features. Rabbits looking curiously from their holes or scurrying into them are a characteristically English touch.[28]

The use of patterns is most evident in scenes of combat where the same form can be used for biblical illustrations of *Kings* I and II, for illustrated manuscripts of Prudentius' *Psychomachia* and for the secular literatures about Roland, Alexander, Trojan heroes and King Arthur. Generally the composition is axial, the mounted knights on the left being mirror images of those on the right. The repeated

manuscript of the *Queste*, ca. 1380–1400, is the first to represent Arthur seated at a round table.

[26] The *British Museum Catalogue of Royal MSS*, II, 140 suggests that the illuminations of Royal 14 E III are 'perhaps of English rather than French origin'. Janet Backhouse, *The Illuminated Manuscript* (Oxford, 1979) reproduces the Queen Mary Psalter miniature in colour, p. 47. The Arthurian feast is used to illustrate Michael Senior, *Sir Thomas Malory's Tales of King Arthur* (London, 1980), p. 146.

[27] See Louis Réau, *Iconographie de L'Art Chrétien*, 3 vols. (Paris, 1956), II, pp. 256–262 on the iconography of David and Goliath.

[28] Cf. English *Apocalypse* MSS such as BL Royal 19 B. XV f. 2ᵛ, ca. 1320–30.

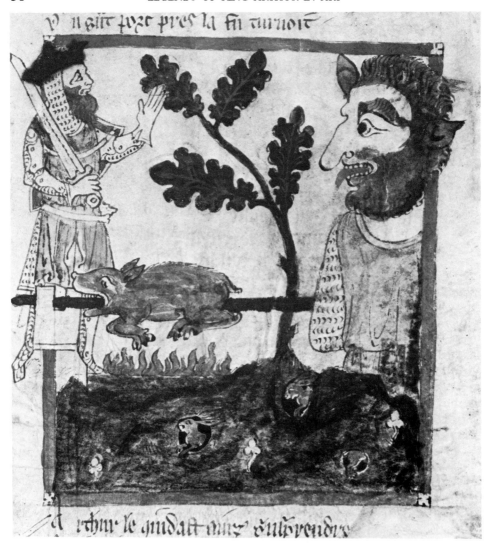

6. King Arthur and the Giant of St Michael's Mount. BL Egerton 3028, f. 49 (*Chronique d'Angleterre*)

rhythms of helmets, lances, and pennons, of horses' heads and legs in carefully crafted manuscripts like BN fr. 95 and BL Add. 10292–4 produce the pleasure of recurrence. In less accomplished poorer manuscripts where the pattern book is too often substituted for textual realization we share Hugo Buchthal's censure of anonymous battle scenes 'repeated quite schematically . . . with exasperating regularity and little individuality or variation'.[29]

---

[29]   Hugo Buchthal, *op. cit.*, p. 17.

Moduli may also provide incidental indicators of a courtly milieu – canopied beds with curtains tied up, sideboards, cushioned benches, elevated thrones. In an elegant miniature, BN fr. 95, f. 291, which shows King Arthur and King Ban discussing a tournament, Guenevere holds a lap dog, an attendant lord feeds a falcon which perches on his gloved left hand and another lord casually dangles a glove. Such details, which may not even be mentioned in the text, are drawn from a storehouse of appropriate motifs. A characteristic which differentiates the better manuscripts from run-of-the-mill productions is the ability to realize significant aspects of plot and to create a sense of specific time and place. Lacking historical perspective, artists did not attempt to place King Arthur and his knights in the sixth-century world which the pseudo-history specified. Arthurian time was their own time; dress, armour, architecture were contemporary. It did not seem incongruous that the stone masons in BL Add. 10292 f. 55^v should carve the date 1316 on the tomb of Nabor and le sire de Karabel (a detail which enables us to date the manuscript) or that 1225 should appear on the stone from which Arthur draws the sword (BL Add. 10292 f. 99). Arthur and his men attack Lancelot's castle with an up-to-date siege machine, a mangonel (BL Add. 10294 f. 81^v and Rylands fr. 1, 2, f. 240^v). Details of this sort delight the modern viewer.

In the early period of Arthurian illustration, pictorial manuscripts of Geoffrey's *Historia Regum Britanniae* and of the chronicle material derived from it are rare. The Douai *Historia*, 880 ca. 1300 has a unique historiated initial on f. 66^v showing Arthur decapitating the Giant of Saint-Michel. A British Library manuscript of Geoffrey's *Prophecies of Merlin*, Cotton Claudius B VII ff. 223^v–34^v, ca. 1250, has on f. 224 a large drawing, tinted brown, green, and grey-blue in which a youthful Merlin reads prophecies written on a long scroll to the enthroned King Vortigern. Both are placed under Early English arches, decorated with trefoils. A striped Corinthian pillar separates them. Beneath the floor, three semicircles show on either side of a pool the two dragons that bring down the king's tower.[30]

The *Flores Historiarum* of Matthew of Westminster, Rylands Chetham 6712, a chronicle written at St Albans from 1250 to 1265, then continued at Westminster until 1326, contains a series of ten coronation portraits, all but one painted at St Albans. A young beardless King Arthur with curly hair is seated on a cushioned chair. His right hand holds the sceptre with three-foiled head while the left touches the clasp on his mantle. Two bishops place the crown, a circlet of fleur-de-lis, on his head (f. 185), as clerics watch.[31] Meyer Schapiro suggests that such a use of frontality, symmetry and central place is a feature of ritual, 'a domain of the real

---

[30] This miniature is reproduced in Nigel Morgan, *Early Gothic Manuscripts* I, 1190–1250 (London and New York, 1982) and in Nikolai Tolstoy, *The Quest for Merlin* (London, 1985), ill. 8 and cover.

[31] See Albert Hollaender's description and reproduction in 'The Pictorial Work in the "Flores Historiarum" of the so-called Matthew of Westminster (Chetham 6712)', *Bulletin of the John Rylands Library*, 28 (1944), 361–381 and *Medieval and Early Renaissance Treasure in the North West*, Exhibition Catalogue, Whitworth Art Gallery (Manchester, 1971), #13.

in which every detail is a sign'. This posture, which characterises representations of Arthur in romance manuscripts, indicates nobility, virtue, and high position.[32]

Arthur with his ancestors and descendants appears in genealogical rolls such as Oxford, Bodley Rolls 3, ca. 1280, a genealogical history from Brutus to Edward I, containing twenty medallions of the Trojan War and two hundred and twenty regal portraits. Arthur appears in Row 12, preceded by Constantinus, Constans, Vortigernus, Aurelius, Ambrosius, and Uter Pendragon and followed by Constantius, Aurelius, and Vortiporsus.

One illustrated manuscript of Peter Langtoft's *Chronicle of England* survives, BL Royal 20 A II, ca. 1307–27, decorated with tinted drawings that Loomis suggests may have been copied from murals.[33] In the picture of Arthur, f. 4, with the Virgin and child on his shield and at his feet the thirty crowns signifying his territories, the colour produces a sense of liveliness: gold crown, red surcoat, green côte, and red shield with a green-gowned Virgin elevated by her golden crown and blue halo so that she barely fits into the space. The illuminator's lack of historical perspective is evident in f. 2 where Brutus and Imogen, who in Geoffrey's text lived eleven centuries before Christ,[34] are wearing thirteenth century dress. With her crown and wimple, red gown, green-lined blue robe and cradled lapdog, this queen could be Guenevere. In the lower picture, Cambere, Locrin, and Albama, the first ruler's three sons, are medieval knights in chain mail. A vivid representation of Merlin, holding a prophetic scroll as he converses with Uther (wearing a smart ermine collar on his surcoat and delicately pointing his left foot), shows the magician as a bearded man with a youthful face. A dubious Igraine looks over a battlemented tower.

BL Egerton 3028, *Chronique d'Angleterre*, mid-fourteenth century, is an abridged version of Wace's *Brut* to which the scribe has added a continuation of English history to 1338, when the Hundred Years War began. The generous pictorial programme provides a half-page squared miniature on most folios, with those of the Arthurian period running from f. 24 to f. 53. Though the colours are muddy and the drawing crude, the artist convincingly conveys a sense of evil: tricky Hengist, snub-nosed and bony-kneed, preparing to kill the bull (f. 19); red-bearded Vortigern, with a villain's arched eyebrows, interrogating Merlin's mother, a slender, long-legged nun (f. 24); the suspicious, unfriendly bishops and nobles who attend Arthur's coronation (f. 37); the Roman ambassadors whose sneers belie the olive branch's message (f. 43); the heavy-browed, hairy-eared, lolling-tongued Giant of Saint-Michel; and purple-bearded Mordred smugly dealing Arthur a mortal wound (f. 53). Blazoned shields abound but with little regard for accuracy, Emperor Lucius' golden double-eagle being exceptional. Arthur is assigned the Plantagenets' Royal Arms, *gules, three leopards or*.

BL Additional 11619 contains an unusual sequence of illustrations in a setting

---

[32] Meyer Schapiro, *Words and Pictures: On the Literal and the Symbolic in the Illustration of a Text* (The Hague and Paris, 1973), pp. 37, 43.

[33] Loomis, ALMA, p. 138.

[34] See the time chart in Geoffrey of Monmouth, *The History of the Kings of Britain*, trans. Lewis Thorpe (Harmondsworth, 1966), pp. 285–288.

that has nothing to do with eponymous history or romance.[35] The manuscript (ca. 1300) is a Latin anthology of moral and religious texts – sermons, a legend of St Gregory, Adso's treatise on the Antichrist, Aesop's fables *et al.* But ff. 6–9[v] contain seven tinted drawings in the usual thirteenth century colours – red, yellow, green, blue, and brown – depicting scenes from the romance of Tristan and Isolde. Originally intended, no doubt, to illustrate Thomas' *Tristan* (which may have been written at Henry II's court about 1175) or even the Middle English *Sir Tristrem* (ca. 1300),[36] the cut down leaves were inserted into this monastic compilation. The subjects are not arranged in chronological order. The first scene (f. 6) shows Tristan, in a traveller's hooded green surcoat, addressing King Mark who is depicted in the schematized three-quarter face position denoting a lower moral status than does a central, frontal posture.

The occasion may be the hero's return from Ireland (Hunt's suggestion). More likely, it represents his first appearance at Mark's court with his two pilgrim guides. The king, wearing a voluminous yellow mantle with a brown lining (fur?), asks, 'Where were you born? What hat tou, belamȝe?' to which the hero replies that he is the son of Sir Roland of Hermonie (*Sir Tristrem*, ll. 529–537). The reverse side is easily identified as the bath episode. Having gone in disguise to Ireland to seek the Princess Isolde as a wife for King Mark, Tristan is recognised as her uncle's killer because of the piece missing from his sword. On the right is the young Isolde (not Brengain, as Hunt thinks) in a green surcoat, her long loose hair, a sign of maidenhood, surmounted by a circlet. On the left is her mother wearing the married woman's barbette and veil. They hold upright between them the notched sword which the princess had drawn from its sheath. The situation is described in *Sir Tristrem*:

> Þe pece þou mizt her se
> Þat fro mi nem was drain.
> Luke þat it so be,
> Sett it cuen o gain.'
> As quik þai wald him sle
> Þer, tristrem, ful fain;
> Soþ þing,
> In baþ þai hadden him slain,
> No were it for þe king   (ll. 1587–1595)

The event which gives the hero the right to claim Isolde is his slaughter of the dragon. The mounted hero's attack with a spear is depicted in f. 7. The flat-topped helm, chain mail hauberk, saddle blanket, and most importantly the shield emblazoned with a lion rampant (green) resemble details in the Chertsey tiles (ca.

---

[35] The illustrations were first described by Tony Hunt, 'The Tristan Illustrations in MS London BL Add. 11619' in *Rewards and Punishments in the Arthurian Romance and Lyric Poetry of Medieval France*, ed. Peter V. Davies and Angus J. Kennedy (Cambridge, Eng., 1987), pp. 45–60.
[36] McNeill, George P., ed. *Sir Tristrem* (Edinburgh, 1886).

1260–80). 7^v shows Tristan slicing through the head of his father's killer, Duke Morgan. The next folio (f. 8) is an early representation of the Tryst beneath the Tree motif. Mark's entire figure, not just his head, is shown in a pear tree (suggested by the textual reference to an orchard), where he has hidden to spy on the lovers' rendezvous. Tristan and Isolde (in a blue gown and red mantle) stand innocently on either side of the tree, having been warned by the king's shadow. Between them is the dwarf Meriadok who in *Sir Tristrem* is not only Mark's spy but also the lovers' go-between. The next two incomplete pictures (ff. 8^v, 9) show sea-voyages, while in the final scene (f. 9^v), an unfinished sketch, the hero presents Isolde to her future husband. If this manuscript is of English provenance, as the inclusion of excerpts from Walter Map's *De nugis curialium* and the jest poem about the simple-mindedness of Norfolk people might suggest, it is the oldest extant set of English illuminations depicting scenes from Arthurian romance.

Despite their enormous influence on the development of Arthurian romance, Chrétien de Troyes' works, apparently, were not popular in illuminated form, judging by the few that have survived.[37] Of the two extant *Yvains*, Princeton University Library, Garrett 125, ca. 1295 is a little earlier than Paris, BN fr. 1433, ca. 1320.[38] Bound with 3000 lines of *Judas Machabée* and 1638 verses of Chrétien's *Lancelot* (*Le Chevalier de la Charrette*), the 6200 lines of the Princeton *Yvain* are decorated with several historiated initials, including one of Kay scolding Calogrenant (f. 40), and seven miniatures, strangely not in chronological order. This illuminator's chief subject is Yvain as a mounted knight-errant carrying a sword and a shield heraldically and sometimes anachronistically embossed *gules, a white lion rampant*. The hero successively attacks a serpent which bites the lion's tail (f. 37); the giant Harpin de la Montagne whom the lion munches from the rear (f. 58); three knights who have seized Lunete (f. 58^v); two demons equipped with spiked clubs of cornel wood wound with brass and round shields as mentioned in the text, ll. 5518–5529; and finally the unrecognized Gawain (f. 38). Stylised trees rising against the *fonds d'or* indicate forest settings. A tree is combined with a Gothic arch in f. 52 which depicts Yvain's marriage to Laudine. In composition, costuming, gesture, facial expression and hairstyle this miniature resembles BN fr. 95, f. 291 closely enough to suggest that they may have been influenced by the same model.

Whoever designed the fourteen pages of miniatures in BN fr. 1433 shows more interest in recreating a sense of Chrétien's gracious castle life. A hospitable red-gowned vavasour stands in the pink gateway of his machicolated castle to greet Yvain; beside him his daughter gathers up her voluminous blue skirt to reveal its

---

[37] On surviving Chrétien MSS see A. Micha, *La Tradition manuscrite des romans de Chrétien de Troyes* (Paris, 1939).

[38] See Robert L. McGrath, 'A Newly Discovered Illustrated Manuscript of Chrétien de Troyes' *Yvain* and *Lancelot* in the Princeton University Library', *Speculum*, 38 (1963), 583–594; Loomis, ALMA, pp. 100–102. On the dating and provenance of fr. 1433 see also J. Porcher, *Manuscrits à peintures en France du XIIIe au XVIe siècle* (Paris, 1955). The Princeton *Yvain* miniatures are reproduced in Norris J. Lacy, ed., *The Arthurian Encyclopedia* (New York and London, 1986), ill. 38–44 (black and white).

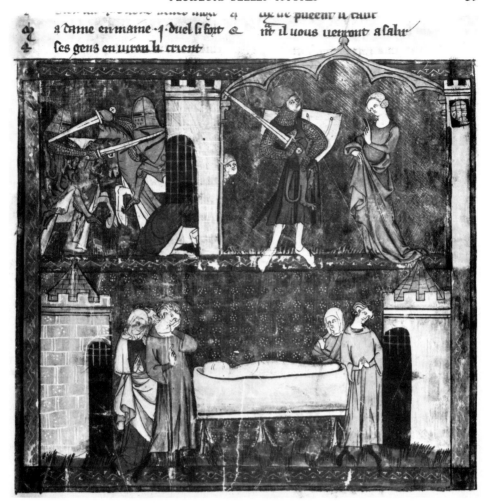

7. Above: Yvain kills Escalados, loses his horse under the portcullis, and encounters Lunete. Below: Laudine and Lunete mourn their dead lord.
BN 1433, f. 69ᵛ (Chrétien's *Yvain*)

red lining and a green cote (f. 67ᵛ). There is also more interest in the romance's magic. The fairy tale castle (f. 65) with its multicoloured towers and blue, gold, and pink roofs is set beside the marvellous forest fountain where Calogrenant (his blazon *or, an eagle noir*) holds up the golden dish that will produce the storm. A large tripartite miniature (f. 69ᵛ) shows Yvain's battle with Esclados beside the gateway where the descending portcullis has trapped the horse. A belligerent hero talks to Lunete as a soldier watches. Beside Esclados' coffin, resembling a pink bathtub, gesturing figures express sorrow (hand to cheek with head inclined) and prayer (clasped hands); f. 85 deals with the sufferings of a mad hero and distressed ladies whom he assists. Yvain can be identified by his shield, *azure, a lion or*, a colour scheme carried out in other costume details; his opponents usually wear red. In f. 90 the hero rescues Lunete from the merrily blazing fire while in f. 104 his adventures culminate in Gawain's recognition. The programme reaches a happy conclusion as Yvain and Laudine, reconciled at last, retire naked to bed, the omnipresent lion stretched out nearby (f. 118).

In both *Yvains* such isolated images as trees and round towers interposed between the frontally placed characters and the backgrounds suggest some degree of spatial depth. The range of colours – pink, grey, royal blue, red, light green and white –, the heavy outlines, nonfunctional drapery, expressive use of gesture, and the 'Gothic sway' stance all characterise the Picard style about 1300.

There is one surviving illustrated *Erec*, BN fr. 24403, ca. 1300–1325, with three mediocre miniatures, one of which shows the Hunt of the White Hart. There are seven manuscripts of *Perceval* (*Conte del Graal*) with narrative cycles: BN fr. 1453, BN fr. 12576, BN fr. 12577, Montpellier 249, Clermont 248, Berne 354 and Mons, Bibl. de l'Université, fonds ancien 331/206. The Mons *Cycle du Graal en vers*, ca. 1290–1310, which like the *Yvain's* was produced in Northern France or Hainaut, contains almost the entire corpus of the verse Perceval and its continuations.[39] It has one defaced miniature (f. 1) and several historiated letters of which the most interesting is f. 474. Here the wounded Hector in a hooded blue robe and Perceval in a rose robe raise their elongated hands in wonder as they see a red-haloed angel emerge from a heavenly cloud. In the right hand he holds precariously by the bottom rim a large goblet (the Grail) while the forefinger of his left hand points downwards. The patterned indigo background gives the effect of a starry sky.

An early fourteenth century *Conte del Graal*, BN fr. 12577 with one large and fifty-one small miniatures is the most extensively illustrated *Perceval*. Loomis notes that the illustrator is unfamiliar with the text, merely following suggestions in the rubrics.[40] As a result, a standard feast scene with a queen as well as a king represents the hall of the Grail Castle. The Grail is a ciborium surmounted by a cross rather than the dish which Chrétien specified. The bearer of the bleeding lance is, correctly, a boy; in Montpellier 249 a girl carries it. Rather than present the hero with iconographic consistency, the painter frequently shows him as a boy wearing the red hooded jacket and thonged leggings of a peasant; he carries a bow and arrows instead of chivalric weapons. The representation is appropriate in f. 1, a two-tiered miniature showing, above, Perceval's forest meeting with Arthur's knights and subsequent departure from home, as his mother swoons in the doorway; below, his reclamation of the stolen goblet after a successful joust with the Red Knight. The 'dümmlingkind' representation is inappropriate in f. 169, Perceval's meeting with his sister, a scene that occurs long after he has put on armour. This manuscript depicts two scenes particularly popular on ivories,

[39] W. Verbeke, J. Janssens, M. Smeyers, eds., *Arturus Rex, Vol. 1, Catalogus, Koning Artur en de Nederlanden* (Leuven, 1987), pp. 207–209.
[40] ALMA, p. 101.

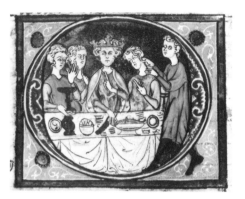

a. Arthur's feast

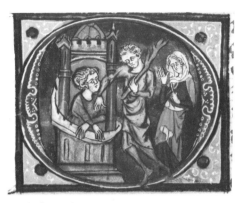

b. Lancelot in prison

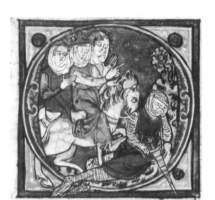

c. The queens find Lancelot
asleep under an apple tree

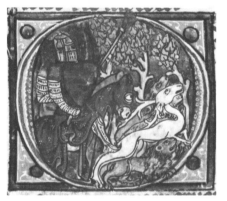

d. The mystical White Hart with four
lions (Christ and the Evangelists)

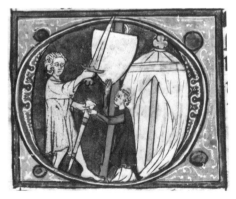

e. Lancelot's madness

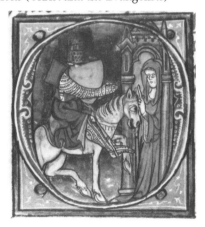

f. Lancelot arrives at a convent

8. Roundels illustrating the Lancelot Cycle. Bodl. Rawlinson Q.b.6, ff. 57, 149^v, 241, 274^v, 311^v, 323^v

Gawain's adventure in the Perilous Bed and his encounter with a lion at the Château Merveil (f. 45).

The most popular of all Arthurian texts with more than one hundred and eighty surviving manuscripts is the *Vulgate Prose Cycle* which consists of five romances arranged according to narrative chronology: *Estoire del Saint Graal, Estoire de Merlin, Lancelot en prose, Queste del Saint Graal, Mort (le roi) Artu*.[41] They were written between 1215 and 1235, soon after the Fourth Lateran Council had made transubstantiation an accepted Catholic doctrine. The cycle was probably the work of several authors under one director. Fernand Lot has proposed that this literary atelier was located in Champagne, a region that was also Chrétien's base.[42] Jean Frappier has suggested that the Cistercian colouring of *La Queste* may be explained by supposing 'that the author of that holy romance had attended the abbey school of Clairvaux, not far from Troyes'.[43] Certainly the region's new Gothic cathedrals at Reims, Troyes, Laon, Soissons and Châlons-sur-Marne used in their art and liturgy the symbolic patterns that the *Vulgate* authors incorporated into their texts and that the illustrators turned back into art.[44]

To deal with such an extensive text, workshops developed programmes (a short cycle and a long cycle) that could be used repeatedly. Even so, the work of producing a fine manuscript like Bonn, Universitätsbibl. 526 with 340 illustrations on 477 folios or BL Add. 10292–4 with a total of 657 miniatures on 695 folios, not to mention borders and rubrics, must have been enormous. The average reader can seldom appreciate the cumulative effect of successive miniatures, since manuscripts are inaccessible to the public and since no more than three or four facsimiles have been published. Nowadays authors and editors sometimes illustrate texts with manuscript reproductions.[45] However, as they choose only the best and most specific examples, a reader's impressions of a particular manuscript are inaccurate. Without seeing the entire programme, one will not realize that *Merlin* manuscripts consist largely of battle scenes and council scenes or that the master of Oxford, Bodleian Rawlinson Q.b.6, by frequently depicting the celebration of mass, emphasises the *Vulgate*'s religious orientation.

---

[41] Useful studies of the *Vulgate* texts are E. Jane Burns, *Arthurian Fictions: Re-reading the Vulgate Cycle* (Columbus, Ohio, 1985); Jean Frappier, *Etude sur La Mort Le Roi Artu* (Paris, 1961), 'Le Graal et La Chevalerie', *Romania*, LXXV (1954), 165–210, and 'The Vulgate Cycle', *Arthurian Literature in the Middle Ages*, ed. R.S. Loomis (London, 1959), pp. 295–318; F. Lot, *Etude sur le Lancelot en Prose* (Paris, 1918); A. Pauphilet, *Etudes sur la Queste del Saint Graal* (Paris, 1921). Apart from the work of the Loomises and Alison Stones, there are few studies of art in French Arthurian MSS but see also Patricia M. Gathercole, 'The Paintings of the Lancelot Manuscripts at the Bibliothèque Nationale', *Romance Notes* XIII/2 (1971), 351–357.
[42] Lot, *op. cit.* pp. 150 ff.
[43] 'The Vulgate Cycle', *Arthurian Literature in the Middle Ages*, p. 306.
[44] Muriel Whitaker, 'Christian Iconography in The Quest of the Holy Grail', *Mosaic*, XII/2 (1979), 11–19.
[45] Manuscript reproductions are used to illustrate Richard Barber, *King Arthur* (Woodbridge, 1986); Christopher Hibbert, *The Search for King Arthur* (London, 1969); John Matthews, *The Grail: Quest for the Eternal* (New York, 1981); Lucy Paton, *Sir Lancelot of the Lake* (London, 1929); Michael Senior, *Tales of King Arthur* (London, 1980); *inter alia*.

All parts of the literary cycle use a common store of motifs related to that secondary world of the imagination which Chrétien had created. The source of tension is the conflict between *la chevalerie terrienne*, which Lancelot, Gawain and Ector particularly represent, and *la chevalerie célestienne* which Galahad, Perceval and Bohort embody. Such shared images as the knights-errant riding in perilous forests, importunate ladies, castles, supernatural ships, enticing pavilions, marvellous swords and emblazoned shields give the material an apparent unity. In fact, the significances are quite different.[46] While the authors introduce hermits, angels, and disembodied voices to explicate the allegory, the artist must dubiously rely on the viewer's ability to interpret signs and to find for himself the explanation.

Because the entire programme of Oxford, Bodleian MS Rawlinson Q.b.6. ca. 1320–30, 214 historiated initials, is available on Bodleian Library Filmstrips[47] and because the historiated initial's restrictive form reduces images to the mimimum requirement, this manuscript can be used as a guide to reading miniatures painted before 1340. The forest setting is indicated by one, two, or three stylised trees, generally set at one side of the circular space but sometimes used to separate figures (f. 8[v] Lancelot learns archery, observed by his tutor and the Lady of the Lake). There may be a fountain, a conventional meeting place (f. 44), or a pavilion (ff. 72, 202, 280[v]) which sometimes has an additional image signifying adventure; e.g. the shield hanging outside the pavilion which the mad Lancelot strikes (f. 311[v]). In the forest there is often a horse tied to a tree, to signify knight-errantry. Deer appear in hunting scenes (f. 28[v]) and as part of the religious allegory, the anagogical White Hart with four lions (f. 274[v]).

In Rawlinson Q.b.6 castles are generally single towers with windows from which characters can watch whatever is going on outside (f. 186[v]). For interior scenes, a wall may be removed (f. 211[v]) or the characters' heads and torsoes may emerge above the walls (f. 123[v]). A table set with food and drink indicates King Arthur's great hall (ff. 57, 132[v]), a bed the private apartments (ff. 211[v], 357[v]). Specific signs distinguish imprisonment from scenes of hospitality. In f. 149[v] a jailer with a large club pushes the prisoner, Lancelot, down into a confined space. Bolted doors in f. 123[v] and f. 186[v] indicate incarceration, as does the barred window (f. 284[v]) through which Lancelot reaches out to pluck a rose. The combination of barred window and climbing rose bush enables us to identify the subject.

A conventional system of signs facilitates character identification. Variations in size, even when the figures occupy the same spatial level, indicate relative import-

---

[46] On the iconography of the Grail Quest, see Chapter 4, 'The Way to Corbenic', in Muriel Whitaker, *Arthur's Kingdom of Adventure: The World of Malory's Morte Darthur* (Cambridge, Eng., 1984).

[47] On the subjects of individual miniatures see Thomas H. Ohlgren, ed., *Illuminated Manuscripts: An Index to Selected Bodleian Color Reproductions* (New York and London, 1977) and *Illuminated Manuscripts and Books in the Bodleian Library* (New York and London, 1978). Thomas E. Kelly and Thomas H. Ohlgren, 'Paths to Memory: Iconographic Indices to *Roman de la Rose* and *Prose Lancelot* Manuscripts in the Bodleian Library', *Visual Resources*, III (1983), 1–13, describes the Bodleian's new filming project which will include all the miniatures in eleven Arthurian prose romances. On the romance holdings see O. Pacht and J.J.G. Alexander, *Illuminated Manuscripts in the Bodleian Library*, Vol. I (Oxford, 1966).

ance. Arthur enthroned (f. 50) is twice as large as his attendants. No attempt is made to maintain realistic proportions between characters and setting. People can be taller than castles and horses taller than trees. Only the impact of each isolated image concerns the illustrator. Kings and queens inevitably wear crowns (even in bed) and their mantles are often ermine-lined. Knights wear carefully painted chain mail hauberks, coifs, and chausses; and their surcoats are red or blue, a colour scheme which sometimes causes a disparity between text and illustration, as in f. 271 where the Black Knight has blue armour and surcoat. The costume is well depicted in f. 241, where the sleeping Lancelot, head supported on his hand, stretches out full length with one elegantly pointed foot extending outside the frame. This illustrator pays little attention to heraldic images except in the case of Galahad, whose white shield with red cross makes him easily recognisable. For castle activities and hunting the men wear gowns. The lady's costume is a long sleeved côte, sleeveless surcoat, shoulder length veil, and sometimes a mantle. There is no differentiation between high-ranking ladies and their attendants or between mortals and fées. A countryman holds his scythe (f. 290), a jailer his club (f. 149v); a physician wears a hooded gown and a round, pointed hat (f. 369). Lancelot, as hero, rides a white horse (f. 28v); his madness is indicated by bare feet and a white shirt (ff. 158v, 311v).

A unique image helps us to identify a character and an adventure. The knight riding in a cart (f. 160) and balancing on a sword bridge above a set of wavy lines representing water (f. 166) can only be Lancelot. The three knights and a damsel gazing at a large sword laid on a bed can only be Galahad, Bohort, Perceval and Perceval's sister. The combination of bed and sword is enough to indicate the Ship of Solomon without any nautical signs.

In literature authors can examine emotional states at length. As Alexander Micha has noted regarding the love of Lancelot and Guenevere in the Vulgate *Lancelot*:

> Chacun des chapitres apporte une couleur ou une nuance nouvelle à l'amour, moments d'abandon ou d'exaltation, bonheurs furtifs, jouissance de la possession, mais aussi tristesses et détresses dues à l'eloignement, doutes, jalousie, dépressions physiques et morales, égarements et folies dont les effets sont décrits avec une précision dénonçant un écrivain assez épris de pathologie.[48]

To translate such emotion into visual form requires a repertoire of gestures with recognizable significances.[49] So that the viewer will not overlook the clues, hands and fingers are unnaturally elongated. Worry and sadness are indicated by resting cheek on hand with tilted head as in f. 148 where Lancelot's companions discuss his absence or in f. 211v where Guenevere, seated on her absent lover's bed,

---

[48] A. Micha, ed. and trans., *Lancelot*, Introduction, p. 15.
[49] The major study is François Garnier, *Le Langage de l'Image au Moyen Age: Signification et Symbolique* (Paris, 1982).

presses one hand to her face while the other dangles limply. Characters in conversation extend their forefingers. A raised hand with open palm means welcome (ff. 50, 132^v). Arms raised with open palms pressed together mean supplication, as in f. 246 where Elaine begs Lancelot to spare her life and in f. 309 where the hero begs the Queen not to banish him. Hands crossed at the wrist mean death or, as in f. 149^v, loss of liberty.

The spareness of these historiated initials demands that each image be examined individually to extract its significance. The lack of depth, the flat, frontal arrangements reduce the text's visual accompaniment to bare essentials that cannot be missed. No forms lie undetected in these forests. The backgrounds of Rawlinson Q.b.6 are gold within the circle, which is surrounded by a rectangle of blue or rose. The gold's luminosity gives the foreground images increased highlighting, their significance magnified by light.

At the end of the thirteenth century and during the earlier fourteenth century vernacular book production was centred in the northern French areas of Picardy, Artois, Flanders and Hainaut. Their ateliers produced extensively illustrated copies of the *Vulgate Prose Cycle*, including the following outstanding examples: Bonn, Universitätsbibl., 526, *Cycle de Lancelot* (1286); London, British Library, Additional 10292–4, *Cycle de Lancelot* (after 1316); London, British Library, Royal 14 E III, *Estoire, Queste, Morte Artu* (ca. 1316); Oxford, Bodleian Library, Douce 215/ Manchester, John Rylands University Library, fr. 1/ New York, H.P. Kraus, Catalogue 165, no. 3, *Cycle de Lancelot* (1315–25); New York, Pierpont Morgan Library, 805, *Lancelot Proper* (ca. 1315); Paris, Bibliothèque Nationale fr. 95; Oxford, Bodleian Library, Ashmole 828/ Yale University Library 229 (ca. 1300).[50] The superiority of these illustrative programmes derives from the exquisiteness of the paintings and their fidelity to the text. The elegant ease and opulence of courtly life are conveyed by miniatures of ladies holding lapdogs and knights playing chess, making love, or jousting outside castle walls as the ladies watch. Feasts are set out in striped pavilions and picnics are spread on the grass beside fountains. The rituals of hospitality are observed as a green rug is laid to welcome visitors (Add. 10293, ff. 279, 359^v) or a squire helps remove a knight's mail shirt (Add. 10293, f. 224). Lovers exchange embraces and kisses, the Morgan miniature of Lancelot and Guenevere's first kiss being especially famous (f. 67). The carnal basis of courtly love is unashamedly asserted as Uther and Igerne (Add. 10292, f. 96^v), Arthur and Morgause (Add. 10292, f. 113), Lancelot and Guenevere (Add. 10293, f. 312^v) and Lancelot and Elaine (Add. 10293, ff. 288, 374) are shown in naked embrace.

The ladies wear gowns of vermilion, blue, indigo and rose, with voluminous skirts elegantly draped and the buttons on their tight sleeves meticulously painted. The chief knights' blazons, lavishly depicted on shields, surcoats, ailettes, banners and horse trappings, are no longer haphazard but relatively consistent

---

[50] For details of size, composition, layout, provenance, and number of illustrations, see M. Alison Stones, 'Manuscripts, Arthurian Illuminated', section 9 in *The Arthurian Encyclopedia*, pp. 369–373.

throughout a text or a group of texts.[51] Literary sources for the arms are rare until the late Middle Ages, though the *Mort Artu* attributes to Lancelot 'un escu blanc a trois bendes de bellic vermeilles et couvertures toutes blanches'. The three bends signify that the hero has the strength of three men. *Argent, three bends gules* is his usual device in Add. 10293–4 and Royal 14 E III. In Douce 215 and Rylands fr. 1, the imaginary arms *argent, two hearts gules* refer to his role as paramount lover.[52] Deriving from the texts of the French romances *Durmart Le Gallois* (ca. 1250), *Escanor* (ca. 1280) and the Second Continuation of Chrétien's *Perceval*, Gawain's arms are *argent, a Canton gules*. Helmut Nickel[53] suggests that they are probably canting arms, punning on Lot, the name of Gawain's father, and lot, a section. Gawain carries this shield in Add. 10293–4, Royal 14 E III and Digby 223. However, in Leiden, Bibl. Ryks-Universiteit 195, *Walewein*, ca. 1350, he bears on his accoutrements a red lion head.

Galahad's arms, *argent à la croix de gueules*, are stipulated in *L'Estoire* where Josephé marks a white shield with a cross drawn in his own blood. Arthur's arms in these manuscripts usually appear as two or three crowns in a red or blue field.[54] It was the workshops of Northern France that originated 'd'armoiries imaginaires'.[55]

A fairytale atmosphere is evoked by the rainbow colours. Horses in fr. 95, Add. 10292–4, Morgan 805 and Rylands fr. 1 may be orange, pink, blue, mauve, dappled blue and grey or white. The Gothic castles and monasteries have towers of pink, blue, orange and green surmounted by crotchets, finials, pennons, golden crosses and lapis lazuli roofs. In Morgan 805, trees with blue and pink trunks defy the viewer to regard the perilous forest as realistic. The fairytale atmosphere is also enhanced by the characters' apparent agelessness. Although in the text people grow old – the *Mort Artu*'s Arthur is ninety-two and Lancelot fifty-five when the Order of the Round Table is destroyed – in the miniatures they remain eternally young, with their small red mouths, rosy cheeks, white skin, expressive eyes, carefully curled hair and slender figures. Only Merlin, the son of a hairy faced, horned, grotesque devil and a beautiful virgin – his engendering is depicted in Add. 10292, f. 78ᵛ and fr. 95, f. 113ᵛ – is physically differentiated from court society. In BL Add. 38117 he is a dwarfish figure, his contorted face, short

---

[51] On Arthurian heraldry see Gerard J. Brault, *Early Blazon: Heraldic Terminology in the Twelfth and Thirteenth Centuries with Special Reference to Arthurian Literature* (Oxford, 1972); Helmut Nickel, 'Arthurian Heraldry', *Avalon to Camelot*, 1 (1984), 11–12 and 'Heraldry', *Arthurian Encyclopedia*, pp. 278–283; Michel Pastoureau, *Armorial des chevaliers de la Table Ronde* (Paris, 1983) and *L'hermine et le Sinople: Etudes d'Héraldique Médiévale* (Paris, 1982); C.W. Scott-Giles, 'Some Arthurian Coats of Arms', *The Coat of Arms*, 8, 84 (1965), 332–39 and 9, 65 (1966), 30–35; George F. Timpson, 'Heraldry in Wolfram's Parzival', *The Coat of Arms*, 4, 31 (1957), 278–81.

[52] Brault, p. 47, n. 2 cites specific illuminations in early MSS which show a common heraldic tradition for Lancelot. There is a useful glossary of heraldic terms, pp. 58–75.

[53] *Arthurian Encyclopedia*, p. 282.

[54] Brault, p. 44. See also C.E. Pickford, 'The Three Crowns of King Arthur', *Yorkshire Archaeological Journal*, XXXVIII (1952–5), 373–82.

[55] Pastoureau, *L'hermine et le sinople*, p. 264.

hair and blue gown setting him apart from the tall, slender aristocrats. His shape-shifting powers are shown as he appears in the guise of a peasant with brown kirtle and club entering Camelot behind a herd of cattle and flock of sheep (Add. 10292, f. 129); in Douce 178 f. 252 he is a boy and in f. 299 a stag. He is a bearded old man with a walking stick and grey cloak in fr. 95.

The good life of *la chevalerie terrienne* must be defended against evil knights and supernatural powers. Most illuminators are quite incompetent when it comes to conveying a quality of strangeness based on magic. The fées are not shown to be dazzlingly superior in beauty and power. Lionel and Bors as fairy hounds (BN fr. 344, f. 196) are ordinary lapdogs that Saraide and her attendant carry in their arms, with no sign of their magic wreaths and chains. The Morgan illustrator, however, is successful in devising adventures that allow heroes to prove their virtue in settings evoking wonder and fear. Deprived of his knightly accoutre-ments, Brandelis, barefoot and half naked, his hands bound at the wrists, watches as Gaheriet dispatches his oppressors; on the right, three knights cudgel a damsel with manacled wrists (f. 223). Outside the Dolorous Tower, Lancelot battles the giant Caradoc, whom he decapitates and throws in a pit while Gawain nimbly escapes over the wall. Magical swords guard a chapel, dragons bar the entrance to the Valley of False Lovers, flames leap up and swords balance on their hilts to protect an unapproachable tomb. Lancelot frees the captives of Gorre by lifting from Josephé's tomb the enormous lid that then hovers in mid-air. Though the lions guarding Baudemagus' blue and red castle look friendly enough, streams of blood vividly convey the damage inflicted by the sword bridge.

Realistic details suggest that some of the illustrators strove to make the roman-ces credible by injecting imagery from ordinary life into the fairytale setting. One servant adds a stick to the fire and another with bellows blows up the flames that will consume the false Guenevere (Morgan, f. 119^v). The Bonn illustrator uniquely depicts a blood-letting with a tourniquet and a stick to support the arm of Perce-val's sister. Fourteenth century building practices are the subject of Royal 14 E III, f. 85; one stonemason hacks a block into shape, another sets a finished block in place, a third climbs to the top of a precarious ladder and a fourth, trowel in hand, listens to the king's instructions. Rivers and seas are stocked with fish that can be identified as eels, carp, perch, skate and salmon.

But the illustrators realise that *L'Estoire del Saint Graal* and *La Queste del Saint Graal* present a different form of the good life from that found in *Merlin* and *Lancelot*, one based on biblical exegesis and the multi-level reading of images. To a far greater degree than in the secular milieu, the view of reality is symbolic.[56] To connect *L'Estoire* and *La Queste*, separated as they are by *Merlin* and the lengthy *Lancelot*, the miniaturists rely on the system of correspondences called typology. The adventures of the Grail quest, which reach a climax in Galahad's mystic vision at Sarras, are part of a historical process that began with the Fall of Man and culminated in the Redemption. Arthurian characters live in the time of grace,

---

[56] See *The Gothic Image*, trans. Dora Nussey (New York, Evanston and London, 1958), p. 29, originally published as *L'art religieux du XIIIe siècle en France* (Paris, 1902).

the time in which man can prepare himself for eternity, and Galahad is the Christ-figure who provides a model of virtuous life.[57]

The miniaturists draw directly from religious art when they depict Adam and Eve in Eden (Douce 215 f. 31^v; Rawlinson Q.b.6 f. 349, Royal 14 E III f. 127^v, 128; Add. 10292 f. 31 and 10294 f. 41^v); Cain slaying Abel (Douce 303 f. 53, 10292 f. 33 where Cain uses as his weapon the English iconographic motif, the jawbone of an ass, and 10294 f. 430); the Annunciation (fr. 95 f. 10); the Crucifixion (Royal 14 E III f. 7; Bonn 526 f. 1); the Deponition and Entombment (fr. 95 f. 6); and the Harrowing of Hell (10292 f. 76). The Old Testament characters represent man's sinfulness and damnation under the Old Law; the New Testament characters effect man's chance of salvation under the New Law.

The authors of *L'Estoire*, which was actually written after *La Queste*, develop a typological patterning based on corresponding characters, events and images, a patterning that is central to the pictorial programme. At the Crucifixion Joseph of Arimathea, a character who joins Judeo-Christian history to Arthurian history, catches Christ's blood in the chalice that, in most pictorial representations, is identified as the Holy Grail. Joseph sets it on the altar when celebrating mass (Royal 14 E III f. 16, f. 18; 10292 f. 8). The table of the Last Supper, Joseph's table and King Pelles' table in the Grail castle are a unified image, paralleling Arthur's table in the secular milieu.[58] Josephé, wounded in the thigh by the angel's spear (10292 f. 74; Royal 14 E III f. 30), is the Maimed King whom Galahad heals to restore the Waste Land (Rawlinson Q.b.6 f. 301) as well as by iconic association Christ, wounded by Longinus' spear which becomes one of the Grail articles. Mordrains, the converted pagan, and Nacien anticipate Perceval for they are marooned on a desert island (Royal 14 E III ff. 34, 36, 45^v; fr. 342 f. 94; 10292 f. 22^v), encouraged by an angelic comforter who arrives in a white ship, and tempted by a demonic lady who disappears in a storm (fr. 95, ff. 43, 44^v, 59). In Royal 14 E III f. 78^v Joseph and his companions are guided by a white hart (Christ) wearing a golden chain (humility) and escorted by four lions (the Evangelists); later Perceval and Galahad see the same anagogic images (10294 f. 45^v). The white shield on which Josephé makes a red cross, using his own blood, is destined for Galahad (Royal 14 E III ff. 85^v, 94^v; fr. 95 f. 108) and the sword which the Grail hero draws from the stone (BN fr. 110 f. 405, Royal 14 E III f. 91^v) recalls the sword in the stone that designated Arthur as king (fr. 95, ff. 158, 158^v, 159^v). Such miniatures help the reader to locate particular events in an often confusing repertoire of adventures. As well, through establishing a pattern of recurrences in a form more easily

---

[57] See Jean Frappier, 'Le Graal et La Chevalerie', *Romania*, LXXV (1954), 165–210, on the knight as an embodiment of medieval idealism. Cf. Paul Zumthor, *Merlin le Prophète* (Lausanne, 1943), pp. 128–9 on the knight's significance as 'l'homme moderne, l'homme 'réel,' celui du milieu social alors vivant-et qui dans la perspective de l'oeuvre est la société prédestinée à qui est réservé de découvrir le secret du Graal'.

[58] The iconographic patterns are similar, both being rectangular until the later fourteenth century when they are sometimes round or semicircular as in BN fr. 343 f. 13, fr. 112, f. 5 and f. 179^v, fr. 120, f. 544^v and fr. 99, f. 563.

recognized than that provided by the text, they impose order and activate memory.

One image that particularly represents an 'ingathering of the images'[59] is the Ship of Solomon, a supernatural vessel free from the temporal and spatial limitations of the real world. Built at Solomon's order (Royal 14 E III f. 51^v), it is a treasury of symbolic artifacts: the blood-red sword of David destined for Galahad as token of his lineage and election; the three spindles made from the Tree of Life, one white as snow to symbolise paradisal purity, one green as grass to symbolise procreation, and one red as blood to symbolise violence. There is a rich bed for the last knight of Solomon's line and a girdle made from the hair of Perceval's sister (the New Testament) to replace the hempen girdle (the Old Testament) – an image uniquely depicted in the Yale *Queste*. The Ship of Solomon, alas, is too great a challenge pictorially. Royal 14 E III f. 125^v typifies the limits of visual realisation: a small clinker-built boat, with words on the top board indicating that it is the Ship of Faith; three upright spindles, correctly coloured, against which leans a large sword, and a plump pillow supporting a crown. As these objects completely fill the ship, it is difficult to imagine where Perceval's sister, Perceval, Bors and Galahad who are approaching in another ship, will find room to board. The subject is also depicted in Douce 215 f. 39, Add. 10294 f. 44, and in Brussels, BR 9627–8 f. 60^v where Galahad actually sleeps on the bed. Other mystical subjects, such as Lancelot's failure to see the Grail at the Perilous Chapel (Bonn 526 f. 426, Rylands f. 195^v, Royal 14 E III f. 99^v) are equally awkward. The difficult concept of transubstantiation is implied by the Bonn illustrator who sets a crucifix inside the Grail chalice.

God's hand is omnipresent, literally pushing Nacien from the burning city (fr. 95 f. 39), holding an instructional scroll (fr. 95 f. 76^v), blessing the dead Joseph (fr. 95 f. 108). As a pillar of flame He strikes down the disobedient like Moys or the Arthurian knight who sit in the Siege Perilous reserved for Galahad (Royal 14 E III f. 76^v, Rylands f. 109^v), destroys pagan castles (10294 f. 47) and separates Bors and Lionel in their fratricidal combat (10294 f. 38^v). These fiery interventions as well as the depictions of horrible fiends (e.g. Rylands f. 190) give the miniatures a dramatic appearance.

With the *Mort Artu* the artists return to the secular world. Images of combat proliferate as Arthur fights Lancelot and Mordred. Resisting the impulse to reproduce repetitive battle scenes, the prolific illuminator of 10294, for example, develops a text-based programme of seventy-three miniatures which emphasize the historical context of Arthur's biography by realizing the contemporary world. Guests hold anticipatory knives as Guenevere graciously offers the fateful fruit (f. 63^v).[60] Lancelot's bloody gown shows where the huntress' arrow has lodged (f. 64). Trapped by Agravain and Mordred, the distraught Queen stands with her

[59] F.W. Locke, *The Quest for the Holy Grail: A Literary Study of a Thirteenth Century French Romance* (Stanford, 1960) illuminatingly examines the theological bases of *Queste* characterisations and images.

[60] This scene, along with Elaine's arrival at Camelot and Lancelot's rescue of Guenevere at the stake, is among the most popular in the *Mort Artu* programme.

crown askew (f. 69ᵛ), as it is again when she waits at the stake in her red gown (f. 90ᵛ). A variety of weaponry is used in the siege of Joyous Gard – a scaling ladder, a mangonel, aquebuses, swords, spears and even a large rock which a defender is about to heave at the enemy (f. 81ᵛ).

The manuscripts show considerable variety in their selection of scenes from the final act. In 10294 f. 87ᵛ the abbess greets a still worldly Guenevere who wears a red dress and pink cloak. In Bonn f. 483 the Queen kneels in supplication, but her self-satisfied mouth and sly eyes support the textual suggestion that she is motivated more by fear and cunning than piety. 10294 f. 89, the only depiction in an Arthurian manuscript of the Goddess Fortuna,[61] utilises the *Hortus deliciarum* formula of a blindfolded, crowned Fortuna turning a wheel with four figures. Arthur at the apex sits enthroned and confident while the other figures, depending on their position, reflect anticipation, apprehension, and despair.

The last battle (f.93) indicates the difficulty of presenting a large number of figures without a mastery of perspective yet the heaped bodies powerfully convey the slaughter's grand scale. Arthur, a large recumbent figure identified by a red crown on his head and white crowns on his blue surcoat, lies on the right while on the left, pierced by his father's spear, is Mordred. Crossed hands indicate that he is dead. Only 10294 and Yale show the return of Excalibur. No manuscript of this period depicts Arthur's departure in the ladies' ship and none shows the Queen's death. Fr. 342 has a charming miniature of Lancelot's admission to the hermitage while his horse, a symbol of chivalric adventure, stands unbridled and unsaddled (f. 233). In BR 9627 f. 155ᵛ tonsured and bearded monks carry a still youthful Lancelot on a golden catafalque.

Though these manuscripts illuminated in France before 1340 may contain too many combat scenes for modern taste, one cannot help being charmed by the elegant gestures and expressive faces, as, for example, Lancelot prepares to test Elaine's boiling bath with his fingertips while she, 'naked as a needle' in Malory's phrase, holds up a restraining hand and the always curious horse looks on (10293 f. 244). The puzzled concern on the courtiers' faces when they view Elaine of Astolat's corpse under its striped pall (Royal 14 E III f. 153ᵛ) and the horror when they look at the boatful of infants whom Arthur has ordered drowned (Add. 38117 f. 97ᵛ) are psychologically convincing. And always in the best manuscripts there is the awareness that love and joy are transient and only death is sure.

Because French ateliers monopolised the production of illuminated Arthurian manuscripts, relatively few works produced in other countries before 1340 are extant. However, the Bavarian State Library in Munich has two works remarkable for their rarity and literary significance if not for their splendour. MS cgm 19 contains Wolfram von Eschenbach's *Parzival* (ca. 1210), a Grail romance in 25,000 lines of rhymed couplets.[62] Based on Chrétien de Troyes' *Perceval* and a continua-

---

[61] See H.R. Patch, *The Goddess Fortuna in Medieval Literature* (Cambridge, Mass., 1927); F.P. Pickering, *Literature and Art in the Middle Ages* (Florida, 1970), pp. 168–222; Philippa Tristram, *Figures of Life and Death in Medieval English Literature* (London, 1976), pp. 128–47.

[62] Wolfram von Eschenbach, *Parzival*, ed. Albert Leitzmann, 5 vols. (Halle, 1905–6), 6th ed. Wilhelm Deinert (Tübingen, 1965), trans. A.T. Hatto (Harmondsworth, 1980); *Vollständiges*

tion, the German romance is original in the conception of the Fisher King, Amfortas, the treatment of courtly love, which is centred on Gawain, the emphasis on family relationships, and the concept of a hero who owes his success not to chance but to 'the reconciliation of courtly teachings and Christian faith'.[63] Meister Hesse's workshop in Strassburg, which flourished 1228–1236, may have produced cgm 19 (ca. 1250). The illustrations painted in three tiers separated by red bands appear on both sides of inserted parchment leaves.[64] Of what should have been a complete narrative programme only two folios remain, those illustrating books XII–XV, a part of the text that tells of Gawain's reconciliation with Gramoflanz and Parzival's encounter with his pagan half-brother Feirefiz.

Characters are identified by labelled scrolls extending from their hands and sometimes arching over their heads. Costumes are the gown and mantle type. Knights have chain mail, flat-topped helms and emblazoned shields. Setting is indicated by a tower, the machicolated Grail castle, and stylised trees with heart-shaped or trefoil leaves. The geometrically patterned pavilions look like tepees. The V shape is repeated in the large triangular shields and in the heavily draped tablecloths of the feasts. Among specific realizations of the text are the broken sword between Parzival and Feirefiz, who have just escaped the sin of fratricide (f. 49v), and the Loathly Lady's long nose and tusk-like teeth (f. 50). A divergence based on a pictorial rather than a textual source is the representation of the Grail as a champagne glass instead of a stone (f. 50).

The range of colours is restricted – dark green on gold backgrounds, red and magenta horses, golden crowns and saddles, blue saddle blankets and an eye-catching red tablecloth for the wedding feast. The dark colours, harsh lines, the awkward gestures and stiff figures make the Parzival society seem more primitive and serious than that depicted in the Munich *Tristan*, where the illustrations are admittedly later in date.

The latter manuscript cmg 51 was produced in the same Strassburg workshop as the *Parzival* for the same scribe worked on both. The text is an abridged version of Gottfried von Strassburg's poem as continued by Ulrich von Türheim (ca. 1236).[65] Later than the text are the illustrations, eighty-four pictures arranged in tiers with two or three scenes on each side of the inserted leaves. The backgrounds are red, indigo or dark green. A draped canopy indicates interior scenes.

Faksimile des Cgm 19 der Bayerischen Staatsbibliothek München, eds. Fridolin Dressler and Heinz Engels, 2 vols. (Stuttgart, 1970).
[63] Otto Springer, 'Wolfram's Parzival' in *Arthurian Literature in the Middle Ages*, pp. 218–50.
[64] The insertion of several leaves presenting a narrative sequence of biblical history uninterrupted by text was a layout that originated in England. It had spread to the continent by the thirteenth century and in Germany was adapted to secular manuscripts.
[65] Pickering, *Literature and Art*, p. 30, notes a disparity between illustration and text because the former attracts the interest of the art historian but the latter, being a retrogressive version of Gottfried's text, deserves the literary critic's rejection. Ulrich's text has been edited by Thomas Kerth (Tübingen, 1979). Text and illustrations are available in *Vollständiges Faksimile des Cgm 51 der Bayerischen Staatsbibliothek München*, eds. Ulrich Montag and Paul Gichtel, 2 vols. (Stuttgart, 1979). On the two Munich MSS see Loomis, ALMA, pp. 131–134.

That these miniatures were probably painted ca. 1300 is indicated by the figures' Gothic elongation and backward sway, the voluminous drapery, and the varied use of gesture. Women have the long, crimped hair and wimpled headdress with fluted cap also found in the Manesse MS, Heidelberg Universitätsbibliothek (ca. 1300–1340). In f. 7, the rhythmic curves of King Mark's right arm as he holds his fleur de lis sceptre, of the musician's bow arm as he plays his viol, of the falcon's body as it bends to the knight's finger, of the dancer's raised arm and swirling skirt, the exuberant nonchalance of the acrobatic listeners and the rippling grace of the pavilion walls give an impression of courtly life that is filled with pleasure and grace.

There are the usual set pieces – feasts (ff. 7, 30); a melée outside a castle (f. 10); ardent lovers abed, not only Tristan and Isolde but also his parents Rivalon and Blanchefleur (ff. 10ᵛ, 90ᵛ); single combats like that between Tristan and Morhault (f. 46). And there are scenes particularly associated with Tristan. His birth utilises Nativity motifs such as that of a lady washing the newborn child in a wooden tub (f. 15). Patterned on the childhood of Christ, the boy's education includes learning to read from a large manuscript on a stand, its letters forming the words *Beatus Vir, Deus, veni sancte Spiritus* (f. 15ᵛ). He puts the stone,[66] throws a spear and harps, accomplishments that provides him with an identifying image and a disguise. The climactic event is the dragon-slaying, differentiated from the other pictures by a more grandiose style. The Romanesque monster with slanted eyes, long ears, blue legs, curled tail in his forest of pink trees is dispatched by a blue-armoured Tristan who cuts out the tongue with a long sword. When the false steward has loaded the beast into a four-wheeled cart drawn by one pink and one blue horse, it resembles the friendly dragon of a children's story.

Later miniatures, evidently by a different artist, are carelessly painted; for example, f. 76 which shows Tristan dropping sticks into the water, as described in ll. 14, 498 –14, 501; a dwarfish hero embracing his lady; and King Mark and Melot precariously perched in a tree to spy on the lovers' tryst. The grotto (f. 90) is meagrely drawn with the lovers awkwardly disposed on either side of the sword. f. 104 returns to the lively, rhythmic style of the early folios. Tristan, disguised as a fool, uses a club to attack his enemies among the heart-leaved trees with their sinuous trunks. The cycle concludes as the dying Tristan receives his last drink (f. 107ᵛ). This manuscript presents a complete sequence of the images that other art forms depict singly or in a more restricted programme.

Thanks to Norman knights and Breton minstrels Arthurian legends were known in Italy even before Geoffrey of Monmouth's *Historia* presented Arthur as a transalpine conqueror.[67] The sculpture over the Porta della Pescheria at Modena's Cathedral, dated 1120–1140, names characters associated with Arthur's Welsh court.[68] Tristanus and Yvanus occur as Christian names in the area of Lake

---

[66] This plebeian sport is not mentioned by Gottfried but is derived from Eilhart von Oberge's *Tristant*, v. 142.

[67] Edmund G. Gardner, *The Arthurian Legend in Italian Literature* (London and New York, 1930).

[68] The Modena archivolt and the Otranto mosaic will be discussed in chapter four.

Constance in the eighth and ninth centuries while Artusius, Walwanus and Merlinus are recorded in the eleventh and twelfth centuries.[69] That the authors of French romance accepted Italy as part of the Arthurian world is illustrated by *Floriant et Florete* (ca. 1280), the hero of which is a Sicilian prince raised by Morgan le Fay.

The transmission of Arthurian legend to Italy has a historical basis, the Normans' conquest in the eleventh century of Apulia, Calabria and Sicily (a sovereignty that lasted from 1030 to 1250) and the Angevins' rule which began in 1264. Emperor Frederich II (1220–1250) was, like Edward I of England, an Arthurian enthusiast who commissioned a *Tristan* to be written at his court and on February 5, 1240 wrote a letter of thanks to a Messinian for sending the king the book of *Palamede*. He was also credited with ordering in Sicily *Les Prophecies de Merlin* (Venice, Marciana fr. App. XXIX [243]), though that manuscript has now been attributed to a Venetian.[70] Nevertheless, these details suggest that French scribes were actively at work in Italy by the thirteenth century.

One of the earliest illuminated manuscripts of the Prose *Tristan*, Paris, BN fr. 760 (ca. 1300) probably originated in southern Italy.[71] Mediocre in style and carelessly written, it suggests rapid production to satisfy popular demand. The illustrations are relatively faithful to the text. f. 16 shows Tristan riding towards the Joyous Gard where Iseult watches from a tower. The Italianate castle has Romanesque arches and an elaborate double door with nail studding, round metal handles and ornamental hinges. In f. 121 King Mark aims a long spear through a doorway so that it will pierce Tristan's back. In contrast to the poetic ending with its story of the black and white sails and the lovers' death in Brittany, the Prose *Tristan* presents a hero treacherously murdered as he plays his harp for Iseult. The illuminator, however, reversing the lovers' roles, depicts the gigantic heroine providing the music and the hero listening with one leg awkwardly crossed over the other. Rubrics identify the characters, MT indicating Monseigneur Tristan. This is a necessary device, says Loomis, because of the 'unimaginative monotony with which the same riding and fighting knights, the same feats and audiences are used over and over again.'

Neapolitan ateliers became productive about 1280 as Charles of Anjou, King of Naples, favoured 'l'apport Septentrional'. B. Degenhart has identified a group of Neapolitan manuscripts (ca. 1290–1320), one of which is London, BL Harley 4389.[72] Based on the first part of Luces de Gaut's Prose *Tristan*, it begins with the

---

[69] E.K. Chambers, *Arthur of Britain*, pp. 133–134.

[70] Gardner, p. 45.

[71] The Prose *Tristan* was the first long Arthurian romance written after the Vulgate Prose Cycle. There are two versions, dubiously attributed to Luces de Gaut and Hélie de Borron. Various versions are published or summarised in Eilhert Löseth, *Le Roman en prose de Tristan* (Paris, 1891). On Italian MSS see F. Avril, M.-T. Gousset, C. Rabel, *Manuscrits enluminés d'origine italienne*, II, xiiie siècle (Paris, 1984) and Loomis, ALMA, pp. 114–118.

[72] B. Degenhart and A. Schmitt, 'Frühe angiovische Buchkunst in Neapel: Die Illustrierung franzosischer Unterhaltungsprosa in neapolitanischen Scriptorien zwischen 1290 und 1320', in *Festschrift Wolfgang Braunfels* (Tübingen, 1978), pp. 71–92.

last adventures of Apollo the Adventurous, Tristan's ancestor, and ends when Galehot hears of his parents' deaths. The thirty-nine miniatures are simply drawn and the painting (which utilises vermilion, indigo, green and magenta) is incomplete. Deep two-masted ships of a Mediterranean type are a favourite motif (ff. 6^v, 15, 17, 18^v, 20^v, 30, 51^v, 55). The scenes are highly conventional with numerous knights, identified by name, approaching numerous castles or engaging in repetitious combats.

Judging by the similarity of shields (emblazoned with a single broad diagonal) and the flat-topped visored helms, Degenhart attributes to the same workshop Udine, Biblioteca Arcivescovile 177, *La Queste del Saint Graal* (1310–20). In f. 27^v a lively Perceval is accompanied by a friendly lion and her cubs who put themselves between the hero and a dragon. The supernatural hart and four lions procede five abreast (f. 91), a variation on a familiar miniature. Quite original is Perceval's dream of two women, one on a dragon, the other on a lion (f. 29). Their mounts identify them iconographically as the Old Law (Synogogue) and the New (Church).

Scriptoria turning out illustrated romance manuscripts also flourished in Lombardy. Chantilly III, *Mort Artu*, with six historiated letters, can be dated 1288 because of an inscription on the last page. A Prose *Tristan*, BN fr. 12599 is similar in its use of historiated initials and colour scheme – orange, blue, brown. After being part of the Saibante collection, it was acquired by Gian Filippi of Verona. More interesting is Oxford Bodleian Douce 178, an *Estoire-Merlin*, early fourteenth century.[73] The *Merlin's* twenty-eight miniatures reflect the Byzantine influence that characterised the North Italian style – clear cut, round faces, statuesque bodies, thin white lines outlining costumes, ornamental hems (f. 313) and buildings with white lines suggesting stonework, as in the representation of Merlin's prison (f. 411^v). Merlin is a grizzled, bearded old man who rides a black horse (f. 195), wears a red or pink gown and in f. 297 where he welcomes Gawain to Benwic's castle, a tall hat.[74]

Guiron le Courtois and *Meliadus*, additions to the Arthurian canon, were derived from the first Arthurian compilation made by an Italian, Rusticiano da Pisa, whose other notable achievement was that he recorded Marco Polo's travels while both men were incarcerated in a Genoese prison. Rusticiano claimed that the source of his *Roman de Roi Artus* was a French book that Edward I of England had left behind when he returned from the Crusades in 1273. The compilation uses the Prose *Lancelot*, *Queste*, *Morte Artu* and *Prophecies of Merlin* as well as the Prose *Tristan* and the *Palamides*. The romances are best known through the printed editions published in Paris in the early sixteenth century – Verard's *Gyron le*

---

[73] Many of the historiated initials are from *Lestoire de Merlin*, Bodleian, Douce 178 reproduced in Senior, *Tales of King Arthur*. They are also available on Bodleian filmstrip.

[74] Other unexceptional products of a Lombard workshop are *Guiron le Courtois*, St Mark's Library, Venice, fr. ix; *Lancelot*, St Mark's Library, Venice, fr. xi; *Tristan*, Modena, Estense Bibl. T.S.I.; *Tristan*, Vatican library Pal. lat. 1964; *Tristan*, Aberystwyth, National Library of Wales, 446 E; *Meliadus*, Paris, BN fr. 1463; *Lancelot*, Paris, BN fr. 354; *Lancelot*, Berlin, Staatsbibliothek, Ham. 49.

Courtoys (ca. 1501) and *Meliadus de Leonnoys*, published by Galliot du Pré, 1528 and Denis Janot, 1532.[75] *Guiron* and *Meliadus* are set in the early days of Arthurian chivalry, a golden age when the most beautiful ladies in the world were the Queen of Scotland and the Lady of Malehaut. The noblest knights included Meliadus, Tristan's father, and Guiron le Courtois, descended from King Clovis and Joseph of Arimathea. Like the *Tristan*, these romances present an amorphous collection of battles, kidnappings, and imprisonments, boring to the modern reader but evidently fascinating to the medieval audience. As the next chapter will reveal, these texts, elaborately decorated, were among the most luxurious of late Gothic manuscripts.

The high point of Italian illumination before 1340 is a *Tristan*, Paris, BN fr. 755 (1320–40). It probably belonged to the Visconti of Milan, a ducal family who had built up a library of one thousand manuscripts by 1499, when the Collection was stolen by the French and deposited in Louis XII's chateau of Blois. The layout of the one hundred and sixty-one folios reveals the Italian preference for large illustrations occupying the lower part of one or even both pages. In expansive tournament scenes ladies watch avidly from the balconies, as the artist evokes a scene combining dramatic activity and erotic emotion. Across the page ride cavalcades of pleasure seeking courtiers, a procession of Christian kings and a lively hunt.

Stylistically, fr. 755 is at the forefront of the new Giottesque style which eventually replaced Byzantine and Gothic conventions. The figures have weight and volume which, together with their dark colouring, differentiate them from the characters depicted in French romances. The diagonally set table in Arthur's pavilion (f. 115) and the diagonally set bed in which the ailing Arthur lies (f. 148) create the effect of three-dimensional rooms into which the viewer can look. The brilliantly painted costumes – red and pink are favourite colours – the varied social scenes, the architecture featuring the golden-brown colour and style of the Mantuan palaces, and the realism of, for example, the handwashing scene presage the deluxe manuscripts of the fifteenth century.[76]

---

[75] Both are available in facsimile editions edited by C.E. Pickford: *Guiron le Courtois* (London, 1977) and *Meliadus de Leonnoys* (London, 1980).
[76] With the exception of the Bonn and Yale *Vulgate Prose Cycle* MSS, I have examined at first hand all manuscripts discussed in this chapter.

CHAPTER THREE

Books for Patrons: Late Gothic Manuscripts

The period of French prosperity congenial to the arts came to an end about 1340. During the Hundred Years' War between England and France that broke out in 1337, the country was ravaged not only by soldiers of various nations but by the French nobles as well.[1] Jean Froissart (ca. 1333–ca. 1400), himself the author of an Arthurian romance, *Meliador*, reported in his *Chronicles*[2] that at the Battle of Crécy (1346) one thousand two hundred and ninety-one French nobles died as well as thirty thousand footsoldiers.[3] Edward III's desire to take ransomable prisoners was frustrated by pillagers and irregulars, Welsh and Cornishmen, who knifed the wounded in order to rob them. As the result of subsequent battles many French nobles, including the king, Jean II, were held prisoner in England, leaving France impoverished and disorganised. Another form of ravishment was the Black Death of 1348 which carried off 'la tierce partie du Monde', says Froissart. The ateliers must have contributed their share of victims.

When the production of illuminated manuscripts revived about 1380, it was affected by a new motivation and a new style. From the end of the fourteenth century until the printed book displaced the manuscript, book production was dominated by the taste and acquisitiveness of aristocratic patrons.[4] What we would today call connoisseurship was an expression of personality. Owning deluxe manuscripts implied taste and wealth, the ability to appreciate and pay for an objet d'art. Furthermore, the patron could gain a kind of immortality by being depicted in the miniatures of a book he had commissioned.[5]

[1] On the Free Companies see C.W. Previté-Orton, *The Shorter Cambridge Medieval History*, 2 vols. (London, 1955), II, pp. 882–4.
[2] Siméon Luce, ed., *Chroniques de J. Froissart* (Paris, 1872); Geoffrey Brereton, trans., *Froissart, Chronicles* (Harmondsworth, 1968).
[3] Brereton, p. 95, n. 1: 'Froissart's total of 1,291 for the dead nobility is reasonably close to the figure of "1,541 good men-at-arms" given by an English eye-witness ... Froissart's "thirty thousand" for these other ranks is usually considered to be at least three times too high.'
[4] C.E. Pickford in *L'Evolution du Roman Arthurien en Prose Vers La Fin Du Moyen Age d'après le manuscrit 112 du fonds françois de la Bibliothèque Nationale* (Paris, 1959) discusses many of these patrons and their collections. See ch. VII, 'Les Mecènes', pp. 272–290.
[5] It goes without saying that the great majority of patrons and artists were men. But Christine de Pisan praises an illuminator called Anastaise whose skill in painting borders

A giant among collectors was Jean, Duke of Berry (1340–1416), son of Jean II, brother of Charles V, Louis of Anjou and Philippe le Hardi, Duke of Burgundy, and uncle of Charles VI and of Jean Sans Peur, Duke of Burgundy. Through his sister Isabella he was connected to the great Milanese ducal family, the Visconti, and through his first wife to the Armagnacs.[6] All these families were bibliophiles. The Duke of Berry was an avid collector of things beautiful and interesting – cameos, coins and medals (both classical antiques and medieval imitations), tapestries and embroideries, jewels and joyaux,[7] panel paintings and hounds – he had fifteen hundred of them in 1388–, castles[8] and books. As a bibliophile he established one of the greatest medieval libraries, acquiring books by purchase, exchange and gift. Not only did he commission books from workshops but he also attached artists to his court as 'peintres et vallets de chambre'. They repaid his patronage by painting him at a New Year's feast in a hall where tapestries showing Trojan heroes alluded to his genealogy (the Limbourg brothers' calendar, f. 1[v] of the *Très Riches Heures du Duc de Berry*). One artist even, in a prophetic image of pious hope, showed him being welcomed by St Peter at heaven's gate (f. 96 of the *Grandes Heures of Jean de Berry*).

In 1402 the Duke hired Robinet d'Etampes to keep up-to-date inventories of his collections. The library records indicate that he owned about three hundred books of which half were illuminated. The inventories reflect both his own taste and that of his time. As Millard Meiss' catalogue of 'reintegrated' French workshops shows,[9] religious works were still the most popular books. In particular, the Book of Hours, a new genre which had developed from a Psalter appendix into a personal book of devotion, provided opportunities for extensive illuminations not limited in size to the width of a column or two. Among secular texts, histories and contemporary works as well as works by Latin authors were rivalling the romances in popularity.[10]

Three surviving Arthurian manuscripts that can be associated with the Duke

was so great that she was unsurpassed by any craftsman in the city of Paris, 'the center of the best illuminators on earth'. Christine, who closely supervised the decoration of her own works, appears as a character in many illustrated manuscripts; e.g. Paris, BN fr. 603, *Cité des Dames*; Brussels, BR 9502, *Epitre d'Othéa*; and Munich, Bayer, Staatsbibl. gall. II, *Cité des Dames*. See Millard Meiss, *French Painting in the Time of Jean de Berry, the Late Fourteenth Century and the Patronage of the Duke* (London and New York, 1967), pp. 3–4.

6   See the genealogical table in Meiss, pp. 350–1.

7   *Joyaux* were small, finely made objects containing precious metals and jewels – small crucifixes, inkstands, nefs, cups, reliquaries and so on. Regarding their relationship to painting, see Meiss, pp. 141 ff.

8   Re pictorial representations of the Duke of Berry's castles, see A. Dean McKenzie, 'French Medieval Castles in Gothic Manuscript Painting', in *The Medieval Castle: Romance and Reality*, ed. Kathryn Reyerson and Faye Powe (Dubuque, Iowa, 1984), pp. 200–14.

9   Meiss, pp. 354–60.

10   Illuminated manuscripts of Boccaccio's *De casibus virorum illustrium* contained Arthurian miniatures; e.g. BL Royal 14 E V shows the fatal conflict between Arthur and Mordred. Similarly dressed in plate armour without coats of arms, each can be identified by his weapon.

show that he was not entirely impervious to the genre's charm. Robinet describes Paris, BN fr. 117–120, *Lancelot Cycle*, as

> Un grant livre appelé le Livre de Lancelot du Lac, escript en francois, de lettre de forme, tres bien historié au commencement et en plusiers lieux, lequel Monseigneur acheta, en janvier 1405, de maistre Regnault du Montet, demeurant a Paris, la somme de 300 escus d'or.[11]

The last volume of the cycle, fr. 120, f. 520 shows the Duke's coat of arms, 'of France the edges engrailed with gules', and the arms of Jacques d' Armagnac who inherited the *Lancelot* and had some of the miniatures repainted in an up-to-date style.[12] The originals suggest the style of the Boucicaut Master's atelier. In fr. 118, f. 85 which shows King Ban and King Bors with their families, the statuesque figures sit stiffly before a truncated wall and a chequered background, their robes schematically draped. Miniatures by another artist showing, for example, Lancelot's attack on the Dolorous Gard (fr. 118, f. 189) and his combat with Meleagant (fr. 119, f. 333) are more animated, with skilled attention to details of architecture and armour, as well as a touch of humour in the latter miniature where the hero escapes from the tower (not the dungeon) by sliding down a rope into a maiden's boat.[13]

Le Brut d'Angleterre, BN fr. 1454, purchased from Jehin Colin in 1413, and containing the Duke's partially erased signature, shows his interest in history. Recently the use of ultra-violet light on a scraped section of the last folio has revealed the distinctive signature Jehan B on Vienna, Österreichischen National-bibliothek 2537, *Roman de Tristan* (ca. 1410).[14] The 492 folios, 19 inches by 14 inches in size, contain 144 miniatures. Dagmar Thoss attributes to the Master of the Duke of Bedford the most accomplished illustrations; for example, the quadripartite miniature on f. 4 showing a shipwreck along a rocky coast where the sea, receding

---

[11] On the Valois inventories see Léopold Delisle, *Recherches sur la librarie de Charles V*, 2 vols. (Paris, 1902).

[12] On Jacques d'Armagnac's Arthurian manuscripts, see Pickford, pp. 272–78 and Loomis, *The Arthurian Legends in Art*, p. 107. Eleven miniatures from BN 117–120 are reproduced in black and white in Lucy A. Paton, *Sir Lancelot of the Lake* (London, 1929) which also reproduces miniatures from Paris, BN fr. 113, fr. 114, fr. 115, fr. 116, fr. 122, fr. 344; Bibl. de l'Arsenal, 3479–3482; London, BL Add. 10293.

[13] BN fr. 117–20 is closely related in style and in the miniature programme to Arsenal 3479–80. See Loomis, p. 105.

[14] Eighty-five brightly coloured miniatures are reproduced in *Tristan and Isolde from a manuscript of 'The Romance of Tristan' (15th Century)*, text by Gabriel Bise, Introduction by Dagmar Thoss (Fribourg-Genève, 1978). For critical discussions see H.J. Hermann, *Französische und iberische Handschriften der ersten Halbe des 15. Jahrhunderts* (Leipzig, 1938), pp. 44–64; D. Thoss, 'Ein prosa Tristan aus dem Besitz des Duc de Berry in der Österreichischen National Bibliothek (Cod. 2537)' in *Codices Manuscripti* 3 (1977), 66–72; *Französische Gotik und Renaissance in Meisterwerken der Buchmalerei*, Catalogue of the Exhibition of Manuscripts and Incunabilia of the Austrian National Library, Vienna, 1978, 103–5. On the Master of Bedford and other miniaturists of the time, see, in addition to Meiss, J. Porcher, *L'enluminure française* (Paris, 1959).

to meet a gradually lightening sky, gives an illusion of three dimensionality and where the delicate drawing of a raised hoof and outstretched hands is complemented by the borders' ivy leaf rinceaux. But too many of the miniatures show large, awkward figures engaged in combat against backgrounds that combine chequering, pink castles and rudimentary landscape forms. Among the miniatures that specifically recreate the text are those showing King Meladius handing the infant Tristan to Curvenal, while an unusually elegant Merlin in pink toga and blue pleated hood watches; the presentation of the horn of chastity to Mark as he sits in a flowery forest with his feet on a cushion; and Tristan's allusive green shield depicting a knight (Lancelot) standing with his feet on the heads of a King (Arthur) and Queen (Guenevere).

For sheer magnitude the Duke's library was inferior to those of his brother King Charles V (1338–1380) and his nephew Charles VI (1368–1422) whose Royal Library in the Palais du Louvre contained 1200 manuscripts. Among the books which Leopold Delisle found listed in contemporary inventories were three *King Arthurs*, five *Lancelots*, eight *Tristans*, four *Merlins*, three verse romances of *Perceval le Galois* and five of those Arthurian compilations which show how the romance repertoire was expanded (and confused) by combining what had originally been distinctly differentiated works; for example, no. 1118, 'Du Saint Greal, de Lancelot, et de Tristan, de Palamedes et Galaad, en trois Coulombez, bien escript et enluminé' and no. 1120, 'Du Saint Graal, de la creacion Adam, la Naissance de toutes choses, Merlin, les Prophecies Sibile, les Prophecies Methode, evesque de Patras, en prose'. Many of the manuscripts were deluxe both in size and in the extent of illumination. The words 'très bien historié et enluminé' or variations of that description frequently appear. ('Historiation' referred to the painted pictures, 'illumination' to such decorations as capitals, rubrics and borders.)

On Charles VI's death his library, now reduced to 800 volumes by gifts, thefts and 'borrowings', – Queen Isabeau made off with several of the most splendid books – was offered for sale. The Duke of Bedford, Henry VI's uncle and titular regent of France, acquired it for the bargain price of 1200 francs, the purchase most likely motivated by a desire to own a prestigious royal possession. It still included two *Lancelots*, three *Grails*, a *Tristan*, two *Merlins*, two of the compilations, a 'romant de la Table ronde' and two *Percevals*. It has been suggested that the Bedford Library might have provided the manuscripts from which Sir Thomas Malory's *Morte Darthur* was 'breffly drawyn oute of Freynshe'.[15]

In Burgundy the Valois princes Philippe le Hardi (1342–1404), his son Jean Sans Peur (1371–1419) and grandson Philippe le Bon (1396–1467) deliberately surrounded themselves with what Jan Huizinga calls 'a nimbus of chivalrous romance'.[16] Philippe le Hardi had a *Merlin*, a *Lancelot*, two *Palamedes*, a *Joseph of*

[15] See Richard R. Griffith, 'The Authorship Question Reconsidered' in *Aspects of Malory*, ed. Toshiyuki Takamiya and Derek Brewer (Cambridge, Eng., and Totowa, NJ, 1981), pp. 159–177. On Jacques d' Armagnac's Arthurian manuscripts as a possible source for a Yorkshire Malory, see William Matthews, *The Ill-framed Knight; a sceptical inquiry into the identity of Sir Thomas Malory* (Berkeley and Los Angeles, 1966), pp. 145–149.

[16] See C.A.J. Armstrong, 'The Golden Age of Burgundy: dukes that outdid kings' in *The*

Arimathea, an illuminated *Lancelot* and several other prose romances as well as a Chrétien collection. Jean Sans Peur added a *Lancelot*, a *Mort Artu* and a *Merlin*, *inter alia*. Peter Cockshaw's examination of the ducal monetary accounts from 1384 to 1419 shows that ambitious merchants and court officials regarded chronicles and romances in expensive bindings as suitable for 'l'occasion des entrennes'.[17] What the patrons did not receive as inheritances or gifts they could commission. The entry regarding a deluxe manuscript that the banker, merchant, and court administrator, Jacques Rapponde, acquired for Jean in 1405 provides insight into the collecting process:

> A Jacques Rapponde, la somme de lllle frans d'or que mon dit seigneur lui a ordonnez estre bailliéz pour avoir fait ung grant livre pour ycellui seigneur tant du rommans de Lancelot du Lac et du Sanc Greal, comme du roy Arthus ystorié de pluiseurs belles ystores, couvert de drap de soye, garni de deux gros fermans d'argent doréz esmailliéz. Duquel livre ycelli Jacques, si comme il afferme, a paié pour parchemin, eluminer, ystorier, relier, couvrir et fermer la somme de IIIIe escus d'or. Et aussi pour la paine et occuppacion qu'il a eue a faire ledit livrre. Pour ce, par mandement de mon dit seigneur donné a Paris le xxie jour de fevrier mil cccc et v ci rendu avec quietance dudit Jaques contenant affirmacion comme dessus IIIIe frans.

Two years later the same Jacques was paid 10 escus for a *Guiron*.[18]

At this time Paris, where Rapponde ordered Jean's books, was still the centre of cultural activities but the English victory at Agincourt (1415) followed by the fall of Paris (1426) initiated a period of artistic sterility which allowed Philippe le Bon to set up a Burgundian court independent of Paris in matters of patronage. Artists now flocked to Brussels, Ghent, Dijon and Bruges where they found not only a 'centre of power politics' but also 'a microcosm of chivalrous, gallant, and wealthy society'.[19]

According to his court historian Chastellain, Philippe wanted to revive the romantic ideal of a knight as one 'sans peur et sans reproche'.[20] In 1430 he

---

Courts of Europe: Politics, Patronage and Royalty, 1400–1800, ed. A.G. Dickens (London, 1977); Otto Cartellieri, *Am Hofe der Herzöge von Burgund* (Basle, 1926), trans. *The Court of Burgundy: Studies in the History of Civilization* (London and New York, 1929); G. Doutrepont, *La Litterature française a la cour des ducs de Bourgogne* (Paris, 1909); J. Huizinga, *The Waning of the Middle Ages: a Study of the Forms of Life, Thought, and Art in France and the Netherlands in the XIVth and XVth Centuries* (New York, 1954) and C.C. Willard, 'The concept of true nobility at the Burgundian court' in *Studies in the Renaissance*, XIV (1967).

[17] Pierre Cockshaw, 'Mentions d'auteurs, de copistes, d'enlumineurs et de libraires dans les comptes généraux de l'état Bourguignon (1384–1419)' in *Scriptorium; Revue internationale des études relatives aux manuscrits*, XXIII (1969), 122–44.

[18] Cockshaw, 138.

[19] *The Courts of Europe*, p. 57.

[20] Contemporary accounts of the Burgundian courts are *Oeuvres de Chastellain*, ed. Kervyn de Lettenhove, 8 vols. (Brussels, 1863–66); Philippe de Commines, *Mémoires*, ed. B. de

founded the Order of the Golden Fleece to embody the code of chivalry as it had been practised by King Arthur and the Knights of the Round Table. What he had in mind was not an organisation devoted to the service of women – he had, after all, been responsible for handing Joan of Arc to the English and for stealing Hainaut from his cousin, Jacqueline of Bavaria. Rather he wanted courtiers who would be as selflessly devoted to him as the knights in the golden age of chivalry had been to Arthur. To provide exemplary models, he had old romances recopied; some of them were translated into contemporary French. The Vulgate *Lancelot*, including Brussels, BR Albert Ier 9627–28, *Tristan*, *Guiron*, prose versions of *Erec et Enide* and of *Cligès*, and the fourteenth-century prose romance, *Perceforest* (Paris, Bibliothéque de l'Arsenal, 3483–3494)[21] all found a place in his library of 900 volumes. Although the Burgundians could read romances, play at Arthurian games,[22] and 'wear the mask of Lancelot and of Tristram', their dream of heroic life was frustrated by technology. Jacques de Lalaing, the paramount Burgundian hero, who modelled his life on knights-errant of romance, was unromantically killed by a cannon ball.

In Italy, too, powerful families like the Visconti and Sforza of Milan, the Aragonese rulers of Naples, the D'Este in Ferrara, the Gonzaga in Mantua and Federigo da Montefeltro in Urbino adopted the pattern of employing their own scribes and illuminators as well as commissioning books from booksellers.[23] An inventory of the Gonzaga library's French books, made on the death of Francesco in 1407, shows the usual representation of Arthurian texts: Chrétien's *Perceval*, a *Merlin*, a *Lancelot*, a *Grail Quest*, four *Tristans* of Luce de Gast and four based on Hélie de Boron, a *Guiron le Courtois*, three volumes of Rusticiano da Pisa's *La Table Ronde*, and a copy of an independent fifteenth-century romance *Papagallus*, in

Mandrot, 2 vols. (Brussels, 1901–3); *Le livre des faits du bon chevalier Jacques de Lalaing*, cd. Kervyn de Lettenhove, in *Oeuvres de Chastellain*, vol. viii and Olivier de La Marche, *Mémoires*, ed. Beaune et d'Arbaumont, 4 vols. (Paris, 1883–88).
[21] This lengthy prose romance combines Arthurian and Alexander materials. The only complete manuscript is Paris, Bibl. de l'Arsenal 3483–94, compiled for Philippe le Bon in 1459–60. London, BL Royal 15 EV, 19E ii and 19E iii are partial manuscripts with illustrations after 1461, according to H.L.D. Ward, *Catalogue of Romances in the British Museum*, I, p. 377. In Royal 15 EV, f. 3, the king receives a volume from a courtier dressed in the short houppelande with wide reveres and the stubby shoes that became popular in the 1480s. For a critical discussion of Perceforest, see Jeanne Lods, *Le Roman de Perceforest: origines, composition, caractères, valeur et influence* (Genève, 1951).
[22] Huizinga, p. 80. In fifteenth century Burgundy, children were given Arthurian names, a phenomenon that recurred in Victorian England.
[23] Re Italian illumination see J.J.G. Alexander, *Italian Renaissance Illumination* (New York, 1977); F. Avril, M.-T. Gousset, C. Rabel, *Manuscrits enluminés d'origine italienne*, II, XIIIe siècle (Paris, 1984); J.W. Bradley, *A Dictionary of Miniaturists, Illuminators, Calligraphers and Copyists with reference to their works, and notice of their patrons*, 3 vols. (London, 1887–1889); P. D'Ancona, *La Miniature italienne du Xe au XVIe siécle* (Paris and Brussels, 1925); E. Pellegrin, *La Bibliothèque des Visconti et des Sforza ducs de Milan au XVe siècle* (Paris, 1955) and Supplement (Paris, 1969); K. Sutton, 'The original patron of the Lombard manuscript Latin 757 in the Bibliothèque nationale, Paris' in *Burlington Magazine*, 124 (1982), 88–92; P. Toesca, *Storia dell'arte italiana* II, *Il Trecento* (Turin, 1951).

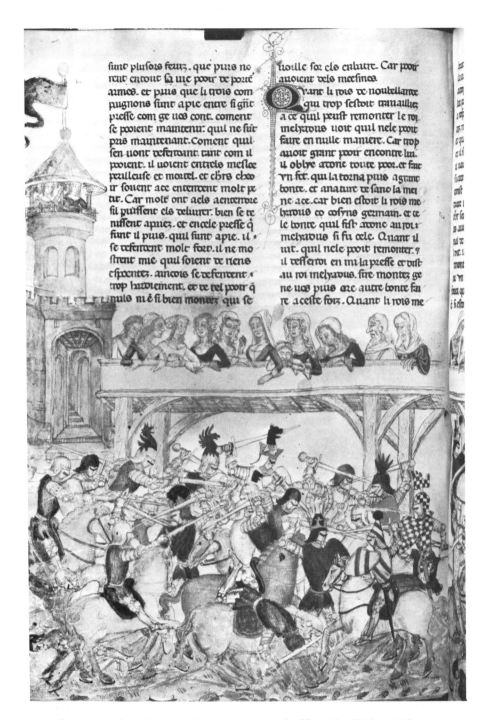

simt plusois feuz. que pius no
rent entout sa uie pour de pour
aimes. et puis que li tois com
pugnons sunt a pie entre si gnt
presse com ge uos cont. coment
se poorent maintenir quil ne sur
pus maintenant. Coment quil
sen uont deferoant. tant com il
porent. il uorent entreis mesce
perilleuse et mortel. et cors cho
ir souent ace entrenoit molt pe
tit. Car molt ont aels a entenoie
sil puissent els deliurer. bien se te
nuffent apriez. et encele presse q
funt il pius. quil sunt apie. il
se deferoent molt foro.il ne mo
strent mie quil soient de riens
espoentes. aincois se deferoent ·
trop haroiement. et de tel poir q
nuis nie si bien monter qui se

liouile for els enlutre. Car pour
auoient dels meesines.
Quant li tois de noubellante
qui trop seroit trauaillie
a ce quil peust remonter le roi
melyaous uoit quil nele poir
faire en nulle maniere. Car trop
auoit grant pour encontre lui.
il oblye a tone toute poor. et fait
vn fet. qui la torna pius a gtant
bonte. et an a tant de sano la mei
ne a ce.car bien estoit li rois me
liaous co cosyns germain. et de
le bonte quil fist a tone au roi
melyaous si fu cele. Quant li
mt. quil nele poir remonter. 7
il deferoi en mi la presse et vist
au roi melyaous. sire montes ge
ne uos pius are autre bonte fai
re a ceste forz. Quant li tois me

9. **Tourneying knights with distinctive armorials. BL Add. 12228, f. 164ᵛ**
(*Roman du Roy Meliadus*)

which King Arthur, advised by a parrot, undertakes various adventures.[24] The Gonzaga collection must have been well known, for in the late fourteenth century many Lombard nobles asked to borrow books, among them Luchino Visconti, who in 1378 requested 'unum romanzum loquentem de Tristano vel Lanzalotto'. The borrowings eventually became intolerable; Franscesco threatened to punish the unscrupulous people who borrowed on indefinite loan or even stole his manuscripts.[25]

During the later Middle Ages most noble families in Western Europe were related by blood and marriage. In addition to those already mentioned, the Valois connections included, for example, the Kings of Aragon; the Emperor Charles IV and his son, King Wenceslas of Bohemia; the English Kings Richard II and Henry V; and the Duke of Bavaria, father of Charles VI's queen. This network facilitated the movement of manuscripts from country to country as they were borrowed, bought, exchanged, copied and inherited. Even when no extensively illuminated Arthurian manuscripts have survived, as in Spain and Portugal, written records attest to their popularity.[26]

Patronage necessarily affected style for, as Marcel Thomas notes, the patrons imposed on their book producers 'a certain tone, a certain courtly elegance, in harmony with their personal tastes'.[27] The princely consumers – to use modern jargon – wanted to be personally identified with their possessions.[28] Border designs now incorporated coats of arms like the Duke of Berry's *azure fleur de lis or engrailed with gules* and his punningly allusive wounded swan and bear.[29] London, BL Add. MS 12228, *Roman du Roy Meliadus*, ca. 1352, bears in the backgrounds of some miniatures the arms of Louis of Taranto who married Queen Joanna of Naples in 1347 and was crowned king in 1352. Furthermore, the romance hero

---

[24] W. Braghirolli, P. Meyer, and G. Paris, 'Inventaire des manuscrits en langue française possédés par Francesco Gonzaga, Ier Capitaine de Mantoue, mort en 1407', *Romania*, 9 (1880), 497–514.

[25] Giovanni Paccagnini, *Pisanello*, trans. Jane Carroll (London, 1973), pp. 45–46.

[26] William J. Entwistle, *The Arthurian Legend in the Literature of the Spanish Peninsula* (New York, 1975). Loomis, pp. 92–93, attributed to a Spanish workshop the illuminations in BN fr. 750, Prose *Tristan*, written by Pierre de Tiergeville in 1278. However, Avril, Grosset and Rabel give its likely provenance as Italy or the Holy Land. On the latter, see J. Folda, *Crusader manuscript illumination at Saint-Jean d'Acre, 1274–1291* (Princeton, 1976). Merlin appears as a character in Cantiga No. 108, one of the Cantigas de Santa Maria written by Alfonso X, King of Castile and Leon (1221–1284). The prophet, in this case, the Virgin's representative, worsts the devil's representative, a Jew, by prophesying correctly that the Jew's son will be born with his face turned towards his back. The scene is depicted in *Cantigas de Santa Maria. Edición facsímil del Códice T.I. l de la Biblioteca de San Lorenzo el Real de El Escorial*, Siglo XIII, 2 vols. (Madrid). I am indebted to Harvey Sharrer for this reference. On the source, *Les Prophécies de Merlin*, see Harvey Sharrer, 'Notas sobre la materia arturica hispanica, 1979–1986', *La Corónica*, 15 (1986–87), 328–40.

[27] Marcel Thomas, *The Golden Age: Manuscript Painting at the Time of Jean, Duke of Berry*, trans. Ursule Molinaro and Bruce Benderson (New York, 1979), p. 8.

[28] See M. Alison Stones, 'Secular Manuscript Illumination in France', in *Medieval Manuscripts and Textual Criticism*, ed. Christopher Kleinhenz (Chapel Hill, NC, 1976), pp. 83–102. Stones notes that ecclesiastics as well as laymen owned secular books.

[29] Meiss discusses Jean de Berry's arms and emblems, pp. 95–98.

carries the Neapolitan arms: *dexter azure fleur de lis or with a red label; sinister the arms of Jerusalem argent a cross with four crosslets or*. Meliadus also wears an emblematic helmet with two peaks, one argent and one azure, to represent Louis and Joanna's joint sovereignty. As manuscripts changed hands, the new owner's arms would be added. BL Royal 20 D IV, *Lancelot*, originally written and illustrated in France ca. 1300, was taken to England between 1360 and 1380. There two miniatures were repainted and the decorative initials were overpainted with the Arms of the Bohun family to which the new owner, Humphrey, Duke of Gloucester, belonged.[30]

In earlier manuscript illuminations a book was depicted as the work of fictional characters like Merlin, who dictates his story to Blaise, and King Arthur, who tells his story to a scribe (Rylands, fr. 2, f. 212 and Royal 14E III, f. 140). In the fifteenth century, however, offering a splendid volume to a patron became the occasion for flattering presentation miniatures, as in BN fr. 100, f. 1, a *Tristan* from Charles V's library.[31] The most famous miniature of this type appears in the *Chroniques de Hainaut*, Brussels, BR 9242, f. 1, where the book's scholar-publisher, Jean Wauquelin, and his patron, Philippe le Bon, are painted so realistically that Panofsky and others attribute this page to Roger Van der Weyden.[32] Also identifiable in the all male court are Philippe's young son Charles; his Chancellor, Nicholas Rolin, donor of the Beaune Altarpiece; and another patron of the arts, Jean Chevrot, who commissioned the Seven Sacraments Altarpiece. The artist, while making clear the Duke's superior height, elegance, and rank, has at the same time managed to flatter other patrons.

Some of these deluxe manuscripts were enormous, running to two, three or four volumes. The two volume *Tristan*, BN fr. 100–101 had 814 leaves; a *Lancelot* cycle manuscript, Paris, Arsenal 3479–80 ran to 1300. The pages could be 52.6 x 34.4 centimetres, as in the third volume of BN fr. 117–20. It is likely that busy patrons might devote more attention to the illustrations than to the text. What they wanted to see depicted were the pastimes that they enjoyed, if they were great nobles, or to which they aspired, if they were wealthy merchants. Less than in the earlier manuscripts are we aware of the knight as a protector of the oppressed and a servant of ladies. Instead, he is engaged with male companions in fighting, tourneying, hunting with hawks and hounds, playing games of chess or cards, and forming part of a cavalcade to ride into the countryside which pro-

---

[30] Lucy Freeman Sandler, *A Survey of Manuscripts Illuminated in the British Isles*, 2 vols. *Gothic Manuscripts [I], 1285–1385* (London and New York, 1986).

[31] See Loomis, p. 104, for discussion.

[32] For a reproduction with discussion see *Medieval Miniatures from the Department of Manuscripts (formerly the 'Library of Burgundy') the Royal Library of Belgium*, commentaries by L.M.J. Delaissé (New York, 1965) and *Les Miniatures des Chroniques de Hainaut (15me siècle), avec une préface de Pierre Cockshaw* (Mons, 1979). Some critics identify the presenter as Simon Nockart. On a suggested relationship to Roger van der Weyden, see Erwin Panofsky, *Early Netherlandish Painting*, p. 466 n. s. See also Georges Dogaer, *Flemish Miniature Painting in the 15th and 16th Centuries* (Amsterdam, 1987), p. 14, 63.

vided, says Raimond van Marle, activities that best represented the ideal life of the nobility.[33]

The idea that art should glorify the patron's life style and person was not limited to miniatures. Tapestries, like paintings, were one of the most popular forms of decoration, being used as wall hangings in castles and pavilions, as bed curtains, and as bench covers. It is not surprising to find numerous references to them in princely inventories, including this one made in 1420 after the death of Jean Sans Peur:

> Neuf grans tapiz et deux mendres de haulte-lice, ouvrez à or, de volerie
> de plouviers et perdriz, èsquelz sont les personnages de feux mon-
> signeur le duc Jehan et madame la duchesse sa femme, tant à pié come
> à cheval.[34]

Manuscripts of *Palamède, Guiron, Meliadorus, Perceforest* and *Tristan* draw on the same pictorial repertoire as tapestries and murals, glorifying the knight's social activities while diminishing the lady's active role. Those delectable damsels who had released knights from apparently inviolable prisons, escorted them through the forest, and, by asking boons at court, provided links between a knight-errant and his adventure fade away. Nor do the manipulative fées and other remnants of Celtic mythology fare better. In an Italian manuscript made for Louis of Taranto, King of Naples, BL Add. 12228, *Roman du Roy Meliadus* (ca. 1352), for example, the miniatures portray a masculine world of self-indulgent entertainment with an occasional giant to add a touch of fantasy.[35] Spreading the scenes across the lower part of the folios and upwards into the margins, the artists treat the pages like walls to be decorated with large scale murals. A king reclines in a tropical grove beside an ornamental fountain (f. 36), a *locus amoenus* image that appears also in ff. 37, 38^v, 61^v, 127, 130^v. King and courtiers listen to a zither player and lutanist in a leafy bower with plump cushions scattered on the ground (ff. 222, 222^v, 223). Their dogs at their feet and their servants at their back, they feast in an arbour (f. 328) or ride off to hunt and hawk (ff. 2^v, 13, 67^v). Their gymnastic versatility is the subject of so many tournament scenes that the several artists involved in the drawing, painting, and gilding evidently gave up in boredom long before the 363

---

[33] Raimond Van Marle, *Iconographie de L'art Profane du Moyen-Age et a la Renaissance*, 2 vols. (New York, 1971), I, pp. 50 ff. and 134–40 re the cavalcade.

[34] George Wingfield Digby and Wendy Hefford, *The Devonshire Hunting Tapestries* (London, 1971), p. 27. René of Anjou may be depicted in the Devonshire tapestries; see. p. 30 and plate 8.

[35] Loomis (pp. 114–5) associates the *Meliadus* with BN fr. 4274, a sumptuously decorated manuscript of the *Statutes of the Order of the Holy Spirit*, 1353. The manuscripts, both produced in Naples, have 'the same details of costume, the scallop-edged tippets, the close-fitting, long-waisted jupons, the white liripipes as well as similar facial types and backgrounds'. f. 2^v of the *Statutes* depicts Louis dressed in the order's white habit, kneeling to the Trinity. The order's insignia was a triple knot. For further details, see Avril *et al.* pp. 74–6.

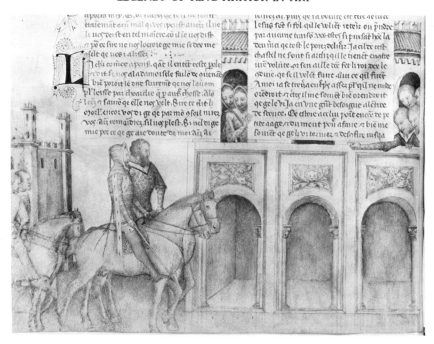

10. Knights ride into a city. BN nouv. acq. fr. 5243, f. 26ᵛ (*Guiron le Courtois*)

miniatures could be completed. As for the courtly ladies, they, too, look bored as
they view from balconies, doorways, and tournament stands the heroes' exploits.

A similar concentration on the recreations of a male-dominated society occurs
in another Italian work, BN nouv. acq. fr. 5243, *The Romance of Guiron le Courtois*
(ca. 1370–1380).[36] This beautiful but fragmentary manuscript was probably decorated in Lombardy, perhaps for Bernabo Visconti. In their study of Italian illumination F. Avril and M.-T. Gousset remark that these miniatures provide 'dans leur
précision documentaire un temoignage de premier ordre sur les moeurs, la mode
et l'armement militaire du temps'. As in BL Add. 12228, the pictures in watercolour or grisaille executed by several artists are spread across the bottom and up
into the text, filling not only the margins but even the spaces between the columns
of text which seem to have become decorated castle walls, pierced by round-
arched windows from which nobles observe the passing parade (f. 26ᵛ). The
acanthus leaf[37] retained from classical architecture decorates doorways and the
roofs are tiled in the Lombard fashion.

Costume also reflects the manuscript's provenance. A change of fashion in the
mid-fourteenth century had replaced the older style surcoat cut in one piece with
garments that had inset sleeves, an improvement that made close-fitting clothes

---

[36] See Avril *et al.* pp. 94–95; Loomis, p. 120; Thomas, pl. I; and Roger Lathuillère, *Guiron Le
Courtois: Etude de la Tradition manuscrite et analyse critique* (Genève, 1966), pp. 77–79.
[37] The Italian acanthus was absorbed into International Gothic style, as the fifteenth-
century manual, *The Göttingen Model Book*, shows.

possible.[38] Whether in armour or court dress, the nobles in nouv. acq. fr. 5243 wear tight, padded jupons (also called cotes-hardies) that exhibit a shapely waist, tight hose that draw attention to a shapely leg, and long shoes or solerets with pointed toes. At the tournament depicted in f. 1, a knight in mi-parti and hood sits with the ladies whose blond plaited hair is wound loosely about their heads in a characteristically Italian fashion.

The art of costume which from 1350 to 1480 produced an unprecedented degree of extravagance was a colourful aspect of the cult of personality.[39] Details of dress could signal not only class but also one's political affiliation and emotional state. At the courts of France and Burgundy there developed, at least for aesthetic purposes, an amorous symbolism according to which blue clothing signified fidelity, green passion, grey and brown sadness. Wearing clothes appropriate to a higher class was regarded as both a sin and a crime while wearing lower class dress or a negative colour like yellow (hostility) was interpreted as an insult.

No miniature provides a better opportunity for discussing the language of costume than 'The Wedding of Arthur and Genoivre', BR 9243. *The Chroniques de Hainaut* (1446) which Jean Wauquelin translated and edited from Jacques de Guise's Latin chronicle at Philippe le Bon's behest, required three folio-sized volumes of 293, 295, and 262 leaves respectively. Only the first volume's illustrations were completed in Philippe's lifetime. The commission for paintings in the second volume, based on Geoffrey of Monmouth's *Historia*, was given to Guillaume Vrelant, the master of a Bruges Workshop.[40] In 1468 a wealthy courtier, Jean de Croy, paid him seventy-two livres for sixty miniatures. Of these, seven depict Arthurian subjects.

The costumes compel the viewer to identify the ideal court of romance with that of the Burgundian Duke, an analogy that was evidently not uncommon in the later fifteenth century. When John Paston III accompanied Margaret of York to Bruges for her wedding to Charles the Rash, he wrote to his mother (July 8, 1468) describing the apparel:

> And they that have jostyd wyth hym [i.e. the Bastard of Burgundy]
> into thys day have ben as rychely beseyn, and hym selve also, as clothe
> of gold and sylk and sylvyr and goldsmythys werk myght mak hem;
> for of syche ger, and gold and perle and stonys, they of the Dwkys

---

[38] Stella Mary Newton, *Fashion in the Age of the Black Prince: a study of the years 1340–1365* (Woodbridge and Totowa, NJ, 1980), p. 3.

[39] On costume, in addition to Newton, see Janet Backhouse, 'Manuscript Sources for the History of Mediaeval Costume' in *Costume, the Journal of the Costume Society*, 2 (1968), 9–14; Huizinga, *op. cit.* especially ch. XIX, 'Art and Life'; Margaret Scott, *Late Gothic Europe, 1400–1500, The History of Dress Series* (London, 1980); Joan Evans, *A History of Jewellery 1100–1870* (London, 1953). On sumptuary laws regulating dress, see E. Baldwin, *Sumptuary Legislation and Personal Regulation in England* (Baltimore, 1926).

[40] Dogaer, *op. cit.*, pp. 15–16, 99–100; James Douglas Farquhar, *Creation and Imitation: the Work of a Fifteenth Century Manuscript Illuminator* (Fort Lauderdale, 1976), and Loomis, pp. 126–7.

coort, neythyr gentylmen nor gentylwomen, they want non; for wyt-
howt that they have it by wyshys, by my trouthe I herd nevyr of so gret
plente as her is. . . .And as for the Dwkys coort, as of lordy[s], ladys,
and gentylwomen, knytys, sqwyirs, and gentyllmen, I herd never of
non lyek to it save kyng Artourys cort.[41]

In composition f. 39^v seems a typical marriage scene with the officiating bishop
at the centre and the bride and groom to his left and right. Their hands are joined
physically and symbolically with the bishop's stole. Unusually, four other couples
in the foreground mirror the ceremony as, with hands joined in the same way,
they each receive a priest's blessing. The guests are symmetrically arranged behind them, twenty to the right of the dividing pillar and twenty to the left. Arthur
and Guenevere wear the Franco-Flemish royal robes of red and blue, the latter
colour having the additional significance of fidelity.[42] Guenevere's scarlet gown is
trimmed with ermine and flecked with gold. With her left hand she delicately
catches up her heavy skirt, revealing beneath a cote of green damask, a material
also revealed beneath her bodice. At the French and Burgundian courts Vert de
Hongrie (a green that the painter made from malachite) was reserved for queens
and princesses. Guenevere's fair hair worn long and loose indicates that she is a
virgin. Arthur's fur-lined robe is split up the side, revealing the stork-like legs that
were greatly admired. On his ermine collar is the insignia of a chivalric order to
which the other bridegrooms belong, as their gold collars show. Arthur's fleur-de-
lis crown alludes to the Burgundian relationship to French royalty.

The couple on Guenevere's left, set even further forward than the hero and
heroine, attracts particular attention. The lady wears the royal colours and her
long train indicates that her rank is higher than that of the other ladies. Moreover,
unlike the other brides whose long hair indicates their virginity, she is married. In
face and dress she resembles a portrait of Philippe's duchess, Isabella of Portugal,
in the *Breviary of Philip the Good*, BR 9026, f. 425 (ca. 1460). And her bridegroom,
with his shaggy haircut, dark eyes, pointed nose and rich sombre dress certainly
looks like Philippe himself as he appears in the same miniature and in Cambridge, Fitzwilliam J. 187, f. 91, *The Book of the Order of the Golden Fleece*. Is Vrelant
memorialising his patron by portraying him and his duchess as the most prominent guests at Arthur's wedding?

If we did not know that the artist worked on these miniatures in the 1460s,
costume details would confirm the date. The split sides of the men's gowns, the
carefully set folds, roomy sleeves, padded shoulders and practical shoes (no
longer extravagantly attenuated) allow freedom of movement. In contrast, the

---

[41] *Paston Letters and Papers of the Fifteenth Century*, ed. James Gairdner, 4 vols. (Edinburgh,
1910), vol. II, p. 318.
[42] Scott, p. 250, says that the 'robe royale' was the name given to a set of garments which
the royal family wore on formal occasions. The style was 'frozen' in the fourteenth century.
Male robes included a cloak and tunic; female a cloak and a gown open at the sides to
reveal the under-dress; cf. Guenevere's costume.

women are constricted by tight-fitting sleeves, high waistbands, and ruthless corsetting to achieve the tiny waists. The effect of female dress in the 1460s was to imprison the body. Among the wedding guests the variety of hats allows for age and preference. For men acorn caps and plush bowlers are comme-il-faut in 1460 but shaggy hats are still worn. Some ladies have the new steeple headdresses while others retain the horned constructions. Turbans, an Oriental feature common in the west after the Fall of Constantinople, adorn both men and women. (The varied headgear reappears on spectators in f. 42, 'Arthur fights Frollo' and f. 45, 'Sports at Caerleon'). Above all, the miniature of Arthur's wedding, with its rich costumes, its fair women with modestly downcast eyes, and its confident men, conveys an impression of a wealthy, fashionable, and virtuous society.

Armour and coats of arms in late medieval manuscripts correspond to those used in contemporary wars and chivalric pageants and games. In the *Chroniques* f. 36[v], 'Arthur's Army and the Saxons' and f. 55[v], 'Arthur's army and the Romans' form-fitting plate armour and bascinets have replaced the chain mail and long surcoats of earlier manuscripts. As Arthur addresses his warriors, armourers can be seen doing repairs in the middle ground. Arthur's armorial, *gules, three crowns or*, is conspicuously displayed on shield and caparison in f. 36[v] and on his shield in f. 49[v], which depicts the fight with the Giant of St Michael's mount.[43] The latter wears old-fashioned chain mail and a red surcoat as an indication of longevity – such a style having gone out of date at least a century earlier. The knights waiting the King's return wear coats of arms that may be individual allusions.[44]

Among the most useful reference works for artists and patrons who organised Arthurian sports and spectacles[45] were the Arthurian armorials which were produced in great numbers between 1440 and 1460. Michel Pastoureau has studied 74 surviving manuscripts depicting the arms, crests and supporters attributed to between 160 and 180 Arthurian characters.[46] While acknowledging the inspirational effect that they had on the pageantry of fêtes and mock tourneys, he proposes that their chief function was as 'aides-memoires' or models for the

---

[43] In French art King Arthur's colours are usually those of French royalty, a golden sign on an azure field, while in art for an English audience they are the Plantagenet colours, a golden sign on gules.

[44] The device with three crescents belonged to the English knight William de Rithre. See Gerald J. Brault, *Early Blazon*, p. 247.

[45] Ruth Cline, 'The Influence of Romances on Tournaments of the Middle Ages', *Speculum*, 20 (1945), 204–211; R.S. Loomis, 'Chivalric and Dramatic Imitations of Arthurian Romance', in *Medieval Studies in Memory of A. Kingsley Porter*, 2 vols. (Cambridge, Mass., 1939), pp. 79–97; and Loomis, 'Arthurian Influence on Sport and Spectacle' in *Arthurian Literature in the Middle Ages*, pp. 553–559.

[46] One of the first rolls of arms was 'Les Noms, Armes, et Blasons des Chevalliers et Compaignons de la Table Ronde' which King René of Anjou compiled with his *Liuire des Tourneys* (ca. 1455). Extant copies include Cambridge, Harvard University Library Hofer 1; and New York, Pierpont Morgan Library 16. See Helmut Nickel, 'Heraldry', *Arthurian Encyclopedia*, pp. 278–283; Edouard Sandoz, 'Tourneys in the Arthurian Tradition', *Speculum* 19 (1944), 389–420; Michel Pastoureau, *Armorial des Chevaliers de la Table Ronde* (Paris, 1983), and *L'hermine et le sinople: Etudes d'Héraldique Mediévale* (Paris, 1982).

illuminators of Parisian and Northern French ateliers.[47] Of course, artists were using 'armes imaginaires' a century before they were codified. By the mid-fourteenth century the addition of crests symbolically endowed the heroes with the lion's courage and nobility, the eagle's power, the fox's trickiness, the boar's defiant valour. Knights with consistent crests and coats-of-arms are a feature of the endless battles and tournaments of later manuscripts; for example, BL Add. 12228, f. 164[v] where extensive chequering on shield, jupon, helm and crest identifies Palamedes,[48] and two bands, Lancelot. Knights further back in the melée sport a wyvern and an eagle, while a dog issuing from a golden crown, Meliadus' crest in the armorials, is here transferred to King Mark.

Gawain's arms change from the canting arms of earlier manuscripts to purple, a double-headed eagle with a golden beak and azure wings (cf. BN fr. 120 *Lancelot*, before 1405). His brothers also carry the double-headed eagle. Guiron's shield is plain gold and Meliadus' plain sinople (red) although in BL Add. 12228 he is honorarily endowed with the arms of King Louis, who commissioned the book. In the armorials Tristan's arms are 'de sinople au lion d'or, armé et lampassé de gueules', as they are in BN fr. 99, 112, 115, 120 and Chantilly 315, 645, 646, 647 but in Vienna, ONB 2537 he has three gold crowns on a green field to imitate Arthur's sign.[49] In late manuscripts like Paris, Bibl. d'Arsenal 3479–3480, *Lancelot* (end of the fifteenth century); BN fr. 99, *Tristan* (1463); BN fr. 115, *Lancelot* (1470–80); and BN fr. 120, *La Mort Artu* (1460–70), the armorial shields, crests, jupons and the horses' sweeping caparisons add an intensity of colour and grace of line that are often the miniatures' most attractive features.

The powerful influence of patrons on the pictorial content does not alone account for the fact that their books have a different appearance from those produced before 1340. The development of the International Gothic Style gave artists a new way of perceiving the world. The Italian conception of three dimensional pictorial space[50] had entered Parisian ateliers about 1325 when Jean Pucelle used oblique lines, modelled figures and fore-shortened frontal settings to give some effect of depth. By 1400, landscapes receding towards the horizon and interiors where the obliquely set furniture and paved floors gave depth began to replace architectural frames and patterned backgrounds. Another element of

[47] Pastoureau localised the initial compilations in Normandy, suggesting that Arthurian armorials were inspired by the arms of particular families such as the Bertrands, Brecquebecs and Fresvilles. Later, families entitled to bear arms might adopt the devices of Arthurian knights. The Duke of Burgundy's chamberlain, Régnier Pot, claimed Palamedes' chequered arms. See Pastoureau (1982), pp. 297–309. Brault, pp. 76–98, illustrates numerous devices.

[48] Chequering indicated confusion, an allusion to Palamedes' Saracen blood. He is a pagan member of a Christian order and an unsuccessful courtly lover whose desire for Iseult brings him into conflict with Tristan.

[49] In *L'hermine et le sinople*, Pastoureau remarks on the instability of Tristan's arms, noting that the variation is partly explained by the plot's demands for disguise.

[50] On the representation of space in book illumination, see Erwin Panofsky, *Early Netherlandish Painting: Its Origins and Character*, I, pp. 21–50; John White, *The Birth and Rebirth of Pictorial Space* (London, 1957), pp. 219–235 and *passim*.

International Gothic was French mannerism, expressed in the sophisticated extravagance of dress and accoutrements and in the exquisiteness of objets d'art. A third element was Netherlandish naturalism which L.M.J. Delaissé believes originated in Dutch ateliers where artists, free from powerful and exacting patrons, could express themselves more spontaneously.[51] Naturalism accounts for the carefully observed butterflies, fruit, flowers, dragonflies and even houseflies in the borders of Oxford, Bodl. Douce 383, *Guiron* (1490–1500) and London, Lambeth Palace Library 6, *St. Alban's Chronicle* (after 1470). It accounts for the fact that knights and ladies are no longer unchangingly fair and youthful. The physiognomies reveal age, boredom, sly malice and hauteur.

A late fourteenth century Visconti manuscript, BN fr. 343 *Lancelot, Queste du Saint Graal, Tristan,* and *la Mort le Roi Artu* (1385–90), exemplifies the beginnings of the new style.[52] In f. 4, King Arthur's red sandstone castle, set diagonally on the right, is massive and enclosed like a fortress with small, sparse, rounded windows on the 'street' side, a rounded doorway filled with spectators (who are viewed from various angles) and a balcony from which Guenevere and her ladies can watch. This is an Italian palazzo, crenellated with the splayed merlons that can still be seen on the Palazzo del Capitano in Mantua. The monarchs' spiked crowns,[53] the sharply pointed beards, the poulaines, the jewelled circlet in Galahad's neat hair, and the haute couture of his close-fitting, mi-parti jupon reflect the mannerism of International Gothic costume. And is it possible that the triple knot so obviously displayed on Lancelot's indigo hose is the insignia of King Louis' Order of the Holy Spirit? Francois Avril believes that the illustrations in this *Lancelot* were based on those of the now fragmentary *Guiron,* BN nouv. acq. fr. 5243, which also belonged to the Visconti.[54]

That the artists have not completely solved the problems of perspective is evident in the depiction of the Round Table as a doughnut which cuts across the feasters' laps in a way that distorts their legs, while the geometrically patterned green curtain behind seems to be tilting the assembly towards the front (f. 3). The Perilous Chapel (ff. 18, 19) is more successful for its chequerboard floor and obliquely set altar and roof deepen the space. The Grail chalice, the elaborate candelabra with acanthus design, the seven tapers, and the Crucifixion triptych provide an image cluster symbolically linking the Grail to the Redemption,[55]

---

[51] L.M.J. Delaissé, *A Century of Dutch Manuscript Illumination* (Berkeley and Los Angeles, 1968), p. 60.

[52] Avril et al., p. 98, note that this manuscript is precisely described in a 1426 inventory of the Visconti library in their castle at Pavia. The unfinished shields in the border of f. 1 were probably intended to bear the Visconti arms.

[53] Meiss, p. 304, suggests that the sharp-pointed crowns, (which are worn by the Magi in Chantilly, Musée Condé MS 65, ff. 51^v and 52), 'may be misunderstandings of the solar rays of the ancient Roman emperors that continue as spikes in medieval crowns'.

[54] Avril *et al.*, p. 98.

[55] The text of *La Queste del Saint Graal* makes clear that the Grail is a symbol of grace which Christ won for mankind through the Crucifixion. See Etienne Gilson, 'La mystique de la Grâce dans la Queste del Saint Grail', *Romania*, L1 (1925), 321–37.

while literally depicting the art of contemporary churches.[56] Isolated trees and rocky slopes darkening on the horizon are features of the inhospitable landscapes indicated in the text, though the artist also uses lush vegetation to give a paradisal effect as in f. 27 where Perceval meets an enticing female. The observant will note the toadstools in the grass.

Fidelity to the text and to relevant iconography is scrupulous in the *Queste* section (ff. 1–60). In f. 4^v the tourneying Galahad wears a red sendal cote-hardie and rides a white horse.[57] He uses the sword drawn from the stone (f. 4) but correctly has no shield, since he will not acquire it until he reaches the white abbey (f. 10^v). In f. 15, which continues the association of white and red, the hero wears an additional sign, a crest consisting of an aureoled angel's head and wings (divine protection). The viewer can easily identify him, even when his visor is closed. Lancelot's personal insignia in f. 6 is the pattern of red hearts pierced by golden arrows which decorates his green jupon; this secular image explains his failure to see the Grail uncovered. In many miniatures the artist successfully applies realism to the text's mystical adventures; for example, in the unique drawing which shows Galahad touching the healing Grail to the Maimed King's bare thigh, the agonized and astounded monarch clutches his chair with credible force. Realism is also apparent throughout the manuscript in the depiction of faces with dark eyes and varied expressions.

One of the most interesting pictorial programmes is found in a Venetian manuscript of *La Tavola Ritonda*, Florence, Pal. 556, (1446).[58] This Italian romance of the later fourteenth century creates a cyclic effect by combining the adventures of Tristan and Isolde, derived from Thomas, the Prose *Tristan* and the *Palamède*, with material about the rule of Uther Pendragon, the Grail Quest, and the downfall of Arthurian society. Its theme is the social effects of ideal love, with Tristano, not Lancilotto, being 'the flower of chivalry'. Bonitazio Bembo's 289 pen drawings are contemporary in style and retrospective in content, for most of the great scenes in the Arthurian repertoire are depicted. As we admire the flamboyant fan-shaped hats, the feathery, embroidered cloaks, the high-waisted gowns (their bombarde

---

[56] A late medieval obsession with opulent display combined with a withdrawal from the material world through mystical contemplation frequently appears in the Grail illustrations of later manuscripts. The artist of Paris, Ars. 5218, *Queste*, 1351, shows his understanding of transubstantiation by drawing inside the chalice a naked Christ with the stigmata clearly revealed. More often the knights adore an elaborate ciborium, a masterpiece of the goldsmith's and jeweller's art; cf. BN fr. 120, f. 544^v; BN fr. 112, f. 179^v; BN fr. 116, ff. 610 and 621, where the Perilous Chapel has disappeared entirely, leaving only a stone altar with Grail, candle and crucifix. See reproductions in John Matthews, *The Grail, Quest for the Eternal* (New York, 1981).

[57] Galahad, a type of Christ, appears at Arthur's court on the Feast of Pentecost, clothed in the colour of Pentecostal flame. White, the other colour associated with this hero, signifies chastity, the essential virtue for success in the Grail Quest.

[58] Filippo-Luigi Polidori, ed., *La Tavola Ritondo o l'istoria di Tristano*, 2 vols. (Bologna, 1864–5); Anne Shaver, trans., *Tristan and the Round Table* (Binghampton, NY, 1983). Eleven of Bembo's drawings are reproduced in Gardner, *The Arthurian Legend in Italian Literature*. See also Loomis, p. 121.

sleeves lined with patterned materials) and the jewelled coiffures, we sense a charm that differentiates this Arthurian society from the self-conscious courtiers of Burgundian manuscripts. The insouciance is produced by idealized faces and by the extraordinary number of animals and birds that infiltrate the scenes, indoors as well as outdoors. As Lancelot (whose name is written on his hat) and Tristan (whose embroidered coat of arms, a rampant lion, identifies him) play chess in the Lady of the Lake's palace, rabbits and a dog scamper at their feet (f. 105). Dogs, monkeys and birds watch jousting knights. Isolde has a cat as well as a dog that watches Tristan drink the love-potion (f. 42^v) and barks warningly when Mark approaches the lovers' bedroom (f. 79^v). The forest shelters rabbits, deer, bears, leopards, porcupines, monkeys, butterflies and birds. The cowherds and shepherds who encounter the mad Tristan have realistic cows and sheep (f. 65).

The artist emphasises Grail iconography, seizing every opportunity to elaborate details sparsely treated in the text. Ribbon-like flames surround Corbenic (f. 147). Anticipating the Pre-Raphaelites in the nineteenth centry, he draws a lily on the ship carrying Perceval's dead sister (146^v) and on the altar of the Grail Chapel (f.150^v). Angels carry the tapers, tablet, bleeding lance and grail, a cookie-jar vessel with rose decoration. Joseph exhibits the figure of a little boy formed from the mass bread (f. 148). We see the death of Guenevere – not as a nun (f. 172); Lancelot's entry into a hermitage which is located in a flowery meadow beside a stream (f. 172); and, uniquely, Arthur's departure for Avalon. Wounded mortally by Mordred, who in the text has won the last battle, he sits upright and alone in a single-masted ship while, in the foreground, a hand flourishes Excalibur, ducks quack, one knight expires and the other, described in the text as Arthur's squire, surveys the scene (f. 171).

La Tavola Ritonda's author and artist devote a good deal of space to Tristan's death, prolonging the final days in the style of a Victorian novelist. F. 159^v shows Mark's fatal attack as Tristan plays chess with Isolde; in f. 161 the hero lies sick in bed; in f. 163^v, he is carried off on a bier; and in 164 the lovers lie buried in one tomb.[59] The joined hands of their effigies and the entwined roses growing from the grave symbolise their eternal union. It would be interesting to know whether the artist originated this depiction which differs in two important details from the Italian text but resembles several Victorian treatments of the subject. The golden effigy of the literary Isolde holds a flower to show that she was the flower of all others in the land and Tristan holds a sword to show that he had set the kingdom free. A year later, says the author,

---

[59] Most miniatures depict the usual Prose Tristan ending. However, BN fr. 103, f. 1, Prose Tristan (ca. 1470) reverts to the poetic ending involving a ship with significantly coloured sails – black to indicate Iseult's refusal to come to Brittany, white to indicate her presence. The artist uses the sail motif to depict in one landscape two events in the love story. In the foreground, the white-sailed ship is about to set out from Ireland with Tristan already drinking the fatal love-potion. In the middle distance the black-sailed ship bears from Brittany to Cornwall the lovers' coffin.

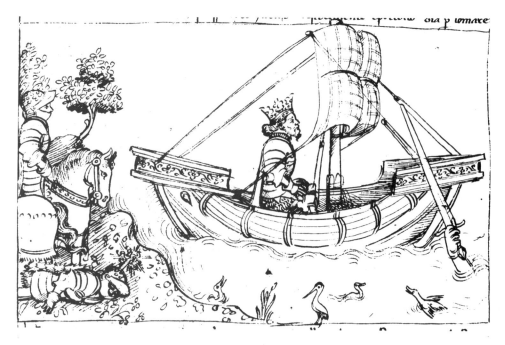

11a. Arthur departs for Avalon. Florence, Cod. Pal. 556, f. 171 (*La Tavola Ritonda*)

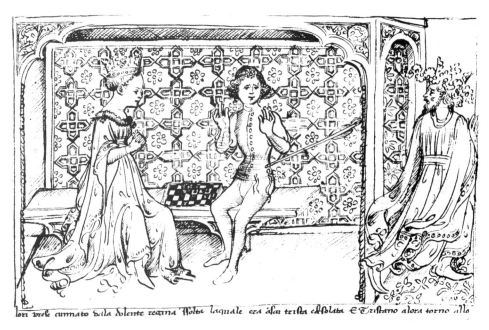

11b. Mark slays Tristan. Florence, Cod. Pal. 556, f. 159ᵛ

out of their grave grew a vine which had two roots, one of which had its start in the heart of Tristano, and the other came out of Isotta's heart. . . . Grapes grew on the vine in three stages, that is, in flower, green, and ripe, to show that, in their delight in each other, they cared nothing for their troubles. And the plant was a grapevine to show that as vines bear fruit that brings rapture to all mankind, so the life of Tristano and Isotta was a tree of love which long afterward comforted and inspired all courtly lovers. (Trans. Shaver, p. 324)

In France, artists who decorate Arthurian manuscripts in the International Gothic style seldom achieve emotional intensity. They seem chiefly interested in the pageantic aspects of heraldry, the challenges of perspective, the depiction of setting, and the creation of brilliant colour. The effect of light, always associated with ideality, was now facilitated by using gum and egg white. As well, there was a greater range of colour than had been available to earlier illuminators. Cennino d'Andrea Cennini provided instructions for making seven shades of red (sinoper, cinabrese, vermilion, red lead, hematite, dragonsblood, and lac), seven greens, six yellows, and various sorts of black and white.[60] Evrard d' Espingues, whose patrons were Jacques d'Armagnac and Jean du Mas, kept a record of the painting materials which he purchased: azur, rose de Paris, vermilhon, verte de flambe, vert de montagne, rouge de minium, massicat jaune, noir de fumée et aultre noir, l'or fin, l'or moulu, and gomme a destemper toutes les colours.[61] Evrard illuminated for Jean du Mas a three-volume *Tristan*, Chantilly 315–317. He may also have had a hand in BN fr. 112, 116, and 120. Loomis disparages his bourgeois taste, expressed in scenes of 'flat ugliness' and 'brutal realism'.

Jean Colombe, whom the Duke of Savoy employed to complete the Duke of Berry's *Très Riches Heures*, left unfinished when the Limbourgs died of the plague in 1416, is said to have painted BR 9246, *Estoire del Saint Graal* (1480). It features what Loomis calls 'a Colombe type of man – with flattened head, frequently emphasized by a flat cap, a face with heavy features and jowl, a thick bushy beard that yet reveals the wide mouth; the figure is not well proportioned and is commonly clad in long robes of thick falling drapery, hatched with gold'.[62] His female type has a high forehead, long hair, and a backward swaying body with the protuberant abdomen referring to the ideal figure of the Virgin Mary, who appears in the *Estoire's* Annunciation (f. 18). Loose gowns and bushy beards spare the illustrator from period costume and individualized physiognomies so that he can concentrate on settings. The landscapes have an Italianate appearance with intensely blue skies receding into a pale horizon, lush grass, tall trees with thin trunks, steep cliffs surmounted by realistic castles, wandering streams that connect the various planes and, in f. 164, an inlet of the sea across which the divine stag leads the elect.

---

[60] *The Craftsman's Handbook*, pp. 20–39.
[61] cited Loomis, p. 110.
[62] Loomis, p. 112.

Architectural settings, too, are realistically drawn – the Corinthian columns and great arches of the abbey containing Josephé's shield (f. 179), the religious frescoes on a castle wall (f. 18^v), the statues in niches of columns and facades (ff. 55, 183), the huge bastion which is split by lightning when the river of blood flows on the cobbled courtyard (f. 84) and the street of fifteenth century houses with steep-pitched roofs that leads to Calvary (158^v). King Mordrain's funeral procession (f. 183) consists of black-habited monks, hooded mourners, tonsured priests, taper-bearing acolytes, and a coffin under a black pall on a catafalque hung with red heraldic shields. In the foreground, two men dig a grave. This is not the world of early Christianity but the 'panoply of grief and departing pomp . . . that establish the lineage and prestige of the defunct' at the end of the Middle Ages.[63] Colombe (or his assistant) indulges in picture painting for its own sake rather than fulfilling an illustrator's obligation to realize the text.[64]

Like the French, Italians and Burgundians, the English upper classes were book collectors – of a kind. In the late Middle Ages they do not seem to have combined collecting with local commissions for illuminated works on secular subjects, preferring, like the Duke of Bedford, to acquire manuscripts on the continent.[65] The 'grete booke called saint Grall bounde in boordes couerde with rede leder and plated with plates of laten' which Sir Richard Roos bequeathed to his niece in 1481/2, was written and illuminated in France. A later owner was Elizabeth Wydville, Edward IV's wife; today we know it as BL Royal 14 E III. Richard II owned 'une Romance de Percivall et Gawyn' but any ambition he might have had for assembling a royal library was terminated by his forced abdication and murder.[66] At no time did the libraries of the English kings rival those of their continental relatives. Kathleen L. Scott's study of a mid-fifteenth-century English illuminating shop shows that its customers included a draper and a stockfishmonger.[67] These were not the wealthy and opinionated patrons who on the conti-

---

[63] T.S.R. Boase, 'King Death, Morality, Judgment and Remembrance' in *The Flowering of the Middle Ages*, p. 239.

[64] New York, Pierpont Morgan M41, *Tristan*, is also painted in the Colombe style. Dated 14 Ap. 1468 (f. 182^v), it is one of only three manuscripts containing the story of Alexander the Orphan. The 80 miniatures are mediocre, showing more interest in landscape than in lively human activities. However, f. 128^v is rather charming. Lancelot in gold and black armour, mounted on a gold-plated horse, rides through a green countryside towards a moated castle while, amid the shrubbery, the naked Elaine waits in her tub.

[65] The fact that several generations of English nobles were involved first in the Hundred Years War and then in the Wars of the Roses must have inhibited artistic production. But see Carol Meale, 'Manuscripts, Readers and Patrons in Fifteenth-century England: Sir Thomas Malory and Arthurian Romance', *Arthurian Literature* IV, ed. Richard Barber (Cambridge, Eng., and Totowa, NJ, 1985), pp. 93–126; various essays in *Manuscripts and Readers in Fifteenth-Century England: the Literary Implications of Manuscript Study*, ed. Derek Pearsall (Cambridge, Eng., 1983); and *English Court Culture in the Later Middle Ages*, ed. V.J. Scattergood and J.W. Sherborne (London, 1983).

[66] See V.J. Scattergood, 'Literary Culture at the Court of Richard II', *English Court Culture*, pp. 29–43; R.F. Green, 'King Richard II's Books Revisited', *The Library*, XXXI (1976), 235–9.

[67] Kathleen L. Scott, 'A Mid-fifteenth-century English Illuminating Shop and its Customers', *Journal of the Warburg and Courtauld Institute*, 31 (1968), 170–196. The middle-class

nent commissioned deluxe volumes. In his essay, 'Painting and Manuscript Illumination for Royal Patrons', J. J. G. Alexander concludes that the paucity of fine manuscripts resulted from the English artists' failure to accept the new treatment of space and the new naturalism. That failure he blames on the lack of patrons to provide encouragement, interest, and financial support.[68]

Certainly the limitations of English secular illumination ca. 1400 are obvious in BL Cotton Nero A.x. Art. 3, a manuscript that couples the jewel of English chivalric romances in verse, *Sir Gawain and the Green Knight*, with illustrations that have been described as 'caricatures', 'infantile daubs', 'naive and crude . . . carelessly painted in dull, muddy colours' and 'crude drawings (with) smudgy colours'.[69] A more tolerant view might accept them as a form of folk art for they have the primary colours (red, yellow, blue), the vivacity, charm and humour of that mode. This style might be appropriate to the anonymous poet's association with Cheshire or Staffordshire. Alternatively, as Gervase Mathew suggests, the miniatures may be copies of 'something grander, something more like the Bohun manuscripts . . . obviously related to the new experiments in the representation of natural scenery and of architectural background which marked sophisticated French court art at the turn of the century'.[70]

Though the poet gives details of architecture and costume so specific that scholars can date the work ca. 1380, the illustrators' realization is equivocal. The careless painter must take some blame. Despite the poet's emphatic assertion that the Green Knight was 'overal enker-grene', the severed head of f. 94 has flesh-coloured skin, blond hair and a blond beard. Arthur, in a blue gown with fur-trimmed bombard sleeves, Guenevere in green, and Gawain and Agravain in red doublets watch from a balcony (not a dais); the three men brandish wicked-looking weapons. In the miniature's lower part, a time-lag scene, Gawain with the battle-axe views his handiwork, while the challenger, mounted on his green horse and bleeding profusely from his severed neck, flourishes his head.

The first seduction scene (f. 125) shows a naked Gawain sleeping on a scarlet bed under a yellow and green striped blanket. The bed is surrounded on three sides (awkwardly drawn) with blue curtains hanging from golden rods. Bertilak's wife chucks the reluctant guest under the chin, a gesture inappropriate for a courtly lady, who was expected to be 'dangerous' (stand-offish), but perfectly

---

Pastons owned *The Death of Arthur beginning at Cassabelaun* and *The Grene Knight* as well as *Guy of Warwick*, a romance of *Richard Coeur de Lion*, Chaucer's *Troilus* and Lydgate's *Temple of Glass*. They were probably not illuminated. See H.S. Bennett, *The Pastons and their England* (Cambridge, 1979 [1932]), Appendix I.

[68] *English Court Culture*, pp. 141–162.

[69] These descriptions come respectively from Loomis, p. 138; J.A. Lee, 'The Illuminating Critic: the Illustration of Cotton Nero A.x', *Studies in Iconography*, 3, 17–46; and Marilyn Stokstad, entry on 'Sir Gawain and the Green Knight', *Arthurian Encyclopedia*, p. 362. See the facsimile edition of Cotton Nero A.x., EETS OS (London, 1923) for black-and-white reproductions. The unique manuscript was written about 1400 in the Northwest Midlands dialect. On the poet and his background, see A.C. Spearing, *The Gawain Poet, a Critical Study* (Cambridge, Eng., 1970), pp. 1–40.

[70] *The Court of Richard II* (London, 1968), p. 117.

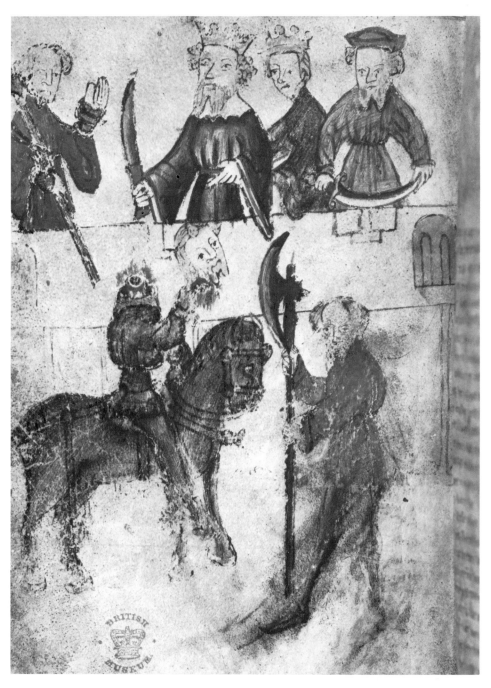

12. Sir Gawain decapitates the Green Knight at Arthur's court. BL Cotton Nero Ax. Art. 3, f. 94

appropriate to an amorously aggressive fée. In a high-necked gown embroidered with rubies and emeralds, her hair confined in a jewelled net, she fashionably represents the International Gothic style ca. 1400. In the first exchange of winnings (f. 126), involving the stag's head, the lord of the castle (alias the Green Knight) resembles the Arthur of f. 94. Gawain, traditionally the 'flower of courtesy', is clad in parti-coloured hose. In the last illustration (f. 129), Gawain, fully armed, rides towards the Green Chapel where the Green Knight waits with his enormous axe. The darkness of the cave mouth, the tangled profusion of plants and the general gloom create a demonic setting appropriate to the text. Though the artists lack technical skill, they succeed in two respects. They choose to illustrate the text's most important episodes and they depict costume with period authenticity, though they ignore such specific details as Gawain's identifying sign, the pentangle.

A lack of sophisticated patrons probably accounts, as well, for the poverty of secular German manuscripts, though the interest in woodcut illustration, well established by the 1460s, may also be relevant. Only five of the seventy-four extant *Parzivals* are illustrated: Heidelberg, Universitätsbibl. pal. germ. 339 (ca. 1440); Dresden, Kgl. bib. 66; Vienna, ONB 2914; and Berne, Stadtbibl. AA. 91.[71] There are also two *Lanzelots*, Heidelberg, Universitätsbibl. pal. germ. 147 and pal. germ. 371 (1420) and two *Tristans*, Heidelberg, Universitätsbibl. pal. germ. 346 (ca. 1460) and Brussels, BR 14697. The two *Wigalois* manuscripts are Leiden, Bibl. Rijksuniv. 537 and Donaueschingen, 17. The workshop of Diebolt Lauber in the Alsatian town of Hagenau is said to have produced the Donaueschingen *Wigalois*, which has twenty-six large, coloured pen drawings, the Brussels *Tristan* containing ninety-two coloured pen drawings, and the *Parzivals* now in Heidelberg, Vienna and Dresden. The three latter share not only similar rubrics and programmes but one remarkable departure from the text, a miniature of Sigune sitting in a tree. Bright colours, vacuous faces with unsmiling red mouths, fixed eyes and curly hair, a lack of interest in landscape, a fascination with headgear and a frequent disregard of text characterise these illustrations. For example, in Heidelberg, pal. 339, Parzival leaves home elaborately costumed in a rose-coloured, plumed hat, a belted, embroidered houppelande and blue hose (f. 99^v), rather than wearing the simple clothes of a countryman.

The most effectively illustrated *Parzival* is the Berne manuscript (1467) which was written on paper and decorated with twenty-eight pictures for a certain Jorg Friburgers von Bern. In ff. 23, 28^v and 29^v the hero's rusticity is conveyed by his fool's costume and his mount, a donkey. Despite the illustrator's limited grasp of perspective, he can create a lively effect, as in f. 118 where Gawain, a large bascinet covering his eyes, walks across the Perilous Bed's rust-coloured bed-

---

[71] For discussion and 41 plates of black-and-white reproductions see Karl J. Benziger, *Studien zur Deutschen Kunstgeschichte Parzival in die Deutschen Handschriften illustration des Mittelalters* (Strassburg, 1914). Elmar Mittler and Wilfred Werner, *Die Bibliothek Palatina: Skizzen zu ihrer Geschichte* (Wiesbaden, 1986) reproduces miniatures from Heidelberg, pal. germ. 339, *Parzival*, and from pal. germ. 345, *Lohengrin*. See also Loomis, pp. 134–138.

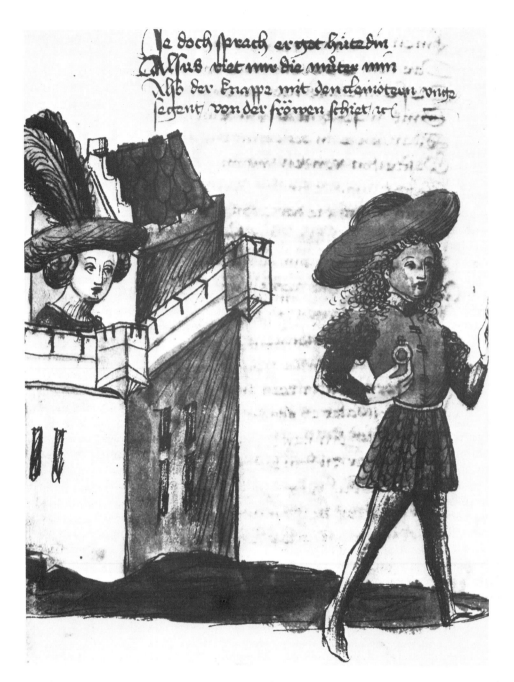

13. Parzival takes the lady's ring. Heidelberg, Universitätsbibl. Cod. Pal. 339, f. 99ᵛ (*Parzival*)

spread while cross-bows discharge arrows and slings discharge rocks from the battlements.

Cod. pal. germ. 371 is one of the two complete manuscripts of Ulrich von Zetzichoven's twelfth-century *Lanzelet*. Written on paper ca. 1420, its illustrations show a limited colour range (rose, green, grey) applied to flamboyant costume. In f. 2 the smartly dressed scribe wears pince-nez to help him write the text correctly. The Heidelberg *Tristant*, based on Eilhart von Oberge's poetic version (the oldest complete *Tristan* romance) is the most extensively illustrated German Arthurian manuscript. Its ninety-three pictures are carefully drawn and painted in an old-fashioned style that pays little attention to setting. The incidents represented include Tristant's voyages to Ireland disguised as a minstrel (ff. 21^v, 23), the dragon-slaying (f. 32), and the tryst beneath the tree. Mark is invisible in f. 63 but appears with his spy in f. 66. Also shown are Tristant's long jump to Isolde's bed under which the spy hides (f. 73^v), Tristant's provision of fish for food during the forest idyll (f. 84^v), Mark's discovery of the sleeping lovers separated by the sword (f. 87), Tristant's madness (f. 102), Isolde's sojourn among the lepers (f. 130^v), Tristant's disguise as Mark's jester (ff. 159, 163^v. 164^v), his death in Isolde's arms (f. 172^v) and the lovers' burial in a pink marble tomb sheltered by entwined trees. In considering these German manuscripts we should bear in mind Loomis' comment that their significance lies in the German instinct for linearism which would find fruition in the art of the woodcut.

Evoking an altogether different world is the creator of the Leiden *Wigalois*, the only important fourteenth-century romance manuscript in German.[72] The text, which Wirnt von Grafenberg wrote ca. 1200–1215, glorifies the son whom Gawain fathers during an Otherworld sojourn. When Wigalois reaches the age of twenty, he seeks his father at Arthur's court and eventually wins a beautiful princess by killing a dragon-sorcerer. The knight's personal symbol is the golden Wheel of Fortune; the original stands in the Otherworld castle. In 1372 a Cistercian monk, 'Jan von Brunswik', copied the romance for his patron, Duke Albrecht von Braunschweig-Grubenhagen (1361–84), decorating it with forty-seven miniatures. *Wigalois* belongs to an earlier romance world of knights-errant, helpful damsels, giants, dragons, blood-red horses, magical artifacts, marvellous beasts, talking birds, and beautiful ladies waiting to be rescued. In both text and pictures the fairy-tale atmosphere is enhanced by colour references. The painter uses blue, lilac, purple-brown, olive green and ochre backgrounds. Costumes are red, white, blue, black and grey. Gold and silver applied to goblets, knife blades, the parrot's

---

[72] J.M.N. Kapteyn, ed., *'Wigalois, der Ritter mit dem Rade', von Wirnt von Gravenberc* (Bonn, 1926); Christoph Cormeau, *'Wigalois' and 'Diu Crône': Zwei Kapitel zu Gattungsgeschichte des nach Klassischen Aventiureromans* (Zurich and Munich, 1977); *Wigalois, the Knight of Fortune's Wheel*, trans. J.W. Thomas (Lincoln, Nebr., and London, 1977). Hans-Jochen Schiewer, in a paper at the 1990 International Arthurian Congress at Durham, noted the connection between this manuscript and the Wienhausen tapestries, made for the same patron (p. 101 below). The choice of subject in the miniatures may show an attempt to extract a religious message from the romance.

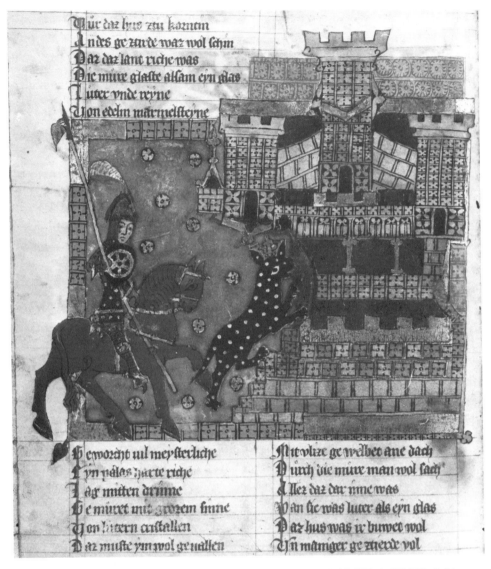

14. Wigalois with the Crowned Beast. Leiden Universiteitsbibl. 537, f. 47ᵛ (*Wigalois*)

cage, the costumes and the hero's heraldic sign produce an opulent effect. An exceptional feature is the imitation of embroidery techniques:

> . . . the representation of castle walls, of throne and spear shafts, no less than of textiles, is made up of little rectangles enclosing a rosette or a four-leaf pattern. Jan scattered rosettes and stars over his backgrounds, and introduced stiffly conventional foliage designs in a way to suggest

appliqué work, an effect enhanced by fine black edging lines that look like stitches.[73]

Two manuscripts produced in Bruges represent the autumnal flowering of deluxe secular manuscripts, though some critics prefer the analogy of over-ripe fruit. The *St. Albans Chronicle*, London, Lambeth Palace Library 6 (after 1470) and *Guiron*, Oxford, Bodleian Douce 383 (1490–1500)[74] are so lavishly illustrated that the seventeenth century term 'miniature' (based on a mistaken etymology) in the sense of 'little picture' is inappropriate. These large, independent paintings, together with the heaped imagery of their borders, contribute such formidable decoration that the ideal proportions between text and illustration give way under the weight of ornament. As well, the late Gothic mastery of perspective creates, as J.J.G. Alexander points out, a 'contradiction between the illusion of depth in the miniature . . . and the flat surface of the page on which the script was written'.[75] The resulting illogicality distracts readers from the text, making them viewers of pictures instead. There is no longer, as in the miniatures painted before 1400, the gradual transition from black or brown text through penwork initials with filigree ornament to miniature and border, a transition that had produced an integrated page. A further disjunction results from the difference of scale between miniature and border images.

The *St. Albans Chronicle* is a version of Peter Langtoft's *Chronicle*, beginning with the arrival of the eponymous founder, Brutus, and ending with the Siege of Calais in 1436.[76] Written in English, it was illustrated by a Flemish artist known as 'The Master of the Dresden Book of Hours', who provided nineteen large and fifteen small pictures. It may have been ordered by one of the English lords accompanying Margaret of York when she married Charles the Rash in 1468. The armorials in the lower border of f. 1, *a shield quartering 1 and 4 argent on a fess, three bizants or, 2 and 3 argent a lion rampant az langued gules,* appear to be the arms of the Purchas family. The text concludes with a Flemish rhyme:

> When ye fleminges were fressh florisshid in your floures
> Sette ye still and bith in pecs.

---

[73] Loomis, p. 135.

[74] Another *Guiron*, BN fr. 363 with one large miniature (f. 1) belonged to the two-hundred book library of Louis de Gruuthuse (ca. 1420–1492), a Bruges noble who also owned BN fr. 103, Prose *Tristan*; fr. 121–123, *Lancelot*; fr. 345–348, *Perceforest*; fr. 356–357, *Guiron le Courtois*; fr. 749, *Histoire du Graal*; fr. 761, *Artus de Bretagne*. On fr. 363 and Bodleian, Douce 383, see Verbeke et al., *Arturus Rex: Koning Artur en de Nederlanden* (Leuven, 1987), Vol. 1, Catalogus, pp. 244–249; R. Lathuillère, *op. cit.*; Loomis, pp. 128–130.

[75] J.J. Alexander, *The Decorated Letter* (London, 1978), p. 21.

[76] M.R. James and C. Jenkins *A Descriptive Catalogue of the Manuscripts in the Library of Lambeth Palace* (Cambridge, Eng., 1930), pp. 15–18; Loomis, p. 128; E.G. Millar, 'Les principaux manuscrits à peinture de Lambeth Palace à Londres', *Bulletin de la Société francaise de reproductions de manuscrits à peintures*, 9 (1925), 15–19; Verbeke et al., Leuven *Catalogue*, pp. 138–140. For extracts from the text, see *Brut*, EETS OS 190, 8 Pt. ii, pp. 534–84.

The nine Arthurian subjects are Vortigern's battle against the Saxons (f. 37^v); Vortigern's meeting with Hengest (f. 40^v); the fight between the red and the white dragons (f. 43^v); Coppa, disguised as a monk, poisons King Aurilambros in a room with diamond-paned windows (f. 49^v); Merlin, wearing an ermine-trimmed cape to indicate his improved status, talks to King Uthred (f. 52); Arthur is crowned inside a barrel-vaulted hall while outside a time lapse battle scene occurs in a landscape vista (f. 54^v); Arthur dispatches the Giant (f. 62^v); Arthur's victorious cavalcade approaches Rome; the Emperor Lucy's head wearing a look of resignation is impaled on a sword (f. 63^v); Arthur fights the last battle against Mordred (f. 66^v). The instructions to the artist, written at the bottom of the pages, E.G. Millar regards as the manuscript's most interesting feature. Those for f. 66^v indicate in part that 'le Roy arthur transperce oultre en oultre le corps de sa lance son adversaire, ne pas ung roy'.

The artists have now solved problems of perspective. In f. 45 spectators at the palace gate are smaller not only because they are less important but also because they are further away, while the workman in the foreground is as tall as the king. A diagonal barrier and dark shading make the dragons' pit seem lower than the courtyard. Figures are shown from behind as in 37^v where a British knight plunges his sword into a Saxon's back. The people are realistic in other ways, too. The men's long, sloppy hair and scraggy beards and the facial expressions ranging from wonder and piety to heavy-lidded boredom and sharp-tongued malice seem to be drawn from life.

However, throughout this manuscript there is an aesthetic conflict between the violent scenes in the foreground and the idyllic landscapes in the background. Arthur and Mordred dispatch one another by a green hill under a bright blue sky. Alured's entrails are wound out of his slit abdomen on a windlass, blood from Becket's shattered pate forms a pool, and the headless neck of a Despencer spurts blood onto the grass while the sun shines gloriously and the rivers gently meander through the summer countryside. The theme of the well ordered land is uncomfortably juxtaposed to the historical 'reality'.

With the Douce *Guiron* we enter a romantic world of jousts, quests and enchanted castles, which realism makes credible and immediate. The armorials on ff. 1 and 17 belong to Engelbert II of Nassau (1451–1504); the collar signifying the Order of the Golden Fleece encloses them. This patron, a courtier of Charles the Rash and Philip the Fair, owned a rich library which included the incomparable *Roman de la Rose*, London, BL Harley 4425, a manuscript that in the nineteenth century would inspire the Pre-Raphaelite poets and painters D.G. Rossetti, William Morris and Edward Burne-Jones. His *Guiron* did not fare so well. Some vandal removed five large and twelve smaller illustrations to make a picture book, and that remnant constitutes the Bodleian manuscript.

Settings and costumes seem to take precedence over plot and character. The scene of Tristan's arrival at le Chastel dessus la Mer (f. 3) conveys a sense of room-space through the slightly oblique setting of three ladies (the Irish queen, Iseult and Brangwain) in front of a tapestry that partially conceals a fireplace. Two musicians with pipe and drum set diagonally in the right foreground, Tristan and a lady in a parallel line near the centre of the floor space, and two retainers in a doorway leading to a room beyond, all of them at an angle to the floor tiles, create an impression of even recession. The space is further extended by a recess containing a two-tiered dresser set with plates and ewers and by windows in the farther room through which courtiers watch the proceedings from outside.

The artists carefully reproduce contemporary dress which featured plumed acorn hats, long velvet gowns slashed to reveal loose-sleeved shirts, and doublets 'so short that the wearers looked like monkeys in short coats, displaying their buttocks', not to mention their appendages.[77] The ladies' low cut gowns of black, scarlet and blue, the gold chains worn as necklaces, and the steeple headdresses convey the elegance of International Gothic. However, the static roles of the women and the infrequency with which they are depicted indicate that 'le génie féminin' is no longer the dominant inspiration. Nor does the pageantry of chivalry interest the artists. Except for Guiron who has a golden shield, there are no armorial identifications. In f. 8, the viewer soon looks past the richly robed courtiers – the King of the Hundred Knights, Hector, Galihault, and Lancelot – to observe the lofty towers of the Chastel de l'Isle Perdue and, facing it across the limpid river, a rocky precipice with a single dead tree as a memento mori; beyond are jousting knights, another castle, green trees, and a sky that responds to the demands of aerial perspective by lightening at the horizon. Then we are into the encroaching border with its realistic carnations, strawberry blossoms and periwinkles, and its little centaur almost hidden in a tangle of acanthus leaves. These borders with their mingling of the natural and the fantastic are a beguiling aspect of an art intended only to delight.

By the end of the fifteenth century, the knight as a political and military entity was dead. In his Epilogue to *The Order of Chivalry* William Caxton lamented the fact that modern knights had nothing to do but 'go to the Baynes and playe atte dyse'. The image of the armed knight seeking adventures that glorify his God, his sovereign and his lady might still serve allegorists like Edmund Spenser but Renaissance artists would find other forms and other interpretations for 'the noble actes of chyvalrye, the jentyl and vertuous dedes that somme knyghtes used in tho dayes'.

[77] Margaret Scott, p. 176.

CHAPTER FOUR

Arts of the Church and Castle

About 1124 St Bernard of Clairvaux wrote an *Apologia*[1] addressed to Guillaume of Saint-Thierry in which he condemned Romanesque luxuriousness because it appealed to man's curiosity rather than to his spirit. Religious art had become an art of superfluity and artificiality in which desire (*cupiditas*), expressed in infinite variety, had replaced the simplicity of nature (*necessitas*). What was the meaning, he asked, of these ugly monsters in pavement mosaics? What were those filthy monkeys doing, those lions, monstrous centaurs, hybrids, fighting soldiers and hunters blowing their horns? Things had come to a sorry pass when it was pleasanter to waste time looking at carvings and paintings than to read God's word. At the same time as St Bernard was denouncing the elaboration of ecclesiastical art, another churchman, Abbot Suger of St Denis, was defending it – a church should be adorned like a bride awaiting her bridegroom. In Romanesque and Gothic churches no part of the structure was so remote or obscure that it could not be decorated, neither the bosses at the intersections of the lofty ribbed vaults, the piers, the capitals of great pillars, the hidden underside of a choir stall nor the well-trodden pavement. And no image that the artist could conceive was banned. The devil himself crouched, chained and malevolent, on Chester Cathedral's north wall.

What may be the oldest surviving example of Arthurian art is the sculpture over the Porta della Pescheria of Modena Cathedral in Northern Italy.[2] That the archivolt represents an Arthurian subject is proven by the names carved in a band above the figures: ISDERNUS, ARTUS DE BRETANIA, BURMALTUS, WINLOGEE, MARDOC,

---

[1] J.P. Migne, ed., *Patrologiae latinae* 182, col. 916. See also Edgar de Bruyne, *Etudes d'esthétique médiévale*, vol. II, pp. 139–141.

[2] See P. Deschamps, 'La légende arthurienne à la cathédrale de Modène et l'école lombarde de sculpture romane', *Monuments Piot*, vol. XXVIII (1925/26), 93 and 'Etude sur la paléographie des inscriptions lapidaires de la fin de l'époque mérovingienne aux dernières années du XIIe siècle', *Bull. monum.*, vol. LXXXVIII (1929), 5–86; G.H. Gerould, 'Arthurian Romance and the Date of the Relief at Modena', *Speculum*, 10 (1935), 355–76; R.S. Loomis, *ALMA*, pp. 32–36, 'The Oral Diffusion of the Arthurian Legend', *Arthurian Literature in the Middle Ages*, pp. 60–62, and 'Geoffrey of Monmouth and the Modena Archivolt: A Question of Precedence', *Speculum*, 13 (1938), 221–231; Jacques Stiennon and Rita Lejeune, 'La légende arthurienne dans la sculpture de la cathédrale de Modène', *Cahiers de Civilisation Médiévale*, 6 (1963), 281–96.

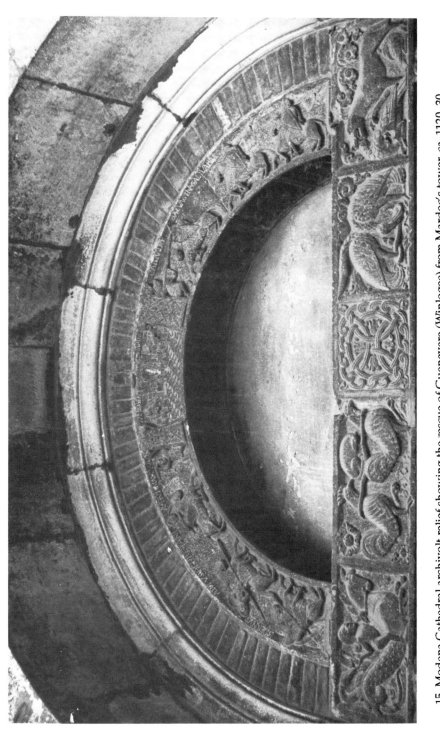

15. Modena Cathedral archivolt relief showing the rescue of Guenevere (Winlogee) from Mardoc's tower, ca. 1120–30

CARRADO, GALVAGINUS, GALVARIUN, CHE. Construction of the cathedral began in 1106 and the portals' decoration, judging by the style of the lettering, was probably executed between 1120 and 1130. At the apex of the rhythmically organised relief is a stone castle, decorated with a shield. It is built beside water (represented by the double-axe pattern of Roman mosaics) and protected on left and right by timber towers. Inside the castle Mardoc holds the distraught Winlogee (Guenevere) prisoner while Carrado with a lance and Burmaltus, a churl with a pick, fend off the attacking knights, Galvaginus (Gawain) and Arthur. Galvaginus is backed by Galvarian, probably his brother in Welsh folklore, and Che (Kay), one of the longest-lived knights of Arthurian tradition. Unlike Galvaginus, Arthur is not followed by a companion but rather by a figure who attacks him from the rear. This unnamed attacker's lack of armour and the ignominious nature of his blow convey his demonic origins. Isdernus (Ider), Guenevere's lover and protector in the French romance *Yder* (ca. 1210), rushes to save the king.[3] This formal arrangement of two mounted groups converging from both sides towards a central castle appears in the Bayeux Tapestry (ca. 1077). The conical helmets with nose pieces, hauberks with mail covering head and chin, and long pointed shields also resemble the Bayeux arms and armour.

The ultimate source of the Modena archivolt must have been a Welsh or Breton folktale in which Guenevere was a fée. K.G.T. Webster's *Guenevere: A Study of her Abductions* throws light on the archetype:

> Guenevere is one of those supernatural beings who are often assigned as wives to the greatest mortals. She appears to be a Persephone – queen of the otherworld and vegetation goddess – as well as a conventional fascinating fairy mistress such as heroes win, or are won by.[4]

In an early Welsh work, Caradoc's *Vita Gildae* (before 1129), King Melwas of the Summer Region (Somerset) kidnaps Arthur's queen, carrying her off to the city of glass, an otherworld image also connected with Glastonbury. This is only one of many analogues,[5] the best known being Meleagant's abduction in Chrétien de Troyes' *Lancelot*. The Celtic names and the fact that it is Arthur himself who goes to rescue the distressed woman suggest that the Modena archivolt embodies a pre-Galfridian and pre-Chrétien stage in the transmission of legendary materials from the Celtic fringe.

Further south in Otranto there is a Norman cathedral with a fantastic mosaic floor of the kind that St Bernard condemned.[6] According to the inscriptions,

---

[3]   Alison Adams, ed., *Yder* (Cambridge, Eng., 1983); Gweneth Hutchings, 'Isdernus of the Modena Archivolt', *Medium Aevum* 1 (1932), 204–5.

[4]   K.G.T. Webster, *Guinevere: A Study of her Abductions* (Milton, Mass., 1954), p. 1. See also T.P. Cross and W.A. Nitze, *Lancelot and Guenevere* (Chicago, 1930).

[5]   Cf. Prose *Lancelot* (Vulgate Prose Cycle), Ulrich von Zatzikoven's *Lantzelet*, Heinrich von dem Turlin's *Diu Crône*, *Li Romans de Durmart le Galois* and Sir Thomas Malory's *Morte Darthur*.

[6]   On the Otranto mosaic see G. Gianfreda, *Il mosaico pavimentale della Basilica Cattedrale di*

Archbishop Jonathan commissioned a priest, Pantaleone, to execute this decorative work in 1165. Composed of marble and coloured stone spread across the middle aisle and two side aisles, the mosaic incorporates human, vegetable, animal, and hybrid images drawn from the Old Testament (e.g. Adam and Eve, Cain and Abel, Noah, Solomon and the Queen of Sheba), the Alexander legends, the zodiac, the occupations of the months, and the bestiary. The north aisle depicts paradise and its patriarchs, while opposite lies hell with 'Infernus Satanus' seated on a three-headed snake. Scenes are compartmentalized by means of leafy branches. Scattered throughout the pavement are drolleries similar to those in manuscript margins. Most of the images are so consistent with iconographical tradition that Pantaleone must have used pattern books.

An original figure, however, is the one labelled REX ARTURUS. Placed between the Expulsion from Paradise and the first murder, the crowned figure holding a club rides a goat-like animal with horns, cloven hoofs, and short tail. Below, but in the same space, a spotted cat attacks the throat of a man lying on his back. This scene may represent the legend of Arthur's combat with the giant cat of Lausanne, the Capalus, known in Welsh folklore as the Cath Palug.[7] Arthur's association with a horned animal is more puzzling; though in the Provençal romance *Jaufré* (ca. 1180–1225) Arthur rides a horned bestia ('non es us taurs'), he certainly is not in control of the animal.[8]

The Otranto figure of a heroic male riding a monster has led Rita Le Jeune to identify an unlabelled sculpture at Modena as Arthur.[9] The Tower of Ghirlandina (1169–79), adjacent to the cathedral, is decorated with eight marble reliefs. One pair showing a king playing a harp and dancing evidently represents David. The second pair depicts Roland. The third, showing a hero astride a goat-like animal, may be Arthur while the companion figure could be identified as Gawain. If these identifications are valid, then the fourth set, showing a queen holding a flower and joining hands with a man in a betrothal or wedding scene, could depict Guenevere.

Since the Normans carried the Arthurian legends to Italy, one would expect to find representations in their native territory. Two piers (1350–1400) in the south aisle of Caen's church of St Pierre show subjects originally derived from Chrétien's romances – Lancelot crossing the sword bridge and Gawain enduring the Perilous Bed. Loomis attributes the designs to the influence of ivory carvings, a popular French art form in the earlier fourteenth century.[10] Enough remains of

Otranto, 2nd ed. (Casamari, 1965); Walter Haug, *Das Mosaik von Otranto: Darstellung Deutung und Bilddokumentation* (Wiesbaden, 1977) and 'Artussage und Heilsgeschichte: Zum Programm des Fußbodenmosaiks von Otranto', *Deutsche Vierteljahrsschrift*, 49 (1975), 577–606; Loomis, *ALMA*, p. 36.

[7] A written version is related in the *Livre d'Artus*, on which see Frederick Whitehead and Roger Sherman Loomis, 'The Livre d'Artus', *Arthurian Literature in the Middle Ages*, pp. 336–8.

[8] Paul Remy, 'Jaufré', *ibid*. pp. 400–405.

[9] Stiennon and Lejeune, *op cit.*, pp. 288–295 and figs. 17–27.

[10] Loomis, pp. 71–2.

the damaged Gawain scene – Gawain's reclining figure, the bed's large wheels, arrowheads, and bells – to substantiate the comparison of this scene with those on the mirror back in Bologna's Museo Civico, the writing tablet in the Musée Arché-ologique, Niort, and several ivory caskets.[11] The design of the Lancelot capital resembles manuscript sources such as BN fr. 122 f. 1 where the hero crawls along the sword, gripping it with hands and knees rather than walking on it. Also in miniatures and the capital but not on the ivories are the lion protecting the castle gate and Guenevere watching from the battlements, her head projecting above the walls, according to manuscript convention.

The Romanesque church of St Efflam in Perros, a Breton village, contains what may be an early depiction of Arthur as monster-slayer.[12] According to local leg-end, St Efflam, a migratory Irish prince who had settled in Brittany, directed King Arthur to a dragon's lair. After a fierce battle, the exhausted king quenched his thirst when the Moses-like Efflam produced water from a rock. The saint then defeated the monster through the power of prayer. The relief (ca. 1100) carved on the second pier of the north aisle shows, from left to right, the coiled monster, an acrobatic nude figure who may represent the battling hero, a man with a crozier, and a prostrate armed man.

An interesting Arthurian carving in a religious setting is a sculpted column in the Spanish cathedral of Santiago de Compostela. This great cathedral, begun in 1078 and consecrated in 1211, enshrined the bones of St James, relics so holy that in the twelfth century a pilgrimage to this site ranked with one to Rome or Jerusalem. The pilgrims' route leading south from Paris through the Pyrenees must have attracted story-tellers who knew the latest romances of courtly love. The Portada de las Platerias on the north front unmistakably exhibits a Tristan carving to which Serafín Moralejo assigns a date early in the twelfth century.[13] Deathly ill from the poisoned wound which Morholt had inflicted, the hero has been placed in a rudderless boat without oars or sails. His horse peers over the side at the seaweed and fish, signs of the marine setting. A long, pointed shield protects the hero's body, as he grips his upright sword which is unmistakably nicked. The missing piece was left in Morholt's skull. Propelled by destiny to Ireland, Tristan is healed by Queen Isolde. On a second trip to acquire the young Isolde as Mark's bride, the nicked sword identifies him as her uncle's killer. In the Norse version of Thomas' *Roman de Tristan*, the hero tells Queen Isolde that when he left Cornwall, he intended going to Spain. What he could not accomplish himself, the story-tellers – 'galeses, bretones, irlandeses y escoceses' – did for him.

What are these sword bridges, perilous beds, fabulous animals and wounded heroes doing in churches? Remembering that the medieval church was a picture book of moral and religious truths, the artist being a submissive interpreter of

---

[11] *Ibid.* p. 72.

[12] *Ibid.* pp. 31–32 and Michel Renouard, *Art roman en Bretagne* (Rennes, 1978).

[13] Serafín Moralejo, 'Artes figurativas y artes literarias en la Espana medieval: Romanico, Romance y Roman', *Boletin de la Asociación Europea de Profesores de Espanol*, XVII, (1985), 32–33, 66–68 and fig. 6.

approved subjects,[14] we should expect some didactic motivation. In each sculpture where the hero can be positively identified, the verbal context includes an evil opponent and an Otherworld journey. The heroes are what Rosemond Tuve calls 'metaphors generalizing on experience'.[15] The knight fighting evil is a model of virtuous living. Tropologically, he is the pilgrim-knight seeking salvation through good deeds. Anagogically, the figure is assimilated into that of Christ the Redeemer, harrowing hell to release the souls that sin and death had bound to Satan. Romance characteristically mingles Classical, Celtic, and Christian mythologies; in each, a perilous passage separates the mundane world from the Otherworld which in the Middle Ages was often depicted as a castle.[16]

The castle surrounded by water on the Modena archivolt suggests the Dolorous Tower of Irish saga, an abode of the dead controlled by the Fomorians. An ugly, evil race who drove the supernatural Tuatha De' Danann into the mounds and islands where they later built their own towers, the Fomorians represent darkness and winter.[17] The ugly jailer Mardoc, the menacing Burmaltus with the pick, and Arthur's unnamed attacker are physically differentiated from the Arthurian knights. Adapted to the Christian context, Arthur becomes a Christ-figure risking his life to rescue Winlogee (the soul?) from the land of the dead.

In the Otranto mosaic the king, with one hand holding the club and the other giving a gesture of victory, clearly controls his demonic mount. His weapon, not a sword but a club, relates him to Hercules whose otherworld journey to rescue Pirotheus and Theseus made him a medieval type of Christ.[18] That the mosaic's designer, Pantaleone, knew classical iconography – there were many Roman ruins in southern Italy – his representation of Satan also suggests; his three-headed snake recalls the three-headed dog Cerberus, guardian of the underworld entrance. By placing Arthur between Adam, the first man, and Abel, the sacrificed man, the pavement artist typologically refers to the Redemption, an association not negated by Arthur's defeat in the battle with the cat. Finally, Arthur's relationship to the Tree of Life which integrates the diverse elements is also a Christological allusion, for typology connected the Tree of Knowledge, the Tree of Life, and the Tree of the Cross, as the Ship of Solomon iconography in La Quête del Saint Graal attests.[19]

---

[14] Emile Mâle, The Gothic Image, p. 392.

[15] Rosemond Tuve, Allegorical Imagery, p. 44.

[16] H.R. Patch, The Otherworld According to Descriptions in Medieval Literature (Cambridge, Mass., 1950). On relevant motifs see Tom Peete Cross, Motif-Index of Early Irish Literature (Bloomington, 1939). On the Celtic Otherworld particularly, see David Bruce Spaan, The Otherworld in Early Irish Literature (Ann Arbor, Mich., 1980).

[17] On Celtic mythology see Myles Dillon and Nora Chadwick, The Celtic Realms (London, 1973); Proinsias MacCana, Celtic Mythology (London, 1970); Alwyn and Brinley Rees, Celtic Heritage: Ancient Tradition in Ireland and Wales (London, 1961).

[18] On Hercules as a Christ figure see Table 27 of Christine de Pisan's Epître d'Othéa, déesse de la prudence à Hector, chef des Troyens (Bruxelles, 1913).

[19] Cf. also Richard Morris, ed., Legends of the Holy Rood; Symbols of the Passion and Cross-Poems in Old English of the Eleventh, Fourteenth and Fifteenth Centuries, EETS OS 46 (London, 1871).

While the Modena archivolt represents an early version of Guenevere's abduction, the Caen capital is based on the final version in which Lancelot is the rescuer. Even in Chrétien's *Lancelot*, the incident is polysemous. Tropologically, there is a psychomachia, a conflict between Good (Lancelot and Bagdemagus) and Evil (Meleagant). Furthermore, the fact that the kingdom of Gorre containing Meleagant's castle is described as 'el reaume don nus n'eschape' – the kingdom from which none escapes – establishes an anagogical level of meaning. The lid of the tomb which Lancelot raises confirms that he is the hero destined to free the prisoners, men and women, in the land which no one, serf or nobleman, may leave and from which none has yet returned. The mutilating sword bridge is the perilous passage which separates the mundane world from the Otherworld. Lancelot's successful rescue of Guenevere, achieved through love, humility, physical suffering, fortitude and faith, makes him a saviour.[20]

Like crossing the sword bridge, the adventure of the Perilous Bed occurs during a journey to a castle that was originally otherworldly. In Chrétien's *Conte du Graal* and its continuations Perceval shares the quest with Gawain. The building containing the Perilous Bed is a Castle of Maidens type, surrounded by a Waste Land, another form of the perilous passage. No coward nor traitor can enter. Its persecuted ladies await a deliverer of Christ-like character:

> Sage et large, sanz coveitise,
> Bel et franc, hardi et leal
> Sanz vilenie et sanz nul mal.   (ll. 7594–6)

> (wise and generous, without cupidity, handsome, brave, and
> loyal, without villainy or evil).

By surviving the perils of the magic bed, the deafening bells, the rain of bolts and arrows, and the fierce lion, Gawain frees the bespelled ladies. He, too, is a saviour whom the inhabitants have long awaited.

In the pilgrim church of Santiago, even Tristan is a not implausible Christ figure. Suffering and dying, he journeys according to God's will, finally reaching Ireland which was the Celtic Otherworld in Welsh myths such as *The Spoils of Annwfn*.[21] His prominent sword and shield recall St Paul's allusion to spiritual arms:

> Take up the great shield of faith, with which you will be able to quench
> all the flaming arrows of the evil one . . . for sword, take that which the
> Spirit gives you – the words that come from God.
>
> (*Ephesians* 6, 15–17)

---

[20] See L.T. Topsfield's discussion of moral and spiritual elements in *Chrétien de Troyes; A Study of the Arthurian Romances* (Cambridge, Eng., 1981), pp. 105–174.

[21] Kenneth Hurlstone Jackson, 'Arthur in Early Welsh Verse', *Arthurian Literature in the Middle Ages*, pp. 15–18.

Tristan has killed the tyrannous Morholt who demanded human tribute; in Ireland he will slay the dragon, the paramount medieval embodiment of destructive malice.

Of all the Arthurian legends none was so popular in religious and secular decoration as that of Tristan and Isolde.[22] Chaucer's contemporary, John Gower, wrote that

> In every mannes mouth it is
> How Tristram was of love drunke
> With Bele Isolde, whan they drunke
> The drink which Brangweine hem betok.
>
> (*Confessio Amantis* VI, 470–3)

As was often the case, one suspects, when men treated this story, Gower used the lovers ironically to illustrate the evil consequences of their acts – in this case, as a warning against drunkenness! Most of the surviving art was created for women who, no doubt, approved both Isolde's power and Tristan's fidelity. It is surprising, then, to learn of an uncritical representation in a male bastion – a Benedictine monastery.

In the Thames Valley near Windsor seventh century Benedictines established a community that Bede called Ceroti Insula – Chertsey. Burnt by the Danes in the ninth century and reconstructed in the eleventh, it became a treasure house of painted glass, monuments and manuscripts. Henry III patronised the Abbey and perhaps its fine Tristan pavement[23] was made from superfluous tiles originally intended for a royal building. The decorative motifs include castles, fleur-de-lis

---

[22] L.F. Flutre's *Table des noms propres dans les romans du moyen age écrits en français ou en provençal* (Poitiers, 1962) lists thirty-six forms of the name in French and Provençal. There are many additional spellings in German, Italian, English *et al.* For consistency's sake I shall normally use *Isolde*.

[23] Elizabeth Eames, *Catalogue of Mediaeval lead-glazed earthenware Tiles in the Department of Mediaeval and Later Antiquities, British Museum*, vol. 1 (London, 1980), pp. 141–71 and *English Medieval Tiles* (London, 1985); J.S. Gardner and Elizabeth Eames, 'A Tile Kiln at Chertsey Abbey', *Journal of the British Archaeological Association*, XVII (1954); Lloyd Haberly, *Medieval English Paving Tiles* (Oxford, 1937); W.R. Lethaby, 'The Romance tiles of Chertsey Abbey', *Walpole Society Annual*, II (1912–13), 69–80; R.S. Loomis, *Illustrations of Medieval Romance on Tiles of Chertsey Abbey*, University of Illinois Studies in Language and Literature (Urbana, 1916); Henry Shaw, *Specimens of Tile Pavements drawn from existing authorities* (London, 1858); Mainwaring Shurlock, *Tiles from Chertsey Abbey, Surrey, representing early romance subjects* (London, 1885). Black and white reproductions are used in Loomis, *op. cit.*; *Arthurian Legends in Medieval Art* figs. 25–59; *The Romance of Tristram and Ysolt by Thomas of Britain*, trans. R.S. Loomis (New York, 1923). Shaw reproduces sixteen roundels in colour, Lethaby and Shurlock the whole available set, with the coloured pages in the latter being particularly fine. The largest part of the tile collection is now in the British Museum, London; as well, the Victoria and Albert Museum, London, the Surrey Archaeological Society Museum, Guildford and the church of Little Kimble, Buckinghamshire have examples.

and crowns. Like other foundations, Chertsey suffered severely at the hands of Henry VIII's despoilers, the Puritans and other marauders.

When the antiquarian Dr Stukeley visited the site in 1752, he found that

> human bones of the abbots, monks, and great personages, who were buried in great numbers in the church, were spread thick all over the garden . . . Foundations of the religious buildings have been dug up, carved stones, slender pillars of Sussex marble, monumental stones, effigies, crosses, inscriptions everywhere. . . . I left the ruins of this place, which had been consecrated to religion ever since the year 666, with a sigh for the loss of so much national magnificence and national history.[24]

In 1853 the men whom a Mr Grumbridge hired to dig the foundations for a new house uncovered a large pavement of decorated tiles, which they apparently wasted a great deal of time admiring! Piled in a shed, many tiles were stolen before Mainwaring Shurlock, an Oxford expert on medieval tiles, salvaged the remainder. To these were added a coffinful excavated from the Chapter House site in 1861 and others found in such distant places as Halesowen near Birmingham. Piecing together this great jig-saw puzzle which included some letter clues, Shurlock discovered that a few tiles illustrated a romance of Richard Coeur de Lion but most of the forty-odd pieces depicted the Tristan romance. A proper Victorian, he could not help commenting:

> Society must have been far lower than our own in morals if the recitation of the original poem could be listened to without repugnance. The subject being well known, it appears strange that a more suitable tale was not chosen for the decoration of tiles intended for the pavement of a church.

The high quality decorated tiles were made by applying white clay to a red body. When they had been glazed with lead glaze and fired, the result was a warm brown tile with yellow figures. The Tristan pictures appeared on roundels nine inches (230 mm) in diameter surrounded by a patterned border. Some borders contained Anglo-Norman inscriptions. Each roundel was set in a square frame of four tiles filled with foliage designs. A complete unit was sixteen inches (405 mm) square. The Chertsey tiles were probably made between 1260 and 1280. In the 1290s, as the 1922 discovery of a tile kiln showed, the patterns were copied in square versions for Halesowen Abbey, West Midlands. They were also used at Hailes Abbey. Three of the Halesowen series survive – a complete tile of Tristan teaching Iswolde to play the harp, a fragment of Mark's head and another showing water lapping against a brick wall.

---

[24] The letter from Dr Stukeley to Dr Ducarel, October 1752, is quoted by Shaw who also gives the Grumbridge story.

Although Loomis cites Thomas' *Tristan* (ca. 1175) as the inspiration, the immediate source was more likely the late thirteenth century Middle English romance, *Sir Tristrem*.[25] The tiles and *Sir Tristrem* agree in several details not found in Thomas. The hero's father is Roland Ris rather than Rivalen. His kingdom is Ermonie ('hermonie' in l. 532) not Lyonesse. A tile fragment bearing the letters ONIE may allude to this thirteenth century designation of Brittany. His family's chief enemy is Duke Morgan, who is not mentioned in the French romances. His blazon, shown on two tiles depicting the battle with Morehaut (so spelled on the roundel inscription), is a single lion rampant. The poem describes the Irish champion striking his opponent 'in þe lyoun' (l. 1040). The Old Norse *Tristan*, based on Thomas, assigns him gold lions – more than one.

The hero's kidnapping by Norwegian merchants is clearly illustrated. As Tristrem plays chess in the prow, a sailor pushes the ship to sea, watched by one of the hawks that had lured the boy onto the ship (ll. 298–350). Set down on English soil he first encounters two palmers (whom he pays to guide him) and then a hunting party. Tristrem instructs the hunters in the etiquette of cutting up a deer, finally exhibiting the stomach on a branch – 'He tiȝt þe maw on tinde' (l. 507). The corresponding tile shows the two palmers, identified by pilgrim badges and scrip, a hunter and the youthful hero holding aloft the stomach on a cleft stick. Having arrived at Mark's court, he is challenged to a harping contest. The tile literally depicts the verbal instruction by showing him sitting 'Bi for þe kinges kne' (l. 560). Later, Mark strikes him on the shoulder – 'He made kniȝt wiþ his hand' (l. 785). In the charming scene where Isolde learns to play the harp (as in other representations of Tristrem's chief sign), the instrument is depicted according to King David iconography in twelfth and thirteenth century manuscripts like Oxford, Bodl. Auct. E., inf. 2, f. 2, an English Bible (ca. 1175).

Fidelity to text is combined with realistic detail when the artist shows Mark holding his nose at the sick man's bedside – 'No man no miȝt for stink/ Com þer tristrem ware'. Voyaging to Ireland in the rudderless boat, 'to a stede þer him was boun'; fever-bright eyes stare from the gaunt, unshaven face as claw-like hands pluck the harpstrings. The English poem's swift movement, reliance on unadorned images, and interest in event rather than characterization facilitated its conversion to pictorial narrative.

The vertical pillars which frame some tiles and the splendidly ornate tower into which the porter (with an oversize key resembling St Peter's) welcomes Rohand are Early English in style. The round mouldings of doors and windows and the pillars' dog-tooth ornament are combined with pointed arches and crenellation. Baron de Cosson, who provided Shurlock with information about the armour, noted that such details as the flat-topped helm, long surcoat worn over chain mail, absence of knee pieces and horse housings, the triangular shape of the

---

[25] The romance only survives in the Auchinleck Manuscript, Edinburgh, National Library of Scotland, Advocates MS 19.2.1. Its first editor, Sir Walter Scott, thought that the 'Thomas' of the text was Thomas of Erceldoune, the supposed author of the Middle English poem. This theory is now rejected. The reference obviously is to Thomas of Britain, the author of *Sir Tristrem*'s source, the Old French *Tristan*.

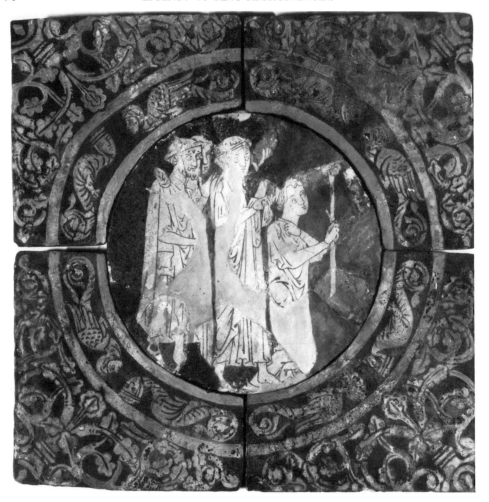

16. Tristram instructs hunters in the etiquette of venery. Chertsey Tile, 1260–80

shield and the ailettes (without blazon) were consistent with those on Henry III's seal (ca. 1275). Servants wear coifs while the upper-class characters wear the round stalked caps with rolled brim that also appear in the slightly later Tristan illustrations of BL Add. 11619 (ca. 1300). The voluminous drapery of the gowns, the incisive lines and the suggestion of actual rounded bodies underneath the clinging cloth relate the figural style to that of thirteenth century illuminated manuscripts such as the Trinity and Paris Apocalypses associated with St Albans. Like the details of armour and architecture, the secular costumes confirm an English rather than a Continental style. These tile mosaics of Chertsey Abbey, fragmented and incomplete, at least suggest the splendour of the decorated pavements which must have been common in both religious and secular buildings until the sixteenth century.

Some of the most interesting decorations in monastic foundations were the misericords.[26] The name, derived from *misericordia* (pity), refers to the shelf placed under a choir stall seat. During lengthy services a monk could tip the seat and support himself by leaning against the edge. If he nodded off, the seat would fall with an embarrassing bang. The oldest set of surviving misericords, at Exeter, dates from the thirteenth century but the chief flowering occurred between the late fourteenth and early sixteenth centuries when carvers spread out from craft centres to decorate not only cathedrals and priories but college chapels and parish churches as well.

On the underside of the choir seat the medieval woodcarver indulged himself with the same wit, verve, imagination and even lubricity as the painter of marginalia displayed. (The Victorian Dean Howsan of Chester had five misericords burned because 'they were very improper'). Characters and incidents drawn from the Bible, the lives of the Virgin and the saints, the iconography of the Seven Deadly Sins and other religious subjects naturally were used. However, secular subjects were far more popular – scenes from daily life, 'social history in miniature', animals, heraldry, foliage, flowers, musical instruments, historical personages, and scenes from romance. The most important scene occupied the centre of the oak block, while a supporter on each side completed the design.

Judging by surviving misericords, the most popular Arthurian subject was an incident from Chrétien's *Yvain* or from the Middle English adaptation, *Yvain and Gawain* (fourteenth century). The Lincoln and Chester cathedrals, New College Chapel, Oxford, and the churches of Boston and Enville all show the scene in which Yvain, having defeated the knight of the magic fountain, tries to follow him into the castle:

> Whan they come to the castel yate,
> In he folwed faste ther-at.
> At either entree was, y-wis,
> Streytly wroght a porte-colys
> Shod wel wyth iren and steel,
> And also grounden wonder wel;
> Under that than was a swike
> That made Sir Ywain to myslike:
> Whan his hors foot touched ther-on,

---

[26] The major studies are M.D. Anderson, *The Medieval Carver* (Cambridge, Eng., 1935); F. Bond, *Wood-carvings in English Churches: (1) Misericords* (Oxford, 1910); Dorothy and Henry Kraus, *The Hidden World of Misericords* (New York, 1975); and G.L. Remnant, *Catalogue of Misericords in Great Britain* (Oxford, 1969). See also Christa Grössinger, 'English Misericords of the Thirteenth and Fourteenth Centuries and their Relationship to Manuscript Illuminations', *Journal of the Warburg and Courtauld Institutes*, 38 (1975), 97–108 and J.L. Purvis, 'The Use of Continental Woodcuts and Prints by the Ripon School of Woodcarvers in the Early Sixteenth Century', *Archaeologia*, LXXXV (1936), 107–28. On individual churches see M.D. Anderson, *The Choir Stalls of Lincoln Minster* (Lincoln, 1967); B.T.N. Bennett, *The Choir Stalls of Chester Cathedral* (Chester, n.d.) which incorrectly identifies the Yvain misericord; and Francis W. Steer, *Misericords at New College, Oxford* (London, 1973).

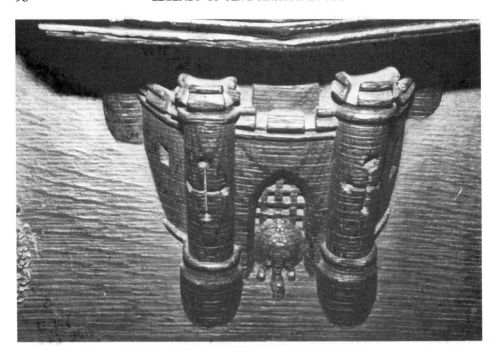

17. Yvain's horse trapped under the portcullis. Chester Cathedral misericord

> Than fel the porte-colys anon
> Betwixe him and his hinder-arsoun:
> Thurgh sadel and stede it smot al doun.
> His spores of his heles it shar.   (ll. 671–683)

In Lincoln and Chester the horse's hindquarters protrude under the lowered portcullis of the towered gateway. The supporters are the heads of knights, each wearing a conical helmet without a visor and a mail aventail. According to M.D. Anderson, the two misericords might have been cut from the same drawing. The Boston misericord is similar.

The model has provided two designs for New College. On the north side #21 shows a similar castle without a horse. The left supporter is a head wearing a conical helmet over a fluted protector while the right supporter, as at Lincoln, wears a helmet with mail aventail. Halfway down the south side #45 shows the horse trapped in an elaborate entrance with crenellations, slit windows in the towers and a row of gatehouse windows decorated with crosses. The supporters are smaller gateways with soldiers' helmeted heads peering over the battlements. Additionally, the gateways are topped with banners, the left one bearing a chevron and the right a saltire.

The finest representation, one suggesting knowledge of the text, occurs at Enville in Staffordshire. Here Yvain's legs and feet with their prominent spurs seem to writhe away to safety as the spiked gate impales the horse. Again the supporters are smaller gateways but instead of merely watching, the soldiers emerge to satisfy the line 'Bitwene the yates now is he tane'.

The most popular Tristan motif in medieval art, the Tryst beneath the Tree,[27] was adapted to the misericord's shape. The literary sources included Béroul, Eilhart von Oberge's *Tristant*, the Norse *Tristrams Saga* and *Sir Tristrem*. To assuage the pain of separation after Tristan's banishment, the lovers arrange meetings under a particular tree (a linden or pine). Informed of the rendezvous, King Mark secretes himself in the tree to spy on them. But seeing his shadow or his reflected face in the stream or fountain at the tree's base, the lovers stage a scene that allays the deceived husband's suspicions. As with the Yvain misericords, the supporters are integral to the subject.

At Lincoln #26 on the south shows Tristan and Isolde standing to left and right of the pool, their hands almost touching Mark's crowned head which looms out of the tree. One dog, perhaps Tristan's Houdain, stands beside the pool while Brangwain, the right supporter, holds another. Iconographically, a lap dog signified a lady's attachment to sensual life but it was narratively appropriate here, perhaps alluding to Petitcru, Tristan's marvellous gift. The left supporter, without a head, may represent Gouvernail. Tristan's padded doublet, low-slung belt decorated with roses, and pointed shoes along with Isolde's low cut bodice and bell-shaped skirt duplicate a style of noble dress that became popular in the 1360s. Brangwain's hooded cape and wimple suggest bourgeois respectability.

The Tryst misericord on the north side of the Chester choir is more sophisticated and accurate; it is also more realistic, since Isolde's little dog laps the water in the pool, presumably disturbing the reflection. The carver's skill is revealed by Tristan's realistic stance as he shows his lady a ring with his right hand while looking over his right shoulder. The supporters are shaded by elegantly contorted trees. Brangwain wears a couvrechief, a style of headdress then fashionable in Bohemia, the Netherlands and England. A moralising French work, *Cy Nous Dit* (Chantilly 1078–79), may provide a reason for the Tryst's acceptability in a church:

> If we guard ourselves from evil thoughts and evil doing, for the love of
> our Lord, who sees all our thoughts, we would keep us in His peace,
> just as the Queen and the knight kept the peace of the king.[28]

Misericord #18 on the south side at Lincoln, showing a knight sleeping with his head in a lady's lap while she holds his horse, may be based on the Middle English romance, *Sir Perceval of Galles*. The Thornton manuscript in Lincoln Cathedral Library contains the only extant copy of the fourteenth century poem. The unique misericord seems to illustrate an incident which occurs after Perceval has defeated the wicked Sultan and married his daughter, Lufamour. Riding into the forest he finds a distressed lady whose husband, the Black Knight, has bound

---

[27] On the motif's literary sources see Helaine Newstead, 'The Tryst beneath the Tree: An Episode in the Tristan Legend', *Romance Philology*, 9 (1956), 269–84.
[28] Chantilly, Musée Condé, MS 1078–79; cited and trans. Loomis, p. 28 .

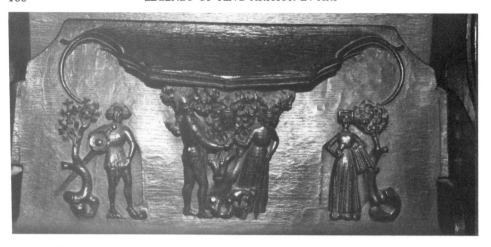

18. The Tryst beneath the Tree. Chester Cathedral misericord

her to a tree because she allowed a stranger (Perceval in his rustic stage) to take
her magical ring. After she has been freed:

> Downe satt the lady,
> And ʒong Percevalle hir by,
> For-waked was he wery,
>   Rist hym wolde he:
> He wende wele for to ryst,
> But it wolde nothyng laste;
> Als he lay althir-best
>   His hede one hir kne.   (ll. 1837–1844)

As the adventure terminates in a scene of forgiveness and reconciliation, a suitable moral could be imposed.

Another art form produced in an ecclesiastical environment was embroidery.[29]
In the later Middle Ages nuns in German convents used their leisure to recreate
not only subjects from the *Legenda aurea*, the *Apocrypha* and other religious works
but also from the romances of Tristan, Iwein and Parzival. As in the case of the

---

[29] The major studies are Marie Schuette, *Gestickte Bildteppiche und Decken des Mittelalters*,
Bd. 1–2 (Leipzig, 1927–30); Marie Schuette and Sigrid Müller-Christensen, *Das Stickereiwerk*
(Tübingen, 1963); English translation by Donald King, *The Art of Embroidery* (London, 1964).
On the Tristan embroideries particularly see Doris Fouquet, *Wort und Bild in der mittelalter-
lichen Tristantradition* (Berlin, 1971) with its extensive bibliography; F. Ranke, *Tristan und
Isold* (Munich, 1925); Hella Frühmorgen-Voss and Norbert H. Ott, *Text und Illustration im
Mittelalter: Aufsätze zu den Wechselbeziehungen zwischen Literatur und bildender Kunst* (Mu-
nich, 1975). This study includes a catalogue of all Tristan art, pp. 140–171. In Loomis, the
relevant pages are pp. 45, 51–55 and *passim*.

pictorial pavement, embroideries allowed the designer to present in narrative sequence a number of scenes taken from literary sources, together with inscribed verbal guides to identity. The German embroideries fall into two types. *Opus teutonicum* designs were embroidered with silk or white linen thread on white linen ground. The use of convent stitch and stem stitch helps to identify monastic work. Linen and wool rather than silk were most common in northern convents, perhaps because the nuns were too poor to afford imported materials. In Southern Saxony the polychrome woollen hangings using silk or linen threads and appliqué figures of blue, red, green, yellow and black must have contrasted vividly with the cloister's stone or brick wall.[30]

An early fourteenth century fragment of embroidery which probably originated in Saxony and is now in the Lüneberg Museum represents the whitework style. The three remaining scenes depict Isolde's recognition that the bathing Tristan is Morholt's slayer, the Tryst Beneath the Tree (with the dog standing on its hind legs), and a scene that Hella Frühmorgen-Voss thinks is Isolde's voyage to join her dying lover. Norbert Ott notes the iconographical resemblance to common religious motifs: a baptism with Bringvain and Ysolt replacing the priest and godfather; the Temptation of Adam and Eve with the lovers taking the place of the Biblical characters on either side of the tree; and the Sea of Genezareth model with a fish-hook and fish beneath the ship.[31]

The Cistercian Abbey at Wienhausen near Celle in Hanover[32] produced three Tristan embroideries which Frühmorgen-Voss calls carpets, Loomis calls hangings and Pickering designates tapestries.[33] Varying in completeness and date, they are referred to as Wienhausen I, II and III. Wienhausen I (ca. 1300–1310) measuring 404 x 233 cm (13 ft 3 in x 7 ft 8 in) consists of four rows of arcaded heraldic shields, many related to the ducal house of Braunschweig-Lüneberg, and three rows of

---

[30] These products of the cloister, however, did not achieve the sumptuousness of romance accounts. In the Middle English romance *Emaré* (ca. 1400), the embroidered cloth which the Emir's daughter made is resplendent with topazes, rubies, agates, and other precious stones. One corner depicts Ydoyne and Amadas with true-love-knots made of carbuncles, sapphires, chalcedony, and onyx set in gold. In another corner Trystram and Isowde are brightened with topazes, rubies, and other stones, because 'They loved hem ryght'. The other model lovers are Floris and Blaunchfleur and the Emir's daughter with the Sultan's son, the latter embroidery including the unicorn, (a symbol of chastity), flowers and birds. The cloth, in the poet's words, is 'stuffed wyth ymagerye'.

[31] ' "Tristan" auf Runkelstein und die übrigen zyklischen dartstellungen des Tristan stoffe' in W. Haug, N.H. Ott *et al., Runkelstein. Die Wandmalereien des Sommerhauses* (Wiesbaden, 1982), pp. 214–18.

[32] The abbey, now an Evangelical convent, still houses the hangings.

[33] For F.P. Pickering's discussion see *Literature and Art in the Middle Ages* (Coral Gables, Florida, 1970), pp. 147–55. He notes that the twenty-two pictures of Wienhausen I 'probably occupied more hours of work than the copying of all the more than twenty extant Gottfried manuscripts. Such a disproportion between invested labour and story almost passes comprehension'. In addition to critical discussions noted in fn. 29, there are Jürgen Ricklefs, 'Der Tristanroman der niedersächsischen und mitteldeutschen Tristanteppiche' in *Niederdeutsches Jahrbuch*, 86 (1963), 33–48 and Jozef Janssens, 'Koning Artur en de Tafelronde' in *Arturus Rex, volumen I. Catalogus*, 87–90. See also p. 81 above.

romance scenes. Horizontal bands with inscriptions in Low German separate the rows. A border of entwined roses and rose leaves symbolising Isolde's beauty frames the left side while the right features a border of oaks and acorns suggesting Tristan's prowess. The strip system of narration was, no doubt, suggested by German illuminated manuscripts.

Each group of scenes shows temporal progression and a consistent pattern of withdrawal and return such as characterises romance texts. The consecutive arrangement of scenes read from left to right, as in a manuscript, and following a linear time scheme integrates the individual scenes into a total story. The first row depicts Tristan's departure from Mark's court, arrival at the island, fight with Morholt, and return to court. The second row presents the hero's first voyage to Ireland, meeting with 'Bringvain' and 'Ysolt', healing, and return. The third row begins with the second voyage to Ireland, going on to the dragon fight, Ysolt's identification of Tristan as her uncle's slayer, the confrontation with the false seneschal, and the voyage to Cornwall, with the lovers in close embrace as Bringvain raises the fatal goblet. The inscriptions do not always match the scenes nor do they conform exactly to any known text, though Eilhart's is the closest. Among the discrepancies, the inscription indicates that Mark opposed the hero's quarrel with Morolt. Doris Fouquet, who has made the most exhaustive study, believes that an oral version of the story current in Northern Germany rather than a literary text was the source.

Red and blue are the dominant colours, being used for backgrounds and for such details as horses, shields, oars and the dragon. Aesthetic effect rather than consistency or realism determines the choice. The tree with heart-shaped leaves in row 4 recalls the foliage of Munich cgm 51, *Tristan*, ca. 1300.

The other Wienhausen embroideries, dated 1330–60 on the basis of costume, illustrate programmes similar to Wienhausen I, the dragon-slaying serving as the central act. Again, there are departures from Eilhart, as when a bird flies into Mark's bedroom carrying not one of Isolde's golden hairs but a leaf, iconography suggesting a Noah's ark model. What survives of Wienhausen II is a section 135 x 164 cm embroidered in bright blue, green, red, black, yellow and white. It is mutilated and worn, having been used to cover the altar steps. Wienhausen III is the most beautifully coloured of the three, combining indigo, pale blue, dark red, straw-yellow, rose, green and white. The largest in size, 254 x 402 cm, it extends the repertoire to include the love grotto, the Tryst, the hero's marriage to the second Isolde, *inter alia*, concluding with the queen's voyage to join the dying Tristan. Intertwined dragons linked tail and neck form a graceful border. Unlike Wienhausen I and II, Wienhausen III acknowledges the conflict between the adulterous lovers and society. By depicting the defeat of the latter's representatives, it condones the love-affair.[34]

---

[34] See Norbert Ott's discussion of this theme in 'Geglückte Minne-Aventiure: zur Szenenauswahl literarischer Bildzeugnisse im Mittelalter. Die Beispiele des Rodenecker "Iwein", des Runkelsteiner "Tristan", des Braunschweiger Gawain und des Frankfurter "Wilhelm-von- Orlens"-Teppichs' in *Jahrbuch der Oswald von Wolkenstein Gesellschaft*, 2 (1983), 1–32.

A Tristan hanging executed in a North German convent about 1370 and now in London's Victoria and Albert Museum is still another depiction of the dragon-slaying sequence. On alternating woollen squares with red or dark blue backgrounds the elegant appliqué men in parti-coloured hose and the lively horses – red, green, or brown – act out their roles beneath triple arcades that link one panel to the next. Details are worked with coloured silk. The mutilated hanging now measures 101 x 241 cm.[35]

Stylistically related to it is a linen tablecloth or quilt embroidered at the Benedictine convent of Würzburg about 1375 and now in the treasury of Erfurt Cathedral. Measuring 93 x 428 cm and featuring the same alternating blue and red colour scheme and the same unifying arcade, it depicts, once again, the dragon-slaying. The programme begins with King Mark's sighting of the swallow carrying the golden hair and ends with the Tryst where both Mark and the dwarf Melot appear. Melot's subsequent punishment is included. An original scene shows the Irish king enthroned with legs crossed in the judgement position, as he condemns the deceitful seneschal. Like the punishment of Melot the scene asserts a courtly obligation to penalise those who attack the mythic society of the elect.

Hartmann von Aue's *Iwein* (ca. 1205) inspired a linen hanging (68 x 490 cm) embroidered with coloured wools of blue, yellow, green and rust.[36] The Malterer family, whose arms appear at both ends, presented it ca. 1310–20 to the convent of St Catherine in Freiburg, where Anna Malterer was a nun. It is now in the Augustinermuseum, Freiburg in Breisgau. The Arthurian lovers, Iwein and Laudine, are associated with other infamous pairs to illustrate the evils of earthly passion, a reminder appropriate to a nunnery whose occupants were brides of Christ. Iwein, wearing a lion helmet, slits Acalon's crowned head as both are threatened by lightning bolts and pommelled by hailstones the size of baseballs. In the second scene Lunete, with a reticulated headdress, presents the hero to an agonized Laudine. The border of wild roses and the lilies embroidered in the interstices (both symbols of the Virgin Mary) produce an elegant effect.

A fourteenth century fragment (155 x 447 cm) discovered in the Kreuzkloster, Brunswick, Herzog, which was a Benedictine convent between 1230 and 1398,

[35] The subjects, excluding the mutilated upper border, are first row: Mark converses with Tristan, squire, swallow with a hair in its beak; squire brings Tristan his sword and shield (which has none of the usual blazons); Tristan rides out with the squire as Mark sees them off; squire asks fleeing seneschal where the dragon is; Tristan attacks the dragon with a lance.

second row: Tristan slays the dragon with his sword; he cuts out the tongue; seneschal rides out to find the dragon; he cuts off its head; he presents the head to the Irish king as the queen and Princess Isolde look on; the tryst beneath the tree. Attached to the right end are two fragments showing Mark's discovery of the lovers in the grotto and another tryst scene.

[36] For discussions see Ott, *Geglückte Minne-Aventiure*, p. 7; Loomis pp. 78–9; Friedrich Maurer, 'Der Topos von den Minnesklaven' in *FM: Dichtung und Sprache des Mittelalters* (Bern/München, 1963), pp. 224–248. Schuette (trans. King) has a colour reproduction, plate IX.

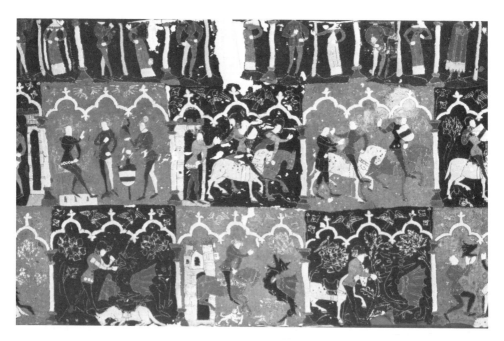

19a. North German Tristan wall hanging showing the swallow with Isolde's hair, the dragon adventure and the tryst, *inter alia*, ca. 1370

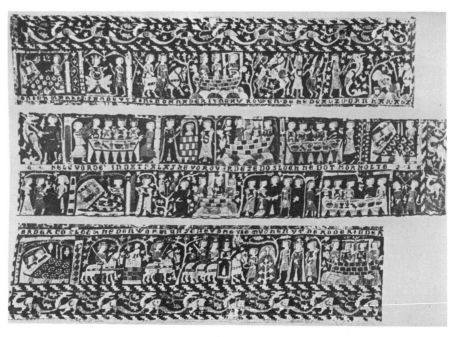

19b. Tristan wall hanging from the Cistercian Convent at Wienhausen (Wienhausen III).

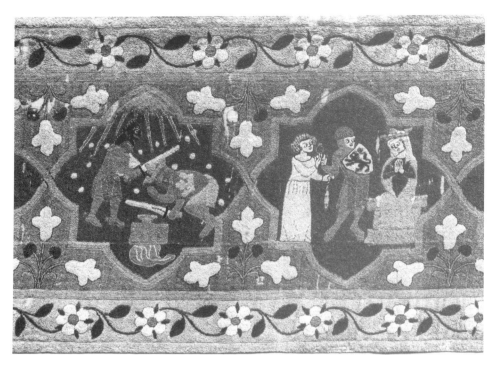

20. *Iwein* scenes on linen wall hanging, ca. 1310–20

indicates that Wolfram's *Parzival* also inspired convent art.[37] The twenty remaining scenes arranged in three rows illustrate Books *X–XIII*, Gawain's adventure with the proud Orgeluse.[38] In row one, the hero accompanies the lady through the forest, watches her depart in a boat, and fights Lischoys Gwelljus. The encounter first with lance on horseback and then on foot with swords resembles Tristan's fight with Morhold in Wienhausen I and II. The second row shows the Perilous Bed episode, complete with slings, crossbows and the lion. In the last row, the hero is reunited with Orgeluse; they are ferried across the river and welcomed to the Chateau Merveil by a group of mounted trumpeters and then by the hospitable hostess, Queen Arnive. As in Wienhausen I, the scenes are so arranged that the most important event of each sequence occurs in the middle of the row. Episodes depicting movement through the forest or across water (an image suggesting an approach to an otherworldly castle) alternate with periods of rest. The cloistered embroiderers evidently misjudged the space required for text since the

[37] Schuette, *Gestickte Bildteppiche*, pp. 8–10; Ott, 10–14; Loomis, 52, 72.
[38] For an English translation see Jessie L. Weston, *Sir Gawain at the Grail Castle* (London, 1903).

inscriptions do not correspond to the adjacent picture. The work is now in the Anton Ulrich Museum, Brunswick.

A wall hanging (76 × 18 cm) housed in the Museum des Kunsthandwerks, Leipzig but originally made in Alsace in 1539 shows that the Tristan embroideries persisted into the Renaissance. The source of the scenes recreated with coloured silks and wools – yellow, black, purple, rose, strawberry red, celadon green and brown – was a chapbook version (1498) of Eilhart's poem. The arms of several Alsatian families assert, as did earlier embroideries, the connection between aristocratic patronage and convent art. Many nuns either belonged to upper class families or, like Chaucer's Prioress, aspired to be considered 'gentle'. The overwhelming popularity of the Tristan story as a source of conventual art may be explained by the nature of its world. Dominated, as Erich Auerbach observed,[39] by a fixed and isolating setting in which women played an authoritative role, the genre provided an idealised analogy to one aspect of convent life. The embroiderers paid little attention to the adulterous love story, selecting, instead, incidents that illustrated Tristan's heroic battles against evil oppressors, first the implacable Morholt with his cruel demand for human tribute, then the dragon, iconographically associated with the devil. The moral and spiritual lessons to be drawn from the story justified producing romance scenes in a religious setting.[40]

Interesting examples of secular Italian embroideries are three Sicilian quilts.[41] Two of them, made as a pair, are now divided between the Victoria and Albert Museum, London and the Bargello, Florence. Countess Guicciardini of Florence owns the third; the quilts were probably made in 1395 for the marriage of her ancestors, Pietro di Luigi Guicciardini and Laodamia Acciaiuili. Inscriptions in Sicilian dialect indicate a programme based on *La Tavola Ritondo*. The Victoria and Albert quilt has been in England for almost three centuries. An inventory listing the contents of the 'yellow nursery' at Southampton House indicates that Rachel, Lady Russell acquired it from the Duke of Bedford in 1711. Measuring 310 × 370 cm (122 in × 106 in), the central portion is divided into six rectangular compartments with additional compartments on three sides as a border. The individual scenes are not arranged chronologically but must be read across the expanse of both quilts and borders. The London quilt shows, reading vertically from left to right,

> Row one: How Amoroldu has come into Cornwall with forty galleys; how Tristainu gives the glove of battle to Amoroldu; how Amoroldu has hired men; how King Languis sends for the tribute to Cornwall.
> Row two: How Amoroldu smote Tristainu by treachery; how Tristainu

---

[39] See 'The Knight Sets Forth' in *Mimesis*, pp. 123–142.
[40] Other examples of Arthurian textiles are listed in the Frühmorgen-Voss catalogue #13–#34 and Schuette, *The Art of Embroidery*, pp. 309–321.
[41] Fouquet, pp. 53 ff; Loomis, pp. 63–5; P. Rajna, 'Intorno a due antique coperte con figurazioni tratte dalle storie di Tristano', *Romania*, 42 (1913), 517–79; Schuette and Müeller-Christensen. On the Victoria and Albert quilt particularly see Averil Colby, *Quilting* (London, 1972), pp. 13–19, 80, 122.

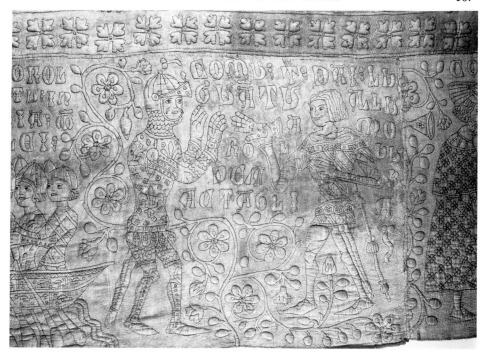

21. Tristainu gives the glove of battle to Amoroldu. Sicilian quilt, 1395

smote Amoroldu in the head; how Tristainu thrust the boat back into the sea.

Row three: Cities of Ireland; how the servant of Amoroldu waited for his master; how Tristainu waits for Amoroldu in the island of the sea Sanc a Vintura. Below rows two and three is a double representation, which would have hung at the foot of the bed: how the messengers have come to King Marcu for the tribute of seven years.

Row four: How Amoroldu has proclaimed the expedition into Cornwall; how King Languis commands that the host go into Cornwall (a double panel); how Amoroldu goes into Cornwall.[42]

The Bargello quilt (205 x 256 cm) combines three events – the sojourn of Tristan and Guviral at King Feramonti's court where the Princess Bellices falls in love with the hero; his arrival at Mark's court and subsequent knighting; and the combatants' journey to the island followed by the joust with lances. The Guicciardini fragment (250 x 250 cm) is largely devoted to fleur-de-lis and to allegorical beasts though a medallion in the centre shows in mutilated form the famous lovers.

The outlines of the important characters – Amoroldu, Tristainu, Languis and

[42] Cf. Colby, p. 15, for diagram with inscriptions in Sicilian and English.

Marcu – are embroidered with brown linen thread on two layers of heavy linen. Natural thread is used for secondary patterns such as the rhythmically decorative grapes and vines, ivy leaves and berries, rose and leaf, and oak leaves and acorns which separate the border scenes. These border devices are extraordinarily similar to those which Aubrey Beardsley devised for the Dent edition of Malory's *Morte Darthur* (1893–4). Could he have seen the quilt in London? Some details of the quilts' execution suggest manuscript convention; for example, the appearance of fish to indicate water and the single-masted ship with billowing sail. Cotton padding between the linen layers raises the quilted pictures. Through meticulous variation in stitching, the embroiderers suggest the differing textures of helmet, chain mail aventail, padded jupon, hair, nail-studded wood, and horse trappings. When Tristan challengingly offers the gauntlet, he wears the fashionable court dress of the late fourteenth century, complete with pointed shoes, buttoned sleeves which widen above the elbows, tasseled liripipe dangling from his hood, and padded chest. His opponent is dressed in the contemporary combination of plate and chain mail with a short, fitted jupon. Tristan's blazon consisting of three horns, while appropriate to his fame as a hunter, actually functions as a compliment to the Guicciardini family whose armorial device this is. The singularly inappropriate fleur-de-lis attributed to the Irish knight may represent the bride's family or the Angevin prince, Louis II who occupied Naples between 1390 and 1399. Since the occasion for creating the quilts was matrimonial, white was a more appropriate colour than would have been the 'rich quilt wrought with coten, with crimson sendel stitched with thredes of gold' that is mentioned in *Arthur of Little Britain*.[43]

In Gothic Europe from the thirteenth to the sixteenth centuries richly decorated consumer goods expressed the increased luxury of the aristocracy and the merchant class. What George Henderson calls the 'Bower of Bliss' mentality created dazzling ornaments, decorated to display all 'that natures worke by art can imitate'.[44] Such objects, often exchanged as New Year's gifts, included the Duke of Berry's Royal Gold Cup with translucent enamel figures in crimson, blue, black, and yellow, telling the story of St Agnes; his ruby carved to represent a rose; and the Duke of Anjou's wine dispenser designed as a hortus conclusus with a Fountain of Youth in which the beautiful people bathed. Thomas of Zerklaere, a thirteenth century German clerk living in Italy, wrote that gloves, looking-glass, finger-ring, brooch, hat, and flowers were suitable gifts for ladies.[45] A miniature in *The Hours of Mary of Burgundy*, Vienna, Nationalbibliothek, MS 1857, shows that they would also appreciate a Book of Hours, a rosary, a bottle of perfume and a jewel box. Carved and painted caskets were receptacles for relics, billet-doux and, most of all, jewels. The Musée de Cluny's Netherlands tapestries include one

---

[43] The French prose romance *Artus de la Petite Bretagne* is best known in the sixteenth-century translation of Sir John Bourchier, Lord Berners.
[44] On Gothic mannerism see George Henderson, *Gothic* (Harmondsworth, 1967), pp. 134–41.
[45] *Queen Elizabeth's Academy*, ed. and trans. F.J. Furnivall, EETS ES 8 (London, 1869), p. 123.

titled 'Le Bain' in which a lady bathes while her attendant maid holds a casket overflowing with the jewels that symbolise her beauty, virtue and wealth.

In comparison with quilts and wall hangings, the pictorial space of objets d'art was limited. The artist used recognisable subjects drawn from literary sources or aristocratic life – the Castle of Love, the Fountain of Youth, the capture of the Unicorn, hunting with hawk and hound, dalliance in a garden, and favourite Arthurian scenes. The ivory back of a Parisian mirror could show a couple meeting beneath a tree containing a crowned head. A Catalan pendant could show a couple about to drink from a goblet. Each representation would trigger a learned response. The pictorial shorthand adapted from the miniatures of illuminated manuscripts included a swag of drapery to represent a bedroom, a tree to represent a forest, wavy horizontal lines for water, a crenellated gateway for a castle. Traces of paint suggest that even the ivories were coloured so that they would express to the maximum degree the Gothic ideal of beauty. As usual, the artists who designed the ivory scenes and the craftsmen who executed them are anonymous, only two names surviving – Jehan le Scelleur and Jehan de l'Image.[46]

By far the most popular decorative motif on the Arthurian objets d'art is the Tryst Beneath the Tree.[47] Its appeal depends on both form and content. It is structurally balanced. The vertical Tristan and Isolde are placed on either side of the tree trunk which splits the pictorial plane into equal parts. The tree's leafy branches, often constrained in a circular shape, balance the fountain. Thus the four points of interest provide a circular progression of contiguous shapes. Added aristocratic signs – Tristan's hawk and Isolde's dog – conform to the pattern. Contrast is provided by the juxtaposed male and female costumes and by the reversal of Mark's head in the fountain mirror. The motif encapsulates the story's central motifs – the love of Tristan and Isolde, the hostility of Mark, and the lovers' success in outwitting the enemy. Symbolically, the motif is ambivalent, suggesting to a woman the lover's fidelity, to a man, the woman's duplicity.

One of the most ingenious adaptations must have been Louis of Anjou's silver gilt salt-cellar:

> The said salt-cellar is set upon a foot of which the pillar is of a tree, in
> which tree is King Mark, and below are Tristan and Ysolt, all carved
> very beautifully, and before them at the aforesaid foot there is a piece
> of crystal in the fashion of a fountain, and within this fountain appears
> the head of King Mark.

A fourteenth century crystal chalice used as a tournament trophy has an enamelled stand which combines the tryst with three other courtly scenes on its octagonal base. Now in the Poldi Pezzoli Museum, Milan, it bears a goldsmith

---

[46] The definitive study is Raymond Koechlin, *Les Ivoires Gothiques Français*, 2 vols. (Paris, 1924).

[47] On representations of the Tryst motif see Loomis, pp. 5–8, 28, 40, 43, 50, 53–56, 59, 63, 65–69; Frühmorgen-Voss, pp. 124–129; Raimond van Marle, *Iconographie de l'Art profane*, vol. II, p. 464 ff.

sign indicating that it came from Montpellier in Southern France. It is a splendid example of Gothic basse-taille enamelling, a technique that allows the high sculpted figures in green, orange, lilac, yellow and grey to stand out brightly against the lower, shaded areas.

A boxwood comb (early fifteenth century) in Bamberg's Historisches Verein, another from eastern France or Switzerland in Boston's Museum of Fine Arts, a leather case in the Namur Museum, circular mirror cases in the Vatican Library and Musée de Cluny, Paris, and a hair parter in Turin are other examples showing the motif's versatility. The Rhenish comb also accommodates lettered ribbons which quote Isolde's warning, 'tristram gardes de dire vilane por la pisson de la fonteine' and the hero's ironical reply, 'Dame, ie voroi per ma foi qu'i fu ave nos monsingor le roi'. Frühmorgen-Voss[48] has identified a literary source for Isolde's trick, which directs Tristan's attention to the water under the pretence of looking at a fish. Dirk Potter's *Der Minnen loep* (1411–12), II, ll. 3620–26 tells the story to illustrate that women can always find a way to escape a trap.

No adaptation is more surprising and touching than that on a triangular fragment of a leather slipper, 159 mm on the base, 23 mm at one end and 79 mm at the other.[49] Found in 1972 in a well located on the property of an Old People's Home in Mechelen, Belgium, the fifteenth century remnant is now in the Archaeological Museum, Mechelen. A heated metal stamp impressed the picture on the moistened leather which must have formed the cuff. The scene presents a mixed iconography. That the man in the long gown, supporting a falcon on his wrist, and the crowned woman are the lovers is confirmed by the words along the rim: 'TRIESTRAM SIEDI NIET D(A)T VISELKIIN – Tristan, see you not that fish?' It is obviously a version of the Dirk Potter text that we know referred to Tristan and Isolde. But the slipper shows no spying king or dwarf; the lovers are innocently playing chess. Since four other slipper fragments (ca. 1340–1400) found in Leiden and Dordrecht also depict the chess game, this would seem to be a common Dutch adaptation. The marriage custom whereby a groom gave his bride a slipper after their first night together probably inspired a version of the subject that signified faithful love service without deception.

Favourite gifts for ladies were boxes of ivory, whalebone, wood and metal often called marriage caskets or coffers.[50] In the earlier fourteenth century Parisian

---

[48] *op. cit.* p. 129.

[49] It was part of the 'Koning Artur en de Nederlanden' exhibition in the Museum of Leuven, July 25–Oct. 25, 1987. See the catalogue, pp. 134–137.

[50] On caskets see Koechlin, pp. 474–505; Loomis, pp. 43–44, 66, 70–72, 73–74; Fouquet, pp. 21–26, 55–57. Frühmorgen-Voss lists boxes illustrating *Tristan*; catalogue pp. 158–161. Articles on individual caskets include Gerard J. Brault, 'Le Coffret de Vannes et la légende de Tristan au XIIᵉ siècle' in *Mélanges offerts à Rita Le Jeune*, vol. 1 (Gembloux, 1969), 653–668; Robert Forrer, 'Tristan et Yseult sur un coffret inédit du XIIᵉ siècle', *Cahiers d'Archeologie et d'Histoire d'Alsace* (Strasbourg, 1933); R.S. Loomis, 'The Tristan and Perceval Caskets', *Romanic Review*, VIII (1917), 196–209; David J. Ross, 'Allegory and Romance on a Medieval French Marriage Casket', *Journal of the Warburg and Courtauld Institutes*, 2 (1948), 112–142. A number of caskets are illustrated in *The Secular Spirit: Life and Art at the End of the Middle*

workshops produced Gothic ivories for such noble patrons as Clemence of Hungary, Jean le Bon, Charles V, Charles VI, Isabel of Bavaria, Robert of Clermont, and the Dukes of Berry, Orléans and Anjou. Cologne was an earlier German centre while in Venice the Embriarchi craftsmen carved the Swan Knight's adventures along with other romance themes. Because of their portability, the coffers were useful articles of international exchange. Of those that have survived intact, some like the coffret of Vannes or the Cracow casket were conserved in cathedral treasuries. In 1913 Robert Forrer's wife found a twelfth century casket among eighteenth and nineteenth century objets d'art displayed in a Parisian shop; the British Museum bought it for £2,050 in 1947. A Brighton junk shop harboured Lord Gort's casket, discovered in 1945.[51]

The Forrer casket is undoubtedly Arthurian, since its scenes reflect recognisable Tristan archetypes. Measuring 14.5 x 9.5 x 7.5 cm, its provenance is a twelfth century Cologne workshop. The five ivory surfaces show scenes in which Tristan and Morholt fight on foot (back); Brangwain offers the love drink to Mark and Isolde in bed (lid); King Mark and Queen Isolde, both crowned, join hands in a castle garden (right side); Tristan and Isolde meet in a garden (left side). On the front is an episode found only in Gottfried, 'the harp and the rote', in which Gandin with his rote-playing wins Isolde from Mark while Tristan with his harping regains her. Reminding us that ivory carving was once a cloister art are the dogtooth borders, twisted pillars, columns with decorated capitals, and round arches of Romanesque architecture, details commonly found on reliquaries. On each plaque vertical towers on the far right and left of the pictorial space emphasize the characters' containment. The warriors' conical helmets with nose pieces (similar to those in the Bayeux tapestry and Modena archivolt), the mail shirts, long swords, great shields decorated with carbuncles, as well as the lady's belted surcoat and loose-sleeved gown are costume details which suggest a date ca. 1200 for the casket. The broccoli-like trees resemble those in BN fr. 110 and BL Add. 38117.

The Vannes marriage casket is made of oak; the lid is fixed to the back with iron hinges and there is an iron handle. Originally it probably rested on wooden feet. The inside is lined with unbleached linen and the outside covered with parchment to provide a surface for the paintings. As in some illuminated manuscripts (e.g. Morgan 805 and BN fr. 1433) differently coloured backgrounds divide each panel in two. Alternating rectangles of yellow vines on a brown background and white saltires and rings on black form the borders. Costume details suggest a date ca. 1170.

Though none of the unmistakable motifs such as the dragon, the harp, the boat, the love potion, or the tryst is illustrated, nevertheless Gerard Brault believes that the various scenes derive from a Tristan romance. He identifies them as follows:

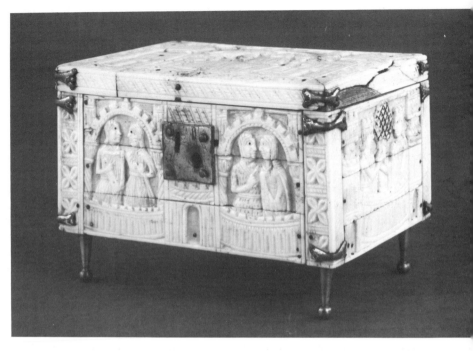

22. Rhenish casket with Tristan scenes, ca. 1200

(1) left end: Two warriors are fighting on foot (Tristan and Morholt). The arms and armour, including nose protector, resemble those on the Forrer casket but Tristan's patterned pantaloons are unusual. Brault relates them to similar costuming in the Romanesque frescoes at the Abbey of Saint-Sabin-sur-Gartempe.

(2) cover: On the left the two mounted knights, Tristan and Govérnal, undertake the second trip to Ireland to acquire Isolde as Mark's bride. On the right, the lady in the tower offering the knight a shield is Isolde, who prepares the hero for the dragon adventure. The only literary source for the scene is Brother Robert's Norse saga.

(3) front: A crowned figure with ermine-lined mantle (King Mark), while hawking in the woods, finds the lovers in their forest refuge. It is not a cave but a striped pavilion that Brault relates to Béroul's little hut. Both men have falcons.

(4) right end: Tristan, disguised as a minstrel, entertains the lady by playing not a harp but a viol, as in the Wienhausen I wall hanging. The slim elongated figures display their costumes to perfection. Tristan's surcoat is split front and back almost to the waist, revealing slender legs and an abbreviated cote. Isolde's narrow sleeves with their

dangling panels were fashionable in the mid-century but had disappeared by 1200.[52]

(5) back: Tristan, disguised as a friar, meets Isolde. This incident only occurs in a thirteenth century German poem, *Tristan als Mönch*. Brault explains this and other discrepancies by positing an oral source.[53] The mixture of Breton and Arabic elements attributed to oral forms of the legend may also account for the dark colours and figural style.

Carved ivory plaques decorate the Parisian caskets, which on the basis of costume are dated 1300–1340. With small variations, the approximate size is 20 x 10 x 8 cm. A consistent arrangement of subjects suggests adherence to workshop models.[54] The lid, which the mounts divide into four equal compartments, usually depicts the Siege of the Castle of Love or a tournament. The front's subjects are the story of Aristotle and Phyllis on the left and the Fountain of Youth on the right. The pictorial space of the right end is divided between the Unicorn Hunt and the Tryst, both scenes illustrating deceit. The left end may illustrate Enyas and the woodhouse, a subject from a lost romance about an old knight who rescues a maiden from a wild man of the woods. Alternatively, Galahad's capture of the Castle of Maidens may appear.[55]

The back's four compartments were usually devoted to Arthurian scenes: Gawain fighting the lion; Lancelot on the Sword Bridge; Gawain on the Perilous Bed; and three maidens waiting to greet Gawain at the castle entrance. The scenes were arranged not according to literary chronology but according to form with vertical figures at the extremities and horizontal figures in the centre. Lancelot is assaulted by diagonal weapons from above so as to parallel formally the attack on Gawain, though there is no justification in the text. Figures on the left side face those on the right, providing a pleasing balance. In the third compartment the lion's paw is embedded in Gawain's shield although in the text the rain of arrows precedes the lion fight. Significantly, Lancelot's shield also bears the lion's paw, an indication that the artist understood the hero of the sword-bridge adventure to be Gawain. Either the artist who devised the scheme was ignorant of the texts or he departed from them for aesthetic reasons. Though many caskets have similar programmes, the Victoria and Albert casket represents the earliest surviving example of the Arthurian sequence.[56]

[52] E.R. Goddard, *Women's Costume in French Texts of the Eleventh and Twelfth Centuries* (Baltimore and Paris, 1927).
[53] On a Welsh fabulator, Bleheris, who flourished between 1100 and 1140 and recited his stories at the court of Poitou, see Helaine Newstead, 'The Origin and Growth of the Tristan Legend' in *Arthurian Literature in the Middle Ages*, pp. 132–3.
[54] See Ross's illuminating discussion of casket types and their iconography.
[55] Loomis proposed this identification in 'A Medieval Ivory Casket', *Art in America*, V (1916), 22 but Koechlin, *op. cit.* p. 505 rejects the suggestion: 'est-il vraisemblable que Galahad, un bien petit seigneur, marche de pair avec ces illustres personnages? Il est loisible de se le demander'.
[56] Other complete examples of caskets with Arthurian scenes include those in the British Museum, London; Metropolitan Museum, New York; The Walters Art Gallery, Baltimore;

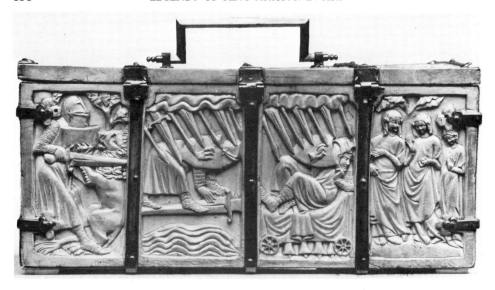

23. Parisian casket of ivory, ca. 1300, showing: Gawain attacking the lion; Lancelot on
the Sword Bridge; Gawain on the Perilous Bed; maidens awaiting Gawain

Caskets devoted entirely to Arthurian subjects were probably quite rare. In
addition to the twelfth century caskets already discussed, there is a Tristan casket
in Leningrad's Hermitage Museum[57] and a Perceval casket in the Louvre. The
former, somewhat controversial, probably derives from Béroul, since it depicts the
substitute bride motif; the reflection in a fountain, rather than a stream; Mark's
discovery of the love grotto; and the equivocal oath. The Perceval casket is based
on Chrétien's *Conte del Graal*. On the left end Perceval with his bow, peasant's
pointed cap and 'skins' (resembling modern ski wear) kneels to three knights who
carry rose-sprinkled shields. The other end shows the hero's arrival at Arthur's
court. In the back's four compartments, Perceval takes leave of his mother, who
collapses despairingly on the drawbridge. He then rides through the forest, carrying the two javelins specified in ll. 1799–1803 and depicted in BN fr. 12577, f. 1. In
the fourth compartment he kisses the damsel in the pavilion. On the casket front,
still dressed in rustic garments, he fights the Red Knight, removes his armour and
has his own wounds tended by a squire. Alternatively, the latter scene shows
Perceval exchanging his peasant wardrobe for chivalric accoutrements. The casket
scenes can be compared with those in Montpellier MS 249. On these Gothic
ivories the ladies' elegantly draped skirts and Gothic sway, the knights' rose-
powdered shields and the maidens' garlands, the nonchalance with which Tristan, hawk on wrist, crosses his right leg over his left knee while Isolde pats her

The Barber Institute of Fine Arts, Birmingham; The Bargello Museum, Florence; the
Cathedral Treasury, Cracow. In addition, fragments of others survive. See Koechlin 1281–87
for details of complete caskets and 1288–97 for fragments.
[57] In addition to the Loomis article, see Fouquet, who discusses two Hermitage caskets, pp.
23–26; and Koechlin, 391 ff., 519 ff.

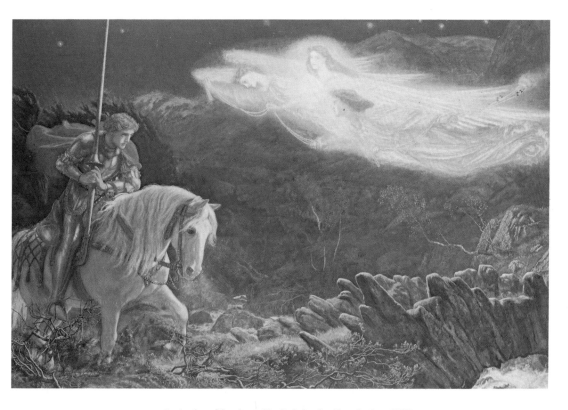

1. Arthur Hughes. Sir Galahad, oil painting 1870

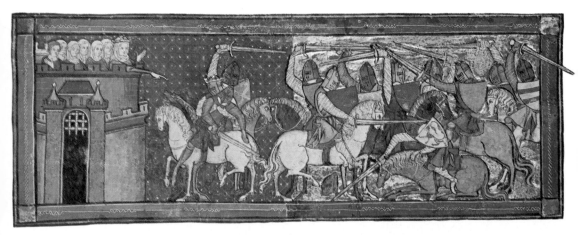

2a. Sir Lancelot fights in a tournament as Guenevere watches.
Pierpont Morgan Library 805, f. 262 (Lancelot)

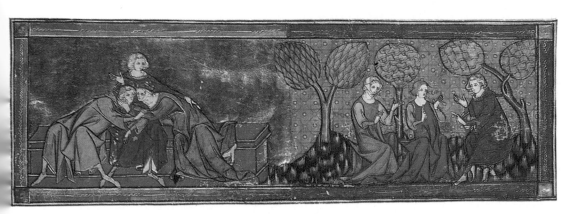

2b. Galeholt watches the lovers' first kiss as the seneschal and ladies converse.
Pierpont Morgan Library 805, f. 67

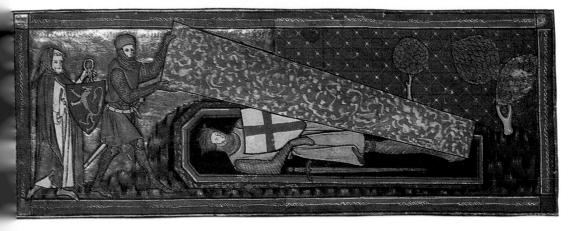

2c. Lancelot raises the lid of Josephé's tomb. Pierpont Morgan Library 805, f. 161v

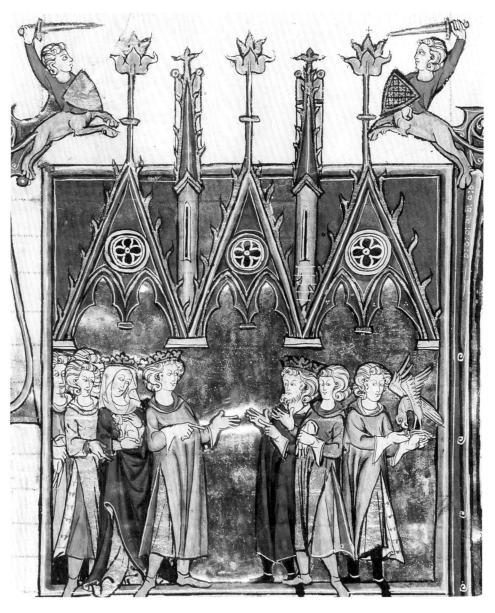

3. King Arthur and King Ban plan a tournament as Queen Guenevere and
courtiers watch. Bibliothèque Nationale fr. 95, f. 291

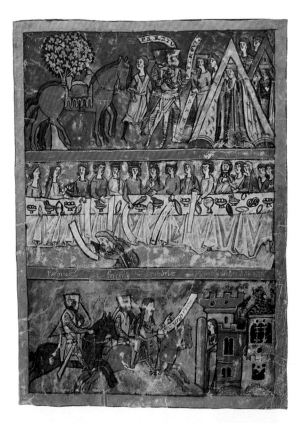

4. Scenes from Wolfram's *Parzival*.
Bayerische Staatsbibliothek,
Munich, cgm 19, f. 50

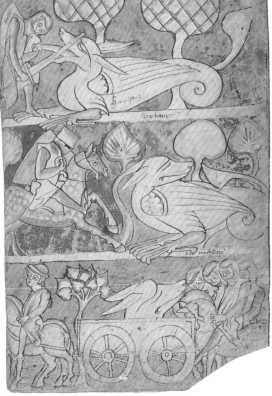

5. Tristan kills the dragon which is
found and claimed by the false
steward. Bayerische
Staatsbibliothek,
Munich, cgm 51, f. 67

6. *Opposite.* Tristan arrives at
le Chastel dessus la Mer.
Bodl. Douce *Guiron*, f. 3

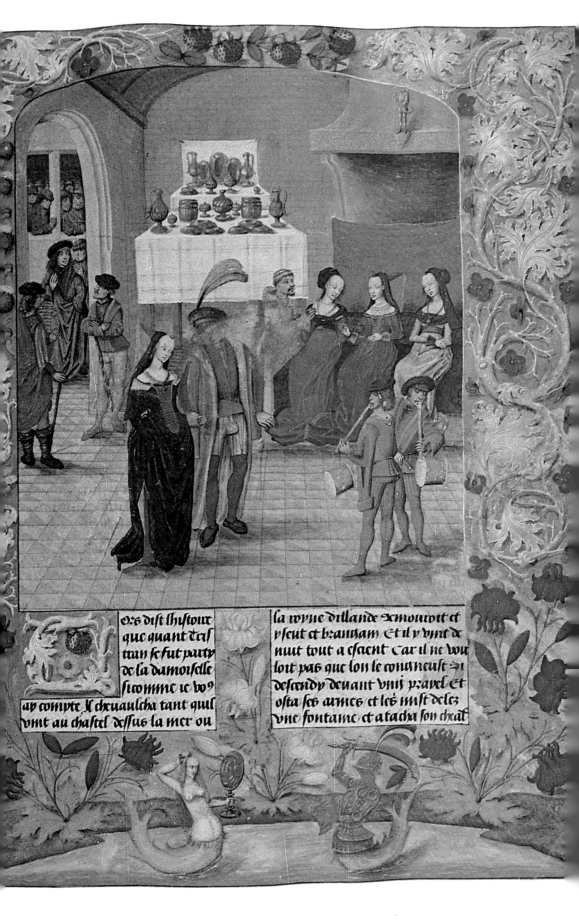

Oꝛs dist lhistoire que quant tri
stan se fut party
de la damoiselle
si comme ie vo⁹
ap compte Il cheuauscha tant quil
vint au chastel dessus la mer ou

la ꝛoyne dillande semontoit et
yseut et brauஅam Et il y vint de
nuit tout a escient Car il ne vou
loit pas que lon le conneust Si
descendy deuant vnij prael Et
osta ses armes et les mist deles
vne fontaine et atacha son cheal

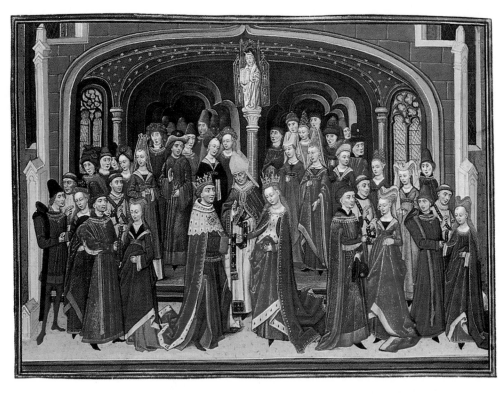

7. The wedding of Arthur and Guenevere in *Chroniques de Hainault*. Brussels, Bibliothèque Royale Albert Ier, f. 39v

8. *Opposite*. Galahad draws the sword from the stone. Bibliothèque Nationale fr. 343, f. 4

qe elatz dont ie ne point. Beuz sire fer
li rois eslaz uos en noieia deus au came
part ausi com il aset espee. Lors regaret
uers la riue griual et uoit ueuir ausi
come abesoing une damoiselle monte
seur un palefroi blac et uenoit uers
aus gritz aleure.

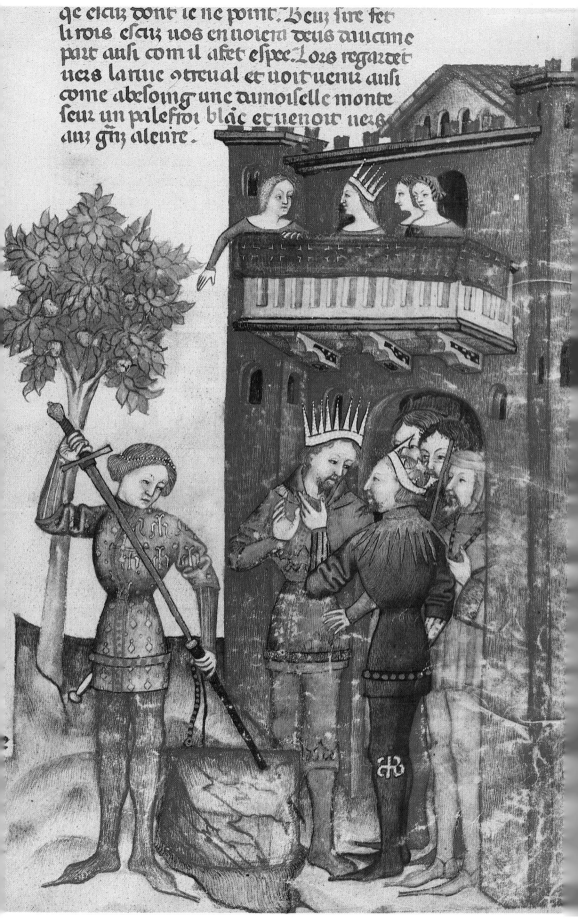

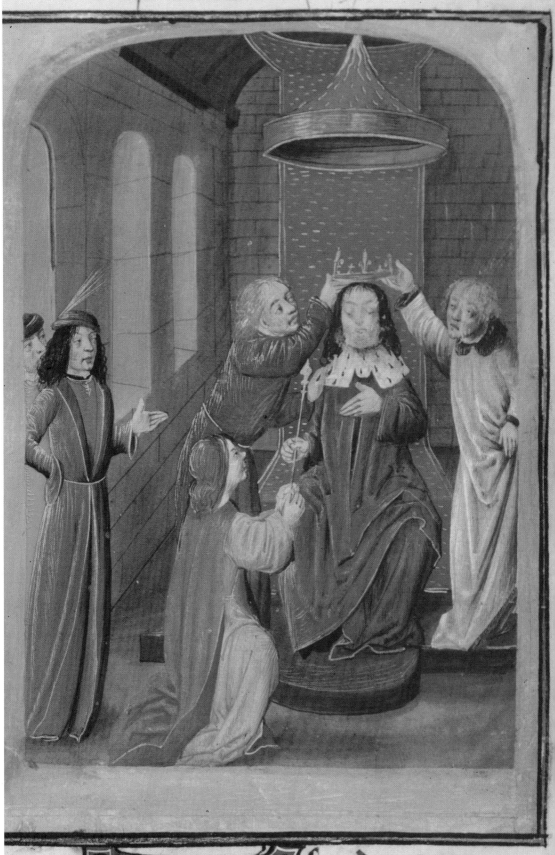

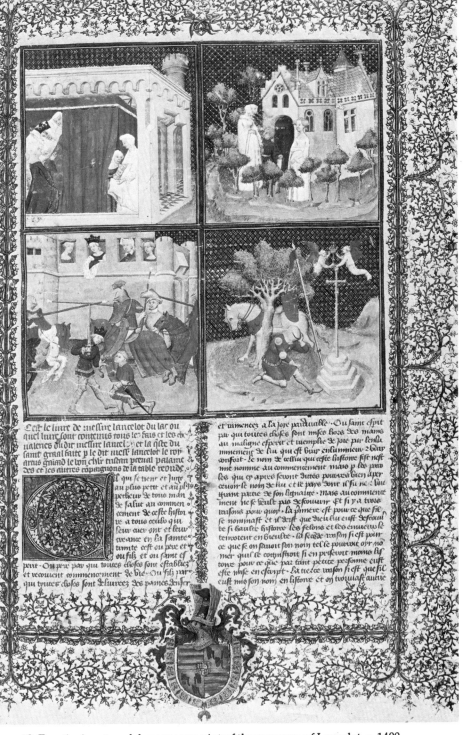

10. Frontispiece to a deluxe manuscript of the romance of Lancelot, c. 1400.
The scenes show Lancelot's birth, his upbringing by the Lady of the Lake,
Lancelot in combat, and his vision of the Grail at the wayside cross.
(Paris, Bibliothèque Nationale, MS Arsenal 3479, f. 1. Photo Giraudon)

9. *Opposite.* Arthur's coronation. *St Albans Chronicle*, Lambeth Palace Library 6, f. 54v

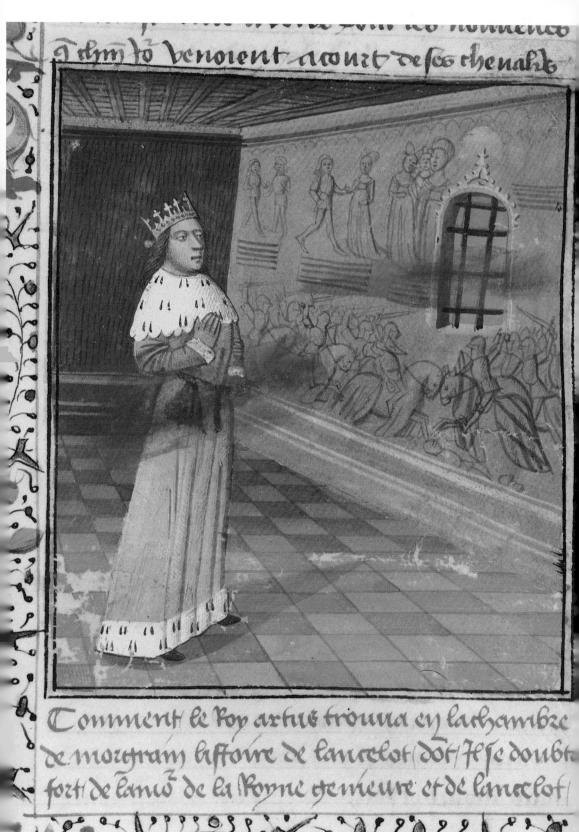

Comment le Roy artus trouua en lachambre de morgram listoire de lancelot dot. Jl se doubt fort de lamo~ de la Royne guenieure et de lancelot

11. Arthur views paintings revealing Lancelot's love for Guenevere.
Bibliothèque Nationale, fr. 112, 193v

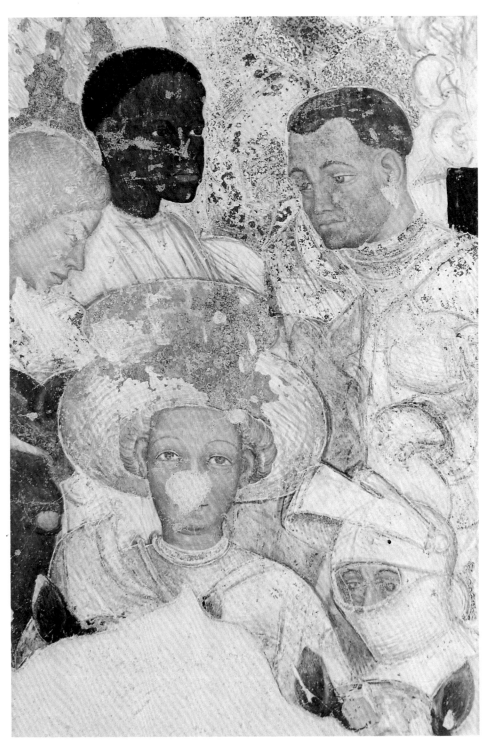

12. Pisanello's fresco of Tristan, Lancelot and Palamedes, Palazzo Ducale, Mantua

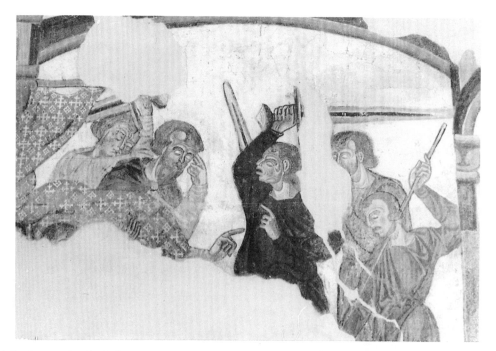

14. Rodenegg Castle, Bolzano,
mural showing Iwein at the
magical fountain

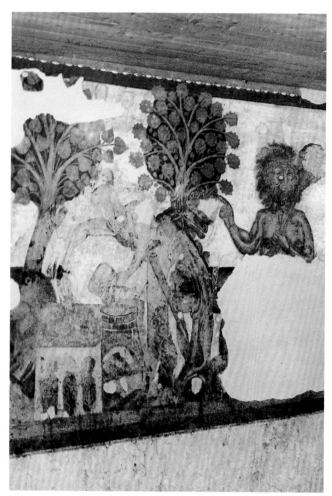

13. Rodenegg Castle mural
showing the search for Iwein

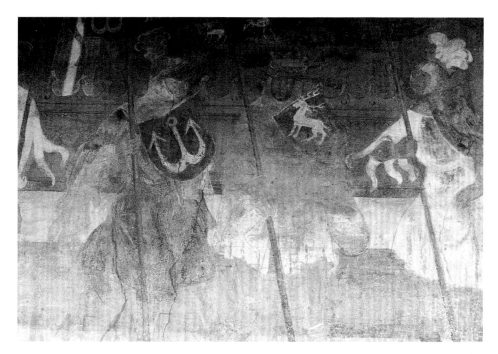

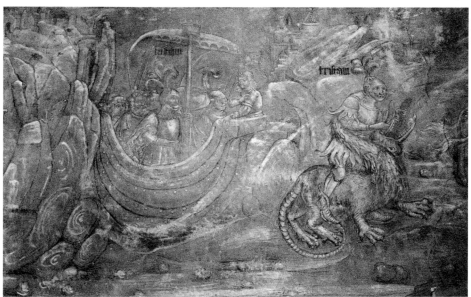

15. Perceval, Gawain and Iwain painted on the balcony of Schloss Runkelstein, Bolzano

16. Tristan arrives in Ireland and despatches the dragon. Runkelstein mural

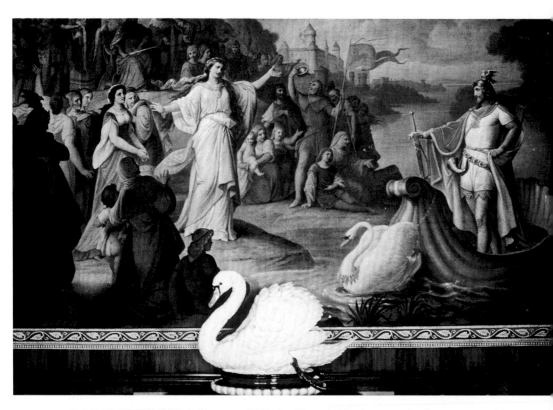

17. Lohengrin's arrival at Antwerp. Wilhelm Hauschild's fresco in the living room of Neuschwanstein Castle, Bavaria

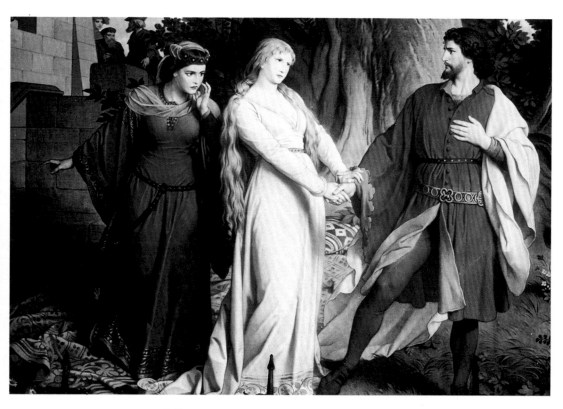

18. Tristan's farewell to Isolde and Brangwain.
Fresco in King Ludwig's bedroom, Neuschwanstein

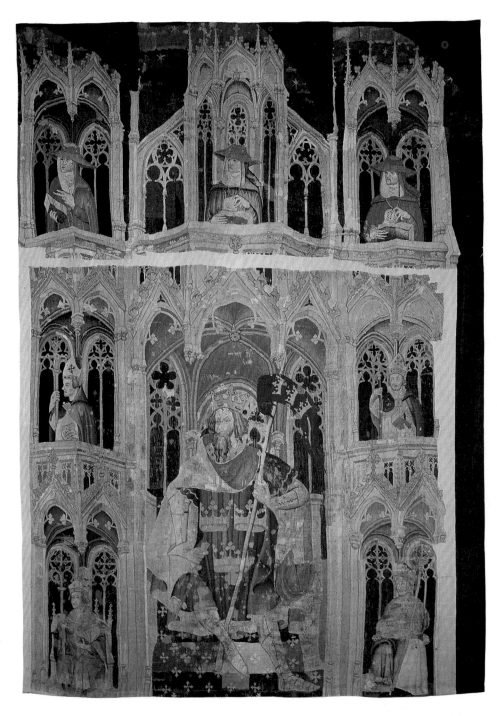

19. King Arthur. Nine Worthies Tapestry, The Cloisters, Metropolitan Museum of Art

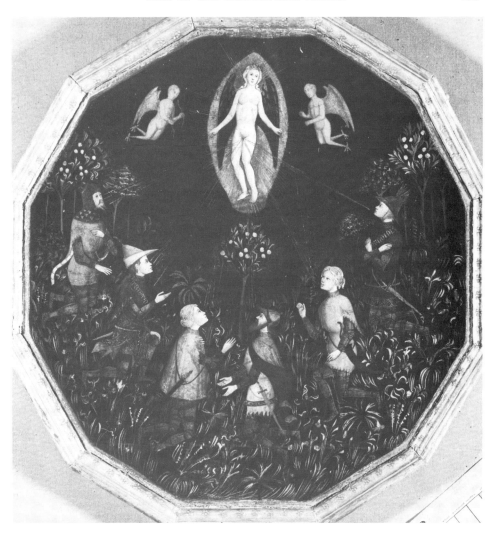

24. Italian maternity tray, 'The Triumph of Venus', ca. 1400

dog, the amiable expressions of the horses and lions charmingly evoke a remote world of love and adventure.

Still, it is ironical that scenes celebrating adulterous love should so frequently appear on gifts for women. How are we supposed to interpret the Italian 'maternity' trays depicting the sensual Garden of Love, which by the fifteenth century had replaced the Castle of Love as a favourite allegorical setting?[58] A twelve-sided tray (ca. 1400) in the Louvre that once belonged to Arconti Visconti combines the courtly motif with classical and Christian iconography. Six fashionably dressed

[58] Van Marle, II, 426 ff.

knights kneel in a paradisal garden,[59] luxuriant with grasses, flowers and fruit trees, their semi-circular arrangement following the tray's shape. Their upraised eyes are focused on a single object. At first glance the mandorla (a conventional frame for sacred personages), the enclosed woman with long, flowing hair, crown and aureole, and the supporters with Fra Angelico wings seem Marian images. But this impression is quickly negated by the nude body whose outspread arms, parted thighs and bent knees imply shameless accessibility. This is Venus,[60] the pagan goddess of love and beauty, supported by cupids with the faces, wings and bird-feet of harpies. The goddess, too, has great angel-like wings.

The worshippers, whose position and gestures parody those of devout Christians and suppliant courtly lovers,[61] are dazzled by rays emanating not from the lady's eyes but from her pudendum.[62] Another relevant analogy, suggested by the mandorla, the stance of the nude body and the rays of light is astrological woman. The Limbourgs illustrate her in the *Très Riche Heures* of the Duke of Berry, Chantilly, Musée Condé MS 65, f.14^v, with a scorpion, sign of *luxuria*, covering her private parts. Those born under the influence of the planetary Venus were predisposed to lechery. The identification of the worshippers provides the final clue to the allegory; they are Achilles, Tristan, Lancelot, Samson, Paris, and Troilus – great warriors whom their lust for women brought low. The words of Chaucer's monk concerning Samson are relevant to all:

> But soone shal he wepe many a teere,
> For wommen shal hym bryngen to meschaunce.[63]

---

[59] On the paradisal garden and the enclosed garden see Derek Pearsall and Elizabeth Salter, *Landscapes and Seasons of the Medieval World* (London, 1973), pp. 56–118.

[60] On the classical, medieval and early Renaissance nude Venus see Kenneth Clark, *The Nude, a Study of Ideal Art* (London, 1956), chapter III. He describes the marriage tray Venus as 'simply a lady of easy manners who has taken off her clothes', rather than a representation of ideal beauty (p. 90). Jean Seznec, *The Survival of the Pagan Gods: The Mythological Tradition and its Place in Renaissance Humanism and Art* (New York, 1953) discusses the goddess' appearance in fifteenth century churches, her metamorphosis into a planet, and the restoration of her classical form in Renaissance art.

[61] In courtly literature the lover commonly prayed to Venus to assist him in gaining the lady whom he desired; cf. Boccaccio's *Il Filistrato*, iii, 74–79 and Chaucer's *Troilus and Criseyde*, III, 1–49. Both passages are rapturous invocations to Venus as planet, goddess of sexual love, and embodiment of the cosmic love which binds the universe. These poets were influenced by Dante's ideas about courtly love. See Colin Hardie, 'Dante and the Tradition of Courtly Love', in *Patterns of Love and Courtesy*, ed. John Lawlor (London, 1966), pp. 26–44 and C.S. Lewis, *The Allegory of Love: A Study in Medieval Tradition* (Oxford, 1936), *passim*.

[62] The artist degrades by parody the courtly love convention that the sight of a lady inspires amorous desire. Cf. Chaucer's description of Troilus' reaction when he sees Criseyde in the temple for the first time:

> And of hire look in him ther gan to quyken
> So gret desir and such affeccioun,
> That in his hertes botme gan to stiken
> Of hir his fixe and depe impressioun.   (I, 295–298)

[63] Geoffrey Chaucer, 'The Monk's Tale' in *The Canterbury Tales*, ll. 2061–2.

The most splendid extant example of a medieval objet d'art given literary significance through its identifiable courtly figures is the Burghley Nef, an elaborate gilded salt cellar formed in the shape of a ship.[64] It was made in Paris in 1482–3, for it bears the mark of Pierre le Flamand and the year-letter for that date. The Victoria and Albert Museum, London, acquired it in 1959. The nef was primarily a status symbol for it marked the host's place at the dinner table.[65] The details of a real ship are artfully reproduced – three masts with the main and foremast carrying main and topsails, the mizzen a lateen sail and the bowsprit a square sail together with rigging and sailors to provide the manpower. There are also soldiers with shields and spears. Battlemented arcading encloses the focsle and the poop (which holds the salt). There are a traditional dragon figure-head and up-to-date cannons, one of which is aimed directly at the mainmast. The whole construction is set in a nautilus shell, a symbol of the sea.

This is not just any fifteenth-century ship. The small images of a courtly man and lady clasping hands as they play chess at the foot of the main mast identify it as the one bringing Tristan and Isolde across the Irish sea to Cornwall. Thomas' *Roman de Tristan*, edited by Bédier, contains the specific reference:

> Au quart jour se jouoit Tristan aux eschès a
> Yseuelt, et faisoit si grant chault que trop.
> Tristan oult soif, si demanda du vin . . .   (II, p. 341)

The lovers wear not fifteenth century dress but the mid-fourteenth century costume familiar from the ivory caskets. Perhaps they were cast from the same moulds which Louis of Anjou's craftsmen had used to make the Tristan objects that he favoured.

Inventories and other documents provide glimpses of lost Arthurian objects – Queen Philippa's gift to Edward III at New Year, 1333, of a ewer with enamelled figures of Caesar, Juda Machabeius, Charlemagne, Arthur, Roland, Oliver, Gawain and Lancelot; statues of Tristan and Isolde 'de auro et rubeis et emeraldis et perlis orientalibus electis et iij grossis emeraldis' which the Earl of Derby offered in 1340 to secure a loan;[66] Louis of Anjou's Tristan goblets that had to be sacrificed to pay his debts; Jean le Bon's Tryst table fountain, to be filled with wine, rosewater or perfume. The description in Chrétien's *Cligès* of a valuable cup created to celebrate a military victory reveals that the craftsmanship of such works was valued even more than their materials yet the intrinsic value of the gold, silver and jewels meant they were broken and melted down to provide ready cash.

[64] Charles Oman, *Medieval Silver Nefs* (London, 1963).
[65] It is depicted in some later manuscripts such as BL Add. 47680, f. 60^v and BN fr. 2813, f. 473^v. The latter illustrates Charles V's party in 1378 for the Emperor Charles IV, an occasion so grand that three nefs were required for the three kings at the table. See the reproduction in Madeleine Pelner Cosman, *Fabulous Feasts: Medieval Cookery and Ceremony* (New York, 1976), p. 36.
[66] Juliet Vale, *Edward III and Chivalry: Chivalric Society and Its Context 1270–1350* (Woodbridge, 1982), p. 45.

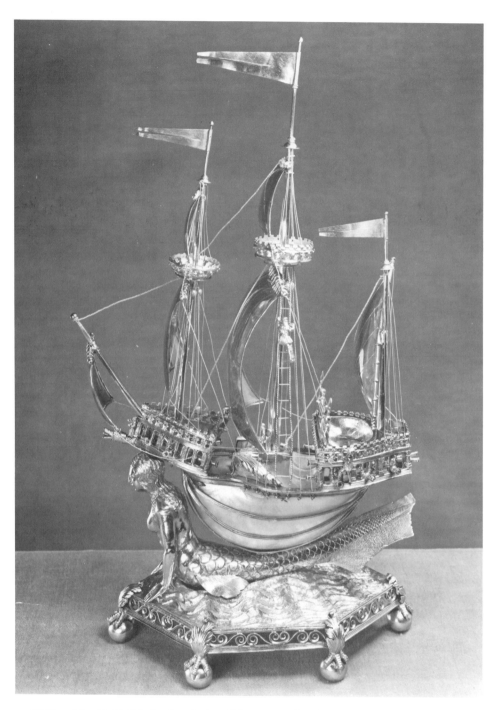

25. Burghley Nef (gilded salt cellar) with Tristan and Isolde, 1482–83

We share Rita Lejeune's curiosity about the golden cup which Jean Renart described in *L'Escoufle* (1200–1202).[67] The Norman crusader, Richard de Montivilliers, presented it to the Church of the Holy Sepulchre in Jerusalem for use at the high altar. What makes this cup an equivocal gift is its decoration. Inside, it is engraved with representations of the swallow bringing Mark Isolde's golden hair, Tristan's ship, and the battle against Morholt. Around the rim on the outside in champlevé enamelling is the forest hunt with Tristan, Governal, Isolde and the dog Houdain procuring food for their exile. On the cover Mark finds the nude lovers sleeping in the grotto, separated by the sword. The stem is the figure of a dwarf. Did the poet actually see such a cup, decorated with a type of enamelling that predominated in the thirteenth century?

In addition to imaginative works of art conjuring up an ideal romantic world, medieval Europe contained Arthurian artifacts that were claimed as the real thing. No doubt, the enthusiasm for relics which followed the Crusaders' plunder of Constantinople in 1204 explains the transfer to secular objects of a supernatural mystique. If a vial of Christ's blood could be displayed at Fécamp, the Virgin's milk at Walsingham, the crown of thorns at St Albans and Joseph and Mary's Nazarene house at Loretto, why could not traces of the equally historical Arthurian society still exist?[68] Richard I, stopping in Sicily on his way to the Crusades, outdid Tancred's generous gift of gold and jewels by bestowing Arthur's best sword 'quem Britones vocaverunt Caliburnum'. Arthur's crown along with a piece of the True Cross was part of the tribute that the Welsh prince Lewellyn surrendered to Edward I after the defeat in 1283. The significance of this act did not escape the monastic chronicler, who wrote, 'sic Wallensium gloria ad Anglos, licet invite, est translata'. Edward's son Alfonso offered it at St Edward Confessor's shrine in Westminster as if it were a sacred relic.

No object possesses a more powerful aura than the chalice in the Cathedral of Valencia. Alfonso V, King of Aragon, acquired it in 1399 from the monastery of San Juan de la Pêna. St Lawrence was said to have brought it to Spain. Even today it is identified as the Holy Grail.[69] It consists of two sardonyx bowls joined by a golden stem. Pearls decorate the golden base while two large emeralds and two rubies stud the mounts. When the chalice was made, probably in the fourteenth century, its materials would have been chosen for their symbolic qualities. According to the lapidaries, sardonyx keeps a man chaste and humble and gracious. In the *Apocalypse* gloss, it signifies those who suffer for the love of God, despising

[67] 'La Coupe de la légende de Tristan dans *L'Escoufle* de Jean Renart' in *The Medieval Alexander Legend and Romance Epic: Essays in Honour of David J.A. Ross*, eds. P. Noble, L. Polak and C. Isoz (Millwood, N.Y., and London, 1982), pp. 119–124.

[68] On Arthurian relics see Christopher Dean, *Arthur of England: English Attitudes to King Arthur and the Knights of the Round Table in the Middle Ages and the Renaissance* (Toronto, 1987), chapter 3, 'Arthur and the Common Folk'; E.M.R. Ditmas, 'The Cult of Arthurian Relics', *Folklore*, LXXXV/I (1964), 19–33 and 'More Arthurian Relics', *Folklore*, LXXXVII/ 2 (1966), 91–104; and Juliet Vale, *op. cit.* pp. 17–18.

[69] Frederic V. Grunfeld, 'The Last Holy Grail', *Connoisseur*, 211 (July, 1982), 98–99. On another 'Holy Grail', the Chalice of Rémi, see Sister M. Amelia Klenke, 'Chrétien's Symbolism and Cathedral Art', *PMLA*, 70 (1955), 223–43.

their flesh. The emerald is a protection against lechery, a sign of purity (as is the pearl) and an assurance of eternal bliss. The ruby is of such 'lordeshippe t. when he þat hym cometh amonge men, all thei shul bere hym honeur & grace & all shul bere hym joye of his presence'.[70] Gold symbolises the divine kingdom. The appositeness of these gems and gold to the characters and motivations of the successful Grail knights, especially Galahad, is obvious.

The Valencia chalice exemplifies the ploy of increasing an object's value by drawing to it a well-known narrative tradition. Identifying it as the Holy Grail transmutes it from a fine but unexceptional vessel into a unique object of supreme significance. The 'value' of this Holy Grail and the other artifacts considered here depends on the viewer's response to signs. Jacques Maritain in *Art et Scolastique* explains how the fine arts go beyond shapes, colours, sounds, and words, taken in themselves as things, to become signs which make known ideas. And the more the artifact is charged with significance, 'plus vast et plus riche et plus haute sera la possibilité de joie et de beauté'.[71]

[70] Joan Evans and Mary S. Serjeantson, eds., *English Medieval Lapidaries*, EETS OS 190 (London, 1933), p. 21.
[71] *Art et Scolastique*, 2nd ed., (Paris, 1927), pp. 92–3.

CHAPTER FIVE

Painted Chambers

The grey stone walls of the medieval castles we see today give little indication that once, like the palace in John Lydgate's *Troy Book*, they were 'painted full prudly with pure gold over' with 'bordis full bright about in þat sale/ Set in cercle of Sedur tre fyn' to decorate the grey marble. Secular murals were inevitably less durable and less practical than the pictorial tapestries and embroidered hangings which from the fourteenth century more commonly adorned the walls of those who could afford them. That any paintings have survived is usually due to a double chance; first, that some centuries ago new construction covered up the old decorations and second, that they were subsequently uncovered in a period that could appreciate their rarity. As recently as 1979, the Neidhart frescoes, the oldest secular mural paintings in Vienna (ca. 1400), were rediscovered because the tenant of the first floor apartment at Tuchlauben 19 decided to make renovations.[1]

Even when their original decorations were not covered with plaster or panelling, few halls continued to serve the original purpose of a 'Festsaal'. The Schmalkalden dining-room deteriorated into a coal cellar as the level of the town rose above the medieval streets. The great hall at the French Castle of St Floret was used as a threshing floor, its flaking frescoes scraped with the tines of hay forks. Manfredi III's great hall in Palermo served as the Inquisition's court room.

When the painting of castle walls became popular in the thirteenth century, Henry III of England (1207–1272) patronised a school of artists at Westminster. Many royal rooms, including the Great Chamber of Westminster Palace, were embellished with pictorial programmes in 'the Court Style', with romance subjects being favoured in the ruler's private apartments.[2] There were Alexander rooms at Clarendon and Nottingham. 'Arthur's Hall' and 'Guinevere's Chamber' in Dover Castle probably took their names from their decorations. Painting was not confined to the walls. The accounts of Mahaut, Comtesse d'Artois, describe

---

[1] Eva-Maria Höhle, Renata Kassal-Mikula, Oskar Pausch, Richard Perger, *The Neidhart Frescoes ca. 1400: the Oldest Secular Paintings in Vienna*, trans. Beatrice Ottersböck (Vienna, n.d.).

[2] The palace was destroyed by fire in 1834 but drawings made earlier in the century survive. On Henry III's painted chambers see Peter Brieger, *English Art 1216–1307* (Oxford, 1957). On English wall painting generally see E.W. Tristram, *English Wall Painting of the Fourteenth Century* (London, 1955).

blue or green ceilings stuck with gold or silver stars, as well as painted ribs and rafters.[3] Literature substantiates the historical records. When the hero of the Middle English romance *Sir Degrevant* was invited to a lady's bedroom, he saw

> Ther was a ryal rooffe
> In the chaumbur of loffe;
> Hyt was buskyd above
>   With besauntus ful bryght.[4]   (ll. 433–6)

And the walls portrayed the three Christian Worthies – Charlemagne, Godfrey of Bologne and Arthur of Britain, 'with here bryght brondus'.

There is ample evidence that the chief source for mural programmes was illuminated manuscripts. For example, when the Parisian artist Jean Coste was summoned by the Duke of Normandy in 1349, the patron lent him an illuminated *Life of Caesar* to provide the main subjects. The Duke's commission was recorded in a letter to his treasurer:

> Envoiez nous tantost a Lery le meilleur paintre de Paris et III ou IIII paintres avecques li, garniz de coleurs pour ouvrer à destrampe, quar nous voulons fair paindre hastivement chambre en nostre chastel du Val de Ruel.[5]

Battle pictures were particularly popular because they could be given a personal relevance. In 1320 when the Countess Mahaut commissioned Pierre de Bruxelles to paint a gallery in her castle at Conflans, she indicated that the decoration should be both narrative and commemorative:

> Et sera l'image du conte d'Artois en tous lieuz là ou il sera, armoiez des armes dudit conte; et les autres ymages des chevaliers nuez de plusieurs couleurs, et leurs escuz, enlieu ou il apperront, seront armoiez de leurs armes.[6]

A commentary inscribed on the wall beneath the images explained the story.

While wall paintings frequently depicted scenes from illuminated manuscripts, the reverse process sometimes occurred. The most famous 'artist' in Arthurian romance is Lancelot.[7] During the two winters and one summer when he was Morgan le Fay's prisoner, he decorated the walls of his chamber with the history of his life and love.[8] It gave him great pleasure to see 'les biaus contenemens de sa

[3]   Joan Evans, *Art in Mediaeval France 987–1498* (Oxford, 1948), pp. 180–1.
[4]   *Sir Degrevant*, ed. L.F. Casson, EETS OS 221 (London, 1944).
[5]   Evans, p. 180.
[6]   J.M. Richard, *Mahaut, comtesse d' Artois et de Bourgogne, 1302–1329* (1887), cited by Evans, p. 181.
[7]   *The Vulgate Version of the Arthurian Romances*, ed. H. Oskar Sommer, vol. 5, pp. 217 ff.
[8]   René, King of Sicily and Duke of Anjou (1409–1480), having been captured by Philip of

dame'. King Arthur's subsequent inspection of the compromising sequence is depicted in several manuscripts; for example, Paris, BN fr. 112, vol. III, 193^v (1470) where the two-tiered arrangement of Lancelot's mural has affinities with the St Floret frescoes and Pisanello's Mantuan designs.

Peter Brieger believes that London, BL MS Cotton Claudius B vii, f. 224 also shows a mural. Vortigern enthroned is painted on a blind arcade while the young Merlin occupies the adjacent space. Striped columns with acanthus leaf capitals indicate the architectural structure. Above the arcading are building stones and the trefoils often found in the Early English style.[9]

The fourteenth century Italian poet Dino Compagni seems to be describing an actual fresco when he writes:

> Dall' altra parte del ricco palazzo
> intagliat'è la Tavola Ritonda,
> le giostre e 'l torneare e 'l gran sollazzo;
> ed èu' Artù e Gineura gioconda,
> per cui 'l pro' Lancialotto venne pazzo,
> March'e Tristano ed Isolta la blonda;
> e sonui i pini esonui le fontane,
> le giostre, le schermaglie e le fiumane,
> foreste e lande e 'l redi Trebisonda.

> (On the other side of the sumptuous palace,/ the Round Table is portrayed,/ jousting and tournaments and great diversions;/ and there are Arthur and gay Guinevere/ with whom brave Lancelot was madly in love,/ Mark and Tristram and the blonde Iseult;/ and there are pine trees and fountains,/ jousting, skirmishes and streams,/ forests and moors and the king of Trebizond.)[10]

In the later Middle Ages, art, life, and literature were so intertwined that it was difficult to distinguish literal reality from the reality of the imagination.

To paint a wall, an activity that Cennini calls the most agreeable and impressive kind of work,[11] it was necessary to cover the surface little by little with fresh mortar mixed with *lait de chaux* which the watercolours would impregnate before the plaster dried. The Comtesse d'Artois' painter, Pierre de Bruxelles, recorded the colours that he used in the chauteaux – azure, the brown of Auxerre, white, yellow ochre, minium (red lead) which Cennini says is made by alchemy, brazil (a red made from wood), vermilion, sinopie (still another red), green, dark blue,

Burgundy, reputedly painted the walls of his Dijon prison. As he was an Arthurian enthusiast, he may have been inspired by Lancelot's example.

[9] Brieger, p. 133.

[10] Quoted by Giovanni Paccagnini, *Pisanello*, trans. Jane Carroll (London, 1973), p. 52.

[11] Cennino d' Andrea Cennini, *Il Libro dell' Arte*, trans. Daniele V. Thompson, Jr., p. 42. Part III deals with fresco painting.

another green – 'voisin du vert', yellow, gold, and silver. He also used two kinds of varnish, a finish which Cennini censures because it 'wants to be obeyed in everything', diminishing the freshness of the colours. In the thirteenth century the development of oil-based paints facilitated a dry wall technique.

The oldest extant series of Arthurian murals is the Iwein cycle executed at Rodeneck (Rodenegg) Castle near Bolzano in the Italian Tyrol.[12] A steep precipice surrounded on three sides by the River Rienz provided an almost impregnable site for the small castle which Friedrich von Rodank built there about 1140. He was a retainer and relative of the local potentate, the prince-bishop of Brixner. In 1491 the Emperor Maximilian presented the property to one of his knights, Veit von Wolkenstein, whose descendants have held it ever since. The frescoes in the old chapel were painted about 1200 or a little after. The construction of a vault later in the century concealed them. They did not see the light of day again until 1972.

Certain stylistic resemblances to frescoes in the Frauenkirche at Brixner led N. Rasmo, the frescoes' restorer, to conclude that the same artist decorated both buildings. He may have been 'Hugo Pictor', court painter to Bishop Konrad von Rodanc who died in 1216.

The literary source was most likely Hartmann von Aue's *Iwein* (completed before 1205) which the artist must have adapted directly since it is unlikely that an illuminated manuscript would have been produced so early.[13] Rather than presenting highlights from the whole romance, the designer achieves unity by limiting the programme temporally and spatially. By excluding the Kalogrenant prologue and the hero's adventurous career after his marriage, the romance is reduced to a single cause-and-effect sequence. The scenes, in damaged condition, are arranged continuously around the room, interrupted only by a doorway and window where trompe d'oeil columns and arcades give an effect of continuity. As in German manuscripts like the Munich *Parzival*, the characters are labelled, with the Latin forms of the ladies' names being used – Luneta and Laudina.

The programme exhibits a familiar romance pattern exemplified by such

---

[12] Studies of the Rodeneck murals include Norbert H. Ott, 'Geglückte Minne-Aventiure. Zur Szenenauswahl literarischer Bildzeugnisse im Mittelalter. Die Beispiele des Rodenecker *Iwein*, des Runkelsteiner *Tristan*, des Braunschweiger Gawan und des Frankfurter *Wilhelm-von-Orlens*-Teppichs', *Jahrbuch der Oswald von Wolkenstein Gesellschaft* 2 (1982/83), 1–32; Norbert H. Ott und Wolfgang Walliczek, 'Bildprogramm und Textstruktur. Anmerkungen zu den *Iwein*-Zyklen auf Rodeneck und in Schmalkalden', *Deutsche Literatur im Mittelalter*, ed. Christoph Cormeau (Stuttgart, 1979), pp. 473–500; N. Rasmo, 'Der Iwein-Zyklus auf Schloss Rodeneck', *Burgen und Schlösser in Osterreich Zeitschrift des österreichischen Burgenvereines* 13 (1977/78), p. 26 ff.; Volker Schupp, 'Die Ywain-Erzählung von Schloss Rodenegg', in *Literatur und bildende Kunst im Tiroler Mittelalter. Die Iwein-Fresken von Rodenegg und andere Zeugnisse der Wechselwirkung von Literatur und bildender Kunst.* (Innsbruck, 1982), pp. 1–29; and 'Kritische Anmerkungen zur Rezeption des deutschen Artusromans anhand von Hartmanns *Iwein*: Theorie – Text – Bildmaterial', *Frühmittelalterliche Studien* 9 (1975), 405–42. Hans Szklenar, 'Iwein-Fresken auf Schloss Rodeneck in Südtirol', *Bibliographical Bulletin of the International Arthurian Society*, XXVII (1975), 172–180.
[13] None of the thirty-two extant *Iwein* manuscripts is illustrated.

heroes as Alexander the Orphan, Gareth, Wigalois, and Libeaus Desconus. The knight-errant rides out to seek adventure, is directed to a significant place, confronts and overcomes a powerful opponent and is rewarded by acquiring a beautiful lady and her property. The picture-story consists of eleven scenes. Iwein rides into the perilous forest where he encounters the Giant Herdsman with his hart, hound and lion. With elongated forefinger, the giant points towards the spring beneath two linden trees. Having tied his horse to a tree, Iwein uses his helmet to dip up water which is poured on the stone. Mounted again, he engages in a lance fight and then a sword fight with the spring's defender, Askalon, who is fatally struck on the head. When Iwein pursues the enemy into the castle, the falling portcullis strikes his horse and breaks his sword sheath. He is rescued by Luneta who gives him a ring of invisibility. With expressions of anguish, Laudina and her retainers attend the burial of her husband. Then the retainers search throughout the castle for his murderer, even striking the curtain in which the hero hides. Luneta takes Iwein to Laudina; the hero makes imploring gestures which soften the lady's heart. It is likely that the cycle concluded with a wedding feast.

Many of the images are familiar pattern-book types – the fight first with spears, then with swords; the horse tied to a tree; the use of pillars, towers and arches to indicate interior scenes. The flat-topped helms, long surcoats and long shields are not unlike those depicted on the Chertsey tiles. Iwein's silver shield bears a lion rampant, his traditional blazon. The Herdsman has the usual giant traits – naked torso, over-large ears, staring eyes, a gnarled club; however, the aureole of red hair increases his dramatic power. The castle retainers who intend to kill the hero have the gaping mouths, hooded eyes and grotesquely modelled faces of the torturers in Crucifixion scenes while Iwein with his luxuriant beard, high forehead and cloak seems a Byzantine saint. Mourning for her dead husband, Laudina resembles a Mater Dolorosa. What all these details suggest is that the painter was using the ecclesiastical iconography which would have been familiar to him if he were the bishop's artist.

The pattern of crosses and squares on the curtain, a pattern repeated on the gown of Perseverentias in the Taufkirche of Brixner, is Byzantine in style, as is Laudina's headdress. The figures are firmly structured, the facial features clearly defined by emphatic lines. The colours – burnt orange, gold, steel blue and dark green – are those of eastern frescoes and manuscripts. It is possible that we see here the influence of twelfth century Venice which David Talbot Rice characterises as 'a Byzantine province so far as the character of the art was concerned'.[14] Despite the familiarity of individual motifs, the artist in adapting ecclesiastical art to a secular subject has produced a total effect of liveliness, originality, and technical competence.

Less than fifty years after the Rodeneck murals presented Iwein's adventures at

---

[14] David Talbot Rice, *Byzantine Art* (Harmondsworth, 1968), p. 534. See also Otto Demus, 'A Renaissance of Early Christian Art in Thirteenth Century Venice', in *Late Classical and Mediaeval Studies in Honor of Albert Mathias Friend, Jr.'*, ed. Kurt Weitznann et al. (Princeton, 1955) and *The Art of Byzantium and the Medieval West: Selected Studies*, ed. W. Eugene Kleinbauer (Bloomington and London, 1976).

the magical spring, this subject appeared in the Thuringian town of Schmal-kalden, now in the German Democratic Republic.[15] In a former manor house called Hessenhoft because the Landgrave of Hesse used it as his steward's residence, the vaulted ceiling and an adjacent wall were painted in seven bands about 31 in wide by 14 ft long (90 x 420 cm). They were rediscovered around 1862 in a former dining-room, as the hospitable welcomer with a raised cup indicates.

A restricted colour scheme – brown, yellow, red and white – was used for the images which were first outlined in brown or black. The influence of manuscript illumination is apparent in the heart-leaved trees, dark brown horses dappled with red and white, gestures executed with forefingers and large, open palms, the frontal, linear positioning and the unrealistic proportions which make humans as tall as towers and trees. The women's costumes, consisting of long-sleeved cotes, mantles and pillbox hats, the knights' arms and armour, and the single Roman-esque towers enclosing the figures to represent interior scenes are somewhat reminiscent of the Munich *Parzival*. Iwain, spelt IWAN on the ceiling, anachronisti-cally carries his rampant lion blazon while Ascalon has a dark red shield with a light-coloured eagle. This device the hero assumes when he becomes the spring's guardian.

In contrast to Rodeneck, this programme has an expanded time scheme which begins at Arthur's court where the rulers are depicted in bed. The final surviving image of Iwein helping a lion to fight a dragon indicates that the decoration must also have illustrated the romance's second part. There Iwein attains a new identity as Knight of the Lion and a new role as defender of the oppressed. On the upper part of the west wall are painted an interior scene (Arthur's bedroom), Iwein's departure, and the meeting with the Giant Herdsman. Above on the ceiling the hero, whose horse is tied to the tree, takes a chained golden bowl to pour water on the raised slab. The fights with spears and swords follow and the successful hero receives the ring of invisibility from Lunete, who leans from a castle tower. In the next band Ascalon's corpse lies on a bed, while a mourning Laudine clasps her hands in anguish; her knights look for Iwein, Lunete speaks encouragingly to the widow and then introduces the hero. The band in the middle of the vault depicts his triumph as Laudine presents him to her courtiers, marries him and takes him into her bed. Under an acanthus leaf border on the north wall a traditional feast confirms the joyful culmination of part one. On the fifth ceiling band, the pictures, running in the opposite direction from those of row four, show how King Arthur produces a hailstorm and Iwein, now the spring's defender, unhorses Kay. The last row, badly deteriorated, shows the hero's farewell as he rides into the forest, where he uses his sword to save the lion.

The artist apparently adopts Hartmann's interpretation of Chrétien's ro-mance.[16] In part one, the individual's self-realizing dream is fulfilled when,

---

[15] Loomis, pp. 77–99 and figs. 159–66; Heinrich Nickel, *Mittelalterliche Wandmalerei* (Leip-zig, 1979), pp. 280–83; Norbert H. Ott and Wolfgang Walliczek, *op. cit.*

[16] On Hartmann von Aue's adaptation of Chrétien's romance, see, for example, Michael S. Batts, 'Hartmann's *humanitas*: A New Look at *Iwein*', *Germanic Studies in Honor of Edward Henry Sehrt* (Coral Gables, Fla., 1968), pp. 37–51; Wolfgang Dittman, "Dune hâst niht wâr,

through prowess and luck, he achieves the beautiful lady and her land.[17] In part two, the knight's social obligations are acknowledged as Iwein uses his prowess to benefit others. Both themes might well have appealed to a landowner's steward just as the chivalric fairy tale in the Tyrolean castle pleased a bishop's retainer. Technically, the Schmalkalden frescoes are much inferior to Rodeneck's.

Two other examples of Arthurian wall paintings in houses rather than castles have been found in Constance, Switzerland,[18] and Lübeck, West Germany.[19] Münsterplatz, no. 5, is known as 'the Distaff House' for its paintings (ca. 1300) on a proletarian theme – the tasks of women engaged in linen production. On the opposite wall, twelve roundels arranged in three rows depict a subject which we encountered on the Louvre marriage tray – male victims of female charms. The literary source was an anti-feminist poem by Meistersinger Heinrich von Meissen. While the inclusion of Arthur in this group is understandable, Perceval's is not, since his love for Blanchefleur did not prevent his success in the Grail quest.

The demolition of a building in Lübeck in 1927 unveiled a series of Perceval murals dated about 1330. Unfortunately, there was insufficient interest to save what remained. William Boht's watercolour copies in the St Annen Museum are the only extant record. As at Schmalkalden the originals decorated a dining hall on the ground floor. Some scenes were derived from Wolfram's *Parzival*. In the best preserved section Parzival's mother talks to her barefooted son with his fool's hood; she watches him depart on a white horse, armed with a bow; he meets a lady seated in a red and white pavilion and reaches Arthur's court where the king sits at the banquet table. The roundels were largely defaced when a second-storey floor was built through them.

Considering the popularity of the Tristan legend, it should not surprise us if the preference shown in various decorative arts extended to frescoes. Chaucer's *Parliament of Fowls* provides a literary analogy. When the dreamer enters Venus' Temple he finds that the walls are 'peynted overal' with the images of famous lovers, including Tristram and Isaude 'and al here love, and in what plyt they dyde' (ll. 284–94). France's most important cycle of extant romance murals is found in the ruined castle of St Floret near Issoire in the Auvergne.[20] When it was constructed in the fourteenth century, its great hall was embellished with Gothic

---

Hartmani' Zum Begriff der *wârheit* in Hartmann's *Iwein'*, *Festgabe für Ulrich Pretzel* (Berlin 1963), pp. 150–61; Hans-Peter Kramer, *Erzählerbemerkungen und Erzählerkommentare in Chrétien's und Hartmann's 'Erec' und 'Iwein'* (Göppingen, 1971); Hugo Kuhn, 'Hartmann von Aue' als Dichter', *Der Deutschunterricht* 5/2 (1953), 11–27.

[17] Cf. Georges Duby, *The Knight, the Lady and the Priest: The Making of Modern Marriage in Medieval France*, trans. Barbara Bray (New York, 1983). The wife's social superiority was the rule in aristocratic marriages.

[18] Loomis, pp. 36–37, 74–75, figs. 10, 149.

[19] Werner Burmeister, 'Gotische Wandmalereien in einem Lübecker Bürgerhause', *Zeitschrift des Vereins für Lübeckische Geschichte und Altertumskunde*, 26 (1932), 113–128; Loomis, p. 75, figs. 150–54.

[20] Paul Deschamps and Marc Thibout, *La Peinture murale en France au debut de l'epoque gothique de Philippe-Auguste à la fin du règne de Charles V (1180–1380)* (Paris, 1963), pp. 222–226 and illustrations; Loomis, pp. 57–61, figs. 92–105.

paintings extending around the room at two levels and even filling window arches and jambs. On each level a three-line commentary based on Rusticiano da Pisa's *Meliadus* (ca. 1270) explained the scenes. They were rediscovered in 1864 by Anatole Dauvergne who identified them as Arthurian. In 1902 and 1909 an artist called Yperman made watercolour copies. Unfortunately, only fragments of thirteen scenes remain from an original forty. On the basis of costume they have been assigned to the reign of Charles V (1364–70), a period appropriate to the knights' pointed helmets, short surcoats and elongated sabatons. Isolde's découpé surcoat which reveals the sides as well as the long sleeves of her gown had gone out of fashion by 1380.

The paintings show the increased interest in armorials that characterised manuscript illumination after 1340. Sir Branor, the hero of the first three scenes, carries a shield parti-argent and sable, a scheme carried out on the caparisons and the pinwheel crests on his helmet and his horse's head. Branor's opponents are differentiated by varied shields – a flaming sun on a green field, an escutcheon on sable, a star and crescent on green, a field parti-white and red crosshatched with green, and *gules a bend engrailed argent*. Tristan's device when he rides adventuring through Logres is *argent a bend gules*, rather than the more usual *lion rampant or on a field gules*. Palamedes carries *argent a chief gules*, and Galahad the usual *argent a cross gules*, ostentatiously displayed on both shield and surcoat. The heroes enact their characteristic roles of rescuing damsels and captured knights against a graceful background of umbrella-like trees with slender trunks, delicately drawn shrubs and flowery sprays.

The treatment of the Tryst beneath the Tree motif shows the artist's skill in adapting his design to the architectural structure. On the window's left jamb is Tristan whose long, wavy hair flipped up at the ends, small full-lipped mouth and brooding eyes give him an effeminate appearance. Facing him on the right jamb is the beautiful blond Isolde in a lowcut gown of green, the colour particularly associated with her, to denote her beauty, youth, and passionate love.[21] She sits in a *hortus conclusus*, as the castellated wall suggests. Her enormously elongated forefingers point upwards to King Mark whose head, surrounded by pine branches, is painted above the window. Below the window there must have been a fountain with its reflecting pool. The inscription is interesting for it utilises the warning device which has been traced to Dirk Potter's 'Der minnon loep' (1411–12). The dialogue at St Floret goes as follows:

> 'tristan, que poysun uoyie? ie ne ui tel molt lonc tans a. dama, ie le bien coneu quar ie lay autrefois ueu.'

> ('Tristan, what fish do I see? I have not seen such for a very long time.'
> 'Lady, I recognized it well, for I have seen it before.')

---

[21] See Margaret Scott, *Late Gothic Europe, 1400–1500*, p. 122. See also for contemporary explication of colour symbolism the Sicily Herald's *Blasons des Couleurs* (Paris, 1503). The work dates from the mid-fifteenth century.

This quotation, predating Dirk Potter by half a century, suggests that the dialogue was already part of a *Tristan* text. As the Tryst does not appear in Rusticiano's version of the *Prose Tristan*, one can only surmise that the artist had a choice of manuscript sources.

Not much later than the St Floret decorations are the scenes painted between 1377 and 1380 in Palermo's Chiaramonte Palace.[22] The great hall of the palace, which King Frederigo III's Grand Admiral built to signify his wealth and power, contained a wooden ceiling. It offered space for an eclectic repertoire – saints, philosophers, characters from the *Troy Book* and the *Apocalypse*, revellers at the Fountain of Youth, Tristan and Isolde. The artists, no longer anonymous craftsmen, worked in their own names and home towns: 'Mastru Chicu pinturi di Naru, Mastru Simuni pinturi di Curiglu, Mastru . . . Darenu pigituri di Palermo'. As Loomis points out, even in their pristine state the paintings must have been difficult to appreciate:

> Unfortunately, the ceiling is over 26 feet from the floor, and many of the painted panels are set in a vertical, not horizontal, plane so that even with opera glasses and a gutta percha neck, it is difficult to study the scenes.

The colours, predominantly red, ochre, brown and black, are said to reflect Spanish influence, not surprisingly since Sicily at this time was ruled by Aragonese princes. A traditional range of episodes is based on the *Tristano Riccardiano*. The idyllic aspects of the love affair are emphasised as Tristan and Mark's wife enjoy a picnic set out on a fringed cloth, exchange bouquets and floral wreaths and play chess. With their pretty faces and neat accoutrements the humans and their horses look like the painted wooden toys that one can still find in Italian markets.

On the outskirts of Bolzano in the Italian Tyrol a porphyry rock rises precipitously along the Talfer River which surrounds it on three sides. Here in 1237, with the Bishop of Trent's permission, two minor aristocrats, Friedrich and Beral von Wangen, built Schloss Runkelstein.[23] In 1274, the castle having been besieged, captured and reduced to ruins, it reverted to the bishopric. More than a century passed before two local capitalists, Niklas and Franz Vintler, acquired it in 1388.

---

[22] Loomis, 61–63, figs. 106–116. Loomis' discussion is based on a study by Gabrici and Levi, *Lo Steri di Palermo* (Milan, n.d.).

[23] Doris Fouquet, *Wort und Bild in der Mittelalterlichen Tristantradition*, pp. 27–29; Walter Haug, Joachim Heinzle, Dietrich Huschenbett, Norbert H. Ott, *Runkelstein: Die Wandmalereien des Sommerhauses* (Wiesbaden, 1982); Egon Kübebacher, ed., *Deutsche Heldenepik in Tirol* (Bozen, 1979); Loomis, pp. 48–50, 79–84, and figs. 60–75, 171–201; Otto von Lutterotti, *Schloss Runkelstein und seine Wandgemälde* (Innsbruck, 1954); Viktor Malfér, *Die Triaden auf Schloss Runkelstein. Ihre Gestalten in Geschichte und Sage* (Bozen, 1967); Norbert H. Ott, 'Geglückte Minne-Aventiure', 8 ff.; Margaret R. Scherer, *About the Round Table* (New York, 1945), pp. 10–13, 40–42; Marisa Viaggi, 'La pittura profana della Venezia tridentina nel. sec. XIV et XV: Le pitture profane a castel Ronculo' in *Studi Trentini di Scienze Storiche*, 29 (1950), 326–57.

Later owners included the Emperor Maximilian, who restored and 'improved' the murals, and the Emperor Franz Joseph, who once more restored the castle before giving it to the city of Bolzano in 1893.

As one climbs the steep, rocky path overhung with hazels and branches loaded with blackberries, the river roaring below, the sun shining above, the butterflies hovering by vetches and morning glory and salamanders darting over the hot rocks, it is easy to imagine that a sense of security combined with pride and joie de vivre inspired Niklas Vintler to build his summerhouse. The tax-collecting, mortgage-holding, and bankrolling of improvident aristocrats that, no doubt, made him unpopular also made him wealthy enough to acquire the castle in 1388. He then rebuilt and expanded it with a moat, defensive walls, cisterns, halls with fireplaces, a library stocked with manuscripts and the other requirements of a late medieval castle where comfort and display were as important as defensibility. Such a newly rich patron demanded decorations that glorified the victories and joys rather than defeats and tragedies of a noble society.

Entering the courtyard through the gate on the south side, one sees on the right (east) the thirteenth century castle with its chapel. On the west rises a three-storey structure where several of the large rooms, including 'the tournament room' have extensive murals. Lords and ladies engage in such courtly pastimes as fishing, hunting, throwing a ball and joining in a round dance. Occupying the north side is the summerhouse. Once the walls and piers of its ground level loggia were covered with grisaille murals illustrating the adventures of Wigalois, the hero of Wirnt von Gravenberg's romance (ca. 1200). Weathering, collapsing walls, and what Loomis calls 'the signatures of countless fools' have virtually obliterated the decorations. Judging by the copies which Graf Waldstein published in 1892, they depicted run-of-the-mill chivalric encounters with importunate ladies and hostile knights. The crowned beast is there but little else of the text's magic. The hero is identified by his wheel crest. Names are inscribed above the characters.

The covered balcony of the second storey is in better condition. A sequence of triumvirates illustrates the medieval delight in classification and correspondences. The larger-than-life figures are the three greatest pagan heroes (Hector, Alexander, Julius Caesar); the three greatest Christian heroes (Arthur, Charlemagne, Godfrey of Bologne); the three best knights (Perceval, Gawain, Iwain); the three noblest lovers (William of Austria and Aglei, Tristan and Isolde, William of Orleans and Amelie); the three greatest swordsmen (Dietrich of Bern with his sword Sachs, Siegfried with Balmuny, Dietleib with Welsun); the three strongest giants (Asperan, King Ortnit, Struthan); and the three giant women (Riel Nagelringen, Vogelgart, the Rahin). At the end of the balcony are three royal dwarfs and a lady who offers a welcoming drink.

Through the middle doors, over which the Vintler, Austrian and Tyrolean coats-of-arms are displayed, we enter the ladies' painted chamber. The walls are covered with fifteen scenes from a *Tristan* sequence based on Gottfried von Strassburg's version. The subdued grey-green of the grisaille background is appropriate to the images of mountain and sea that dominate this Tristan landscape. Although they were surrounded by magnificent alpine scenery, the painters stuck to the broken terrace type which characterised landscape painting from Roman times to the fifteenth century.[24] The great piles of rock are strongly marked with vertical lines to suggest cliffs and precipices. They loom over rock-strewn beaches and stormy seas, looking as if at any moment they will crash upon the frail humans. Not only do the cliffs and oceans provide transitions from one scene to the next but they also symbolise the unregenerate world which constantly challenges heroes.

The artists' selectivity has ensured that the climactic moments of achievement are recorded, Tristram's fatal stroke on Marolt's[25] skull but not the fight with lances and swords; his surgery on the dragon's tongue but not the vicious battle. Copious splashes of red paint indicate the bloodiness of the fray. The scenes flow continuously around the room so that the rocky shore of the island where Tristram beats Marolt to his knees becomes the point of embarkation when the hero, in full armour, departs with a retinue for Ireland. Another stretch of crags and boulder-strewn beach separates that ship from an almost identical one which carries him in the next scene towards the dragon. Isolde discovers the unconscious hero on another rocky shore. His sword lying between them seems to presage the grotto episode, which is not depicted. Set within a triple-arched castle room, the bath scene shows the naked hero, with curly hair and a short beard that Maximilian's restorers probably added. Isolde, wearing a magnificently voluminous gown, a crown on her long, loose hair, confronts him while Bragene grips her right hand to deflect the sword. Next a third ship, complete with trumpeters, embarks from a precipitous harbour. As the Irish rulers watch from the castle balcony, Tristram in the bag-shaped hood popular in the 1380s passes the princess the fateful goblet.

The remaining scenes, badly scratched and faded,[26] show Isolde's wedding to Mark, her reconciliation with Bragene after the attempted murder, and the lovers' success in outwitting Mark and his dwarf. The programme concludes with a final ship scene as Isolde prepares to be carried by the squat pilgrim. Then barefoot, dressed only in a kirtle, she can swear the ambiguous oath while holding a red hot iron bar (coloured red). The officiating bishop wears a most dubious expression! This concluding episode of the pictorial text affirms that God Himself approves the faithful lovers.

The adjacent room in the summerhouse, overlooking terraced vineyards, has a brighter aspect because of a predominantly red and light blue colour scheme. The source of the major surviving decorations is a romance about Garel, another of Gawain's sons, whose adventures are recounted in *Garel von dem Blühenden Tal* (1260–80), *Garel of the Flowering Valley*, by an Austrian poet, Der Pleier. The plot

[24] Derek Pearsall and Elizabeth Salter, *Landscapes and Seasons of the Medieval World* (London, 1973), pp. 30–32.
[25] 'Tristram', 'Marolt' and 'Isalde' are the spellings in the inscriptions.
[26] The collapse of the north wall in 1868 caused additional damage to both the Tristan and Wigalois programmes so that it is necessary to rely on drawings which I. Seelos made. See I.V. Zingerle and I. Seelos, *Freskenzyklus des Schlosses Runkelstein* (Innsbrück, 1857) and Loomis' reproductions.

concerns Arthur's war against Ekunaver of Konadic, after a challenge from the
giant Karabin. Garel, according to the conventional pattern, has a series of successful confrontations which culminate in his rescue of a beautiful, wealthy lady
who becomes his bride. The most interesting fresco shows a group of men seated
about a round table that is set outside the castle. The feasters wear blue, white, or
red houppelandes decorated with epaulettes and dagged sleeves. Loomis suggests that the inspiration for this scene, which in the literary context celebrates
Garel's arrival at Arthur's court, was the contemporary enthusiasm for Arthurian
games known as 'Round Tables'.[27]

In the later Middle Ages an interest in literature and art concerned with love
and combat was an accepted sign of gentility – or at any rate, of social aspirations.[28] Chaucer's middle class Canterbury pilgrims, the Franklin and the Wife of
Bath, both entertain the company with romances centred on the theme of *genti-
lesse*. The Franklin proposes that this quality belongs not only to the aristocrats,
Arveragus and Dorigen, but also to the 'lusty squier' and the philosopher. Speaking through her character, the Loathly Lady, the Wife asserts, 'He is gentil that
dooth gentil dedis'. The Vintlers may have thought that pictorial narratives of
romance texts constituted 'gentil dedis', a testament to their quality. There must
also have been a temptation for the 'upwardly mobile' citizens to identify with
heroes whose involvements in love and combat always ended successfully in the
pictorial 'text'.

While the painted chambers so far discussed were commissioned by *nouveau
riche* entrepreneurs and minor aristocrats, one evocation of Arthurian romance,
the finest to have survived, was ordered by a rich, powerful and cultured duke. In
the twelfth century the Gonzagas were peasants. By 1433, following two hundred
years of land acquisition, a coup d'état in 1328 that unseated the Bonacolsi family,
and the payment to the Emperor Sigismond Hohenzollern of 1200 gold florins,
Gianfrancesco Gonzaga found himself Marquis of Mantua.[29] Gianfrancesco and
his son Ludovico seem to have combined attributes of medieval patrons with
those of Renaissance courtiers for their tastes were both chivalric and humanistic.
The Gonzaga library containing many Arthurian manuscripts has already been
described.[30] They rebuilt Mantua in the International Gothic style and evidently in
the fourteenth century showed an interest in Arthurian art for their palace contained a Saleta Lanzaloti. They waged war as condottieri against neighbouring
states, participated in chivalric games, and through enlightened patronage estab-

[27] See R.S. Loomis, 'Arthurian Influence on Sport and Spectacle', *Arthurian Literature in the
Middle Ages*, pp. 553–559.
[28] Cf. Jacques Coeur, the son of a Bourges fur-seller who became the most powerful man at
the court of Charles VII. Between 1443 and 1453 he built a fine mansion in Bourges; on the
vault of the treasure chamber was carved the 'Tryst beneath the Tree'.
[29] On the Gongaza family see Selwin Brinton, *The Gonzaga, Lords of Mantua* (London, 1927);
Rita Castagna, *Mantua, History and Art* (Florence, 1987).
[30] W. Bragirolli, 'Inventaire des manuscrits en langue française possédés par F. Gongaza',
Romania (1880), 497–515. See Chapter 3 above.

lished their court as a centre of art and culture. The scholar Vittorino da Feltre was persuaded to found a Mantuan school, La Giocosa, which Ludovico attended.

Mantua also claimed religious importance for according to legend a vial of Christ's blood was buried there. A sixteenth century chronicler, Stefano Gionta, has the story:

> In the reign of Tiberius, being the third year after Jesus Christ's death, that same Longinus came to the city of Mantua who had once pierced the Saviour's side . . . Lodging in an alms-house on that very spot where is now to be seen S. Andrea, and because the land was full of pagans, he buried in the orchard of the alms-house that vessel where was the Precious Blood, and went forth again to exhort the people to worship Jesus Christ.[31]

Given the medieval facility for making connections, the Grail castle (Corbenic), which contained the lance of Longinus and the chalice into which Christ's blood had fallen would find a counterpart in Mantua.

Gianfrancesco Gonzaga's most significant aesthetic achievement was his patronage of Antonio Pisano (Pisanello) who was born about 1395 and died between 1450 and 1455.[32] The two men may have met in 1415 when Gianfrancesco, in proper Arthurian fashion, jousted against the Marchesa di Farrara in Venice's Piazza San Marco. By 1422 Pisanello was a citizen of Mantua and from 1424, although he accepted commissions from other patrons, he was the Gonzagas' court painter. Sometime in the late 1440s he was instructed to decorate what came to be called the Sala del Pisanello in the Corte Vecchia of the Palazzo Ducale, using the expanded *Prose Tristan* as his literary source. Images were drawn on three walls of a room measuring 17.4 x 9.6 m. The commission was never finished. In 1480 the room's timber ceiling collapsed and as a result of the subsequent reconstruction, the Pisanello frescoes disappeared for almost five hundred years. In 1969 Giovanni Paccagnini brought them to light again after an amazing piece of research. His own words reveal the excitement of pursuit:

> On this side of the room, after part of the superimposed layers of eighteenth- and sixteenth-century *intonaco* was removed, an older, very dirty, decorated surface was discovered, which could be construed as part of a fifteenth-century frieze painted on the wall up to the level of the lost wooden ceiling. It was seen that this frieze continued along the wall when the superimposed *intonaco* was removed, bringing to light a dusty surface which, after cleaning, revealed the outline of a frescoed frieze of incomparable elegance. Ribbons, flowers and leaves fluttering

---

[31] Stefano Gionta, *Il Fioretto delle chroniche di Mantova, Amplicato Fine al Presente Anno MDCCXLI*, quoted by Selwyn Brinton, p. 7.
[32] The most detailed study of the artist, with particular attention to his Arthurian murals, is Giovanni Paccagnini's *Pisanello*. My discussion is greatly indebted to this work. See also E.L. Goodman, 'The Prose Tristan and the Pisanello Murals' in *Tristania*, III/2 (1978), 23–35.

in serpentine rhythm stood out against the dark background, winding round faintly-outlined figures of animals: a dog, a fawn and an eagle, all known to be heraldic devices of the Gonzaga family.

Under the frieze appeared mounted knights with pig-faced basinets and lances, trumpeters, standard bearers, bareheaded condottieri, until at last an elaborate (though incomplete) battle scene was uncovered, followed by a mountain landscape where single knights wandered and wild animals roamed. Above them were isolated castles and a crowded city with Gothic churches, palaces and tile-roofed houses.[33] As well as the upper wall decoration, large sinopia drawings on the lower walls were recovered.

Because of the murals' incomplete state, it is possible to study the artist's technique which reflected new developments of fifteenth century painting. The basis of the successful mural, as Cennini insisted, was drawing – from small sketches of particular subjects to full size cartoons which were transferred to the walls as charcoal drawings and then outlined with black or red paint.[34] This stage was called the *sinopia*. Pisanello and his assistants covered the sinopia with a layer of plaster, the *intonaco*, and while it was still wet, the artist drew on it freehand with a fine brush dipped in *verdaccio* (made with one part black and two parts ochre). Then the entire background was painted black to make the figures more prominent.

Some decorative designs such as the frieze were transferred by using perforated paper patterns (spolveri). Gold and silver leaf was affixed to highlight the patterns of lances and swords, details of armour, gilding on leather, and the decoration of hats and gowns. Finally, the colours of landscape, faces, costumes and caparisons were painted in *mezzo fresco* onto a moistened surface or *al secco*. The latter was a less propitious technique since the disintegration of the binding material (egg yolk or egg) caused flaking. Pisanello's imagination was so fertile and his technical facility so accurate that at each stage he revised and changed his original plan so that, as Paccagnini remarks, 'Even though the battle scene matured over a long formative process it gives the impression of spontaneity and effortlessness'.

Clues to the particular source are provided by the fragmentary inscriptions which Paccagnini identifies as Calibur as dures mains, Arfassart li gros (cuer), Malies de l'Espine, Meldons l'envoissiez, all of them knights who took part in the *Prose Tristan* Grail quest.[35] The preliminary painting depicts the Tournament of

---

[33] The recovered murals and sinopia drawings are now displayed in the former Sala dei Principe, the adjacent Sala dei Papi and the first room of the appartments Guastalla.

[34] Many of Pisanello's drawings are now in the Louvre, Paris, including some related to the Arthurian murals; e.g., #2277, Gonzaga crest with dog, #2444, horse seen from behind, and #2324, head of a negro.

[35] As the same knights also appear in the *Prose Lancelot* story of Bohort's visit to King Brangoire's castle, some critics, including Joanna Woods-Marsden, *Arthurian Encyclopedia*, p. 427, believe that it is the textual source. (Cf. Sommer, vol. IV, pp. 266–8). Paccagnini rejects the attribution because of insufficient correspondences between text and image.

Louverzep, the last great chivalric gathering before the Quest of the Holy Grail.[36] In the literary accounts it is significant for several reasons. It is arranged so that King Arthur can meet the famous beauty, Isotta la Blonde. (Pisanello shows her, beautiful and demure, watching from a canopied balcony.) It recognises Tristan as the supreme hero. It reinforces the hostility between Tristan and Palamedes (who also loves Isotta) and by pitting Tristan and Lancelot against one another and, together, against King Arthur's forces, it presages the coming disintegration of the Round Table. Louverzep is a particularly bloody tournament with many deaths and injuries.

But it is hardly necessary to identify a particular textual incident. This is not narrative; it is historical record, painting from life to show the tragic results of condottieri battles in some of which the two Gonzaga brothers, Ludovico and Carlo, fought on opposite sides. One anguished knight sprawls on his face, revealing the soles of sabatons and the padding under his armour. Another lies on his back, his foreshortened legs contorted in pain. A third, pierced through the back with a lance, sinks on hands and knees. The armour is thoroughly up-to-date with cumbersome pauldrons (shoulder armour) and helmets with movable visors which are sometimes raised so that we may see the knights' straight noses, thin eyebrows, and eyes filled with pain and weariness. Only the flamboyant panaches evoke the extravagance of International Gothic style.

Among the combatants and their horses (often protected by scaled armour), one group of three particularly draws attention. The dark-skinned face with thick red lips and brooding eyes, clearly based on a Pisanello sketch of a negro, is Palamedes, the pagan knight. The equally melancholy dark-haired man beside him must be Lancelot whom Tristan defeated. In the forefront is the heroic Tristan with curled blond hair and a great fur hat similar to that which the bridegroom wears in Jan van Eyck's 'Arnolfini Marriage Portrait' (1434). He complacently acknowledges his superiority with a half-smiling mouth though the eyes remain wary. The psychological complexity of these faces reflecting a variety of emotions is unequalled in any other examples of medieval Arthurian art.

Paccagnini suggests that the melancholy Lancelot is to be identified with Carlo Gonzaga, the contentious brother, while the successful hero, Tristan, represents Ludovico. The fair-haired young man on Palamedes' right (Dinadan?), may be a Mantuan courtier, Belloto Cumano, who was immortalised in one of Pisanello's famous medals.

The contemporary relevance of the depicted event is emphasised by other Gonzaga allusions. Two bareheaded knights under the heraldic frieze are portraits of the artist's patrons, Gianfrancesco and Ludovico. One of their famous dwarves, decked out in armour and wearing the ducal colours of red, white and green, rides into the fray as if participating in a Mantuan pageant. When the knights depart on the Grail quest, the subject of the second programme, the ladies watch from a balcony decorated with Gonzaga devices including a heraldic dog. The moated castle beside a river is Ludovico's castle of S. Giorgio on the River Mincio.

---

[36] See Löseth, pp. 283–4.

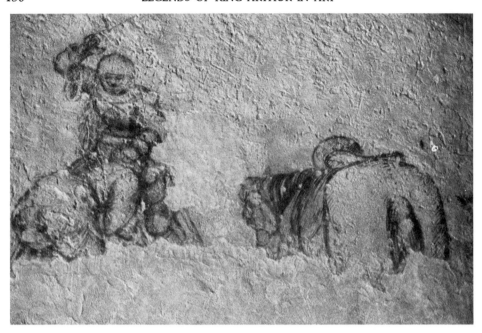

26. Lancelot at the River Marcoise. Pisanello fresco, Palazzo Ducale, Mantua, ca. 1450

The mysterious strangeness of Pisanello's wooded mountains is appropriate to the Grail landscape where each knight rides alone, taking the way that seems best. In the foreground of the sinopia, Lancelot's great stallion holds back from the river Marcoise just before a mysterious attacker kills him. In the middle distance, two unsuccessful knights, Malies de l'Espine and Meldons li envoissiez, wander away, their backs turned on the castle which, isolated on its mountain peak, must be Corbenic. The pavilion recalls Perceval's temptation by the devil woman who enticed him into her silken bed.

Unlike the creators of the other castle programmes, Pisanello depicts not the chronological narrative of a fictional plot but rather a historical record of contemporary people, places and actions thinly disguised as romance. These murals are the supreme record in Arthurian art of a society that lived its chivalric myth.

CHAPTER SIX

King Arthur Among the Worthies

The Renaissance ideal of princeliness, partly inspired by Baldassare Castiglione's *Il Cortegiano* (1528), combined proficiency in the arts and in several branches of learning with prowess on the battlefield. Hamlet, Prince of Denmark, with his 'courtier's, soldier's, scholar's, eye, tongue, sword' was recognisably a Renaissance type. For rulers with imperialistic ambitions and genealogical pretensions the *topos* of the Nine Worthies – or Nine Heroes – was attractive.[1] It had originated ca. 1310 when a jongleur, Jacques de Longuyon, contributed a digression, *Les Voeux du Paon* (*The Vows of the Peacock*), to *The Romance of Alexander*.[2] To glorify the feats of his hero Porris, the poet asserted that no man had equalled him in prowess, not even the nine noblest men who ever lived. In keeping with the medieval love of order, correspondences and number symbolism, the nine were subdivided into three groups of three. The three 'honest heathens' were Hector, Alexander and Julius Caesar; the three Hebrew champions, Joshua, David and Judas Maccabeus; the three Christian heroes, Arthur, Charlemagne and Godfrey of Boulogne. Subsequently, a tenth hero was sometimes added – Bertrand du Guesclin, Frederick Barbarossa, Robert the Bruce, or even Henry VIII.

Nine Worthy Women were soon assembled to balance the male warriors. None was an Arthurian heroine. Both series were incorporated into *Le Chevalier Errant* which Tommaso, Duke of Saluzzo, wrote in the early fifteenth century. A miniature illustrating that manuscript, Paris, BN MS fr. 12559, f. 125,[3] is a useful guide to the iconography which enables one to identify each character.[4] Since the Worthies' virtue derives from their warrior status, they are normally depicted wearing armour and carrying weapons. The kings wear crowns and the Jews sometimes have such oriental headdresses as turbans. Coats of arms appear on

---

[1] The major study is Horst Schroeder, *Der Topos der Nine Worthies in Literatur und bildender kunst* (Göttingen, 1971) with 43 plates.

[2] For text and translation see John Barbour, *The Buik of Alexander, or, the Buik of the most Noble and Valiant Conquerour Alexander the Grit*, ed. R.L.G. Ritchie, Scottish Text Society, NS 12, 17, 21, 25 (Edinburgh and London, 1921, 1925, 1927, 1929).

[3] It is reproduced in Schroeder, pl. 1; Loomis fig. 13; Hibbert, p. 20 (colour).

[4] Another text, Sébastien Mamerot's *Histoire des neuf preux et des neuf preues*, was beautifully illustrated by Jean Colombe, Vienna, Österreichische Nationalbibl. 2577–78 (1460–72).

shields, battle standards and surcoats though there is no absolute consistency.[5] In the Tommaso illustration Hector carries a red standard with a golden lion. Julius Caesar's golden shield is emblazoned with a sable double-headed eagle while Alexander's red shield bears a *silver lion rampant* (sometimes seated in a chair) carrying a battle-axe. Joshua has a green basilisk on a silver shield and carries a quiver; sometimes his blazon is a flaming sun. David has a golden harp and Judas Maccabeus a raven. Arthur's heraldic sign, well established in romance manu-scripts, is three golden crowns on an azure (or red) field; they signify his domi-nion over England, Scotland and Brittany.[6] Charlemagne's dimidiated shield alludes to his dual role as French monarch and Holy Roman Emperor – the right side has golden fleur-de-lis on an azure field while the left is emblazoned with half of the imperial double-headed eagle. Godfrey of Boulogne, the Crusader King of Jerusalem, exhibits on his white jupon and standard a golden cross potent between four crosslets.

In the later Middle Ages some texts treated the Worthies as examples of the *sic transit gloria mundi* motif. In *The Parlement of the Thre Ages* the allegorical figure, Old Age, introduces them to prove that worldly joys are vanity.[7] The fourteenth century alliterative *Morte Arthure*[8] contains a highly developed iconography which combines two favourite *topoi*. Arthur and his eight companions, bound to the Goddess Fortuna's Wheel, are predestined victims of her deceitful fickleness. However, these negative associations had little effect on the visual arts.

In the late Middle Ages and Renaissance the Worthies rivalled Tristan and Isolde as subjects of inspiration, appearing in manuscript illuminations, printed books, tapestries, stained glass, painted walls and ceilings, enamels, goldsmiths' work, series of woodcuts and engravings, sculptures, pageants and even playing cards. As early as 1336 they were portrayed in a pageant at Arras; the text survives in Paris, Bibl. d'Arsenal MS 5269, *Récits d'un bourgeois de Valenciennes*. Princely inventories provide tantalising glimpses of vanished works.[9] Charles V had two large flagons of silver gilt with the Nine Heroes in relief, as well as two tapestries made by his order in 1379–80. On July 19, 1388 Philippe le Hardi ordered from Pierre de Beaumetz tapestries of Ten Heroes and Nine Heroines, for which he paid 2600 francs on April 7, 1390. On December 25, 1389, he paid Dourdin 3400 francs for tapestries of Nine Heroes and Nine Heroines with gold and silver threads.

---

[5]   See Schroeder, pp. 261–291, for tables of each character's coat of arms in a wide range of visual representations.
[6]   See Karl Lippe, 'Armorial Bearings and their Meaning' in *The Alliterative Morte Arthure, a Reassessment of the Poem*, ed. Karl Heinz Göller (Cambridge, Eng., 1981), pp. 96–105.
[7]   *Parlement of the Thre Ages*, ed. M.Y. Offord, EETS NS #246 (London, New York, Toronto, 1959). See also the Roxburghe Club *Parlement* ed. Sir Israel Gollanz (London, 1897) for the editor's quotation of 12 Nine Worthies texts from the thirteenth to sixteenth centuries.
[8]   *Morte Arthure*, ed. Edmund Brock (London, 1871; rpt. 1961). See Anke Janssen, 'The Dream of the Wheel of Fortune' in *Reassessment*, pp. 140–152.
[9]   J.J. Guiffrey, 'Inventaire des tapisseries de Charles VI' in *Bibliothèque de l'Ecole des Char-tres* vol. 48, 1887, pp. 90, 91, 424; *Nicolas Bataille, tapissier parisien du XIVe siècle; sa vie, son oeuvre, sa famille* (Paris, 1884); *Histoire générale de la tapisserie*, pt. I, France (Paris, 1878–85); Jules Labarte, *Inventaire du mobilier de Charles V, roi de France* (Paris, 1879).

Louis d'Anjou and the Comte de Hainaut also purchased sets while Philippe le Bon inherited from his father tapestries 'fait richement à or'. The Duke of Berry, always at the forefront of taste and fashion, had a nef and two gold basins with Heroes and Heroines in red enamel; and a 1416 inventory notes a Heroes tapestry of Arras work, made with gold, silver, and wool of several colours. Worthies tapestries were among the treasures which the Duke of Bedford acquired in 1423 when he purchased Charles VI's library.

In his *Les Voeux du Paon*, Jacques makes worthiness depend on conquest. But Arthur's imperialism is subservient to his skill as a giant-killer:[10]

> D'Artus qui tint Bretaingne va le bruit tesmoingnant
> Que il mata Ruiston. j. jaiant en plain champ,
> Qui tant par estoit fort, fier et outrecuidant
> Que de barbes a roys fist faire. i., vestemant,
> Liquel roy li estoient par force obeïssant;
> Si volt avoir l'Artus, mais il i fu faillant!
> Sur le mont saint Michiel en r'ocist. i. si grant
> Que tuit cil du païs en furent mervellant.
> En plusours autres lieus, se l'istoire ne ment,
> Vainqui li rois Artus maint prince outréement.
>
> (ll. 7548–7557)

A translation in the Scottish *Buik of Alexander* (1438), dubiously attributed to John Barbour, follows:

> Arthur, that held Britane the grant,
> Slew Rostrik, that stark gyant,
> That was sa stark and stout in deid
> That of kingis beirdis he maid one weid,
> The quhilk kingis alluterly
> War obeysant to his will all halely;
> He wald have had Arthouris beird,
> And failzeit, for he it richt weill weird.
> On mount Michaell slew he ane,
> That sik ane freik was neuer nane,
> And ma gyantis in vther places sua,
> Bot gif the story gabbing ma.   (ll. 9981–9992)

Geoffrey of Monmouth's assertion in *Historia Regum Britanniae* that the demonic Giant of Saint-Michel was a foreign invader from Spain gave the *topos* additional value in the Protestant England of Henry VIII, Elizabeth I and James I.

Among surviving representations of King Arthur as Worthy, depictions in an architectural setting are most durable. The earliest is a painted stone statue (ca.

---

[10] Geoffrey of Monmouth, *Historia Regum Britanniae*, X, 3 and X, 4.

1325) in the Hall of the Hanseatic League, the Rathaus, Cologne.[11] The king, with a crown surmounting his helmet, wears complete chain mail over which is a long surcoat blazoned with three crowns on the front and sleeves. The device is repeated on the shield dangling from his wrist. His right hand, raised to lift his visor, touches his temple in a gesture that would later develop into the military salute. He stands like a cathedral saint in an arcaded niche against a blue background gilded with stars. Such an architectural structure both isolated and emphasized the figure, lending it dignity and importance. The bearded monarch's middle-aged face shows the weariness and fortitude of one who has laboured long. That the Worthies still appealed to German merchants in the sixteenth century is indicated by the complete set of statues which Albert von Soest executed between 1580 and 1584 for Lüneberg's Rathaus.[12] Arthur with curly hair, beard and moustache stands behind Godfrey of Boulogne, achieving independence by looking in the opposite direction. The faces are portrait-like in their individuality.

The towers of Pierrefond, Louis d'Orlean's early fifteenth century castle, were named for the Heroes and decorated with sculptures of which fragments remain.[13] There were similar sculptural programmes in Enguerrand VII's great hall at Courcy and on the keep of Maubergeon, near Poitiers, which Guy de Dammartin built for the Duke of Berry before 1385. However, the best extant evidence of the Duke of Berry's interest is the Nine Heroes tapestry now in New York's Cloisters Museum.[14] Assembled from ninety-five fragments, it represents two-thirds of a set of three large tapestries, each more than 21 x 16 ft (4.27 x 2.97 m), made in Flanders about 1385. Each one showed a group of enthroned heroes surrounded by smaller figures in an architectural setting of Gothic arches, niches, traceried windows, ribbed and embossed ceilings, galleries, gables with crockets and finials and slender columns all presented in rich shades of red, blue, green and sand.[15]

It was the kind of art work that inescapably conveyed its owner's wealth, taste,

[11] Loomis, p. 38 and fig. 11; Scherer, *About the Round Table*, pp. 30–31;

[12] Schroeder, pl. 38.

[13] Jean Adhémar, *Influences antiques dans l'art du Moyen Age francais* (London, 1939) notes the Pierrefond, Maubergeon and Courcy examples as well as giving information about tapestries.

[14] Phyllis Ackerman, 'Tapestries of Five Centuries, The French Gothic Looms', *International Studio*, LXXVI (1922) 40–45; Alfred de Champeaux and P. Gauchery, *Les travaux d'art executés pour Jean de France, duc de Berry* (Paris, 1894); Joseph Jobé, ed., *The Art of Tapestry* (London, 1965); James J. Rorimer, *The Cloisters, The Building and the Collection of Medieval Art in Fort Tryon Park* (New York, 1963), pp. 26–83; J.J. Rorimer and M.B. Freeman, 'The Nine Heroes tapestries at The Cloisters', in *Metropolitan Museum of Art Bulletin*, NS Vol. VII (May, 1949), pp. 243–260 and *The Nine Heroes tapestries at The Cloisters, a picture book* (New York, 1960); Francis Salet and Geneviève Souchal, *Chefs-d'oeuvre de la tapisserie du XIVe au XVIe siècle*; Catalogue of an exhibition held at the Grand Palais, Paris, and the Metropolitan Museum of Art, New York, February 7 to April 19, 1974 (Paris, 1973).

[15] The surviving Heroes in the Cloisters tapestry are Alexander, Julius Caesar, Joshua, David, and Arthur.

power and good breeding.[16] The Arthur panel, 4.27 x 2.97 m, shows the crowned king, with stringy brown hair and curled beard, seated on a throne, its blue cover embroidered with patée fitched crosses.[17] He wears fourteenth century plate armour, a blue surcoat with three large yellow crowns, and a lined red mantle. His left hand holds a dagger and his right an emblazoned pennon. The aquiline nose, wary eyes and severe expression imply vigilance. Above him to right and left in the same architectural space are cardinals with Bibles, archbishops with crosses and bishops with crosiers to emphasize his fame as *christianissimus rex*.

James Rorimer has noted the resemblance of the architecture to stained glass formerly in the Sainte Chapelle of the Duke's palace in Bourges, where the tapestries may have been woven. The similarity of this tapestry to the Apocalypse series at Angers, made for the Duke's brother Louis of Anjou, suggests that the master weaver, Nicolas Bataille, might have been responsible for both sets. They have the same weave, the same colour scheme, the same golden tan stonework, the same architectural structures. Both fulfilled the purpose which Geneviève Souchal attributes to medieval tapestries: 'rendre tangible la puissance d'un prince'.

Arthur and Godfrey of Boulogne appear in another Cloisters tapestry, an early sixteenth century Flemish piece depicting the Life of Charlemagne.[18] Unusually, the British king wears court dress – a voluminous red houppelande with white lining slit high on the left side to reveal a jupon and hose. Compared with the fourteenth century depictions, his face is remarkably youthful, an effect achieved by smoothly flowing shoulder length hair, wide eyes and sweet mouth.

A wool and linen Gobelin (ca. 1490) in the Historisches Museum, Basle, Switzerland,[19] also shows a youthful Arthur in court dress consisting of a short rose-coloured, fur-trimmed gown, slit at the sides, wrinkled hose, low pointed shoes, a tasselled collar, a belt supporting a scabbard and an acorn hat decorated with a sunburst. His pink pennon blazoned with white crowns is attached to a grounded spear. The tapestry was probably made for a rich knight, Mathias Eberler of Baseler, whose coat of arms is woven into the background. Along with the armed Judas Maccabeus and Charlemagne, Arthur stands against a flowery background which includes climbing roses, tulips and daisies. His decorative scroll reads, 'Kunig artus min macht und min miltikeit das ich alle lant erstreit' ('King Arthur. My power and my generosity [brought it to pass] that I conquered all lands'). The courtly and paradisal iconography makes the hero an embodiment of the peace which the successful warrior should establish.

A series of Gobelins in the Chateau de la Palisse may have been woven for the 1498 wedding of Jean I de Chabannes and Françoise de Blanchefort. An aging

---

[16] Ten of the fourteen banners on turrets in the Hebrew Worthies' tapestry and shields in the vaults above David and Joshua show the Duke of Berry's coat of arms *azure fleur de lis or engrailed with gules*, a sign of his ownership.

[17] Salet and Souchal note that the seated figures that André Beauneveu painted in a Psalter for the Duke of Berry are similar in design.

[18] It is reproduced in Scherer, p. 28.

[19] Loomis, fig. 15.

Arthur, armed and mounted on a lavishly caparisoned horse, is set in a hilly landscape dotted with castles. Two servants in smart liveries accompany him on foot. The representation was probably inspired by the equestrian statues so popular in the Renaissance. The statue's portrait character has been skilfully transferred to another medium, as has the sense of authority which the horse at rest implies. A similar equestrian style, with costumes updated to the period of composition (1525–1540), appears in the series of tapestries made for the Castle of Chaurey and now in the castle of Langeais in the Loire Valley.[21]

Murals often shared the subject matter and style of tapestries which they intentionally imitated. In the North Italian Castle of La Manta both long walls and the end wall of the great hall are covered with representations of the Nine Worthies and the Nine Worthy Women.[22] An acanthus leaf border above and a band containing descriptive verses below mimic a wall hanging's edges. Between these horizontal lines, thin-trunked trees from which hang identifying shields divide the space into compartments. Each life-size figure stands in a flowery meadow which together with the luxuriant fruit trees produces a paradisal effect. Arthur, with short, dark hair and Italianate face, holds an upright sword. His inscription, translated by Loomis, reads:

> I was king of Britain, Scotland, and England. Five hundred kings I conquered, who held their lands from me. I have slain seven great giants in the midst of their land. I went to conquer still another on Mont S. Michel. I saw the Holy Grail. Then Modred made war on me, who slew me some five hundred years after God came to earth.[23]

This expanded version of Jacques de Longuyon's biography combines details from chronicle and romance. The first-person narration resembles the speeches devised for pageants and similar entertainments. The La Manta paintings (ca. 1430), commissioned by Valerano Provana, a bastard son of the Duke of Saluzzo who wrote Le Chevalier Errant, are both decorative and commemorative for the artist has complimented Valerano by depicting him as Hector while his wife Clemensia becomes Penthesilea.

A badly preserved mural in the Castle of Valeria, Sion, Switzerland, is notable because Arthur's shield displays both his traditional charges. The Virgin and Child of Godfrey's Historia is impaled with the three crowns.

Sixteenth century wall paintings in the parish church at Dronninglund, Denmark, provide another variation. Instead of being seated in an enclosing and isolating niche or standing at regular intervals in a landscape, the paired and mounted heroes energetically engage in violent jousts – Hector against David,

---

[20] Schroeder, p. 91 and pl. 24.
[21] Schroeder, pp. 92 ff. and pl. 25. See also Diana B. Tyson, 'King Arthur as a Literary Device', Bibliographical Bulletin of the International Arthurian Society, XXXIII (1981), 242, n. 17.
[22] See reproductions in Loomis, p. 39 and fig. 14; Scherer, p. 30 and Schroeder pls 3 & 4.
[23] The chronology resembles that of the Vulgate Queste del Saint Graal where the Grail Quest is said to begin four hundred and fifty-four years after the Crucifixion.

Gottfried against Judas Maccabeus, Charlemagne against Joshua, and Alexander against Arthur.[24] They were almost certainly copied from a set of Flemish wood-cuts ca. 1500 now in Brussels, BR Albert I[er]. In both, Alexander rides an elephant, alluding to his conquest of India, while Arthur is mounted on a snarling camel. This bizarre iconography may be due to confusion with Judas Maccabeus.

Another progeny of the same woodcut is a Flemish roundel of grey and yellow glass which the art historians of New York's Metropolitan Museum of Art attribute to the early sixteenth century.[25] Arthur's posture astride the camel, the arrow in the animal's side, the knobby legs and open mouth with prominent teeth are all reproduced exactly. While theoretically the exotic animals recall the Heroes' connection with universal history, their appearance may have contemporary relevance. Many princes of the late Middle Ages and Renaissance kept menageries. (An image of the Duke of Berry's cheetah was woven into his Worthies tapestry.) When Francis I made a triumphal entry into Caen in 1532, the procession included the Nine Worthies on mounts that alluded to bestiary tradition but drew their chief importance from being spectacular. Joshua rode an elephant, David a camel, Judas Maccabeus a stag, Hector a unicorn, Alexander a griffin, and Julius Caesar a dromedary. Only the Christians rode natural mounts, horses.

It is not impossible that a woodcut series provided the initial idea, for in the fifteenth and sixteenth centuries the Worthies were a prime subject for illustration on large sheets that could be cheaply produced and easily transported. A.M. Hind has identified five extant examples printed on the continent before 1500.[26] The technique of engraving, which developed about the same time, increased the degree of ornamentation. The Nuremburg Master, Virgil Solis (1514–1562), transferred to his Worthies series (ca. 1540) the same intricacy of patterning that he devised for decorating sheaths, daggers, pendants, coats of arms, vases, friezes and cups. His Heroes in elaborate Renaissance armour are framed in triumphal arches through which may be glimpsed such landscape details as grass, trees, castles, a distant town, clouds, and hills, varying from one plate to another. Arthur, his back turned, appears to walk away from the viewer, dragging the enormous emblazoned shield (which is each design's most prominent feature). His frame incorporates busts of naked-breasted women, a cupid proffering roses, and two squawking egrets.[27]

An extraordinary use of King Arthur for self-glorification and genealogical aggrandisement was devised by Maximilian I (1459–1519), the Habsburg ruler

---

[24] See Schroeder pl. 9–19 for reproductions of the murals and of three related woodcut series. Placed in a church, the murals seem to advocate that Christians should engage in militant attacks on infidels and Jews.

[25] Though the provenance of this glass is unknown, Schroeder has described two more examples of German fifteenth-century glass *in situ* – a complete set of Worthies in the Rathaus, Lüneburg (ca. 1420) and the three Christians in Augsberg (ca. 1535–40).

[26] Arthur M. Hind, *An Introduction to a History of Woodcut with a detailed survey of work done in the fifteenth century*, 2 vols. (London, 1935), I, pp. 94, 157. See also Loomis, p. 140.

[27] See Schroeder, plate 34 and reproductions in the Department of Prints, Victoria and Albert Museum.

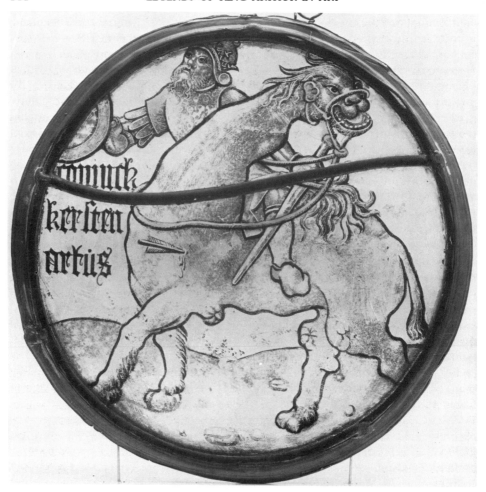

27. King Arthur on a camel. Flemish glass of the early sixteenth century

who established Austria as a first class dynastic power. Though his interest in military activities, learning and the arts made him Castiglione's type of Renaissance man, he liked to think of himself as 'the last of the knights'. His restorations at Schloss Runkelstein were undertaken both to preserve a painted record of medieval story and to establish a translation centre where new copies of medieval epics and romances could be produced. He engaged some of the best artists of his time, including Albrecht Dürer, Hans Burgmair, Albrecht Altdorfer, Leonhard Beck and Hans Schäufelein to celebrate his Arthurian activities – successful military expeditions, tournaments, hunts, cavalcades – for he believed that whoever prepared no memorial for himself when he was alive would be forgotten with the sound of the bell that tolled his passing. A memorial based on the ostentatious glorification which the Roman triumphal processions had exhibited was the

collection of one hundred and thirty-seven woodcuts, *The Triumph of Maximilian I,*
with a text dictated by the Emperor.[28] The triumphal procession included funerary
statues representing emperors, kings, archdukes and dukes whose coats of arms,
lands and ancestry Maximilian claimed. Among them is King Arthur,[29] bearded,
venerable, craggy faced, dressed in the extravagant armour that imitated court
dress. His shield bears the oldest known representation of the arms of the Kingdom of England – *three lions passant guardant.* When he was dying, Maximilian
promised Henry VIII his title of Holy Roman Emperor on the grounds that both
were descended from the British king.

   Dürer was employed to design sculptures of King Arthur and King Theodoric
(another supposed ancestor) for the Emperor's tomb in Innsbruck's Hofkirche.[30]
The splendid bronze statue executed in the workshop of Peter Vischer in Nurem-
berg shows the patron's obsession with details of armour. (He is credited with
inventing the fluted armour now known by his name.) Arthur is dressed in
complete mail, exactly tailored as fifteenth century knights demanded. He has the
new style of conical helmet with hinged visor and mezail, a gorget, chain mail
shirt, gauntlets, pointed sollerets, leg armour with knee caps, and an elaborately
embossed corselet. His left hand rests on his sword, the scabbard supported by a
medallioned belt while his right hand touches his shield. It bears not the familiar
crowns but the royal arms of England which quartered *gules three lions passant
guardant or* with *azure three fleurs-de-lis or.* Devised by the Plantagenets, these arms
persisted until the death of Elizabeth I.

   In Tudor Britain the image of Arthur as one of universal history's noblest men
was combined with others that derived from his place in the roll of English kings
and his importance as a national hero. Henry Tudor (1457–1509), the Lancastrian
Earl of Richmond, attained the English throne by defeating the Yorkist king,
Richard III, at the Battle of Bosworth Field (1485). His marriage to Edward IV's
daughter Elizabeth established a peace which the double Tudor rose symbolised.
Henry's claim derived from his great-grandfather who was the son of Edward
III's brother John of Gaunt and his mistress, later his wife, Catherine Swynford.[31]
Henry's grandfather was Owen Tudor, a noble of Anglesey, who traced his family
to Cadwalader, the last British king of Geoffrey's *Historia.*[32] Henry's father

---

[28] *The Triumph of Maximilian I,* trans. Stanley Appelbaum (New York, 1964); Alfred
Aspland, ed., *The Triumphs of the Emperor Maximilian I,* with Woodcuts Designed by Hans
Burgmair, Reproduced by the Holbein Society, 3 vols. (Manchester and London, 1873–5).
[29] Aside from his Trojan genealogy, Maximilian based his right to Britain on the promise of
Perkin Warbeck (1474–1499), the pretender who claimed to be one of the 'Princes in the
Tower', Edward IV's son, Richard.
[30] The drawings, now lost, were noted in a letter written by Lazarus Sprengler.
[31] Their children were legitimised by an Act of Parliament in Henry IV's reign. On Henry
VII's pedigree see Ralph A. Griffiths and Roger S. Thomas, *The Making of the Tudor Dynasty*
(Gloucester, 1985), pp. 190 ff.
[32] On the Trojan genealogy see Sidney Anglo, 'The British History in Early Tudor Propaganda', *Rylands Library Bulletin,* 44 (1961–2), 17–48; Roberta Florence Brinkley, *Arthurian
Legend in the Seventeenth Century* (Baltimore and London, 1932); Mary E. Griffin, 'Cadwalader, Arthur, and Brutus in the Wigmore Manuscript', *Speculum* 16 (1941), 109–20; George

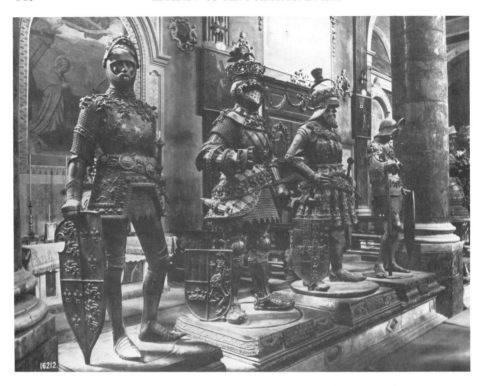

28. Bronze statue of King Arthur; Maximilian's tomb, Hofkirche, Innsbruck

Edmund was the son of Tudor and Henry V's widow, Katherine of Valois, whose 'marriage' was not officially recognized. Clearly Henry's genealogy could stand the infusion of ancient British blood which the Cadwalader link provided.

The Arthurian genealogy served three purposes. It guaranteed dynastic respectability, provided a precedent for imperial claims, and encouraged eulogies identifying successive Tudors as the expected Welsh saviour – *rex quondam, rex futurus*.[33] Henry arranged that his first child should be born at Winchester, which Malory had identified in his *Morte Darthur* as Camelot; to make the connection

Gordon, 'The Trojans in Britain', *Essays of the English Association*, IX (1924), 9–30; Charles B. Millican, *Spenser and the Table Round, a Study in the Contemporaneous Background for Spenser's Use of the Arthurian Legend* (Cambridge, Eng., 1932).

[33] Cf. Geoffrey of Monmouth, *Historia* xii, 18. The writer of the Jesus College, Oxford MS LXI adds an allusion to Geoffrey's *Prophetiae Merlini*; when Arthur returns 'The mountains of Armorica shall erupt and Armorica itself shall be crowned with Brutus' diadem. Kambria shall be filled with joy and the Cornish oaks shall flourish'. See Geoffrey of Monmouth, *The History of the Kings of Britain*, trans. Lewis Thorpe, pp. 282–3, n. 1. London, BL Sloane 2578 exemplifies the use made of Merlin's prophecies in the Tudor period. Protestant in sympathy and condemnatory of Queen Mary who had just married Philip of Spain (1554), it foresees the return of Edward VI, the deliverer and saviour who will be a new Arthur. I am indebted to Sharon L.J. Jaech for this reference.

unmistakable, the prince was christened Arthur. The Tapestry of Roses woven for the occasion was decorated with three crowns on an azure field.[34] The king also utilised the red dragon symbol, the particular sign of Uther Pendragon and Arthur, by creating a new herald, Pursuivant Rougedragon.[35] And his new residence, Richmond, was adorned with large statues of ancient kings – Brutus, Hengist and Arthur.

Though parsimonious by nature, Henry VII appreciated the propaganda value of lavish spectacles, pageants, masques and other public entertainments which demonstrated a ruler's wealth and magnificence.[36] Pageants with painted scenes and written speeches could convey political attitudes, nationalistic sentiments and even intellectual concepts. Since books of drawings, engravings, and woodcuts together with printed records of the oral texts were compiled for particular occasions, the subject is not irrelevant to the study of Arthurian art. Roy Strong remarks that 'the pageants themselves looked like medieval paintings and manuscript illuminations come to life'.

An early example of Arthur's usefulness to subjects wishing to ingratiate themselves occurred in 1486, soon after Henry's coronation, when he visited Worcester. His identification with famous warriors culminated in the citing of King Arthur, who had been the 'Welcome Defence to England as a Walle'. Henry was hailed as the fulfiller of Geoffrey's prophecy that Cadwalader's descendants would ultimately triumph. Prince Arthur's name encouraged allusions which achieved spectacular expression when he was betrothed to Katherine of Aragon in 1501. On entering London, the princess was treated to 'uj goodly beautiful pageauntes', including one in Cheapside:

foragayne Soperlane was set the iiij pagent, In maner of an heven, whereyn was paynted the xij signes, and ouer theym was Arthure, clene armed, in his Golden Chare.[37]

---

[34] A piece of the tapestry in use as a bedside mat was found in the same Warden's bedroom at Winchester that held the unique manuscript of Malory's *Morte Darthur*. See W.F. Oakeshott, 'The Finding of the Manuscript' in *Essays on Malory*, ed. J.A.W. Bennett (Oxford, 1963), pp. 2–3.

[35] Arthur inherited the red dragon sign from his father, Uther Pendragon, whose title was suggested by the victorious red dragon under Vortigern's tower and by the dragon-shaped star that foretold his defeat of the Saxons (*HRB* vii, 3 and viii, 15). It became specifically the symbol of Wales.

[36] On Tudor pageantry see Sidney Anglo, *Spectacle, Pageantry, and Early Tudor Policy* (Oxford, 1969); Robert Withington, *English Pageantry. An Historical Outline*, 2 vols. (Cambridge, Mass., 1918); Roy Strong, *Splendour at Court: Renaissance Spectacle and Illusion* (London, 1973) and *The Cult of Elizabeth: Elizabethan Portraiture and Pageantry* (London, 1977).

[37] British Library Cotton MS Vit. A. xvi, f. 191[v] cited by Withington, p. 167, n. 6. See Sidney Anglo, *Spectacle, Pageantry, and Early Tudor Policy*, pp. 56–97, on the interpretation of the allegorical pageants. For another account of the marriage festivities, see A.H. Thomas and I.D. Thornley, *The Great Chronicle of London* (London, 1938), pp. 313 ff.

By 1502 Prince Arthur was dead; his bride and titles passed to his brother who became Henry VIII.

Henry VII's accumulated wealth and a natural inclination toward chivalric display enabled his son successfully to manipulate the politics of spectacle.[38] The supreme example of princely magnificence occurred when Henry and his rival Francis I met in France at the Field of the Cloth of Gold (1520).[39] The entertainment included a Nine Worthies masque. While in France, Henry also met the third member of the triumvirate – the Emperor Charles V. For these entertainments a circular theatre was built, its outer gateway surmounted by King Arthur holding the Round Table with his heraldic crowns at his feet. The accompanying inscription read:

> Moy Artus roy chef de la table ronde
> Principal chef de tous cueurs vallereux
> Vueil recevoir de volunte parfonde
> Tous nobles cuers par effect vertueux
> Princes puissans preux et audacieux
> Aymans honneur soubz vostre seigneurie
> Suyvez mes faitz et ma chevallerie.

The supporting iconography together with appropriate mottoes – a shield showing two hands grasping a sword, a crowned king with the old arms of England, Hercules with a club and a scroll inscribed with the Emperor's device, a red dragon with the arms of England and a black eagle with the Imperial arms – neatly balanced the emblems of each monarch. The entire decoration illustrates the use of chivalric images to express dynastic power and prestige.

Two years later when Charles visited England, King Arthur was trotted out again in his roles as English king and ruler of a great empire. The fifth pageant presented during the royal entry to London was both nationalistic and diplomatic:

> Also att the Condytt in Cornhyll dyd stande a pageant off a goodly
> Castell well and rychely garnysshede and arayde where satte the ryght
> noble and victorious emprowr Kynge Arthur w^t a crowne imperiall in
> complett harnes and a swerde in hys hande w^t the rounde table before

---

[38] On chivalry as a source of Renaissance idealism, see Arthur B. Ferguson, *The Chivalric Tradition in Renaissance England* (Washington, London and Toronto, 1986) and *The Indian Summer of English Chivalry: Studies in the Decline and Transformation of Chivalric Idealism* (Durham, N.C., 1960). On a particular form of chivalric spectacle, see Frances A. Yates, 'Elizabethan Chivalry: The Romance of the Accession Day Tilts', *Journal of the Warburg and Courtauld Institutes*, XX (1957), 4–25; Alan Young, *Tudor and Jacobean Tournaments* (Dobbs Ferry, N.Y., 1987).

[39] Anglo, 137–169; Joycelyne C. Russell, *The Field of the Cloth of Gold: Men and Manners in 1520* (London, 1969). The occasion was recorded in a great painting now at Hampton Court.

hyme. Whiche was accompanyed w^t all the noble prynces thatt were wnder his obeisaunce that is to say on the ryght hande, Skater Kynge off Scotlande, Aloth Kynge of Denmarke, Walganus Kynge of Gutlande, Guyloin Kynge off Northwalys, Achilles Kynge off Iselande, Cander yerle of Cornwall and Eueraldus yerle of Sarylbury. And wppon the lefte hande of Kynge Arthur sate fryste Madad Kynge of Irelonde, Cadwar Kynge of Southwalys, Cador Kyng of litill brytyn, Andher Kynge off Orkeney, Gunwado Kynge off Norwey, Morwidus yerle off glocester and Cutsall yerle of Chester. Also ther was a childe goodly apparelde whiche saluted the emprowr in laten versis laudyng & resemblyng hym in noblenes to the seyd Arthur.[40]

Though Henry had lost to Charles in their rivalry for the title of Holy Roman Emperor, he did not easily abandon his imperial claim.

Another politically motivated entertainment was an excursion to see King Arthur's Round Table in Winchester Castle. In his *Chronicle* of 1463 John Hardyng had remarked that the Round Table began at Winchester and ended there and 'there it hangeth yet'. Studies undertaken in the 1970s, when the table was taken from the wall to be repaired, have considerably amplified the historian's brief account.[41] The table, eighteen feet in diameter and weighing more than a ton, was probably made by a millwright who knew the 'clasp-arm' technique for strengthening mill wheels. Fifty-one thin prefabricated planks form the surface. The underside, strengthened by a massive beam and radials, has square grooves where legs were inserted. Carpenters' marks in Roman numerals provided guidance for the original assembling of 121 pieces of oak. Dendrochronology indicates that the table was made between 1250 and 1280 while carbon dating has given a time about 1255. It most likely was built in the reign of Edward I (1272–1307), an Arthurian enthusiast who had opened the Glastonbury tomb in 1278 and looked upon the two caskets painted with pictures of Arthur and Guenevere.[42]

Henry VIII was struck by the brilliant idea of painting the table traditionally associated with the earlier king so that it would iconographically convey a political message. The surface was divided into twenty-four pie-shaped segments (the number associated with the Knights of the Garter). Each was inscribed on the outer rim with the name of a Round Table Knight; most were drawn from Malory's *Morte Darthur*. The segments were painted in the Tudor colours, alternatively green and gold. Gerard Legh's *The Accedens of Armory* (1562)[43] describes

---

[40] The entry was described by the Tudor historians John Stow, Edward Hall and Richard Grafton. The fullest description is Cambridge, Corpus Christi (Cantab) MS 298 (no. 8), 132 ff. See Withington, pp. 175–179.

[41] Martin Biddle and Beatrice Clayre, *Winchester Castle and the Great Hall* (Winchester, 1983).

[42] C.A. Ralegh Radford, 'Glastonbury Abbey' in *The Quest for Arthur's Britain*, ed. Geoffrey Ashe (London, 1968), pp. 119–138.

[43] Legh specifically discusses the arms of the Nine Worthies. On f.38 he refers to King Arthur's designated blazon – 'his Shielde Azure xiii crownes or, 3333+1' – which increases

contemporary colour symbolism. Green meant 'joyful with worldly riches' while gold[44] indicated wisdom, riches, magnanimity, joyfulness and elation of mind, virtues not inappropriate to the young Henry. At the centre, within a circle inscribed 'Thys is the rownde table of Kyng Arthur w(ith) xxiiii of hys namyde knyghttes', is the Tudor rose, the white rose of York on the larger red rose of Lancaster. Rising above the emblem, an orb in one hand and sword in the other, Arthur sits enthroned under a type of canopy that first appeared in the plea rolls of 1515. His gold and red velvet crown is surmounted by a cross. His ermine-trimmed red mantle covers a dark blue gown – the traditional royal costume. The iconography of the orb, cross and upright sword signifies his roles as imperial ruler and 'Defender of the Faith' (one of Henry VIII's titles.) That the image of Arthur in Tudor England represented far more than the successful giant-killer of the continental characterisation is emphasized by the table's association of the prince with the most famous heroes of chivalric romance. His nobility consists of physical courage and prowess used for honour, justice, the defence of the Church, and the establishment of peace. (At his assumption of sovereignty, Malory's King Arthur swears 'to stand with true justyce fro thens forth the dayes of his lyf'.) His duties as a prince are the duties which he shares with his knights and the whole mystique of knight-errantry is assimilated into his position as head of the Round Table fellowship.

Though William Cave's repainting in 1798 and a Victorian repainting have turned the king's hair grey, x-ray photography has revealed that the original face strikingly resembled Henry's own as it appeared on a Confirmation Charter issued to the Bishop of Exeter, January 12, 1511[45] and in a portrait by an unknown artist painted ca. 1520.[46] In 1515 the Venetian ambassador described the monarch as the 'handsomest potentate I ever set eyes upon; above the usual height with an extremely fine calf to his leg, his complexion very fair and light, with auburn hair . . . and a round face so very beautiful that it would become a pretty woman'. The Round Table, which still hangs in Winchester Castle, is the most important English example of didactic Arthurian art until the Victorian Age.

During the sixteenth century civic displays connected with ceremonial entries continued to rely on allegorical images. When Henry VIII's daughter, Queen Mary, and her husband, Philip of Spain, entered London in July, 1554, the Grace church conduit was adorned with a painted canvas later preserved in the Church

his kingdoms by ten, emphasizing his imperial status. On the symbolic and emotional connection between a bearer and his shield see Sara Stevenson, *The Heraldic Ideal in England 1560–1610*, University of London doctoral dissertation (London, 1972).

[44] A French heraldic treatise written by Le Feron in 1555 attributed thirty-six separate meanings to gold including justice, strength, temperance, purity, splendour, right, obedience, generosity, constancy, gravity, joy, charity, riches, humility, and chivalrous love.

[45] Erna Auerbach, *Tudor Artists: A Study of Painters in the Royal Service and of Portraiture on Illuminated Documents from the accession of Henry VIII to the death of Elizabeth I* (London, 1954); see plate 5.

[46] It is now in the National Portrait Gallery, London.

of St Benet. The comment of an observer, John Elder, proves the connection between illustration and text:

> . . . painted verye ingeniouslye the nine Worthies with many notable proverbes and adges, written with fayre Roman letters on every side thereof.[47]

At least two books combining these pageantic elements have survived, the Commonplace books which Thomas Trevelyon, a London scrivener, assembled in 1608 and 1616. The pictures on the nine pages devoted to the Worthies were probably copied from another book or a set of woodcuts. In the 1608 version all are depicted (in colour) as warriors in variegated armour. They stand like *tableaux vivant* in a landscape consisting of flanking trees and grassy slopes. Each holds a grounded spear with identifying pennon, green for pagans, blue for Hebrews and red for Christians. Eight to twelve lines of verse similar to those used in murals and pageants complete the characterisation. The 1616 version, following a favourite design of woodcuts and engravings, places the Worthies under triumphal arches.

The theory that there was a connection between pageants, pageant books and mural programmes received confirmation when renovations in 1931 at a sixteenth century house, 56 High Street, Amersham, Bucks, revealed the remains of nine painted panels.[48] Three of them were on the south wall and six on the west wall, each about 5 ft 6 in high (1.68 m) and 2 ft 6 in (0.76 m) or 2 ft 9 in (0.84 m) wide. The full length figures dressed as warriors in medieval or pseudo-classical armour held grounded lances with pennons. Although the remains of accompanying verses were indecipherable, Francis Reader used iconography to identify most of them as various Worthies. This identification Horst Schroeder confirmed and expanded by comparing the panels to Trevelyon's 1608 Commonplace book. He found that 'the illustrations of the Nine Worthies in Trevelyon's first manuscript are virtually the same as the Amersham panels'. Either one series was copied from the other or they had a common source.

There is considerable evidence that in the period from about 1520 to 1620 the Worthies were one of the most popular subjects for domestic decoration among all levels of British society. The Amersham house probably belonged to a merchant. Harvington Hall, a moated Elizabethan residence near Kidderminster, was the home of Roman Catholic gentry. There a coat of whitewash and the owners' determined obscurity in an effort to escape religious persecution preserved a series of mural drawings until their discovery in 1936. The life sized figures,

---

[47] Camden Society No. 48 (1850), p. 147, cited by John L. Nevinson, 'A Show of the Nine Worthies', *Shakespeare Quarterly*, 14 (1963), 103–7.

[48] On the Amersham wall paintings, see Francis W. Reader, 'Tudor mural Paintings in the lesser Houses of Bucks', *The Archaeological Journal*, 89 (1933), 116–73; John L. Nevinson, *op. cit.*; Horst Schroeder, 'The Mural Paintings of the Nine Worthies at Amersham', *The Archaeological Journal*, 138 (1981), 241–47. The latter reproduces the Amersham murals and the 1606 commonplace book illustration, plates XVIII–XVIV.

energetically engaged in combat, are skilfully drawn with black outline. Guy of Warwick, a supposed ancestor, replaces King Arthur. The date 1576 is scratched on a window at the end of the decorated gallery (which was 47 ft long, 4 ft 6 in wide and 7 ft high). Like the Amersham panels, these were probably the work of travelling artists of limited skill who, forced out of the Roman Catholic Church's employ after the Reformation, catered to the middle classes and minor gentry by providing bright, clear, uncomplicated pictures.

In 1864 the Vicar of Amberley announced to a meeting of the British Archaeological Institute that in the 'Queen's Room' of the Bishop of Chichester's episcopal residence, Amberley Castle, there were life-size half length panel paintings of the Worthy Women, wearing fanciful armour that had been gilded and silvered.[49] Dating from the early sixteenth century, they were probably the work of a Flemish artist, Theodore Bernardi, who came to England in 1519. Though the corresponding male figures have not survived, the Vicar's description gives us an impression of a more sophisticated approach to the basic pageant and engraving type. Each figure, boldly painted with thick black outlines, was seen through an arch which evoked the military triumphs of Roman emperors.[50] A two line description was written below. The costume, a mixture of mail and plate, gilt foliage, jewels, bosses and chains was 'antique'. A shield dangled from the left arm while the right hand grasped a weapon. The complexions were shaded with slaty or purple tint, the cheeks and lips were painted bright pink and the eyes blue. The colours seemed to have been applied in tempera. The vicar concluded that the work was intended to imitate tapestry.

Painted ceilings had a better chance of survival since they were less subject to contact. A farm building in Binnal, Shropshire had busts of the Worthies, all depicted as kings, dated about 1610. Each hero was sheltered by a canopy and identified by a shield bearing his name. They also adorned ceilings at Earlshall in Scotland[52] and Crathes Castle, Banchory, Kincardineshire, where the 1602 painting is described by Schroeder as the most beautiful depiction of its kind in the British Isles.[53] The identified source for the iconography is a set of engraved portraits made in 1594 by Nicolas de Bruyn.[54]

---

[49] George A. Clarkson, 'A Series of Paintings in Amberley Castle', *The Archaeological Journal*, 22 (1865), 65–68; Edward Croft-Murray, *Decorative Paintings in England 1532–1837*, 2 vols. (London, 1962), pp. 23–25.

[50] Trevelyon's 1616 book also used this setting instead of the landscapes found in the earlier version. The change shows the influence of continental Renaissance engravings and woodcuts like the Virgil Solis series ca. 1540. H.C. Marillier, 'The Nine Worthies', *Burlington Magazine*, 61 (1932), 13–19 pointed out an interesting adaptation from a specific source which proves the interdependence of various media. A set of Worthies tapestries made by the Brussels weaver Jacques Geubels ca. 1590 was based on Antonio Tempesta's engravings which in turn were adapted from Rubens' designs of the Roman Emperors.

[51] Schroeder, *Der Topos*, pp. 101 ff.

[52] Marillier, 14.

[53] Schroeder, *Der Topos*, pp. 102 ff.

[54] The engraver (ca. 1570 – ca. 1635) worked in Antwerp and Amsterdam. Casts and drawings based on his Worthies set were used for a number of plaster and painted ceilings

The designer had to fit nine figures into a space divided vertically into six areas. He solved the problem by devoting a full space to the first of each triad while his companions shared the adjoining one. Their costumes consist of mantles and tightly fitted body armour. As evidence of Scottish humanism some carry books rather than weapons, a change in iconography consistent with the Renaissance ideal of nobility. As well as the conventional verse inscriptions there is an exhortation directing young noblemen to pattern their lives on the heroes – clear evidence that these figures still had an exemplary function. Nationalistic bias also affects the design. The primary Christian is not Arthur but Charlemagne, the representative of Scotland's ally France, whose pact of friendship is specifically mentioned.

Aston Hall, Birmingham, which the seventeenth-century antiquarian, Sir William Dugdale, describes as 'a noble fabric which for beauty and state much exceedeth anything in these parts', had a handsome plaster ceiling in the Great Drawing Room (ca. 1620). High relief figures of the Worthies under triumphal arches stand in niches.

The antique Italian style of architecture, which Inigo Jones had superbly mastered, favoured the use of the Worthies in outdoor settings, too. At Chillingham Castle in Northumberland, an arcade on the east side of the courtyard, attributed to Inigo Jones, has projecting stairs where the Worthies in classical garments form a procession to the terrace.[55] The coat of arms on Arthur's oval shield shows a crown within a circle of fleur-de-lis. Also dating from the early seventeenth century are the stone statues in antique armour which Sir Edward Phelips set up in front of his Somerset mansion, Montacute House. An expert describes them as 'coarse and almost grotesque figures' that indicate the void between English sculpture and that of the Continent.[56]

These surviving examples of the decorative arts together with numerous printed texts[57] confirm a widespread British interest in the Nine Worthies topos during the Renaissance.[58] And in English records, Arthur is regarded as the great-

---

in England and Scotland; e.g. Canonbury (1599), Bromley-by-Bow (1610); Balcarres, Fife; Glamis Castle, Angus (1620–21); Muchalls, Kincardineshire (1624); Craigievar, Aberdeenshire (1625–6). The Christian Worthies are generally omitted in Scotland. I am indebted to my colleague John Orrell for this information.

[55] Cadwallader John Bates, *The Border Holds of Northumberland* (Newcastle-upon-Tyne, 1891), pp. 301 ff; Nikolaus Pevsner, *The Buildings of England: Northumberland* (Harmondsworth, 1957), pp. 124–26. Pevsner, who ignores the Inigo Jones attribution, comments that the statues on their corbels seem too small for their position. He adds a note (p. 125), 'Mr. Hussey has drawn attention to the similarity of the statues to those above the columns of the porch of 1625 at Gibside in County Durham'.

[56] Margaret Whinney, *Sculpture in Britain 1530–1830* (Harmondsworth, 1964), p. 3.

[57] For example, Robert Fletcher, *The Nine Worthies* (1606); Thomas Fuller, *The History of the Worthies in England* (1662); Stephen Hawes, *The Passetyme of Pleasure* (1506); Richard Johnson, *The Nine Worthies* (1592); David Lloyd, *The Worthies of the World, etc.: An Abridgement of Plutarch's Lives* (1665), *inter alia*.

[58] Shakespeare's *Love's Labour's Lost* (ca. 1593) provides evidence that the Worthies pageant had filtered down to the village level. When the locals entertain the gentry in a country house, the bashful Nathaniel is so nervous that he forgets the lines in which he identifies

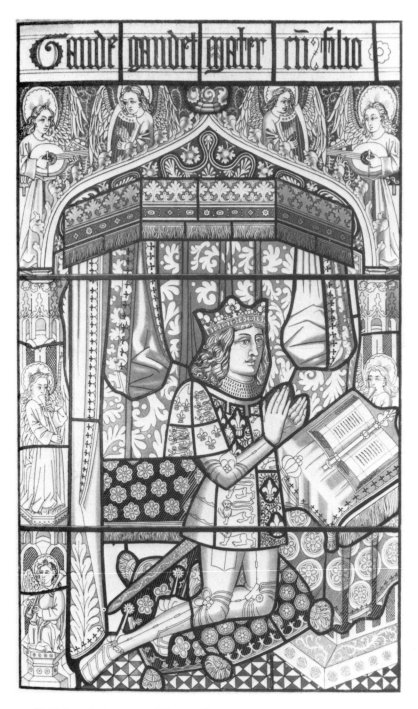

29. Prince Arthur, son of Henry VII. Stained glass window in Malvern
Priory, 1501

est of all. John Coke's 'The Debate betwene the Heraldes of Englande and Fraunce' (1550), after listing the territories which constituted the empire, concludes, 'This myghty conquerour for this valiauces most glorious and marcial actes is the fyrst & chyefe of the nyne worthies beyng christened and was the most lyberall, coragious, worthiest, famous and redoubted prynce of the earth'.[59] There speaks the fervent nationalism that Tudor art encouraged.

An alternative model set Arthur among Christian kings, English kings and national heroes. John Thornton's Great East Window at York Minster, depicting world history from the Creation to the Last Judgment, shows Arthur in the row of ecclesiastics and kings. Walter Skirlaw, Bishop of Durham, commissioned the window in 1405. The antechapel of All Souls' College, Oxford, contains a magnificent stained glass series which John Glazier made in 1440–47 for the Old Library.[60] Under a row of English saints – Dunstan, Edmund and Odo – King Arthur with golden sceptre, orb, and crown accompanies Archbishop Chichele and Henry VI, the college's founder. Each labelled figure stands on a chequered floor surmounted by an architectural canopy.

A rare example of late fifteenth century secular glass is the parade of English kings in St Mary's Hall, Coventry.[61] They appear in the lower lights of a fine Perpendicular window at the north end. In the company of William the Conqueror, Richard the Lion-hearted, Henry III, IV, V and VI (the latter given the place of honour in the centre), are 'Constantinus Anglicus, Imperator xptnimus' (i.e. Christianissimus) and 'Rex Arthurus conquestor inclitus'.[62] A combination of military fame and Lancastrian genealogy determined the choice of memorial figures in this Hall of the City Guilds. The virtually identical poses indicate the use of a single master cartoon varied by differing facial expressions, coats of arms, colours and accoutrements. Dressed in a red surcoat with three large crowns as a border, the dark-haired Arthur carries a gold-hilted upright sword and a jewel-studded triple crown surmounted by a cross, no doubt an allusion to his legendary role as Holy Roman Emperor. The crown on his head is rich with gold and pearls.

Constantine, who, according to the genealogy of Malory's Morte Darthur, was Arthur's grandfather, gains a place in the parade of kings because he had proclaimed himself Roman Emperor at York in 306 A.D. Constantine's coat of arms is complexly allusive. In the second and third quarters are the sable eagle on a gold field, the blazon of the Holy Roman Emperor's eldest son, the titular King of the Romans. The other quarters are charged with a cross, denoting his establishment

himself as Alexander. Costard chides, 'You will be scraped out of the painted cloth for this: your lion, that holds his poll-axe sitting on a close-stool, will be given to Ajax: he will be the ninth Worthy' (Act V, sc. ii, ll. 575–580).
[59] Quoted by Millican, Spenser and the Table Round, p. 34.
[60] Philip Nelson, Ancient Painted Glass in England 1170–1500 (London, 1913).
[61] Loomis, p. 40, fig. 16; Bernard Rackham, 'The glass-painting of Coventry and its neighbourhood', Walpole Society, XIX (1930–31), 89–110; Nelson, op. cit. p. 200.
[62] A more complete roll call – from Brutus to Henry VIII – was painted on the ceiling of the Great Hall, Kirkoswald Castle, Cumberland. See Edward Croft-Murray, op. cit., p. 16.

of Christianity as the Roman Empire's official religion. In each quarter is the Greek letter Beta, the sign of the Paleologus family, the last of the Byzantine Emperors. Constantine carries the True Cross with three nails, recovered by his mother St Helena. This beautiful window may have been executed at the royal workshop in Westminster to commemorate Henry VII's visit to Coventry in 1487.[63]

A set of greenish-white windows made in England ca. 1530 combines the Worthies and the Christian Kings. The coats of arms resemble those in the fifteenth century heraldic manuscript London, BL MS Harleian 2169 (ca. 1420) which appeared as a printed book in the sixteenth century. Each figure is depicted in the antique armour-ceremonial arch form. Arthur, with shoulder-length hair, fleur-de-lis crown, and ermine-lined mantle, is unusually boyish. His shield with three impaled crowns dangles from his arm.[64]

A discussion of glass from the Tudor period should not exclude the unique east window in All Saints parish church, Langport, Somersetshire. In keeping with the church's dedication, ten saintly figures identified by their personal symbols are assembled in two rows. The village's proximity to Glastonbury no doubt accounts for Joseph of Arimathea who, according to an evangelisation myth, established Christianity in Britain and who, according to the Grail legends, brought there the Holy Grail and the lance of Longinus. In the window the saint holds two cruets, an allusion to John of Glastonbury's story that Joseph had two white and silver vessels filled with Christ's blood and sweat.[65]

Arthur's historicity was a controversial question in fifteenth and sixteenth century Britain. Though works like Polydore Virgil's *Historia Anglica* (1534–55) denounced the falsity of Geoffrey's Arthurian history, antiquarians like John Leland (1506–1552) and William Camden (1551–1623) sought out artifacts that might substantiate the ancient king's existence. At St Edward the Confessor's shrine in Westminster Abbey, Leland examined Arthur's seal, 'a monument most cunningly engraven, auncient and reverent'.[66] The red wax seal mounted on a circular silver plate was inscribed on one side with the words PATRICIUS ARTVRIVS BRITTANNIÆ GALLIÆ GERMANIÆ, DACIÆ IMPERATOR. On the other side the king

---

[63] The smaller lights in the tracery which contain shields of royal arms and of local families indicate the Renaissance enthusiasm for heraldry. Henry Peacham in *The Gentleman's Exercise* (1612) gives a moral justification for studying the subject: '. . . when I came into an old decaied Church or Monastery (as we have plenty in England) or Gentleman's House, I might rather busie myselfe in viewing Armes, and maches of Houses in the windowes or walls, then lie bootes and spurres upon my bedde in mine Inne, or overlooke mine Hostes shoulder at Irish'; quoted by Stevenson, p. 25.

[64] They are described by S.H. Steinberg, 'The Nine Worthies and the Christian Kings', *Connoisseur* 104 (Sept., 1939), 146–49.

[65] In addition to C.A. Raleigh Radford, *op. cit.* see also James P. Carley, 'Glastonbury and the Grail Legend', *Avalon to Camelot*, I, 3 (Spring, 1984), 4–8 with a reproduction of the Langport glass, and Valerie M. Lagorio, 'The Evolving Legend of St. Joseph of Glastonbury', *Speculum* 46, (1971), 209–231.

[66] John Leland, *Assertio inclytissimi Arturii Regis Britanniae* (1544), trans. Richard Robinson, *The Assertion of King Arthure* (1582); reprinted in Christopher Middleton, *The Famous Historie of Chinon of England*, ed. William Edward Mead, EETS OS 65 (London, 1925).

inuested with purple, royally sitteth vpon a halfe circle, such one as we see the raine boe is. Hauing a crowne vpon his heade he shineth like the sunne. In his right hand riseth up a scepter wrought with a Flower-deluce at the toppe: and his lefth hand holdeth a globe adorned with a crosse. His beard also groweth comely, large, and at length, and even that is a maiestie.

Leland believed that King Henry II had taken the seal from Arthur's Glastonbury tomb and given it to the Abbey. He concluded that nothing 'more evidently approveth that Arthure was living, then the same Seale doth'.

William Camden's *Britannia*,[67] an account of his antiquarian researches, was first published in 1586. The edition of 1607 was printed in folio so that it might include a life-size reproduction of the drawing which the author had made at Arthur's tomb in Glastonbury. It showed, as Camden described it,

a broad crosse of lead grossly wrought: which being taken forth shewed an inscription of letters . . . The letters being made after a barbarous maner, and resembling the Gothish character, bewray plainly the barbarism of that age, when ignorance (as it were) by fatall destinee bare such sway, that there was none to be found, by whose writings the renowne of Arthur might be blazed, and commended to posteritie.

What the letters said was HIC JACET SEPVLTVS IHCLITVS REX ARTVRIVS IH IHSVLA AVALOHIA ('Here lies the famous King Arthur in the island of Avalon'). The forms of the letters, according to C.A. Ralegh Radford, are 'proper to the eleventh century or earlier' rather than to the late twelfth century when the monks discovered the tomb in the presence of Henry II.[68]

---

[67] The subtitle of Philemon Holland's 1610 translation reads, 'A chorographical description of the most flourishing kingdomes, England, Scotland, and Ireland and the islands adioyning'.
[68] Other versions of the Latin epitaph on the Glastonbury tomb are those reported by Giraldus Cambrensis in *De Principis Instructione* (1193–96): 'Hic iacet sepultus inclitus rex Arthurus cum Wenneueria uxore sua secunda in insula Auallonia' and by Ralph of Cogge-shall in the *Chronicon Anglicanum*: 'Hic iacet inclitus rex Arturius in insula Avallonis sepul-tus'. On the subject of the Glastonbury tomb see also Richard Barber, 'Was Mordred Buried at Glastonbury? An Arthurian Tradition at Glastonbury in the Middle Ages', *Arthurian Literature* iv, ed. Richard Barber (Cambridge, Eng., 1985), pp. 37–63; Antonia Gransden, 'The Growth of Glastonbury Traditions and Legends in the Twelfth Century', *Journal of Ecclesiastical History* 27 (1976), 37–58; W.A. Nitze, 'The Exhumation of King Arthur at Glastonbury', *Speculum* 9 (1934), 355–61; and John Withrington, 'The Arthurian Epitaph in Malory's "Morte Darthur" ' *Arthurian Literature* vii, ed. Richard Barber (Cambridge, Eng., 1987), pp. 108–111. In March 1983, Derek Mahoney was released from prison in Enfield, having served time for refusing to reveal where he had hidden an ancient cross. He had found the relic, thought to be the Glastonbury cross, in the bed of a dredged lake at Forty Hall.

In 1485 when William Caxton wrote his justificatory Prologue to Malory's *Morte Darthur*, the cited evidences of Arthur's historicity included 'his sepulture in the monasterye at Glastyngburye', 'his seal in reed waxe closed in beryll' at St Edward's shrine in Westminster Abbey, 'at Wynchester the round table' and his status as 'Fyrst and chyef of the thre best crysten' – among the 'IX worthy, the best that ever were'.

CHAPTER SEVEN

The Illustration of Early Printed Books

In 1471 Margaret, Duchess of Burgundy, ordered the Governor of the English Merchant Adventurers in Bruges to finish his translation of Raoul Le Fèvre's *Le Recueil des Histoires de Troyes*. Because of that command, William Caxton (ca. 1422–91)[1] learned the technique of printing, urged on by considerations that he describes in an epilogue:

> And for as moche as in the wrytyng of the same my penne is worn, myn hande wery & not stedfast myn eyen dimmed with ouermoche lokyng on the whit paper and my corage not so prone and redy to laboure as hit hath ben and that age crepeth on me dayly and febleth all the bodye and also be cause I have promysid to dyuerce gentilmen and to my frendes to adresse to hem as hastely as I myght this sayd book Therefore I have practysed & lerned at my grete charge and dispense to ordeyne this said book in prynte after the manner & forme as ye may here see and is not wreten with penne and ynke as other bokes ben to thende that euery man may haue them attones ffor all the bookes of this storye named the recule of the historyes of troyes thus empryntid as ye here see were begonne in oon day and also fynyshid in oon day.[2]

The only extant copy of Caxton's *History of Troy* has a frontispiece made from an engraving (1470) which shows a kneeling man (Caxton?) presenting two volumes to a slender lady whose height is attenuated by a steeple headdress. The intertwined initials C (Charles) and M (Margaret) on a canopy indicate that the recipient is the Duchess whom Caxton described as 'the right hye myghty and vertuouse Pryncesse hys redoubtyd lady'.

---

[1] On Caxton's life and work, see N.F. Blake, *Caxton: England's First Publisher* (London, 1976); George D. Painter, *William Caxton, A Quincentenary Biography of England's First Printer* (London, 1976); *William Caxton: An Exhibition to Commemorate the Quincentenary of the Introduction of Printing into England*, 24 September 1976 – 31 January 1977, British Museum Publications (London, 1976).
[2] W.J.B. Crotch, ed., *Prologues and Epilogues of William Caxton*, EETS OS 176 (London, 1928) pp. 7–8.

The appearance of block books in Western Europe ca. 1430 and Johann Gutenberg's perfecting of the printing press in the early 1450s made it possible to produce books more rapidly, more consistently and in greater numbers than was possible in manuscript workshops.[3] For a time illuminating and printing proceded side by side as printers deliberately attempted to produce the effects of manuscripts by printing on vellum (a material less receptive to ink than was paper), providing elaborate borders and painting illustrations by hand. A *Merlin* (1498) which the leading French publisher, Antoine Vérard (fl. 1485–1512), presented to Henry VII is a deluxe book of this kind (British Library, C22C6). The full folio frontispiece demands attention not only by means of its subject, the bearded, horned devil's engendering of Merlin on a naked, long haired, modest-looking woman, but also by its colours – a blue bedspread embroidered with golden roses, magenta bed curtains and canopy, vivid green shrubbery and blue sky seen through the window. The book's twenty half-page paintings are stock-in-trade chivalric scenes which make no specific reference to Merlin. Battles, feasts, cavalcades, regal conferences, and a hunt are enjoyed by neat, pretty males as lifeless as cardboard cutouts. The old fashioned costumes suggest that the iconographical source was earlier manuscript patterns.

Since fifteenth century Augsburg was a centre for producing playing cards and woodcut pictures, it is not surprising that the oldest extant printed Arthurian romance with illustrations was produced there or that the romance was *Tristan und Isolde* (1484). Its publisher, Anton Sorg, was a woodcut enthusiast whose edition of Reichenthal's book on the Council of Constance had eleven hundred cuts. His *Tristan*, based on a prose version of Eilhart von Oberge's poem, is decorated with fifty-nine small pictures which, without being elaborate, are faithful to the text.[4] Though the expressions are unvaried, the cutting of the faces is competent. Details of costume (crowns, pointed shoes, jupons) and the minimal settings resemble those in the *Tristan* MS pal. germ. 346, painted a quarter of a century earlier and also based on Eilhart.

Like Sorg's *Tristan*, a *Wigalois*[5] which Johannes Knoblauch printed in Strassburg in 1519 suggests that modest books for a middle-class public might be more profitable than time-consuming deluxe editions requiring handwork. The *Wigalois* is a 'Volksbüch' which with its boldly set, condensed text and simple but lively woodcuts is not unlike the chapbooks popular in eighteenth-century England. The hero bears Fortune's Wheel on his shield and helmet. Benign kings, plump ladies, valiant knights in plate armour with lamboys and pauldrons, the naked

---

[3] On early printing and book illustration see David Bland, *A History of Book Illustration* (London, 1969); Robert Brun, *Le Livre français illustré de la Renaissance: étude suivie du catalogue des principaux livres à figures du XVIe siècle* (Paris, 1969); A.M. Hind, *Introduction to a History of the Woodcut*, 2 vols (London, 1935); Alfred W. Pollard, *Early Illustrated Books: A History of the Decoration and Illustration of Books in the fifteenth and sixteenth Centuries* (London, 1917 [1893]) and Loomis, pp. 141–144 and figs 395–420.

[4] Loomis, figs 395–403.

[5] A facsimile edition was published by Georg Olms (Hildesheim and New York, 1973).

giantess Ruel with her club, and a fire-breathing dragon (similar to those in the Wienhausen embroideries) are frontally disposed before trees and towers.

Le Triumphe des Neuf Preux (1487) which Pierre Gérard printed at Abbeville suggests that a woodcut series could be the source of book illustrations.[6] The one exception to the fierce archetypal conquerors standing with feet apart in the usual landscape of grass tufts, bushes and stylised flowers is the tenth Worthy, Bertrand du Guesclin. William Morris, who owned a copy of the book, remarked that 'this bullet-head must have followed a true tradition of the living man'.[7]

Jean Le Bourgeois of Rouen and Jean Dupré of Paris produced the first printed Prose Lancelot, a two-volume edition entitled Le Livre des vertueux faix de plusieurs nobles chevaliers (1488). Already the practises of using the same all-purpose scenes in various works, of repeating the same cut in one work, and of circulating blocks from one print shop to another were established in the trade. The half-page cuts at the beginning of Parts I and II of the Rouen volume – a 'Combat with Long Swords' – had been used in Abbeville for La Cité de Dieu (1486–87). But at least the full folio frontispieces were specifically designed for this work. In a room defined by Corinthian columns and Roman arches an aged King Arthur sits at his Round Table under a baldachin with three impaled crowns. Gawain is on his right and Lancelot on his left, separated from the king by the empty Siege Perilous. Sharing the feast of chickens and other birds on salvers are two unidentified knights wearing gowns with wide reveres and slit sleeves over their plate mail. Servants and dogs occupy the foreground and armed knights with blazoned shields the background while Guenevere, looking decidedly cantankerous, watches from a balcony. No faces express the joys of the court; from king to dogs, all look dissipated, proud, grumpy or bored. In the frontispiece of Volume II, the central scene shows Lancelot, armed with a sword and a shield emblazoned with a flaming sun, as he attacks the dragon from the Corbenic tomb. Peripherally, he arrives at the castle, assists the naked Elaine to step from the boiling bath and, at the conclusion of the sequence, bids her farewell beside a tree from which hang challenging shields.

A feast also opens Volume III; the particular Pentecostal feast when Galahad came to Camelot, as the presence of the hero and the Holy Grail attest. Just as the Flemish illuminators expanded a picture's content by providing additional scenes in border roundels or by combining several stages of a story in a single picture plane, this designer has used windows and machicolated walls to compartmentalize associated events. We see at the top of the picture (perspective being incompetently handled) Lancelot's knighting of his son, a damsel escorting Lancelot to the nunnery, and Galahad kneeling before the Grail. In the middle distance on the left, a monk leads Galahad, in complete mail, through the castle gate which is bisected by an interior pillar. No logical progression of peripheral scenes justifies the iconographic density. The elaborate borders with empty shields (awaiting a

---

[6] Hind, Vol. II, pp. 623–4 and fig. 371.
[7] M.R. James, Catalogue of Manuscripts and Early Printed Books from the libraries of William Morris, Richard Bennett Bertram, fourth Earl of Ashburnham and other sources now in the Morgan Library, 3 vols (London, 1907), II, 9.

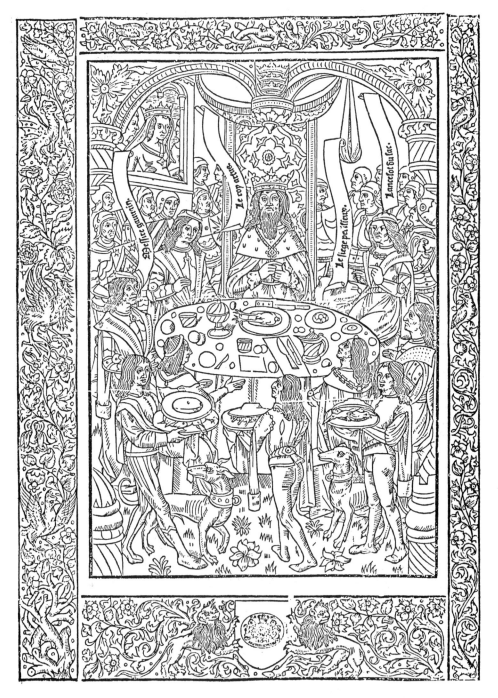

30. Arthur's feast at Camelot. Woodcut from the first printed *Prose Lancelot*, 1488

patron's coat of arms), acanthus leaves, climbing roses, columbines, and such fantastic animals as wyverns and phoenixes imitate fifteenth century Flemish manuscripts.

Antoine Vérard, a former calligrapher and miniaturist whose scriptorium catered to aristocratic patrons, was the leading printer and seller of secular texts. He produced a three-volume *Lancelot* (1494; reprinted 1504), *Tristan* (1494, 1499, 1506), *Merlin* (1498), and *Guiron le Courtoys* (ca. 1501).[8] Many of his books reveal the rather shady practices of a commercially minded entrepreneur who did not blink at vulgarising the product to save money. His designers were not encouraged scrupulously to fulfill what Edward Hodnett defines as the illustrator's function, 'the composition of identifiable characters in action within a setting suggested by the text'.[9] Vérard began using woodcuts in 1485 and until 1492 he had the services of a competent designer, Pierre Le Rouge. After the 1494 *Lancelot*, large new blocks were rare.

In volume one of the *Lancelot*, some of the 13 large and 140 small woodcuts (including initials, borders, and headpieces) do relate to the text, as we see King Arthur receiving the keys of the Dolorous Tower and Lancelot holding up Caradoc's severed head or stealing away with his grandfather's head into a forest. The setting, which shows a competent use of perspective, includes the sculpted tomb, lions scrabbling for bones, a hermit outside his cell, a cross, and a cliff that suggests the wildness of the Grail landscape. A well known artist, Jacques de Besançon, painted some of the woodcuts for a deluxe edition, covering the print with rich, gold-streaked colour to soften the knife's hard edges and produce an effect similar to the work of late medieval miniaturists like Jean Colombe. For volume three, however, only one new block was cut. The others had already illustrated different texts. From Vérard's edition of Ovid's *Metamorphoses* which he entitled *La Bible des Poètes* (1493–4) came 'Scylla with the head of Nesius', (f. 7), 'Glaucus and Circe', (ff. 80 and 213^v) and 'the arming of Achilles and the suicide of Ajax', (f. 198). Three cuts from the *Bataille Judaique of Josephus* (1492) were also used with minor adaptations, such as replacing the high priest's mitre with a crown.[10]

The *Tristan* received even fewer decorations specific to the text. The publisher used, often inappropriately, some of the *Lancelot* cuts, including the one showing the hero with Caradoc's head – a favourite, evidently, since it also appeared in the 1494 edition of Boethius' *Consolation of Philosophy* (*Le Grant Boèce de Consolation*). A Spanish version of Vérard's *Tristan*, translated by Philippe Camas, was published

---

[8]   A facsimile series by the Scolar Press under the editorship of C.E. Pickford has reproduced the 1488 *Lancelot du Lac*, 2 vols (London, 1973); the 1498 *Merlin*, 3 vols (London, 1975); the *Gyron le Courtoys* ca. 1501 (London, 1977); the 1516 *L'Hystoire du Sainct Greall*, 2 vols (London, 1978); the 1489 *Tristan* (London, 1976); the 1532 *Meliadus de Leonnoys* (London, 1980).

[9]   Edward Hodnett, *Image and Text: Studies in the Illustration of English Literature* (London, 1982), p. 17.

[10]   *Catalogue of Books Printed in the Fifteenth Century now in the British Library*, introd. Victor Scholderer (London, 1949).

in 1528 in Seville. Almost every chapter has a rectangular illustration one column wide, separating the title and plot summary from the text. The conventional scenes, frequently repeated, are sometimes enlivened by touches of realism. A courtly couple rides into a forest where a wild boar feeds on acorns. A hound sniffs its way towards a swimming duck. A naked man (Tristan) in a rowboat encounters three Spanish galleons near a rocky shore.

Vérard's *Guiron*, prefaced by an armorial of 169 named knights of the Round Table, was printed on vellum with illuminations (Paris, BN Resere Vélins 622) and in the less expensive paper-woodcut format. Typical of the disregard for accurate iconography is Arthur's Coronation where fleur-de-lis emblazon his pennon and shield.[11]

When William Caxton introduced printing to England in 1476, the motives influencing his choice of books were nationalism and didacticism. He evidently realised that the printed book could assume the responsibility for popular moral teaching that had once been alotted to ecclesiastical art. In comparison with the Burgundians among whom he had lived for thirty years, English knights seemed a poor lot. In his epilogue to the *Order of Chivalry* (1485?), he vividly conveys the chivalric decline that dynastic struggles had hastened. He also offers a remedy:

> O ye knyghtes of Englond where is the custome and usage of noble chyvalry that was used in tho dayes? What do ye now but go to the baynes & playe atte dyse.[12] And some not wel advysed use not honest and good rule ageyn alle ordre of knyghthode. Leve this, leve it and rede the noble volumes of saynt graal, of lancelot, of galaad, of Trystram, of perseforest, of percyval, of gawayn, & many mo. Ther shalle ye see manhode, curtosye, gentylnesse.[13]

Caxton undertook to provide exemplary models by translating (where necessary) and publishing books of chivalric practice and the lives of the Worthies who represented 'a succession of great chivalric moments' in the progression of world history.[14] Of this series Sir Thomas Malory's *Morte Darthur* (1485)[15] was the climax:

---

[11] Other Arthurian books printed on the continent were Michel Le Noir's *Merlin* (Paris, 1505 and 1507); Jehan Jeannot's *Merlin* (Paris, 1510); a *Merlin* co-produced by Jehan Mace of Rouen, Michel Angier of Caen and Richard Mace of Rouen in 1528; *Guiron* published by Jean Petit and Michel Le Noir ca. 1515; Galiot du Pré's *Perceforest* (Paris, 1528) which had as frontispiece the arms of the University of Paris; Philippe Le Noir's *Merlin* (Paris, 1528); and *L'Hystoire du Sainct Greaal* published in Paris by Jehan Petit, Galiot du Pré and Michel Le Noir (1516) and consisting of 'L'Hystoire', 'Perlesvaus', and parts of 'the Vulgate Queste' and 'Lancelot'.

[12] The public baths, which also served as brothels, were centres of dissipation. Caxton adds that the knights who hang about in such places don't know one end of a horse from the other.

[13] *Prologues and Epilogues*, pp. 82–3.

[14] See J.R. Goodman, 'Malory and Caxton's Chivalric Series, 1481–85', *Studies in Malory*, ed. James W. Spisak (Kalamazoo, 1985), pp. 257–274 and Blake, *op. cit.*, pp. 180–1.

[15] The major editions are Eugène Vinaver, *The Works of Sir Thomas Malory*, 3 vols (Oxford,

For herein may be seen noble chyvalrye, curtosye, humanyte, frendly-
nesse, hardynesse, love, frendshyp, cowardyse, murdre, hate, vertue,
and synne. Doo after the good and leue the euyl, and it shal brynge
you to good fame and renommee.[16]

Not everyone was prepared to regard the *Morte* as a moral work. The humanist
Roger Ascham, tutor of Henry VIII's children, denounced it because 'the whole
pleasure standeth in two speciall poyntes, in open mans slaughter, and bold
bawdrye: in which booke, those be counted the noblest Knightes that do kill most
men without any quarrell, and commit fowlest aduoulteres by subtlest shiftes'.
His diatribe proves the work's popularity with the Tudor royal family:

> Yet I know, when Gods Bible was banished the Court, and Morte
> Arthure receiued into the Princes chamber. What toyes, the dayly read-
> ing of such a book may worke in the will of a yong ientleman or a yong
> mayde, that liueth welthily and idelie, wise men can iudge, and honest
> men do pitie.[17]

The fact that this first edition was unembellished probably reflects the publisher's disinterest in illustration *per se*. Of his hundred surviving productions, only
nineteen have woodcuts. In the earliest, *The Mirror of the World* (1481), the wood-
blocks have been crudely cut by inexperienced English artisans from drawings
that imitate the illuminations of a Bruges manuscript. After 1486, Caxton imported blocks from the continent, blocks that were inherited by his successor, the
Alsatian Wynkyn de Worde,[18] on Caxton's death in 1491.

Unlike his employer, de Worde seldom published a book without illustrations,
though he was not particularly concerned with achieving uniformity of effect
through consistency of design and relevancy of content. As a businessman, he
appreciated the fact that pictures made a work more saleable. When he reissued
the *Morte Darthur* in 1498, Caxton's text was enlivened by twenty-one woodcuts,

---

1947; 2nd ed. 1967), based on the Winchester Manuscript, and James W. Spisak, ed., *Caxton's Malory. A New Edition of Sir Thomas Malory's Le Morte Darthur Based on the Pierpont
Morgan Copy of William Caxton's Edition of 1485*, 2 vols (Berkeley and Los Angeles, 1983). For
critical discussions see J.A.W. Bennett, ed., *Essays on Malory* (Oxford, 1963); Larry D.
Benson, *Malory's Morte Darthur* (Cambridge, Mass., 1976); R.M. Lumiansky, ed., *Malory's
Originality, A Critical Study of Le Morte Darthur* (Baltimore, 1964); Beverly Kennedy, *Knighthood in the Morte Darthur* (Cambridge, Eng., 1985); James W. Spisak, ed., *Studies in Malory*
(Kalamazoo, 1985); Toshiyuki Takamiya and Derek Brewer, eds, *Aspects of Malory* (Cambridge, Eng., 1981); and Muriel Whitaker, *Arthur's Kingdom of Adventure; The World of
Malory's Morte Darthur* (Cambridge, Eng. and Totowa, N.J., 1984).
[16] *Caxton's Malory*, pp. 2–3.
[17] *The Scholemaster* (1570) in *English Works of Roger Ascham*, ed. W.A. Wright (Cambridge,
Eng., 1970 [1904]), p. 231.
[18] On de Worde see Edward Hodnett, *English Woodcuts 1480–1535* (1934, rptd. Oxford,
1973); James Moran, *Wynkyn de Worde, Father of Fleet Street* (London, 1960); Henry R.
Plomen, *Wynkyn de Worde and His Contemporaries from the death of Caxton to 1535* (London,
1925).

each of which takes up the full width of the folio page and half its length.[19] Critics have usually taken a rather denigratory tone when describing these woodcuts. Pollard calls them 'very ambitious but badly executed';[20] Hind says they are 'crudely cut in thick line, with regular patches of parallel shading . . . remarkable and somewhat bizarre'.[21] T.F. Dibden, the cataloguer of the Spencerian library which formerly contained the Rylands copy comments:

> They are very little superior to the clumsiest embellishments which distinguish the volumes of the two Coplands; yet to the curious antiquary they have a certain degree of value, and to the bibliographer such a volume, remarkable for the beauty of its execution, as well as the rarity of its appearance, cannot fail to be held in very considerable consideration.[22]

At least two illustrators are involved in the design of this edition. The less important one is imitative, relying on simplified versions of manuscript miniatures. His design for Book X resembles the tournament encounter of Arthur and Tristram as depicted in Paris, BN fr. 99, f. 561. But Iseult and her ladies, watching from a stand in the miniature's upper centre, are omitted in the woodcut. This cut was not repeated in de Worde's 1529 Malory; it had already illustrated scenes in Raoul le Fèvre's *Hystoryes of Troye* (1502 and 1503); *King Ponthus* (1505?); *King Ponthus* (1511); and *Cronycles of Englonde* (1515). 'How Syre Launcelot rode on his adventure' (Book XI) shows Arthur seated at a Round Table so small that there is room for only two courtiers. One goblet and a leg of lamb designate a Pentecostal feast. In the foreground a hermit with elongated forefinger asks why the Siege Perilous (against the wall) is empty. The scene is a simplified version of the long-lived Last Supper archetype.

As Edward Hodnett suggests, the major illustrator is original and entertaining:

> Of all the hands that come under our eyes in English books, the *Arthur* cutter is the most markedly individual and the most amusing. His heavy 'mourning' borders, his diving black birds, the heavy-lidded eyes of his narrow-chested women and long-legged men, and particularly his heavy outlines and habitual use of white line in fur, hair, foliage and in the patchy, enlarged thumb-print shading trimmed at

---

[19] The unique copy is in the John Rylands Library, Manchester. A facsimile was published by Basil Blackwell (Oxford, 1934) and Houghton, Mifflin, (Boston and New York, 1934.) For a description of the woodcut series, see Edward Hodnett, *English Woodcuts*, pp. 309–12.

[20] Pollard, p. 23.

[21] Hind, p. 728.

[22] *Bibliotheca Spenceriana, or a Descriptive Catalogue of the Books Printed in the fifteenth Century, in the Library of George John, Earl Spencer* (London, 1815), VI, 403; quoted by H. Oskar Sommer, ed., *Malory's Morte Darthur*, 3 vols (London, 1889), II, 5.

the edges as though by shears – his idiosyncracies are as good as a signature.[23]

Familiar with the text, he devises illustrations that are faithful to Caxton's titles. Merlin slinks into a formidably rocky cave, urged on by a towering Nimue, whose malign expression betrays the engraver's inability to cut facial details gracefully. A long-haired Gareth supports himself on the shoulders of two men. In one of the most elaborately composed scenes, two gentlewomen (not one, as in the text) attend to the new-born Tristram beside the body of his mother who is already dead, as the arms crossed at the wrist indicate. Beyond the stylized trees of the forest can be seen the realistic architectural detail of a parish church, its tower surmounted by a steeple in the English perpendicular style. The subject of Guen-evere's maying, however, he found too daunting; Book XIX is introduced by the conventional knight-in-the-cart scene.

This artist cares for both historical authenticity and textual accuracy. Illustrating Mordred's attack on the Tower of London, he includes cannons which emit flames and cannonballs, archers, and spear-carrying foot soldiers. Gawain and Ector (Book XVI) wear the fluted armour associated with Emperor Maximilian, gothically elaborate in its gardes-de-bras, demi-greaves and lamboys. Sallets, a type of helmet popular between 1450 and 1510, appear in the cuts for Books XVI, XIX, and XXI.

By the end of the fifteenth century, the elegant sophistication of dress recorded in late medieval manuscripts had given way to the 'bulky look'. A deliberate effect of untidiness was achieved by shaggy hats, wrinkled hose, fluffy shoulder-length hair and short, broad doublets. The stubby shoes worn by Mordred and his cannoneer, Balin, Galahad, La Cote Male Tayle, Gareth's supporters, and Lancelot are the complete antithesis of the impractically elongated pointed footwear that only began to disappear in the 1480s.

While the ladies' dresses still feature trains (a sign of aristocratic rank since they imply the presence of servants to carry them), the headdresses have changed from spiring steeples and wide banner types held out by wires to hoods so long that they have to be split vertically so that the pieces can fall before and behind the shoulders. The ladies standing sideways on the far left in the illustrations of Book I and Book III perfectly illustrate this effect.[24] That the ladies were still more elegantly constrained than the men is evident in the first woodcut where the courtier on the left (the Duke of Cornwall) achieves the chunky effect by wearing a ridiculously short, wide-sleeved doublet with exaggerated lapels. Above, a large hat like the 'luggit' bonnet which James IV of Scotland acquired in 1489 is set rather tipsily on his head.

The flamboyant opulence of Tudor court dress is delightfully conveyed in Thomas Warley's description of a young gallant:

---

[23] *English Woodcuts*, p. 14.
[24] Cf. the painting of Elizabeth of York (1465–1503), Henry VII's queen, in London's National Portrait Gallery.

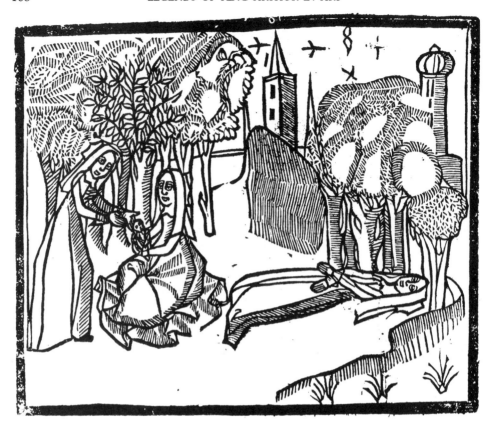

31. The Birth of Tristram. Woodcut by the *Arthur*-cutter for Wynkyn de Worde's
Malory, 1498

> Robert Whethill brags freshly in the Court in a coat of crimson taffeta,
> cut and lined with yellow sarcenet, a shirt wrought with gold, his
> hosen scarlet, the breeches crimson velvet, cut and edged and lined
> with yellow sarcenet, his shoes crimson velvet and likewise his sword-
> girdle and scabbard, a cloak of red frisado, a scarlet cap with feathers
> red and yellow. He hath many lookers-over.[25]

This luxuriousness of colour and cloth the illuminator could convey. But the
Arthur cutter does his best for his characters by careful attention to the texture of
furs, plumes and jewelled crowns, to a generosity of drapery and pleating, and to
a contemporary stylishness. The emphasis is on the real and tangible; the magical
and mystical are largely ignored.

Wynkyn de Worde reprinted his illustrated *Morte* in 1529 using the same woodcuts with the exception of those for Books VI, X, XVI, and XXI. Each of the reused

[25] Muriel St. Clare Byrne, ed., *The Lisle Letters*, selected and annotated by Bridget Boland
(Harmondsworth, 1985), pp. 240–1.

blocks is marred by wormholes. In 1557, William Copland printed *The Story of Kyng Arthur, and also of his noble and Valiante Knyghtes of the Rounde Table*[26] using de Worde's text. William (fl. 1556–69) was probably the brother of Robert Copland (fl. 1508–47), a London printer, bookseller, and stationer whose illustrated books depended almost entirely on de Worde cuts. William looked to the same source, though it is impossible to determine whether the blocks were legitimately borrowed or plagiarized by tracing the illustrations in de Worde's Malory and having them cut onto blocks. In any case, those for Books II, IV, V, VII, IX, XI (where de Worde's right hand cut is used on the left), XII, XIII, XIV, XVII, and XIX duplicate the 1498 edition, while X, XX, and XXI reproduce the 1529 variations. While not identical, the wedding scene for Book III resembles de Worde's in composition, though the number of attendants is reduced and the architectural background features pillars.

Some cuts are completely irrelevant; for example, that for Book XVI shows a wolf devouring a child while a troop of soldiers lurks behind a mountain. Outside the picture plane is a Romanesque castle. In Book IX Lancelot's dragon has become a monster with three human heads whose mouths spew forth the kind of scrolls that in illuminated manuscripts had been filled with identifying inscriptions. The dissociation between picture and text also occurs in Book XXI where Mordred sits enthroned with crown and sceptre at the siege of the Tower of London. His surcoat bears the double-headed eagle, Julius Caesar's coat of arms in the Worthies series, and a symbol of the Holy Roman Emperor. The elaborate floral and faunal borders surrounding the pictures may suggest a desire for aesthetic sophistication, but the effect of quality is sacrificed to convenience and cheapness. Many woodcuts are placed at the bottom of the page to fill up the space, double cuts differ in size, and the de Worde cuts are heavy and smudged, giving an effect of darkness and imprecision.

The last Tudor Malory was Thomas East's *The Story of Kynge Arthur, and also of his Knyghtes of the Round Table* (1585). The text was based on Copland, as are some cuts including the St George-and-the-dragon frontispiece showing a knight in sixteenth-century armour holding a red cross shield. To provide many illustrations at mimimal expense, East used whatever cuts he could get his hands on, with no regard for consistency of size or style. The blocks are of thirteen different sizes, ranging from those for Books I and II which are one column wide to those for Books XX and XXI (b) which take up half a page. Though many of the cuts are modelled on the de Worde Malory illustrations, adaptations have occurred. Gareth now wears a peasant's hooded kirtle. Balin wears cuisses, greaves, and solerets rather than hose and chunky shoes. The Protestant religion having been firmly established, Perceval's aunt and ladies who are clearly not nuns stand outside a castle, not a priory. The vicissitudes which a block might undergo are evident from J. Payne Collier's comment on the cut associated with Book XV[27]:

---

[26] The British Library has three copies, two of them imperfect.
[27] Quoted by Sommer, II, i, n. 3, from J. Payne Collier, *A Bibliographical and Critical account of the Rarest Books in the English Language*, 2 vols (1865), p. 31.

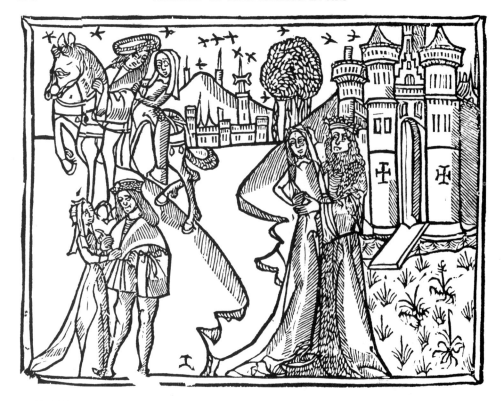

32. Uther, Igraine and the Duke of Cornwall. Woodcut by the *Arthur*-cutter for Wynkyn
de Worde's Malory, 1498

A few of the woodcuts of East's edition are considerably older than the
date when he printed; one of them was used by W. de Worde in 1520
before Christopher Goodwyn's poem 'The Chaunces of a Dolorous
Lover'. The block then came into the hands of W. Copland and having
been used by him in his reprint of the 'Morte Darthur' it was subsequently in the possession of East, who applied it to the same purpose
in his reprint preceding the 16th (sic) book. Thus W. de Worde's 'Dolorous Lover' served the turn, in the hands of Copland and East, to
represent a dead man in a white shirt an hundred winters old.

These later editions are often technically superior to those of de Worde. The
faces show a greater range of expression and the physiognomy is less likely to be
marred by skewed mouths and drooping eyes. The fantastical landscape features
of the *Arthur*-cutter are smoothed and the perspective is more realistic, but the
adaptations are not necessarily improvements, as the print of Merlin's incarceration attests. Without the lowering rocks, the diving birds, the sharp points of
mountain, castle, and steeple, and the towering fay's malevolent features, the
mood of evil and doom is quite removed. The energy of the early woodcuts has

been dissipated – one reason, perhaps, that Thomas East's *Kynge Arthur* was the last illustrated Malory for almost three hundred years.

In addition to the loss of colour and refinement occasioned by the shift from painting to woodcut, there are other important differences between medieval and Renaissance Arthurian illustration. Thirteenth and fourteenth century manuscripts were permeated with the rituals and attitudes of courtly love. Elegant lovers were depicted listening to music, playing chess, meeting in the forest, exchanging kisses, and even reclining naked in bed. Wynkyn de Worde devotes two woodcuts to Launcelot and Guenevere. To illustrate the subject of Book XVIII, 'how Launcelot fyl to hys olde loue ageyn', a lovers' meeting outside the castle gate is shown. Guenevere's crown, train, and long, loose hair signify her royalty and the artist-cutter has managed a suggestion of Gothic sway through the costume's insistent diagonals. Her elongated forefinger raised in admonition captures the illuminators' gestural language. The doleful Lancelot appears to stand on tiptoe with barely suppressed passion, displaying a shapely pair of legs beneath his abbreviated houppelande. For the following book, a two stage cut presents Lancelot's arrival in the cart and his entrance into the castle while Guenevere and an attendant watch from a window. For XVIII Copland substitutes a plump king with crown and sceptre greeting a troup of knights outside a castle and East substitutes a cavalcade of ladies for the knight in the cart. All allusions to courtly love have disappeared.

Neglected also by Copland and East – for the reason that England was no longer a Roman Catholic country – is the iconography of the Grail Quest. Wynkyn de Worde used four cuts depicting monks and nuns and six showing churches, chapels and monasteries. Copland uses half this number and East eliminates the religious entirely. The perilous forest, that numinous place of adventure where knights-errant demonstrated their prowess and nobles pursued the pleasures of the wilderness, is reduced in the two scenes requiring a forest setting – the birth of Tristram and Launcelot's madness – to sparse vegetation near a city. Except for the obligatory cut of Merlin's entombment, Celtic magic is ignored. What remains is a monarch-oriented, castle-centred view of Renaissance England, where the celebration of royal marriages, the reception of ambassadors, the entertainments of tournament and hunt, and the successful waging of wars are major interests.

The earlier books of the *Morte Darthur* present an idealised secular world of knight-errantry, courtly love and magic far removed from ordinary human experience. The pivotal books concerned with the Quest of the Holy Grail are an allegory of the Christian life. The final books have the effect of a chronicle, recording contemporary events with temporal and spatial specificity. They are concerned with intrigues, betrayals, flagrant adulteries and civil wars, with 'Slander and Strife'. Malory's dominant imagery centering on physical loss and decay is appropriate to the theme of courtly disintegration. The illustrators, however, subvert the Malorian joy, the Malorian tragedy and the medieval view of life as a progression towards heaven or hell. Increasingly, they restrict their content to the secular and the contemporary.

East's 1585 edition is the most overtly complimentary to the royal family. He

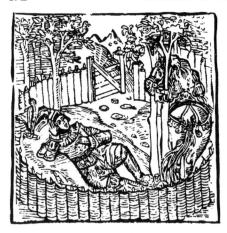

33. The Dolorous Lover woodcut used by
Copland and East to represent a dead monk

removes the lettering which had identified the mounted knight in Copland's
frontispiece as St George, allowing the viewers to see a resemblance to Henry VIII.
Book III's 'The Wedding of Arthur and Guenevere' is illustrated by a copy of
Richard Pynson's 'Traduction & marriage of the princess' (1561), a design that
commemorated Prince Arthur's union with Katherine of Aragon. And in the
woodcut for Book I, the royal arms of England – *gules three lions passant guardant or*
quartered with azure fleur-de-lis – appear on the king's shield. The object of
Malory's Tudor illustrators was neither the creation of a wish-fulfilling dream
world nor the demonstration that *la chevalerie célestienne* was superior to la *chevalerie terrienne*. In the context of Tudor nationalism and imperialism they affirmed the power and glory of the temporal sovereign.

In English literature, the greatest Arthurian work of the sixteenth century was
Edmund Spenser's *The Faerie Queene*. It was written at the height of English
optimism when poets thought it proper to glorify 'the worthy gests of noble
Princes', and in particular, of Elizabeth whom Spenser addresses as 'the most high
Mightie and Magnificent Empresse'.[28] A letter to Sir Walter Raleigh prefixed to the
1590 edition explains his purpose:

> The generall end therefore of all the booke is to fashion a gentleman or
> noble person in vertuous and gentle discipline . . . I chose the hystorye
> of King Arthure, as most fitte for the excellency of his person, being
> made famous by many mens former workes, and also furthest from the
> daunger of envy, and suspition of present time.

[28] On the imperial theme at Elizabeth's court, see Roy Strong, *Splendour at Court: Renaiss-
ance Spectacle and Illusion* (London, 1973) and *The Cult of Elizabeth: Elizabethan Portraiture and
Pageantry* (London, 1977). See also Robin Headlam Wells, *Spenser's Faerie Queene and the
Cult of Elizabeth* (London, Canberra and Totowa, N.J., 1983).

His real intention was to celebrate the queen whose 'rare perfection in mortalitie' mirrored divine virtue.[29]

In the context of Arthur's biography, the linear chronology occupies the time between the hero's emergence from childhood and his acquisition of the throne. As 'Prince Arthur', he has not yet achieved his fame but, the letter to Raleigh suggests, Spenser could count on his audience's bringing to their reading such connotations as those of the Tudor ancestor, the chivalric hero, and the famous conqueror whom Malory described as 'the Noble Kynge Arthure that was Emperoure hymself thorow dygnyté of his hondys'.[30] Having dreamed of the Fairy Queen, Prince Arthur undertakes a quest to achieve her, proving his virtue en route by delivering a succession of victims.

Dynastic celebration is effected through Britomart, descendant of the Trojans and ancestor of Elizabeth; to her the prophet Merlin reveals the great deeds her family descending through Cadwallader will accomplish. The British line will be restored, culminating in a Virgin Queen. Prince Arthur learns his genealogy by reading a chronicle of British kings from Brutus to Uther Pendragon. It is the persistent Tudor myth once more.

The elaborate pictorialism on which Spenser's allegory depends did not inspire contemporary artists. The 1590 edition contains one woodcut.[31] A multiplumed Red Cross Knight (his coat of arms decorating his shield and the horse's caparison) spears a rather innocuous dragon that is nothing like the monster of the text:

> His body monstrous, horrible, and vast,
> Which to increase his wondrous greatness more,
> Was swollen with wrath, and poison, and with bloody gore.
>
> (Bk I, canto XI, vs. 8)

It is a St George-and-the-dragon type most likely introduced to compliment the Order of the Garter. The ceremonies connected with that medieval order, says Roy Strong, 'offered the Elizabethan age something it badly needed – a reinforcement of medieval hierarchical principles and an affirmation of chivalrous ideals'.[32] An

---

[29] Rosemond Tuve, *Allegorical Imagery, Some Medieval Books and Their Posterity* (Princeton, 1966), chapter two, discusses the Allegory of Vices and Virtues as it relates to *The Faerie Queene*.

[30] Henry VIII exploited Arthur's *imperium* in the Act of Supremacy to justify Britain's separation from Rome. Richard Hakluyt coupled the chronicles of the Elizabethan empire builders Sir Humphrey Gilbert, Sir John Hawkins, Sir Francis Drake *et. al.* in *The Principal Navigations, Voyages, Traffiques, and Discoveries of the English Nation* with 'Certaine Testimonies concerning king Arthur and his Conquests'. See Charles Bowie Millican, *Spenser and the Table Round, A Study in the Contemporaneous Background for Spenser's Use of the Arthurian Legend* (Cambridge, Mass., 1932).

[31] The unique copy is in the Rare Books Division of the New York Public Library. The woodcut appears facing page 185.

[32] See 'Saint George for England: The Order of the Garter' in *The Cult of Elizabeth*, pp. 164–186.

edition of Spenser's poetry published in 1611[33] had ornamental headpieces with images from the border repertoire – acanthus leaves, crowned lions, wyverns, and drolleries involving rabbits, apes, stags and hounds engaged in human activities. There were the obvious Gloriana emblems of Tudor roses and phoenixes rising from the flames but no illustrations of the texts. The truth was, as Joseph Addison remarked in his 'Account of the Greatest English Poets' (1694):

> But now the mystic tale, that pleased of yore,
> Can charm an understanding age no more . . .
> We view well-pleased at distance all the sights
> Of arms and palfries, battles, fields and fights,
> And damsels in distress and courteous knights;
> But when we look too near, the shades decay,
> And all the pleasing landscape fades away.

[33] *The Faerie Queen: The Shepheard's Calendar: together with Other Works of Englands Arch-Poet, Edm. Spenser.* Printed by H.L. for Mathew Lownes, 1611.

CHAPTER EIGHT

The Art of Moral Buildings

When Thomas Warton wrote his 'Observations on the Fairy Queen of Spenser' (1754), he commented that 'chivalry is commonly looked upon as a barbarous sport or extravagant amusement of the dark ages'. This denigratory attitude the Age of Reason also applied to Gothic architecture, which John Evelyn condemned in his *Account of Art and Architecture* (1707) as 'Congestions of Heavy, Dark, Melancholy, and Monkish Piles, Without any just Proportion, Use, or Beauty'. Gothic ruins were acceptable in 'picturesque' landscapes where, covered with ivy, mosses and ferns, they became 'a work of nature, rather than of art'.[1] They could inspire the lugubrious philosophizing of pre-romantic poetry, as in Warton's 'The Pleasures of Melancholy':

> Beneath yon ruined abbey's moss-grown piles
> Oft let me sit, at twilight hour of eve
> Where through some western window the pale moon,
> Pours her long-levelled rule of streaming light,
> >   Or let me tread
> Its neighboring walk of pines, where mused of old
> The cloistered brothers: through the gloomy void
> That far extends beneath their ample arch
> As on I pace, religious horror wraps
> My soul in dread repose.

Such emotive medievalism based on architecture Sir Walter Scott, S.T. Coleridge, John Keats, Thomas Love Peacock and other Romantics exploited to create fictional pasts.

A.W. Pugin, a young English architect and a convert to Roman Catholicism,

---

[1] On Gothic and the picturesque see William Gilpin, *Observations, relative chiefly to Picturesque Beauty, made in the Year 1772, on . . . the Mountains, and Lakes of Cumberland, and Westmoreland*, 2 vols (London, 1796) and Charles L. Eastlake, *A History of the Gothic Revival*, ed. J. Mordaunt Crook (Leicester, 1970 [1872]). Other critical discussions are Kenneth Clark, *The Gothic Revival: An Essay in the History of Taste* (London, 1974 [1928]); Christopher Hussey, *The Picturesque: Studies in a Point of View* (London, 1927); David Lowenthal, *The Past is a Foreign Country* (Cambridge, Eng., 1985).

restored moral significance to Gothic architecture when he published *Contrasts: or, a Parallel between the Noble Edifices of the Middle Ages and the corresponding Buildings of the Present Day; showing the Present Decay of Taste* (1836). By juxtaposing engraved scenes from England's medieval past with the same sites as they existed in his own time, Pugin affirmed that the moral and spiritual superiority of medieval society was proven by its architecture.[2]

The theory of Gothic's moral superiority was disseminated by the influential art critic and social reformer, John Ruskin, who arrived at the same conclusion as Pugin by studying Venice's medieval architecture. A good building resulted from the Gothic workman's freedom of expression – 'every jot and tittle, every point and niche of it, affords room, fuel, and focus for individual fire'.[3] 'The Nature of Gothic', the most famous chapter in *The Stones of Venice*, warned industrial society against enslaving the workman and reducing him to 'an animated tool' through the dominance of the machine. The very perfection of classical architecture, a perfection that machinery facilitated, was a sign of moral and aesthetic inferiority: 'art is valuable or otherwise only as it expresses the personality, activity, and living perception of a good and great human soul'.[4] Architects like G.E. Street gladly embraced this moral justification of Gothic Revival, partly because it dissociated the style from Roman Catholic connotations. 'We *are* medievalists and rejoice in the name', Street exclaimed. 'We are medievalists in the sense of wishing to do our work in the same simple but strong spirit which made the man of the thirteenth century so noble a creature'.[5]

An opportunity to practise Gothic Revival theories in an important secular building arose when fire destroyed the Old Palace of Westminster on October 16, 1834. The New Palace of Westminster, consisting of a House of Commons and a House of Lords, was to be built in the English and Christian Gothic Perpendicular Style rather than in the foreign and pagan Classical. The chief architect was Charles Barry, assisted by A.W. Pugin who designed the decorative wood-carving, ornamental metal work, stained glass and encaustic tiles.

In 1841 a Fine Arts Commission was appointed, chaired by Prince Albert (newly married and under-employed) to supervise the decoration.[6] The Commissioners were motivated by two principles: a desire to create public art that would be accessible to people of all classes and a desire to create a national art that would

[2] Nineteenth century examples of this technique of juxtaposition include William Cobbett, *A History of the Protestant Reformation in England and Ireland*, 2 vols. (London, 1829); Robert Southey, *Sir Thomas More: or Colloquies on the Progress and Prospects of Society*, 2 vols. (London, 1829); and Thomas Carlyle, *Past and Present* (London, 1843).

[3] *The Stones of Venice* in *The Complete Works of John Ruskin*, ed. E.T. Cook and Alexander Wedderburn, 39 vols (London, 1903–12), 9, p. 291.

[4] Ruskin, *Works*, 11, p. 201.

[5] *The Ecclesiologist* (Cambridge Camden Society) XIX, NS xvi (1858), 234, quoted by J. Mordaunt Crook, *William Burges and the High Victorian Dream* (Chicago, 1981), p. 55.

[6] T.S.R. Boase, 'The Decoration of the New Palace of Westminster, 1841–1863', *Journal of the Warburg and Courtauld Institutes*, (July, 1954), 319–58; Maurice Bond, *Works of Art in the House of Lords* (London, 1980); R.J.B. Walker, *A Catalogue of Paintings, Drawings, Sculptures and Engravings in the Palace of Westminster*, 7 vols (London, 1959–67).

celebrate England's history and literature. They decided that fresco should be the favoured medium for reasons set forth by the German Nazarene Peter van Cornelius, whom they had consulted:

> It is difficult to impress upon the mind of a nation . . . a general love of art unless you were to use as an instrument Painting upon a large scale and Fresco was particularly suited for this purpose: it was not to be expected that the lower classes of the community should have any just appreciation of the delicacies and prior characteristics of painting in oil; and that they required large and simple forms, very direct action, and in some instances, exaggerated expression.[7]

Following competitions which required artists to submit chalk or charcoal cartoons illustrating subjects from British History[8] or from the works of Shakespeare, Spenser and Milton, three painters received commissions to decorate the House of Lords. William Dyce (1806–64),[9] who studied the art of fresco in Germany and Italy, was instructed to paint the Queen's Robing Room with scenes from Sir Thomas Malory's *Morte Darthur*.[10] If Victor Hugo's *Notre Dame de Paris* (1831) inspired the interaction of literature and art in nineteenth century France,[11] Malory's *Morte*[12] was the most important literary source of Victorian medievalism, providing political, social, moral, religious and aesthetic ideals for an unprecedented industrial age.[13] King Arthur was the beginning of the national mythology.

The letters which Dyce addressed to Charles Eastlake, the Commission Secre-

---

[7] H.T. Ryde, *Illustrations of the New Palace of Westminster* (London, 1849), p. 57.
[8] See Roy Strong, *And when did you last see your father?: the Victorian Painter and British History* (London, 1978).
[9] On this Scottish painter see Marcia Pointon, *William Dyce 1806–1864: A Critical Biography* (Oxford, 1979); David and Francina Irwin, *Scottish Painters at Home and Abroad 1700–1900* (London, 1975). My major source has been a manuscript in the Aberdeen Art Gallery, *Life, Correspondence and Writings of William Dyce, R.A., 1806–1864, Painter, Musician, and Schooler* (sic.) by his son James Stirling Dyce. Copies of many letters are included.
[10] According to James Dyce, while his father was painting a fresco at Osborne, he suggested to Prince Albert that 'the stories of King Arthur and in particular, Sir Thomas Malary's (sic.) "Morte d'Arthur" would supply to English painters subjects of legendary antiquity, and national chivalrous character and would surpass those of the Niebelungenlied, of which so much has been made by the Germans'. Dyce suggested that the commission be given to Daniel Maclise.
[11] Editor's forward p. vii, Emile Mâle, *Religious Art in France: the Twelfth Century*, ed. Harry Bober, trans. Marthiel Mathews (Princeton, 1978).
[12] On available editions of Malory, see Barry Gaines, 'The Editions of Malory in the Early Nineteenth Century', *The Papers of the Bibliographical Society of America*, 68 (1974), 1–17.
[13] General studies of Victorian medievalism include Alice Chandler, *A Dream of Order, the Medieval Ideal in Nineteenth-Century English Literature* (Lincoln, 1970) and Mark Girouard, *The Return to Camelot: Chivalry and the English Gentleman* (New Haven and London, 1981). Joanna Banham and Jennifer Harris, eds, *William Morris and the Middle Ages, a collection of essays, together with a catalogue of works exhibited at the Whitworth Art Gallery, 28 September – 8 December, 1984* (Manchester, 1984) is an invaluable reference. Debra N. Mancoff's unpub-

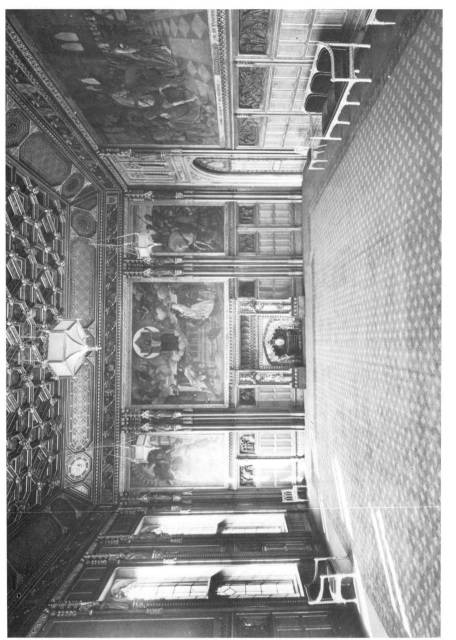

34. The Queen's Robing Room, Palace of Westminster

tary, reveal the difficulties of adapting a literary subject to a fixed architectural setting and at the same time satisfying the commissioners and their royal chairman.[14] Dyce accepted Arthur's historicity but he did not want to be mired in Druidism and sixth-century history.[15] Nor did he want to be limited to the biography of Arthur. On 20 July, 1848 he wrote, 'The question, then, is: whether I ought to adopt such a plan as would enable me to introduce adventures of all the great personages of the Romance, or confine myself to the 'Mort d'Arthur': – in other words – whether the Series of works ought to be historically consecutive, or to consist of a number of pictured adventures of Arthur and his Knights, forming a series only with respect to their allegorical or moral signification'. Personally, he favoured the latter approach:

> I should propose to consider the Companions of the Round Table as personifications of certain moral qualities and select for representation such adventures of Arthur and his Knights as best exemplified the courage magnanimity, courtesy temperance fidelity, devoutness and other qualities, which make up the ancient idea of Chivalric greatness.

When Prince Albert replied that the illustrations should be selected from 'the *widest* circle of the Legend of Arthur', Dyce reminded him that the chief part of the *Morte* 'turns on incidents which, if they are not undesirable for representation under any circumstances, are at least scarcely appropriate in such an apartment' (15 August, 1848). He was willing to expand the repertoire by treating Arthur's character among the Nine Worthies, though he had not decided whether they should be 'represented by statues or by pictures on the walls or in the windows'.[16]

The letter of 25 July is chiefly devoted to complaints about the spaces which the frescoes would fill:

> I do not know what the reasons were which induced the architect to fix the particular spaces laid down in the lithographed plans: but it seems to me very disadvantageous to the effect of the works that all the

lished dissertation, *The Arthurian Revival in Victorian Painting*, 2 vols, presented to Northwestern University, Evanston, Ill. in 1982, contains useful art historical information.

[14] Copies of the Dyce-Eastlake exchanges are in the Aberdeen Art Gallery. Prince Albert's letters relevant to the Dyce frescoes are in the National Art Library, Victoria and Albert Museum, London, file 86GG18. File 86CC47 contains letters which Eastlake, as Secretary of Her Majesty's Commissioners on the Fine Arts, wrote between 1 July, 1852 and 7 September, 1860.

[15] His reading in preparation for the pictorial programme included Robert Southey's 1817 edition of Malory, based on Caxton's first edition, accompanied by commentary and notes; Edward Davies, *The Mythology and Rites of the British Druids Ascertained by National Documents* (1809); John Dunlop, *History of Prose Fiction* (1814, rptd. 1845) which included summaries of Old French Tristan material; and Algernon Herbert's *Attila and Britannia after the Romans* (1836–1841). Dyce frequently shared his researches with the Commissioners.

[16] Letters 50, 25 July, 1848 and 51, 15 August, 1848 discuss at some length the treatment of the Nine Worthies 'as representatives and chief of the highest order of Chivalry'.

compartments with one exception should be upright. As a general rule, I should say it was impossible to make a graceful composition consisting of many figures in an upright space, unless the figures are so diminished in size, as to render the picture (so far as the figures are concerned) an oblong.

The Commissioners passed on the complaint without effecting a change.

The first fresco, completed in 1851, was 'Religion: The Vision of Sir Galahad and his company' (3.42 x 4.43 m), painted above Barry's and Pugin's polychromatic fireplace on the north wall. Dyce had originally offered 'The Departure of the Knights on the Grail Quest', a lively chivalric cavalcade intended to represent the virtue of Piety, while avoiding 'the particular adventures of the St. Greal, which, regarded either as Arthurian myths or as Christian allegories, appeared to me to involve matters of religious and antiquarian controversy, which had better be avoided' (23 November, 1848). The watercolour version[17] has a brilliance of colour and a pageantic grace that the artist never achieved in his frescoes. Probably the commissioners rejected it because, with its sorrowful and aged king and its faithless lovers, it implied chivalric failure. 'The Vision' depicts Bors, Perceval, Galahad and Perceval's sister at the chapel in the Waste Forest where, during the celebration of Mass, they see a white hart transformed into a man who 'sette hym upon the aulter in a ryche sege', while the four lions became the evanglists' signs – a man, a lion, an eagle and an ox.[18]

A heavy cloud border (imitated from manuscript illumination) indicates the visionary nature of the experience. The half-naked Christ, enthroned in an Italianate Renaissance chair, holds up his hands to reveal the stigmata. The other characters wear thirteenth-century costumes, that of Perceval's ascetic sister being unsuitably rich and elegant. Though some of the 'popish' images which appeared in the sepia and chalk study have been omitted or subdued, the effect is still hieratic. These are undoubtedly 'dignified figures taking part in heroic and morally enlightening actions'[19] such as the German Romantics and Prince Albert approved but the result is unemotional and static.

'Religion' was flanked on the left by 'Courtesy' (3.42 x 1.78 m) and on the right by 'Generosity' (3.42 x 1.78 m). Dyce chose Tristram and Launcelot to represent aspects of courtesy which he defined as 'not only courtesy of speech and manners, and other accomplishments of social life, but mercy, generosity, and a certain

---

[17] A pencil, pen, watercolour and bodycolour version (23.4 x 44.1 cm) is in the National Gallery of Scotland, Edinburgh.
[18] The Aberdeen Art Gallery has a sepia and chalk study (23.5 x 30.6 cm) as well as a study of jousting knights. Dyce's literary source was *Morte Darthur*, XVII, 9. My citations and quotations refer to James W. Spisak, ed., *Caxton's Malory, a new edition of Sir Thomas Malory's Le Morte Darthur based on the Pierpont Morgan copy of William Caxton's edition of 1485* (Berkeley, Los Angeles and London, 1983). The artist based his Grail on the print of 'a chalice which is now in Spain'. Could this have been the Valencia Chalice discussed in Chapter Four?
[19] William Vaughan, *German Romantic Painting* (New Haven and London, 1980), p. 215.

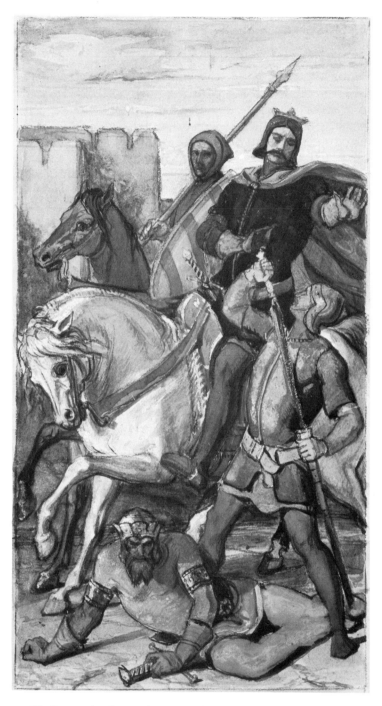

35. Generosity: Launcelot spares Arthur's life. William Dyce's
watercolour version of the Robing Room fresco

modest considerateness in warfare'. With Brangwain as chaperon, Tristram, 'the Romantic personification of social courtesy', harps before the modest Isolde, whose hand rests on the harp which he has taught her to play. His traveller's garb, including scrip, is his disguise in the enemy's household. Through the Romanesque arch we see a huntsman and a young man with a falcon, images alluding to the hero's role as the originator of hunting and hawking rituals. Eastlake praised the fresco as being superior to the Germans in colouring but inferior in 'magnitude of design or multitude of figures' and in 'the grasp of thought which such comprehensive themes suggest'.

'Generosity' illustrates the virtues of courtesy, mercy and loyalty which made Malory's Launcelot 'the flower of earthly chivalry'. The particular incident occurs during King Arthur's siege of the Joyous Gard. As Bors is about to despatch the monarch whom he has unhorsed, he is restrained by Launcelot's order to 'touche hym no more, for I wille neuer see that most noble kynge that made me knyghte neyther slayn ne shamed'. This is one of Dyce's most successful characterisations.[20] The great knight's face reflects nobility, compassion and enormous sadness. It is also one of the artist's most successful treatments of colour. The King's scarlet jupon, golden armlets, and jewelled crown, Bors' scarlet jupon and green hose, Launcelot's royal blue jupon and scarlet-lined green mantle together with his correctly blazoned shield and white horse successfully emulate the stained glass designers' use of contrasting colours to clarify forms.

By 1853 Dyce had begun to decorate the west wall with 'Mercy: Sir Gawain swears to be merciful and "never be against ladies" ' (3.42 x 3.11 m). The source, Malory, III, 13, describes Gawain's accidental slaying of a lady who comes between him and his opponent, the lady's husband. As a penance, Guenevere makes him swear always to defend ladies and never to refuse mercy.[21] This fresco reveals Dyce's weariness with the Westminster commission for the careless figure drawing and the lack of a consistent period sense are obvious. He claimed to adhere to 'the Lombard or Byzantine style, of which our Saxon and Normans are modifications, and of which we have specimens of a more ornate description on such remains as the Shrine of Edward the Confessor in Westminster Abbey Church'. The throne's spiral columns, pointed back and decorative inlays are more Raphaelesque than Anglo-Saxon. Historically inexplicit garments camouflage the femininity of the stolid women.

During the fifteen years spent on the project, the artist complained bitterly about the dampness of the walls, the dirtiness of the surface (which Prince Albert tried to remedy by rubbing with stale bread), the English climate, which allowed one to paint in fresco only during summer, the difficulty of climbing up and down ladders, the tedium of painting chain mail, and his own poor health. A further source of irritation is suggested in his advice to C.W. Cope, another Westminster

[20] Cf. the watercolour version in the National Gallery of Scotland, Edinburgh and the charcoal on paper study, Whitworth Art Gallery, Manchester.
[21] Mancoff, p. 361, notes its topicality: 'In addition to the obvious statement on the protection of the fair sex, special obligation to a female sovereign is suggested'.

painter: 'When you are about to paint a sky seventeen feet long by some four or five broad, I don't advise you to have a Prince looking in upon you every ten minutes or so'.[22] That the irritation was not all on the artist's side is evident from the P.S. of a letter from Balmoral, August 18, 1860: 'I think you ought to point out to Mr Dyce how much injury his dilatoriness has done, & is doing to the cause of the Fine Arts & other artists'.

Dyce's last fresco, left unfinished at his death in 1864 and completed by Cope, was 'Hospitality: the Admission of Sir Tristram to the Fellowship of the Round Table' (3.42 x 6.64 m). It was intended to satisfy Prince Albert's desire for a depiction of the Round Table 'with the king & his knights about him as the historical or rather mythological type of the whole'. The space is crowded with the figures that a Victorian would imaginatively (rather than historically) associate with a medieval court: a king histrionically brandishing his sword, a minstrel with his harp, singers, beautiful ladies, knights in full armour and a champion on a white horse galloping into the castle's great hall.

Despite the irritations, despite the inadequate grasp of the fresco medium which made frequent restorations necessary, Dyce's Robing Room programme had great significance. It affirmed that Arthurian chivalry could provide valid models for Victorian society. It established Malory's *Morte Darthur* as an essential link in the chain of national historiography, and it was the first example of an Arthurian pictorial cycle that took account of historical perspective.

Running around the Robing Room below the paintings were frieze panels of oak. In 1867 H.H. Armstead, a sculptor who had worked on the Albert Memorial, confirmed that he would provide reliefs in wood and stone for £1900.[23] While Dyce's frescoes are episodic and hortatory, Armstead's eighteen bas-reliefs are narrative. Based on Malory, they illustrate two story lines. The biography of Arthur, including his birth, success in the sword test, wars, marriage, encounter with the giant, last battle and withdrawal to Avalon, occupies panels one to eight and ten to twelve. Scenes from the 'Quest of the Holy Grail' are carved on panel nine and on thirteen to eighteen. The figures in their heavily draped robes, together with their wide-nostrilled war horses, are statuesque, dignified and ponderous like those in a Roman frieze. Only the serpentine figurehead of Arthur's ship in 'How King Arthur gate his Sword Excalibur' and of the Otherworld barge add what J.L. Tupper called 'a weird working of fancy hitherto the sole heritage of Blake'. In its totality the Robing Room is an opulent example of decorated Victorian Gothic, somewhat dark but imbued with a sense of power and glory.

The revival of large scale mural painting was further stimulated by the Oxford Union murals of 1857.[24] Built in 1856 as a combined debating hall, library and

[22] Prince Albert also annoyed the artist with his incessant suggestions for improving the designs. In a letter of 9 November, 1853 Eastlake passed on the royal critique of 'Mercy': the knight's head 'wants to be relieved of the background' and the legs would be improved by adding a sandal.

[23] R.J.B. Walker, *op. cit.* Pt. III, *Sculpture* (London, 1961) gives the subjects' literary sources, and relevant correspondence.

[24] References include John Christian, *The Oxford Union Murals* (Chicago, 1981) with a

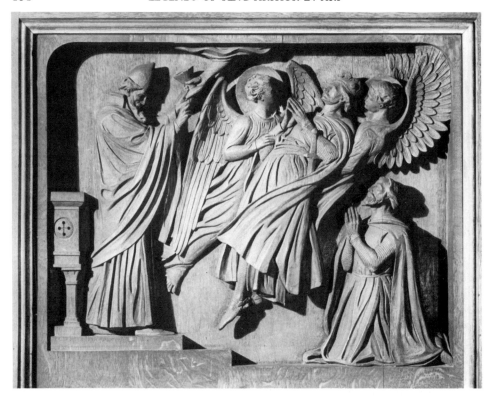

36. Sir Galahad's Soul Borne to Heaven. H.H. Armstead's Robing Room bas-relief

reading room, the Union provided an opportunity for 'a new notion of "art-architecture" involving richly associational decorative sculpture and painting'.[25] The architect, Benjamin Woodward, adopted the Venetian Gothic style which Ruskin recommended. The new House of Commons provided a close analogy for in both chambers benches were arranged facing inwards from opposite sides, the seat for the Speaker or President was placed at one end and there was an observers' gallery. The Union's apsidal ends, exposed beams, a clerestory consisting of two circular six-foil windows in each of ten bays, buttresses, and red and white banded voussoirs combined Venetian Gothic with 'Glastonbury Kitchen' Early English.[26] Alexander Munro's relief carving of King Arthur and his knights filled the tympanum over the Frewin Court entrance. Designed by Dante Gabriel

microfiche of 84 colour illustrations; W. Holman Hunt, *Oxford Union Society: The Story of the Painting of the Pictures on the Walls and the Decorations on the ceiling of the Old debating hall (now the library) in the years 1857–8–9* (Oxford and London, 1906); J.D. Renton, *The Oxford Union Murals*, 2nd ed. (privately printed, 1983); Rosalie Mander, 'Rossetti and the Oxford Murals, 1857', *Pre-Raphaelite Papers*, ed. Leslie Parris (London, 1984).

[25] Eva Blau, *Ruskinian Gothic: The Architecture of Deane and Woodward 1845–1861* (Princeton, 1982), pp. 82–92.

[26] In *The Saturday Review*, 26 December, 1857, Coventry Patmore approved the adapted

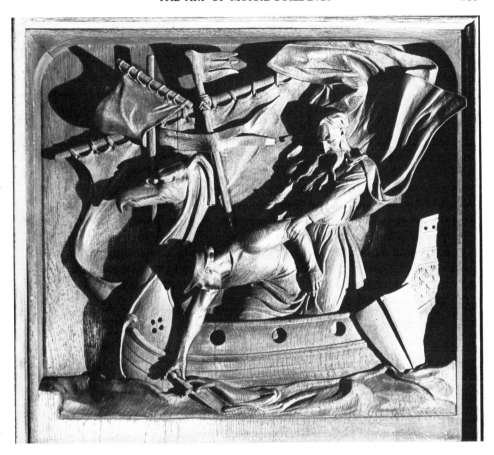

37. How Arthur attained Excalibur. H.H. Armstead's Robing Room bas-relief

Rossetti, it shows the Pentecostal Feast which initiated the Grail Quest. At a doughnut-like table similar to that in BN fr. 343, f. 3 Arthur sits enthroned with orb and sword while his kneeling knights look upward at the angel-borne Grail. Typical Pre-Raphaelite symbols are the table's provisions – a peacock, signifying Pride, the questers' paramount sin, a fish, an early Christian sign for Christ based on the letters of the Greek word, and bread and wine, the Mass elements signifying Christ's body and blood. Like medieval sculptures, this one was brightly painted.

How the group of English artists known as the Pre-Raphaelites became involved in the project has been described by Dante Gabriel Rossetti:

> thinking of it only as his beautiful work and without taking into consideration the purpose it was intended for . . . I offered to paint figures

Venetian Gothic as 'incomparably better fitted for secular purposes than the contemporary Northern manner, which was continually tending to the entire abolition of the wall'.

of some kind in the blank spaces of one of the gallery window bays and another friend who was with us – William Morris – offered to do the second bay. Woodward was greatly delighted with the idea; as his principle was that of the medieval builder to avail himself in any building of as much decoration as circumstances permitted at the time, and not prefer uniform bareness to partial beauty. He had never before had a decided opportunity of introducing picture work in a building.[27]

Morris and Rossetti were joined by Edward Jones (later Burne-Jones), Val Prinsep, Arthur Hughes, John Pollen, and R.S. Stanhope. Morris and Jones were Oxford friends who shared an enthusiasm for a 'treasure' of life-long significance, as Georgiana Burne-Jones describes:

> It was Southey's reprint of Malory's *Morte d'Arthur*: and sometimes I think that the book never can have been loved as it was by those two men. With Edward it became literally a part of himself. Its strength and beauty, its mystical religion and noble chivalry of action, the world of lost history and romance in the names of people and places – it was his own birthright upon which he entered.[28]

The artists, several of them quite inexperienced, were caught up in 'the High Victorian Dream'. Art, medievalism, and beautiful women, whom they referred to as 'stunners', were their enthusiasms and Rossetti was 'the planet around which we all revolved'.[29] Having agreed with the Union building committee to give their time freely if the Union would pay for the materials, lodging, travel and food (including great quantities of soda water), the painters began 'the Jovial Campaign' during the Long Vacation. Burne-Jones later remembered the Oxford time as 'blue summer then and always morning and the air sweet and full of bells'.

The chosen technique was not fresco but distemper, executed in the manner of Rossetti's watercolours. The punning phrase 'O tempera, O Morris' attached to William's inexpert effort was apt for all. The dampness of the brick and mortar walls and the inadequate preparation of the surface were fatal to preservation. The chosen subject was the *Morte Darthur*, suggested, perhaps, by Morris and Burne-Jones or even Rossetti, who had declared the *Morte* and the Bible the greatest books in the world.[30] The text was to provide not allegorical models of

---

[27] Oswald Doughty and J.R. Wahl, eds, *Letters of Dante Gabriel Rossetti*, 4 vols (Oxford, 1965–67), II, pp. 405–6.

[28] Georgiana Burne-Jones, *Memorials of Edward Burne-Jones*, 2 vols (London, 1904), I, p. 116. Christian, *op. cit.*, p. 26, suggests that they would also have known the Arthurian material from Kenelm Digby's *The Broad Stone of Honour* (1823), Matthew Arnold's 'Tristram and Iseult' (1852), Alfred Tennyson's early poems, and Charlotte Yonge's *The Heir of Redclyffe* (1853).

[29] *Memorials*, I, 164.

[30] The entry for 1 April, 1855 in *The Diary of Ford Madox Brown*, ed. Virginia Surtees (New Haven and London, 1981) records that he and Rossetti had been 'Talking about King Arthur, in praise of, & how it would illustrate'.

virtue in the Dyce manner but inspiration of a kind that Burne-Jones described to a friend of later years:

> What is the highest thing I know? Beauty. And when imagination is added thereto, we are close to the secret of all things, the hidden recesses of God. And for daily use we'll say pretty, and for imagination for daily use we will say fancy, and the big words shall be used for the feast of Pentecost.[31]

Although Rossetti wrote to Gilchrist that there was 'a perfect scheme . . . for the whole series',[32] the failure to complete the project makes it difficult to determine what it was. Nevertheless, there are connections that knowledge of the text clarifies. Rossetti told Charles Eliot Norton, 'the series commences with Pollen's picture . . . and ends with Hughes's';[33] that is, with the acquisition and return of Excalibur. Malory has two Excaliburs. The sword in the stone, which yields only to the destined hero, confirms Arthur's right to the throne. When that sword is broken in a fight with King Pellinore, it is replaced by another which the king receives as an Otherworld gift that signifies his temporal reign:

> So they rode tyll they com to a laake that was a fayre watir and brode. And in the myddis Arthure was ware of an arme clothed in whyghte samyte, that helde a fayre swerde in that honde.   (I,25)

In Pollen's mural, which closely follows the text, the brandished sword has a scarlet scabbard, a protective amulet that prevents an enemy from wounding the king. The Lady of the Lake, wearing a golden robe and circlet of flowers, walks on the water. Arthur reaches from the boat to grasp Excalibur while the red-robed Merlin watches. Their horses are tied to trees on shore. A Pre-Raphaelite addition is the flight of water-birds, no doubt painted from nature.

Hughes' subject, 'Arthur carried away to Avalon and the sword thrown back into the lake', differs from the other murals in its subdued tonality. As Tennyson does in his 'Morte d'Arthur' (1842), a possible source, Hughes chooses a night setting for the dark-robed queens and agonised Bedivere. The only luminosity derives from the arm clothed in white samite, the golden barge, Arthur's golden armour and circlet and Morgan's golden buttons.[34]

'Merlin and Nimue' (Burne-Jones), 'Sir Gawaine and the Damsels at the Foun-

---

[31] Letter to Mrs H.M. Gaskell, n.d., Fitzwilliam Museum, Cambridge, Department of Manuscripts, Burne-Jones papers, XXVII, 30.31.

[32] *Letters*, II, 406.

[33] *Letters*, I, 337.

[34] Lady Pauline Trevelyan disagreed with Ruskin's view that Hughes' mural was not decorative enough and that a moonlight effect was unsuitable. She thought that the effect was 'pleasant & reposeful among all the blue skies, red haired ladies, and sunflowers. Several of the mourning ladies are very pathetic'. Virginia Surtees, ed., *Reflections of a Friendship. John Ruskin's Letters to Pauline Trevelyan 1848–1866* (London, 1979), pp. 277–8.

tain' (Stanhope), and 'Sir Pelleas and the Lady Ettarde' (Prinsep) are narratively related. Malory's Nimue or Nyneve is the fée who beguiles the enamoured Merlin into teaching her the arts of magic, then uses her knowledge to incarcerate him under a rock.[35] She is motivated by a desire to guard her virginity and by fear of the 'devyls son'. Burne-Jones uses the two windows that interrupt the wall space to compartmentalize his subject and dramatize the opposing powers. Her long dark hair loose to indicate her maidenhood, Nimue stands on the left, playing a lute to facilitate the spell. Merlin confronts her from the right while the rocky prison rises between them. The artist would return to the subject in a famous oil painting, 'The Beguiling of Merlin'.

Book IV of the *Morte* also contains the Stanhope and Prinsep subjects. Riding in the forest of Arroy, noted for its strange adventures, Gawain, Yvain and Marhault find three ladies at a fountain – an old lady with a golden garland to suggest honour and wealth, a thirty-year-old lady with a circlet of gold to suggest courtly sophistication, and a fifteen-year-old damsel with a garland of fresh flowers to symbolise youth and beauty. After choosing a companion, each knight rides off to seek adventures. Stanhope simplifies the subject by eliminating Yvain and Marhault. The damsel kneels before Gawain in a reversal of courtly love etiquette. However, this Gawain is not a model of *courtoisie*. He behaves so badly that his lady could 'sey but lytyll worshyp of hym'. He commits a flagrant offence against honour when, having promised to intercede for Pelleas with the haughty Ettard, he sleeps with her. The benevolent Nimue bespells Pelleas so that he loves and marries her while Ettard, now love-stricken, is rejected, as Prinsep shows.

Morris, too, treats the pains of love, choosing Palomydes' jealousy of Tristram. Like Pisanello, the artist gives the pagan knight black hair and a swarthy skin. The mural suffers from technical shortcomings which Morris concealed as best he could by covering a large part of the space with apple trees and sunflowers. He went on to decorate the roof with vegetation, beasts and grotesqueries that inspired a local versifier:

> Here gleams the dragon in the air;
> There roams along a dancing bear;
> Here crocodiles in scaly coats
> Make love to birds with purple throats . . .[36]

The most accomplished mural was Rossetti's,[37] described in the letter to Norton:

---

[35] She is also known as the Damsel of the Lake. Malory distinguishes her from the Lady of the Lake, who gives Arthur his sword and scabbard and subsequently is decapitated by Balin because of a family feud. Nimue becomes Arthur's supernatural protector after Merlin's disappearance.

[36] See K.L. Goodwin, 'William Morris' "New and Lighter Design" ', *Journal of the William Morris Society*, II/3 (1968).

[37] There are numerous studies in London's Tate Gallery, Oxford's Ashmolean Museum, Birmingham City Art Gallery and Museum, and Cambridge's Fitzwilliam Museum. The

My own subject (for each of us have as yet done one only) is Sir Launcelot prevented by his sin from entering the chapel of the San Grail. He has fallen asleep before the shrine full of angels, and, between him and it, rises in his dream the image of Queen Guenevere, the cause of all. She stands gazing at him with her arms extended in the branches of an apple-tree . . . The works you know are all very large, – the figures considerably above life size, though at their height from the ground they hardly look so . . . There is no work like it for delightfulness in the doing, and none I believe in which one might hope to delight others more according to his powers.

The subject enabled him to use the Christian symbolism and typology learned from studying original works and reproductions of Netherlandish painters like the Van Eycks, Dürer woodcuts, and illuminated manuscripts in the British Museum.[38] He adopted the medieval artists' 'principle of disguising symbols under the cloak of real things' so that 'the whole universe "shone" as Suger would say, "with the radiance of delightful allegories" '.[39]

On the right, scarlet-gowned Launcelot, with Burne-Jones' face, sleeps beside the well where hang the shield and helmet which he will soon lose because of his unworthiness. On the left kneels the Damsel of the Sanct Grael, holding a long-stemmed cup and basket of bread (the mass elements). Above her hovers the traditional symbol of the Holy Spirit, the white dove, which bears a golden censer, as Malory describes, in the *Morte's* Grail processions. The chapel steps are strewn with a lily (purity), poppy (forgetfulness) and rose (sexual passion). There are also a bell, one of Rossetti's favourite symbols of religious devotion, and attendant angels with splendid blue and magenta wings.

Jane Burden, the artist's future mistress and Morris' future wife, was a model for the Queen, though the head also shows traces of Elizabeth Siddal. Voluptuously alluring in her gown of green (symbolising carnal love), Guenevere stretches her arms along the branches in a parody of the Temptation and Crucifixion. The apple tree signifies the fall of man, tempted by the woman's apple (which Guenevere holds) while the Cross, its anti-type, symbolises man's redemption. In medieval legend the tree of the Cross grew from a seed of the Edenic apple. To emphasise the mural's typological connections, a green serpent hangs suspended

---

Ashmolean watercolour of the uncompleted mural (71 x 107 cm) may be a copy by H. Treffry Dunn, who painted the same scene on carved mirrors which originally belonged to Algernon Swinburne. They are now in Wightwick Manor. On the mural and various studies see Virginia Surtees, *The Paintings and Drawings of Dante Gabriel Rossetti (1828–1882), a Catalogue Raisonné*, 2 vols (Oxford, 1971), I, nos 91–93 H and II, nos 117–123.

[38] The British Museum manuscript collection in 1857 included the Cotton, Harley, Sloane, Royal, Landsdowne, Hargrave, Burney, Kings, Arundel and Egerton manuscripts, as well as the additional series begun in 1756. By 1854 its numbering had reached 19720. Ruskin had an extensive collection which he readily made available. See Julian Treuherz, 'The Pre-Raphaelites and Medieval Illuminated Manuscripts', *Pre-Raphaelite Papers*, pp. 153–169.

[39] Erwin Panofsky, *Early Netherlandish Painting*, I, pp. 141–2.

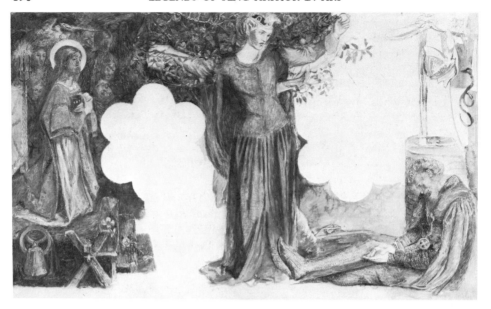

38. Sir Lancelot's vision of the Sanc Grael. Dante Gabriel Rossetti's watercolour study for the Oxford Union mural

above the hero's head. Coventry Patmore in the *Saturday Review* 4 (26 December, 1857) waxed enthusiastic about the 'mysteriousness' of Rossetti's colouring:

> The colour is as sweet, bright and pure as that of the frailest waif of cloud in the sunrise; and yet, if closely looked into, there is scarcely a square inch of all those hundred square feet of colour which has not half-a-dozen different tints in it.

Ruskin described Rossetti's mural as 'the finest piece of colour in the world'.[40] Though he did not think much of the drawing, the murals' brilliance also struck William Bell Scott who visited the Union in 1858:

> They are poems more than pictures – being large illuminations and treated in medieval manner, not studied from nature . . . the colour is all positive, like medieval work, the execution of stippling like a miniature.[41]

For various reasons, the group dispersed without completing the programme. In June 1859, to Rossetti's disgust, the Union hired William Riviere and his son,

---

[40] *Memorials*, I, 168. Today the colour is best appreciated by studying the Ashmolean watercolour.
[41] William Bell Scott, *Autobiographical Notes*, ed. W. Minto (London, 1892), II, p. 42.

Briton, to fill the three empty panels for a payment of £150. By choosing scenes from the life of Arthur, Riviere altered the Pre-Raphaelite scheme both chronologically and thematically. 'The Education of Arthur by Merlin' was derived not from Malory but from Spenser's *Fairie Queene*, Bk. I, canto IX, vs. 5. The youth lies at the feet of the wizard, iconographically defined by his wand, hourglass, skull, illuminated manuscript and a prophetic parchment showing Excalibur in a clenched hand, a crown, a snake, and a crescent moon. 'Arthur's Wedding, with the incident of the White Hart' and 'King Arthur's first victory with the sword' were the other subjects. These murals, executed in what John Christian calls 'Michelangelo's Grand Manner', were competent but uninspired. Rossetti sarcastically described them as 'wonderful exceedingly'.

The murals rapidly deteriorated. In 1906, when they were photographed, they were so fragile that 'a mere breath upon the surface, while insufficient to blow away the cobwebs, was yet enough to make the tattered fragments of the painting fall down in dust'.[42] Further restoration and cleaning occurred in 1935–36[43] and in 1984 but even today they are difficult to see because of the debilitating light from the clerestory.

A kind of moral architecture relying not on the ornate splendours of High Gothic but on the simplicity of Early English received its first domestic expression in 1859 when Philip Webb built a house for William Morris and his bride Jane Burden. Stefan Muthesius calls Red House at Bexley Heath, Kent 'the most famous building of the later nineteenth century . . . the beginning of simplicity in modern architecture, at least in domestic design'.[44] In the draft of a lecture given in 1894,[45] Morris wrote:

> If I were asked to say what is at once the most important product of Art, and the thing most to be longed for, I should answer, a beautiful House.

Set in an orchard of apple and cherry trees, Red House was a place 'after his own heart', 'a most noble work . . . more a poem than a house . . . but an admirable place to live in too'. The real estate agent's advertisement, when the house was put up for sale in 1866, mentions such medieval features as 'an old English Oriel Window', 'a Fine Hall, entered through a Porch with a Lofty Gothic Arch' and a 'charming Greensward, with Well, canopied in the Old English Style'.[46] There

---

[42] C.J. Holmes, introduction to W. Holman Hunt, *Oxford Union Society* (1906).

[43] Derek Patmore, 'The Wall Paintings in the Oxford Union Library', *Studio*, III (1936), 324–5.

[44] Stefan Muthesius, *The High Victorian Movement in Architecture 1850–1870* (London, 1972), p. 203. See also Philip Henderson, *William Morris, His Life and Friends* (London, 1967), pp. 58 ff.; Ray Watkinson, 'Red House Decorated', *Journal of the William Morris Society*, VII/4 (1988), 10–15; *Memorials*, I, pp. 146, 208–213; Harris and Banham, *William Morris and the Middle Ages*, 109–124.

[45] 'On the Illuminated Books of the Middle Ages'.

[46] *The Collected Letters of William Morris*, ed. Norman Kelvin, 2 vols (Princeton, 1984–1987), I, p. 43.

were also flagged floors, exposed beams, a minstrel's gallery and a garden inspired by an illuminated *Roman de la Rose*, probably BL Harley 4425. The designers' chief purpose was to create a setting in which such decorative features as
stained glass windows, embroidered wall hangings, painted furniture, wood
carvings, hand made screens and murals would show to advantage.

In the summer of 1860 Georgiana and Edward Burne-Jones arrived to assist
with the interior decoration. For the drawing room they 'fixed on' the Middle
English romance 'Sir Degrevaunt',[47] perhaps because its painted and sculpted
chamber was a literary forerunner of the Red House interior. Or it may have
seemed appropriate because the romance's hero was not only an Arthurian
knight-errant but also a bridegroom and English property owner. Burne-Jones
designed seven pictures, three of which he painted on the wall in tempera. The
historical accuracy of the costumes was a major concern, with Rossetti's copy of
Bonnard's *Costume Historique* being a likely source for the knight's dagged houppelande.[48] Myldore wears a late fourteenth century surcoat with low cut sides and
gored skirt similar to the costume which Morris had designed for Jane ca. 1857.[49]
Indeed, the bride with her luxuriant dark hair, sensuous lips and sulky expression
looks remarkably like Morris' wife, while the groom resembles William himself.

In his bachelor days at Red Lion Square, where, said William Allingham, all the
talk was of 'medievalism' and of 'beauty of form and colour',[50] Morris had already begun to design his own furniture on which he painted knights and ladies.
In the Red House the furniture included a great settle from Red Lion Square, a hall
cupboard and a dining room buffet, all 'intensely medieval', in Rossetti's phrase.[51]

[47] It was among the Thornton Manuscript romances which the Camden Society published
in 1844. The three scenes painted in the Red House wall are still *in situ*, under glass. A
pencil on blue paper study squared for transfer (27 x 26.7 cm) belongs to Birmingham City
Museum and Art Gallery, a second drawing (22.2 x 34.3 cm), which includes the bridal
guests, belongs to the Royal Institute of British Architects while the Fitzwilliam Museum,
Cambridge has a watercolour (30 x 47 cm). See *Burne-Jones: the paintings, graphic and
decorative work of Sir Edward Burne-Jones 1833–98*, catalogue of an Arts Council of Great
Britain Exhibition, Hayward Gallery, London, 5 November, 1975 – 4 January, 1976; Southampton Art Gallery, 24 January – 22 February, 1976; City Museum and Art Gallery, Birmingham, 10 March – 11 April, 1974, nos 63–65. See also *Morris & Company in Cambridge*,
Cambridge, 30 September – 16 November, 1980, nos 15–16.
[48] The complete title of this work which indicates the Continental fascination with medievalism is *Costumes des XIIIe, XIVe, et XVe siècles extraits des monuments les plus authentiques
de peinture et de sculpture (dessines engravés par Paul Mercuri) avec un texte historique et
descriptif* par C. Bonnard, 2 vols (Paris, 1829–30). See Roger Smith, 'Bonnard's *Costume
Historique* – a Pre-Raphaelite Source Book', *Costume* VII (1973), 28–37. Rossetti bought 'a
most stunning copy – perfectly new' for three pounds, according to a letter to F.G. Stephens
written before September 18, 1849.
[49] The pink gown of finely woven wool and its white surcoat with deep cut sides and
gored skirt are now in the William Morris Gallery, Walthamstow.
[50] *William Allingham, A Diary*, ed. H. Allingham and D. Radford (Harmondsworth, 1985
[1907]), p. 75.
[51] See Clive Wainwright, 'Pre-Raphaelite Furniture' in *The Strange Genius of William Burges
'Art-Architect', 1827–1881*, ed. J. Mordaunt Crook (London and Cardiff, 1981). The Medieval

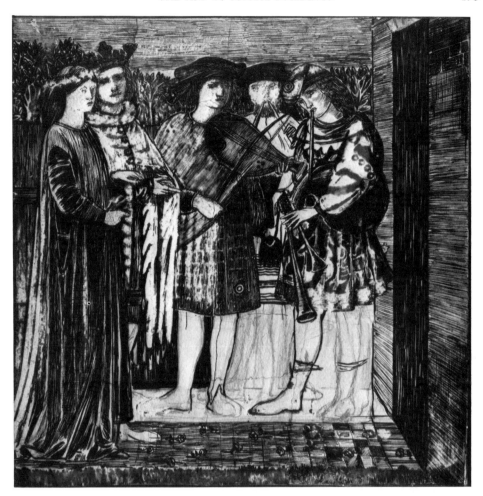

39. The Wedding Procession of Sir Degrevaunt. Edward Burne-Jones' study for a Red
House wall painting

On the cupboard's pictorial doors were three figures in a garden.[52] A woman sits
on the ground, partly supported by a man who kneels beside her, offering her
some fruit. On the right another woman stands with one hand on a tree while
with the other she raises her skirt in a typically medieval gesture. Ray Watkinson
identifies them as Georgiana Burne-Jones, Edward Burne-Jones and Lizzie Siddal
cast as La Belle Iseult, Tristram and Brangwain. They are simultaneously in the
garden of Red House and of the Joyous Gard where they enjoyed 'alle manere of

Court at the International Exhibition of 1862 popularised painted furniture that imitated
medieval types.
[52] The composition can best be seen in the drawing, formerly in the Janet Camp Troxell
Collection. See Watkinson, 14.

myrthes that they could deuyse'. So the Pre-Raphaelites memorialised life as art just as fifteenth century painters had done to flatter their patrons.

The most important result of the Red House experience was the founding of the firm Morris, Marshall, Faulkner and Co. for reasons that Morris described to Andreas Scheu:

> At this time the revival of Gothic architecture was making great progress in England and naturally touched the Pre-Raphaelite movement also; I threw myself into these movements with all my heart: got a friend to build me a house very medieval in spirit . . . and set myself to decorating it; we found, I and my friend the architect especially, that all the minor arts were in a state of complete degradation especially in England, and accordingly in 1861 with the conceited courage of a young man I set myself to reforming all that and started a firm for producing decorative articles.[53]

In 1862 Walter Dunlop, a Bradford merchant described as one of those men of culture who 'leaven the lump of the money-getters', leased Harden Grange near Bingley in Yorkshire.[54] Immediately he made extensive additions, including an entrance hall and staircase that he wished to adorn with stained glass. He offered the commission to Morris, who was at the forefront in the revival of medieval crafts. Paul Lawson has described the procedure that would have been followed in executing the Harden Grange work:

> First he would consult with the client in order to establish the kind of window-opening to be filled and the subject or design required. An artist – usually one of the circle – would then be commissioned to produce a cartoon or preparatory drawing. Next the different pot metals would be selected (a procedure in which Morris played a decisive part) and cut to size. The glass-painter, a skilled craftsman using staining agents, would then transfer the cartoon image to the glass on the side to be viewed. When the glass had been fired the pieces would be joined together by means of lead cames, and the window was then ready to be fixed into the opening.

Morris's own ideas about the differences between glass-paintings and oils or frescoes are contained in a pamphlet for the Foreign Fair at Boston, 1883:

---

[53] Philip Henderson, ed., *The Letters of William Morris* (London, 1950), pp. 185–6. For another account see *Memorials*, I, 213.

[54] On the Harden Grange stained glass, see A. Charles Sewter, *The Stained Glass of William Morris and his Circle*, 2 vols (New Haven and London, 1974); Herbert E. Wroot, 'Pre-Raphaelite Windows at Bradford', *Studio*, LXXII (1917), 69–73; Paul Lawson, 'The Tristram and Isoude Stained Glass Panels', *The Bradford Antiquary*, 3rd ser. 1 (1985), 50–55; Banham and Harris, 178–186.

Absolute blackness of outline and translucency of color are then the
differentia . . . The drawing and composition have to be much more
simple, and yet more carefully studied, than in paintings which have
all the assistance of shadow and reflected lights to disguise the faults
. . .

After these we ask for beautiful color. There may be more of it, or less,
but it is only rational and becoming that the light we stain should not
be changed to dirt or ugliness. Color, pure and sweet, is the least you
should ask for in a painted window.

Morris probably suggested the subject. Tristram and Isoude, a story of frus-
trated love, seems to have had a personal relevance. When he painted his Oxford
Union mural, the model for Sir Palomydes was Algernon Swinburne, for La Belle
Iseut Jane Burden, the beautiful Oxford 'stunner' to whom both Morris and
Rossetti were attracted, and for Tristram, Morris himself. In 1857, as well, his pen,
ink and a pencil sketch 'Iseult on the Ship' showed Jane as the anguished queen
and in 1858 she was the model for his only surviving painting, known as 'Queen
Guinevere' or 'La Belle Iseult'. The latter identification is now preferred on the
grounds that the dog in the painting is Petitcru.[55] By 1862, Morris had married
Jane but increasingly it was Rossetti who played ardent lover while Morris found
himself the rejected husband.[56]

When the Bradford Art Galleries and Museum acquired the Tristram panels in
1917, Dunlop's niece passed on a summary of the *Romance of Tristram* apparently
prepared by Morris and sent to Dunlop for approval. Along with the resumé is a
list of specific subjects suitable for illustration. While Malory was chiefly interested in Tristram as knight-errant and successful jouster and tourneyer, Morris
totally excludes material unrelated to the love story. As the costumes, armour,
furniture and weapons indicate, his Arthurian Age is the late fourteenth or early
fifteenth century. The colours, which Morris designated (thus providing a unifying element) were chiefly dark green, white, ruby red, gold and brown. For
identification and narrative continuity, plot summaries in Caxton-like language
were included at the bottom of each panel.

To provide cartoons for the thirteen panels Morris turned to several of the
Oxford Union group. Arthur Hughes designed 'The birth of Tristram' (68 x 60.5
cm), allowing Victorian sentimentality to determine his treatment; the dying
Elizabeth sits up to look at her naked son whom the attendant holds.[57] Rossetti

---

[55] A letter which Rossetti wrote William Bell Scott in June, 1857 refers to another painting,
now lost: 'Morris has as yet done nothing in art but is now busily painting his first picture,
Sir Tristram after his illness in the Garden of King Mark's Palace, recognised by the Dog he
had given to Iseult, from the *Morte d'Arthur*. It is being done all from nature of course, and,
I believe will turn out capitally' (*Letters*, I, p. 325).

[56] According to Norman Kelvin (I, p. xxx) Rossetti and Jane were lovers from 1867 or 1868
to 1875.

[57] The source, Malory's Bk. VIII, 1, recounts how Queen Elizabeth, knowing that she was
about to die, requested, 'Now lete me see my lytel child for whome I haue had alle this

chose 'The fight between Sir Tristram and Sir Marhaus' (68 x 61 cm). The rite de passage scene which establishes Tristram as a hero features archetypal attributes – blond hair, golden armour and a white horse. The love potion scene takes place in the ship's cabin as Malory describes and Morris specifies. Isoude wears an elaborate headdress of layered veils on a horn-shaped wire structure similar to one in the fifteenth-century manuscript BL Harley 4431. Her 'cote-hardie, open up sides and kirtle to go under' resembles one of the costumes that the artist had a seamstress make up as drawing models. The sideboard with its display of dishes was an interior feature in fifteenth-century manuscripts, too. Morris must have utilised his knowledge of heraldic colour symbolism when he chose the costume colours. White signifies faith and innocence, Tristram's red hood suggests prowess, green represents new love, while Isoude's white and green together signify virtuous youth.

Between the Rossetti panels is Val Prinsep's 'The departure of Tristram and La Belle Isoude from Ireland' (68 x 61.5 cm). Costume is the central interest. King Anguisshe's luxurious ermine-trimmed houppelande, patterned with stylised flowers and peacock feathers and inset with bombarde sleeves, and his ornamental gold chain evoke the Burgundian court's opulent display.

Edward Burne-Jones was the Morris firm's most important designer. 'The marriage of Tristram and Isoude Les Blanches Mains' (68 x 60.5 cm) formally resembles marriage scenes in manuscripts and early printed books while the altar frontal and reredos with rose motif are the kind of church furnishings that were profitable products of the Morris workshops. 'The madness of Tristrem' (68 x 60.5 cm) traditionally represents the hero's dementia by movement from court to wilderness, his exchange of aristocratic garments for a shirt, his naked limbs, pallor and sunken eyes and cheeks. There is an allusion to the Orpheus myth in the images of peasants, a hound and a pig entranced by Tristram's harping.[58] The next panel, 'The attempted suicide of La Belle Isoude' (68 x 60.5 cm), shows a *hortus conclusus*, a setting Morris also uses in 'The recognition of Tristram by La Belle Isoude'. The garden with its fence, large trees, roses and ornamental fountain may derive from the British Museum *Roman de la Rose*, Harley 4425, a favourite with both artists. George Boyce noted in his diary for April 14, 1860 that Burne-Jones had shown him this manuscript 'filled with the most exquisite illuminations, as fine as could well be in colour and gradation'.

Morris also designed 'Tristrem and Isoude at King Arthur's court' (77 x 61 cm). This scene, where the four elegantly costumed characters listen in an enclosed garden to a minstrel's harping, confirms the inscription's words that at Camelot the lovers 'lived for long with great joy'. Ford Maddox Brown's violent representation, 'The death of Tristram' (77 x 61 cm), is based on the account which Malory had inserted into the catalogue of knights at the Healing of Sir Urry: 'that

sorowe. And whanne she sawe hym she said this: A, my lytel sone, thou hast murthered thy moder, and therfore I suppose thou that arte a murtherer soo yong, thou arte ful lykely to be a manly man in thyn age'.

[58] There is also an easel version (59 x 56.5 cm) with a different background. The helpful lady's castle is gone; a tablet giving the relevant Malory text hangs from a tree.

traytoure kynge slew the noble knight sir Tristram as he sate harpynge afore hys lady, La Belle Isode, with a trenchaunte glayve . . . And La Beall Isode dyed sownyng uppon the crosse (i.e. corpse) of sir Trystram, wherof was grete pite'. Like Burne-Jones in panel 7, Brown gives Mark red hair and a sinister face. Tristram's white gown is embroidered with sunflowers, a symbol of glory. His golden chain's medallion bears the image of a blindfolded Cupid with bow and arrow. Through the open window peer Brangwain and Governail, while the heroine's little dog watches from the settee, which with its rush seat and carved back is suitably 'medieval'.[59]

The final narrative panel, Burne-Jones' 'The tomb of Tristram and Isoude' (68 x 60.5 cm), is the only one not based on Malory. Its literary source may have been Matthew Arnold's 'Tristram and Iseut' (1852):

> In Cornwall, Tristram and Queen Iseult lay
> In King Marc's chapel in Tyntagel old.

The marble lovers lie side by side on a tomb carved with decorative reliefs that recapitulate the story. Enclosed medieval fashion within arches are scenes of the young hero in the forest, the arrival of the ship, the drinking of the love potion, Isoud's attempted suicide and Tristram's marriage. The two hounds guarding the tomb (symbols of fidelity) John Christian has traced to Dürer's St Eustace engraving.[60] Using a print lent by Ruskin, Burne-Jones copied the hounds into his sketchbook ca. 1862–3. The final panels, both 71 x 71.5 cm, are Morris' figural subjects with Latin inscriptions. In 'Queene Guinevere and Isoude Les Blanches Mains', the representation of the Breton princess is identical to the one in an unfinished embroidery for Red House. 'King Arthur and Sir Lancelot' incorporates what was originally a Gideon design.[61]

The foliate backgrounds in several of the panels became a trademark of the firm's work while the use of allegorical images is a characteristic Pre-Raphaelite device for increasing significances. Sometimes these appear as attributes or accompaniments, like the red apple (sexual temptation) which Isoude holds in panel 8, the Cornish choufs sable on Mark's shield in panel 7, and Isoude les Blanches Mains' bridal bouquet of yellow pansies, which in Victorian flower language symbolised both thoughts and love in vain. Sometimes the symbols are background details; for example, the curtain's pattern of swans symbolising death

---

[59] Bradford Art Galleries and Museum at Cartwright Hall possess a pen, ink, pencil, black chalk and wash study (23.5 x 22.25 cm), Cecil Higgins Art Gallery, Bedford a watercolour, and Birmingham Museums and Art Gallery an oil version made in 1864 for George Rae.

[60] John Christian, 'Early German sources for Pre-Raphaelite designs', *Art Quarterly*, XXXVI, 1–2 (1973), 56–83.

[61] Madox Brown originally prepared the cartoon now in London's Victoria and Albert Museum to represent St Dunstan in armour with a pair of tongs at his feet. In 1862 it became the source of a Gideon window in the north aisle, St Martin's Church, Scarborough. A watercolour in the National Gallery, Edinburgh, 'King Howell of Brittany and Isoude his daughter', ca. 1862, was probably not part of the Harden Grange programme.

and the soul's passage to the Otherworld (panel 10), and the horn, harp, and eagle above the tomb. Morris's suggestion in his resumé that the horn and harp might ornament the glass is explained in the inscription, 'Now Tristram invented all manner of words that they use in hunting and the writing of notes in music: He was a mighty hunter & a great minstrel'. When Dunlop died in 1903, the owner of Harden Grange sold the panels. They are now regarded as the best example of the firm's early stained glass.

Idealistically disposed to providing beautiful furnishings for modest homes, Morris found himself decorating millionaires' mansions. In 1890 the company received its largest order, to supply furniture, wallpaper, textiles, woodwork, carpets, metalworks and mosaics for Stanmore Hall near Harrow. Its new owner was W.K. D'Arcy who had made one fortune from Australian goldmines and would make another from the Anglo-Persian Oil Company. This was not a house where one would find the harmony and contentment associated with truthful architecture. Morris dismissed it scornfully as 'a house of a very rich [man] – and such a wretched uncomfortable place! A sham Gothic house of fifty years ago now being added to by a young architect of the commercial type-men who are very bad'.[62] Without Morris' active supervision, the company installed a hand-painted staircase with 'tones like those of embroidery', a refectory table with trestle legs, a chimney piece with shelves on which were repoussé dishes, and much more, creating what a contemporary journalist called 'an air of gaiety without vulgarity'.[63] The set of tapestries adorning the dining-room added to an effect that was 'almost entirely Gothic with strong French influence apparent'.

Morris had long believed that truth and beauty in the decorative arts could be achieved by studying medieval sources. In *The Lesser Arts* (1877) he expressed his attitude to such models:

> if we do not study the ancient work directly and learn to understand it, we shall find ourselves influenced by the feeble work all around us ... Let us therefore study it wisely, be taught by it, kindled by it, all the while determining not to imitate or repeat it; to have either no art at all, or an art which we have made our own.[64]

Just as the Harden Grange panels reflected his desire to revive medieval glass techniques so the Stanmore Hall tapestries were the most beautiful products of his high-warp weaving. Disgusted by the 'upholsterer's toy' tapestries of the Gobelins factory and the Royal Windsor Tapestry Works, Morris first mastered the craft by studying 'an old technical work on the subject, written in French somewhere in the seventeenth century'.[65] In 1881, he set up looms at Merton Abbey where large

---

[62] J.W. Mackail, *The Life of William Morris*, 2 vols (London and New York, 1899), II, p. 245.
[63] J.S. Gibson, 'Artistic Houses', *Studio*, 1, 6 (Sept. 1893) 215–226.
[64] *Collected Works*, XXII, pp. 15–16.
[65] Kelvin, *Letters*, I, p. 526 and Aymer Vallance, 'The Revival of Tapestry-Weaving. An interview with Mr. William Morris', *Studio*, 2–3 (1893–4), 98–101.

tapestries could be created using natural dyes made on the premises. His work-men, whom he trained himself, were 'artists, not merely animated machines'.

Burne-Jones was the 'only man at present living' who possessed the require-ments of a good tapestry designer: a feeling for decorative art, a strong sense of colour, an ability to draw the human figure, especially the hands and feet, a skill in using the stitch of the work.[66] For pictorial tapestries the artist made original studies 'not above 15 inches high' which were enlarged by photography in squares, fitted together, and revised. J.H. Dearle, the workshop manager, usually did the 'ornamental accessories, the patterns of brocades in the draperies, the flowers and foliage'.[67]

Malory's 'Tale of the Sankgreal' was the artist's chosen subject for the Stanmore Hall tapestries. Since his Oxford days when he had advised his friend Cornell Price, 'Learn Sir Galahad by heart. He is to be the patron of our order' until the end of his life, the world of King Arthur was 'such a sacred land to me that nothing in the world touches it in comparison'.[68] Above all it was the Quest of the Holy Grail that contained the meaning of life. In 1898 when he was dying, he wrote to Sebastian Evans (for whose *High History of the Grail* he had provided a frontispiece):

> Lord! how that San Graal story is ever in my mind and thoughts continually. Was ever anything in the world beautiful as that is beauti-ful? If I might clear away all the work that I have begun, if I might live and clear it all away, and dedicate the last days to that tale – if only I might.[69]

He had already depicted scenes from the Grail Quest in four stained glass panels (46 x 32.5 cm) which the Morris Company made in 1886.[70] Originally intended for his London home, they were subsequently installed, as his grand-daughter Angela Thirkell describes, in their country home at Rottingdean near Brighton:

> Above the bold-faced sink was a stained-glass window of jewelled brilliance, containing 4 scenes from the story of the San Graal; . . . The Holy Grail above a housemaid's sink, both needed, both a part of daily life. It is easy to laugh a little, but there was a splendid disregard of external values in this juxtaposition and it was a summing up of the best part of the Pre-Raphaelite attitude to life.[71]

[66] An important letter to Thomas Wardle, written November 14, 1877 (*Letters*, I, pp. 409–11) summarises his views.
[67] Vallance, 101.
[68] *Memorials* II, p. 247.
[69] *Memorials* II, p. 333. A copy of the *Morte Darthur* acquired in 1895, now in the Ashmolean Museum, Oxford, he bound with white leather and painted with a scene similar to the Evans woodcut design.
[70] Sewter, I, pp. 588–91, II, pp. 104–5.
[71] A.M. Thirkell, *Three Houses* (London, 1931), p. 123. The glass panels remained in the

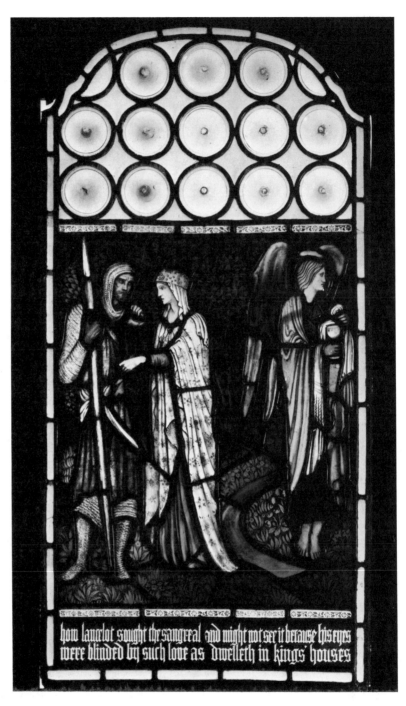

how lancelot sought the sangreal and might not see it because his eyes were blinded by such love as dwelleth in kings' houses

40. How Lancelot sought the Sangreal. Burne-Jones' stained glass panel for his Rottingdean House

As in 'La Queste del Saint Graal' and Malory, individual knights represent human types whose success in attaining divine grace (which the Grail symbolises) is related to their conduct in the sin-filled, dangerous world. An angel holding a chalice conveys the judgement of a quester's moral and spiritual state. Inscriptions explain the subjects. The figures, elongated in the Gothic style and dressed in thirteenth century costumes, are set on patterned grounds that recall the Harden Grange panels and the firm's floral wallpapers. A winding stream widening into a river of light links the four. In 'How Lancelot sought the sangreal and might not see it because his eyes were blinded by such love as dwelleth in King's houses', the hero, with the lined face of a middle-aged man and the red surcoat denoting passionate love, gazes into Guenevere's eyes as she offers his shield. Her white surcoat, worn over a blue gown, is patterned with roses. The angel, separated from the lovers by a stream, turns away his face. The second panel depicts Gawain, the worldly man 'blinded by thought of the deeds of kings'. He dreams by a fountain as a richly dressed lady plays her harp to represent earthly pleasures. The red-winged angel turns his back on them.

The third panel is inscribed 'How Galahad sought the Sangreal and found it because his heart was single so he followed it to Sarras the City of the Spirit'. The Grail Knight stands on a rocky promontory before twisted trees, the hostile landscape representing the difficulties of the ascetic life. The angel turns his face towards the hero who will enjoy the full mystical vision. The last panel shows the Romanesque temple in Sarras, both the earthly Jerusalem where Galahad is crowned king and the heavenly Jerusalem where the faithful see God. The Grail, set on an altar, is guarded by three angels – red, blue and green.

The panel subjects were taken up again in the tapestries,[72] a medium that the artist enjoyed because 'big tapestry's beautifully half way between painting and ornament'.[73] He created the six designs in 1890–91; the weaving took four years.

The series begins with 'The Summons' (2.63 x 5.18 m), placed on the upper wall adjacent to the fireplace. The miniaturists' device of removing the castle's outside

Rottingdean house until 1920 when they were given to the Victoria and Albert Museum. Sepia and gouache studies are in the William Morris Gallery, Walthamstow.

[72] See Emmeline Leary, *The Holy Grail Tapestries designed by Edward Burne-Jones for Morris & Co.* (Birmingham, 1985); Linda L.A. Parry, 'The Tapestries of Edward Burne-Jones', *Apollo*, 102, 324–28; Susan Moore, 'The Marxist and the Oilman, Morris & Co. at Stanmore Hall', *Country Life*, Nov. 14, 1985, 1494–1496; Banham and Harris, 187–193. 'The Arras Tapestries at Stanmore Hall', *Studio*, 15 (1899), 98–104 includes photographs of the tapestries *in situ*. The Duke of Westminster bought the Stanmore Hall set in 1920; the second, third and sixth panels were sold at auction in 1978. In 1895–96 Morris & Co. wove 'The Arming and Departure', 'The Failure of Sir Gawaine' and 'The Attainment' for the drawing room at Compton Hall, Wolverhampton; they are now in the Birmingham Museum and Art Gallery. Another series was woven in 1898–99 for D'Arcy's business partner, George McCulloch; its 'Summons' panel became part of the Birmingham collection as did 'The Ship' and a verdure woven for Mary Middlemore. Still another copy of 'The Summons' and 'The Attainment' went to Henry Beecham of Lympne Castle, Kent; they are now in the Stadtsmuseum, Munich. Dimensions given in the text refer to the Birmingham tapestries.

[73] Mary Lago, ed., *Burne-Jones Talking: His Conversations 1895–1898 preserved by his studio assistant Thomas Rooke* (Columbia, Miss., 1981), p. 105.

wall allows one to view the interior. Arthur sits at an elongated table where ten chairs (including the empty Siege Perilous) are so placed that the feasters' faces may be seen as they turn towards the Grail maiden. The mille fleurs tapestry behind the knights mirrors the foreground of English flowers – tiger lilies, tulips, carnations, daisies, harebells, cornflowers, and columbines – woven in the Flemish style. (Morris's tapestry workers always had fresh flowers before them while working.) Though the diagonal floor boards create some recession, there is considerable foreshortening as the designer attempts to make the figures impressive from the floor below. Red, blue and moss green are the predominant colours.

Henry Dearle's verdure dados (approximately 1.5 m high), which were hung below four of the pictorial tapestries, summarize the narrative content in Gothic lettering.[74] Deer drink from a stream in the flowery meadows but the chief feature is the heraldry. Using the armorial printed with the 1520 *Guiron* and *La devise des armes des Chevaliers de la table ronde*, Morris himself designed the shields, introducing not only the usual blazons of Arthur, Galahad, Gawain, Lancelot, Iwain and Tristram but more exotic devices belonging to non-Malorian knights like Sir Wolf Ganesmor le noir and Sir Jambourg du chastel. Burne-Jones remarked that he would like to have given Galahad a gold cup on a silver ground rather than the red cross 'which is so dull for him'.

'The Arming and Departure of the Knights' (2.59 x 4.45 m) was fitted into a corner where two walls came together. In the text, the departure is a scene of lamentation. Tears fall from the king's eyes as he foresees that 'my true felaushyp shall neuer mete here more ageyn'. The queen and ladies had 'such sorowe and heuynesse that there myght no tonge telle it'. The tapestry scene is less emotional and more ritualistic as virgin ladies with garlands in their hair hand up various parts of the knights' accoutrements. As in the Rottingdean panel, Guenevere presents Launcelot's shield.

'The Failure of Sir Gawain' (2.59 x 3.23 m) shows the sinful knight, accompanied by Iwain (not Ector), riding up to the wilderness chapel but an angel bars their entry. Horses occupy a large part of the pictorial space. The artist considered that 'a horse is such a fine ornament in a picture – when a knight and his horse look like one animal'. Aware that his steeds were often awkward, he added, 'I can't do them anything like as well as some chaps, but I'll get through them somehow'.[75] In 'The Failure' not only are the horses disproportionately high, but the tops of the knights' coifs are cut off. Paired with this tapestry (they were placed on either side of a window) is 'The Failure of Sir Lancelot'. The letter to Mrs Gaskell explains that Lancelot was

> eaten up not by coveting of glory but eaten up he was, and his heart set
> on another matter. So he is foiled – dreams he comes to the chapel and

---

[74] Burne-Jones' letter to Mrs H.M. Gaskell (*Memorials*, pp. II, 208–209) explains the subjects. The damsel of the San Graal 'appears and summons all the knights to the adventure, and suddenly writing comes on the empty chair'.
[75] *Burne-Jones Talking*, p. 81.

has found it, but a ruined and broken one – and still he cannot enter, for one comes and bars the way.

Instead of sleeping by the cross, as in the text, Lancelot dreams beside a well. It may be the boiling well in the perilous forest, 'a sygne of lechory that was that tyme muche used' or it may be the fair well representing God's grace, from which Malory's knight is unable to drink. The darkness surrounding the chapel has moral and spiritual connotations, countered only by the brightness which illumines the Grail and flows out to highlight the angel's surplice, the knight's red surcoat and the shield. When he painted an oil version in 1895, Burne-Jones commented, 'Launcelot's very hard to get right. But when I've tingled it up with bright points of light, and buzzed about it and given it atmosphere I'll get it right at last'.[76]

'The Ship' effects the transition from Logres to Sarras, 'the land of the soul'. It is anchored off a mountainous coast where rocks, sand, coarse grass and seashells imply both a realistic seascape and a spiritually arid society which no longer serves the Grail. The sequence culminates in 'The Attainment' (2.59 x 9.12 m) which covered the upper part of the end wall, above built-in serving tables and a door. Eliminating the city of Sarras, Burne-Jones sets the Grail chapel in a wilderness bordered by a paradisal garden of English flowers which we realize are being used symbolically – the columbine (dove of the Holy Spirit), the daisy (innocence), the primrose (keys of heaven), the carnation (Christ's passion), the lily of the valley (purity). These spring flowers symbolize the Resurrection and Redemption of which the Grail is another sign. The spatial division is tripartite. Bors, the bull with one black spot representing one lapse from chastity, stands furthest from the chapel. In front of him kneels Perceval whose positioning and costume, a golden surcoat with jewelled baldric, show his higher value. Three angels occupy the centre, their great flame-coloured pinions (executed in a style perhaps taken from Blake) denoting divine love. They hold eucharistic candles, the bleeding lance of Longinus, and the golden dish of the Paschal Lamb. Surrounded by tall lilies, a symbol of purity associated with the Virgin Mary in medieval Annunciations, Galahad kneels at the chapel entrance, gazing at the uncovered Grail, which three more angels guard and worship. The lily motif also decorates his helm's golden crown which signifies his kingship in Sarras. Not a dove but a Pentecostal wind blowing the curtain above the altar indicates the Holy Spirit. The chalice was copied from a reproduction of the eighth-century Tassilio Chalice in Kremsmünster Abbey, Austria. Gold, jewels, and the bright colours of costumes and flowers express the transcendent reality that was central to Burne-Jones' aestheticism.

---

[76] *Ibid*, p. 85. The artist's view of women and their tastes is revealed in another comment: 'While "Aurora" was a "ladies" picture, . . . "Lancelot" is "the gentleman's picture". No sentiment appeals to them. I don't know why ladies shouldn't care about it, but they don't. Perhaps they think it's ridiculous to make such a fuss about a mere peccadillo. They don't approve of the morals of it. But, Lord, it doesn't matter. The great point is, not that they should understand us, but that they should worship us and obey us . . .' (pp. 98–99).

The Gothic Revival was not confined to Britain. German Romanticism had anticipated the Victorian view of the medieval period as a Golden Age of faith, order and heroic actions.[77] The Nazarenes had revived the principles of Dürer and Raphael, the paramountcy of colour, and the feeling for nature, ideas that the Pre-Raphaelite Brotherhood would promote in England. Artists like Ludwig and Julius Schnorr, Peter van Cornelius and Moritz von Schwind decorated public buildings with what William Vaughan describes as 'high-minded allegorical cycles', under the patronage of Ludwig I of Bavaria. Ludwig's grandson, another Ludwig (1845-1886),[78] grew up in Hohenschwangau, a medieval castle restored in the Gothic Revival style with pointed arches, frescoed walls – and a billiard room. Its Hall of the Swan Knight introduced the child to Teutonic legend long before he met Richard Wagner. The romantic paintings by Christian Ruben, Michael Neher and Lorenz Quaglio tell the story of Parzival's son, Lohengrin. Brightly dressed nobles in fifteenth-century costumes strike heroic poses in a Bavarian landscape of castles, mountains and lakes. The swan, symbol of eternal bliss and immortality, an image that would become one of Ludwig's obsessions, symbolically linked Bavarian royalty to the twelfth-century Knights of Schwangau, one of whom was immortalised by the Codex Manesse.

On May 13, 1868 Ludwig, by now king, wrote to Richard Wagner announcing his intention of rebuilding the ruined castle Vorderhohenschwangau in the genuine style of the old German knights' strongholds. It would be called Neuschwanstein. Today the pinnacled and turreted exterior of this fairy tale castle is familiar to tourists not only in Germany but also in Disneyworld. It was not planned by an architect but by a stage designer, Christian Jank. The natural setting of snow capped mountains, gorges and waterfalls the king imaginatively equated with the rocky landscape of the *Ring* cycle and *Parzival*.

Far from embodying the Ruskinian principles of truthful construction and an honest use of materials that considers their natural textures and colours, Neuschwanstein is a labyrinth of deceit. The throne room's columns are imitation porphyry, the Singers' Hall 'tapestry' is only painted cloth, chandeliers are gilded brass and everywhere are faux marble walls, paint imitating mosaic interlace and stucco masquerading as stone. The interior's architectural style is hybrid – Gothic in Ludwig's bedroom, Romanesque and Byzantine elsewhere. The throne room (lacking a throne) was modelled on Constantinople's St Sophia and on the Great Hall of the Grail Kings in order to assert the sacral nature of Ludwig's kingship. The Singers' Hall was adapted from the festival hall of the Wartburg Castle in

[77] Paul Frankl, *The Gothic: Literary Sources and Interpretations through Eight Centuries* (Princeton, 1960), pp. 447–478; W.D. Robson-Scott, *The Literary Background of the Gothic Revival in Germany: A Chapter in the History of Taste* (Oxford, 1965); William Vaughan, *German Romantic Painting* (New Haven and London, 1980).

[78] See Wilfred Blunt, *The Dream King, Ludwig II of Bavaria* with a chapter on Ludwig and the Arts by Dr Michael Petzel (London, 1984); *Designs for the Dream King: The Castles and Palaces of Ludwig II of Bavaria* (London, 1978), catalogue of an exhibition at the Debrett Cooper-Hewitt Museum, New York, with introductory essay by Simon Jervis.

Thuringia and, like it, was a model for *Tannhauser* settings on the operatic stage. In Ludwig's lifetime these rooms never fulfilled their particular purposes.

'Form without function and splendor without taste, slavish imitation of other places and other eras carried out by inferior artists', wrote Oliver Bernier.[79] High-minded Victorians would have regarded the castle as immoral for other reasons, too. The artist-workmen were allowed no freedom, no chance of expressing 'their sense of the beauty and mystery of life', as Morris recommended. Every detail was dictated, even the requirement of finishing on Good Friday, 1884 a wall painting of Parzival meeting the Good Friday pilgrims. Furthermore, in a period when art was seen, not least by the Germans, as a vehicle for improving the public's moral standards and providing what Charles Kingsley called 'the towns-man's paradise of refreshment',[80] the art of Neuschwanstein was elitist and exclusive, created for the private indulgence of a single individual. Such art, said Morris, was 'contemptible and dishonourable, a rag of luxury and folly'.[81]

Arthurian motifs from the stories of Tristan, Parzival and Lohengrin are scattered throughout – swan-shaped vases, taps, door handles and basins, a tiled stove decorated with a clay Tristan and Isolde, a painted bookcase showing Gottfried von Strassburg, Tristan and Isolde, Wolfram von Eschenbach, and the Grail. The two poets reappear above the dining-room doors – Ludwig had ordered his artists to take their subjects from medieval literature, not from Wagner's operas. The living-room, reached by way of an artificial grotto, has Wilhelm Hauschild's Lohengrin frescoes: the knight's arrival in Antwerp, Elsa's welcome and the account of her troubles, the hero's combat with Teliamund, and his abandonment of Elsa and their children because she has broken the tabu. The most ostentatious piece depicts the Grail procession in Montsalvat. Above the light-giving chalice (resembling a bird-bath) hovers the dove, as Amfortas, the crowned Grail Maiden, the lance-bearer, assembled knights and ladies and the silent hero watch in wonder. With their decorated borders, solid figures, and insistent primary colours, the paintings imitate tapestries, sustaining the air of illusion (or delusion) that permeates the building.

In the passage to the Singers' Hall Spiess, Piloty, Munsch and Kolmsperger depicted the adventures of Parzival's father, Gahmuret, and his friend, Gawain; for example, the winning of Queen Herzeloide, Gawain's fight with the lion at Klingsor's enchanted castle, and Gawain's wedding. In the Hall itself the ten large murals tell Parzival's story though they must vie for attention with Romanesque arcades, polychrome interlace panels, arches painted to imitate dog-tooth stone carving, jewelled chandeliers, gigantic candelabra, and smaller paintings of allegorical figures and minor characters. The dümmlingkind hero wears brown fus-

---

[79] 'Ludwig's Castles: Forms of Fantasy', *The New York Times*, April 6, 1986, xx, 9, 27.
[80] 'Politics for the People' (May 6, 1848 and May 20, 1848), reprinted in Robert L. Peters, ed., *Victorians on Literature & Art* (New York, 1961), pp. 182–185.
[81] See his address, 'A Socialist's Protest Against Capitalist Brutality: Addressed to the Working Classes' (1883) in May Morris, ed., 2 vols *William Morris: Artist, Writer and Socialist* (London, 1936), II, pp. 382–406.

tian, thonged leggings and a fool's hood when he hunts in the forest, kisses his youthful mother goodbye and attacks the Red Knight. After that he is a proper Teutonic hero – fair haired, beardless, almost corpulent, dressed in chain mail and a scarlet gown, striking attitudes as if engaged in an operatic performance. The hall of the Grail Castle, arcaded, pillared, adorned with golden stairs, inlays and decorated tiles, clearly resembles Ludwig's throne room which, in turn, was modelled on the hall of the Grail Castle. Such insidious circularity bespeaks the lack of invention only too obvious in the pictorial programmes.

But the heart of Neuschwanstein is Ludwig's bedroom where, above the bed's Gothic canopy, the pinnacles of a reading chair and the washstand's Swan finials, Spiess has illustrated scenes from *Tristan*.[82] Herman Kurtz had translated Gottfried's and Thomas' poetry into modern German in 1847 but the artist's choice of subjects is closer to the Wagnerian than to the medieval. Excessive ornamentation is again the prevailing stylistic feature – abhorrent to Ludwig would have been the view of Morris and Webb that one should do without pattern unless it were really beautiful.

In the love potion scene, the plump blond heroine, wearing a white gown embroidered with gold, a jewelled crown and a string of pearls, which she nervously twists, sits on a gold and purple cushion set on a fringed and embroidered hanging which covers a lion-headed, claw-footed chair. Her elbow rests on a carved table with gold inlay and her feet on a gold and purple tasselled cushion, placed on a patterned rug. The red-gowned hero, darkly handsome with flashing eyes, curly hair and beard, offers the love potion in a dragon-adorned horn. Behind them, from a carved valance a patterned curtain of Arabic inspiration is drawn back to reveal a stormy sky and a sea of incredible blue. Even the boards which represent the ship's side are intricately grained. Here and in three other scenes, where the lovers embrace, the low cut neckline and the dress material, clinging to breasts and thighs, emphasize the woman's voluptuousness. By contrast, Isolde of the White Hands watches, dark, demure, and plain, while her husband, hand theatrically shading his eyes, scans the horizon for the Queen's ship and, finally, dressed in full armour, expires in his mistress' embrace. The darkness of the panelling, the deepness of the windows which admit little light, the tragic story depicted on the walls were appropriate for not only was 'Mad' King Ludwig, like the lovers, 'night-consecrate' but also he was doomed.

Michael Petzel comments that the King's castles were 'more than a mere illusory world into which he withdrew to protest against the bourgeois world which showed no understanding of him: they were his very life, in which dream and reality were blended and history lived again – not merely on a stage'.[83] Ludwig II of Bavaria is an extreme but not unique example of those who make art a substitute for life.

---

[82] Ludwig had sponsored the first performances of Wagner's 'Tristan und Isolde' on June 10, 1865 in Munich, with Ludwig Schnorr von Carolsfeld, Wagner's ideal heroic tenor, as Tristan.
[83] *The Dream King*, p. 182.

CHAPTER NINE

Tennyson and the Artists

On the nineteenth-century revival of Arthurian legend the greatest single influence was Alfred Tennyson (1809–1892), a son of the manse who by 1860 had become the most popular living poet that Britain had ever known.[1] 'The Lady of Shalott' appeared as early as 1832 and was republished in the *Poems* of 1842 which also included 'Sir Galahad', 'Sir Launcelot and Queen Guinevere', and 'Morte d'Arthur'. In 1859 Edward Moxon published the first *Idylls of the King* – 'Enid', 'Vivien', 'Elaine' and 'Guinevere'. 'The Holy Grail', 'The Coming of Arthur' and 'Pelleas and Ettare' followed in 1870, 'The Passing of Arthur', 'Gareth and Lynette' and 'The Last Tournament' in 1872 and the last 'little picture', 'Balin and Balan', in 1885. His chief source was Malory's *Morte Darthur*. The story of Enid and Geraint he found in Lady Charlotte Guest's translation of the Welsh *Mabinogion*.[2]

Though some critics questioned the usefulness of reviving 'a forgotten cycle of fables which never attained the dignity or substance of a popular mythology', the literate, prosperous middle class who constituted Tennyson's public enthusiastically welcomed works combining moral uplift and sensuous romanticism.[3] The poet's friend, Arthur Hallam, approved the pictorialism:

[1]   On Tennyson's life, sources, extracts from correspondence, notebooks, diaries, records of conversations, recollections of friends *et al.* see Hallam Tennyson, *Alfred, Lord Tennyson, a Memoir*, 2 vols (London, 1897), hereafter cited as *Mem.* For the texts see *The Poems of Tennyson*, ed. Christopher Ricks (London, 1969) and *Idylls of the King*, ed. J.M. Gray (New Haven and London, 1983). Relevant criticism includes J. Phillip Eggers, *King Arthur's Laureate: A Study of Tennyson's 'Idylls of the King'* (New York, 1971); J.M. Gray, *Thro' the Vision of the Night. A Study of Source, Evolution and Structure in Tennyson's Idylls of the King* (Edinburgh, 1980); *Tennyson: The Critical Heritage*, ed. John D. Jump (London, 1967); *Tennyson*, ed. D.J. Palmer (London, 1973); David Staines, *Tennyson's Camelot: The Idylls of the King and its Medieval Sources* (Waterloo, 1982). The Tennyson Research Centre in Lincoln has a varied collection including letters, manuscripts, and books from Tennyson's library.

[2]   *Mabinogion*, ed. Lady Charlotte Guest, 3 vols (London, 1838–49). 'Gereint son of Erbin' parallels Chrétien de Troyes' *Erec*. For a discussion of the relationship see Idris Llewelyn Foster, 'Gereint, Owein, and Peredur' in *Arthurian Literature in the Middle Ages*.

[3]   See M. Shaw, 'Tennyson and his Public 1827–1859' in Palmer, pp. 52–88.

> . . . poetry cannot be too pictorial, for it cannot represent too truly, and when the object of the poetic power happens to be an object of sensuous perception, it is the business of the poetic language to paint.[4]

While W.M. Rossetti denied that Tennyson was an art 'connoisseur' or that he had 'any particular insight into matters of pictorial art as such',[5] the evidence supports Horsley's description of him as the painter's poet.

He provided extensive visual detail in describing objects such as Excalibur, Lancelot's shield, Arthur's dragon-ornamented throne and his decorated hall. These details were not intended to be read on the literal level only. On the keystone of Camelot's gate Gareth sees a statue of the Lady of the Lake, her arms extended 'like the cross', her hands dripping with purifying water; a sword, a censer, and a sacred fish contribute to the allegory. Surmounting the whole structure are three Queens (Faith, Hope and Charity, as well as the Three Graces). Tennyson might protest, 'They have taken my hobby, and ridden it too hard' or 'I hate to be tied down to say, "This means that"',[6] yet he admitted to 'the thought within the image'.

His depiction of characters in moments of emotional significance such as the Lady of Shalott's sight of Sir Lancelot, Galahad's vision of the Grail, Merlin's submission to Vivien, Arthur's castigation of Guenevere and the king's departure for Avalon provided artists with scenes that could be plucked from the narrative stream. He created settings in a Pre-Raphaelite way, focusing on individual details without organising them into a single consistent perspective. Botanical forms were observed from nature, though the particular selection might depend on the image's value as symbol. On the basis of verbal description, an artist could re-create a setting like Earl Yniol's castle:

> Then rode Geraint into the castle court,
> His charger trampling many a prickly star
> Of sprouted thistle on the broken stones.
> He look'd and saw that all was ruinous.
> Here stood a shatter'd archway plumed with fern;
> And here had fall'n a great part of a tower,
> Whole, like a crag that tumbles from a cliff,
> And like a crag was gay with wilding flowers:
> And high above a piece of turret stair,
> Worn by the feet that now were silent, wound
> Bare to the sun, and monstrous ivy stems
> Claspt the grey walls with hairy-fibred arms,
> And suck'd the joining of the stones, and look'd

---

[4] *Mem.* I, p. 501.
[5] William Michael Rossetti, *Dante Gabriel Rossetti, His Family Letters*, 2 vols (New York, 1970 [1895]), p. 190.
[6] *Mem.* II, pp. 426–7.

A knot, beneath, of snakes, aloft, a grove.

('The Marriage of Geraint', ll. 312–325)

These visual details are crucial to mood and plot because they rouse in the reader/viewer's mind curiosity about the past and future.

Finally, Tennyson shared with Pre-Raphaelites like Rossetti and Burne-Jones the ability to create a secondary world of the imagination inhabited by a mythic society of knights and ladies who performed their roles in castles, perilous forests, enclosed gardens and wasteland chapels. Using recounted vision and dream, he added a psychological 'inner world' comparable to that of the medieval Grail knights whose cycle of waking and dreaming life was both mundane and transcendent.

Because the 1842 *Poems* had been a financial success, Edward Moxon proposed reissuing the collection with wood-engraving illustrations. On 27 February, 1854 he wrote that he had made some progress in procuring illustrators – Sir Edwin Landseer, Mulready, Creswick, Millais and Schart, who would provide 'a few gems from the antique'. As well, he intended to 'call upon Stanfield, Maclise, Horsley, and Frost – all excellent in their respective lines, and all men who can draw on wood'.[7] Several of them had contributed to S.C. Hall's *Book of British Ballads* (1842). It was probably Tennyson who suggested that Pre-Raphaelite artists be included. Millais had already painted a Tennysonian subject, 'Mariana'.

Early in 1855 Moxon called on D.G. Rossetti 'wanting me to do some blocks for the new Tennyson', he wrote to William Allingham. Rossetti is probably the first Arthurian illustrator to record his view of the artist's relationship to his text:

(I) fancy I shall try the 'Vision of Sin' and 'Palace of Art', etc. – those where one can allegorize on one's own hook on the subject of the poem, without killing for oneself and everyone a distinct idea of the poet's. This I fancy, is *always* the upshot of illustrated editions – Tennyson, Allingham, or any one – unless where the poetry is so absolutely narrative as in the old ballads, for instance.[8]

For Gleeson White, fifty years later, the Moxon Tennyson marked 'the genesis of the modern movement'.[9]

Of fifty-five illustrations, six were Arthurian. Daniel Maclise, an Irish artist who advocated the Round Table ideal of fellowship as a model for contemporary society, was assigned the 'Morte d'Arthur'. His first design illustrated the dying king's recollection of how

---

[7] A considerable number of letters exchanged by Moxon and Tennyson are housed in the Tennyson Research Centre. See *Tennyson and Lincoln: A Catalogue of the Collections in the Research Centre*, ed. Nancie Campbell, 2 vols (Lincoln, 1971).

[8] *Letters of Dante Gabriel Rossetti*, ed. O. Doughty and J.R. Wahl, 4 vols (Oxford, 1965), I, pp. 238–9. The standard reference on Rossetti's art is Virginia Surtees, *The Paintings and Drawings of Dante Gabriel Rossetti (1828–1882), A Catalogue Raisonée*, 2 vols (Oxford, 1971).

[9] *English Illustration: The Sixties* (London, 1897), p. 105.

> In those old days, one summer noon, an arm
> Rose up from out the bosom of the lake,
> Clothed in white samite, mystic, wonderful,
> Holding the sword . . .

Identified by the dragon on his helmet and shield, Arthur sits alone in a swan-prowed boat, awkwardly clasping his hands. Waterlilies in the foreground suggest time and place, but detracting from that realistic detail is the lake spirit's resemblance to a grounded whale. A similar boat with a swan figurehead to indicate its Otherworld destination bears away the recumbent king, along with three queens and a crowd of shadowy attendants who suggest sorrow through gesture and stance. (Swans, waterlilies and dragon crests became the most shopworn images in the Arthurian repertoire.)

Rossetti also depicts weeping queens, nine of them as Geoffrey of Monmouth specified in the *Vita Merlini*. His woodcut relates to a tapestry scene in 'The Palace of Art':

> Or mythic Uther's deeply-wounded son
> In some fair space of sloping greens
> Lay, dozing in the vale of Avalon,
> And watch'd by weeping queens.

Crowded into the foreground – 'You *can* cram!' said Ruskin – the nine women with thin, Siddal faces, long, sexually provocative hair and differentiated crowns almost obscure the monarch. The artist achieves the same concentrated effect of pictorialism and mystery when illustrating the 'secret shrine' in 'Sir Galahad':

> The stalls are void, the doors are wide,
> The tapers burning fair.
> Fair gleams the snowy altar-cloth,
> The silver vessels sparkle clean,
> The shrill bell rings, the censer swings,
> And solemn chaunts resound between.

Alastair Grieve[10] notes that Rossetti's images are derivative; the treatment of the singers placed below the chapel floor he has drawn from his 'Giotto Painting Dante', the bell comes from 'Fra Pace' and the brightly lit interior amid surrounding gloom from 'Hesterna Rosa'. In a watercolour version, 'Sir Galahad at the Ruined Chapel' (1859; Birmingham City Museum and Art Gallery), vibrant reds and yellows emphasize the red-headed knight's glory and the Grail's brilliance. Both the woodcut and the painting show an obsession with medieval accessories

---

[10] Alastair Grieve, *D.G. Rossetti's Stylistic Development as a Painter*, University of London doctoral dissertation, 1968, p. 119.

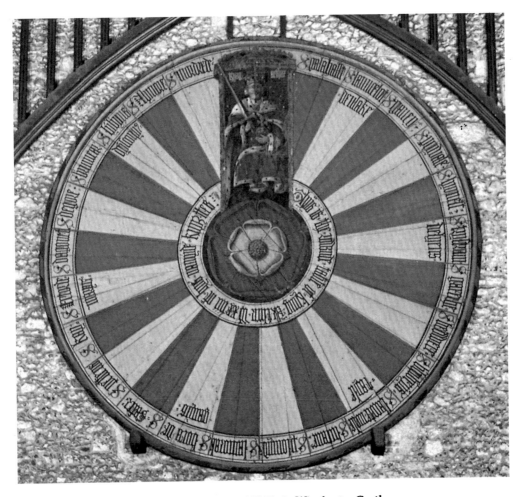

20. Arthur's Round Table in Winchester Castle.

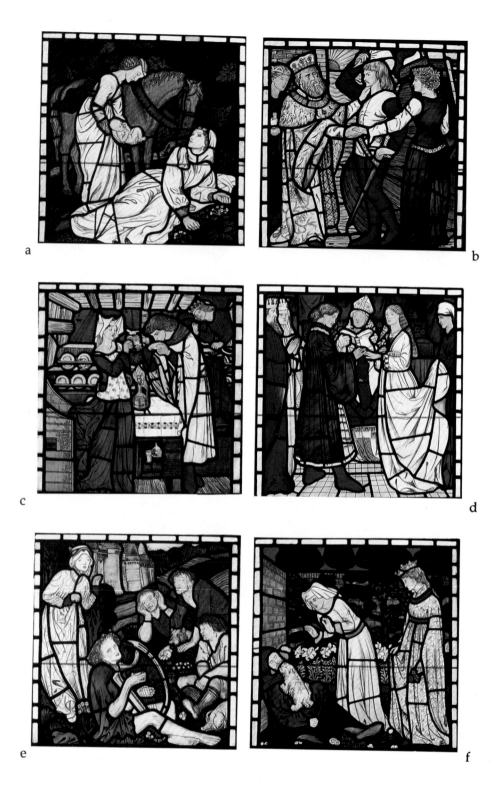

a

b

c

d

e

f

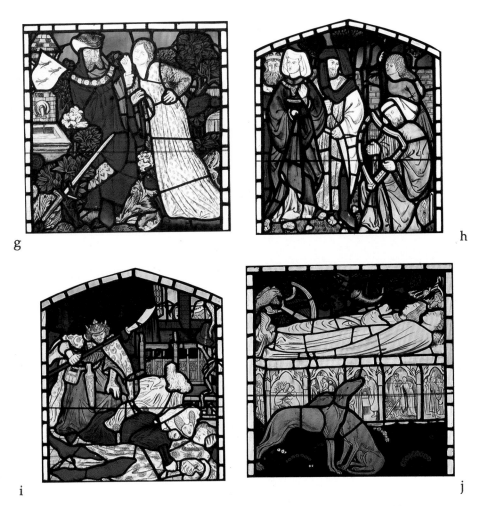

g

h

i

j

21. & 22. The Tristan stained glass for Harden Grange executed by
Morris & Company, 1862

a. Arthur Hughes. The Birth of Tristram
b. Val Prinsep. The departure of Tristram and La Belle Isoude from Ireland
c. Dante Gabriel Rossetti, Tristram and La Belle Isoude drink the love potion
d. Edward Burne-Jones. The marriage of Tristram and Isoude Les Blanches Mains
e. Edward Burne-Jones. The Madness of Tristram
f. William Morris. The recognition of Tristram by La Belle Isoude
g. Edward Burne-Jones. The attempted suicide of La Belle Isoude
h. William Morris. Tristram and Isolde at King Arthur's court
i. Ford Maddox Brown. The death of Tristram
j. Edward Burne-Jones. The tomb of Tristram and Isolde

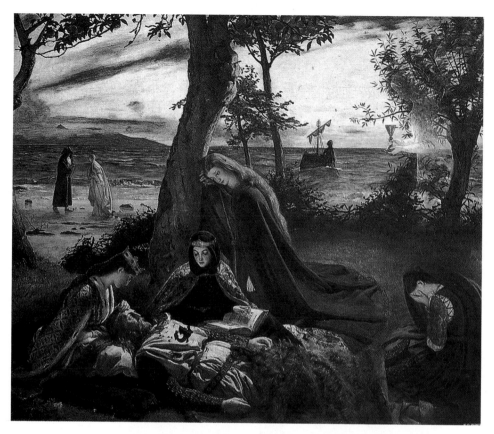

23. James Archer. La Mort D'Arthur, oil painting 1860

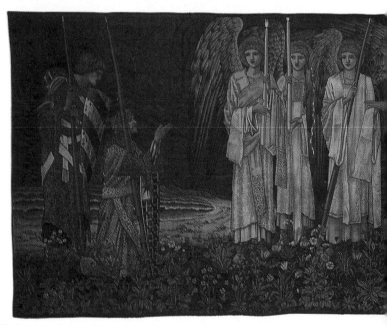

25. Edward Burne-Jones. The Attainment of the Holy Grail.
Stanmore Hall tapestry executed by William Morris & Co. 1898–9

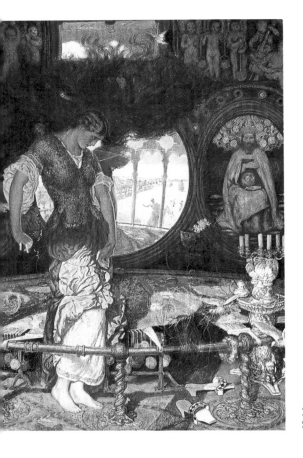

24. W. Holman Hunt. The Lady of
Shalott, oil painting 1886–1905

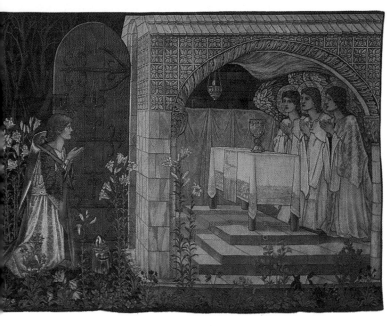

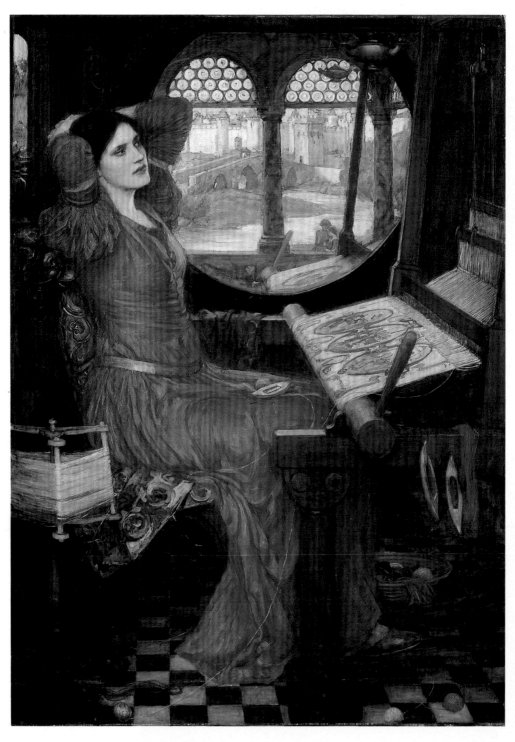

26. J. W. Waterhouse. ' "I am half Sick of shadows" said the Lady of Shalott', oil painting 1860

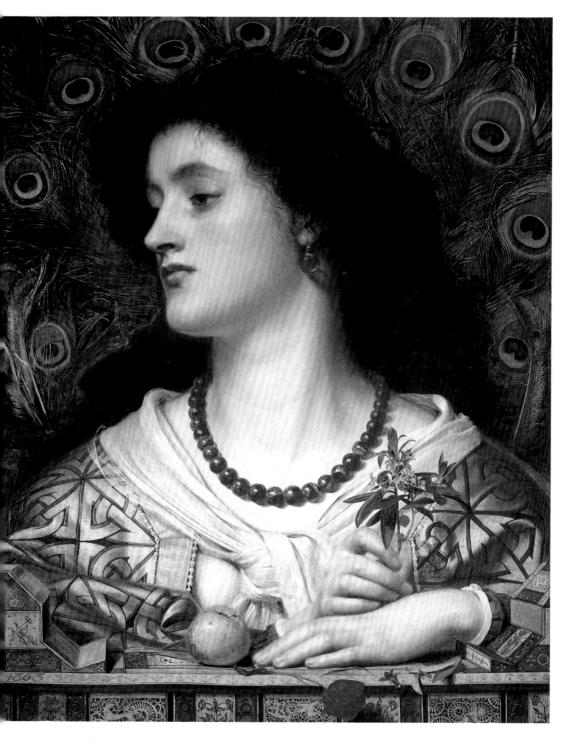

27. Frederick Sandys. Vivien, oil painting 1863

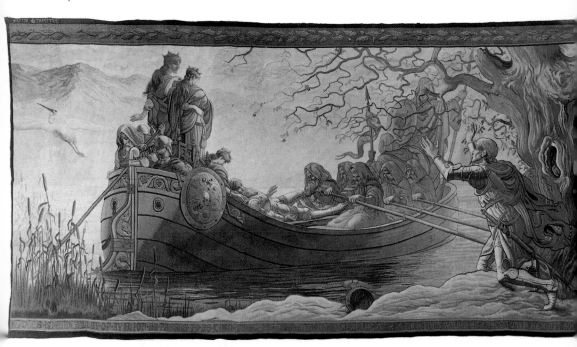

28. Herbert Bone. The Passing of Arthur. Woven by the Royal Windsor
Tapestry Manufactory 1879

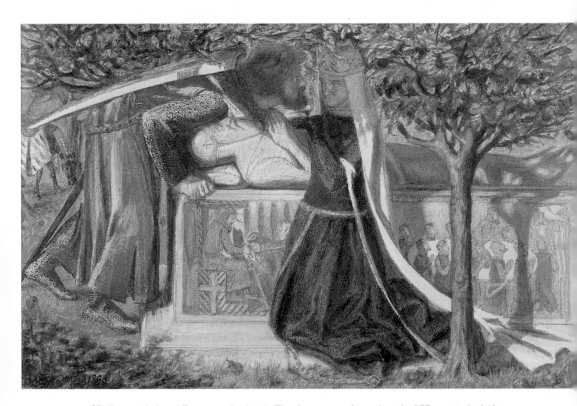

29. Dante Gabriel Rossetti. Arthur's Tomb, watercolour dated 1855, copied 1860

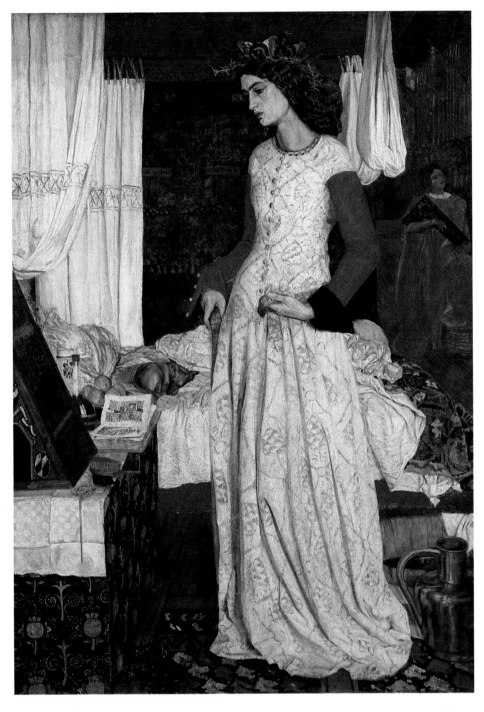

30. William Morris. La Belle Iseult (also called Queen Guinevere), oil painting 1858

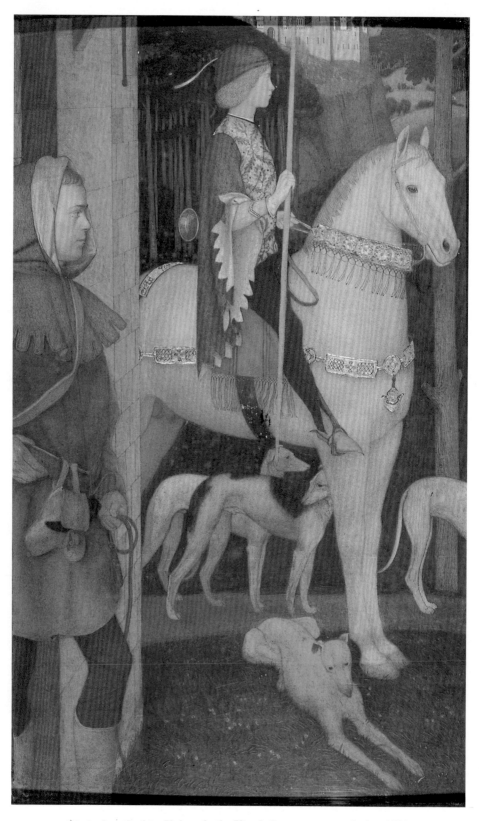

31. Arthur Gaskin. Kylwych, the King's Son, tempera painting 1901

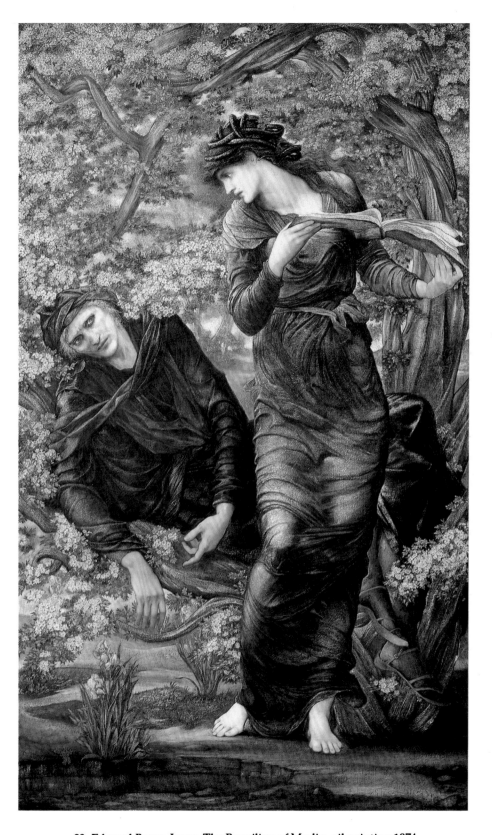

32. Edward Burne-Jones. The Beguiling of Merlin, oil painting 1874

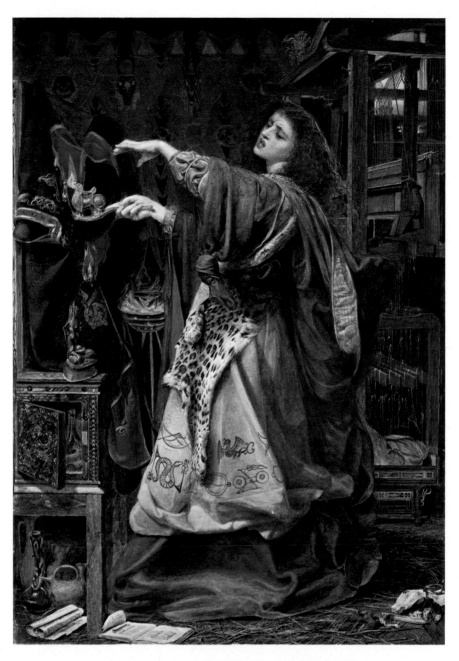

33. Frederick Sandys. Morgan-le-Fay, oil painting 1862–3

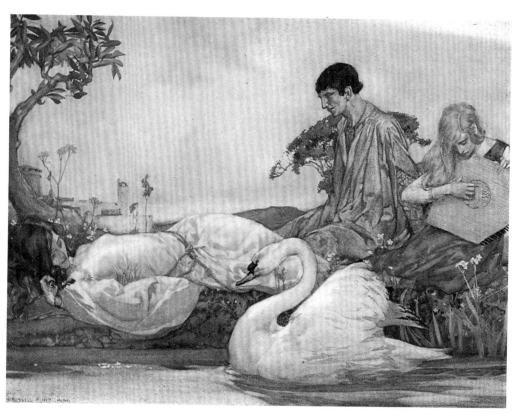

34. William Russell Flint. Alisander and Alice la Beale Pilgrim in the land of Benoye from Malory's *Morte D'Arthur* (London: Warner, 1910–11)

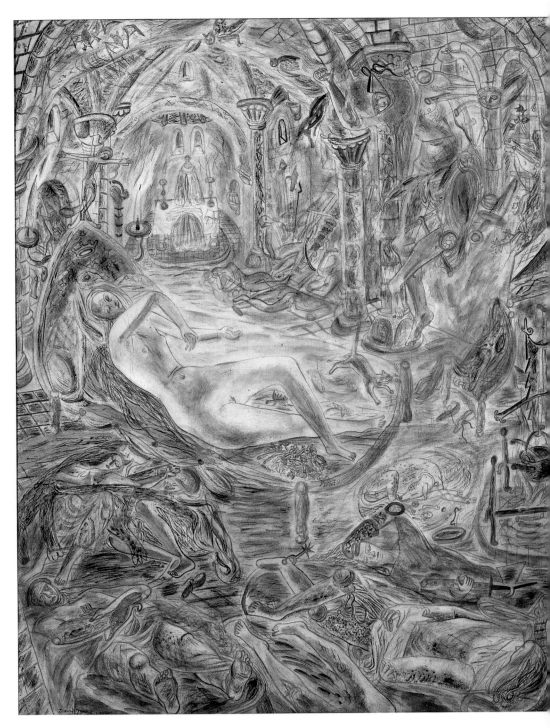

35. David Jones. Guenever, water colour 1940

from the bentwood railing and holy water stoup to the decorative crosses, chain mail hauberk, and white horse.

Rossetti's third subject, surrendered by Hunt after the former's complaint that other artists had snapped up the best topics, recreated the final scene of 'The Lady of Shalott':

> Out upon the wharfs they came,
> Knight and burgher, lord and dame,
> And round the prow they read her name,
>   The Lady of Shalott.
>   . . .
>
> But Lancelot mused a little space;
> He said, 'She has a lovely face;
> God in his mercy lend her grace,
>   The Lady of Shalott'.

The maiden lies on her barge, enclosed by roof and candles. She wears a patterned dress and a cloak with jewelled fastening. A bundle of garments, her face in the shadows, she is peripheral to the composition while it is Lancelot (with William Morris's face) who, unnaturally enlarged and elaborately costumed, occupies most of the picture plane. He gazes into the lady's face with the rapt attention that Galahad directs on the Grail chapel. The lack of distinction between erotic and spiritual rapture is a Rossettian characteristic.

The Moxon Tennyson's best known illustration is William Holman Hunt's design for 'The Lady of Shalott'. On the literal level the poem is a fairy tale about a beautiful lady in an island tower whose only view of the outside world comes from reflections in a mirror. She weaves 'the mirror's magic sights' into a tapestry. When, dazzled by the brilliant Sir Lancelot, she looks directly on the real world, a curse comes on her and she dies. On the allegorical level, the poem is interpreted as encapsulating the artist's dilemma in general and Tennyson's in particular.[11] The creative personality must choose between using art in the service of humanity (a social and tropological motivation) or single-mindedly pursuing art-for-art's sake. Tennyson's own comment suggests that the sexual content should also be considered: 'The new-born love for some thing, for some one in the wide world from which she has been so long excluded takes her out of the region of shadows into that of realities'.[12]

Hunt illustrates the lines describing what happens when the lady turns to the real world:

---

[11] See Leona Mosk Packer, 'Sun and Shadow: The Nature of Experience in Tennyson's "The Lady of Shalott" ', *The Victorian Newsletter* 25 (Spring, 1964), 4–8. On interpretations of the allegory and its relationship to the poet, see also Jerome H. Buckley, *Tennyson, the Growth of a Poet* (Cambridge, Mass., 1960) and E.D.H. Johnson, *The Alien Vision of Victorian Poetry* (Princeton, 1952).

[12] *Mem.* I, p. 117.

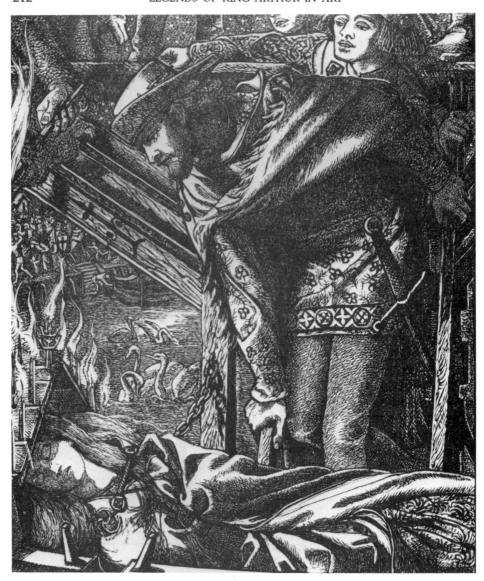

41. The Lady of Shalott. Dante Gabriel Rossetti's woodcut for **Alfred Lord Tennyson**, *Poems* (London: E. Moxon, 1857)

> Out flew the web and floated wide;
> The mirror crack'd from side to side,
> 'The curse is come upon me', cried
> The Lady of Shalott.

To make the drama work the artist must depict the exact conjunction of three events, a simultaneity that he can actually convey more accurately than the poet can.

Hunt was attracted to the subject as early as 1850 when he composed a pen and ink drawing.[13] As the Lady stands facing away from the cracking mirror with its images of Sir Lancelot, the window tracery and her own back, she is imprisoned by the loom's whip-like threads. As in late medieval illumination, the narrative content is expanded by the border of roundels about the mirror. They depict, clockwise from the top, a tower beside the river, the lady at her loom, her act of looking out the window, and the mounted Sir Lancelot with his 'helmet and plume'. The remaining mirror-roundels, all cracked, convey her tragic fate, as she writes her name on the prow, sits in the boat and floats down the river to Camelot where the townspeople view her corpse.

In the Moxon illustration and in the large oil painting developed from it (1886–1905), the artist uses allegorical images to contrive an expansion of meaning.[14] The circularity of loom, mirror and exploding threads is retained but the roundels are replaced by two oval plaques showing the crucified Christ, a new moon behind His arm, and Christ in Majesty. The lady has chosen emotional experience, which the binding threads suggest is a trap, rather than dedication to spiritual values. She is 'human soul' refusing its 'accepted responsibility'.

The most remarkable detail of the heroine's appearance is her hair which Tennyson complained was 'flying all over the shop'.[15] Hunt later explained that it was meant to convey the realization that the moment of catastrophe had come. Tennyson's view was that 'an illustrator ought never to add anything to what he finds in the text'.

The later oil version is so loaded with icons – irises, shoes, a lamp on a sphinx-legged base, doves, vases of flowers et al. – that the artist prefaced a 1909 edition of the poem with an explanatory essay.[16] The red-framed plaques now picture the Virgin and Child (humility) and Hercules attaining the apples of the Hesperides after slaying the dragon, an act representing courage. The tapestry design records the good and evil influences at Arthur's court. On the right is Arthur enthroned,

---

[13] For reproduction and comment see *The Pre-Raphaelites*, catalogue of the exhibition at the Tate Gallery, London, 7 March – 28 May, 1984 (London, 1984), #168.

[14] Two versions of the painting are the large oil (6 ft 2 in x 57 ft 2 in) at the Wadsworth Atheneum, Hartford, Conn. and the smaller oil (17½ in x 13⁷⁄₁₆ in) in the City Art Gallery, Manchester. *Ladies of Shalott: A Victorian Masterpiece and Its Contents*, catalogue of an exhibition by the Department of Art, Brown University, Providence, Rhode Island 23 February – 23 March, 1985 provides an extensive treatment of Hunt's paintings and related works.

[15] W. Holman Hunt, *Pre-Raphaelitism and the Pre-Raphaelite Brotherhood*, 2 vols (London, 1905), pp. 124–5. See also George Somes Layard, *Tennyson and his Pre-Raphaelite Illustrators* (London, 1894), p. 41. This critic regarded departures from the text as unethical. For another account of the Moxon Tennyson see Richard L. Stein, 'The Pre-Raphaelite Tennyson', *Victorian Studies* 24 (Spring, 1981), 279–301.

[16] Alfred Tennyson, *The Lady of Shalott*, with introduction by W. Holman Hunt explaining his painting's symbolism (London, 1909). See also Miriam Neuringer, 'The Burden of Meaning: Hunt's Lady of Shalott' in the Brown exhibition catalogue, pp. 61–70.

supported by Christian virtues, dutiful knights and Galahad with the Grail. On the left 'the lady has already pictured the brilliant but idle and vain-glorious Sir Lancelot, who brings no offering but lip-service'. While the knight reflected in the mirror rides through a sunlit landscape, the lady's head and torso in its peacock-feather bodice are already submerged in shadow, though her rose-coloured skirt, petticoat and bare feet, together with the vari-coloured balls of wool, are still bright with reflected light. The smaller version was painted, Hunt said, 'to determine the colour scheme', which consists of variations on the favourite medieval colours – red, green and blue. The tonal richness results from his technique of layered glazes. Probably the most complex Arthurian oil painting ever devised, Hunt's 'Lady of Shalott' avoids the 'poorness in individuality' that he deplored and strives to convey 'an elevated idea of the object to the spectator', the aim which he consistently pursued.[17]

Writing to Tennyson about the 1857 edition, Ruskin commented, 'Many of the plates are very noble things, though not, it seems to me, illustrations of your poems'.[18] On 3 or 4 April, 1859, Ruskin described to Margaret Bell a visit to Holland House where he found 'Watts lying back in his armchair . . . with Tennyson's PRB illustrated poems on his knee. Tennyson standing above him – explaining over his shoulder why said illustrations did not fit the poems'. In the discussion that followed, the poet insisted on exact truth to what the writer said, while Watts and Ruskin argued that 'the poet *must* be content to have his painter in partnership – not a slave'.[19]

Between 1860 and 1869 alone fifty or sixty paintings on Arthurian subjects were exhibited and though some derive from Malory, Tennyson's influence in popularising the material was paramount. Artists assumed the viewer's knowledge of the stories to which the titles of their works alluded. The 'Morte d'Arthur', later incorporated into 'The Passing of Arthur' idyll, retains the Malorian images of Excalibur, Bedivere, the mysterious arm emerging from the lake, the black-hooded ladies and their waiting ship. Tennyson adds the winter landscape emotively required by the tragedy and by a time scheme based on the seasonal cycle.

E.H. Corbould's watercolour 'Morte d'Arthur' (1864) and Frank Dicksee's 'The Passing of Arthur' (1889) are workmanlike recreations of the departure scene though one critic thought that Tennyson's 'long glories of the winter moon' might have provided a more mysterious illumination than the ship's lantern. Arthur Hughes, responding to Alice Boyd's request in 1891, painted a small oil version of

---

[17] Hunt discusses his views in a letter to John Lucas Tupper written June 20, 1878. See *A Pre-Raphaelite Friendship: The Correspondence of William Holman Hunt and John Lucas Tupper*, ed. James H. Coombs, Anne M. Scott, George P. Landow, Arnold A. Sanders (Ann Arbor, Mich., 1986), p. 246.

[18] *Works*, 36, p. 265.

[19] *The Winnington Letters of John Ruskin*, ed. V.A. Burd (Cambridge, Mass., and London, 1969), p. 150. Other illustrated editions include *The Lady of Shalott*, ill. Howard Pyle (New York, 1881); *A Dream of Fair Women and Other Poems by Alfred Lord Tennyson*, ill. Edmund J. Sullivan (London, 1899) which has a line drawing of the reapers who hear the lady singing and, to illustrate 'Sir Launcelot and Queen Guinevere', the lovers riding by a stream; *The Lady of Shalott*, ill. Charles Keeping (Oxford, 1986).

his Oxford Union mural, getting 'more of sleep and more of kingliness in Arthur'.[20] James Archer's oil, 'La Mort d'Arthur' (1860; City of Manchester Art Galleries) shows Arthur in Avalon, a green meadow with an apple orchard at the edge of the sea. Queen Morgan le Fay holds his bandaged head while three other beautiful ladies, whom Malory identified as the Queen of North Wales, the Queen of the Waste Lands and 'Nynyve, the chyff lady of the laake', mourn around him. Hovering above them a diaphanous figure approaches carrying the Holy Grail which in the fifteenth century *Morte Darthur* had healed the mad Lancelot, Bors, and the sick knight at the Perilous Chapel. In the middle distance Merlin converses with a lady, while further off the barge rides at anchor as the symbolic sunrise colours the eastern sky.[21]

While Arthur represented the ideal of heroic death suffered in serving humanity, Galahad embodied purity, a virtue that for the Victorians had specifically sexual connotations. Virginity before marriage and absolute fidelity after were the accepted 'norms'.[22] No lines of *The Idylls* were more frequently quoted to the younger generation than those describing Arthur's chivalric ideal:

> To lead sweet lives of purest chastity,
> To love one maiden only, cleave to her,
> And worship her by years of noble deeds.
>
> ('Guinevere', ll. 471–473)

Arthur goes on to assert that high thought, amiable words, courtliness, ambition, love of truth, and manliness all depend on purity. With the exception of Rossetti, G.F. Watts (1817–1904)[23] was the first Victorian to paint Sir Galahad. Living at Little Holland House with Henry and Sara Prinsep, the latter a famous London hostess, the artist met everyone of note, including Tennyson. But he had not read 'Sir Galahad' when in 1862 he painted fifteen-year-old Arthur Prinsep as a dreamy knight in plate armour standing beside a white horse in a luxuriant forest. There is nothing aside from the title – neither heraldic image nor radiant Grail – to identify the figure with the legend. The image was intended to express Watts' aesthetic theory, which was, in fact, medieval:

---

[20] 'A Pre-Raphaelite Gazette: The Penkill Letters of Arthur Hughes to William Bell Scott and Alice Boyd 1886–97', ed. William E. Fredeman, *Bulletin of the John Rylands Library* 49/2 (1967) and 50/1; rpt. *Pre-Raphaelite Studies* (1965–71), pp. 31–2.

[21] Archer's painting inspired T.A. Blaikie to write two sonnets, published in the *Magazine of Art*, 7 (1884), 433–34. For this reference I am indebted to W.E. Fredeman, 'The Last Idyll: Dozing in Avalon', documentation for a lecture at the 'Passing of Arthur' Conference, Barnard College, November 15, 1986. For critical responses to nineteenth century Arthurian painting see G.W. Whiting, *The Artist and Tennyson*, Rice University Studies 50 (Summer, 1964), 1–84.

[22] Walter E. Houghton, *The Victorian Frame of Mind 1830–1870* (New Haven and London, 1957), pp. 341–393.

[23] For biographical information see Wilfred Blunt, 'England's Michelangelo,' *a biography of George Frederic Watts* (London, 1975); W. Gaunt, *Victorian Olympus* (London, 1952); Mary Watts, *George Frederic Watts, the Annals of an Artist's Life*, 3 vols (London, 1912).

a great picture should be a thing to live with, to respond to varying moods . . . and to awaken the highest of our subtle mental and intellectual sensibilities . . . . it must have also the power to sustain the awakened and elevated spirit in that pure atmosphere that we only breathe in our happiest and least earthly moments.[24]

That Tennyson's lines, 'His strength was as the strength of ten/because his heart was pure' became attached to Watts' painting confirmed his aesthetic theory. When he was asked some thirty-five years later to supply a version of 'Sir Galahad' for Eton College Chapel, he readily agreed for reasons that he explained to H.E. Luxmoore, one of the Eton masters:

I recognize that from several points of view art would be a most valuable auxiliary in teaching, and nowhere can lessons that may help to form the character of the youth of England be more important than in the great schools where statesmen, and soldiers, and leaders of thought receive their first impressions.[25]

The idea of using the images of medieval knighthood to promote contemporary morality and religion also inspired the Scottish painter Sir Joseph Noel Paton (1821–1902) whom a critic described as 'more concerned with the enforcing of his view than with the painting of a picture'.[26] Armour and angels were his favourite allegorical images. Reputed to have the greatest private collection of armour in Scotland, he drew arms and armour with scrupulous accuracy.[27] He had already painted 'Sir Lancelot of the Lake' (1860) and the 'Death Barge of King Arthur' (1865)[28] when he began a series of Galahad pictures. In 'Sir Galahad's Vision of the Sangreal' (c. 1880)[29] and 'Sir Galahad and his Angel' (1884), the hero, protected by hovering angels, rides, sword or lance in hand, through a mountainous wasteland. A small oil 'How an Angel rowed Galahad over the Dern Mere' (ca. 1885–86) was reworked as the allegorical 'Beate Mundo Corde' (1890, the Pre-Raphaelite Trust). Lighted by a yellow-green sunset, the youthful hero in full armour along

[24] *Annals*, I, p. 315.

[25] *Annals*, II, p. 263. Watts' original 'Sir Galahad' is in the Fogg Museum of Art, Harvard University, Cambridge, Mass. It was reproduced as a stained glass window (1919) for St Paul's, Fairlie, Ayrshire, for Grahamstown in South Africa and for at least six other places. It appeared on the cover of an early twentieth century periodical, *Honour*, because Galahad was the 'type of perfect manly courage and purity'. On the painting's widespread distribution and influence see Marc Girouard, *The Return to Camelot*, passim.

[26] Alfred Thomas Story, 'The Life and Work of Sir Joseph Noel Paton', *The Art Journal*, Easter, 1895, 95–128.

[27] Malcolm Baker, 'A Victorian Collector of Armour, Sir Joseph Noel Paton', *Country Life*, 25 January, 1973, 232–6.

[28] A sepia of this work in the Glasgow Art Gallery and Museum was engraved in 1866 by the Glasgow Art Union to be handed out as a prize.

[29] This painting and 'Sir Galahad and his Angel' are reproduced in Girouard, plate XVIII and No. 104 respectively.

with his steed, a symbol of power, strength and prudence, is rowed across a mountain lake by a rosy-winged angel. The subject may have been suggested by Tennyson's lines:

> Sometimes on lonely mountain-meres
> I find a magic bark;
> I leap on board: no helmsman steers:
> I float till all is dark.

When the painting was exhibited at London's Doré Galleries in 1908, the catalogue entry noted:

> More is meant than meets the eye. It is a piece of definite and earnest symbolism . . . . The stately, beardless knight, standing there with his right hand on the red-cross shield and his helmet surmounted by great golden wings, is youth itself – youth in the splendour of visible beauty, of just perfected strength.

Drowning in the murky water beside the spiritual ship are Pleasure, a golden-haired, rose-adorned figure with a lute, 'her face forever unseen', and Despair, tearing poppies from her tresses. The connection which Paton made between the iconic figure of the knight and what the Victorians called 'muscular Christianity' is unmistakably figured in a sketchbook drawing. A Galahad-like knight, spear in hand, stands with his left foot on the chest of a slain barbarian; the subscription reads, 'Life's no Resting, but a Moving. Let thy life be Deed on Deed'.[30] The message was equally applicable to Captains of Industry, public school boys, and all those aspiring to the bourgeois dream of success and respectability.[31]

No nineteenth century poetry inspired a greater amount of art than 'The Lady of Shalott'[32] and its related Idyll, 'Elaine'.[33] These heroines share much the same

[30] Scottish National Gallery, Edinburgh.

[31] Other 'Sir Galahad' pictures are Edward Burne-Jones' pen and ink on vellum drawing (1858, Fogg Museum); Arthur Hughes' oil, 'The Meeting of Sir Galahad with the Grail' (1870, Walker Art Gallery, Liverpool); Robert Martineau, 'The Knight's Guerdon' (1864, Ashmolean Museum, Oxford) which illustrates the lines 'How sweet are looks that ladies bend / On whom their favours fall'; Herbert Gustave Schmalz, 'Sir Galahad' (1881); Charles Edward Johnson, 'Sir Galahad' (1888); Byam Shaw, 'Sir Galahad' (1905). Works exhibited at the Royal Academy are listed in Algernon Graves, *The Royal Academy of Arts*, 8 vols (London, 1905).

[32] 'Lady of Shalott' paintings not discussed in the text include those by H. Darvell (1855), James Smetham (before 1859), Walter Crane (1862), H.M. Paget (1881), Peter MacNab (1887), Byam Shaw (1898) and Edmund Joseph Sullivan (1899). John Everett Millais produced a drawing (1854) and Walter Crane a series of drawings (1858–9) now in the Houghton Library, Harvard University.

[33] 'Elaine' paintings, some of them probably inspired by Malory rather than Tennyson, include Henry Wallis' oil imitating stained glass (1861), C. Goldie's head of Elaine (1861), William Millais' 'Elaine, the Lily Maid of Astolat' (1862), R. Gibbs' oil (1875), Charles Edwin Fripp's watercolour, H.G. Schmalz' 'Elaine' (1885), Edward Blair Leighton's oil of the barge

iconology, with Lancelot's shield replacing the loom in *Idyll* imagery and a dumb, Charon-like boatman being added to the limited company of figures.

As early as 1861 a critic complained in *The Art Journal*: 'We are well nigh satiated with 'Elaine' – and most sincerely hope that this young lady will be allowed at least one season's respite'. His hope was unfulfilled. Excluding book illustrations, at least eighty recorded versions of the Lady of Shalott/Elaine subject were produced before World War I, though the location of many is now unknown. Some of Elaine's qualities were inherited from Malory. She is his most psychologically credible woman and his chief vehicle for exploring the nature of love. The extraordinary poignancy of her plea – 'fayre knyght and curtoyse knyght have mercy uppon me, and suffir me not to dye for youre love' – and her defiant questioning of her fate – 'I do none offence, though I love an erthely man, unto God, for He fourmed me thereto' – produce a tragic intensity that the artists can only transmit as pathos.

How are we to account for the Lily Maid's extraordinary popularity? What attracted Victorian males, I suspect, was the iconic depiction of an 'ideal' relationship between the sexes. The handsome, successful masculine figure engages actively in the real world outside the castle – every Englishman's home – while the woman, impregnable, inviolate, secluded in her tower, engages in domestic activity. Also attractive was the image of a young, beautiful, innocent, 'high born maiden' who in dying for love was a sacrifice to male power and glory. Her beauty is even enhanced by death, as in a painting by Toby E. Rosenthal (1849–1917) who festoons the death barge with garlands as if it were a bridal coach. A white gown frequently emphasised the bride-of-death motif, though some artists preferred the crimson of sacrifice or blue of fidelity.

The material was extraordinarily adaptable, allowing an artist to exploit particular strengths and visions. Since Tennyson gave no details of the Lady's appearance, the subjective embodiment of beautiful woman could have hair that was dark, blond or red, straight or curly, short or long – the latter being preferred in death-voyage scenes. It fanned out around the head or trailed in the water, emphasizing a sexuality that was also implied by the shapes of thighs and legs moulded under the richly patterned covering. That technical skill sometimes betrayed imagination the critical comments make evident.[34] E.H. Corbould's 'Elaine the Lily Maid of Astolat' (1861), for example, is a 'flagrant sin' against the text with Elaine 'a vulgar-faced, sensual-lipped female' while in R.S. Lauder's 'The Lady of Shalott' (1854) the 'creamy face, verging to a deep claret colour, may have been like the Lady of Shalott, but it is certainly not common in living humanity'.

Because there is no psychological drama in the death-voyage paintings – all passion spent, as far as the maid is concerned – landscape frequently provides

---

arriving at Camelot (1899), J.M. Strudwick's 'Elaine with Lancelot's shield' (1891), George Benton's 'Lancelot and Elaine' (1900), Marie Johnson's miniature (1902), Ernest Normand's frieze design (1904) and Barry Sleigh's 'Elaine' (ca. 1904).

[34] Whiting, *The Artist and Tennyson*, Chapter VI, passim.

justification for choosing the subject. Arthur Hughes' 'The Lady of Shalott' (1873) presents an expansive river scene where sunlight pours on grasses, reeds and flowers as well as on awe-struck country women and the floating maiden. The iconic realism of willows and swans had previously been used in a pencil study (1864) where these death images claustrophobically enclose the Lady, who is about to escape into reality by loosening the boat's chain. In John Atkinson Grimshaw's 'Elaine' (1877) Camelot's Neo-Gothic skyline, the dragon-prowed barge and shadowy boatman are reduced to silhouette by the fading sunset, a favourite death metaphor. Moonlight, an effect in which Grimshaw specialised, glimmers on barge, corpse and wooded shoreline in 'The Lady of Shalott' (1878).

G.H. Broughton's 'The Road to Camelot' (1898, Walker Art Gallery, Liverpool) is one of the rare paintings that ignores the lady. It is a literal recreation of the text's 'market girls', 'damsels glad' in pseudo-medieval gowns, 'long-hair'd page in crimson clad' and, beyond the river, 'knights riding two and two'. Aesthetic indulgence rather than significant emotion characterises the work, which is lively, pretty and superficial. Aside from his lack of seriousness, Broughton drew Ruskin's disapproval on grounds of his technique which was like the work of 'a converted crossing sweeper, with his broom, after it was worn stumpy'.

Representations of the Lily Maid in her tower were often treated as genre scenes. In William Maw Egley's oil (1858, City Museum, Sheffield) the luxurious furnishings and many-paned windows with their fine view are more important than the psychological crisis. That the subject even offered opportunities for satire five issues of *Punch* published in March, 1866 reveal. Both the poetry and the already numerous paintings are parodied in George du Maurier's 'A Legend of Camelot'.[35]

No Victorian artist was more captivated by the Lily Maid than J.W. Waterhouse (1849–1917) who painted her at least seven times over a period of thirty years.[36] Psychological portraiture was his speciality, though he did not ignore the uses of impressionistic landscape and allegorical images to create what John Dixon Hunt has called (quoting D.G. Rossetti's 'The Sonnet') 'a moment's monument'. His first Lady (1888, Tate Gallery, London) presents the penultimate scene in the narrative chronology, the death voyage's beginning. Wearing an expression of anticipated doom, the heroine sits in the boat, her blond hair lightly blown by the wind that ripples the water. Such details of setting as the decaying steps and the subdued light of a rainy autumn contribute to the melancholy atmosphere and the sense of life running out. Everything trails in the water – the long medieval sleeve of her white gown, the chain that she languidly releases into the turgid

[35] There are other examples of Victorian satire on the *Idylls*. A. Forestier's drawing 'The Last Idyll', *Illustrated London News*, October 22, 1892, p. 509, shows the dying poet surrounded by a moonlit company of *Idylls* characters including a hortatory King Arthur and a long-haired Lily Maid who raises over his head her flowery spray. Based on 'Tennyson's fanciful "Idylls"', William Brough (1826–1870) wrote a 'Christmas Extravaganza', *King Arthur, or the Days and Knights of the Round Table*, produced at the Haymarket, London, December 26, 1863. Ellen Terry, briefly G.F. Watts' wife, was Tristram.
[36] Anthony Hobson, *The Art and Life of J.W. Waterhouse R.A. 1849–1917* (London, 1980).

river, the willows, the dead leaves, the broken reeds. Of three candles,[37] two have already gone out and the third barely lights the crucifix. Nor does the lantern's pallid flame provide any radiance. The impressionistic treatment of nature, particularly obvious in the foreground, aroused censure as being unsuitably foreign but R.E.D. Sketchley[38] welcomed the new style:

> the identification of the real and the ideal is not to be accomplished by painting a poetical subject from beginning to end out of doors; (where) it is the irrelevant detail which is most apt to catch the eye.

He also rejoiced that the subdued colours did not approximate the 'missal-like intensity of Pre-Raphaelitism'.

The second 'Lady of Shalott' (1894; City Art Gallery, Leeds) with its circular forms (mirror, loom, tapestry roundels, decorated floor) and its imprisoning loops around the lady's skirt inevitably suggests Hunt's treatment of the 'curse is come upon me' subject. But rather than showing her in the act of turning from mirror to window, Waterhouse depicts his dark-haired beauty directly facing the imagined window (which admits little light) and the spectator; her expression and stance convincingly convey the mixed emotions of curiosity, apprehension, and fascination. She stands out dramatically against the room's darkness where only the bright Lancelot in a green countryside and the tapestry's roundels are illuminated.

The first in narrative order but last to be painted is ' "I am Half-Sick of Shadows," said the Lady of Shalott' (1915, Art Gallery of Ontario, Toronto). Waterhouse uses the same brunette model and shadowy, claustrophobic room as in his previous painting, though the loom is realistically detailed and the mirror reflects not only the lovers (who have sparked the Lady's dissatisfaction) but the walled city of Camelot beside the river. The lady's troubled face reveals her realisation that security and diligence do not make a life. Again the dark interior, which seems too small for the figure, conveys an air of forboding while the mirror's bright landscape images the lure of romance.

Two years earlier Sidney Meteyard (1868–1947) had illustrated the same line of poetry in a composition tonally restricted to shades of blue.[39] His lady seems bored and lethargic as she lets one arm dangle over the chairback; and she distances herself from the tapestry in which an almost completed Lancelot rides past

---

[37] Layard, op. cit. p. 61 quotes a letter from Waterhouse:
> With respect to the lighted candles in my picture, I made use of them merely as a means of completing the composition, my excuse being that lighted candles might have been used by the Lady of Shalott as a kind of *devotional* office before her death. I remember seeing in an engraving from a medieval manuscript a bier covered with candles.

[38] R.E.D. Sketchley, 'The Art of J.W. Waterhouse, R.A.', *The Art Journal*, Christmas, 1909, 1–31.

[39] This painting together with the Wadsworth Atheneum Hunt, the Tate Waterhouse, and Grimshaw's 'Elaine' are all reproduced in colour in Christopher Wood, *The Pre-Raphaelites* (London, 1981).

sheaves of wheat. The foreground of banked camellias (inevitable reminders of Alexander Dumas' heroine) and the dark mirror in which the lovers faintly glimmer effect a mood of sensuality combined with doom.

It is as illustrators of Tennyson's poetry that women artists first appear in the history of Arthurian art. Although we do not know even the name of the lady who in 1852 provided woodcuts for a benefit edition of 'The Lady', we know a good deal about another early illustrator, Elizabeth Siddal (1829–1862). She was a milliner's assistant who became Ruskin's protegée – a letter of May, 1855 invites her to 'come up and look at a missal or two' – and D.G. Rossetti's model, mistress and wife. One of her first works, dated 1853, was a pen, ink and pencil drawing in which, to the accompaniment of cracking glass and breaking threads, a seated lady looks over an open cupboard and crucifix to the empty Camelot road outside. According to Deborah Cherry, the drawing shows 'gender difference' by its refusal to present woman as 'helpless, cursed, dying, dead'.[40] Instead, we see a woman who is 'pure, chaste, calm . . . not offered as a victim or a spectacle for the masculine gaze'. In fact, several nineteenth-century artists like Sophie Anderson and Margaret W. Tarrant preferred the corpse, though Mary L. Gow's 'Elaine' (1876) and Ellen Montalba's 'Elaine' (1880) show chamber scenes.

It was only in 1981 that a truly feminist interpretation was achieved, Shelah Horvitz's drawing, ' "I am Half-Sick of Shadows" '.[41] Paradox is the basis of the conception. The lady is naked to suggest both her craving for sexual experience and her vulnerability. She draws up her knees and binds them with muscled arms to protect her virginity. Her mood is one of desperation. With its rough stone walls, plank floor and slit of a window the tower room is prisonlike yet it contains a richly carved Gothic chest, symbol of 'a beauty unseen'. The enormous mirror reflects Guenevere, with Jane Burden's face – a 'thoughtless coquette;' a naked Lancelot, doer not thinker; and, between them, King Arthur, 'the largest face in the picture because he is the greatest mind'. Horvitz makes no apology for departing so radically from the text:

> . . . my intention was not to illustrate Tennyson's poem but to take it as inspiration, as my starting point. Had I written the story, the Lady would not have died. Indeed, she would have braved the curse, journeyed down river to find Lancelot, become his love, and resumed weaving in Camelot, where she could experience life and thereby become a better and deeper artist.

The 1842 *Poems'* themes of self-sacrifice, male purity and female virtue, adumbrated through Arthurian personae, Tennyson explored more complexly in his serial poem, *The Idylls of the King*. The central allegory concerned 'Sense at war

[40] *The Pre-Raphaelites*, Tate exhibition catalogue, pp. 266–7.
[41] Shelah Horvitz, 'My Lady of Shalott', *Journal of Pre-Raphaelite Studies*, III/2 (1983), 64–68. See also Jack T. Harris's response, 'I have never seen a naked Lady of Shalott', *Journal of Pre-Raphaelite Studies* V/I (1984), 76–87.

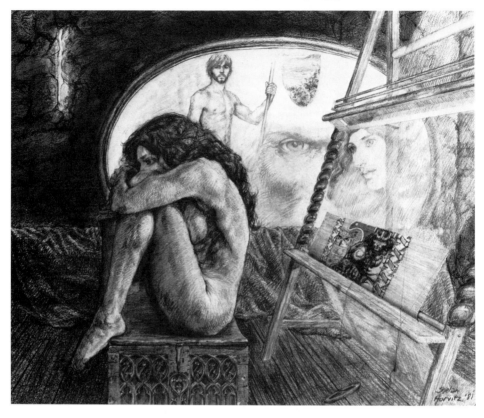

42. Shelah Horvitz. 'My Lady of Shalott', 1981

with Soul'. Tennyson considered that Henry Alford's interpretation came closest
to his conception:

> This higher soul of man in its purity, in its justice, in its nobleness, in its
> self-denial, we understand Mr. Tennyson to figure forth by the King . . .
> On the pragmatical issue we recognize the bearing down in history
> and in individual man, of pure and lofty Christian purpose by the
> corruptions of superstition, by human passions and selfishnesses.[42]

Arthur, 'ideal manhood closed in real man', is the hero (Soul), Lancelot and
Guenevere are the destroyers (Sense). The symbolic significances are underlined
by physical attributes. Arthur has 'a golden head', hair like 'a sun that ray'd from
off a brow/ Like hillsnow high in heaven'. He also has a curly golden beard,

---

[42] Henry Alford, 'The Idylls of the King', *The Contemporary Review*, XIII (January, 1870),
104–125.

steel-blue eyes, and a clear face. Lancelot, in contrast has 'night-black hair', 'large black eyes' and a face that is scarred and lined:

> The great and guilty love he bore the Queen
> In battle with the love he bore his lord
> Had marr'd his face and mark'd it ere his time.

But the illustrators of Tennyson's *Idylls* preferred the romantic to the didactic mood. At Moxon's invitation, the Alsatian Gustave Doré provided thirty-six drawings to be reproduced as steel engravings in folio editions of *Elaine* (1866), *Enid* (1866), *Guinevere* (1866) and *Vivien* (1867). Though the artist's friend Blanchard Jerrold claimed that 'Doré was at home in Tennyson's exquisite dreamland',[43] the poet, as usual, was less than pleased.[44] The *Athenaeum*'s critic suspected that 'M. Doré has never read Tennyson', a suspicion that was correct, since the French artist did not understand English.

Doré's strength was his ability to create a landscape imbued with the wildness and strangeness appropriate to romance. While Tennyson's idea of wilderness came from Cornwall and Wales, Doré derived his from the more rugged scenery of the Vosges and Savoy where he found the castle-topped crags that became his signature. His serpentine roots and dead branches predate Arthur Rackham's mastery of this mood-inducing device. The Alsatian, a notorious magpie, could have found both the forest settings and 'the flickering fairy circle (that) wheel'd and broke' (frontispiece, *Guinevere*) in the works of the German romantic, Moritz von Schwind (1804–1871), in particular, his 'Elfentanz im Erlenhain' (now in Munich's Schack-Galerie). Doré effectively evokes an emotional relationship between character and setting, as in 'The Remorse of Lancelot' (*Elaine*, ill. 9) where the grey waters of the Thames, the mist and the wind-blown reeds create a feeling of desolation. He can also use setting to provide a sense of momentous occasion. In the 'Finding of King Arthur', (*Guinevere*, ill. 7), a naked baby lies cradled on the sand while storm clouds roll, sea gulls wheel, and the surf pounds on the dark cliffs. The bearded, barefoot bardic Merlin, clutching a harp, looks on.

Too often, however, the towering cliffs, dark forests, and ruined castles dwarf the humans, making them seem inconsequential. And too often the setting becomes a stage. In 'Lancelot Relating his Adventures' (*Elaine*, ill. 3) the characters are theatrically placed in a pseudo-Gothic hall, those in the foreground illuminated by an external spotlight while those on whom the light from the windows should fall are placed in shadow. The chiaroscuro effect is acceptable dramatically but not rationally. Tennyson's central interest, the personalities of the women who represent 'The True and the False', is of little concern to Doré. Vivien, appearing in only four scenes and individualized in only one, 'Vivien and Merlin Repose', is a lazy-looking gypsy. Elaine and the similarly depicted Enid with their Saxon braids, languid attitudes and vapid expressions are quite at variance with their strong-minded literary prototypes. And in Guinevere's scenes of significant emo-

---

[43] *Life of Gustav Doré* (London, 1891), p. 145.

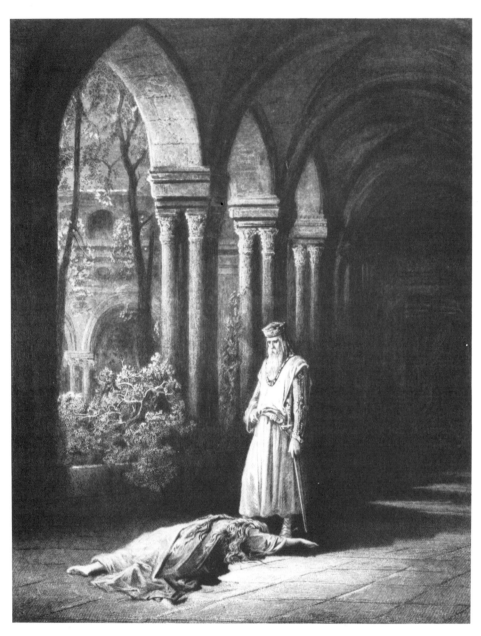

43. The King's Farewell. Gustave Doré's illustration for Tennyson's *Guinevere*
(London: E. Moxon, 1866)

tion, 'The Parting', 'The Dawn of Love' and 'The King's Farewell', we are shown only her back. The four idylls failed to provide opportunities for the caricature, grotesquerie and sublimity that were Doré's forte. Moreover, they presented moral situations with which the artist could not or would not deal.

Even as Tennyson's Arthurian poems were appearing, a new technique was developing that claimed the status of art. 'A new world slowly widens to our sight – new sky, new earth, new flowers, a very heaven compared with the old earth' – Joseph Durham A.R.A. is talking about photography. The daguerreotype and the wet collodion process made possible Pre-Raphaelite truth-to-nature. The 'little bit of little landscape effect, all blurred and uncertain . . . is superseded by large pictures with minute foregrounds, regular planes of distance, and perfectly clear skies', marvelled Lady Eastlake.[45] Reproductions of romantic Arthurian places like Tintagel could now be circulated, with accompanying Tennysonian quotations, and models could pose for photographers as for painters.

One of the earliest art photographers, Henry Peach Robinson (1830–1901), deliberately adopted Pre-Raphaelite attitudes and subjects.[46] As soon as the first *Idylls* appeared in 1859, a lugubrious girl with long hair and a white skirt was set to gaze on a lion-blazoned shield in what is obviously a Victorian parlour for 'Elaine watching the shield of Lancelot'. In 1861 he photographed 'The Lady of Shalott', composing the floating heroine in a manner closely resembling Millais' drowning 'Ophelia'. Waterlilies decorate the foreground; trees and plants along the riverbank are clearly reflected in the shining water. Matthew Arnold's 'Tristram and Iseut' inspired Robinson's third Arthurian study, 'Sleep' (1867). Using his own children to represent those of Tristram and Iseut of the White Hands, the photographer suggests the analogy between sleep and death by pallidly lighting the faces. In all these photographs there is too great a discrepancy between the realism of the settings and the quasi-medieval characters to make them succeed as art.

In 1874 the publishing firm Henry S. King & Co. wanted illustrations for the 'Peoples'' or Cabinet edition of Tennyson's works. Tennyson approached his Isle of Wight neighbour, the pioneer photographer Julia Margaret Cameron (1815–1879) with the request, 'Will you think it a trouble to illustrate my *Idylls* for me?' to which she replied 'Now *you* know, Alfred, that *I* know that it is immortality to me to be bound up with you'.[47] She had spent most of her life in India but when her

---

[44] *The Letters of Emily Lady Tennyson*, ed. James O. Hoge (University Park, Penn. and London, 1974), p. 206 note 2. See also *Lady Tennyson's Journal*, ed. James O. Hoge (Charlottesville, Va., 1981), entry for 10 March, 1868: '. . . the world thinks that we are enriching ourselves by Doré's editions whereas we have not received a penny as yet for the use of the poems tho' (Moxon) promises something when thousands of each is [sic] sold'.
[45] Michael Bartram, Introduction, *Pre-Raphaelite Photography*, catalogue of an exhibition organised by the British Council (London, 1983), pp. 5–6.
[46] See Margaret F. Harker, *Henry Peach Robinson: Master of Photographic Art 1830–1901* (Oxford, 1988) and Robinson's own work, *Pictorial Effect in Photography, Being Hints on Composition and Chioroscuro for Photographers* (1869).
[47] On her life and work see Helmet Gernsheim, *Julia Margaret Cameron: Her Life and Photographic Work* (Millerton, N.Y., 1975); Charles W. Millard, 'Julia Margaret Cameron and

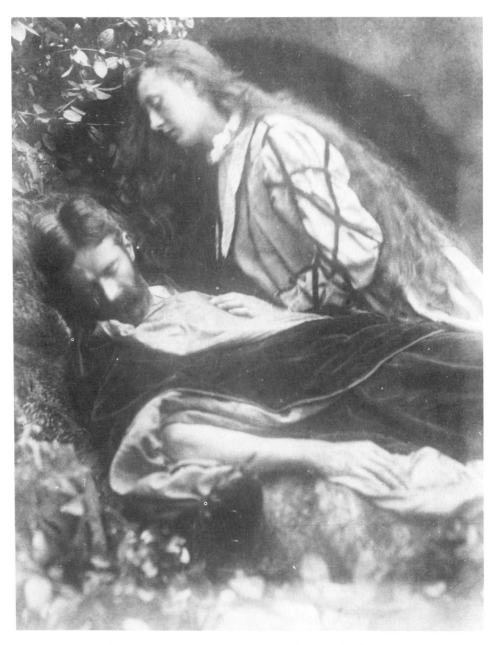

44. Gareth and Lynette. Julia Margaret Cameron's photograph. *Illustrations to Tennyson's 'Idylls of the King' and Other Poems*, 1874–75

husband, the jurist Charles Cameron, retired in 1848, they settled in England where, as one of the seven Pattle sisters, Mrs Cameron had numerous relatives and friends. Mary Watts described her as epitomising 'all the qualities of a remarkable family, presenting them in a distilled form'.[48] William Allingham in his diary entry for October 3, 1863 about a visit to the Tennysons, noted, 'Mrs. Tennyson in white, I can sometimes scarcely hear her low tones. Mrs. Cameron, dark, short, sharp-eyed, one hears very distinctly'.[49] In her religious faith, devotion to an elderly husband and willing acceptance of matriarchal duties, she seems an ordinary Victorian woman. But she had the energy, imagination and commitment to a new art form, photography, that make some modern critics describe her as a genius.

Using the wet collodion method, she produced in a few months a series of fifteen photographs illustrating the *Idylls*, as well as some for other poems. Only 'Maud', 'Elaine' and 'Arthur' appeared, as woodcuts, in the Cabinet edition. The entire series she hoped to have published in large albums of full-sized prints made from her negatives and to this proposal King agreed. Two albums appeared, the first in January 1875 with twelve *Idylls* photographs, and the second in May, 1875, with the rest of her Tennysonian studies, including three *Idylls* subjects. The albums were gift books, intended to be looked at rather than read. The relevant lines of text she copied out by hand, underlining the most important parts.[50]

Mrs Cameron made a credible correspondence between the reader's word-based image of a literary character and the individual face chosen as model. Her own venerable husband with his long white hair and beard was an excellent Merlin and dumb boatman. Her niece, May Prinsep, was a dewy Lynette and Elaine while May's fiancé, Andrew Hitchens, played Gareth. On 10 October, 1874,

Tennyson's "Idylls of the King" ', *Harvard Library Bulletin* XXI/2 (April, 1973), 187–201; Mike Weaver, *Julia Margaret Cameron 1815–1879*, catalogue of an exhibition arranged by the John Hansard Gallery, the University, Southampton and toured by the Arts Council of Great Britain, March 7, 1984 – October 6, 1985 (London, 1984); *Lord Tennyson and his Friends, with Reminiscences* by Anne Thackeray Ritchie and H.H.H. Cameron (London, 1893); Joanne Lukitsh, 'Julia Margaret Cameron's Photographic Illustrations to Alfred Tennyson's *Idylls of the King*', *Arthurian Literature* VII, ed. Richard Barber (Cambridge, Eng., 1987), 145–157. The Tennyson Research Centre has letters.

[48] *Annals* I, 205.

[49] *A Diary, 1824–1889*, p. 87.

[50] Sets of both volumes are located in the Houghton Library, Harvard; the International Museum of Photography at George Eastman House, Rochester; the Victoria and Albert Museum, London; the BBC Hulton Picture Library, London; the Gernsheim Collection, University of Texas; and the collection of Janet Troxell. The Metropolitan Museum, New York, Tennyson Research Centre, Lincoln, Royal Photographic Society, Bath, Jerrald Moore and J. Hillelson have single volumes. See Millard, 190, note 22 and Lukitsh, p. 157. Lincoln also has a miniature volume dedicated to Victoria, Crown Princess of Germany, the Princess Royal. Photographs 1–17 illustrate the *Idylls*. There are minor variations in the photographs from one collection to another; for example, 'The Corpse of Elaine in the Palace of King Arthur' and 'King Arthur wounded lying in the barge' which Lukitsh reproduces from the Eastman collection are not identical to those in the Hulton Collection. In the November 29 letter to Ryan, Cameron claimed, 'I have taken 180 pictures to obtain 12 successes'.

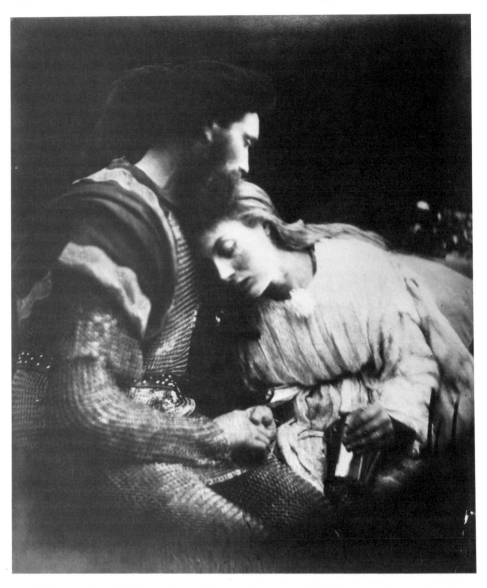

45. The parting of Sir Lancelot and Queen Guinevere. Julia Margaret Cameron's photograph. *Illustrations to Tennyson's 'Idylls of the King' and Other Poems*, 1874–75

Cameron reported to Charles Tennyson, 'I have taken Gareth in the cave with honeysuckle outside, he asleep & Lynette leaning over him'. For Arthur she used William Warder, an Isle of Wight porter. The choice suggests that the Tennysonian ideal – 'mystic mythical a real embodiment of conscience'[51] – was not to be found in the Camerons' upper middle class circle. A gardener and parlour maid were also pressed into service and if the supply of relatives and servants failed, passing tourists might be co-opted. One of the latter, a potential Guinevere, was found in an exhausted condition – 'I have been lying on the floor for the last two hours, clutching the porter's ankle', she explained.

But months passed and still she could find no Sir Lancelot. One day she and Tennyson paid a visit to the theologian William George Ward. On entering the room her eye lit on a knightly figure illuminated by the light of the fireplace. 'Alfred', she cried, 'I have found Sir Lancelot!' In ringing tones, the poet replied, 'I want a face well worn with evil passion'. There was embarrassment all round when the putative Lancelot turned out to be the Roman Catholic Bishop – future Cardinal – Herbert Vaughan. Evil-looking models were in short supply. If the beautiful Vivien was insufficiently malignant, it was because the model was so virtuous, the photographer explained. Only the weak-faced Sir Galahad, about whose waist Perceval's sister binds the belt made from her hair, seems somewhat miscast.

Though signs are needed to identify characters, Mrs. Cameron does not crowd the space. Arthur, Galahad and Elaine have their respective dragon, cross and lily. Enid wears a pearl necklace with pendant hearts (purity and love) while her hand rests on a lute, a motif that might have been borrowed from Arthur Hughes' oil 'The Brave Geraint' (ca. 1860). Merlin is provided with a hollow oak, hauled over from Tennyson's property, but other natural details such as the moon and the waves of 'So like a shatter'd column lay the King' were painted onto the photographic plates. There are anacronistic anomalies like the signet ring and wedding ring on Merlin's left hand or the Prussian helmets which Lancelot and Arthur wear when they view Elaine's corpse. And in a number of compositions the homemade costumes and exaggerated posturings produce the comic effects of amateur theatricals, a characteristic that has led to the denigration of the whole corpus.

Mrs Cameron's greatest accomplishment was the creation of mood. This was partly the result of faulty photographic technique which blurred outlines and distorted perspective. Another amateur photographer, Charles Dodgson (Lewis Carroll) accused her of purposely manipulating focus and calling the results a triumph of art. Her aesthetic sensibility made her choose moments charged with the emotions of love, longing and sorrow. Her husband's treatise, 'An Essay on the Sublime and Beautiful' (1835), no doubt encouraged her to believe that sorrowful feelings and the objects which produced them were beautiful. Her desire was 'to arrest all the beauty that came before me'. At her best, she composed

[51] The phrase occurs in a letter to Sir Edward Ryan, 29 November, 1874, cited by Lukitsh, p. 148.

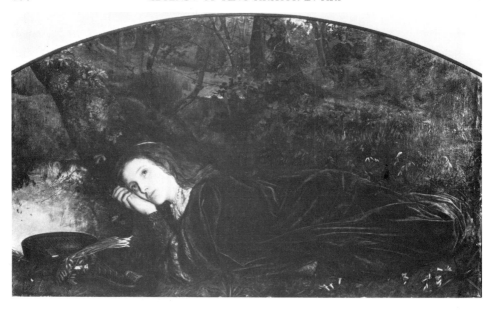

46. Arthur Hughes. The Rift in the Lute, oil painting ca. 1862

photographs that elicited the kind of response once reserved only for painting. Of 'The Parting of Lancelot and Guinevere' a reviewer in *The Morning Post* wrote on 11 January, 1875:

> 'Sir Lancelot' is the flower of mediaeval chivalry – a knight towering above all others in stature as in renown, yet the gentlest, tenderest, most courteous of all in the Arthurian Legends. The prostration and *abandon* of overwhelming grief are pictured with a touch of poignant pathos in the look and attitude of the sorrow-stricken queen, who sinks hopelessly upon his breast.

Cameron's own comment in a letter of 6 December, 1874, summarises her aesthetic creed: 'At last yesterday I achieved the picture with as much power and pathos as one can bring into a photograph consistently with what I think the great principle of high art, reserve and composure expressive of subdued passion'. Julia Margaret Cameron's career was glorious but brief. In 1875 she and her husband returned to their old home in Ceylon where she died four years later.[52]

Too many of the paintings which the *Idylls* inspired have a greeting-card pretti-

---

[52] Among many other illustrated editions are *Tennyson's Enid* illuminated in the style of the 14th Century (London, 1862?); *Illustrations of Alfred Tennyson's Heroes and Heroines*, ill. in colour lithograph by Marcus Stone, G.G. Kilburne, R. Sauber, I. Warry, R. Kemm and Fanny Bowers, with pen and ink drawings by J. Pauline Sunter (London, Paris, New York, 1893); *Geraint and Enid*, ill. Byam Shaw (London & Edinburgh, 1906); *The Idylls of the King*, ill. Eleanor F. Brickdale, an extensively illustrated book with full page watercolours which also

ness and sentimentality that rarely approaches Cameron's psychological realism. Enid is almost as popular as Elaine for she projects the ideal of wifeliness – beautiful, loving, obedient, protective, loyal and, in Tennyson's word 'simple'.[53] She is the kind of woman described in Ruskin's influential lecture 'Of Queens' Gardens', which Walter Houghton calls 'the most important single document I know for the characteristic idealization of love, woman, and the home in Victorian thought'.[54] Arthur Hughes (1832–1915),[55] a Pre-Raphaelite follower whose sense of beauty Ruskin praised as 'quite exquisite', in the early 60's painted three oils on romance subjects – 'The Knight of the Sun' (1860), once entitled 'The Death of Arthur', but now related to a non-Arthurian legend; 'The Brave Geraint' or 'Geraint and Enid' (c. 1860; Lady Anne Tennant); and 'The Rift in the Lute' (ca. 1862; Gordon Bottomley Bequest, Carlisle Art Gallery). The latter title alludes to Vivien's song which in turn alludes to Arthurian decline:

> It is the little rift within the lute,
> That by and by will make the music mute,
> And ever widening slowly silence all.
> ('Merlin and Vivien' ll. 388–390)

A recumbent lady who may be identified as 'Vivien, like the tenderest-hearted maid' (l. 375) stretches out in the forest beside her anacronistic lute (a Victorian rather than medieval form of the instrument). Although Robin Gibson proposes that 'without the necessary documentation . . . the significance of details such as the approaching huntsman hero will probably never be known', the image was surely suggested by Merlin's response to Vivien's song:

> Far other was the song that once I heard
> By this huge oak, sung nearly where we sit:
> For here we met, some ten or twelve of us,
> To chase a creature that was current then
> In these wild woods, the hart with golden horns.
> ('Merlin and Vivien', ll. 403–407)

The magician's explication of what differentiates the sexes – 'Man dreams of Fame while woman wakes to love' – is not inconsistent with the painter's characterisations.

---

appeared in a limited edition of 350 signed copies (London, New York, Toronto, 1911); *Tennyson's Guenever and Other Poems*, ill. Florence Harrison (Glasgow, 1912).
[53] Paintings based on *Enid* include J. Hallyar, 'and the sweet voice of a bird' (1860); J.B. Bedford, 'Enid Hears of Geraint's Love' (1862); F.M. Miller, 'Enid' (1866); E.H. Corbould, 'Enid's Dream' (1873), H.M. Paget, 'Enid and Geraint' (1879); G.F. Watts, 'Enid' (1879); Mrs Samuel Nicholl, 'Enid' (1880); Alice M. Scott, 'Enid, and seeing her so sweet and serviceable' (1881); Helen Blackburne, 'Enid' (1885); F. Sydney Muschamp, 'Enid – then breaking his command of silence' (1885) and Madeline M. McDonald, 'Enid' (1896).

Hughes worked up a study for this painting to create 'The Brave Geraint', the title being the first three words of 'The Marriage of Geraint':

> The brave Geraint, a knight of Arthur's court,
> A tributary prince of Devon, one
> Of that great Order of the Table Round,
> Had married Enid, Yniol's only child,
> And loved her, as he loved the light of Heaven.

Because of his uxoriousness, he neglects his courtly rites and duties until his people 'Began to scoff and jeer and babble of him/ As of a prince whose manhood was all gone'. This is the cause of the sorrow and perplexity reflected on Enid's face. To the 'Lute' composition of a reclining woman (this time wearing a wedding ring) Hughes has added the seated Geraint, effecting a triangulation that leads from the sheathed sword (chivalric inactivity) and lute (pleasure) lying on the forest floor in the foreground to the top of the hero's head and the distant trees which are cut by the picture's arched top. The figures are set in a woodland landscape composed of details that would certainly have been painted out of doors in the Pre-Raphaelite way – the bole of a large tree, a weedy stream, and a bank of bluebells in the dappled glade. The subdued tones complement the heroine's melancholy.

Sir Joseph Noel Paton's 'Hesperus' (Glasgow Museum and Art Gallery), a romantic painting of lovers meeting in a wild landscape beneath the evening star, has been related to 'Gareth and Lynette'. Hesperus is the third of four brothers whom the hero must defeat on his assigned quest. Tennyson describes this enemy as 'wrapt in harden'd skins/ That fit him like his own', a symbol of bad habits that have become a second nature. This characterisation is the antithesis of the painter's. The strongest evidence against the identification, however, is the fact that the Paton work is signed and dated 1857 while Tennyson did not begin 'Gareth and Lynette' until August, 1869 and did not send it to press until 9 July, 1872. Nor is there anything in Malory's 'Tale of Gareth' to suggest the scene.

After so many virtuous, suffering damsels, the 'Vivien' (1863, Manchester City Art Galleries) of Frederick Sandys (1832–1904) is a refreshing diversion. Tennyson's character represents corrupting Sense, the conqueror of Reason (Merlin) and the most malignant enemy of Soul (Arthur). Vivien exults in lasciviousness as the paramount expression of the life-force. Sandys presents the head and shoulders of a Rossettian fatal woman with a mass of dark hair, brooding eyes, and long, white neck. Her attributes convey neither narrative context nor historical period. They are timeless aspects of an idea. The background consists of peacock feathers (vanity), with twelve eyes (the zodiacal number associated with the occult) and, flanking the fée, two serpents (evil). She holds a sprig of poisonous daphne and before her are an apple (temptation) and red rose (passionate love). Her yellow dress with its red cabbalistic designs denotes jealousy, deceit and hate while her necklace and earing of coral signify the 'evil eye'. The essence of enchantress resides in these images. Alerted by the aureole-effect of the peacock eyes, however, and by the rose-patterned, machicolated wall behind which Vivien stands, we may realise that each image can be associated with the Virgin Mary. The peacock and daphne represent immortality; the wall belongs to the *hortus conclusus*, a symbol of virginity; the rose without thorn refers to her innocence, beauty and love; the apple to her role as Eve's antitype who trod underfoot the demonic serpent; the golden dress with its chi-rho monograms, and the halo of twelve eyes (stars) denote she is the Virgin of the Immaculate conception and the Queen of Heaven, while the coral jewellery is a protection against passion. Is Sandys playing a typological game learned from Rossetti's Oxford Union painting?[56]

The Victorian Arthuriad also inspired sculpture and various forms of the decorative arts. Thomas Woolner (1825–1892), an original member of the Pre-Raphaelite Brotherhood, had followed the gleam to the Australian gold fields in 1852, inspiring Ford Madox Brown's mournful painting, 'The Last of England'. Woolner returned two years later with a desire for sculptural portraiture rather than a pocketful of nuggets. Having established his reputation in 1857 with a bust of Tennyson, he busied himself thenceforth with busts and medallions of eminent Victorians such as Cobden, Newman, Carlyle, Browning and Queen Victoria. He also made occasional forays into romance. His marble statuette, 'Elaine with the shield of Lancelot' (1868), Holman Hunt 'positively abominated – it was so posturing and so bad in form'[57] but the 'Guinevere', a half life-size marble statue of a classical figure with the Gothic sway of a thirteenth-century Virgin, was more successful. Tennyson was so delighted with the 'simple and elegant figure . . . standing coronetted, holding a rose, and to her feet draped in a simple robe' that an engraved reproduction was used as frontispiece in an 1888 edition of the *Idylls*.[58] A half-lifesize marble statuette of Enid followed in 1881.

Sir William Reynolds-Stephens (1862–1943) incorporated a narrative element into his bronze and ivory statuette, 'Guinevere's Redeeming', (1905, Castle Museum, Nottingham) by adding four reliefs at the base. The heroine is dressed in a nun's habit and adorned with a large crucifix on a chain. Her finely carved ivory face with downcast eyes wears a contemplative expression. On the base's back, a relief labelled 'AS QUEEN' shows her enthroned and 'AS LOVER' in seated embrace with Lancelot. The reliefs at the front illustrate her repentance 'BY GIVING DOLE' to a half-naked old man and 'BY PRAYER' as she kneels at a prie-dieu. The relevant lines from Tennyson are

---

[54] Houghton, p. 343, note 7.
[55] See Robin Gibson, 'Arthur Hughes: Arthurian and related subjects of the early 1860s', *Burlington Magazine*, CXII (1970), 451–456; Virginia Surtees ed., *Sublime & Instructive. Letters from John Ruskin to Louisa, Marchioness of Waterford, Anna Blunden and Ellen Heaton* (London, 1972); W.E. Fredeman, ed., *The Penkill Letters*.
[56] In 1857 Sandys became a close friend of D.G. Rossetti who strongly influenced the younger man's style. In the 60s Rossetti was painting bust length female figures in a confined space. A coral necklace was a recurrent motif.
[57] *A Pre-Raphaelite Friendship*, p. 151.
[58] F.G. Stephens, 'Thomas Woolner', *The Art Journal*, 1894, 84.

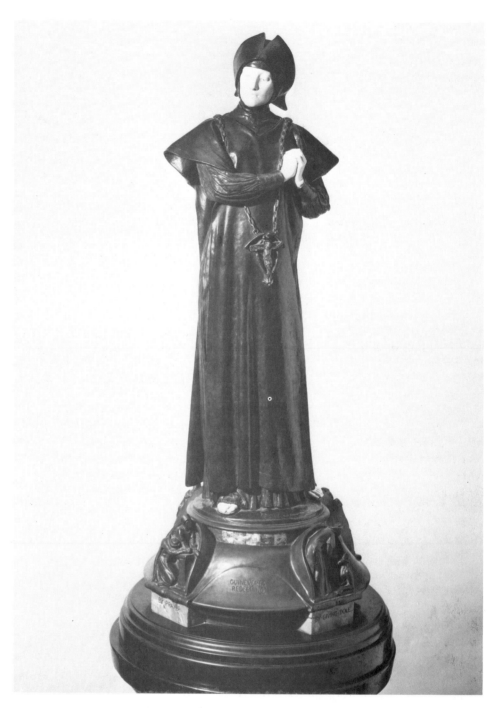

47. Sir William Reynolds-Stephens. Guinevere's Redeeming, silver, bronze and shell statuette, 1905

And so wear out in almsdeed and in prayer
The sombre close of that voluptuous day.

(The restoration of English sisterhoods enabled Victorian artists to use contemporary models when depicting medieval monasticism.) Reynolds-Stephens' penitent nun was preceded by two other Arthurian sculptures, 'Lancelot and the Nestling' (1899) and 'Guinevere and the Nestling' (1900).[59]

A young architect, J.M. Allen, adapted scenes from the *Idylls* to stained glass; Thomas Hughes had Guinevere, Vivien, Elaine and Enid on his staircase. John Duncan painted 'The Taking of Excalibur' on the Common-Room wall of Ramsay Lodge, Edinburgh (1897). Walter Cave's oak settee, shown in the 1896 Arts and Crafts exhibition (now the property of the Victoria and Albert Museum, London), had six scenes from romance which Cave's wife painted. Two were drawn from Tennyson's *Idylls*. In 'How Elaine le blanc broidered a cover for the shield of Lancelot du Lac' the tower setting (with a lily growing from the floor) is paired with a river scene – barge, oarsmen, corpse with golden pall, trees, swans and Camelot's towers. The scene entitled 'How Sir Lancelot brought the Lady Guenever to the Court of Arthur' proves that the inspiration is Tennyson not Malory.

Tennyson's use of imagery was often likened to the pictorialism of tapestry. The American poet, Henry Wadsworth Longfellow, writing to James T. Fields about the 1859 edition, lauded the poems as 'rich tapestries . . . worthy to hang by the Faerie Queen'.[60] In 1876 Coleridge Kennard M.P. commissioned the Royal Windsor Tapestry Works[61] to create a 'Court of King Arthur' series. The eight or possibly ten pieces designed by Herbert Bone were woven as a continuous frieze with a narrow selvedge providing vertical divisions, an upper border of flowers and leaves, and a lower border inscribed in Gothic capitals with relevant quotations. Classically draped gowns are combined with fifteenth-century armour. 'The Marriage of Arthur' (1879, 12 ft 3 in x 6 ft 3 in) is a vivid ceremonial scene with a church in the middle distance and Windsor Castle beyond. Also figured are a trumpeter, peacock, clergy, knights, kneeling townspeople and a woman strewing narcissi, pink roses and may (repeated in the border) to honour the bride and groom. The inscription reads, 'Blow trumpet for the world is white with may;/ Blow trumpet, the long night has rolled away!/ Blow through the living world –

---

[59] Other sculptures are Susan R. Canton's 'Gareth and the Star of Evening' (1881), W.S. Frith's 'Elaine' (1877) and an ivory and bronze bust, 'The Lily Maid of Astolat' (1903) by Clovis Delacour.

[60] *Mem.* I, 445.

[61] Queen Victoria was the patroness and her son Prince Leopold the factory's first president when it was established in 1876. It followed the Gobelin method of weaving that Morris denounced. Never popular – perhaps because, as Morris said, 'They had no Burne-Jones' – it closed down in 1890. See Beryl Platts, 'A brave Victorian venture: the Royal Windsor Tapestry Manufactory', *Country Life*, November 29, 1979, 2003–2006 and G.B. Cullingham, *The Royal Windsor Tapestry Manufactory 1876–1890, An Illustrated Handlist of Tapestries Woven at the Old Windsor Works* (Windsor, 1979). 'The Marriage of Geraint' belongs to the Queen, 'Merlin and Vivien' and 'Guinevere' to the Ossendryver Galleries, Wilton, Conn. and the 'Passing of Arthur' to Vigo-Sternberg Galleries, London.

let the King reign!'. 'Gareth and Lynette' or 'The Monster' (1879–80, 4 ft 10 in x 6 ft 3 in) is woven in subdued tones to illustrate 'In the half light through the dim dawn advanced the monster'. 'Geraint and Enid' (1879–80) shows the hero in plumed cap and tunic bowing to Enid and her parents before a dilapidated Romanesque castle – 'Like a blossom vermeil white fair Enid all in faded silk'. Convolvulus flowers and foliage are the border pattern. 'Merlin and Vivien' (1879–81, 2 ft 10 in x 6 ft 3 in) depicts in autumnal browns, yellows and greens the wild forest of Broceliande where the magician sits with drooping head as Vivien extends above him a sinuous arm – 'For Merlin told the charm and slept'. Interwoven oak leaves are the border device.

The fifth tapestry presents that inevitable scene, 'The Arrival at Camelot of the Dead Elaine' (1879, 12 ft 1 in x 6 ft 3 in). She lies with her head on a plump pillow, her white dress covered by a lily-embroidered yellow pall. The red gowned king directs Perceval, with a mastiff, and Galahad, with a shield, to carry her onto the landing. Beyond the machicolated wall, bentwood fence and garden Sir Lancelot gazes sadly. An upper border of lilies parallels the lower border's inscription, 'The Lily Maid lay smiling like a star in blackest night then turned the tongeless man and pointed'. 'The Holy Grail' (1880–86, 6 ft x 6 ft 10 in) shows a turreted convent where Perceval's sister in nun's habit girds on Galahad's sword – 'I round thee bind my belt go forth for thou shalt see what I have seen and break thro' all'. For 'Guinevere' Bone uses a richly furnished chapel, its altar frontal reading 'Misere Mei Domine', as background for the queen's grovelling scene. A crimson cushion, the King's crimson mantle and his golden surcoat brighten an otherwise sombre tapestry. The border is formed of the roses which Victorians liked to associate with Guinevere. The inscription reads, 'Lo I forgive thee as eternal God forgives. Farewell'. 'The Passing of Arthur' (ca. 1880, 12 ft 1 in x 6 ft 3 in) has a wintery atmosphere with its bare-branched oak, shrivelled bullrushes and misty water. The departing crane, like the queens in the barge, promises immortality. Oakapples and acorns decorate the upper edge while the lower one reads, 'To the island valley of Avilion he passes to be king among the dead and after healing of his grevous wound he comes again. Herbert Bone inven'.

In considering the range of Arthurian art which Tennyson's poetry inspired, one cannot help asking, 'Where is Arthur?' Aside from 'Passing of Arthur' scenes, some of which derive from Malory, there are only a few unexceptional works like R. Norburg's 'King Arthur and the Diamond Crown' (1874) and Joseph Walter West's 'The Coming of Arthur as a Boy' (1894). It was Sir Galahad who represented inspired attacks on evil and it was Sir Lancelot who represented the ideal of a gentleman – even Queen Victoria preferred him to Arthur. What the romantic artists and their public evidently liked best of all were the mystical, medieval resonances of beautiful, suffering women that provided an escape from materialistic industrialism.

CHAPTER TEN

Fair Women and Noble Knights

In the earlier part of Queen Victoria's reign, the written word, available at reasonable prices through books, journals and newspapers, attracted a large public over whose minds and emotions it had enormous influence. In November, 1859, Woolner reported to Emily Tennyson:

> Gladstone was reading some of the 'Idylls' to a few friends . . . and at one portion both Gladstone himself and Lord Granville . . . burst into tears before all the company – which does show that they are susceptible of tender sentiments.[1]

In contrast to literature, the condition of the Fine Arts was deplorable, 'having little or no connexion with the industrious masses, and dove-tailing not in with them who compose, almost exclusively, the natural system of society'. That was the opinion expressed in *Douglas Jerrold's Shilling Magazine* 6, July 31, 1847.[2] However, the time was at hand when artists would no longer be 'dependent on the state, or those who derive power from its regulations'. The Industrial Revolution produced a new moneyed class anxious to indicate its wealth and taste by collecting art. In 1871, F.G. Stephens could write, 'The so-called middle-class of England has been that which has done the most for English art. While its social superiors "praised" Pietro Perugino, neglected Turner, let Wilson starve, and gave as much for a Gaspar Poussin as for a Raphael, the merchant princes bought of Turner, William Hunt, Holman Hunt, and Rossetti.'[3] The new collectors liked bright colours, moral improvement, beautiful, well-clothed women, and literary subjects – exactly what the Pre-Raphaelites were willing to provide. Reviled in the fifties, these artists eventually prospered.

Despite the emotional response of Gladstone and his friends to the *Idylls*, Tennyson's treatment of the Arthurian legends was not universally approved. One would expect Algernon Swinburne's sarcasm: 'Mr. Tennyson has lowered the

---

[1]   Amy Woolner, *Thomas Woolner, R.A. Sculptor and Poet: His Life in Letters* (New York, 1971 [1917]), p. 178.
[2]   'The Place of the Fine Arts in the Natural System of Society', *Douglas Jerrold's Shilling Magazine*, 6, 72–81.
[3]   'English Painters of the Present Day, XXXI – William Holman Hunt', *Portfolio*, 2, 38.

tone and deformed the outline of the Arthurian story, by reducing Arthur to the level of a wittol, Guenevere to the level of a woman of intrigue, and Launcelot to the level of a "correspondent".[4]

But the respected scholar F.J. Furnivall said much the same thing in his introduction to the Roxburghe Club edition of *La Queste del Saint Graal* (1864):

> To anyone knowing his Malleore . . . to come on Arthur rehearsing to his prostrate queen his own nobleness and her disgrace, the revulsion of feeling was too great, one could only say to the 'Flower of Kings', 'If you really did this, you were the Pecksniff of the period'.

Some artists pointedly divorced their paintings from Tennysonian associations by choosing Malorian titles; for example, James Archer's 'How Sir Launcelot and His Eight Fellows of the Round Table Carried Queen Guinevere from Almesbury to Her Tomb at Glastonbury' (1868); William Bell Scott's, 'King Arthur Carried to the Land of Enchantment' (1847); Frederick Sandys' 'King Pelles' Daughter Bearing the Vessel of the Sanc Graal' (1862); and Simeon Solomon's 'Death of Sir Galahad while taking a potion of the Holy Grael'.

One of the most ardent Malorians was Dante Gabriel Rossetti. As early as 1853, he used *Morte Darthur* language to report the demise of the Pre-Raphaelite Brotherhood: 'So now the whole Round Table is dissolved'.[5] When we notice how many members of the Hogarth Club (which met from 1858 to 1862) were associated with Arthurian art – Morris, Burne-Jones, Madox Brown, Hunt, Ruskin, Arthur Hughes, Val Prinsep, Watts, Fripp, Webb, Woodward, Bell Scott, Hungerford Pollen, for example – we may conclude that his enthusiasm was infectious. A reminiscent Val Prinsep recalled a dinner at Rossetti's in 1858 or 1859:

> To be at that feast was like entering a new world! The past was mixed so frequently and with such sincerity with the present that I found some saying of the man who prepared the paints at the 'Union', whose walls we were to decorate, mentioned at the same time and nearly in the same sentence as a joke of Sir Dinadan, who I was to learn was the maddest wag among the knights of King Arthur.[6]

The form of Pre-Raphaelitism associated with Rossetti differed markedly from that of Hunt and Millais. It was not 'Christian Historical' or 'Moral Historical' or 'Modern Moral'. Nor did the artist for long seek 'truth to nature' by painting outdoors where one might be 'dreadfully cold' like Hunt or threatened by both a bull and a charge of trespassing like Millais. Romantic medieval subjects and the cult of female beauty furnished 'the narrow chamber of the individual mind'.

---

[4] *Under the Microscope* (London, 1872), p. 41.
[5] Doughty and Wahl, *Letters*, I, #131.
[6] 'A Chapter from a Painter's Reminiscence. The Oxford Circle: Rossetti, Burne-Jones and William Morris', *The Magazine of Art* 27, (1904), 167–72.

William Blake (1757–1827) had already broken down the academic tradition in painting by abandoning the three-dimensional elements in favour of a linear and emblematic style which Rossetti adopted.[7] He may also have learned from the earlier poet/painter techniques for expressing visionary experience through clearly depicted images rather than shadowy forms. Both were indebted to Gothic illuminations and German woodcuts for brightness of colour, clarity of line, the frontal treatment of space and allegorical imagery. What differentiated them was that Blake's imagination was mythic while Rossetti's was romantic. The latter's claustrophobic medieval world depended on courtly costume, heraldry, heavy Gothic furniture, arms and armour, objects representing daily life in the fourteenth or fifteenth century, as well as the powerful reds, greens and blues of thirteenth century glass and the patterned backgrounds of illuminations and tapestries. In an artificially constructed setting enclosed by walls, the artist places one or two characters tense with passionate feeling. Reviewing the 1857 watercolours exhibited at the Tate Gallery in 1916, Roger Fry commented:

> The ordinary world of vision scarcely supplied any inspiration to him. It was only through the evocation in his own mind of a special world, a world of sure romance, that the aspects of objects began to assume aesthetic meaning.[8]

Rossetti's first type of beautiful woman, Elizabeth Siddal, conveyed a purity and remoteness that were archetypally medieval. W.M. Rossetti described her as

> truly a beautiful girl; tall, with a stately throat and fine carriage, pink and white complexion, and massive straight coppery-golden hair. Her large greenish-blue eyes, large-lidded, were peculiarly noticeable . . . One could not have seen a woman in whose whole demeanour maidenly and feminine purity was more markedly apparent.[9]

Ruskin's father thought by her look and manner she might have been a countess. Rossetti drew her as Guenevere in 'Arthur's Tomb', as the weeping Queens (though his sister Christina was also a model) and the Lady of Shalott in the Moxon *Tennyson*, as the angelic faces and as Guenevere in studies for the Oxford Union murals. She is the angel of the Grail in 'Sir Galahad, Sir Bors and Sir Perceval viewing the Sanc Grael'. In 1862 she posed as the Princess Sabra for a watercolour, 'St. George and the Princess Sabra'. A few days later she died from an

---

[7]   Dante Gabriel and William Rossetti helped prepare Alexander Gilchrist's *Life of William Blake, 'Pictor Ignotus'* (1863) for the press.

[8]   *Burlington Magazine*, XXIX (June, 1916), 100.

[9]   'Dante Rossetti and Elizabeth Siddal written by W.M. Rossetti with facsimiles of five unpublished drawings by Dante Rossetti in the collection of Mr. Harold Hartley', *Burlington Magazine*, 3/1 (May, 1903), 273. See also studies reproduced in A.I. Grieve, *The Watercolours and Drawings of 1850–1855* (Norwich, 1978).

overdose of laudanum. Her husband immortalised her once more as Beata Beatrix, Dante's ideal love. His private hieroglyph for Elizabeth was a dove.[10]

If Siddal was *la princesse lointaine*, Jane Burden Morris was the *femme fatale*. After visiting the Morrises on March 10, 1869, Henry James admitted to his sister that he could hardly distinguish the individual from the type, the real woman from the painting:

> Oh ma chère, such a wife! Je n'en reviens pas – she haunts me still. A figure cut out of a missal – out of one of Rossetti's or Hunt's pictures – to say this gives but a faint idea of her, because when such an image puts on flesh and blood, it is an apparition of fearful and wonderful intensity. It's hard to say whether she's a grand synthesis of all the pre-Raphaelite pictures ever made – or they a 'keen analysis' of her – whether she's an original or a copy. In either case she is a wonder. Imagine a tall lean woman in a long dress of some dead purple stuff, guiltless of hoops (or of anything else, I should say) with a mass of crisp black hair heaped into great wavy projections on each of her temples, a thin pale face, a pair of strange sad, deep, dark Swinburnian eyes, with great thick black oblique brows, joined in the middle and tucking themselves away under her hair, a mouth like the 'Oriana' in our illustrated Tennyson, a long neck, without any collar, and in lieu thereof some dozen strings of outlandish beads – in fine complete. On the wall was a nearly full-length portrait of her by Rossetti, so strange and unreal that if you hadn't seen her you'd pronounce it a distempered vision, but in fact an extremely good likeness.[11]

Rossetti depicted her as a series of heroines increasingly dark and demonic – Guenevere in 'Sir Launcelot in the Queen's Chamber', Yseult in the Harden Grange glass and the corresponding water-colour, 'Sir Tristram and La Belle Yseult Drinking the Love Potion' (a work which Burne-Jones thought 'splendid, one of his very best'),[12] La Pia de' Tolomei, Mariana, Pandora, Proserpine, Astarte Syriaca, Mnemosyne and many others. In works featuring other models, even those created by other artists, the head was adapted to the Jane Burden style of ideal woman, defined by a mass of hair, brooding eyes, long neck, sensuous, unsmiling mouth, still, almost lethargic body, and air of remote sexuality. This effect of voluptuous mysteriousness men found irresistible. The painter of Manchester's industrial slums, L.S. Lowry (1887–1976), whose 'Pre-Raphaelite Passion' led him to collect fourteen Rossettis, described his response to the women:

---

[10] For catalogue information, and black and white reproductions of Rossetti's art see Virginia Surtees, *The Paintings and Drawings of Dante Gabriel Rossetti*.

[11] Percy Lubbock, ed., *The Letters of Henry James*, 2 vols (New York, 1920), I, pp. 17–19.

[12] Lago, ed., *Burne-Jones Talking*, p. 107.

. . . his women are very wonderful. I can't find anything quite like them . . . They're very queer creatures and I like him for it . . . What he puts into the individual is all him.[13]

He admitted to Mervyn Levy:

I don't like his women at all, but they fascinate me, like a snake. That's why I always buy Rossetti whenever I can.

Lady Eastlake's reaction to the new style was unequivocal – 'female horrors with thin bodies and sensual mouths looking as if they were going to be hung, or dead and already decomposed'.[14]

In addition to fostering images of woman that could represent everything from Soul to demon, Rossetti, like Hunt, Millais, Burne-Jones and Morris, initially relied on a symbolic realism of medieval origin. Lacking an audience that could read a large number of traditional images typologically and allegorically, artists limited themselves to those that their contemporaries might be expected to understand – lilies, doves, chalices, angels with splendid wings, enclosed gardens, knights in armour, and beautiful women in trailing gowns. The unified sensibility that they so much admired in medieval art was not easily achieved. While every detail in a Van Eyck is part of a consistant iconographic programme integrated into a scene of almost photographic realism, Pre-Raphaelite pictures are often awkwardly fragmented and inappropriately figured.

William Morris's only surviving easel painting, 'Queen Guenevere' or 'La Belle Iseult' (1858, Tate Gallery, London), depicts Jane Burden in a medieval role. The picture plane is crowded with images, some intended to create an historical ambience, others symbolising aspects of the narrative source, Malory's *Morte Darthur*. The little dog on the rumpled bed (which the lovers have recently vacated) may be, on the narrative level, the 'little brachet' that Sir Tristram gave Iseult when she first came to Cornwall. Malory tells us that the dog would never depart from her unless Tristram was nearby (IX, 20). Iconographically, it symbolises fidelity, a quality relevant to both Iseult and Guenevere who, says Malory, had a good end because she was a faithful lover. The illuminated missal reflects Morris's delight in that art form; beginning in 1856 he made his own illuminated books so skilfully written and decorated that Ruskin thought him the equal of any thirteenth-century draughtsman. Other decorative details contributing to a medieval effect are the embroidery frame, the snake-like golden ribbon, the candle, the figural tapestries and the embroidered bed curtains caught up as they are in numerous miniatures. The water jug (which also appears in the Red House 'Sir Degrevaunt' panels) is a conventional symbol of the Virgin Mary. Empty – the queen has evidently finished bathing – it signifies the Virgin's anti-type Eve, who

---

[13] Sandra Martin, 'Introduction', *A Pre-Raphaelite Passion, The Private Collection of L.S. Lowry*, catalogue of an exhibition at the Manchester City Art Gallery, 1 April – 31 May, 1977.
[14] 'Quarterly Gazette' quoted by Diana Holman Hunt, *My Grandfather, His Wives and Loves* (London, 1969), p. 134.

lacked saving grace. Morris is reputed to have written on the back of the painting, 'I cannot paint you but I love you'. The face is so characteristically Rossettian that one suspects Morris' mentor had a hand in the work.

Morris' passionate medieval world – heroic, sensuous, mystical and dominated by women more powerful and interesting than the noble knights – was evoked in a volume of poems, *The Defence of Guenevere* (1858). *The Saturday Review*'s critic disparagingly likened the characters and settings to those in illuminated manuscripts, 'all cold, artificial, and angular . . . it is a mercy to have got rid of them'.[15] One poem, at least, was suggested by a Rossetti watercolour, 'Arthur's Tomb' (1854 or 1855, Tate Gallery, London). To increase the drama of the lovers' last meeting, Rossetti shifts the scene from Almesbury, where Guenevere has become a holy nun, to Glastonbury, King Arthur's burial place according to the Christian rather than Celtic legend. As Lancelot, in surcoat of red (passionate love), leans over the effigy, Guenevere draws back. The relevant *Morte Darthur* text reads:

> 'Madame, I praye you kysse me, and never no more.' 'Nay,' sayd the quene, 'that shal I never do, but absteyne you from suche werkes.'
>
> (XXI,10)

The surrounding orchard alludes to the medieval equation of Glastonbury with Avalon, the 'insula pomorum'. The tomb's pictorial panels, which show Arthur knighting Lancelot and the Grail's appearance at the Pentecostal feast, recapitulate the hero's dual disloyalty to his king and his God. The figures' flatness reminded Ruskin of 'a knave of Clubs and a Queen of Diamonds'[16] but form and colour successfully convey intense emotion.

Two of Rossetti's 1850s designs were intended for the Oxford Union. The pen and ink drawing 'Sir Galahad, Sir Bors and Sir Perceval receiving the Sanc Grael' (1857, British Museum) actually has circles to represent the windows. In its watercolour version, 'How Sir Galahad, Sir Bors, and Sir Perceval were fed with the Sanc Grael; but Sir Perceval's Sister died by the Way' (1864, Tate Gallery, London) a brilliant effect is produced by the dazzling lily at the Grail Maiden's feet, the white dove with its golden censer (a detail from Malory), the flame-winged angels, the golden haloes, curtains and candelabra and the costume details highlighted in red and gold. Rossetti's mysticism depended on intensely perceived sensory impressions – as did that of such medieval mystics as Richard Rolle and Dame Juliana of Norwich. The images evoke not only light but scent (incense, lilies, the flowery meadow), touch (the linked hands, the grasped Grail, the dead woman's folded palms) and taste (the mass elements).

A variety of iconographic references, incompletely assimilated, is apparent in 'Sir Launcelot in the Queen's Chamber' (1857, Birmingham City Museum and Art Gallery). Inscribed in gold on the original frame are the words, 'How Sir Launcelot was espied in the Queen's Chamber, and how Sir Agravaine and Sir Mordred

---

[15] Peter Faulkner, ed. *William Morris, the Critical Heritage* (London, 1973), pp. 42–47.
[16] 'The Art of England', Cook, 33, p. 299.

came with twelve knights to slay him' – Caxton's title for Bk. XX, ch.3. The fierce, moustached hero peers at the attackers beyond the enclosing wall of decorated boards that traps the lovers between the low ceiling and rumpled bed. Guenevere's ladies wear Van Eyckian headdresses that can be dated ca. 1440–1460 but her own gown with its elaborate peacock-feather shawl and her crown casually dangling from the bed frame are unhistorical. As in medieval art, the elongated hands convey emotional states. Lancelot grasps his sword with his right hand while defiantly pushing the wall with his left. The attendant ladies cover their faces in fear. Guenevere despairingly clutches her throat. The rampant garden, no longer an orderly *hortus conclusus*, invades the bedroom. Jane Burden is again the model, as she is in another drawing, 'Jane Burden as Queen Guenevere' (1858, National Gallery of Ireland, Dublin).

In the *Contemporary Review*, October, 1871, Robert Buchanan savagely attacked Rossetti and his associates for their 'fleshliness' and 'grotesque medievalism'. But Walter Pater justified sensory intensity and escape into the past because they startle us into 'a sharp and eager observation':

> Every moment some form grows perfect in hand or face, some tone on hills or sea is choicer than the rest; some mood of passion or insight or intellectual excitement is irresistibly real and attractive for us for that moment only . . . To burn always with this hard gem-like flame, to maintain this ecstasy, is success in life.[17]

While the passionate Iseult and Guenevere were one form of Arthurian fatal woman, the fée was another – beautiful, powerful, and uninhibited by moral considerations when contriving pleasure or revenge. The chief source of baleful magic in the *Morte Darthur* is Arthur's half-sister, Morgan-le-Fay. She is paradoxical for she combines the destructive aspects of the Celtic hag, the Morrigan, with the healing powers of the white goddess Matrona. Constantly plotting against Arthur, she sends him a magical mantle of great splendour that will reduce its wearer to coals (Bk. IV, ch. 16). The subject of Frederick Sandys' self-conscious oil, 'Morgan-le-Fay' (1864, Birmingham City Art Gallery), is the making of this mantle.[18] In style the picture is obviously Rossettian – vivid, claustrophobic, icon-studded, impassioned. The central figure, for whom the girl Keomi was the model, has Burden's agonised face, thick dark hair, long neck and sensuous mouth. The *Art Journal's* critic described her as 'a petrified spasm'. Her exotic costume in barbaric colours features cabalistic signs and a leopard skin. A tall loom on the right, a tapestry with fantastic animal heads, and a Victorian Gothic cabinet from which hangs the bespelled garment effect a sense of enclosure. Scattered about the room are various stage properties, some, like the illuminated

[17] Review of Poems by William Morris, *The Westminster Review*, New Series, vol. XXXIV (1868), 300–312.
[18] For reproductions of Sandys' work see *Frederick Sandys 1829–1904*, catalogue of an exhibition at the Brighton Museum and Art Gallery, 7 May – 14 July, 1974.

book of spells and the zoomorphic lamp, denoting necromancy, others, like the strewn rushes, intended to convey medieval social history. The sunrise glow beyond the loom suggests that the cloak's creation has been an act of darkness.

Sandys' 'La Belle Yseult' (1862) of which there are several versions is also ·derivative in form and iconography. The painting of a bust-length woman holding an identifying object (a silver goblet), sumptuously costumed and surrounded by symbolic flowers, resembles the gallery of beauties that Rossetti created in the sixties. The acolyte's technique was superior to Rossetti's; Burne-Jones complained that if anything was wrong in a picture, 'he *wouldn't* get it right, wouldn't bother . . . he hated trouble or anything that ran counter to his mood, and was quite without any stern morality about his work.'[19]

Burne-Jones' fascination with enchantresses persisted for forty years, from his Oxford Union Nimue to the stately fées who await Arthur's wakening in Avalon. A gouache 'Morgan Le Fay' (1862, London Borough of Hammersmith Public Libraries) was originally designed as an embroidery for Ruskin and later used as Medea in a stained glass 'Legend of Good Women' series for Peterhouse College, Cambridge. The rich blues and greens were likened to Tintoretto's work which Burne-Jones was studying at the time. The fée holds in one hand a serpent-ornamented globe and in the other a poisonous plant, one of those recorded in an 1862–3 sketchbook.

His personal Arthurian myth, however, was the story of Merlin's enchantment. Inscribed on the inner frame of a gouache 'Merlin and Nimue' (1861, Victoria and Albert Museum, London) is Malory's slightly modified text: 'A great wonder wrought by enchantment which went under a stone so by her subtle craft and working she made Merlin to go under that stone to let her wit of the marvels there but she wrought so that he came never out for all the craft that he could do'. The enchantress' plum-coloured velvet gown, tawny cloak, luxuriant hair, sensuous mouth, elongated neck and worldly-wise eyes constitute a familiar type. Other iconographic details related to the battle of the sexes are the book of spells, which Nimue now possesses, the small dog tugging at Merlin's gown, the poppies of sleep, and the stone slab with padlock and key. The distant water reminds us that Nimue's alternative designation was the Damsel of the Lake. Even in this early stage of his career the artist can convey palpable desire and fear. Like Malory, he treats this fée as unmalignant but capable of using the man's weakness in order to protect her virginity.

Burne-Jones' masterpiece on the theme of the male-female struggle for supremacy was the large oil 'The Beguiling of Merlin' (1874, Lady Lever Art Gallery, Port Sunlight). F.R. Leyland commissioned it for the Prince's Gate residence where Whistler had created the Peacock Room. This time the source was not Malory but the Old French *Roman de Merlin*. In 1865–9 the Early English Text Society published the fifteenth-century English translation, thus providing an accessible version. Having promised Merlin sexual favours in return for instruc-

[19] Lago, *Burne-Jones Talking*, pp. 46–7.

tion in the arts of magic, Niniane lulls him to sleep beneath a white thorn bush in Broceliande, then encloses him within a tower of air.

Burne-Jones' fée, holding the book of spells, towers over the infatuated magician who cowers under her powerful gaze. Linearity rather than colour determines the presentation. The serpentine forms of her snaky headdress are repeated in the folds of the indigo dress and in the hawthorn's sinuous roots, trunk and branches which like tentacles surround the failing man. In Celtic myth hawthorns mark faerie trysting places. The murky pool is edged with irises, the artist's private symbol of passion. The model for Merlin was the American journalist W.J. Stillman whose face, damaged in a childhood accident, was unusually white and queer. The enchantress was Maria Zambaco, a beautiful Greek with 'glorious red hair and almost phosphorescent skin', according to her cousin, Luke Ionides. The artist loved her passionately; the ending of their relationship made her suicidal and him so depressed that he could not work.[20] Many years later, in 1893, he confided to Helen Gaskell, 'I was being turned into a hawthorn bush in the forest of Broceliande – every year when the hawthorn buds it is the soul of Merlin trying to live again in the world and speak – for he left so much unsaid.'

The artist returned to the subject in a series of watercolour roundels (1882–98, British Museum) based on the visual images that flower names suggested. 'Witch's Tree' reworks the 'Beguiling' elements – delicate blossoms, sinuous branches enclosing a sleeping, white-bearded mage, and the fairy queen whose music sustains the enchantment. In his maturity Burne-Jones had learned to use myth as an expression of a psychological problem – that of the artist reduced to impotence by a woman's supremacy and his own lust.

Woman's powerful and mysterious beauty also attracted members of the New Sculpture movement which began about 1880.[21] Like Burne-Jones, these artists required images that could function as symbols of ideas and emotions for they were unwilling to be judged by the academic standard of 'truth to nature'. One of the first of the 'new' sculptors, Alfred Gilbert (1854–1934), regarded Burne-Jones as a model because his personality and production were so intimately wedded. George James Frampton (1860–1928), whose 'Peter Pan' in Kensington Gardens and statues of Queen Victoria in Calcutta, Winnipeg and Leeds, *inter alia*, made him one of the most successful establishment sculptors, developed his personal symbolist style, 'an inward world of thought and feeling', under Pre-Raphaelite influences. An innovative aspect of his art was his combination of various materials in a way that linked sculpture to the decorative arts. A figure's body might be bronze or painted plaster, the flesh carved ivory, the costume ornaments silver, gold and jewels.

Since Morris' aim of beautifying the home could be served by statuettes and low relief panels, sculptures for private as well as public purposes were profitable

[20] See Penelope Fitzgerald, *Edward Burne-Jones: A Biography* (London, 1975), pp. 117–162.
[21] Susan Beattie, *The New Sculpture* (New Haven and London, 1983); Benedict Read, *Victorian Sculpture* (New Haven and London, 1982); Sandy Nairne and Nicholas Sewta, eds, *British Sculpture in the Twentieth Century*, a catalogue of an exhibition at the Whitechapel Art Gallery, London, 1981.

in the 1890s. In 1895–6 Frampton designed for Astor House, Temple Place, West-minster[22] a series of nine silver gilt panels representing heroines of the *Morte Darthur* together with Tennyson's Enid. After being exhibited at the Royal Acade-my, they were set in the mahogany door of the 'Renaissance' Great Hall which served Lord Astor as living room and office. They are arranged in groups of three, the outer figures in profile facing the frontally positioned central lady. The Lady of the Isle of Avelyon and the Lady of the Lake with Excalibur flank Elaine. Morgan le Fay and La Beale Isoude look towards Guenevere who holds the rose that Tennyson's queen preferred to the lily. The final trio is Lyonors, Enid and Alis la Beale Pilgrim, Alexander the Orphan's beloved. Beneath a Romanesque arch that encloses and isolates her, each sits on 'twelfth-century' furniture decorated with armed knights. But the ladies have fashionable fin-de siècle coiffures, bare arms, and art nouveau dresses.

After 1900, Frampton was occupied with numerous public commissions but he still created some idealised heads which, says Susan Beattie, were 'increasingly vapid in quality, their smoothed-out modelling devoid of psychological tension'.[23] Still 'Enid the Fair' and 'La Beale Isoude' (1908, Christopher Wood Gallery, Lon-don) are rather charming, though only the titles identify them as Arthurian.

The fascination with beautiful women must not obscure the fact that the Vic-torians were a nation of hero-worshippers.[24] The sagacious Thomas Carlyle urged his countrymen to rekindle their 'spiritual lightning' by finding appropriate models:

> Hero-worship, done differently in every different epoch of the world,
> is the soul of all social business among men; that the doing of it well, or
> the doing of it ill, measure accurately what degree of well-being or of
> ill-being there is in the world's affairs.[25]

Malory's *Morte Darthur* was one usable source for the Round Table Knights' chivalric oath was relevant to the industrial kingdom of adventure and the expan-ding empire. Spenser's *The Faerie Queene* was another text that provided a gallery of active knights each representing a specific virtue. Chivalric subjects permitted the artist to paint a kind of costume that was ennobling. Speaking of contempor-ary dress, G.F. Watts complained:

> A well-dressed gentleman ready for dinner or attired for any ceremony
> is a pitiable example – his vesture nearly formless and quite foldless if
> he can have his will. His legs, unshapen props – his shirt front, a void –
> his dress coat, an unspeakable piece of ignobleness.

---

[22] Temple Place on the Victoria Embankment was built in 1895 as William Waldorf Astor's residence and offices. It is now the head office of Smith and Nephew. The door panels are still *in situ*.

[23] *op. cit.*, p. 232.

[24] See Walter Houghton, *The Victorian Frame of Mind*, pp. 305–340.

[25] Thomas Carlyle, *Past and Present*, ed. Richard D. Altick (New York, 1965), p. 39.

In contrast, 'mediaeval armour perhaps surpasses any other effort of human ingenuity' for it expresses an 'unaffected, unconscious artistic excellence of invention approaching more nearly to the strange beauty of nature'.[26]

Leigh Hunt in the *New Monthly Magazine*, June, 1833 likened Spenser's 'masterly, poetical pictures' to the works of the Old Masters – 'of the Titians in colouring and classical gusto, the Rembrandts in light and shade, the Michael Angelos in grandeur of form and purpose, the Guidos in grace, the Raphaels and Correggios in expression . . . and even the homely Dutch painters in landscape'. Hunt published two anthologies of Spenserian passages suitable for painting. In the century from 1770 to 1870 at least one hundred and seventy-five *Faerie Queene* subjects were exhibited, most of them based on Book I.[27]

John Hamilton Mortimer (1741–79), whose specialty was painting the exploits of bandits, presented the belligerent 'Sir Arthegal, the Knight of Justice with Talus, the Iron Man' (1778, Tate Gallery, London). For Henry Fuseli (1741–1825), a Swiss painter and author who moved to England in 1763, epic poetry was the best source of sublime subjects for it enabled the artist to express 'one general idea, one great quality of nature or mode of society'.[28] His early watercolours included 'The appearance of the Fairy Queen to the Dreaming Arthur' and 'The Cave of Despair'. Some of his Spenserian illustrations such as 'The Vision of Prince Arthur' (1788) were engraved for Macklin's Poets' Gallery, along with John Opie's 'The Freeing of Amoret' and Richard Cosway's 'Sans-Loy Killing the Lion'.

When Sir John Soane commissioned Charles Eastlake to paint 'Una delivering the Red Cross Knight from the Cave of Despair' (1830, Sir John Soane's Museum), the Spenserian material was becoming stale. The knight in a salmon pink surcoat lies murkily at the feet of a half-naked Despair. His saviour Una, in Saxon dress, is bathed in yellow light. Above her flutter three putti, the winged children whom Michelangelo and Blake used to represent the state of purity preceding knowledge. G.F. Watts' faith in Art's moral function appears in 'Una and the Red Cross Knight' (1869, Lady Lever Art Gallery, Port Sunlight) and 'Britomart and her Nurse' (1878, Birmingham City Museum and Art Gallery). The model for the Red Cross Knight is the same dreamy-faced, curly-headed Arthur Prinsep who was 'Sir Galahad'. In the Britomart painting, an Annunciation lily in a pot denotes her purity. The prophetic mirror behind the figures recalls the probable source of several 'literary' pictures, including Hunt's 'Lady of Shalott' and Frederick Shields' 'The Vision of Britomart'. It is 'The Arnolfini Marriage' (1434), the Jan van Eyck masterpiece that the National Gallery in London acquired in 1842.

An academic artist who was a direct contrast to the Pre-Raphaelites and their circle though equally attracted to chivalric subjects was Sir John Gilbert (1817–

---

[26] 'The Present Condition of Art' in M.S. Watts, *Annals*, III, pp. 151–3.
[27] See Richard D. Altick, *Paintings from Books: Art and Literature in Britain 1760–1900* (Columbus, Ohio, 1985), pp. 346–353.
[28] Ronald Paulson, *Book and Painting: Shakespeare, Milton and the Bible: Literary Texts and the Emergence of English Painting* (Knoxville, Tenn., 1982), pp. 128–9.

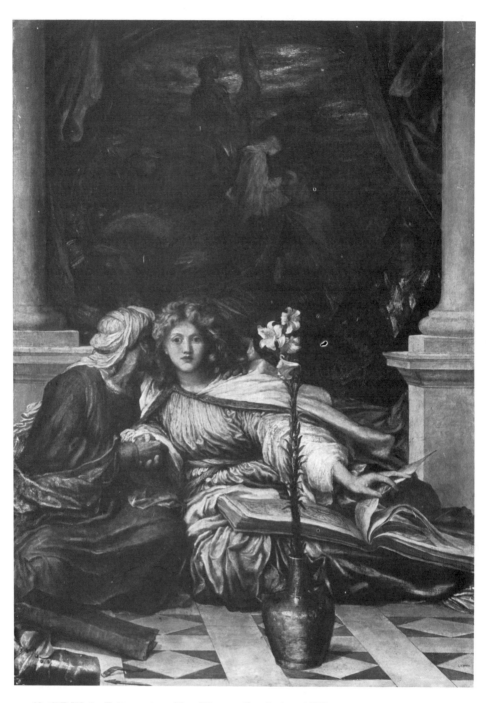

48. G.F. Watts. Britomart and her Nurse, oil painting, 1878

1897). According to his obituary in *The Illustrated London News*[29] 'he represented, in fact, what the word "art" in the Victorian era has really implied'. In 1857 the *Art Journal* described him as 'the most widely known artist in the world'. In the 829 drawings that he provided for the Routledge Shakespeare (1856–58), his women were particularly praised: 'Mr. Gilbert is almost the only popular artist who draws a pretty woman. He never scares us with a Pre-Raphaelite fright, starved upon parish allowances.'[30] He shared the academic distrust of the new style, finding Rossetti's work 'too far gone in a kind of madness' for him to understand. On April 22, 1870, as President of the Royal Watercolour Society, he welcomed the Royal Family to the annual exhibition. But ten years later his work was out of fashion: 'It is really no use painting', he records in his diary, 'nothing sells. Noone comes near me. There is such an utter stagnation that it is quite oppressive and disheartening. *Never* in my recollection have things been so *utterly bad.*'[31]

Whether painting the battles of Tewkesbury and Agincourt or 'The Slain Dragon' (1886, Walker Art Gallery, Liverpool), a Spenser subject with awe-stricken peasants in a Sussex countryside, Gilbert regarded himself as a historical, not a romantic artist. That he shared with G.F. Watt and Sir Joseph Noel Paton a belief in art's didactic function is evidenced by 'Onward', (1890, Manchester City Art Galleries), an oil of a knight holding aloft a banner as his horse leaps forward.

'Sir Lancelot du Lake' (1886, Guildhall Art Gallery, London) was based on a ballad in Thomas Percy's *Reliques of Ancient English Poetry*. Derived from the *Morte Darthur*, Bk. VI, 7–9, it recounts the hero's battle against the villainous Sir Tarquin. The armour is carefully drawn as are the lively warhorses recollected from youthful drawings of the Royal Horse Artillery exercises on Woolwich Common. A vaguely Saxon costume suffices for the watching damsel. The oak tree's burden of copper basin and the shields of captured knights are long-lived narrative motifs. Misty mountains, a stormy sky, and subdued earth tones contribute to the ominous atmosphere. In the centre foreground, Lancelot, actively combating evil and defending womanhood, is the antithesis of static Pre-Raphaelite males.

Translations of medieval sources such as the Welsh *Mabinogion* expanded the artist's repertoire, though the Victorians tamed and prettified the primitive heroes. Lady Charlotte Guest's 'Kilhwch and Olwen' vividly details the young man's appearance as he sets out for Arthur's court:

> And the youth pricked forth upon a steed with head dappled grey, of
> four winters old, firm of limb, with well-formed hoofs, having a bridle
> of linked gold on his head, and upon him a saddle of costly gold. And
> in the youth's hand were two spears of silver, sharp, well-tempered,
> headed with steel. . . . A gold-hilted sword was upon his thigh, the
> blade of which was of gold, bearing a cross of inlaid gold . . . his war

[29] Gilbert was this periodical's most important graphic artist, executing 30,000 illustrations from the commencement of his employment in 1842.

[30] *The Times*, 26 December, 1860.

[31] *Diary*, 30 June, 1880. I am indebted to Jan Speirs, Curator, Guildhall Art Gallery for this reference.

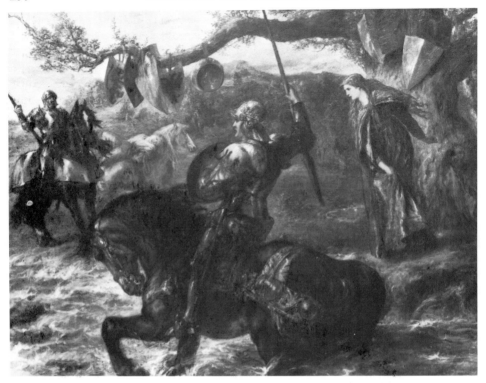

49. Sir John Gilbert. Sir Lancelot du Lake: 'She brought him to a river then', oil painting, 1886

horn was of ivory. Before him were two brindled white breasted grey-hounds, having strong collars of rubies about their necks. . . . About him was a four-cornered cloth of purple, and an apple of gold was at each corner, and every one of the apples was of the value of three hundred kine. And there was precious gold of the value of three hundred kine upon his shoes, and upon his stirrups, from his knee to the tip of his toe.[32]

In the pictorial version, 'Kilhwych, the King's Son', Arthur Gaskin (1862–1928), lacking models of early Welsh costume, dresses the hero in red hose and a fashionable fifteenth century houppelande with dagged sleeves. With his spear, staghounds and golden-trapped horse, Kilhwych seems prepared to play a pageantic role in an artificial world.

Through the establishment of new exhibition spaces like the Grosvenor

---

[32] *The Mabinogion*, trans. with notes by Lady Charlotte Guest (London, 1877; rptd. Cardiff, 1977), pp. 219–20.

Gallery[33] which provided alternatives to the conservative and political Royal Academy, Burne-Jones' style became increasingly influential in the last quarter of the century. His reputation soared not only in England but on the continent, where he had exhibited several paintings, including 'The Beguiling of Merlin', at the Paris Exposition Universelle in 1878. Walter Crane (1845–1915), an eminent illustrator of children's books and a companion of William Morris' socialist activities, described the effect of Burne-Jones' painting on younger artists like himself:

> The curtain had been lifted and we had a glimpse into . . . a twilight world of dark mysterious woodland, haunted streams, meads of dark green with burning flowers, veiled in dim and mystic light, and stained with low-toned crimson and gold.[34]

The French Symbolists, in particular, seized the Burne-Jones method of making psychological reality accessible.

In *Les Fleurs du Mal* (1857), Charles Baudelaire (1821–1867) had already revived the medieval use of symbols as agents of duality – the one world directly perceived by the senses, the other reached by dreams, visions, and spells that allowed one to escape from bourgeois materialism. Baudelaire's system of correspondences substituted imagination for God:

> It is imagination which has taught man the moral implication of colour, line, sounds and scents. At the beginning of the world it created analogy and metaphor.[35]

Fées were usable agents of metamorphosis. John Keats' 'La Belle Dame Sans Merci' had revived the Celtic view of an Otherworld that was both a retreat of sumptuous indulgence and a place of the dead:

> I saw pale Kings and Princes too
> Pale warriors, death-pale were they all;
> They cried, 'La belle dame sans merci
> Thee hath in thrall.'

The beautiful, powerful fée, free from ethical compulsions, could metaphorically represent the transcendent and exotic.

---

[33] See *Mem.* II, pp. 69–72 and Martin Harrison & Bill Waters, *Burne-Jones* (London, 1973), passim. W.S. Gilbert's satiric lines in *Patience* (1881) suggest the Gallery's association with the Aesthetic Movement:
> A pallid and thin young man
> A haggard and lank young man
> A greenery-yallery, Grosvenor Gallery
> Foot-in-the-grave young man.

[34] *An Artist's Reminiscences* (London, 1907), p. 84.

[35] *Salon review* (1859) quoted by John Milner, *Symbolists and Decadents* (London, 1971), p. 30.

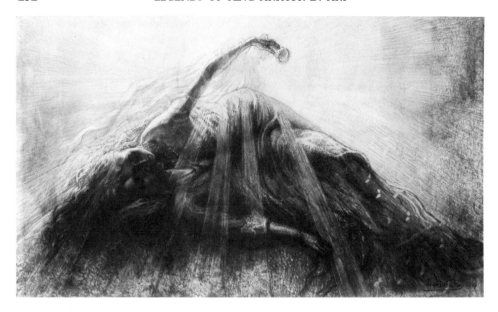

50. Jean Delville. Tristan and Yseult, drawing, 1887

Brittany had never lost its devotion to Arthurian legend. As recently as 1880, Thomas Louet donated to the parish church of Ile-Aux-Moines, Morbihan a stained glass window depicting St Arthur.[36] To Paul Gaugin (1848–1903), Odilon Redon (1840–1916) and Paul Sérusier (1864–1927) the country seemed an ancient, spirit-filled garden with Broceliande its Sacred Wood. Sérusier[37] filled the forests of his oil paintings with fées treated as part of the landscape's reality. A group of peasants see flower-decked women beyond the stream in 'La Vision près du Torrent ou Le rendez-vous des fées' (1897, Collection Danion, Quimper). 'Les Elfes' (1906, private collection) and 'Danses d'elfes' (1908) show them dancing, their feet bare (like Nimue's) and their long fair hair adorned not with snakes but flowers. 'La Rencontre avec la fée' (1916) appears to be a Merlin-Nimue subject. In a setting of trees and rocks, a beautiful woman in fifteenth century costume bespells an aged, dark-cloaked man. In 'Le Petit chien d'Yseult' (1912) the dull gold tones of the fifteenth century dress, hair and skin, the dark forest background, the heroine's doleful expression as she pats Tristan's gift, the indulged dog on its cushion, convey the dolour of a deserted lover. Legend expresses the artist's tragic sense of life by reminding him of lost paradises.

Another source of Symbolist painting was Wagnerian opera, an art form that transported the hearer/viewer to a mystical otherworld remote from sooty cities and the mutable, rapacious natural world. In Baudelaire's view, 'No other musician rivals Wagner in *painting* depth and space, material and spiritual.' Wagner

[36] Karl Heinz Göller, 'Arthur: Saint and Sinner', *Avalon to Camelot*, II/I (1986), 11–12.
[37] For critical comment and reproductions see Marcel Guicheteau, *Paul Sérusier* (Paris, 1976).

himself enunciated an assessment of his aesthetic aims that seemed close to Symbolist aspirations:

> The most exalted work of art should replace real life, should dissolve reality in an illusion, thanks to which it would be reality itself which would appear to us as illusory. The nothingness of the world – here we would freely discover it, without bitterness, smiling![38]

The vagaries of the new cult occupied the pages of the *Revue Wagnerienne*, published in Paris between 1885 and 1888. Here writers and artists could develop a philosophical framework for their aestheticism with Wagner as catalyst.

Jean Delville (1867–1953), a Belgian who promoted the Rosicrucian philosophy of Joséphin Péladan, was one of the most accomplished among those who sought to 'unite the emotions of literature, the Louvre and Bayreuth in a state of harmonious ecstasy'.[39] His drawing 'Tristan and Yseult' (1887, Musées Royaux des Beaux-Arts, Brussels) presents a state of illumination transcending both yearning and pain. From the empty goblet in Yseult's raised hand stream rays of sublime light. They shine upon the triangle of the supine bodies, motionless with ecstacy, upon the curve of Yseult's cheek, the strands of trailing hair, the lace of Tristan's cuff. His face is already shrouded in shadow; the butterflies on her gown symbolise their transcendent souls. One can hear in the background the Liebestod's triumphant conclusion.

It was in *Parsifal* (1882), however, that Wagner recreated the most profound mystical experience available to Western man. He wrote not only the music but the text which had occupied his mind for thirty years. His sources for the Grail legend were Wolfram von Eschenbach's *Parzival*, a modern French translation of Chrétien de Troyes' *Perceval* and its continuations, some nineteenth century critical studies, and Comte de Villemarque's *Contes des anciens Bretons*, which made him aware of the legends' Celtic origins. His central characters were Parsifal, the innocent fool destined to be the saviour; Amfortas, the 'Fisher King' wounded by the spear of Longinus, which he had failed to guard; Klingsor, the evil enchanter whose magical garden is a sexual trap and Kundry, the 'Loathly Lady'. The Grail is not Wolfram's stone but the chalice of the Last Supper, a vessel of divine grace, conceived as in the Old French *La Queste del Saint Graal*.

Jean Delville's charcoal drawing 'Parsifal' (1890, Coll. Deville, Brussels) shows the hero in a state of transfiguration. Having restored the spear to the Grail castle, Monsalvat, and having healed Amfortas, he uncovers the shrine. The imagined chorus sings

---

[38] Lucy Beckett, *Richard Wagner: Parsifal* (Cambridge, Eng., 1981), p. 110. For reproductions of Symbolist art based on Wagnerian opera see Philippe Jullian, *The Symbolists*, trans. Mary Anne Stevens (Oxford, 1973). See also Philippe Jullian, *Dreamers of Decadence: Symbolist Painters of the 1890s* (London, 1971); and *Le Symbolisme en Europe*, catalogue of an exhibition at the Musée Boymans-von Beuningen, Rotterdam, 1975, with an introductory essay by Hans. H. Hofstätter.

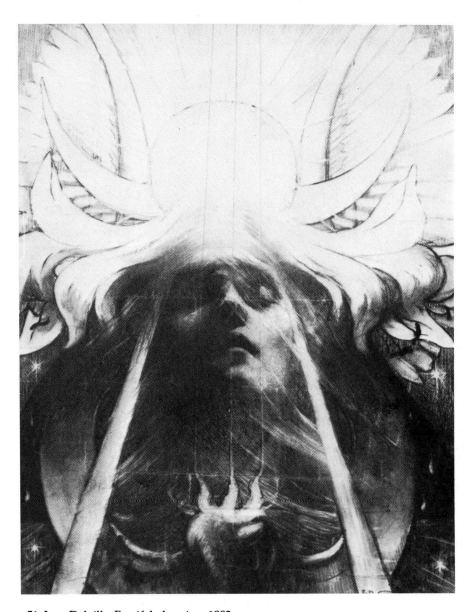

51. Jean Delville. Parsifal, drawing, 1882

Höchsten Heiles Wunder!
Erlösung dem Erlöser!

(Highest wonder of salvation!
Redemption to the redeemer!)

Parsifal is illuminated by the flames of the Grail-Sun. His eyes closed in contemplation, his hair swept by the divine wind, he is a focus of supernatural energy and order expressed in tautly symmetrical form.

Princus Marcius Simons (1867–1909), an American who also exhibited Wagnerian subjects at Péladan's Salon de la Rose + Croix, combines Parsifal's mystical adoration of the Grail with detailed architecture in the oil painting 'The Chapel of the Holy Grail' (Coll. Camord, Paris). Like Max Brückner's oil, 'The Temple of the Grail', this work seems based on a set design for a Bayreuth production. The splendid chalice encircled by angels lights up Romanesque arches, Corinthian columns and carved balconies of such immensity and grandeur that the kneeling hero is almost overlooked.

Jacques-Emile Blanche's lithograph in the *Revue Wagnerienne*, 'Parsifal' (1886, Bibliothèque Nationale, Paris), is a mediocre depiction based on the opera's first act. The naive hero, with his wide-set, childish eyes, full lips and peasant's smock appears in the foreground. He carries the bow which he has just used to kill the wild swan, an act of thoughtlessness corresponding to his disregard for his mother and his subsequent failure to heal Amfortas by asking the spell-breaking question. Behind the boy, outlined against the forest, is Kundry, the fatal woman who destroys the Grail knights by seducing them.

Jan Toorop (1858–1928) more dramatically expresses the struggle between chastity (the source of spiritual enlightenment) and sexual indulgence in his charcoal and crayon drawing, 'Kundry et Parsifal' (ca. 1895, private collection). In Klingsor's magical garden the hero again encounters Kundry, transformed into a beautiful lady who reclines on a couch of flowers. Parsifal's nakedness suggests the degree of temptation but as his glance falls on the chalice and its cross, he forcefully pushes himself away from her vicinity with his large, splayed hand. The scene is analogous to Perceval's temptation in *La Queste del Saint Graal* and Malory where the sight of his sword's cross-shaped hilt saves him from fornication. Toorop's treatment is highly decorative and linear with swirling flowers providing a medieval-style background that negates perspective.

Parsifal's successful defence of his chastity enables him to regain the bleeding spear, kill Klingsor and turn his garden into a Wasteland. Now Parsifal can heal Amfortas' bleeding wound. The hero's return with the lance is Odilon Redon's subject in a lithograph, 'Parsifal' (1892, Bibliothèque Nationale, Paris). The most important Symbolist artist, Redon believed that mystery is always equivocal. The work of art should allow several interpretations so that the viewer may choose one that suits his own state of mind. Regarding this lithograph, the viewer must decide both the particular event in the narrative line and the particular emotion which the dark eyes convey. Even period is indeterminate for the crescent-shaped helmet is unrelated to specific time or place.

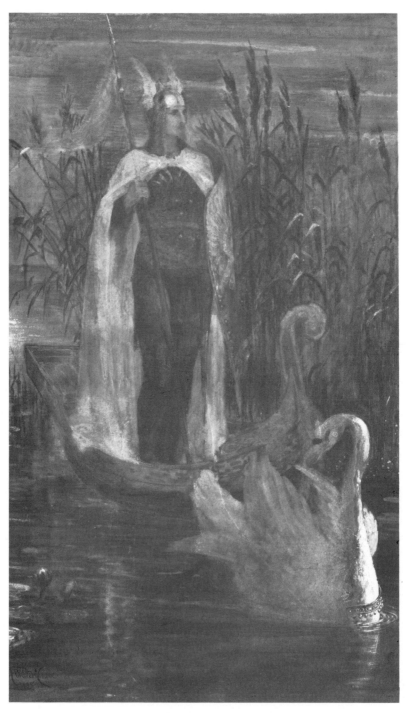

52. Walter Crane. The Swan King, coloured chalk drawing, 1895

Though Wagnerian music dramas were performed at Covent Garden during the latter part of the century, there was no cult of enthusiasts comparable to those on the Continent. Aubrey Beardsley's wickedly satiric black and white print 'The Wagnerites' (1894, Victoria and Albert, London) suggests that the German composer's devotees were cynical society women and Jews; yet Beardsley himself was particularly inspired by the *Ring Cycle* and *Tristan and Isolde*. The print entitled 'Isolde', one of his rare experiments with colour, shows, against an apricot background, an elongated woman wearing a Victorian tea gown and wide brimmed straw hat adorned with poppies. She leans eagerly towards the love chalice which is caressingly held between her palms.

In 1893 Walter Crane travelled to Bayreuth where he saw *Lohengrin*, *Tannhauser* and *Parsifal*. One result was 'The Swan King' (1895, Forbes Magazine Collection, Old Battersea House, London), a coloured chalk attempt at recreating the effect of the swan-music that he had heard 'stealing on the silence in the darkness in a way that reminded one of a creeping mist over the lowlands, on the silver windings of a river flowing ever nearer, until it reached one's feet in full flood'.[40] The shape of the large swan in the foreground (having hermaphroditic connotations for the Symbolists) is insistently repeated both in the water's reflection and in the boat's construction. Against a decorative background of tasseled reeds, japonesque in their delicacy, the hero stands with spear, shield and winged helmet.

When the Parsifal music was performed at the Royal Albert Hall in 1884, Burne-Jones, who did not usually like Wagner, was entranced: 'He made sounds that are really and truly . . . the very sounds that were to be heard in the Sangraal Chapel'.[41] By now the artist was working on a picture, originally commissioned by George Howard, that was to occupy his heart, mind and hand for the rest of his life, 'The Sleep of Arthur in Avalon' (1881–98, Museo d'Arte, Ponce, Puerto Rico). The notebooks of his assistant, Thomas Rooke, record the progress and setbacks in creating this work which Burne-Jones called 'my chief dream now . . . I think I can put into it all I most care for'.[42] On July 10, 1896 he was painting the blue hanging on the palace wall, on July 15 an Amazon with a shield, on May 25, 1897 Morgan Le Fay's white dress, and the next day a pink harper and a green dulcimer player. Over the years he painted and obliterated nude 'Hill Faeries', a battle scene, the bottle green waters lapping the shore of the Otherworld island, and a rocky barrier. No painting gave him greater trouble in composition because no painting was so important in conveying Idea.

The subject is the ancient myth of King Arthur's survival in Avalon. Mortally wounded in battle against the forces of evil and chaos, the King is carried by fées to a 'locus amoenus'. Eventually healed and invigorated by his supernatural sleep, he will waken and return to Britain at a moment of crisis which the blowing of a horn or the ringing of a bell will announce. Allegorically, Arthur represents

---

[39] Jullian, *The Symbolists*, p. 31.
[40] *An Artist's Reminiscences*, p. 424.
[41] *Mem.* II, p. 43.
[42] *Mem.* II, p. 125.

the artist, in particular Burne-Jones, who devoted his life to appreciating and recording beauty. Avalon 'where I have stiven to be with all my might' is the ideal place where one's intentions can be perfectly realized – 'I have designed many pictures that are to be painted in Avalon – secure me a famous wall, for I have much to say'.[43]

Arthur is also his old friend, William Morris, who died in 1896. Graham Robertson, a visitor to the 'Avalon' studio, noted the physical likeness to Morris in Arthur's 'glorious head on a crumple of clothes'. Both men had battled Philistines in defence of beauty, not as selfish indulgence but as a source of joy and hope for all. Like Arthur, they seemed to have battled in vain. Writing on 'Painting and Popular Culture' in *Fraser's Magazine* 101 (1880), T.C. Horsfall asserted that the works of artists like Burne-Jones, despite their noble subjects, 'have no relation to the knowledge, and therefore none to the thought and feeling, of most of the people who see them'. The commonest hedgerow in the country and the flowers grown in the smallest house in the smokiest town are more efficacious in 'making us feel . . . that life is worth living' than any beautiful things that artists produce.

'Arthur in Avalon' is the ultimate expression of the 'beauty in repose' motif, poignant with belief that sleep will end in renewal. Surrounded by beautiful women whose loose gowns deliberately avoid historical specificity, the king rests his head in the lap of his sister, who wears a white dress indicating her beneficence. Her hands are raised as if she were executing a spell of healing. The jewelled crown is ready to be taken up again as are the shield, helm and sword that the fées guard. The flowers which adorn the foreground of the *hortus conclusus* have symbolic values – yellow iris, the artist's personal icon for love, columbines for grace, poppies for sleep. The musical instruments, as in the Rottingdean panels and 'The Witch's Tree', suggest pleasure and bespelling. The reliefs on the palace's golden canopy show scenes from the 'Quest of the Holy Grail', not only the central book among the artist's literary sources, but also the personal myth of pursuit and achievement. The single lamp shining above the king's bed affirms that he is not dead but sleeping. The predominant colours are the rich reds and greens of stained glass and tapestry. This great oil painting (111 in x 254 in) is the artist's and the century's last evocation of 'a magical land that I dream about'.

---

[43] *Mem.* II, p. 169.

CHAPTER ELEVEN

The Book as Art Object

William Morris's revival of the medieval decorative arts brought him near the end of his life to the printed book.[1] He considered that the most beautiful books ever produced were French illuminated manuscripts of the thirteenth and fourteenth centuries which vividly combined the story-telling and decorative functions of art.[2] Because early printed books imitated manuscript traditions, modern book designers could use them as models. To avoid the ugliness which characterised most nineteenth century books (and which signified for Morris a decadent society), a publisher should insist that every element of the 'architecture' be treated as part of an organic whole. The type must be black and bold like that of Schoeffer of Mainz or Mentelin of Strassburg, the words well spaced, the paper and ink of the best quality, and the decorative elements – initials, title pages, borders, frames and illustrations – in harmony with the printed page. The result would be 'a visible work of art' that was 'beautiful taken as a whole – alive all over, and not merely in a corner here and there'.[3]

Despairing of finding all the desired attributes in the books of contemporary publishers, in 1891 Morris established the Kelmscott Press. The hand-operated machinery was housed in a room at 14 Upper Mall, Hammersmith. The 'Note by William Morris on His Aims in Founding the Kelmscott Press' (1896) begins:

> I began printing books with the hope of producing some which would have a definite claim to beauty, while at the same time they should be

[1]   Morris' views on the subject have been collected in *The Ideal Book, Essays and Lectures on the Arts of the Book by William Morris*, ed. William S. Peterson (Berkeley, Los Angeles and London, 1982). A friend and fellow socialist, Emery Walker, particularly aroused his interest through an illustrated lecture given at the first Arts and Crafts Exhibition, 15 November, 1888.

[2]   Morris had a considerable collection of illuminated manuscripts and early printed books, including Wynkyn de Worde's *The Golden Legend* (1527); he borrowed from Quaritch de Worde's *Recuyell of the Histories of Troy* when he was looking for sample types. Much of his collection is now in the Pierpont Morgan Library, New York. See M.R. James, *Catalogue of Manuscripts and Early Printed Books from the libraries of William Morris, Richard Bennett Bertram, fourth Earl of Ashburnham and other sources*, 3 vols (London, 1907).

[3]   'The Woodcuts of Gothic Books' (1892).

easy to read and should not dazzle the eye, or trouble the intellect of the reader by eccentricity of form in the letters.

The books would affirm the Master's socialist theories; like beautiful buildings and beautiful furnishings they would depend on artistic freedom and good working conditions.[4] While the medieval artist-craftsman was the model, Morris did not reject technology that freed his employees from monotonous tasks; for example, photography was used to transfer the artist's design to the woodblock, which was then cut by hand.

Although both Morris and his chief illustrator, Burne-Jones, planned that an edition of Malory should follow their great *Chaucer* (1896),[5] the former's death on 3 October, 1896 forestalled the fulfillment of their ambition. The press's only medieval Arthurian romances were *Syr Perecyvelle* and *Sire Degrevaunt* with Burne-Jones' woodcut frontispieces. Two Kelmscott artists decorated Arthurian works for other publishers. Walter Crane (whom Morris regarded as an ideal artist-illustrator because he could design an entire page comprising picture, ornament and type) was invited to supply woodcuts for *The Story of the Glittering Plain* (1894). At the same time Crane was fulfilling a commission from George Allen to decorate a six volume edition of Spenser's *Faerie Queene* (1894–7).[6] Allen, whose reissue of Ruskin's works had been commercially successful, hoped that the same audience would buy a well-illustrated Spenser, an author whom Ruskin constantly cited and praised.

Allen's was not the first illustrated *Faerie Queene*. In 1751 J. Brindley had published a three volume edition with thirty-two copper-plate engravings designed by William Kent (1685–1748). Kent was one of those all-round artist-craftsmen of whom Morris would have approved – an architect, interior decorator, furniture designer, painter, book illustrator and a landscape gardener whose layout of Cirencester Park included a castellated woodshed known as 'King Arthur's Castle'. The *Faerie Queene* pictures, so finely engraved that they have the texture of tapestry, feature realistic landscapes and neo-Gothic buildings with occasional lapses into the classical (battlements on Ionic columns) and chinoiserie (parasol, bridge and pagoda-like tower in plate 19, 'Guyon leaves the Palmer and crosses the Idle Lake with Phedria'). The bare-footed Merlin is gowned like a Greek philosopher. The ladies, too, are classically draped, revealing a good deal of flesh, but Prince Arthur wears fifteenth century armour and a dragon-crested helmet.

---

[4] One of the first Kelmscott books was Ruskin's 'On the Nature of Gothic' (K.P. 1892), which Morris called 'one of the very few necessary and inevitable utterances of the century'.

[5] See the two-volume Basilisk Press edition (London, 1975) with commentary by Duncan Robertson.

[6] Allen produced 1000 copies on handmade paper, using the text of the 1590 Quarto. The Editor's Preface noted, 'The object has indeed been as modest as the original demand for the book, namely, to furnish an accurate, reliable, and up-to-date text for the genius of the illustrator to decorate'.

As Timon and Merlin educate the youth, Queen Elizabeth watches from a full moon (plate 13).

The 1894 *Faerie Queene* is one of the most extensively decorated literary texts to be embellished by a single hand. Any area not devoted to print is filled with design. There are one or more full-page illustrations for each canto, as well as headpieces, endpieces, borders and title pages. Crane believed that 'books which have been considered by their printers and designers as works of art as well as of literature give double pleasure since they satisfy more than one sense'.[7] In *An Artist's Reminiscences* he reflects on the challenge that the long allegorical poem presented:

> To follow the poet through the six books and endeavour to embody the
> extraordinarily rich invention and complexity of allusion as well as to
> depict the incidents and characters of the story, was no light undertak-
> ing, but the task was a congenial one, and I commenced with a light
> heart.[8]

He consciously adopted the medieval use of images to convey not only 'extra-ordinary beauty but deep symbolical, historical, constructive and racial meaning'.[9] As in fifteenth century manuscripts like the Bodleian *Guiron* or in medieval tapestries, border incidents expand the contents of the central picture. Duessa enthroned and gazing into a mirror iconographically represents the para-mount sin, Pride, while the remaining deadly sins, humans riding appropriate animals, encircle her in the pomegranate border. Monsters, the most obvious signs of evil, are appropriate both to 'the art of pictorial statement' which is related to the allegorical narrative and to the 'art of decorative treatment', an aspect of illustration equally attractive to Crane.[10] Duessa's dragon has demonic associ-ations as does the opponent whose serpentine coils enclose the Red Cross Knight. The significance of the hero's 'most glorious victory' is signalled by the border design – on the left, Eden's serpent-twined Tree of the Knowledge of Good or Evil; on the right the Tree of Life (Arbor Vitae).

The fair-haired Prince Arthur, whether rescuing the oppressed or studying his genealogy, embodies such Victorian ideals as duty, loyalty to a lady-regnant,

---

[7] *William Morris to Whistler: Papers and Addresses on Art and Craft and the Commonwealth* (London, 1911), p. 75.

[8] *An Artist's Reminiscences* (London, 1907), p. 429. *The Faerie Queene* inspired other exam-ples of Crane's art; e.g. 'The Red Cross Knight in Search of Una' (1869), a drawing of a knight on horseback in a landscape based on a Derbyshire clough, and 'Britomart by the Sea' (1895), a watercolour developed from the headpiece of Book III in his illustrated edition. As well he provided sixteen full-page colour plates for Henry Gilbert's *King Art-hur's Knights* (1911).

[9] 'Ornament and its Meaning' in *Ideals in Art. Papers theoretical, practical, critical* (London, 1905), pp. 102–9.

[10] See *Of the Decorative Illustration of Books Old and New* (London, 1984 [1896]), pp. 5, 217–231.

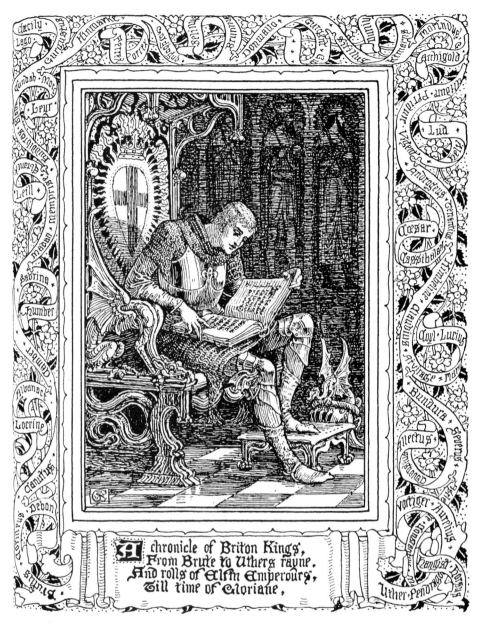

A chronicle of Briton Kings,
From Brute to Uthers rayne.
And rolls of Elfin Emperours,
Till time of Gloriane,

53. Prince Arthur. Walter Crane's wood engraving illustrating Edmund Spenser, *The Faerie Queene* (London: George Allen, 1894–97)

courage and muscular Christianity. The dragon motif on his throne and helm is dynastic, not malign.

Wood-engraving is an appropriate technique for illustrating *The Faerie Queene*, since it is congenial to the sixteenth-century text and sufficiently flexible to permit complex detail. Crane meets the requirements of 'the ideal book' with the blackness of the Gothic lettering incorporated into the designs; the recognition of the page's rectangular shape in the picture's shape; the title page's ornamentation which focuses on lettering but alludes in a symbolic way to the literary contents; the proportions of the ornate borders, wider on the outside of the page than towards the centre of the double-page spread; and the decorative connections between the frieze-shaped panel headings and the initial letters. In the endpieces, one of his particular delights, he avoids anti-climax by providing 'some lingering echo, some recurring thought suggested by the text'.

Another Kelmscott artist was Charles M. Gere (1867–1957) whom Morris employed to illustrate his romance, *The Well at the World's End*. In a letter of November 7, 1893 he advised Gere to take as his inspiration 'illuminations in 13th and 14th century books . . . woodcuts and so on'. After Morris's death Gere worked for C.H. St. John Hornby (1867–1946), a partner in W.H. Smith and Son and owner of the Ashendene Press, which he founded in 1894.[11] Hornby called it 'the hobby of my leisure hours', a pursuit that allowed him to indulge 'my own personal taste in illustration . . . books which gave scope for a certain gaiety of treatment in the use of coloured initials and chapter headings'. Having taken tea at Kelmscott House on 13 March, 1895, he departed 'in a state of elation and high resolve', convinced that the great fifteenth-century printers provided the best models.[12]

Of the forty major books produced in forty years, the most important was the 1913 edition of *The Noble and Joyous Book Entytled Le Morte Darthur Reduced into Englyssh By Syr Thomas Malory Kt*.[13] Southey's reissue of Caxton, including the preface, provided the text which was printed on 504 folio size pages. The decoration included border rubrics, alternating red and blue initials, red chapter headings, two full page woodcuts, and twenty-four smaller woodcut illustrations designed by Charles Gere, and three by his sister Margaret. W.H. Hooper, a Kelmscott alumnus whom Hornby described as 'almost the last of the old school of woodengravers', cut the designs as far as Book X, Chapter 59. J.B. Swain did the remainder.

---

[11] On the press and its founder, see Colin Franklin, *The Private Presses* (London, 1969); C.H. St. John Hornby, *A Descriptive Bibliography of the Books Printed at the Ashendene Press MDCCCXCV–MCMXXXV* (London, 1935); Will Ransom, *Kelmscott, Doves and Ashendene* (San Francisco, 1952).

[12] Sir Sidney Cockerell reported the visit in *The Spectator*, May 10, 1946; reprinted in *An Anthology of Appreciation* (London, 1946).

[13] The complete title read *The Noble and Joyous Book entytled Le Morte Darthur not wythstandying it Treateth of the Byrth, Lyf, and Actes of the Sayd Kyng Arthur, of his noble Knyghtes of the Rounde Table, theyr mervayllous conquestes and adventures, thachyevyng of the Sangreal and in thende the dolorous deth and departying out of thys worlde of them al whiche book was reduced in to Englysshe by Syr Thomas Malory Knyght.* Eight copies were printed on vellum and one hundred and forty-five on paper.

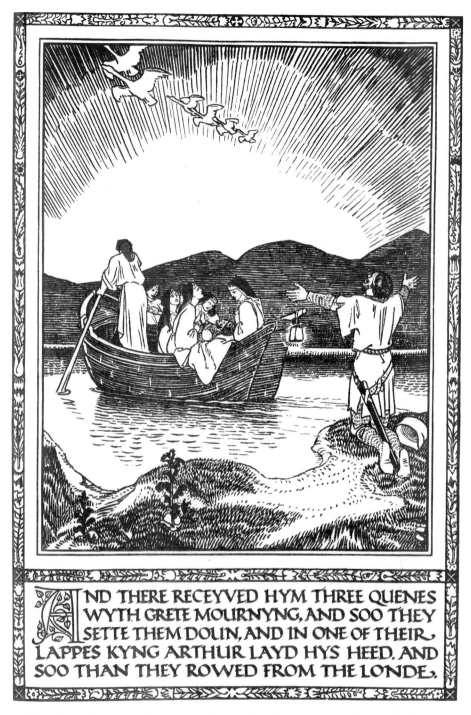

AND THERE RECEYVED HYM THREE QUENES WYTH GRETE MOURNYNG, AND SOO THEY SETTE THEM DOUN, AND IN ONE OF THEIR LAPPES KYNG ARTHUR LAYD HYS HEED. AND SOO THAN THEY ROWED FROM THE LONDE.

54. Arthur's Departure for Avalon. Charles Gere's wood engraving for Sir Thomas Malory, *Morte Darthur* (London: Ashendene Press, 1913)

Hornby regarded the *Morte* as 'a gentleman's book', an attitude common in the later Victorian and the Edwardian periods. Malory's Round Table Knights were desirable models for British youth since they combined distinctiveness of class and an ideal of public service with the social and moral attributes of courtesy, fellowship, courage, piety, truth, protectiveness towards women, and loyalty to a monarch. In particular Launcelot represented 'that highest type of manhood, the Christian gentleman'.[14] Gere's illustrations acknowledge Launcelot's paramount-cy. The 'flower of chivalry' appears in eleven of twenty-seven woodcuts – sleeping under the apple tree where he is captured by the crowned fées, slaying the ghost-knights at the Perilous Chapel, lying in his madness by a well, weeping into his hands after healing Sir Urry, riding in a cart towards the castle gate as his arrow-pierced horse trails behind. There is no hint of adulterous passion, even the entrapment scene being remarkably chaste as a retinue of women chaperones the queen.

The weakness of Gere's designs is that they are both stolid and inconsistently derivative. The chain-mail armour, horse litter carrying Guenevere's corpse, and hand surrounded by light which offers the chalice to imprisoned Grail Knights may derive from early fourteenth century manuscripts. The millefleur tapestry in Elaine's bedroom, the flagon-filled cupboards on the Irish ship and the Entombment mosaic in the Grail Chapel are most likely drawn from ninetenth century painting. Burne-Jones' *Chaucer* illustrations, no doubt, suggested the constricted spaces of interior scenes, the nightgown-like garments of the Avalon queens, and such obvious symbols as the flight of swans at Arthur's departure. One misses the leafy borders of the Kelmscott volumes. Gere clearly gave story-telling priority over decoration.

The most original response to the Kelmscott books came in 1892 when J.M. Dent decided to bring out editions of the classics similar to Morris'.[15] Since he would use line-block illustrations which could be reproduced by a photo-mechanical method rather than hand-engraved wood blocks, his books would be considerably less expensive than those of the Kelmscott Press. Having asked a bookseller friend, F.H. Evans, if he knew of a likely illustrator for Malory's *Le Morte Darthur*, with which he planned to begin the series, Dent was one day invited to call around at Evans' book shop and take a look at some drawings by a clerk in the Guardian Life and Fire Insurance Office. His first meeting with Aubrey Beardsley is described in his memoirs:[16]

[14] Waldo Cutler, *Stories of King Arthur and his Knights* (1905), p. xix.
[15] My discussion of Beardsley is excerpted from Muriel A.I. Whitaker, 'Flat Blasphemies – Beardsley's Illustrations for Malory's Morte Darthur', in *Mosaic, A Journal for the Comparative Study of Literature and Ideas*, published by the University of Manitoba Press, VIII/2 (1975), 67–75.
[16] Quoted by F.J. Martin Dent in the 'Publisher's Note' prefacing the Fourth Edition of Malory's *Le Morte Darthur* with Aubrey Beardsley's designs (London, 1972).

The young artist, Aubrey Beardsley, was then barely nineteen years of age,[17] and when I saw him I was shocked at his emaciated appearance. Alas! even at that time it was evident that without great care he could not be long for this world. He was a strange boy, 'weird'[18] is the right description. . . . He was keen about his art and about the commission to decorate Malory's book. It was soon arranged that he should prepare a first drawing for approval, and in a few weeks he produced a picture which in my poor judgment will always remain a masterpiece, 'The Achieving of the Sangreal', a marvellous design of which I am still the proud possessor. The book startled the critics considerably, but though much adverse criticism came from the 'orthodox', Joseph Pennell at once realised the new 'value' of its art and praised the work to excess, and Beardsley was soon imitated by many young artists of the time. They 'discovered' that 'colour' and 'balance' in black and white which has ever since been a feature of modern work.

What Dent had in mind and what the Sangreal illustration suggested he would get was the soulful medievalism of Morris and Burne-Jones with a dash of japonesque in the form of bare branches, oriental flowers, and asymmetrical arrangements. In a letter to G.F. Scotson Clark, written ca. 15 February, 1893, Beardsley gave his version of the enterprise:[19]

Last summer I struck for myself an entirely new method of drawing and composition, something suggestive of Japan, but not really japonesque. Words fail to describe the quality of the workmanship. The subjects were quite mad and a little indecent . . . quite a new world of my own creation. . . . My next step was to besiege the publishers, all of whom opened their great stupid eyes pretty wide. They were frightened, however, of anything new and so daringly original. One of them (Dent – lucky dog!) saw his chance and put me on to a large *édition de luxe* of Malory's *Morte Darthur*. The drawings were to be done in medieval manner and there were to be many of them. The work I have already done for Dent has simply made my name. Subscribers crowd from all parts. William Morris has sworn a terrible oath against me for daring to bring out a book in his manner. The truth is that, while *his* work is a mere imitation of the old stuff, mine is refreshing and original. Anyhow, all the good critics are on my side, but I expect there will be more rows when the book appears (in June).

[17] Actually, as F.J.M. Dent points out, he must have been twenty.
[18] The adjective suggests some of the names which would be attached to him – 'Wierdsley Dauberey', 'Awfully Weirdly', 'Dawbaway Weirdsley'.
[19] Henry Maas, J.L. Duncan, W.G. Good, eds. *The Letters of Aubrey Beardsley* (London, 1971), p. 43.

Indeed, Morris was so annoyed at what he called Beardsley's 'act of usurpation' that he contemplated a lawsuit. 'A man ought to do his own work', he complained. Certainly the influence of Morris and Burne-Jones was very evident in such early illustrations as 'Merlin Taketh the Child Arthur into His Keeping', with its central figures in the style of early woodcuts, its crowded landscape, bat's-wing armour, briars and bentwood lines as well as its border of densely intertwined grape-vines and acanthus leaves. But long before Beardsley had completed the 585 chapter headings, borders, initials, ornaments and full or double-page illustrations, he had passed so far beyond both the style and content of his initial offerings that it was an effort to maintain consistency and interest. In the borders and initials, the extravagant and inhibiting *entrelacement* of naturalistic foliage was replaced by the energy of the whiplash line and the greater abstraction of floral motifs such as characterized Art Noveau; in the set pieces, the illustration was often strung out over two pages in order to meet more easily his commitment to the publisher. Exhausted by the drudgery of the *Le Morte Darthur* drawings, Beardsley complained that Malory's book was 'very long winded'. It was with considerable difficulty that Dent and Beardsley's mother pressured and cajoled him into completing the work, despite the attraction of the £250 fee.

So great is the discrepancy between text and illustration that is is doubtful Beardsley read more than the opening books of the *Morte*. Many episodes that he chose to illustrate he could have known from Tennyson, Swinburne and Wagner. Malory is full of action as his knights energetically engage in tournament, battle and the testing adventures of the Perilous Forest. Beardsley's knights, in contrast, are as wan and pale as the victims of *La Belle Dame Sans Merci*. They mope about in flowery meadows, using their swords as walking sticks, gaze raptly at lilies and phallic floral arrangements, emerge Tom-Thumb-like from columbines, or peer languidly over their shoulders at satyrs. Of the fifteen full-page illustrations depicting Round Table heroes, seven show knights in recumbent positions and none shows anything but passive contemplation. Their armour is so fantastically elaborated and classically draped as to be quite unsuitable for chivalric action. Though the knights occupy centre stage in Malory's text, they must share the interest in the illustrations with angels, satyrs, fatal women and androgynous nudes.

What chiefly differentiates the two artists is their attitude to evil. Malory's first publisher, William Caxton, had no reservations about the moral quality of *Le Morte Darthur*:

> And I, according to my copy, have done set in imprint, to the intent that noble men may see and learn the noble acts of chivalry, the gentle and virtuous deeds that some knights used in those days, by which they came to honour; and how they that were vicious were punished and oft put to shame and rebuke. . . . Do after the good and leave the evil, and it shall bring you to good fame and renown.
>
> (xxxv)

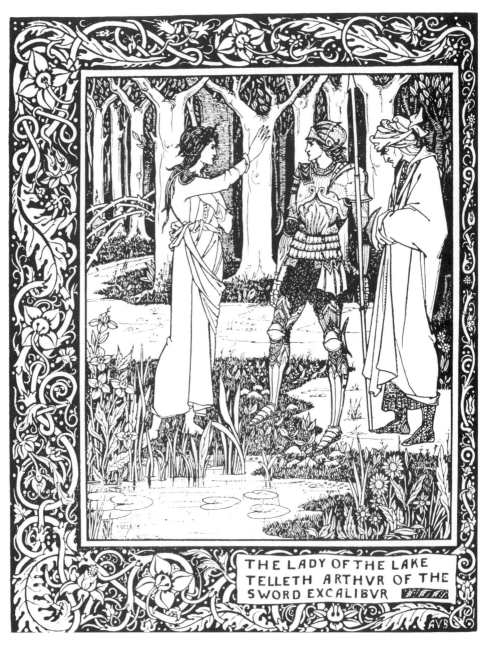

THE LADY OF THE LAKE
TELLETH ARTHVR OF THE
SWORD EXCALIBVR

55. The lady of the lake telleth Arthur of the sword Excalibur. Aubrey Beardsley's illustration for Malory's *Morte Darthur* (London: Dent, 1893)

The struggle between good and evil which is the basis of the tropology and anagogy is present in many episodes. Though Malory never directly states the didactic purpose which Caxton imputes to him, nevertheless his treatment of chivalry supports Caxton's view that 'al is wryten for our doctryne'. The archetypal patterns of quest and combat represent the application of chivalric ideals to human problems.

Malory does his best to play down the adulterous 'courtly love' of his sources. Tristan is far more important as a knight-errant than as the lover of Isolde. Gareth must be married to Lady Lyoness before he can enjoy the reward for his prowess. The sexual relationship between Launcelot and Guinevere is not made explicit until the story is far advanced and in the end both lovers achieve sanctity and salvation.

Beardsley, in contrast, is the inheritor of the 'romantic agony'. Though one need not go so far as Roger Fry who dubs him the Fra Angelico of Satanism[20] or Alice Meynell who protests that he never devises a picture 'without busying his imagination to express an infernal evil',[21] one recognizes his affinity to Baudelaire, Gautier, Huysmans, and Poe as well as to Swinburne, Wilde, and the decadent poets of the nineties for whom horror could be a source of delight and beauty while religion was a source of blasphemy and perversion. In Beardsley's illustrations, sin is fascinating, provocative, and irresistible or in some cases just boring. Sex in a variety of forms is its basis.

Conditioned as we are to unisex and liberation, Beardsley's hermaphrodites, his feminine males and hoydenish females do not shock us as they did the Victorians. Nor are we likely to be disturbed by his world-weary angels. Yet we recognize the provocative sensuality half-hidden in the murky forest or exhibiting itself complacently in the walled gardens. And the form which evil takes is that of the importunate female, the homosexual male bent on seduction, the leering or alluring satyr.

As Mario Praz has pointed out, 'the Romantics made of the Fatal Woman an archetype which united in itself all forms of seduction, all vices, and all delights'.[22] In Malory, it is the knights who are aggressive. The ladies have little to do but inspire prowess and hand out the tournament prizes. The two Elaines who attempt by positive action to persuade Launcelot to marry them end up abandoned with a child or floating down to Camelot on a funeral barge. Despite their supernatural powers, even the fées – Morgan, Hallowes and Anneure – are constantly thwarted in their attempts to acquire the great knights as lovers. Beardsley's effeminate knights, however, are completely subjugated by the blowsy, aggressive females with their bulging breasts and thighs or the Medusa-locked enchantresses, heavy-lidded, bored, and contemptuous. Arthur himself is given the Medusa locks and contemptuous mien of a Beardsley woman while Merlin who in Malory's work is the chief architect of Arthur's political success now is port-

[20] *Vision and Design* (New York, 1924), p. 236.
[21] *The Pall Mall Gazette*, 2 November, 1904.
[22] *The Romantic Agony*, trans. Angus Davidson (London, 1933), pp. 209–210.

rayed in a foetal position, confined in a roundel that suggests the wizard's dependence. These role reversals would have been unthinkable to Malory – a degenerate parody of chivalric romance.

Even in the set pieces it is the fatal women who attract the artist's attention. Nimue with a flourish of her elongated hand consigns a slinking Merlin to his rocky prison. A demonic damsel offers Arthur the mantle which will reduce its wearer to coals. Morgan and her companion fées apprehend the sleeping Lancelot to incarcerate him in the Castle Chariot. The witch Hallowes entices Launcelot to the Perilous Chapel while he, with a gesture of self-destruction suggesting castration, directs his sword point towards his own thigh. La Beale Isoud crouches beside the dying Tristram like a vampire with her solid black robe, hunched shoulders, and down-drawn mouth. In the most dramatic of all Beardsley's Arthurian drawings, 'How Sir Tristram Drank of the Love Drink', the promise of joy symbolized by Tristram's raised goblet is countered by the premoniton of pain and death in Isoud's Medusa locks. In the final full page illustration, 'How Queen Guenever Made Her a Nun', the massive use of black so characteristic of the artist's mature poster style combines with an unholy expression and a strange beaked hood to make the queen seem more witch than nun.

Chapter headings and borders feature classical and aesthetic images. Horned satyrs, coy fauns, naked androgynes, roses and lilies, poppies, peacocks and swans, sunflowers and sundials are recurrent symbols of mingled beauty and pain, drugged sleep, ephemerality and perversity. Having outgrown the adolescent enthusiasm for romance that is apparent in the earlier designs, Beardsley becomes a satirist, determined to épater le bourgeois. His castles are towered and pinnacled Neo-Gothic railway hotels or such fantastically elaborate imitations of fairy tale castles as 'Mad' King Ludwig designed. In the garden of the Joyous Gard the flowering branches are tied onto the shrubs as if to point out the artificiality and transience of all love, not only that experienced by Sir Tristram and La Beale Isoud. The border consists of pears that are unmistakable female torsos, with lop-sided breasts and pubic hair. One chapter heading shows a naked sybarite with the face of Oscar Wilde, languidly sniffing a bunch of grapes.

In illustrating Le Morte Darthur, the artist wields a double-edged pen. On the one hand, he satirises Arthurian romance by converting chivalric action into erotic contemplation and by making the ladies enthrall and enervate the knights. On the other, he ironically subverts the Victorian idealisation of woman by substituting for the angel in the house the fatal Venus whose lips divided, vein by vein, the body of the knight Adonis in Swinburne's poem. The medieval ideal of Christian knighthood which had been combined with the Puritan work ethic to produce muscular Christianity is mocked by an art which questions the wisdom of pursuing any ideal except that of proficiency in illustration.

A decorative artist who did not merely imitate Beardsley but evolved from his example an individual style was Jessie Marion King (ca. 1875–1949). An instructor in book design at the Glasgow School of Art, she was commissioned to illustrate Morris's early exercise in literary medievalism, The Defence of Guenevere and other Poems, which John Lane reissued in 1904. Her full-page line drawings with hand-

lettered titles (quotations from the text), headpieces and endpieces are an outstanding example of Art Nouveau. To Beardsley's repertoire of motifs – the
poppy, multifoliate rose, bramble, burning taper, rococo furniture and sardonic
angel face – she adds crucifixes wound with roses and orbed with stars, angel
wings like ragged ribbons, and high stone walls that, like the patterned backgrounds of medieval miniatures, encourage a two-dimensional perception. While
Beardsley's images are firmly outlined to imitate woodcuts, King's lines dissolve
into circles, dots and lopsided stars. The artificiality of pure decoration denudes of
naturalism the trees, shrubs, flowers and clouds, making them images in a dream
world which is unpolluted by Beardsley's cynicism.

The ladies have towering, elongated bodies, abundant hair, remote expressions
and a sideways stance. Skirts, sleeves and cloaks billow under the impetus of the
whip-lash line. But King's Guenevere lacks blatant sensuality and demonic energy. Enclosed within a small room or walled garden, the melancholy queen uses
her imagination to escape the pain of capture, trial and judgment, while offering
her beauty as a proof of innocence:

> 'say no rash word
> Against me, being so beautiful . . . see my breast rise.
> Like waves of purple sea, as here I stand;
> And how my arms are moved in wonderful wise,
> This little wind is rising, yea now look you up,
> And wonder how the light is falling so
> Within my moving tresses: will you dare,
> When you have looked a little on my brow,
> To say this thing is vile?'

As in Beardsley's depiction of Guenevere the nun, an illustration for 'King
Arthur's Tomb' utilises the massive blackness of nun's habit, black headband and
flower, thorny branches and blackbirds streaming by to encroach symbolically on
the white space which contains Launcelot, kneeling by the tomb, a rose in his
hand. Generally, the artist prefers what Walter Pater calls 'the mystery of white
things'. Empty spaces evoke the magical and mystical. King's particular excellence is her merging of waking and dreaming. Imagination, memory and vision
make the dream world accessible. In 'The Defence of Guenevere' the queen asks
her accuser, Gauwaine, to imagine that on his deathbed he must choose between
two cloths, one red, one blue (representing heaven and hell). In the illustration,
the white-gowned 'God's angel' carrying the cloths on decorated wands illuminates the bedroom with beams that disintegrate into dots and stars. Only the
ebony bedpost carved with roses and beaded interlace is substantial.

When the hero of 'Sir Galahad, a Christmas Mystery' wakens from sensuous
dreams, he sees censorious angels, the foremost holding a scarf embroidered with
the exhortation, 'Galahad, rise and be arm'd'. In 'The Chapel in Lyoness' another
Grail knight, Bors, dreams that a beautiful lady, defined by roses and stars, bends
over him, obscuring the cross. The line's nervous intensity conveys the nervous

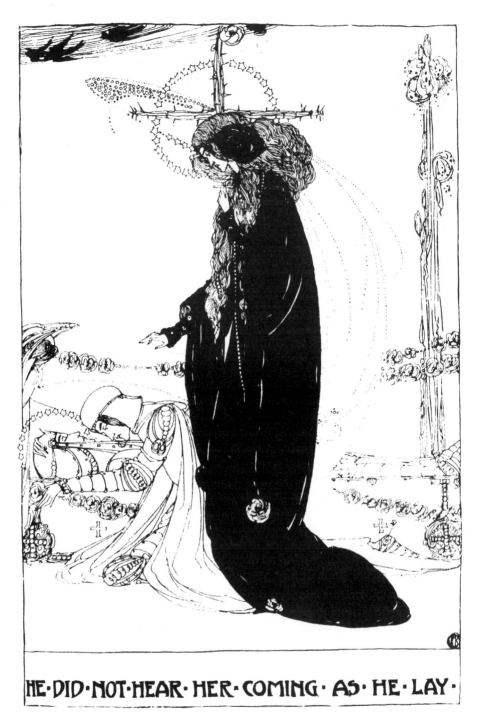

HE·DID·NOT·HEAR·HER·COMING·AS·HE·LAY·

56. King Arthur's Tomb. Jessie M. King's illustration for William Morris, *The Defence of Guenevere and Other Poems* (London: John Lane, 1904)

intensity of the central characters. Arthur Symons said that the ideal of decadence was 'to fix the last fine shade, the quintessence of things; to fix it fleetingly; to be a disembodied voice and yet the voice of a human soul'.[23] This kind of idealism King achieves in illustrations that complement their text as closely as did the best medieval miniatures.

About twenty years after Morris began promoting the concept of the book as a 'thing of beauty' a triumvirate of French publishers, Henry Floury, Ambroise Vollard and Henry Kahnweiler, turned their attention to the *livre d'artiste*, fine limited editions illustrated by important artists and sculptors.[24] Their approach was not identical to Morris'. While the Englishman insisted on the equal excellence of typology, book materials and decorative elements, even in modest books, the French emphasised superlative illustration by known artists. Their ideal was not 'un livre parfait' but 'un livre grandiose'. The woodcut technique, which had fallen into disuse in the sixteenth century, was revived as was the format of the 'handmade' illuminated manuscript with its clear text, borders, historiated capitals and other *mise en page* decorations.

In 1909 there appeared the first of thirty-six examples of the *livres d'artiste* that Kahnweiler published. *L'enchanteur pourrissant* by Guillaume Apollinaire (1880–1918) illustrated by André Derain (1880–1954) combined an avant-garde text and fauve woodcuts. In the subscription notice[25] the author described the artist as 'le plus précis réformateur de l'esthétique plastique a gravé sur le bois des images, des lettrines et des ornements qui font de ce livre une pure merveille artistique'. At the same time he indicated that his own aim was to express 'les racines s'étendent très loin, jusqu'aux profondeurs Celtiques de nos traditions'. Originally published in 1904 in the review *Festin d'Esope, L'enchanteur pourrissant* was a prose-poem inspired by the *Roman de Merlin* legend of Merlin's fatal love for Viviane and his incarceration in Broceliande. The son of a pure maiden and a devil, Apollinaire's Merlin combines his mother's mortality and ability to be deceived with his father's perversity, supernatural knowledge and indestructible *daemon*. Though his flesh has decayed, his spirit survives to converse with Viviane, the embodiment of evil beauty, and with other visitors to his grave. On Christmas Eve a phantasmagoric procession of repulsive animals, fatal women, the Chapalu (a monster-cat of Arthurian folklore which Derain depicts in ill. 5 as a bat-winged horse), witches, philosophers, sphinxes, the three false kings, and other tormentors mock him, implore him, and paradoxically comfort him. He complains, 'Il y a trop de personnages divins et magiques dans la forêt profonde et obscure, pour que je sois dupe de cette fantasie de Noël funéraire'.

After the visions of the winter solstice, spring transforms the landscape – 'le

---

[23] 'The Decadent Movement in Literature', *Harper's New Monthly Magazine*, November, 1893.
[24] On the genre see Gérard Bertrand, *L'illustration de la poésie à l'époque du cubisme 1909–1914: Derain, Dufy, Picasso* (Paris, 1971); W.J. Strachan, *The Artist and the Book in France: the 20th Century, Livre d'artiste* (London, 1969).
[25] Quoted by Jean Hugues in the introduction to *50 Ans d'Edition de D.H. Kahnweiler* (Paris, 1959).

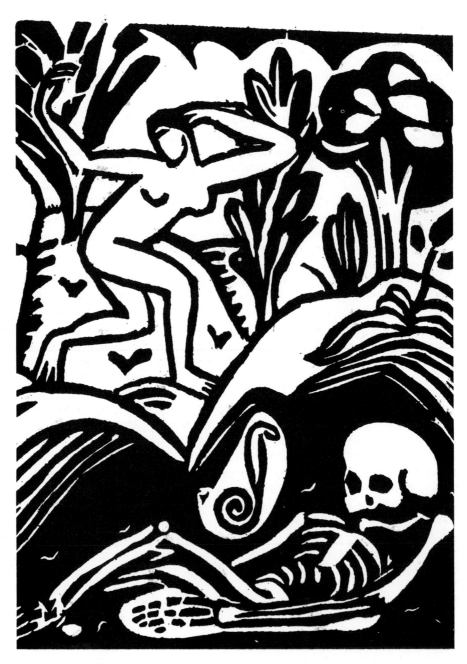

57. Viviane dances on Merlin's Tomb. André Derain's woodcut illustration for
Guillaume Apollinaire, *L'enchanteur pourrisant* (Paris: Kahnweiler, 1909)

soleil eclaira une forêt fraîche et florale'. The knight Tyolet, a second Orpheus who may symbolise the poet's death and resurrection,[26] emerges from a castled city to charm the forest creatures. (Fish, a duck, a butterfly, pigeons, horses, a snake and a deer brighten Derain's dark forest in the corresponding illustration.) The paradise soon becomes a battlefield as the animals rapaciously destroy one another. The work concludes with dialogues on the nature of love as male and female experience. The magician's suffering has uniquely transformed him: 'J'avais la conscience des éternités différentes de l'homme et de la femme'.

Derain felt no obligation to recreate the text literally, risking the woodcut's reduction to a 'forme d'art auxiliaire'. His task was to express the spirit and underlying significance. The 'old fashioned' woodcut technique was historically appropriate to Arthurian romance, yet Derain's style of illustration produced a 'dissonance baroque'.[27] Rather than recreating an impression of medieval Brittany, he resorts to a naive primitivism[28] that makes the time and place of his woodcuts independent of the text. His forest is a jungle of vines, serpentine roots and exotic, tulip-like flowers with only an occasional hawthorn blossom as a subtle allusion to the original myth. And his humans are Gauginesque nudes whose grotesque movements convey powerful emotions, although their identity as characters is not always clear. In the second full-page illustration a nude woman with rigid black hair and Oriental face stands in a wilderness garden. The flower which she provocatively holds suggests passion, beauty, seduction. Is she Lilith, Delilah, Viviane or simply a symbol of what Apollinaire called 'l'éternité de la femme'? In the tenth large woodcut it is Viviane who dances on the hilly mound covering Merlin's skeleton, which is guarded by a worm-serpent. Here her actions express, in Gérard Bertrand's words, 'la soif de vengeance et la nostalgie de l'amour'.

The complexity of vegetation contrasts with the simplicity of the humans, producing a tension between the worlds of man and nature that is also found in the text. At the same time, the plant forms unify the twelve full-page woodcuts, the nine designs set into the text, the seven ornamental letters and the three chapter headings. The other unifying element is the atmosphere of violence, created in the text by descriptions of battle, rape, murder, and cannibalism and in the illustrations by the barbarous rhythms and brutal contrasts between the whiteness of massive, awkward bodies and the blackness of gracefully undulating plants. In the short term this *livre d'artiste* was commercially unsuccessful; only forty-five of the one hundred copies were sold in five years. But it revived in France the art of the woodcut and initiated a genre which subsequently attracted Rouault, Dufy, Matisse, Picasso, Dali, Cocteau, and Le Corbusier.

William Russell Flint (1880–1969) rejected the austere woodcut and two-dimensional black and white print in favour of early Pre-Raphaelite colour and opulence. A noted water-colourist specializing in 'the nude in sunlight',[29] he was

[26] Anne Hyde Greet, *Apollinaire et le livre de peintre* (Paris, 1977), p. 147.
[27] For a detailed commentary on the illustrations, see Bertrand, pp. 15–40.
[28] An important influence on Derain's concept of primitivism was Paul Gaugin whose *Noa-Noa*, an account of his first year in Tahiti, was published in 1897.
[29] Percy Bradshaw, *W. Russell Flint*, 'The Art of the Illustrator' series (London, 1918), p. 11.

invited to provide forty-eight colour illustrations for a four-volume deluxe edition of Malory's *Morte Darthur*.[30] Published by Philip Lee Warner for the Medici Society, the volumes appeared in 1910–11. With its beautiful ladies and medieval settings the romance stimulated Flint's delight in pictoral beauty. But, like Beardsley's, his illustrations are unreliable guides to the text for the artist largely ignores the adventures of knight-errantry in order to present ladies in provocative poses for which there may be no literary justification.

Regarding his nude 'Melusina' he commented:

> A beautiful woman is one of the marvels of creation, and adequate portrayal a matter of extreme difficulty. The artist's spirit must be pagan or gay, but his workmanship must be deadly serious. Early slavery at 'the antique' left me, I suppose, with a feeling for classic form, and I have been remarkably lucky in getting models with what might be called Artemisian figures.[31]

The words explain his treatment of Morgan le Fay, Nimue, Tristram's step-mother, Alys, Guenevere at the stake, and even such virginal characters as Elaine of Corbenic in the boiling bath – Launcelot shades his eyes from the sight of her nakedness – and Perceval's saintly sister who, scantily draped, sensuously fondles her hair.

Flint's drawing is faulty. He is incapable of conveying through gesture and facial expression the intense emotions that Malory's words suggest. The successful Grail knights who contemplate the full mystery with open mouths and rolling eyes seem mad rather than transfigured. Looking on Guenevere's still corpse Launcelot appears to be shrinking from a foul smell. In the scene of Isolde's attempted suicide, the sinuous tree in which the sword is fixed has more grace than do the rigid bodies of husband and wife. But beguiled by the Cerulian Blue skies, the elegant, long-sleeved gowns painted with Crimson Lake, Indian Yellow and Burnt Sienna, the ecclesiastical furnishings of the Neo-Gothic chapels, the carved Romanesque pillars, the golden-winged angels and magic serpents, the evocative harps and swans, we may overlook the fact that Balin's spear pierces King Pelles' armpit rather than his thigh.

Theatricality is substituted for psychological realism. Lady Lyonnesse receives Gareth in a *hortus conclusus* with a dazzling machicolated wall beyond which is a

---

See also Arnold Palmer, *More Than Shadows: A Biography of W. Russell Flint, RA, PRWS* with *136 illustrations of his works* (London and New York, 1943); *The Water-Colours of W. Russell Flint*, special issue of *Studio* (1920) with forward by Malcolm C. Salaman.

[30] The full title reads *Le Morte Darthur. The Book of King Arthur and his noble knights of the Round Table by Sir Thomas Malory, Knt.* Five hundred copies were printed on handmade Riccardi paper and twelve on vellum. Each painting was reproduced separately, then attached to the page and covered with a translucent leaf giving the relevant Malorian quotation. Later the edition was republished for general sale in a two-volume set (1920) with 36 illustrations and a one-volume edition (1927) with 24.

[31] Quoted in Palmer re plate 103.

landscape of fields, forests, mountains and a castle. Within the garden erotic images are concentrated: doves (Venus's bird) carved on the chair's finials, a standard rose bush with red roses, a lady (Lynette) with a hoop reclining on the grass, and, enthroned, the crimson-gowned Rossettian heroine who plays with her loose auburn hair. The hero, excluded from the garden and relegated to a shadowy corner, peers over the wall like a Peeping Tom. The scene is independent of the text which indicates that the lovers' meeting place was Gringamore's castle hall. Flint's world reflects the 'mannerly ease and comfort' of Chrétien de Troyes' woman-centred castles rather than the energetic masculinity of Malory's forests and tournament grounds.

Reviewing Volume I of the *Morte* for the *Burlington Magazine*,[32] the critic had high praise for the printing but deplored 'spoiling so perfect a piece of typography by coloured illustrations so grotesquely inconsistent with the style of the book as a whole'. The critic of Volume II, Roger Fry, was equally vitriolic:

> Alas! the illustrations are of the same distressing Lyceum-stage kind as heretofore and completely dispel the visions which the perusal of Malory in a beautifully printed edition might be expected to arouse. Woodcut, whether plain or coloured, is the only possible accompaniment to such type.[33]

The review of volumes III and IV concluded, 'Nothing taxes the invention of an artist more than the illustration of a long and well-known theme, and the *Morte Darthur* is one of the worst worn; it is worn out.'[34]

But only four years later there appeared yet another Malory, this time illustrated by Arthur Rackham (1867–1939), who has been called 'Le Peintre-Sorcier'. From Pre-Raphaelite beauty and Beardsleyesque satire he fashioned an individual and influential style. *The Romance of King Arthur and His Knights of the Round Table* (1917)[35] was Alfred W. Pollard's abridgement of Malory. In a lengthy Preface, the editor outlined the history of Arthurian romance and analysed various characters, showing their relevance to contemporary life. While King Arthur was dismissed as a 'typical sportsman . . . weak in his own life and weak in suffering the outrages of his nephews', Launcelot was glorified:

> He is perhaps the most splendid study of a great gentleman in all our literature, generous to friend and foe, courteous to everyone, eager to set himself ever harder adventures, unwilling to be praised above his fellows, always bearing himself with an easy dignity which lets him use very straight speech and yet is no whit impaired. He is more than a

---

[32] *Burlington Magazine*, 18 (Oct.–Apr. 1910–11), 358.
[33] *Burlington Magazine*, 19 (Apr.–Sept. 1911), 365.
[34] *Burlington Magazine*, 21 (Apr.–Sept. 1912), 121.
[35] The limited edition consisted of 500 signed copies, bound in vellum with pictorial stamping in gold on the cover and spine. There was also a trade edition.

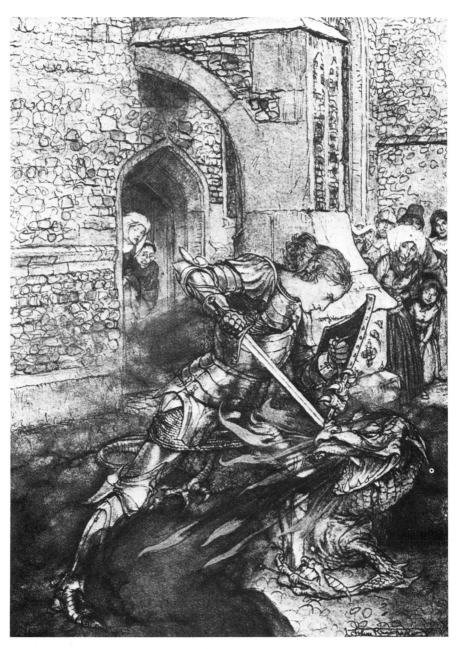

58. Lancelot and the fiendly Dragon. Arthur Rackham's illustration for Malory's *Morte Darthur*, ed. A.W. Pollard (London: Macmillan, 1917)

great gentleman; he is a very subtle study of a soul in which spirit and flesh, aspiration and evil habit, strive for the mastery.

Rackham provided eighty-six illustrations, including sixteen full-page water-colours mounted on white paper, and Beardsley-inspired chapter headings with effeminate knights in elaborate armour, peacocks, sunflowers, stylised foliage and heraldic beasts. Pre-Raphealite traits include landscape details drawn from nature. A plank props up the gnarled apple tree where Launcelot sleeps. Hawk on hand, a damsel converses with Percival beside a reedy English lake. May trees blossom about the beautiful Guenevere as she and her company, accurately cos-tumed in fifteenth-century style, set out on their fatal expedition. The realism of landscape and costume applies also to architecture and physiognomy. The varied textures of wood, plaster and stone lend credibility to the arrival of Elaine's barge. A crowd consisting not only of Arthur and Guenevere with their courtiers and fool but also of pompous, sharp-nosed merchants and their beady-eyed women watches Galahad draw the sword from the stone.

Rackham's originality lies in his ability to recreate the milieu of medieval romance by insinuating the supernatural into the mundane. This is a world where evil is palpable and the possibility of metamorphosis ever present. A minor inci-dent in the text, Launcelot's fight with the Corbenic dragon is elevated to an archetypal combat between mailed hero and mailed monster. Diagonals increase the sense of conflict. The shield parallels the outstretched leg and spewed flames while the sword provides a right angle cross. The dragon's zig-zag pose foretells its crumpled descent to the stony courtyard. As Eliot harps before King Mark in a banquet scene, the rapacious expression of the half-starved dog gnawing its bone is duplicated in the King's foxy face with sharp nose and hairy pointed ears. The ominous questing beast with its sinuous ochre body, cold eye and flicking tongue replicates a tree root terminating in a gaping mouth and cold eye. Rackham's conception of the Perilous Forest was definitive. Trees that advance bare branches shaped like grasping hands, serpentine roots, striated trunks with eye-like knots, turgid waters and thorny thickets keep appearing in the work of twentieth cen-tury illustrators, including Virgil Burnett[36] and Alan Lee.[37]

Contributing to the 'faerie' effect is the use of line drawings washed with watercolour, a style suited to the new three-colour printing technology. At times aestheticism outweighs stylistic consistency as in the winter landscape where the tiny figures of the arrow-pierced Launcelot, the huntress, the deer and the tenta-tively brushed trees seem part of an Oriental hanging. But what Derek Hudson[38] calls 'the ironies of incongruous juxtaposition' are powerfully used in 'How

---

[36] See Virgil Burnett's line drawings for *Sir Gawain and the Green Knight*, trans. Theodore Silverstein (Chicago and London, 1974) and his lithographs for the Folio Society's *Sir Gawain and the Green Knight*, trans. Keith Harrison (London, 1983).
[37] See his forty-five watercolour illustrations for *The Mabinogion*, trans. Gwyn and Thomas Jones (London, 1982) and the Arthurian section of David Day's *Castles*, ed. David Larkin (New York, 1984).
[38] *Arthur Rackham, His Life and Work* (New York, 1975 [1960]), p. 44.

Mordred was slain by Arthur and how by him Arthur was hurt to death'. The Goya-like iconography of dark foreground and lurid sky, bat-like combatants, ominous birds of prey, fragmented weapons and heaped corpses conveys Malory's sorrow at 'the dolorous deaths'. Simultaneously, the painting represents Rackham's dreadful vision of a World War I battlefield where the Victorian 'golden age' was being destroyed.

Like Tennyson's illustrators, Rackham believed in the artist's right to self-assertion:

> An illustration may legitimately give the artist's view of the author's ideas; or it may give his view, his independent view, of the author's subject. But it must be the artist's view; any attempt to coerce him into a mere tool in the author's hands can only result in the most dismal failure. Illustration is as capable of varied appeal as is literature itself; and the only real essential is an association that shall not be at variance or unsympathetic. The illustrator is sometimes expected to say what the author ought to have said or failed to say clearly. . . . Sometimes he is wanted to add some fresh aspect of interest to a subject which the author has already treated interestingly from his point of view. . . . But the most fascinating form of illustration comes of the expression by the artist of an individual sense of delight or emotion aroused by the accompanying passage of literature.[39]

Few modern illustrators have equalled Rackham's ability to express not only the awarenness of evil but also the beauty and virtue of the Arthurian world.

In competition with colour illustration, black and white wood engravings remain popular in books conceived as art objects. One advantage of the form is that it enables the artist to take responsibility for the final product since he or she uses the graver to draw directly on the wood. Thus the artist can show respect for the medium, ensuring that his work will be 'primarily a thing of Beauty itself and not a reproduction of something else'. The commercial producer, aiming at 'mere representation' in quantity forms an assembly line, with disastrous results, as Eric Gill thought:

> In the matter of drawing and illustration and engraving, degradation is inevitable when one man draws, another touches up the drawing, another photographs, another touches up the negative, another prints it on the metal, another etches, another touches up the etching, another mounts it, another proves it and another keeps the accounts and to crown all, another takes the profits.[40]

---

[39] Hudson, pp. 87–88.
[40] Eric Gill, foreword to R. John Beedham, *Wood Engraving*, reprinted as *Foreward to a Treatise Upon the Craft of Wood Engraving* (Vancouver, 1967), pp. 3–4.

When Robert Gibbings (1889–1954) acquired the Golden Cockerel Press in 1924, he fulfilled his ambition 'to do some decorations for really first class books'. Not since Albrecht Dürer produced his *Apocalypse* (1498) had a single person so completely combined the functions of artist, designer and printer.[41] Gibbings pursued his profession in the idyllic setting of a Berkshire garden 'with birds singing in the apple trees'.[42] As described in his *Sermons for Artists*, his creation of wood-engravings was a mystical experience:

> When out of the riot of forms and colours in nature the artificier is able to co-ordinate the elements of a more comprehensible design, then it is that for brief moments he reaches harmony with the universal spirit. Sometimes in those seconds of insight time stands still, events past, present, and future remain stationary like resting cattle spotted on the surface of a field.[43]

A commission from the Limited Editions Club of New York to illustrate a deluxe, three volume edition of Pollard's Malory[44] stimulated his ability to design rhythmic arrangements of botanical forms and chivalric images that take account of the woodblock's grain and of the historiated capital's shape. His style admirably simulates the continuum of Malory's isolated castles and perilous forests where only images directly related to chivalric adventure, courtly life and the spiritual quest appear. Mounted knights with raised spears or swords lope through the forest, charge opponents or acrobatically unhorse one another, their exuberance faithfully conveying Malory's zest for chivalric action. A king graciously takes a queen's hand. A ship with a large cross on its sail carries three Grail knights over a sea contained within fronds which spring from a capital N and a chalice. Though heraldry is an important decorative element, the arbitrary devices do not identify particular knights.

The few illustrations depicting specific events generally suggest the abnormal and macabre. Having been tricked into sleeping with Elaine of Corbenic, the naked Launcelot draws his sword as the equally naked lady escapes down the elongated frond of a phallic plant. The cannibal Giant of St Michael's Mount gnaws a limb while three trussed infants are barbecued over the fire. The lack of transition between black and white flattens the designs and contributes to abstract simplifications.

[41] Albert Garrett, *A History of British Wood Engraving* (Tunbridge Wells, 1978), p. 204. On Gibbings see also Thomas Balston, *The Wood-Engravings of Robert Gibbings* (London, 1949). Many of the Malory illustrations are reproduced in Patience Empson ed., *The Wood Engravings of Robert Gibbings*, introd. Thomas Balston (London, 1959), pp. 181–97.
[42] Malcolm C. Salaman *The Woodcut of Today at Home and Abroad* (London, 1927), p. 38.
[43] Quoted Empson, p. xxi.
[44] The title page reads 'Le Morte Darthur. The Story of King Arthur and of his noble knights of the Round Table written by Sir Thomas Malory, first printed by William Caxton, now modernized by A.W. Pollard, illustrated with wood engravings by Robert Gibbings and printed at the Golden Cockerel Press, London, for the Limited Editions Club, New York, 1936.' The work was published in 3 volumes.

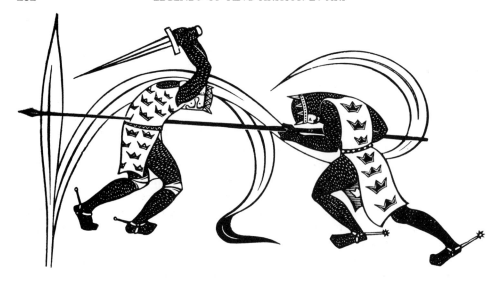

59. The Last Battle. Robert Gibbings' wood engraving for Malory's *Morte Darthur* (London: The Golden Cockerel Press, 1936)

Gibbings' primary purpose is not to provide comprehenive illustrations of the narrative but to furnish ornaments that harmonise with the type. Yet in his best design he does combine narration and decoration. As Mordred and Arthur exchange death blows, visual tension develops between the combatants and the plant motif that binds them together. The human bodies follow the plant's curving line while the horizontal spear formally provides a right angle connection with the stem. The duplicated iconography of the crown on heads and surcoats further unites the men in a uniquely momentous act. Only a knowledge of the text enables the viewers to identify the true king.

From the inception of the technique, many woodcuts were coloured. Wood-engravers like Gibbings, Eric Gill and Gwen Raveret, however, generally preferred black-and-white for its purity. The amount of work involved in a colour print, in which a different block had to be cut for every colour, must also have been a consideration. Dorothea Braby (1909–) thought that the colour print was 'the most laborious and roundabout way in existence in which to create a small coloured picture. Unless the print has something special to say, the amount of work entailed is hardly justified'.[45] Nevertheless, she accepted a commission to provide six colour engravings for Gwyn Jones's prose translation of *Sir Gawain and the Green Knight* which the Golden Cockerel Press published in 1952.[46] The

[45] *The Way of Wood Engraving* (London and New York, 1953), p. 70.
[46] The fourteenth century poem was first published in 1839 when it appeared in a collection of Gawain romances which Sir Frederic Madden edited for the Ballantyne Club. Because of its difficult dialect, it continued to be neglected for another century. Only when translations and retellings in modern English made the work accessible did it attract illustrators.

colour range is restricted to two shades each of rose and green, suggesting the antitheses basic to the text's aesthetic pattern – warmth and coldness, natural and supernatural, courtliness and barbarity, sensuous castle life and rigorous forest hunts.

What Gwyn Jones describes as 'the gracious and aristocratic air, the polished manners and good breeding' of the characters Braby conveys through fifteenth-century costumes (similar to those which the Limbourgs painted in the Duke of Berry's *Très Riches Heures*), graceful stances, and the sinuous lines of skirts, banners, a stream and horses' tails. The Green Knight is not a macabre giant but, as the poet describes him, a well-proportioned man with broad back and small waist. A minstrel playing a lute, a serving boy in tight hose and doublet carrying a heaping plate of fruit, a canopied bed where the bare-breasted lady caresses the hero's arm suggest the pleasures of castle life. But the wild hunt passing outside, the snake-like girdle at the foot of the bed, the dog preparing to attack a bone as Gawain and Bertilak exchange kiss and fox pelt (both symbols of deceit) convey an underlying menace which is realised in the final print. Wintery branches reach out skeletal fingers, the horse neighs in terror, and the enormous axe which the Green Knight is about to raise occupies the foreground.

For this deluxe edition, the inks were especially made and the paper ordered two years in advance. Christopher Sandford's leather binding was chosen to match particular inks. In addition, the artist consulted the translator about every pictorial detail. In contrast to *L'enchanteur pourrissant* and Gibbing's Malory, this book is the product of close team work.

To a greater degree than do commercial products, the fine book allows the artist to express personal tastes, skills and conceptions in an opulent manner. For example, the Victorian calligrapher and illuminator, Alberto Sangorski, inscribed on vellum an extract from Canto I of *The Faerie Queene* (London, n.d.), decorating the pages in a late medieval style. The full-page medallion frontispiece shows the Red Cross Knight and Una riding through a flowery meadow against a backdrop of mountains. The rectangular border reproduces an Italianate acanthus design. Robert Riviere and Son (the same artists who completed the Oxford Union murals) bound the quarto volume in blue crushed morocco with gilt decoration and a design featuring the Red Cross Knight's coat-of-arms. Ivory watered satin lined the covers. A green velvet case with padded silk interior completed the art work.

In a fine edition of Tennyson's *Morte Darthur* produced between 1978 and 1981, a Canadian artist, Annegret Hunter-Elsenbach, is responsible for the calligraphy (Gothic lettering in ebony ink), the watercolour illustrations in funereal indigo, mauve and black, the endpapers' patterning of dead and broken reeds, the leather binding and the design of the silken case with its brown velveteen lining. Each full-page illustration is interleaved with a Japanese-style paper in which are embedded strands of straw-coloured fibre. Forming their own broken-reed patterning, they suggest the winter-death metaphor which dominates the poet's and the artist's conceptions. The burgundy and black leather triangles of the cover direct us to Excalibur, its blade parti-coloured white and black leather, its pommel inset with gold, its discs of green, red, blue and topaz imitating the text's jewels:

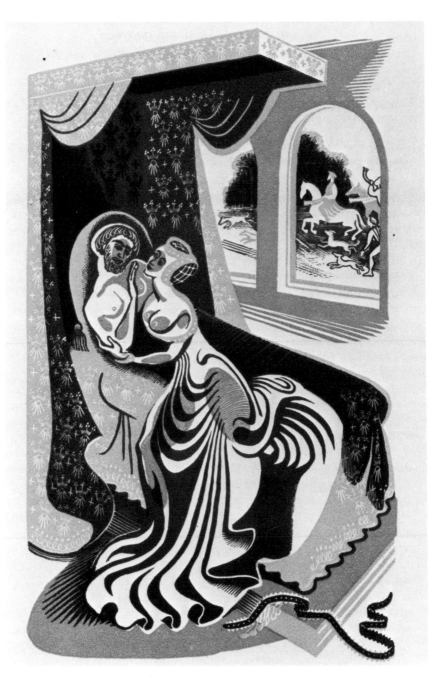

60. Bercilak's lady tempts Sir Gawain a third time. Dorothy Braby's colour engraving for *Sir Gawaine and the Green Knight*, tr. and ed. Gwyn Jones (London: Golden Cockerel Press, 1952)

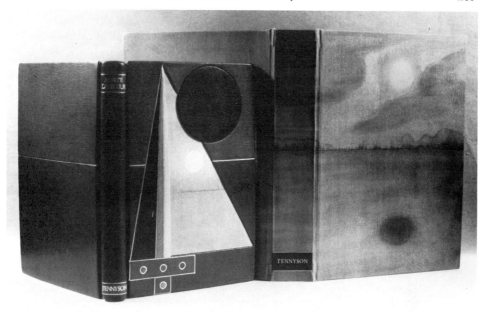

61. Annegret Hunter-Elsenbach, bindings and case for Tennyson's *Morte Darthur*, 1981

> For all the haft twinkled with diamond sparks,
> Myriads of topaz-lights, and jacinth-work
> Of subtlest jewellery.

Triangles and sword combine to form 'the barge with oar and sail' that carries the king to Avalon, under the full moon, a black leather circle in the cover's upper righthand corner. The main sail is a silken representation of a lake and sky, ghostly under the white moon. As well as representing a sail, the triangle provides the setting for Excalibur's final appearance. The desolate landscape in understated blues and misty greys and greens appears again on the case where the sky's white moon is darkly mirrored in the water. Shoreline evergreens and leafless willows strongly suggest a lake in the Canadian wilderness.

The Kelmscott Press, which published books for only seven years, had a profound effect not only on private presses but also on commercial publishers who realized that well-designed machine-made books, using good quality materials, could aspire to be works of art. One example of such an enterprise is the Folio Society of London which reprints classic texts with newly commissioned illustrations. In the three-volume *Sir Thomas Malory's Chronicles of King Arthur* (1982) Edward Bawden's linocuts imitate woodcuts but their assumed crudeness evokes a primitive society rather than the courtly milieu of the text. Joan Freeman's fine wood-engravings for Lady Charlotte Guest's *The Mabinogion* (1980) capture the atmosphere of medieval Wales with a mingling of barbarous confrontations and heroic rituals. For the Folio Society's *Sir Gawain and the Green Knight*, translated by

Keith Harrison (1983), Virgil Burnett provides five sepia-toned lithographs which present an Arthurian world without laughter or delight. The most original design surrealistically illustrates Gawain's 'heavy dreams' on the morning of the third temptation. Under a crescent moon, Bercilak's castle is not the pinnacled refuge that glimmered and glowed through the bright oaks but an ugly pile of stones enclosed by brambles which, like the girdle in which the hero is tangled, convey the idea of entrapment.

It is appropriate to end a discussion of the book as art object by quoting once again the words of William Morris. The final sentence of his lecture, 'The Ideal Book', reads:

> The picture-book is not, perhaps, absolutely necessary to man's life, but it gives us such endless pleasure, and is so intimately connected with the other absolutely necessary act of imaginative literature that it must remain one of the very worthiest things towards the production of which reasonable men should strive.

CHAPTER TWELVE

Arthurian Art in America

In *A Connecticut Yankee in King Arthur's Court* (1889) Mark Twain attacks monarchy, hierarchy, Catholicism, the decadent English, Arthurian romance, and senseless admiration for the past. His modern American hero, transported through time to the fourteenth century, finds 'not a man who wasn't a baby to me in acquirements and capacities'. He is confident that his superior knowledge and skills will effect 'the destruction of the throne, nobility abolished, every member of it bound out to some useful trade, universal suffrage instituted, and the whole government placed in the hands of the men and women of the nation'. Chivalry was impractical, irrational, and inconsistent with technological achievements.[1] The plantation owners of the South who perpetuated the eighteenth-century idea of gentility based on land ownership along with a romantic sense of honour suffered inevitable defeat in the American Civil War. As for living in 'a gimcrack of a Gothic castle – there can be nothing more grotesque, more absurd, or more affected'.[2]

In the post-bellum period, however, rapid industrialisation, the massive immigration of East Europeans, and political instability made Old World medievalism seem an attractive refuge from modernism. The Victorians had found in their medieval past patterns of heroism, aestheticism, social responsibility, artistic freedom and spirituality. Now for some Americans the Middle Ages were 'the nearest aproach to the Christian Commonwealth man has thus far achieved',[3] and chivalric romance provided an entré into a 'pictured, illuminated Past'. The cowboy, a product of America's westering movement, was a modern knight who defeated villains, maintained order and rescued damsels in distress.[4] P.V.E. Ivory's paintings 'Knight Errant of the Plains' (1909) and 'It's You or Me Bill' (1917), Frederic

---

[1] On American attitudes see John Fraser, *America and the Patterns of Chivalry* (Cambridge, Eng., 1982) and Beverly Taylor and Elisabeth Brewer, *The Return of King Arthur* (Cambridge, Eng. and Totowa, N.J., 1983), chapter 6.
[2] David Lowenthal, *The Past is a Foreign Country* (Cambridge, Eng., 1985) p. 111, citing a *New York Mirror* review of William H. Ranlett, *The American Architect* (1846). On the conflict between Ancients and Moderns, see Lowenthal, pp. 105–124.
[3] Ralph Adams Cram, *Architecture in Its Relation to Civilization* (Boston, 1918), p. 21.
[4] Kirsten H. Powell, 'Cowboy Knights and Prairie Madonnas: American Illustrations of the Plains and Pre-Raphaelite Art' in *Great Plains Quarterly* 5/1 (1985), 39–52.

Remington's 'The Last Cavalier' (1895), and Owen Wister's novel *The Virginian* (1902) relied on a chivalric association to glorify the heroes of a supposedly unhierarchic society. Wister's essay, 'The Evolution of a Cow-Puncher', which *Harper's* published in 1895, laid claim to a tradition stretching

> from the tournament at Camelot to the round-up at Abilene. No doubt
> Sir Launcelot bore himself with a grace and breeding of which our
> unpolished fellow of the cattle trail has only the latent possibility; but
> in personal daring and in skill as to the horse, the knight and the
> cowboy are nothing but the same Saxon of different environments.

The knight even provided a model for industry as in John Alexander White's mural series 'The Crowning of Labour' at Pittsburg's Carnegie Institute. Personifying the City of Pittsburg (as the crest on the black breastplate indicates), the knight rises from a cauldron of iron and steel to be crowned by a goddess.

Paramount influences on North American art in the late nineteenth and early twentieth centuries were Pre-Raphaelitism and its offshoots, the Aesthetic Movement and the Arts and Crafts Movement. From mid-century, such ideas as the 'cult of beauty' and 'truth to nature' had circulated among Harvard intellectuals as the result of the Rossettis' friendship with Charles Eliot Norton.[5] As early as 1855 W.J. Stillman (1828–1901), 'the American Pre-Raphaelite' (and Burne-Jones' model for 'The Beguiling of Merlin'), established *The Crayon: A Journal Devoted to the Graphic Arts and the Literature Related to them*. The Civil War ended its publication but not before it had conveyed the Ruskinian ideal of art's moral beauty.

Avenues of influence were varied. Most American artists made trans-Atlantic journeys, studying in famous studios, meeting their mentors, and viewing exhibitions. John La Farge (1835–1910) determined to become a professional artist after seeing the 1857 Pre-Raphaelite Exhibition in Manchester. Mary Gertrude Mead, who had seen nine of G.F. Watts' paintings at the International Exhibition in Paris, urged an American showing, not to enhance the artist's reputation but 'for the sake of the people here . . . I want them to come that the people may hear the voice of a great teacher . . . they are hungering for a sight of such pictures as yours'.[6]

The public lecture was another source of instruction. In 1882 Oscar Wilde crossed the continent lecturing on 'The English Renaissance and Decorative Art in America' and pleading that handicrafts be encouraged and museums and art schools established to develop standards of taste. Unfortunately, his effete appearance (long hair and short pants) and his complaints about the Americans' ugly wallpaper, horse hair sofas, creaking rosewood furniture, thick coffee cups and soup plates painted with moonlight scenes aroused hostility and derision. Walter Crane, who had supplied a Newport mansion, 'Vinland', with a frieze of Long-

---

[5]   David Howard Dickason's *The Daring Young Men: the story of the American Pre-Raphaelites* (Bloomington, 1953) is the best study of the subject.
[6]   Mary Watts, *Annals*, II, p. 221.

fellow's 'The Skeleton in Armor', showed his works, socialized with his admirers, and presented lectures in 1891.

As in Britain, industrialists began collecting art as evidence of their wealth and taste. Samuel Bancroft Jr., a rich cotton manufacturer who discovered Rossetti's work while on an 1880 business trip to the Midlands, subsequently assembled a significant Pre-Raphaelite collection at Wilmington, Delaware. Equally influential was G.L. Winthrop's collection, bequeathed to the William Hayes Fogg Museum of Art at Harvard; the collection included Watts' 'Sir Galahad', Burne-Jones' 'Perseus and Andromeda' and Rossetti's 'The Blessed Damozel'.

Painters adopted aestheticism, botanical accuracy, symbolism, and, not least, bright colour. Writing in *New Path* (June, 1863), a journal of art criticism that succeeded *The Crayon*, T.C. Farrer praised the English poet-artists with their mistletoe-green, duck's egg blue, rose-amber of the pomegranate flower and other rainbow hues. They had confounded 'the scientific decorators who were sure of what colors would go together and what colors wouldn't'. However, North Americans were less interested than the British in Arthurian subjects, the Lady of Shalott-Elaine material being a rare exception. John La Farge produced a small oil, 'The Lady of Shalott' (ca. 1862, New Britain Museum of American Art) in which he showed Tennyson's heroine 'lying, rob'd in snowey white', 'a gleaming shape', 'dead-pale between the houses high' as she floats into Camelot. Hands folded on her breasts, she reclines in a shallow, unadorned boat while the sky apocalyptically lightens behind her.

Homer Watson (1855–1936), Canada's first native-born landscape painter to gain an international reputation, normally confined himself to scenes from pioneer life; for example, 'The Wheatfield' (1878–81) and 'Clearing the Land' (1880). When Queen Victoria's daughter, wife of Canada's Governor-General, purchased 'The Pioneer Mill' (1880), the headline in the Toronto *Globe* read, 'Country boy paints picture bought by Princess Louise'. (That country boy subsequently had the thrill of seeing his painting in Windsor Castle). Watson's single departure from Canadian landscape painting was 'The Death of Elaine' (1877, Art Gallery of Ontario, Toronto), a large oil based on Tennyson's lines:

> and the dead
> Steered by the dumb went upward with the flood –
> In her right hand the lily, in her left
> The letter-all her bright hair streaming down –
> And all the coverlid was cloth of gold
> Drawn to her waist, and she herself in white
> . . .   she did not seem as dead
> But fast asleep, and lay as tho' she smiled.

In composition Watson's painting closely resembles Doré's illustration for the Moxon *Elaine* (1868).[7] The barge, with its boatman and transfigured maiden float-

---

[7]   As early as 1873 when he was eighteen, Watson was poring over Doré's etchings in his father's books.

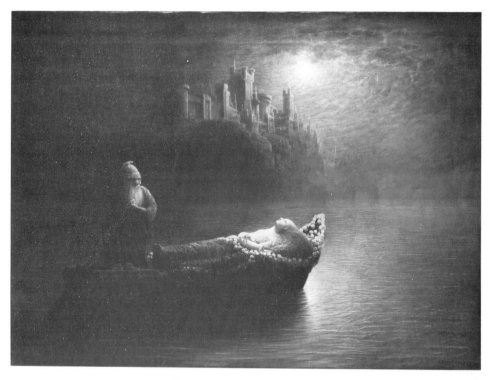

62. Homer Watson. The Death of Elaine, oil painting, 1877

ing on the rippling river occupies the foreground while the upper part of the picture space is devoted to towered Camelot and the moonlit sky. As in Toby Rosenthal's 'Elaine' (1874, Art Institute of Chicago), the black barge is garlanded with pink roses, symbols of transient beauty.

Watson exemplifies the response to a medieval subject of those who, born in the New World, have never seen a castle, monastic ruin, illuminated manuscript, Gothic artifact or literary landscape. Instead they must rely on what W.L. Morton calls 'landscapes of the mind . . . cultured landscapes formed by what the mind, not the seeing eye alone, takes in'.[8] Though Morton is writing of Manitoba, his words are applicable to Watson's Ontario:

> Thus my actual landscape, the one the neighbours had made and worked in with apparent content, and my literary landscape . . . were in conflict. I had no single vision for both, but had to re-focus like one passing from dark to light.

As Watson walked along the river bank near his home, he later recalled,

[8]   'Seeing an Unliterary Landscape', Mosaic 3/3 (1970), 1–10.

I would look at the vista in the valley of the Grand thinking with a romantic notion that an old ruin or a castle on the banks of the Grand would lend an old-world air to it. These ideas were the outcome of the desire of a country boy to travel. You have a sort of storied outlook; one born in the backwoods is apt to have this.[9]

It is the Grand, not the Thames, that bears Elaine's death barge on its grey-green waves, as it is Toronto's neo-Gothic buildings – perhaps the old University College – that provide the model for Camelot. Gerald Noonan suggests that an unfulfilled love for Cassy Muir, the fiancée of his friend James Kerr-Lawson, inspired Watson's single excursion into medievalism, a representation of an unsuccessful lover.[10]

Another example of nineteenth-century Arthurianism in Canada is extraordinary for its textual form. Arthur G. Doughty (b. 1860), who emigrated to Montreal in 1886 and eventually became Dominion Archivist, published a shorthand version of Tennyson's *Idylls of the King* (1889) which he urged the government to subsidize.[11] His intention was

to present to Canadian students a work not only valuable as an educational one but one which from its illustrative nature would act as an inducement to the study of a branch of literature which is indispensible to success in almost every phase of commercial life.

To make the book attractive, sepia reproductions of seven watercolours were interspersed between the pages of lines and curves. These were the work of Henry Sandham (1842–1910), a Canadian painter, illustrator and photographer whose painting style resembles that of John Gilbert.

North American art in its various forms was still largely imitative. As late as 1934 Thomas Craven wrote, 'The only outlet, the sole means of escape, for the American painter, lies in the discovery of the local essence, after which we may hope for a viable native school and eventually for a sublimation of its forms'.[12] As the north-east became increasingly a producer of machine-made consumer goods, the American version of the Arts and Crafts Movement flourished in protest against the assembly line. William Morris was idolized, quoted and copied. The first issue of *The Craftsman* (1901–1918),[13] published by the United Crafts of East-

---

[9] Jane Van Every, *With Faith, Ignorance and Delight, Homer Watson* (Aylesbury, 1967), p. 40.
[10] I am indebted to Dr Noonan for allowing me to read his unpublished paper, ' "The Death of Elaine" and Homer Watson's Affair of the Heart'.
[11] Robert J. Hayward, 'Sir Arthur Doughty, Shorthand, and Alfred, Lord Tennyson' in *Archivaria* 21 (Winter 1985–86), 103–110.
[12] Thomas Craven, *Modern Art, the Men, the Movements, the Meaning* (New York, 1934), p. 265.
[13] Dickason, pp. 170–181. See also 'Turn of the Century American Periodicals and William Morris', *William Morris Society Newsletter*, January 1988, (U.S.) pp. 5–10 for brief selections.

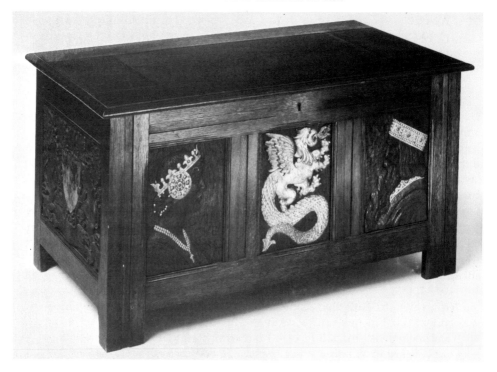

63. King Arthur chest designed by Sidney Richmond Burleigh and carved by Julia Lippett Mauran, ca. 1900

wood, New York, was devoted to 'the great decorator and socialist' whose principles were to be the American guild's guide:

> The lesson to be learned from the vision is that a real art, created by the people for the people, is able not only to beautify, but also to simplify life, to unify the interests of all sorts and conditions of men, and finally to realize the meaning of the word Commonwealth.[14]

The echoes of the Anglican Book of Common Prayer and the American Declaration of Independence contribute to the loftiness of aim. The American view of art's relationship to labour is reiterated in the second issue:

> In our own country and colonies we must profit by the experience of England, lest with us industrialism also secure its sacrifice of human happiness, energy and joy. The trades and crafts must be raised from the disrepute into which they fell through the divison of labor. The laboring class must be wisely guided by State and School until self-respecting and thoroughly enlightened, they shall be heard to declare:

[14] Irene Sargent, 'Two Friends: Morris and Burne-Jones', *The Craftsman* 1/1 (October, 1901).

'We are men and nothing that is human is foreign to us.' In this work, art must be the prime factor, and a practical knowledge of drawing be made the basis of all the handicrafts. Thus, through the widened avenues of perception, Beauty will pass to relieve fatigue, to create pleasure for the toiler, and to show things in their proportions and relations: in a word to reincarnate the citizen spirit of the Middle Ages in a community purified by Science from all superstitions.[15]

An advantage of the Arts and Crafts Movement for North Americans was that it could justify aesthetically handicrafts that the pioneers had produced through necessity. In contrast to Neo-Gothic architecture, stained glass and tapestries, the hand-made furniture, wood carving, woven rugs and pottery were 'native' crafts. Not that Old World designs were prohibited. An oak chest (ca. 1900, Museum of Art, Rhode Island School of Design) designed by Sidney Burleigh, constructed by Potter and Company, Providence, Rhode Island, and carved by Julia Lippitt Mauran, exemplifies the combination of American craftsmanship and English literary sources. The chest measuring 55.8 x 56 x 125.6 cm has eight panels containing hand carved profiles of Arthurian characters and their associated signs, finished with green, gold, red and cream paint. On the front, Queen Guenevere and King Arthur face one another on either side of the royal dragon. On the back appear the coats of arms, helmets and banners denoting Galahad, Perceval and Tristram. The end panel on the left is devoted to Launcelot by means of his oak-encircled name, dragon coat of arms and helmet. The corresponding panel on the right represents Galahad by means of a chalice and his coat of arms.

Architectural decoration and book illustration provide the most notable examples of Arthurian art in America. Though republican taste preferred classical buildings, the influence of Britain's Gothic Revival was apparent after the Civil War. In the 1880s the young Ralph Adams Cram,[16] who would become 'the High Priest of the Gothic Revival', watched the construction of the Boston Public Library, located directly in front of the Gothic Trinity Church. Fifty years later he recalled this extraordinary juxtaposition:

On the one hand, an almost brutal, certainly primitive, boldness, arrogance, power; on the other, a serene classicism, reserved, scholarly, delicately conceived in all its parts, beautiful in that sense in which things have always been beautiful in periods of high human culture.

The Library was to be equally beautiful inside, embellished by the sculptures of St Gaudens and the paintings of John Singer Sargent, Puvis de Chavannes and Edwin Austin Abbey (1852–1911).[17]

---

[15] Irene Sargent, 'The Rise and Decadence of the Craftsman: An Historical Note', *The Craftsman* 1/2 (November 1901).
[16] See Robert Muccigrosso, *American Gothic: The Mind and Art of Ralph Adams Cram* (Washington, 1980) and Ralph Adams Cram, *My Life in Architecture* (Boston, 1936).
[17] The standard biography is E.V. Lucas, *Edwin Austin Abbey, Royal Academician, The record of his life and work*, 2 vols (London, 1921).

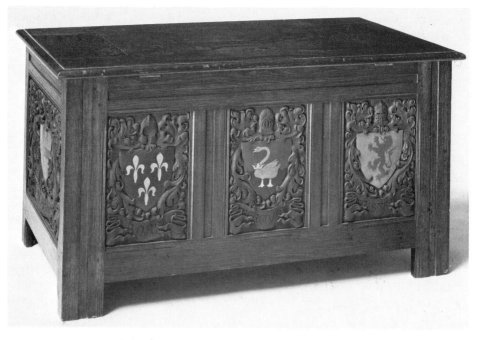

64. King Arthur chest, back view

Born in Philadelphia – Henry James described him as 'irremediably native' –
Abbey became interested in British painting and decorative arts in 1876 when he
first saw the work of Watts, Leighton, Morris and de Morgan at Philadelphia's
Centennial Exhibition. Two years later he moved permanently to England. He
had produced only two oil paintings before the evening in 1890 when in the
company of the architect Charles McKim and Sargent he dined in a private railway car with the Boston Public Library's trustees. These gentlemen hoped to
make Boston 'the earliest of the seats of public pilgrimage' in the United States by
commissioning civic murals that would rival those of Florence, Venice and
Assissi.[18] For $15,000.00 Abbey was to paint a frieze 180 feet by 8 feet in the
library's Delivery Room.

The subject that he chose was the Legends of the Holy Grail since they were
morally satisfying and common to several literary traditions. Having studied
English, French and German versions, he compiled his own narrative programme
which Henry James subsequently explicated.[19] The grail 'conveyed, among many
privileges, the ability to live, and to cause others to live, indefinitely without food,

[18] Ernest F. Fenollosa, *Mural Painting in the Boston Public Library* (Boston, 1896).
[19] Henry James prepared an outline of Abbey's version of the legends, in consultation with
Mrs Abbey. The first five paintings were privately exhibited in London in 1895. Paintings 6
to 15 were publicly exhibited at the Guildhall in London, 28 October to 9 November, 1901,
attracting 57,000 viewers. See Edwin Austin Abbey, *The Quest of the Holy Grail, a series of
paintings done for the Public Library of the City of Boston* with 5 plates (New York, 1895); Henry

as well as the achievement of universal knowledge, and of invulnerability in battle'. The 'achievement' of the Grail was 'the proof and recompense of the highest knightly purity'. Malory, Tennyson and the American poet Richard Hovey had established Galahad as the paramount Grail knight in the American consciousness. But Chrétien's *Perceval* and Wolfram's *Parzival* had features congenial to Protestant morality. Sharing Tennyson's preference for the married state rather than the celibacy exalted by the *Vulgate Prose Cycle*, Abbey appropriated Blanchefleur from the Perceval tradition to be the hero's beloved.[20] The frieze's fifteen scene narrative, then, combined *Vulgate* – Malory material with *Perceval-Parzival* elements.

The first four scenes are basically Malorian. 'The Infancy of Galahad' (panel 1) shows a nun holding the baby who reaches out towards the angelic Grail-bearer and the dove with its golden censer. A Pre-Raphaelite hanging embroidered with golden lions and phoenixes (signs of Christ) helps the artist to simulate the frontal positioning and two-dimensional space of fourteenth-century miniatures. 'The Oath of Knighthood' (panel 2) recreates the convent chapel (decorated with the Celtic sign of eternity) where Galahad's knighthood is conferred by his father Launcelot. As Launcelot and Bors attach his spurs and candle-bearing nuns watch, the hero in his identifying scarlet robe prays. Panel 3 elaborately describes Galahad's arrival at Arthur's court, where he is presented by a 'good olde man and an aunciente, clothed all in whyght'. The aged King Arthur rises from his Renaissance throne with its ornate baldachin; the knights at the rectangular table stare in amazement; an angel lifts the cloth from the Siege Perilous, revealing the words, 'This is the seat of Galahad'; a cohort of aureoled angels fills the background, as in Rosetti's Grail paintings. In contrast to the brightness of the arrival, the scene of 'The Departure' (panel 4) is gloomy; only the heraldic devices in shields and banners contribute colour highlights.

Then Abbey shifts to the *Parzival* material. Amfortas' golden bed on its catafalque of red and black marble dominates the Grail castle's great hall. Wounded for his sin of taking up arms in the cause of illicit love, the Fisher King must look at the radiant Grail with its blood-stained cover. It will keep him in living torment until the hero asks the spell-breaking question. The white-robed, crowned bearer is followed by red-robed Herodias with John the Baptist's head, two knights with seven-branched candelabra, and the youth with the bleeding spear (panel 5). Next day, having failed to ask what the Grail procession means, Galahad returns to the forest where he meets the vituperative Loathy Lady (panel 6). Panels 7, 8, and 9 are based on Malory's Castle of Maidens adventure during which Galahad defeats seven knights representing the Seven Deadly Sins, receives the key of the castle, and releases twenty beautiful women (an opportunity to paint fair faces and vari-coloured medieval gowns).

James, *Corporation of London Art Gallery Descriptive Catalogue of the Loan Collection of Pictures* (London, 1901); A.G. Temple, *Guildhall Memories* (London, 1918).
[20] In Chrétien de Troyes' *Perceval*, the hero and Blancheflor share a bed for three nights, embracing passionately without consummation, before Perceval continues his quest. In Wolfram's *Parzival*, the hero marries Condwiramurs before his first visit to the Grail Castle.

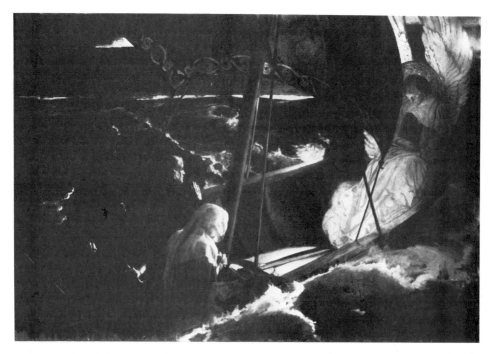

65. Edwin Austin Abbey. The Voyage to Sarras, painting in the Delivery Room, Boston Public Library, 1895–1902

Balancing these three panels are another three from *Perceval-Parzival*: the hero's abandonment of his rose-crowned bride (panel 10); the second visit to the Grail Castle, a scene in which Amfortas escapes into death as an angel removes the Grail (panel 11); and the saviour's departure through a green countryside, the Waste Land having been restored to fertility (panel 12). The quest's final stage follows the *Vulgate-Morte Darthur* narrative. The three successful Grail Knights voyage to Sarras in the Ship of Solomon which also contains the red, green and white spindles from the Tree of Life, Galahad's white shield with red cross, and in the prow, the Grail's guardian angel (panel 13). Galahad's sword and shield are superimposed on battlements labelled 'Sarras' (panel 14). The ultimate vision of the golden chalice unveiled is Galahad's alone (panel 15). But this scene's chief feature is an Art Nouveau Cosmic Tree. Its golden arabesques, which screen the angels, presage the immutable brilliance of Galahad's heavenly destination.

During the ten years that Abbey took to create the frieze panels, he filled his studio with such stage props as costumes, armour, books, artifacts, casts, and models. The result, said Henry James, was 'the most romantic place in a prosaic age. I retain a great impression of the mystic and wonderful and white samite process going on there'.[21] Having located his Arthurian age in the twelfth century,

---

[21] See Lucas, p. 360 re James' letter to Mrs Abbey.

Abbey was not content with locally fabricated columns used to observe the effect of light. A journey to the Auvergne provided inspiring views of cathedral architecture and casts of Romanesque capitals. The latter appear as architectural features in the Grail Castle's great hall.

Like Dyce in the Queen's Robing Room, Abbey was concerned that the design be compatable with the shape, size and position of the space to be decorated. After his appointment as 'Visitor' to the School of Painting at the Royal College of Art, South Kensington, he wrote a report on mural decoration in which he urged that students should spend a year under the Professor of Architecture; without exact knowledge, the painting becomes 'merely an easel picture'. Rather than dividing the library frieze into panels of equal size, Abbey carefully adjusts proportion to subject and treatment. Panels I and II are 6 feet long by 8 feet high so that the larger-than-life angels may dominate the space. Close-ups involving only two or three characters are 4 ft x 8 ft (panel 6) or 7 ft x 5 ft (panels 8, 10). Panel 14 is 9 ft 9 in x 2 ft for it is a mere border above a door. In contrast, the crowded, architecturally detailed scenes such as panel 3 (24 ft x 8 ft) and panel 4 (19 ft x 8 ft) are lengthened to permit pageantic display. The largest of all in the pictorial programme is panel 5 (33 ft x 8 ft). In this scene Abbey displays his skill in colour, architectural detail, costume and tonal qualities, ranging from the brilliant light of the Grail procession to the gloom in which the bespelled courtiers must dwell.

The paintings were attached to the walls by a process called marouflage; the canvas, rolled onto the leaded wall like wallpaper, became solidly fixed. Viewing the final paintings from floor level, Abbey discovered that many details could no longer be discerned. The haloes of the forty angels in panel 3, for example, had to be built up in relief and regilded to overcome the blackness that distance conferred. However, he objected strongly when floodlights were installed to increase visibility, saying, 'The room is not an art gallery . . . and the light in the Delivery Room is just what I should prefer it should be . . . *Now* if it is vulgarised and cheapened by rows of electric footlights I shall be disgusted and disheartened'.

On 14 July, 1902, the trustees of the Boston Public Library passed a resolution expressing

> their great satisfaction with the subject he has chosen and the attractive manner in which it has been executed. They hope that the fine results of Mr. Abbey's genius in making so beautiful this room of the Library by the representation of a romance dear to the poetical and religious heart of Christendom may open new fields for his gifts, and in these days of engrossing outward activities lead many, by the enjoyment of this painting, to some deeper and more generous interest in Art and Literature.

Another famous building that the firm of McKim, Mead and White designed was J. Pierpont Morgan's marble library on East Thirty-sixth Street in New York.[22]

[22] William Walton, 'The Recent Mural Decorations of H. Siddons Mowbray', *Harper's Weekly*, 122 (April, 1911), 726–37.

H. Seldon Mowbray was commissioned to provide thought-provoking mural decorations appropriate to the architectural mouldings of the vaulted entrance. An octagonal plate glass skylight twenty-three feet above the floor illuminated the space. The great semicircular lunettes over the cornices of three walls are devoted to the Epic Muse, the Lyric Muse and, above the entrance, a tabernacle of the muses, richly carved and ornamented with gold. The tabernacle is flanked by representations of Dante's *Divine Comedy* and Malory's *Morte Darthur*. Girt with Excalibur, Arthur wears chain mail, a long surcoat with an Art Nouveau border of stylised flowers, and a floral-patterned chain with swan insignia. His right hand grasps the lance of Longinus and his left encircles the jewelled Grail. These attributes are iconographically inappropriate since the king neither undertook the Grail Quest nor approved of it. Beside him stand Launcelot and Guenevere accompanied by a lady with a lyre and a youth with a falcon, signs of courtly pleasures. The lunettes were completed in 1906.

While the classical-Renaissance style was considered appropriate for civic buildings, Gothic was suited to universities, since these institutions had originated in the Middle Ages. The president of Princeton University, Woodrow Wilson, assured the alumni in 1902:

> By the very simple device of building our new buildings in the Tudor Gothic style we seem to have added to Princeton the age of Oxford and Cambridge; we have added a thousand years to the history of Princeton by merely putting those lines in our buildings which point every man's imagination to the historic traditions of learning in the English-speaking race.[23]

Ralph Adam Cram, who from 1907 to 1927 was Princeton's supervising architect, was a dedicated Ruskinian. He believed that beauty was a sign of 'right feeling, right thinking and right living', the basis of true civilization.

Princeton's Graduate College (1913) and new chapel (1928), an enlarged version of Oxbridge chapels, are fine examples of Cram's Collegiate Gothic. For a Gothic chapel stained glass windows were the most appropriate decoration. Cram awarded the commission to Charles Connick (1875–1945) who had begun his artistic career as a cartoonist for a Pittsburg newspaper. Having studied the craft of stained glass, he rejected the opalescent product which John La Farge had popularized, favouring instead a medieval type of translucent glass.[24] Cram considered Connick to be united in spirit and technique with the masters of Chartres and Paris. Indeed, thirteenth century glass was his ideal because the workers imparted to it 'a gracious spirit of devotion'. Like them Connick believed in his work's moral and spiritual value.[25] Of the glass which he designed for a children's hospital – a series of medallions where Sir Galahad and Joan of Arc appeared with Tom Sawyer and Huckleberry Finn – Connick wrote, 'We all gloried in the

[23] Muccigrosso, p. 87.
[24] John Gilbert Lloyd, *Stained Glass in America* (Jenkintown, Penn., 1963), pp. 66–69.
[25] Charles Connick, *Adventures in Light and Color* (New York, 1937).

thought that our windows would, in their honest functioning, bring smiling lights into tired little eyes, and that they might set alive some creative impulses to survive memories of sickness and pain'.

For the bay of Princeton's Proctor Hall dining-room he designed a Holy Grail window. The commission had originally gone to an English artist, Florence Camm (1874–1960), who created a Malory window design. But the outbreak of World War I prevented transatlantic shipping of the panels. They were eventually purchased for the Cleveland Museum of Art, at Cram's urging. The three-tiered design presents varied scenes, with the Quest of the Holy Grail providing the climactic event of Arthur's reign. The bottom row shows Merlin's reception of the infant Arthur, the sword-in-the-stone test, the Grail's appearance at the Penecostal feast in Camelot's Gothic hall, Launcelot's generous act of sparing the King's life, the return of Excalibur (watched by swans), and the three queens guarding the purple bier as the ship sets out for Avalon. Unusually, Arthur's dream of the fight between the bear and dragon (a vision prophesying his victory over the Roman Emperor) is also depicted. The second tier has the usual Achievement of the Grail sequence, but testifying to the artist's close reading of Malory are panels showing Galahad healing the Maimed King and feasting with Grail knights from other countries. The top light shows, for the first time since the middle ages, I think, a transubstantiation scene where the Christ Child is manifested to the kneeling Joseph of Arimathea.

As Camm's designs had been submitted to the Proctor Hall competition before the war, they probably influenced Connick's schemes. His Grail Window is divided into three tiers with three sets of paired lancets in each. On the lowest level Galahad and the Grail appear at Camelot, the quest begins and the knights engage in adventures. Gareth, Uwain and Gawaine attack the Castle of Maidens; Bagdemagus loses the white shield; Launcelot dozes at the Perilous Chapel. Bors rescues the virgin from the Black Knight; Perceval rescues the lion from the snake; and Launcelot escapes the lions guarding Corbenic. Each knight has a specific blazon which Pierre de Chaignon La Rose of Cambridge provided. The second tier includes Galahad's lonely questing, Perceval's vision of the white hart with lions, and the sacrifice of Perceval's sister. Miracles associate Galahad with Christ–the restoration of Mordrain's sight, the healing of the Maimed King and the Sarras cripple, and the prisoners' sustenance. The final scene shows Galahad's farewell. Inscriptions in Malorian language identify each subject. Large figures of Joseph of Arimathea, an angel with a lance, and knights with banners direct the eye to the top tier where Christ with raised Grail welcomes Galahad to heaven.

Even though the mode is visual, Connick skilfully alludes to other senses. Jagged, angular pieces of glass suggest the 'crakynge and cryienge of thunder' accompanying the Grail's appearance at Camelot (xiii, 7). Angels with censers explain why 'there was al the halle fufylled with good odoures'. Colours are used symbolically in a religious and heraldic context with white and violet glass signifying spirituality while red-violet glass denotes the violent 'black knights' – the Seven Deadly Sins. Like Morris, Connick had a clear view of the medium's distinctiveness:

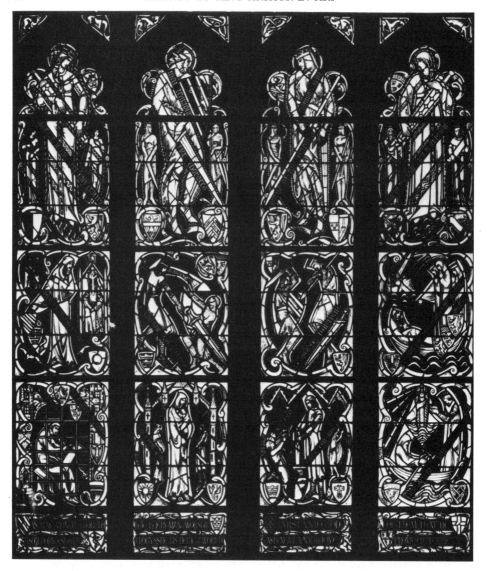

66. Charles Connick. Malory window in Princeton University Chapel, lower tier, 1931

A stained-glass window can never be a picture. It is essentially a flat
decoration through which light must play. Whatever its richness and
detail, its component parts of glass and lead determine its simplicity
and directness and its tendency toward the silhouette rather than the
subtleties of tone which are associated with pictorial art in general, and
especially with painting.

Each window in the Milbank Choir of Princeton's Chapel[26] depicts a narrative of man's search for God–Dante's *Divine Comedy*, Malory's *Morte Darthur*, Milton's *Paradise Lost* and Bunyan's *Pilgrim's Progress*. The English programmes are to be read from bottom to top to signify man's aspiration for God. The structure of the Italian allegory is controlled by the circles, mountain and heavenly plain of Dante's cosmology. All panels culminate in the Mystic Rose enclosing the vision of Christ. Connick has contrived that the colours in the chapel windows become richer in tone as one progresses from west to east, so that in every part of the building the windows are 'balanced in light'.

His colour symbolism he retrieved from the Middle Ages. Blue, 'the most active, the most magical, the most mysterious of all colours in light' signified fidelity and divine wisdom. Red represented the active life and love – hence its appropriateness to Arthurian heroes like Launcelot and Galahad. Green was spring, hope and victory; in the Malory window it is also associated with fées like Nimue. Golden yellow was fruitfulness, the goodness of God, heavenly treasure but in a paler form it could denote treachery. White was faith, innocence, joy, life. Tristram wears white armour in three 'aspiration' panels. Antithetical black was despair, sorrow, mystery and death. In *Adventures in Light and Color* (1937) Connick wrote that the four epic windows had provided 'glowing and colorful inspiration for boys and girls everywhere . . . Vibrations of color-in-light are sure to quicken a glow in the eyes of sensitive children, regardless of age, color or condition of servitude'.

The Malory window is divided into three tiers illustrating 'The Life and Death of King Arthur', 'Aspirations of Chivalry' and 'The Quest of the Holy Grail'. Individual panels in the first two tiers are read in narrative order from left to right, the 'story' panels being surmounted by elongated representations of major characters related to the biography of Arthur (Morgan, Mordred, Arthur, the Lady of the Lake) and the adventures of secular chivalry (Tristram, Arthur and eight Knights, Guenevere, Launcelot). The third tier is read from bottom to top with a light devoted to each major figure of spiritual chivalry – Bors, Perceval, Perceval's sister, Galahad. Shields of depicted characters occupy the corners of each panel.

A diagonal ribbon indicates the particular subject in Malory's or Caxton's words; for example, 'How Arthur gate Excalibur'; 'Merlyn warned The Kynge' and 'To Auylyon to hele me of my greuous wounds' in the biography of Arthur series. In the second tier Connick uses Dyce's conception, illustrating chivalric virtues by association with particular characters and incidents. The virtues are those which Caxton designates in his preface – Friendship, Gentleness, Noble Acts, Quest, Faithfulness, Courtesy, Mercy and Prowess. That Connick knew his Malory thoroughly is suggested by his inclusion of minor episodes as well as such familiar topics as Launcelot's rescue of the Queen (Prowess) and Gareth's endur-

---

[26] The major study is Richard Stillwell, *The Chapel of Princeton University* (Princeton, 1971). For a detailed description of the Malory window, together with the relevant texts from *Morte Darthur*, see pp. 59–75. The description of the Holy Grail Window in Proctor Hall comes from Connick materials which C.W. Whall collected. They are now in the Victoria and Albert's National Art Library, Box IV, 89.

ance of Lynet's mockery (Gentleness). Dinadin's rescue of a lady whom Sir Breuse Sance Pitie has victimised illustrates 'Noble Acts' and Lamorack's refusal to kill Sir Belliance represents 'Courtesy'. Specific textual details are incorporated into the picture planes – the cloth of gold about the infant Arthur, Elaine's red sleeve on Launcelot's helmet, Alexander the Orphan's bloody doublet, Pelleas' circlet won for Ettarde, the Questing Beast with its serpent's head and leopard's body.

The theme of progress towards perfection which the narrative panels illustrate is substantiated by the ornaments separating the tiers. These are grotesques and unnatural beasts at the bottom to represent Arthur's Dark Age origins. Leaves and natural beasts in the middle section represent secular chivalry while flowers and Grail quest symbols indicate the highest type of chivalry, as do the white and red colours which dominate the top tier. Uniting the individual lights is the thematic inscription running through the lowest sections, a quotation from one of Malory's most original additions: 'As May month flowereth and flourisheth let every man of worship flourish his heart in this world, first unto God and next unto the joy of them that he promised his faith unto'. And in the lowest panel on the left the knight-prisoner writes his *Morte*, surrounded by his manuscript sources.

Alistair Duncan attributes the popularity of stained glass decoration during the late nineteenth century to the increased interest in applied arts generally.[27] The Arts and Crafts Movement's demands for 'a fresh start' meant renewing medieval techniques for making pot glass and abandoning the kind of window where the picture was painted onto clear glass. America's most innovative and influential Art Nouveau decorator was Louis Comfort Tiffany (1848–1933). The extraordinary colours and rich details, particularly of his landscapes in glass, produced a sense of overwhelming beauty. Among hundreds of windows that Tiffany's Glass and Decorating Company provided for religious, institutional and domestic settings are some Arthurian subjects.

A head of Joseph of Arimathea, originally part of 'The Entombment' Memorial window dedicated to the artist's father, was reproduced as a single panel. It was exhibited at the Grafton Galleries in London and then installed at Tiffany's Long Island mansion, Laurelton Hall, while a mosaic version decorated the stairway of the New York showrooms. The brooding, compassionate face was that of the designer's father, Charles Lewis Tiffany. A triptych memorial window (1917) commissioned by the Women's Relief Corps of the North and the United Daughters of the Confederacy of the South for the National Headquarters of the American Red Cross in Washington shows characters from *The Faerie Queene*. In the left window eight larger-than-life figures are grouped about a grounded shield bearing the Red Cross Association's symbol, which is also the sign of the Red Cross Knight, Galahad and St George. The majestic ladies, who appear in Spenser's Book I, are Celia, a holy woman devoted to helping the poor and weak, and her three daughters Fidelia (with a golden chalice), Speranze, and Charissa (embracing a child). Their companions are Repentance with a bowl of cleansing water, Mercy, and Una

---

[27] Alastair Duncan, *Tiffany Windows* (New York, 1980), p. 9.

who has guided the knight to this place of salvation, symbolised by the anchor on the central banner. The centre window shows a specific act of charity. The prostrate Guyon (Temperance) accepts a drink of water as his rescuer, Prince Arthur, mounted on a white charger, watches. In the third window, Una, crowned and adorned with flowers, is surrounded by modest ladies, the red cross shield and banners with red crosses and a heart. The knights wear fifteenth century plate armour while the ladies are gowned in the loose, all-purpose costumes that can function in both religious and secular designs without reference to specific time or place. The figures are solidly set in Tiffany's characteristic Art Nouveau landscapes – slim, leafy birches, which formally parallel the verticals of spears and banners; plump clouds that stream across the irridescent sky and foreground flowers sumptously displaying their colours.

Galahad is a popular subject, appearing with King Alfred in a window at St Mark's School, Southboro, Mass. Adapted from G.F. Watts' painting, he is also depicted in the Ogden Cryder Memorial, St Andrew's Dune Church, Southampton, N.Y. (1902), rounder of face and wider of eye than the Prinsep prototype. The plate armour is more ornamental with rose-decorated poleyns and multi-sectioned sabatons. The most remarkable change concerns landscape, no longer a realistic English forest but a more glamorous Art Nouveau setting. Reduplicated tree trunks which emphasise linearity have become the chief structural ornament. The foreground plants, sharpened and freed from their natural forms, energetically fill the space to the lower frame and superimpose themselves on the horse's flank. The painting's subdued blues and greens have exploded into brilliance.

A sketch represented in 'Tributes to Honour' as a model for a memorial shows a kneeling Galahad, inviolate in Symbolist rapture despite his imprisonment by the tyrant of Sarras. In this design, Tiffany has abandoned plate armour for an unrealistic chain mail costume with a reptile's scale-like patterning. Mistily hovering above the curly head is the Grail chalice and red-cross shield with a superimposed flower.[28]

Probably the most influential form of Arthurian didacticism was the illustrated Malory intended for juvenile readers. As early as 1860 Lucas W. Collins was complaining in *Blackwood's Magazine* that British schoolboys could tell you more about Sir Bagdemagus and King Pellinore in a week than they could of Diomed and Hector at the end of a school half-year:

> The truth is that the style of these romances recommends itself at once
> to the schoolboy mind, healthfully active and energetic; with very little
> love-making, few of the finer flights of fancy, and no moral reflections,
> there are plenty of terrific encounters and hard blows.

---

[28] Other Grail windows are the Willet Stained Glass Studios' 'Quest for the Grail' in the Fort Lincoln Cemetery, Washington, D.C., and a Parsifal window in the Allegheny Cemetery, Pittsburgh. The Chapel of Mercersburg Academy, Pennsylvania, has Arthurian windows by Florence Camm and her brothers. Florence Camm's 'Sir Galahad in Meditation' (ca. 1917) is in the Cleveland Museum of Art.

The first edition intended specifically for boys, Sir James Knowles' *The Story of King Arthur and His Knights of the Round Table* (1862) did show concern for moral values. In addition to modernizing the style, abridging, and unifying, Knowles 'suppressed and modified where changed manners and morals have made it absolutely necessary to do so for the preservation of a lofty original ideal'.[29] The suppression and modification applied particularly to Roman Catholicism and adultery, with unspecified treason and the jealousy of Mordred explaining the Round Table's disintegration.

In post-bellum America, a former Confederate officer, Sidney Lanier, clung to chivalric idealism as a means of revitalising the South. 'The days of chivalry are not gone, they are only spiritualized . . . the knight of the 19th century fights, not with trenchant sword, but with trenchant soul', he wrote.[30] *The Boy's King Arthur* (1880) adopts Knowles' pattern of expurgation, modernisation and moral example, as Lanier urges his readers to learn from 'generous' Sir Tristram, 'stainless' Sir Galahad, 'gentle' Sir Percival, 'meek' Sir Gareth, 'brilliant' Sir Palamides, 'persevering' Sir la Cote Mal Taile and above all the 'majestic manhood' of Sir Launcelot.[31] Of Lanier's Malory, 'the very first book I knew', John Steinbeck recalled, 'I think my sense of right and wrong, my feeling of noblesse oblige, and any thought I may have against the oppressor and for the oppressed came from this book . . . I don't know any book save only the Bible and perhaps Shakespeare which has had more effect on our morals, our ethics, and our mores than . . . Malory'.[32]

An even greater influence than Lanier in shaping the American chivalric imagination was Howard Pyle (1853–1911).[33] He emerged in the 'Golden Age of Illustration' when the enormous popularity of periodicals provided artists not only with a good livelihood but also with a chance of influencing taste and morals. Between 1876 and 1887 Pyle's pictures were reproduced by the old

[29] Preface, *The Story of King Arthur and His Knights of the Round Table compiled and arranged by J.K. Knowles*. G.H. Thomas, a painter and illustrator of ceremonial subjects and group portraits, provided six garishly coloured illustrations. Lancelot Speed illustrated a 1912 reprint and Louis Rhead an American edition of 1923.

[30] *Poems and Poem Outlines, Centennial Edition of the Works of Sidney Lanier*, ed. Charles R. Anderson (Baltimore, 1945), I, xlii quoted by Taylor and Brewer, p. 164.

[31] *The Boy's King Arthur being Sir Thomas Malory's History of King Arthur and his knights of the Round Table* (London, 1880), illustrated by Alfred Kappes, Introduction, xxiv–xxv.

[32] *A Life in Letters* (New York, 1975), p. 540.

[33] References include Rowland Elzea, *Howard Pyle* (New York, 1975); Susan E. Meyer, *America's Great Illustrators* (New York, 1978); Henry C. Pitz, *The Brandywine Tradition* (Boston, 1969), 'The Brandywine Tradition', *American Artist* 30 (December, 1966), 44–49 and 74–76, and *Howard Pyle: Writer, Illustrator, and Founder of the Brandywine School* (New York, 1975). *The Brandywine Heritage: Howard Pyle, N.C. Wyeth, Andrew Wyeth, James Wyeth* is a catalogue of an exhibition, The Brandywine River Museum, Chadds Ford, Penn., 1971 with foreward by Richard McLanathan. *The Children's Literature Association Quarterly*, 8/12 (Summer, 1983) is devoted to Pyle. See especially Patricia Dooley, 'Romance and Realism: Pyle's Book Ilustrations for Children', 17–19. The major collections of Pyle's papers, manuscripts, library and related materials together with those of N.C. Wyeth are in the Delaware Art Museum, Wilmington.

method of tracing a pen-and-ink design onto a block of boxwood and having an engraver cut it. But the rotary press, the process of photo-engraving and new methods of colour reproduction greatly decreased the time required to make a printing plate and concomitantly increased the demand. Pyle produced over 3300 published illustrations. He also affected standards by teaching art, first in Philadelphia, then at his homes in Wilmington, Delaware and Chadds Ford, Pennsylvania. His students included N.C. Wyeth, Frank Schoonover, Maxfield Parish and Jessie Willcox Smith. As a result, says Henry C. Pitz,

> a large segment of American illustration was showing the Pyle imprint, and the sycamores, the tree-shaded banks, the stone houses, and the round hills of the Brandywine were appearing in the pages of America's books and magazines.[34]

His style was a curious blend of realism and romance, the result of such diverse influences as his Quaker upbringing in the Brandywine River valley, Swedenborgian mysticism, and the literary pictorialism of Millais, Burne-Jones, Rossetti, Maddox Brown, Houghton, Tenniel and and other British artists published in *Punch, The Illustrated London News,* and children's periodicals of the fifties. The use of the heavy black line he learned from Dürer while Beardsley must have inspired the eclectic headpieces and endpieces of his Arthurian books as well as ventures into the mysterious and sinister. When Pyle came to devise complete books, in contrast to magazine illustration, Walter Crane's page designs provided a model for composition and decoration.

He believed that literary ideas could be depicted convincingly if the artist surrendered himself to the world of imagination without losing his grip on reality. For his medieval illustration he studied S.R. Meyrick's *A Critical Inquiry into Antient Armour* (1824) and Georg Hirth's *Kulturgeschichtliches Bilderbuch.* The resemblance between his ladies' wide-sleeved, narrow-waisted gowns and those worn by Margaret, Henry VI's queen and her attendants suggests that he had at hand Henry Shaw's *Dresses and Decorations of the Middle Ages* (1843), a frequently republished reference. It was also a possible source for his ornamental swords in a sixteenth century style. He could recreate the past so vividly that, as he said, 'I forget the present and see the characters and things of those old days about me'.

Pyle's first Arthurian work was his 'decoration' of Tennyson's *The Lady of Shalott* which Dodd Mead & Co. published in 1881. Despite a conscious imitation of the illuminator's style (ornate capitals, zoomorphic interlace, Gothic script and a profusion of acanthus leaves), the book is a failure aesthetically. As colour technology at that time was incapable of producing anything but flat primary colours and insipid green, there is no medieval brilliance. The desire to recreate the social scene produces a preponderance of images inconsistent with the aristocratic milieu – a woman with a tambourine, a monk with his breviary, a haymaker, a shepherd, a girl with a stool and milkpail. In Part II, Launcelot is a

---

[34] *American Artist* 30: 49.

fair-haired Saxon with a winged helmet of gold while in Part III he is a dark Tartar on a wild-eyed steed. A distracting feature is the repetition across the illustrated page on the left of the verses printed on the right.

Early in the new century Pyle turned to King Arthur and his Knights, producing four illustrated volumes: *The Story of King Arthur and His Knights* (1903), *The Story of the Champions of the Round Table* (1905), *The Story of Sir Launcelot and His Companions* (1907) and *The Story of the Grail and the Passing of Arthur* (1910). Though Malory was his chief source, he also used Middle English metrical romances like 'The Wedding of Sir Gawain and Dame Ragnell' as well as the *Mabinogion*. The 'Foreword' to the first volume reveals his didactic fervour:

> For when, in pursuing this history, I have come to consider the high nobility of spirit that moved these excellent men to act as they did, I have felt that they have afforded such a perfect example of courage and humility that anyone might do exceedingly well to follow after their manner of behaviour . . . For I believe that King Arthur was the most honorable, gentle Knight who ever lived in all the world.

Pyle adopts a pseudo-archaic English prose style intended to suggest Caxton's Malory. The opening sentence of Book 1, chapter l, *The Story of King Arthur and His Knights*, reads, 'It happened that among those worthies who were summoned unto London Town by the mandate of the Archbishop as above recounted, there was a certain knight, very honorable and of his estate, by name Sir Ector of Bonmaison – surnamed the Trustworthy Knight, because of the fidelity with which he kept the counsel of those who confided in him, and because he always performed unto all men, whether of high or low degree, that which he promised to undertake, without defalcation as to the same'. Throughout, he expands the text with numerous sensory details which complement the dense pictorial equivalents. The full page illustrations imitate the woodblock unadorned by the elaborate borders which isolated image from text in his earlier books. Gothic lettering indicates the subject.

The 'Foreword' makes chivalry seem the central concern and there are some depictions of jousting knights, the horses and riders so generously swathed in caparisons and surcoats, so loaded with excessively plumed helmets and heavy swords, as would have rendered them immobile in the real world. Without their helms they are frowningly severe (Uther), Orientally devious (Kay), shifty-eyed (Gawaine), naively innocent (Pellias) and stoically resolute (Launcelot). Only occasionally, as when Tristram leaps from the castle into the sea or when Arthur prepares to pull the sword from the stone do flailing limbs or clenched hands convey an expenditure of energy. For the most part the characters are frozen in an imagined time of narrow, lofty castles, patterned columns, fluted flagons and chairs decorated with full-breasted sphinxes.

It is the almond-eyed ladies with their long black tresses, heavy jewellery and rich gowns who provide the chief interest. They are often presented as portraits – passive embodiments of beauty, though they also may be shown fixed in a significant confrontation. Guinevere nonchalantly dangles a rose as she turns her back on the jousters. Vivien kneels motionless at Merlin's feet, only her serpent crest indicating her malevolence. The Belle Isoult is as sadly remote as Rossetti's heroines. In narrative scenes tension is produced by effects of light and darkness, Pyle's nearest approach to reality. As Gawaine and Ettard sit 'bedight with extraodinary splendor, and . . . illuminated by a light of several score waxen tapers', Pellias, wearing a black friar's cowled habit, lurks in the shadows. The gloom of Leodegrance's 'closet' is relieved by the brightness of the 'gardener's boy', Arthur. Technically derivative, the illustrations verify priorities explicated for Pyle's students – 'pictures are the creations of the imagination and not of technical facility . . . I subordinate that technical training entirely to the training of the imagination'.[34]

A star pupil at the Howard Pyle School of Art was N.C. Wyeth (1882–1945).[35] He would become the patriarch of a three generation family of artists but when he was accepted into Pyle's colony in 1902, he was still dubious about his ability. Like Pyle, he was a popular magazine illustrator yet he resented the commercial spirit's deviousness and niggardliness. He saw history not as a collection of facts but of experiences which persisted from period to period with only the setting changed. As aids to authenticity he collected costumes and props of various places and periods, particularly Colonial America and medieval England. His other interest was the natural world; when amalgamated with human life it produced 'a cosmic relationship which if not felt leaves us superficial and at bottom useless to ourselves and the world'.[36]

The world he knew best and depicted most often was the Brandywine Valley, which Henry C. Pitz describes as a

> lovely ribbon of stream, meadowlands and encircling hills; a delight to the artist's eye . . . But it is not merely these fields, waters, grass and stone houses; it is these things touched by history and talent.[37]

Wyeth regretted that he could not bring to his romances and other books with foreign settings 'knowledge substantiated by facts as far as is possible – and above all else after a personal investigation of the country'.[38] He compromised by setting romance characters in American landscapes.

Among more than three hundred books that Wyeth illustrated was Lanier's *The Boy's King Arthur* (1920). He prefers to present men engaged in physical activity rather than passive women. A tremendous sense of speed and expended energy is conveyed by the figures of Gawain and his brothers attacking Lamorak

---

[35] In addition to Pitz, Meyer and McLanathan noted above, see also Susan E. Meyer, 'N.C. Wyeth' in *American Artist* 39 (February, 1975), 35–45, 78–89 (part of 'Three Generations of the Wyeth Family'); *The Wyeths. The Letters of N.C. Wyeth*, ed. Betsy James Wyeth (Boston, 1971).
[36] *American Artist* 39, 40.
[37] Henry C. Pitz, 'The Brandywine Tradition', 43.
[38] Letter, Jan. 31, 1921 to his father.

he Lady Guinevere

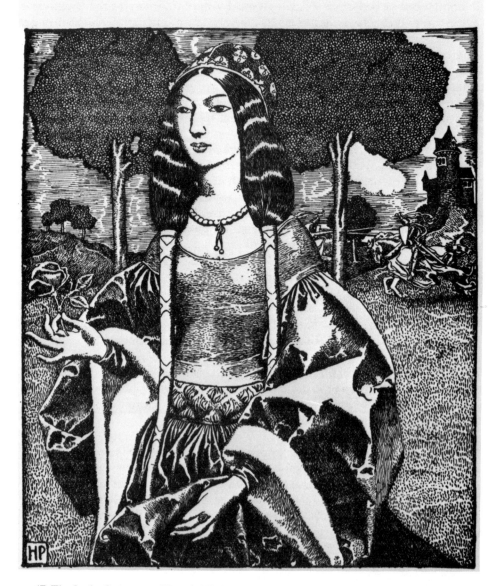

67. The Lady Guinevere. Howard Pyle's illustration for *The Story of Arthur and His Knights* (New York: Scribner, 1984)

from both sides with swords and battleaxe; by Mark's glave descending to murder Tristram; by Guenever's streaming hair as she rides behind her rescuer to the Joyous Gard. Best of all are the destriers, muscled images of power that strain like farmhorses and stir up the dust as Launcelot unseats Mador. Wyeth's experience as a hard-working farm boy gave him 'a vivid appreciation of the part the body plays in action'. Realistic details drawn from his own terrain are the brown meadow grasses beside the creek where Launcelot challenges Tarquin; the shadow-dappled boulders, sycamore trunks and little waterfall of the mad Launcelot's forest refuge; and the golden light of an autumn sunset that tinges Launcelot, the queen, their grey horse and the flowery meadow embroidered with Queen Anne's lace and other wildflowers.

Colour enables Wyeth to convey more varied moods than Pyle's black and white could emcompass. Early morning mist mysteriously merges water and sky so that the proffered Excalibur, the swans, and Arthur and Merlin in the golden-prowed boat emerge like the vivid cut-outs of a collage. Gold, sapphire and crimson convey the pleasures of Lyoness' castle while the greyness of poplar trunks and faded browns of meadow stalks foretell Lamorak's imminent death. There is a similar mood-inducing colour scheme in the oil painting 'He Blew Three Deadly Notes' (1917), enlarged from an illustration for Book III, 'Of Sir Gareth of Orkney'. Astride a black destrier trapped in green and gold, the Green Knight sounds the horn of challenge suspended from a sycamore. The subdued landscape with its pale sky, straw coloured shrubs and grass and dusty country road implies humiliation and defeat.

Wyeth is a congenial illustrator of Malory's text for he shares the medieval author's tragic sense of life. In a letter to his mother, December 5, 1908, he wrote that life was

> enshrouded in a glow of deep, tragic red. Why tragic, I don't know, but for some reason or another *anything* that I appreciate keenly and profoundly is always sad to the point of being tragic. Whether it is a lone tree on a hillside bathed in the fading light of the afternoon sun, or the broad stretch of a green meadow shining and sparkling after a shower, or be it even the birds joyously singing in the spring trees . . . it is all so sad, because it is all so beautiful – so hopeless.

Despite Pre-Raphaelite influences on American Arthurian Art, the image of woman as a symbol of power is absent. Henry Adams wryly commented that 'American art, like the American language and American education, was as far as possible sexless'.[39] The dynamo was more attractive than the goddess. Yet Americans could not abandon completely the Arthurian dream and when a hero appeared in the shape of John F. Kennedy, he had to be given his Camelot.[40]

---

[39] *The Education of Henry Adams* (New York, 1931 [1918]), p. 385.
[40] The line of descent was Malory's *Morte Darthur* by way of T.H. White's *The Once and Future King* (1958) and Alan Jay Lerner and Frederick Loewe's Broadway musical, *Camelot*.

CHAPTER THIRTEEN

Myths for the Age of Anxiety

With the death of Queen Victoria in 1901 and the accession of her 59 year old son as Edward VII, the model of masculine sovereignty was reestablished. The subject of C.E. Butler's 'King Arthur' (1903, Christopher Wood Gallery) is a slim youth in plate armour, painted in the act of placing the crown on his head. Physically he bears no resemblance to the stout monarch yet he embodies the mystique of kingship and confidence in a great future associated with the new reign. That the British ideal of patriotic public service as a masculine duty had spread through the Empire is evident in the words that Earl Grey, the Canadian Governor-General, addressed to Toronto schoolboys on Empire Day, 1909:[1]

> Empire Day is the festival on which every British subject should rever-
> ently remember the British Empire stands out before the whole world
> as the fearless champion of freedom, fair play and equal rights; that its
> watchwords are responsibility, duty, sympathy and self-sacrifice; and
> that a special responsibility rests with you individually to be true to the
> traditions and to the mission of your race.

In the Edwardian Age Arthurian idealism was not the preserve of a public school elite. Lord Baden-Powell's Boy Scouts, the American Knights of King Arthur, and the Alliance of Honour linked the definition of a gentleman to the virtues of a knight in ways that included working-class boys.[2]

William Dyce's idea that the Round Table Knights were relevant to the modern age continued to influence the decoration of buildings, particularly schools. Between 1903 and 1910 Mrs M. Sargent-Florence, sister of Oakham School's headmaster, covered eight wall spaces in the Elizabethan Hall with frescoes illustrating 'The Tale of Gareth'. Although the first scene, which shows the bare-legged boy's farewell to his mother in her Italian Renaissance castle, is Tennysonian, subsequent details like Gareth's black armour and the dangling bodies of the Red Knight's victims show that Malory was also a source. The artist intended to

---

[1] Robert M. Stamp, 'Empire in the schools of Ontario: the training of young imperialists', *Journal of Canadian Studies* (Aug. 1973), 32–42.
[2] Mark Girouard, *The Return to Camelot*, chapter 16, 'Chivalry for the People'.

present the patient, courteous, brave and humble hero as a suitable model for Oakham schoolboys. To this end she introduced the faces of students among the crowds. The castle hall of the hospitable Green Knight is the same hall that the frescoes decorate; its 1904 chimney piece featuring Endeavour as a winged figure discharging an arrow is the identifying image.[3]

Chivalric myths were the vernacular of the decorative arts. Walter Crane's 'England and France Exhibition Piece' (1908, Victoria and Albert Museum), a tapestry of woven wool and cotton, makes extensive use of the Galahad/St George iconography, Tudor roses, heraldic trumpets hung with Union Jacks, and jousting knights in fifteenth century armour. The latter image recurs on Crane's dragon-bordered Pilkington lustre dish (1907, Sotheby and Company). Phoebe Anna Traquair's silver box (1908, Victoria and Albert Museum) is embossed with an enamel plaque depicting 'The Passing of Arthur'. Traquair also pioneered the revival of manuscript illumination and lettering; among the texts that she copied onto vellum and decorated was an extract from Morris's *Defense of Guinevere*.[4] Sir Alfred Gilbert, one of the 'new' sculptors, created from gold, ivory and polychrome a series of fantastic knights (1903) that led critics to accuse him of breeding mischief in the sculpture schools. A wide range of household articles from umbrella stands to inkwells allowed chivalric display in ordinary homes.

The idea of the male as a modern knight, a metaphor which the educational system, sports activities, clubs and manufacturing sustained, was excruciatingly tested in 'the bloodiest war of all'. World War I put chivalry at the service of recruitment and propaganda. E.A. Marsland's study of war poetry in English, French and German[5] reveals that patriotic verse was permeated with references to shining helmets, swords, armour, 'storied scutcheons', *Eisenkelten* and guerdon. When the war ended, mythologies were needed to distance the horror and justify the pain. The figure of Galahad took on a new meaning. He was neither the medieval Catholic who proved through asceticism the superiority of *la chevalerie celestienne* nor even Tennyson's social activist who had no need to pursue the vision of the Grail uncovered since he enjoyed the beautific vision from the beginning. He now represented all war's victims who had 'the strength to overcome the bad and the grace to remain unsullied'.[6]

Since the sacrifice of the men and women who died for their country and countrymen seemed an expression of chivalry, medieval knights figured in war memorials. The Boer War provided a precedent. Clifton College, which Girouard cites as a good example of public school chivalry, prepared three hundred boys for service in South Africa. Alfred Drury's lofty statue of a knight with the face of an

---

[3]   On the school's history see John Barber, *The Story of Oakham School* (Wymondham, 1983). Glenalmond, a Scottish public school, had a 'Gareth' window dedicated to the school doctor. Gareth had Launcelot's virtues without his adultery.

[4]   Anthea Callen, *Angel in the Studio: Women in the Arts and Crafts Movement 1870–1914* (London, 1979), pp. 122–3, 185–6.

[5]   E.A. Marsland, *The Nation's Cause: French, English and German Poetry of the First World War* (London, 1990).

[6]   Mary E. Southworth's characterization in *Galahad, Knight Errant* (Boston, 1907).

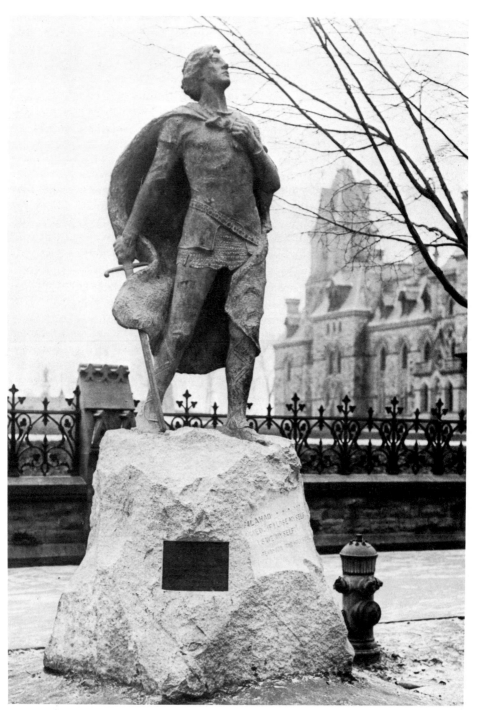

68. Ernest W. Keyser. Sir Galahad statue on Wellington Street, Ottawa, 1905

English schoolboy commemorates the forty-four who died. Clifton's Great War Memorial windows are specifically Arthurian. King Arthur, girt with Excalibur and holding his spear and shield, stands in a Gothic niche. The corresponding figure, Galahad, holds his sword front and centre so that the image combines the iconography of battle (courage and service) with that of the cross (sacrifice and faith).

In 1919 Wilhemina Geddes (1887–1955),[7] an Irish artist who was part of 'An Túr Gloine' (the Tower of Glass) workshop, received a commission from the Duke of Connaught, a Canadian Governor-General. He wanted to commemorate in St Bartholemew's Church, Ottawa his staff members who had died in the Great War. In the three-light window above the altar, Galahad appears among the soldier saints. This is not Ottawa's only representation of the Grail Knight as a symbol of sacrifice. On Wellington Street the parliament buildings E.W. Keyser's 1905 sculpture of Henry Albert Harper depicts him as a bareheaded Galahad grasping his sword. Harper lost his life in the nearby river while trying to rescue a drowning girl. His friend, the future Prime Minister W.L. MacKenzie King, not only raised the subscription money but also had the words of Tennyson's Galahad carved on the memorial's base: 'If I lose myself, I save myself'. Harper had shouted them as he leapt into the icy water.

Despite the tragedy of war, chivalry as an ideal was not discredited in the post-war period. Arthurian societies such as The Fellowship of the Round Table flourished. In Tintagel, romantic site of Arthur's conception and birth, a parodic 'moral building' was opened on the Feast of Pentecost, 1933. King Arthur's Hall of Chivalry was the realised dream of a custard millionaire, Frederick T. Glasscock, who built it to house meetings of a chivalric society. The Fellowship of the Round Table was to revive the Ideal of Chivalry, 'to join all the peoples of the world in Fellowship and Love, and make the Kingdom of God upon this earth an accomplished fact'.[8] Every part of the building symbolised an aspect of the virtues associated with Arthur, 'the fountain head of Chivalry'. The granite building stones represented his strength, other vari-coloured stones the Fellowship's beauty. On the polyphant floor the Round Table was depicted in red porphyry and the Cross in white elvan. Surrounded by a corridor accessible through arches, the Hall of Chivalry was programmed to convey a symbolic movement from darkness to light. Tennyson's lines in 'The Coming of Arthur' describe the progress which chivalry could effect:

> And Arthur and his knighthood for a space
> Were all one will, and thro' that strength the King

---

[7]   Peter Cormack, *Women Stained Glass Artists of the Arts and Crafts Movement*, catalogue of an exhibition held at the William Morris Gallery, 7 December 1985 – 2 March, 1986 (Waltham Forest, 1985), 2, 19–23; Nicola Gordon-Bowe, 'Wilhemina Geddes . . . Ireland's Extraordinary Artist', *Stained Glass* 76/1 (Spring, 1981), 41–43.

[8]   The society published a magazine, *Excalibur*, which contained poems, short stories, information about the legends, hortatory articles with such titles as 'Endeavour, Enthusiasm, Enchantment', and reports of Branch meetings.

> Drew in the petty princedoms under him,
> Fought, and in twelve great battles overcame
> The heathen hordes, and made a realm and reigned.

Polished shields of various stones were placed around the hall, black and other dark colours at one end, white at the other. Overshadowing the thrones on the dais was an ancient uncut stone, supporting an anvil in which was set Excalibur. The anvil represented Arthur's strength, the sword Christian Faith.

What redeems King Arthur's Hall are the splendid windows of Veronica Whall (1887–1967).[9] Her father, Christopher Whall, was a teacher, designer and pioneer of the Arts and Crafts Movement in stained glass. The shortage of labour which the war occasioned in his studio enabled Veronica to participate in designing windows, while the post-war demand for memorials provided her with a permanent occupation. The Tintagel commission required the design and execution of seventy-three windows. Those in the corridor bear the heraldic devices of the Round Table knights. High on each side of the great hall are nine windows (the number signifying the multiplied Trinity) based on emblems of the chivalric virtues; for example, a lily represents Purity, a heart and crimson rose Love, a flaming torch Truth, a sword and laurel Honour, a golden anchor and double rainbow Hope, a vine Obedience, and an oak-wreathed anvil Strength. Dark colours such as purple and indigo dominate the 'dark' side where one enters. The glass lightens as one moves forward to the climax of golden red. Veronica Whall shared Charles Connick's emphasis on the centrality of light in the artist's conception:

> The three things technically essential to the making of a stained glass window are glass, lead, and – light . . . light is our medium, and light is our colour . . . We have to mix it with our colours; we have to harness it; to tie it down; to make it stop where we want it, – or let it pour through; a stupendous, living, ever-changing force.[10]

At either end triple windows based on Malory show not only Whall's skill in managing colour to achieve aesthetic and didactic effect but also her attention to details that unite past and present, myth and reality. Characters are Gothically elongated to emphasise theme. At the dark, secular south end the left light shows Arthur in purple hose and gown withdrawing Excalibur. Dark cypresses, buff towers, tombstones, cliffs and a pale sky are landscape elements that seem to prophesy the ultimate failure of worldly glory. The central light's theme is the struggle between good and evil. From his cave Merlin (Wisdom) surveys the land, seeing on his right the Lady of the Lake whose gown symbolises Faith. With her feet in purifying water, she flourishes the cross-shaped Excalibur. On the left

---

[9] *Women Stained Glass Artists*, pp. 2, 17–19.
[10] 'Glass, Lead, and Light', *Stained Glass*, xx, 1 (Spring/Summer 1935), 10–14, quoted Cormack, p. 2.

Morgause in blood-coloured gown and purple cloak cradles the infant Mordred, child of incest and Arthur's nemesis. The right hand light depicts the knights' departure on the Grail Quest. Launcelot's azure shield and the Queen's blue gown imply amorous fidelity. We recall Malory's verdict on the Queen – she was a true lover and therefore she had a good end. The horse's hairy fetlock, drawn from life, is a realistic detail resulting from the artist's study of horses in the flesh.

At the opposite end the windows create an apocalyptic effect with their 'gold pink' glass. Here the Grail Quest is pursued and completed. On the left Galahad and Dindrane, Perceval's sister, board the Ship of Solomon under a fiery sky. The central scene shows the Grail hovering above Galahad while Perceval and the Damsel mime adoration and joy. Shimmering pink, bright green and white contribute a radiance which is enhanced by the 'fiery tongues' effect about the knight's head. Pools of light glisten on the Romanesque chapel's stone steps. The final window is both retrospective and prophetic. Arthur, robed in scarlet, magenta and gold, knights Launcelot but Guenevere, whose champion he is to be, turns aside her head in an act that foreshadows her eventual rejection of physical love. Roundels contain the bleeding spear and blood-red poppies, a symbol of the Great War.

Furnishings include a Round Table with places for thirteen knights, a Last Supper association. On the surrounding walls are William Hatherell's ten oil paintings based on Malory. Undistinguished in colour and technique, they present static tableaux of familiar subjects such as the acquisition of Excalibur, Galahad's arrival at court, Launcelot's failure at the Perilous chapel, his rescue of the condemned Queen, the last battle and the departure for Avalon.

After the war the Western imagination was haunted by a more ancient legend than that of Galahad. According to Sir James Frazer and Jessie L. Weston,[11] the Waste Land myth was originally a vegetation myth that linked the fertility of a land and its inhabitants to the health of its ruler. In Grail legends the land's restoration depended on a hero who could heal the king wounded by the Dolorous Blow. T.S. Eliot's *The Waste Land* (1922) used the image to symbolise modern man's physical, intellectual, moral, spiritual and aesthetic impoverishment. No longer living in harmony with the natural world, the individual futilely sought a unified life. Disillusioned and decadent, his only response was passive endurance, submission and suffering. Such phrases as 'I will show you fear in a handful of dust', 'here is no water but only rock', 'dry sterile thunder without rain' and 'If there were the sound of water only/ Not the cicada/ and dry grass singing' present objective correlatives of the post-war psyche. Through the use of myth as form and symbol and the technique of allusion James Joyce and T.S. Eliot brilliantly developed 'a way of controlling, of ordering, or giving a shape and significance to the intense panorama of futility and anarchy which is contemporary history'.[12]

---

[11] Sir James G. Frazer, *The Golden Bough, A Study of Magic and Religion* (London, 1890); Jessie L. Weston, *From Ritual to Romance* (Cambridge, Eng., 1920).
[12] See Eliot's review of Joyce's *Ulysses*, 'Ulysses, Order and Myth', *The Dial* (1923), 480–3.

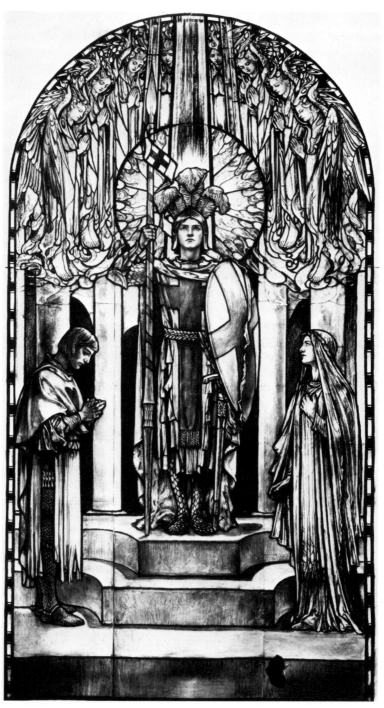

69. Veronica Whall. Cartoon for Sir Galahad window, King Arthur's Hall, Tintagel, 1931

Their method provided a *modus operandi* for this century's most inventive Arthurian artists.

David Jones (1895–1974)[13] was, like William Blake, a poet, painter, craftsman and mystic.[14] His service on the western front with the Royal Welsh Fusiliers (1915–1918) was so horrendous that in later life he suffered a series of break-downs. The war and his conversion to Catholicism dominated his life and art. His war poem *In Parenthesis*, which Faber published in 1937 at Eliot's urging, contains many Wasteland descriptions; Part 4 is sub-titled 'King Pellam's Launde'. Myth was David Jones' tool for ordering chaos. In particular, the Arthurian legends provided the link between Romano-British history and myth, a dual reality. In a review of *Arthurian Torso*[15] Jones argued that the post-war generation possessed a better 'historic sense' than had the Victorians because 'we have been forced to live history as Tennyson's generation was not'.[16] What particularly attracted him to the 'Matter of Britain' was that it synthesised not only native Welsh materials and medieval romances but also 'the complex of the ancient deposits . . . the un-plumbed deeps and recessions below and beyond the medievalized and chris-tianized story'. In particular, Malory's *Morte Darthur* not only gathered 'recessions from the past' but projected itself forward so that other works of art and nature, conditioned by it, seemed Malorian.[17]

After studying at the Westminster School of Art, Jones in 1921 moved to Ditch-ling, Sussex, where he lived with Eric Gill and his family as part of a craft guild, the Ditchling Guild of St Joseph and St Dominic. As a result he learned the art of wood-engraving. In 1927 he produced ten copper-engravings for Douglas Clever-don's edition of Coleridge's *Rime of the Ancient Mariner*, delighting in 'the lyricism inherent in the clean, furrowed free, fluent engraved line' which reminded him of Anglo-Saxon illuminations.[18] Cleverdon hoped that an illustrated Malory would follow. On February 14, 1929, Jones indicted that he was thinking about the

---

[13] Relevant reproductions, essays, and criticism include David Blamires, *David Jones, artist and writer* (Manchester, 1971); Douglas Cleverdon, *The Engravings of David Jones: A Survey* (London, 1981); H.S. Ede, 'The Visual Art of David Jones', *Agenda, David Jones Special Issue*, 5/1–3 (1967), 153–8; Arthur Giardelli, 'Trystan ac Essyllt by David Jones', *Agenda, David Jones Special Issue*, 11/4–12/1 (1973–4), 50–53; René Hague, ed. *Dai Greatcoat: A Self-Portrait of David Jones in his letters* (London, 1980); Paul Hills, 'The Romantic Tradition in David Jones', *The Malahat Review*, 27 (1972–3), 125–37; Robin Ironside, *David Jones* (London, 1949); David Jones, *Epoch and Artist* (London, 1959) and *The Dying Gaul and Other Writings* (Lon-don, 1978); Kathleen Raine, *David Jones and the Actually Loved and Known* (Ipswich, 1978). Particularly useful is Paul Hill's catalogue for the David Jones exhibition at the Tate Gallery, 21 July – 6 September, 1981 (London, 1981).
[14] Jones defined a mystic as 'that human being who is more *directly* in union with God than are most of us', *Dai Greatcoat*, 45.
[15] Jones's review essay of Charles William's and C.S. Lewis's *Arthurian Torso* appeared in *The Tablet*, 25 December, 1948. It is reprinted as 'The Arthurian Legend', in *Epoch and Artist*, pp. 202–211. Together with 'The Myth of Arthur' in the same collection, pp. 212–259, it represents the best guide to the ideas, attitudes and symbols that inspired his Arthurian art.
[16] *Epoch and Artist*, p. 205.
[17] Malory was 'the normal and national source' of the legends.
[18] *Dying Gaul*, p. 188.

project but on May 16, 1929 another letter to Cleverdon expressed his doubts about carrying out the commission because of difficulty in finding an appropriate iconography. Only one dry-point drawing and a title page were completed before illness ended the work. The title page of *Morte Darthur* (1933), drawn on a wood-block, contains images later used in other works; for example, the wounded knight, the riderless horse, and the chalice with a spear emerging diagonally. Paralleling the spear are a branch of the Glastonbury thorn, barbed and blossoming, and beams of light descending from clouds.

'Lady with wounded knight by seashore' (1930) is a death of Arthur scene combining three models – Malory's account of the barge's black-hooded ladies – 'and in one of their lappis Kyng Arthure layde hys hede'; Layamon's account in the *Brut* of Argante (Arianrhod in Jones's mythology), the queen of Avalon who will heal the king; and the pietà tradition of Mary embracing her son's corpse. The two mounted knights on the left and the toppling knight on the right are combatants in the last battle between Arthur and Mordred. The King's death wound has been delivered not by a sword but by a weapon that represents Layamon's 'walspere brade' and the lance of Longinus. The sun setting over the sea is a death symbol. The riderless horses are those that Malory described as going 'where they wolde' because their masters, having become monks, 'toke no regarde of no worldly rychesses'. In Jones' subjective, associative imagination the animals in 'Ponies on a hill slope' (1926) and 'Hill Pasture, Capel-y-ffin' (1926) are their descendants 'shrunken in bulk . . . but holding themselves with breeding, black in colour, and primitive in contour'. The horses have formal as well as symbolic usefulness – 'to break the rigidity and immobility of the design and get a lateral flowing movement across and also to indicate a series of distances and give recession'.[20]

In the same year Jones produced a pencil and monochrome body colour drawing, 'Merlin appears in the Form of a Child to Arthur Sleeping' (1930). This is one of several drawings and watercolours specifically based on the *Morte Darthur*, a work which Jones compared to the Latin Vulgate Bible 'in the sense that it can be called a true version, the *precise* originals of which are no longer available'. Early in his reign when the kingdom is still beset by rebels who question his legitimacy, Arthur follows a hart, an Otherworld agent that brings him in contact with the supernatural. After seeing the questing beast, the king sits drousing by a fountain, a faerie place. Merlin, disguised first as a child, then as an old man, tells him that his parents were Uther and Igraine, that he has incestuously conceived a child and that he will die honourably in battle. Jones' composition strongly resembles that of a Beardsley drawing based on the same chapter (I, 19), 'How King Arthur saw the Questing Beast and thereof had great marvel'.[21] In both, Arthur reclines on a rocky platform beside a stream. His legs are crossed and he supports himself in

---

[19] *Epoch and Artist*, p. 251.
[20] *Dai Greatcoat*, p. 138.
[21] While a student at Camberwell School of Art, 1909–14, Jones was introduced to the work of Sandys, Beardsley and other Pre-Raphaelites.

one case against the beast's body, in the other against the Puckish Merlin. He is surrounded by isolated images that create a particular ethos. Beardsley's are demonic – a dragon-like monster, a spider, a satyr, a water snake and a tree snake. Jones' are signs of Christ based on the medieval bestiary – a deer, leopard, unicorn, hound and lion. Paul Hill's suggestion that Arthur's pose derives from a 'Man of Sorrows' model is not inconsistent with the allegorical images.

David Jones was always concerned that there be a balance between the real and the symbolic, and between the literary content and the form – 'happiness comes when the forms assume significance with regard to this juxtaposition to each other'. He feared getting 'bogged down with a most complex "literary" and "literal" symbolism at times. Subject is *everything* in one sense and nothing in *another*.[22] Two watercolours, 'Guenever' (1940, Tate Gallery) and 'The Four Queenes' (1941, Tate Gallery) he thought 'successful and authentic' though not 'psychologically balanced'. 'Guenever' is an excellent example of modern art that functions in a medieval way through images that are both artifacts and symbols. In its literal-literary mode it illustrates a scene from the 'Knight of the Cart' adventure (*Morte Darthur*, XIX, 6). Launcelot arrives at Meleagant's castle to rescue the kidnapped Guenevere and her unarmed retinue. After finding a ladder and climbing to the bedroom window, the hero converses with the lady, telling her that he wishes to come in:

> 'wolde ye so, madame,' seyde sir Launcelot, 'wyth youre harte that I were with you?'
> 'Ye, truly,' seyde the quene.
> 'Than shall I prove my myght,' seyde sir Launcelot, 'for youre love.'

He then gains admittance by breaking the iron bars with his bare hands.

In the painting's foreground are the wounded knights. They represent a long line of war's victims: an effigy-like mailed Crusader with legs crossed to indicate death in battle; a Tommy with bayonet fixed to his rifle; an ancient Briton in his barrow; figures huddled in an air-raid shelter. At the centre of the picture plane the naked Guenevere voluptuously reclines. Naked except for his shield and knee cops, Launcelot hangs on the ladder. His position is that of the Christ on the crucifix above the Queen's head – hands open to display the stigmata, legs crossed, eyes closed, head dropping forward, side pierced. This is both Christ the Bridegroom of the exegetes' *Song of Songs*[23] and Christ the Redeemer. Now Guenevere's allegorical role can be recognised. The crown and seven stars on the bed's headboard, the roses and the burning candles are Marian images that combine with the *Song of Songs* allegory to denote the Church, Christ's Bride. The sexual act about to take place symbolises the sacrament of the mass for which the altar in the recess is prepared. The interpretation would seem blasphemous were it not for Jones' insistence that

---

[22] *Dai Greatcoat*, pp. 137–8.
[23] For particular parallels cf. ch. 1, vss. 13–16; ch. 2, vss. 8–10, 16–17; ch. 4, vss. 1–7.

what the artist lifts up must have a kind of transubstantiated actualness. Our images, not only our ideas, must be valid *now*. Obviously
there are almost infinite ways and modes by which this is achieved or
attempted.[24]

Actualness he achieves by crowding the space with tactile images – fire irons,
an iron soup pot with ladle, Launcelot's discarded sword, the dish and gnawed
bone of a sleeping dog, a cat and circling bats. The food and drink that have
satisfied the hungry creatures are anagogically the mass elements, symbols of
grace. The watercolour's predominant blue is the colour of both secular and
religious fidelity. Philip Lowery[25] describes Jones as 'a superlative "interjoiner"
who can bring many parts together to make *one*'. All the objects seem 'real, made,
used, craftsman's things'. The 'fragment technique' which Louis Bonnerot notes in
the writings[26] is equally evident in the art, though the tenuous lines and understated colours make determining form a difficult matter.

'Gwener' (1959), another watercolour of a long-haired naked woman reclining
on a bed, is based on Jones' identification of the Queen with Venus whom he
characterised as the goddess of fidelity. His letter to Valerie Wynne-Williams is
worth quoting in some detail to explain the iconography and to show how his
allusive mind worked:

> As you know Aphrodite rose from the sea and there is the association
> between the seafoam – born goddess and Mars the war god so there is
> a sea battle in which Gwener, Venus, Aphrodite (call her what you like)
> lies on what I suppose would be called in Welsh a Lleithig ... The wall
> of the ystafell is meant to resemble the usual form of Roman or classi-
> cal building, layers of stone between layers of tiles or brick [revealed]
> where the covering plaster was cracked or fallen away ... The gulls as
> they sweep in become doves as they approach the goddess, because
> the dove was one of the creatures sacred to her. As you know, Eros or
> Cupid was the son of the Goddess and he carried a bow that dis-
> charged arrows. I decided that his bow should be a cross-bow and his
> arrows would be bolts, hence the cross-bow left under the couch and
> the bolts left on the coverlet mixed up with the flowers, lilies of the
> valley, love lies bleeding, roses and what not.

He adds that Gwener's bandaged thigh alludes to her wounding at Troy, the cat is
an attribute of a Nordic goddess, and the high-heeled shoe comes from Lady
Llanover's watercolour studies of Welsh costume.

---

[24] *Epoch and Artist*, pp. 210–11. There was a precedent for this treatment in Eric Gill's
engraving for 'Nuptials of God', a prose poem published in *The Game* (1923). The Church,
symbolized by a naked woman, embraces Christ on the Cross. The accompanying lines
read, 'The Rood His marriage bed,/on which He doth enfold/His spouse naked'.
[25] *Agenda*, 11/4–12/1, 33.
[26] ibid. 76–98.

Yet another component of his goddess cluster is Olwen, the *Mabinogian* heroine whom he identifies with Mary in 'Y Cyfarchiad I Fair', 'The Greeting to Mary', ca. 1963. The watercolour contains representations of animals and birds that Culhwch must acquire before he can marry the Giant's daughter. His quest is an allegory of Christ's passion.

'The Four Queens find Launcelot Sleeping', the other wartime watercolour that pleased David Jones, is not obviously anagogic. Rather it reveals his interest in the possibilities of metamorphosis, in the use of a variable time point, and in the evocation of 'the particular genius of places, men, trees, animals'. The literary source is *Morte Darthur* VI, 3 where Launcelot falls asleep under an apple tree, a point of communication with the Celtic Otherworld. The four queens intend to bespell him and force him to choose one of them as a lover. The scene is washed with green, a fairy colour and a forest colour.[27] These ladies inhabit two states for they are queens in Arthur's courtly world and fées in the world of adventure. Launcelot also occupies two states, the mundane world where he falls asleep and the dream world where he thinks of Guenevere, symbolised by the sexual image of the swan. The apple tree has three levels of existence – the 'real', the faerie and the spiritual for with the props supporting its branches it recalls the Tree of Charity in William Langland's fourteenth century allegory, *Piers Plowman*.[28] Taken with the tall spear and its cross-decorated banner, it comprises an image cluster that implies connections with the Tree of Knowledge, the Tree of Life and the Tree of the Cross. Significantly, while this tree is loaded with ripe fruit, those in the background are bare of leaves.

Complexities of time are another facet of the watercolour. Jones approved the Tate Gallery's catalogue note:[29]

> The apple trees are associated with wire netting in the artist's mind, irrespective of the fact that there was no wire netting in the Middle Ages, while the recumbent figure of Launcelot reminds him of the bodies of soldiers on the battlefields of the 1914–18 war: Launcelot wears a German helmet but his feet rest on a dog, an association with mediaeval tomb sculpture.

The Romanesque chapel is both medieval and contemporary, an appropriate feature of an Arthurian setting and a recollection of the chapel of Capel-y-ffin, the place that suggested the hills' contours. The dolmens and the horse carved out of the chalk (as at Uffington) push back the time frame to the Iron Age. Jones'

---

[27] Exhibition catalogue #138, pp. 123–4.
[28] The props, representing the Trinity, are used to beat off the devil who would steal the apples. Jones refers to *Piers Plowman* as 'a glorious poem and no mistake' (letter to H.J.G., 15 February, 1957). It was one of the works he read as a young man (letter to H.J.G., 1 September, 1956). See *Dai Greatcoat*, pp. 171–173 and Colin Wilcockson, ed., *Letters to William Hayward* (London, 1979); pp. 64–65.
[29] Quoted in the Hill catalogue, p. 65.

conclusion to 'The Myth of Arthur', an essay written in 1940–42, casts light on his deliberate layering:

> The mythological deposits seem to say to us: God is wonderful in his masters of illusion, in the transmogrifications, in the heroes who sustain the folk and the land.
> The historical fragments perhaps say to us: God is wonderful in the Dux . . . in the defence of the province.
> The Romance authors say . . . God is wonderful in the achievements of feats, in lover and beloved . . .

How to relate aesthetic form to present time was a recurrent problem. In a letter to Harman Grisewood, August 24, 1947, Jones complains that the modern age is 'fundamentally alien to sign and symbol'. A candle or a wood fire is more aesthetic than a gas-fire or electric light bulb. Two 1932 watercolours attempt to synthesise myth and reality, with the titles providing clues. On the surface 'The Chapel Perilous' (Tate Gallery) is a landscape of Helen Sutherland's country place, Rock Hall in Northumbria. There was a beautiful garden going down to a lake, a wood beyond and a view of the Norman Church in the village of Rock. Bamburgh Castle, Launcelot's Joyous Garde, was nearby. That juxtaposition may have led the artist to imagine the church with its surrounding graveyard as the Perilous Chapel where Launcelot defied ghost knights, an earthquake and the fée Halowes in order to save a wounded knight (*Morte Darthur*, VI). 'The Queen's Dish' (1932) seems a straightforward still life with silver cup, a dish with an apple, and a fruit knife. Once we have become familiar with the sign language, we are compelled to read the images as allusions to the Fall and Redemption, to the Last Supper, and to the Mass.

David Jones likened the Grail Legends to a deep-rooted shrub cultivated, preserved and grafted by medieval romance writers. Jessie L. Weston, whose *From Ritual to Romance* he read enthusiastically in 1929, provided the mythological comprehensiveness that suited his vision. In the wood-engraving 'He Frees the Waters' (1931), he incorporates her explanation of the Lance and Cup symbols:

> They are sex symbols of immemorial antiquity . . . the Lance, or Spear, representing the Male, the Cup, or Vase, the Female reproductive energy. Found in juxtaposition, the Spear upright in the Vase . . . their signification is admitted by all familiar with 'Life' symbolism and they are absolutely in place as forming part of a ritual dealing with the processes of life and reproductive vitality.[30]

The woodcut depicts the legend that the unicorn purified poisoned water by plunging his horn into the pool so that other animals could drink safely. At the allegorical level the animal, who in the bestiary story was caught by a virgin and

---

[30] Weston, *op cit.* p. 75.

murdered by a hunter's spear, represents Christ. As the horn is plunged into the pool (the revitalising sexual act), the lance simultaneously connects the animal's wound with the chalice which stands on an altar cloth. Thus through complex iconographical references the erotic union of the fertility rite is transformed into a Crucifixion, an Atonement, and a celebration of the mass. Additional allusions to Christ are the rays of the Bethlehem star that fall on the unicorn's back; the second instrument of the Passion, the sponge on its stick; and the lopped tree resembling the Cross in the Evesham Psalter (British Library, MS Add. 44874, f. 6). Strong diagonals in the woodcut's composition emphasise the sense of a violent thrusting.

Almost the last of the watercolours is 'Trystan Ac Essyllt' (ca. 1962, National Museum of Wales, Cardiff). Mark's nephew and the Irish princess stand on the deck of the ship which carries them to Cornwall. Malory describes the particular moment:

> Than they loughe and made good chere and eyther dranke to other frely, and they thought never drynke that ever they dranke so swete nother so good to them. But by that drynke was in their bodyes they loved aythir other so well that never hir love departed, for well nother for woo.   (VIII, 24)

Jones explained, 'Essylt I saw as emerging triumphant, whereas Trystan, having drunk of the love potion which brings about the whole tragedy, realises what all this means'.[31] The preliminary study (ca. 1959–60) shows the knight's awareness of doom. But Essylt, too, seems extraordinarily vulnerable with her wind-tossed hair, bare shoulders, wrinkled forehead and bare feet placed uncomfortably close to the sword's sharp point. A letter of May 22, 1962, illuminates the effect Jones was aiming at:

> Chaps refer to the 'mystery' or 'subtlety' or 'illusiveness' or 'fragility' or 'waywardness' or 'complexity' or 'fancifulness' etc. etc. Well, Christ almighty! What else is there in a bunch of flowers or a tree or a landscape or a girl or a sky . . . one must somehow, if possible, capture *something* of these qualities if the thing is going to be any damn good.

Almost every image has been chosen for its relevance to details of character, plot, and setting. His desire for absolute accuracy, particularly regarding the ship and tackle, made the drawing 'the hardest thing I've tried to do'. Even the constellation Arcturus, the Bear, juxtaposed to the bear on the pennant, is correctly placed for St Bridget's Day, which recognised an early Irish Christian and a Celtic fertility goddess. Jones believed that 'the imagination takes off best from the flight deck of the known'. Yet he did not ignore entirely his 'Lesbian rule' – 'the rule adapts itself to the shape of the stone'. The ship's frame timbers are drawn outside

---

[31] British Council tape edited by Peter Orr, quoted by Hills, catalogue #141, p. 126.

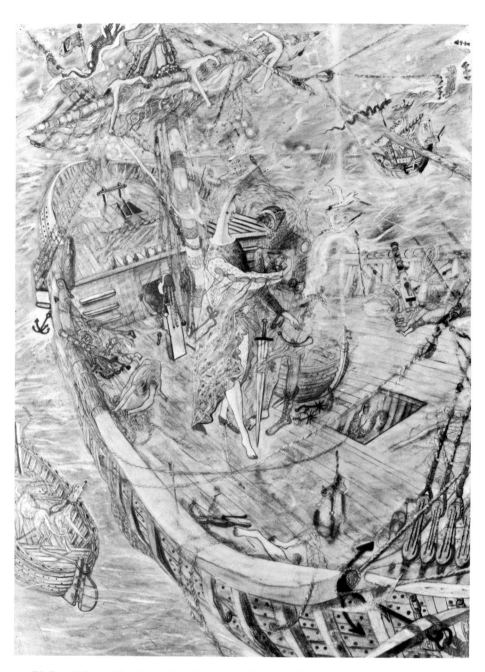

70. David Jones. Trystan ac Essyllt, watercolour, ca. 1962

the planks to create a rhythm of verticals that contrast with the lines of deck and quarterdeck.

Literalness combined with mystery may explain Malory's attraction. The medieval author provided a version of the Grail quest which was relevant to Jones' definition of art as a thing which 'shows forth' existing realities under another form. And the *Morte* conveyed with data that were 'accurate, experiential and contactual' the tragedy of war which Jones had experienced. The contemporary world frighteningly resembled Arthur's fallen kingdom where 'the *status quo* is not restored, the wrongs go unrighted, the aggressed are aggressed to extinction, the "noble fellowship" is dissolved for ever, no recovery at all'.[32]

Kathleen Raine's description of David Jones as 'the recorder of a new Dark Age' aptly applies to another modern artist, Anselm Kiefer.[33] Born in 1945, he grew up amid the physical and psychological devastation which marked Germany's defeat in World War II. How to deal as an artist and a German with 'the terror of history' and particularly with the Nazi experience was his central concern. Myth provides one mode of synthesising the Teutonic people's heroic past and the shamefully unheroic present. In Kiefer's drawings and paintings the wasteland is a recurrent landscape type, a German 'scorched earth' that is literal, moral and spiritual. Black clods, hovering fires, and infernal smoke ('Maikäfer flieg' ['Cockchafer Fly'], 1974), a ravaged forest ('Glaube, Hoffnung, Liebe' ['Faith, Hope, Love'], 1976), a wintery field where real sand is an ingredient of the painting's material ('Wege: märkischer Sand' ['Ways: March Sand'], 1980) are unsettling reminders of human suffering and cultural deprivation.

Another kind of wasteland appears in a series of paintings dated 1973 – an attic of lumber and beams empty except for a significant object. The attic is real in that it is the room in his home (an old schoolhouse) that Kiefer used as his studio. It is a polysemous space evoking ambiguous associations. The yellowish wood with its black grain marks not only the tree's death but also the evolution over centuries of natural forms, a process which parallels the evolution of human institutions. The stalwart beams are reminders of the Teutonic forests where gods and heroes tested and were tested. They are symbols of ancient German virtues – strength, endurance, reliability, respect for order. They also are death images, their gallow-tree shapes holding associations of murder and suicide. The beams and

---

[32] *Epoch and Artist*, p. 258.
[33] On the artist and his work see Bazon Brock, 'The End of the Avant-Garde? And so the End of Tradition: Notes on the Present "Kulturkampf" in West Germany', *Artforum* 19/10 (Summer, 1981), 62–74; Michael Compton, *New Art at the Tate Gallery* (London, 1983), pp. 20–29; Jürgen Harten, *Anselm Kiefer*, catalogue of the exhibition at the Städtische Kunsthalle, Düsseldorf, 24 March – 5 May, 1984 (in collaboration with the Musée d'Art Moderne de la Ville de Paris); Mark Rosenthal, *Anselm Kiefer*, catalogue of an exhibition at the Art Institute of Chicago, 5 December, 1987 – 31 January, 1988, and the Philadelphia Museum of Art, 17 October, 1988 – 3 January, 1989 (Chicago and Philadelphia, 1987). On modern German artists including Kiefer see Christos M. Joachimides, Norman Rosenthal, Wieland Schmied, eds, *German Art in the 20th Century: Painting and Sculpture 1905–1985*, catalogue of an exhibition at the Royal Academy of Arts, London, 11 October – 22 December, 1985 (Munich and London, 1985).

floorboards are not dusty or decaying. The attic, we may imagine, has been a room in the House of German Art which has held the state-approved junk of the Nazi era, raising it high above the 'Degenerate Art' of Post-Impressionists, Marxists and Jews.[34] Now the space has been cleared, scrubbed and purified, like Odysseus' hall after the slaughter of the suitors.

Into the empty space the artist can introduce images infused with power and magic. Woden's great sword Nothung appears ('Notung', 1973). The fires of the Trinity burn on three chairs without consuming them ('Vater, Sohn, heiliger Geist', 1973). The serpent of Wisdom joins the Trinity ('Quaternität', 1973). The attic is a wasteland pregnant with the possibility of restoration.

Four paintings of 1973 are entitled 'Parsifal'. In each a particular artifact – two ancient, two modern – is set in a varying representation of the attic space that symbolises the mind-shift effected by successive images. Each contains isolated words or quotations, which may seem nothing more than patterning unless one recognises the literary context. The words are the device that sets up a dialogue between the heroic past and the empty present. Rather than introducing people into his space, Kiefer relies on the viewer to recall a whole range of events in which the named characters participated. Thus the viewer must take responsibility for interpretation.

In 'Parsifal I' (Tate Gallery; 127⅝ in x 86½ in; oil on paper laid on canvas) a crib is set before a single window which admits a frosty blue light. Falling across the bed and nearby boards, it contrasts with the dark shadows which dominate the rest of the set. To the right is the word 'Herzeleide'. The name of Parsifal's mother spurs an identification of the crib with Parsifal, the Dümmlingkind raised in the wilderness to isolate him from the chivalric world that had killed his father. The wooden attic, darkly secure, represents the primitive forest retreat which, nevertheless, the light of chivalry penetrates. Parsifal abandons his mother to fulfill his destiny but not without enduring the guilt of having caused her death.

'Herzeleide' (1979), a watercolour and charcoal painting, provides further evidence as to her significance. Here she is a country woman in modern dress, presented in profile as she looks into a mirror shaped like a palette. A form often imposed on other images, the palette is Kiefer's personal symbol for art's function. Herzeleide, then, is a nurturing creator, an earth-mother, white goddess type comparable to David Jones' Guenevere, Venus and Virgin Mary. In 'Parsifal I' she is both creator and victim, a metaphor, perhaps, for Kiefer himself.

The largest 'Parsifal' for the Tate gallery triptych (117¾ in x 167⅝ in, oil and blood on paper laid on canvas) shows a broken and bloody spear thrust into the floorboards' swirling grain. Unnaturally lighted by a distant window, it is confined between diagonal beams which support the roof. This is the most densely annotated scene. At the upper centre are written the words 'Gamuret' (Parsifal's father) and 'Fal parsi', a broken form of the hero's name that denotes his original failure at the Grail castle. To the right of centre are the names of the suffering Grail Kings, the wounded Amfortas and his aged grandfather Titurel, whom the Grail

---

[34] See Henry Grosshans, *Hitler and the Artists* (New York and London, 1983).

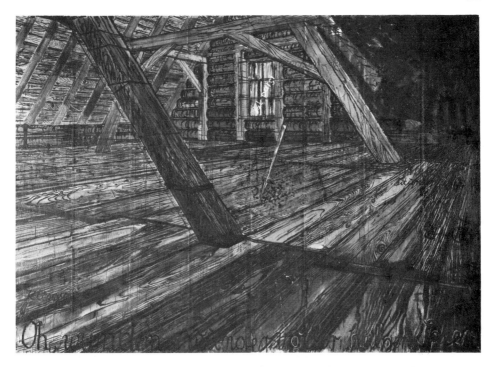

71. Anselm Kiefer. Parsifal, oil and blood on canvas, 1973

keeps alive. At a lower level the cast of characters is completed by 'Kundry', the cursed temptress and 'Klingsor', the equally suffering magician who inflicted the Dolorous Blow, punishment for Amfortas' sin. Along the lower edge is a quotation from Wagner's 'Parsifal' – 'oh wunden-wundervoller heiliger Speer' ('O lance of wounds and wonder'). The bleeding spear (real blood is one of the painter's ingredients) is both the lance of Longinus which pierced Christ's side and the Grail relic which Amfortas lost and with which he was wounded. If Parsifal can recover it, it will wonderfully heal and release the Maimed King and Titurel, restore the Wasteland and effect Kundry's salvation. In the opera Parsifal imagines that he hears Christ calling, 'Erlöse, rette mich/aus schuldbefleckten Händen!' ('Redeem, rescue me from guilt-defiled hands!').

Corresponding to the crib painting in size is a third 'Parsifal' (Tate Gallery; 127⅝ in x 86½ in; oil and blood on paper laid on canvas). Here the serpentine swirls of the floorboards are pierced by two swords, streaked red with the real blood that drips from the superscribed names, 'Parsifal' and 'ither'. The latter, demeaned by the use of a small rather than a capital letter, is the Red Knight whom the hero slays at the beginning of his quest and whose armour he wears. The clear window's light falls on Parsifal's weapon, a sign that it is, like the swords of Arthur, Galahad and Woden, imbued with mythic power. In an interview (December, 1986), Kiefer asserted that when Germany is in trouble, she looks for a hero to find the magic sword. The painting implies that Germany can be revitalised by Parsifal's sword (the artist's redemptive tool) but not by the bullying Ither's weapon.

The fourth 'Parsifal' (Kunsthaus, Zürich, 118 in x 210 in) provides the most positive image of redemption. This Holy Grail is not a splendid jewelled goblet on an altar but a humble enamel washbasin set on a stool. For the first time the attic set is symmetrical. The beams seem the pillars of a cathedral, the uprights behind the basin a reredos, the floor's diagonals an aisle. Above the Grail, which is filled with blood, are lines from the opera's finale:

> Höchsten Heiles Wunder!
> Erlösung dem Erlöser!

> (Miracle of the highest salvation! Redemption to the redeemer!)

Amfortas' name in the left foreground associates him with the act of redemption.

When Kiefer's paintings were exhibited at the Venice Biennale (1980), the German critics scathingly condemned his promotion of an 'obsolete' mythology. Bazon Brock suggests that German suspicion of the avant-garde results from a national inability to accept the use of myth as a device for social criticism. Yet if one understands the myth, one realises that the 'Parsifals' not only acknowledge violence but also offer a glimmer of hope.

An alternative to Kiefer's magic realism was the escapist fantasy that developed in the sixties 'to resolve an insecurity through what we call the dream or fantasy level of the mind', as Christopher Booker puts it.[35] One literary focus for fantasy, a genre that demands the intrusion of the marvellous, was the Arthurian material. Except in film, the visual arts were far less inventive and prolific than were the forms of fiction.[36] James Houston, a Canadian author, artist and former civil servant, designed an 'Excalibur' for Steuben Glass of New York. It consists of a cut crystal stone with a sterling silver sword blade and a hilt of 18 karat gold. Commissioned by the British Branch of the International Arthurian Society, the Royal Worcester Manufactory created in 1979 a collection of six porcelain plates featuring James Marsh's designs. The shape of the plate, 23 cm in diameter, combined with clean lines and bright colours, suggests roundels in fifteenth century manuscripts. The Grail knights are carried to Sarras and the King to Avalon in high-pooped sailing vessels. Merlin, his bare legs humiliatingly exposed, is bespelled beneath an apple tree. The feasters who turn their gaze on Galahad sit at a Winchester Round Table. Launcelot and Meleagant joust in an Italian landscape where a stream meanders from castle to horizon. In a flowery glade, watched by a deer and bluebirds Tristan and Isolde recline, separated by the sword. To celebrate

---

[35] Christopher Booker, *The Neophiliacs, a study of the revolution in English life in the Fifties and Sixties* (London, 1969), p. 57. On fantasy and the desire to be 'carried away' see pp. 57–80.
[36] See Raymond H. Thompson, *The Return from Avalon; a Study of the Arthurian Legend in Modern Fiction* (Westpoint, Conn. and London, 1985).

the quincentenary of Caxton's Malory, the British Post Office issued stamps designed by Yvonne Gilbert. Merlin in the guise of a pilgrim whispers into the ear of King Arthur, who looks like Peter O'Toole (17 pence). A strong-faced Lady of the Lake stands thigh deep in reedy water (22 pence). Launcelot rides through the forest with Guenevere leaning on his shoulder (31 pence). And Galahad prays, illuminated by divine radiance (34 pence).

The only living Arthurian painter who can be called prolific is Harold Hitchcock (1914–). As a conscientious objector, he spent World War II with a bomb disposal unit atached to the Royal Engineers. Painting provided an escape both from his surroundings and his spiritual malaise. What is unusual about his works is that they are produced under the impetus of pictorial automatism. Ian Williamson describes the process:

> Without preliminary drawing or sketches, and frequently with his eyes closed, the artist submits himself to the inner feeling, allowing his vision to emerge . . . the hand is only an instrument used to produce a sense of visual splendor – a true metamorphosis of feeling into medieval fantasy.[37]

The hero's (i.e. painter's) journey into the subconscious dreamland represents, in Joseph Campbell's words, 'a retreat from the desperation of the waste land to the peace of the everlasting realm that is within'.[38] The Jungian archetypes of 'personalized myth' that appear in the paintings include white birds, white horses, deer, sailing ships, bright flowers, angels and knights set in a golden age landscape of towering elms, clear water, and pristine classical buildings. Arthur's England is one of the peaceable kingdoms of Hitchcock's subconscious,[39] an earthly paradise firmly interposed between the artist and the external world.

Gareth's perception of the city, as Tennyson describes it, seems to have inspired 'Camelot' (1969):

> Far off they saw the silver-misty morn
> Rolling her smoke about the royal mount,
> That rose between the forest and the field,
> At times the summit of the high city flash'd;
> At times the spires and turrets half-way down
> Prick'd thro' the mist
>
> ('Gareth and Lynette', ll. 186–191)

The canvas is largely devoted to a Turneresque dissolving of sunlight and mist. Gothic arches merge into trees and air. Bands of forest rise diagonally beside a

---

[37] Ian Williamson, *Harold Hitchcock: A Romantic Symbol in Surrealism* (New York, 1982), p. 57.

[38] Joseph Campbell, *The Hero with a Thousand Faces* (Cleveland and New York, 1956 [1949]), especially 'Myth and Dream', pp. 3–24.

[39] On the influence of Theosophy and Subud, see Williamson, pp. 44–52.

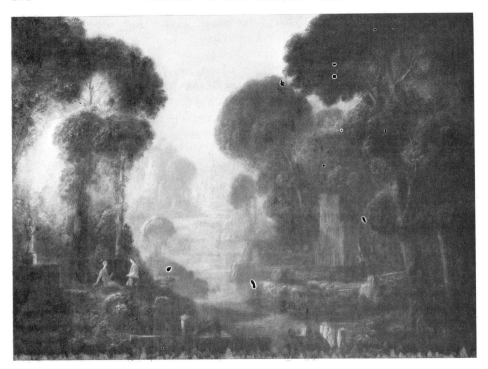

72. Harold Hitchcock, *The Isle of Merlin*, (Christopher Wood Gallery)

cone of colours – gold, bronze, green and azure. Shadowy people stand on the
shore looking towards great ships with amber sails. On the far right a damsel
guides the hero on his white horse through the flowery forest. Read archetypally,
the ships and knight-errant represent the transcendent journey while Camelot is
the achieved goal. In 'Arthur and Guinevere' (1971) a slender dark-haired couple
stand serenely outside a Gothic church. Arthur holds a lance, a phallic symbol.
Elms of disproportionate height frame a Claudian landscape of Roman arches,
pastures and a white horse suffused in a theatrically blue light. A Jungian reading
is encouraged by the sunlit earth altar between the portico and the elm tree's
roots. It symbolises the self to which the ego must submit for complete realisation.

'Arthur and Guenevere at Avalon' (1971) repeats the stage set, which defies
historical specificity by combining a Tower of Pisa, Corinthian pillars, Romanesque arches and Gothic stained glass. The royal pair is dwarfed by their enclosing arch. Sailing ships, exotic red and blue flowers, an anchor, and spear-like
fenceposts are infused at the extremeties in magenta warmth that contrasts with
the centre's cool light. A mandorla indicates that the King and Queen enjoy a state
of perfection. 'The Coronation of Arthur' (1984, Christopher Wood Gallery), unusually emphasises the human element. The oil presents two states of existence.
The mundane life of rural England is expressed through a peasant who pushes a
wooden cart, a woman holding a sheaf, a child catching a bird, and a farmhouse.

Hitchcock associates the spiritual life of Arthur's kingdom with knights, angels playing lutes, and the cross-like Excalibur on which the King takes his coronation oath.

'Medieval Glastonbury' (1985, Christopher Wood Gallery) introduces images that connect the place with Joseph of Arimathea and the Grail, a vessel that Hitchcock associated with Christianity and alchemy. White and red blooms, a red cross and monastic architecture link setting and character. An aureoled Grail Maiden with roses welcomes Galahad (designated by a hovering dove). A Madonna in Marian blue, peasants with baskets of fruit (symbols of fertility rites), the Loathly Lady and a figure holding the lance of Longinus complete the cast. Other paintings, too, rely on the mystique of place name to evoke appropriate associations. 'The Road to Avalon' (1971), 'The Isle of Merlin' (1983), 'The Isle of Avalon' and 'Tintagel' (1984) repeat the formula of Roman arches, mounted knights, companionable couples, sailing ships and *locus amoenus* landscapes.

In Hitchcock's construct the passionless humans play a subordinate role to nature. Plants he considers the most important earthly forms for they express

> not only the beauty but also the thoughts of God's world, with no intent of their own and without deviation. Trees in particular were mysterious and seemed to me direct embodiments of the incomprehensible meaning of life.[40]

Light, a symbol of the spiritual, is the other notable aspect of the art. Like Rossetti and Millais, Hitchcock achieves brilliance by painting on a white ground and like Turner, he creates paradisal light with dissolving forms and refraction. But his efforts at sublimity cannot succeed because his scenes lack a necessary strain of terror. No encroaching time decays his buildings, no frost will ever kill his blossoms nor any violent passion disturb his graceful people.

Of the many artists, known and anonymous, whose works we have noticed in the course of this study, none was more sensitive about critical intrusions than David Jones. He complained to Harman Grisewood that

> the whole business of critics endlessly nosing around for 'influences' is a bore and virtually useless and deceptive, and gives quite a false impression of how an artist works. Trying to rack my brain for 'influences' makes me more and more convinced of this. It's more the whole conditioning 'civilizational' situation into which one was born that determines the 'form'.

Through nine centuries Arthurian art has expressed the tastes and beliefs, the fears and aspirations, both public and private, of individual artists who belong to differing societies. As 'conditioning "civilizational" situations' demand appropriate myths, King Arthur perpetually returns and finds a kingdom waiting.

[40] *ibid.*, p. 73

Selected Bibliography

Abbey, Edwin Austin. *The Quest of the Holy Grail: a series of paintings done for the Public Library of the City of Boston.* New York, 1895.

Adams, Henry. *The Education of Henry Adams.* New York, 1931 [1918].

Aho, Gary. 'Turn of the Century American Periodicals and William Morris', *William Morris Society Newsletter* (Jan., 1988), 5–10.

Alexander, J.J.G. *The Decorated Letter.* London, 1978.

———. *Italian Renaissance Illumination.* New York, 1977.

Alford, Henry. 'The Idylls of the King', *The Contemporary Review* XIII (Jan., 1870), 104–25.

Allingham, H. and D. Radford, eds. *William Allingham, A Diary.* Harmondsworth, 1985 [1907].

Altick, Richard D. *Paintings from Books: Art and Literature in Britain 1760–1900.* Columbus, Ohio, 1985.

Anderson, M.D. *The Choir Stalls of Lincoln Minster.* Lincoln, 1967.

———. *The Medieval Carver.* Cambridge, Eng., 1935.

Anglo, S. 'The British History in Early Tudor Propaganda', *Rylands Library Bulletin* 44 (1961–2), 17–48.

———. *Spectacle, Pageantry, and Early Tudor Policy.* Oxford, 1969.

Appelbaum, Stanley, trans. *The Triumph of Maximilian I.* New York, 1964.

Armstrong, C.A.J. 'The Golden Age of Burgundy: dukes that outdid kings', *The Courts of Europe: Politics, Patronage and Royalty, 1400–1800,* ed. A.G. Dickens. London, 1977.

'The Arras Tapestries at Stanmore Hall', *Studio* 15 (1899), 98–104.

Ashe, Geoffrey. *The Discovery of King Arthur.* New York, 1985.

———, ed. *The Quest for Arthur's Britain.* London, 1968.

Auerbach, Erich. 'The Knight Sets Forth', *Mimesis, the Representation of Reality in Western Literature,* trans. Willard R. Trask. Princeton, 1953.

Avril, F., M-T. Gousset, C. Rabel. *Manuscrits enluminés d'origine italienne, II, XIIIe siècle.* Paris, 1984.

Backhouse, Janet. *The Illuminated Manuscript.* Oxford, 1979.

———. 'Manuscript Sources for the History of Mediaeval Costume', *Costume, the Journal of the Costume Society* 2 (1968), 9–14.

Backhouse, Janet, Mirjam Foot and John Barr, eds. *William Caxton: An Exhibition to Commemorate the Quincentenary of the Introduction of Printing into England.* London, 1976.

Balston, Thomas. *The Wood-Engravings of Robert Gibbings.* London, 1949.

Banham, Joanna and Jennifer Harris, eds. *William Morris and the Middle Ages: A collection of essays together with a catalogue of works exhibited at the Whitworth Art Gallery.* Manchester, 1984.

Barber, John. *The Story of Oakham School.* Wyndmondham, 1983.

Barber, Richard. *King Arthur, Hero and Legend.* Woodbridge, 1986.

———. 'Was Mordred Buried at Glastonbury? An Arthurian Tradition at Glastonbury in the Middle Ages', *Arthurian Literature IV,* ed. Richard Barber. Cambridge, Eng., 1985.

Bartram, Michael. *Pre-Raphaelite Photography.* Catalogue of an exhibition organised by the British Council. London, 1983.

Bates, Cadwallader John. *The Border Holds of Northumberland.* Newcastle-upon-Tyne, 1891.

Baumgartner, Emmanuèle. 'La couronne et le cercle: Arthur et la Table Ronde dans les manuscrits du Lancelot-Graal', *Texte et Image, Actes du Colloque international de Chantilly.* Paris, 1984.

Beattie, Susan. *The New Sculpture*. New Haven and London, 1983.

Beckett, Lucy. *Richard Wagner: Parsifal*. Cambridge, Eng., 1981.

Bennett, B.T.N. *The Choir Stalls of Chester Cathedral*. Chester, n.d.

Bennett, H.S. *The Pastons and their England*. Cambridge, Eng., 1979 [1932].

Bennett, J.A.W., ed. *Essays on Malory*. Oxford, 1963.

Benson, Larry D. *Malory's Morte Darthur*. Cambridge, Mass., 1976.

Benziger, Karl J. *Studien zur Deutschen Kunstgeschichte: Parzival in die Deutschen Handschriften illustration des Mittelalters*. Strassburg, 1914.

Bernier, Olivier. 'Ludwig's Castles: Forms of Fantasy', *The New York Times*, April 6, 1986, xx, 9, 27.

Bertrand, Gérard. *L'illustration de la poésie à l'époque du cubisme 1909–1914: Derain, Dufy, Picasso*. Paris, 1971.

Biddle, Martin and Beatrice Clayre. *Winchester Castle and the Great Hall*. Winchester, 1983.

Bise, Gabriel. *Tristan and Isolde from a manuscript of 'The Romance of Tristan' (15th century)*, with an introduction by Dagmar Thoss. Fribourg-Genève, 1978.

Blake, N.F. *Caxton: England's First Publisher*. London, 1976.

Blamires, David. *David Jones, artist and writer*. Manchester, 1971.

Bland, David. *A History of Book Illustration*. London, 1969.

Blau, Eva. *Ruskinian Gothic: The Architecture of Deane and Woodward 1845–1861*. Princeton, 1982.

Blunt, Wilfred. *The Dream King: Ludwig II of Bavaria with a chapter on Ludwig and the Arts by Dr. Michael Petzet*. London, 1984.

———. *'England's Michelangelo': a biography of George Frederic Watts*. London, 1975.

Boase, T.S.R. 'The Decoration of the New Palace of Westminster, 1841–1863', *Journal of the Warburg and Courtauld Institutes* 17 (1954), 319–58.

Bond, F. *Wood-carvings in English Churches: (I) Misericords*. Oxford, 1910.

Bond, Maurice. *Works of Art in the House of Lords*. London, 1980.

Bonnard, C. *Costumes des XIIIe, XIVe, et XVe siècles extraits des monuments les plus authentiques de peinture et de sculpture (dessins engravés par Paul Mercuri) avec un texte historique et descriptif*. 2 vols. Paris, 1829–30.

Braby, Dorothea. *The Way of Wood Engraving*. London and New York, 1953.

Bradley, J. W. *A Dictionary of miniaturists, illuminators, calligraphers and copyists with reference to their works, and notice of their patrons*. 3 vols. London, 1887–1889.

Bradshaw, Percy. *W. Russell Flint. 'The Art of the Illustrator'* series. London, 1918.

Braghirolli, W., P. Meyer and G. Paris. 'Inventaire des manuscrits en langue française possédés par Francesco Gonzaga, Ier capitaine de Mantoue, mort en 1407', *Romania* 9 (1880), 497–514.

The Brandywine Heritage: Howard Pyle, N.C. Wyeth, Andrew Wyeth, James Wyeth. Catalogue of an exhibition at the Brandywine River Museum, Chadds Ford, Penn., 1971 with a foreword by Richard McLanathan.

Branner, Robert. *Manuscript Painting in Paris during the Reign of Saint Louis: A Study of Styles*. Berkeley, Los Angeles and London, 1977.

Brault, Gerard. *Early Blazon: Heraldic Terminology in the Twelfth and Thirteenth Centuries with Special Reference to Arthurian Literature*. Oxford, 1972.

———. 'Le coffret de Vannes et la légende de Tristan au XIIe siècle', *Mélanges offerts à Rita Le Jeune*. 2 vols. Gembloux, 1969.

Brinkley, Roberta F. *Arthurian Legend in the Seventeenth Century*. Baltimore and London, 1932.

Brock, Bazon. 'The End of the Avant-Garde? And so the End of Tradition: Notes on the Present "Kulturkampf" in West Germany', *Artforum* 19/10 (1981), 62–74.

Bromwich, Rachel. 'Celtic Elements in Arthurian Romance: a General Survey', *The Legend of Arthur in the Middle Ages*, ed. P.B. Grout, R.A. Lodge, C.E. Pickford and E.K.C. Varty. Cambridge, Eng., 1983.

Brun, Robert. *Le Livre français illustré de la Renaissance: étude suivie du catalogue des principaux livres à figures du XVIe siècle*. Paris, 1969.

Buchthal, Hugo. *Historia Troiana: Studies in the History of Medieval Secular Illustration.* London and Leiden, 1971.

Buckley, Jerome H. *Tennyson, the Growth of a Poet.* Cambridge, Mass., 1960.

Burd, V.A., ed. *The Winnington Letters of John Ruskin.* Cambridge, Mass. and London, 1969.

Burne-Jones, Georgiana. *Memorials of Edward Burne-Jones.* 2 vols. London, 1904.

Burne-Jones: the paintings, graphic and decorative work of Sir Edward Burne-Jones 1833–98. Catalogue of an Arts Council of Great Britain Exhibition. London, 1975.

Burns, E. Jane. *Arthurian Fiction: Re-reading the Vulgate Cycle.* Columbus, 1985.

Callen, Anthea. *Angel in the Studio: Women in the Arts and Crafts Movement 1870–1914.* London, 1979.

Campbell, Nancie, ed. *Tennyson and Lincoln: A Catalogue of the Collections in the Research Centre.* 2 vols. Lincoln, 1971.

Carley, James P. 'Glastonbury and the Grail Legend', *Avalon to Camelot* I/3 (1984), 4–8.

Cartellieri, Otto. *Am Hofe der Herzöge von Burgund.* Basle, 1926. *The Court of Burgundy: Studies in the History of Civilization.* London and New York, 1929.

Chambers, E.K. *Arthur of Britain: the Story of King Arthur in History and Legend.* London, 1927.

Chandler, Alice. *A Dream of Order: the Medieval Ideal in Nineteenth-Century English Literature.* Lincoln, Nebr., 1970.

Christian, John. 'Early German Sources for Pre-Raphaelite Designs', *Art Quarterly* 36/1–2 (1973), 56–83.

———. *The Oxford Union Murals.* Chicago, 1981.

———. *Burne-Jones.* Catalogue of an exhibition at the Hayward Gallery, London, 1975–6, Southampton Art Gallery and City Museum and Art Gallery, Birmingham, London, 1975.

Clark, Kenneth. *The Gothic Revival: an Essay in the History of Taste.* London, 1974 [1928].

Clarkson, George A. 'A Series of Paintings in Amberley Castle', *The Archaeological Journal* 22 (1865), 65–68.

Cleverdon, Douglas. *The Engravings of David Jones: A Survey.* London, 1981.

Cline, Ruth. 'The Influence of Romances on Tournaments of the Middle Ages', *Speculum* 20 (1945), 204–11.

Cockshaw, Pierre. 'Mentions d'auteurs, de copistes, d'enlumineurs et de libraires dans les comptes généraux de l'état Bourguignon (1384–1419)', *Scriptorium: Revue internationale des études relatives aux manuscrits* 23 (1969), 122–144.

Colby, Averil. *Quilting.* London, 1972.

Compton, Michael. *New Art at the Tate Gallery.* London, 1983.

Connick, Charles. *Adventures in Light and Color.* New York, 1937.

Coombs, James H., Anne M. Scott, George P. Landow, Arnold A. Sanders. *A Pre-Raphaelite Friendship: The Correspondence of William Holman Hunt and John Lucas Tupper.* Ann Arbor, 1986.

Cormack, Peter. *Women Stained Glass Artists of the Arts and Crafts Movement.* Catalogue of an exhibition held at the William Morris Gallery. London, 1985.

Cram, Ralph Adams. *Architecture in its Relation to Civilization.* Boston, 1918.

———. *My Life in Architecture.* Boston, 1936.

Crane, Walter. *An Artist's Reminiscences.* London, 1907.

———. *Ideals in Art: Papers theoretical, practical, critical.* London, 1905.

———. *Of the Decorative Illustration of Books Old and New.* London, 1984 [1896].

———. *William Morris to Whistler: Papers and Addresses on Art and Craft and Commonwealth.* London, 1911.

Croft-Murray, Edward. *Decorative Paintings in England 1532–1837.* 2 vols. London, 1962.

Crook, J. Mordaunt. *William Burges and the High Victorian Dream.* Chicago, 1981.

Cross, Tom Peete. *Motif-Index of Early Irish Literature.* Bloomington, 1939.

Cross, Tom Peete and W.A. Nitze. *Lancelot and Guenevere.* Chicago, 1930.

Cullingham, G.B. *The Royal Windsor Tapestry Manufactory 1876–1890: an Illustrated Handlist of Tapestries Woven at the Old Windsor Works.* Windsor, 1979.

D'Ancona, P. *La Miniature italienne du Xe au XVIe siècle.* Paris and Brussels, 1925.

Dean, Christopher. *Arthur of England: English Attitudes to King Arthur and the Knights of the Round Table in the Middle Ages and the Renaissance.* Toronto, 1987.

de Bruyne, Edgar. *Etudes d'esthétique médiévale.* 3 vols. Genève, 1975.

Degenhart, B. and A. Schmitt. 'Frühe angiovische Buchkunst in Neapel: Die Illustrierung französischer Unterhaltungsprosa in neapolitanischen Scriptorien zwischen 1290 und 1320', *Festschrift Wolfgang Braunfels.* Tübingen, 1978.

Delaissé, L.M.J. *A Century of Dutch Manuscript Illumination.* Berkeley and Los Angeles, 1968.

Delisle, Leopold. *Recherches sur la librairie de Charles V.* 2 vols. Paris, 1902.

Denomy, Alexander J. 'Courtly Love and Courtliness', *Speculum* 27 (1953), 44–63.

de Portal, Frederic. *Des couleurs symboliques dans l'antiquité, le moyen age et les temps modernes.* Paris, 1857.

Deschamps, P. 'La légende arthurienne à la Cathédrale de Modène et l'école lombarde de sculpture romane', *Monuments Piot,* 28 (1925–26).

Deschamps, Paul and Marc Thibout. *La Peinture murale en France au debut de l'époque gothique de Philippe-Auguste à la fin du règne de Charles V (1180–1380).* Paris, 1963.

Dickason, David Howard. *The Daring Young Men: the story of the American Pre- Raphaelites.* Bloomington, 1953.

Ditmas, E.M.R. 'The Cult of Arthurian Relics', *Folklore* 85/2 (1966), 91–104.

Dogaer, Georges. *Flemish Miniature Painting in the 15th and 16th Centuries.* Amsterdam, 1987.

Dooley, Patricia. 'Romance and Realism: Pyle's Illustrations for Children', *The Children's Literature Association Quarterly* 8/2 (1983).

Doughty, Oswald and J. R. Wahl, eds. *Letters of Dante Gabriel Rossetti.* 4 vols. Oxford, 1965–67.

Doutrepont, G. *La Litterature française à la cour des ducs de Bourgogne.* Paris, 1909.

Duncan, Alastair. *Tiffany Windows.* New York, 1980.

Dupin, Henri. *La Courtoisie au moyen age (d' après les textes du XIIe et du XIIIe siècle).* Paris, 1906.

Dyce, James Stirling. *Life, Correspondence and Writings of William Dyce. R.A., 1806–1864, Painter, Musician and Schooler (sic); unpublished manuscript in the Department of Manuscripts, Aberdeen Art Gallery, Aberdeen.*

Eames, Elizabeth. *Catalogue of Mediaeval Lead-glazed Earthenware Tiles in the Department of Mediaeval and Later Antiquities, British Museum.* Vol. 1. London, 1980.

———. *English Medieval Tiles.* London, 1985.

Eastlake, Charles L. *A History of the Gothic Revival,* ed. J. Mordaunt Crook. Leicester, 1970 [1872].

Ede, H.S. 'The Visual Art of David Jones'. *Agenda, David Jones Special Issue* 5/1–3 (1967), 153–58.

Eggers, J. Phillip. *King Arthur's Laureate: A Study of Tennyson's 'Idylls of the King'.* New York, 1971.

Elzea, Rowland. *Howard Pyle.* New York, 1975.

Empson, Patience, ed. *The Wood Engravings of Robert Gibbings.* London, 1959.

Entwistle, William J. *The Arthurian Legend in the Literature of the Spanish Peninsula.* New York, 1975.

Evans, Joan. *Art in Medieval France 987–1498.* Oxford, 1948.

Evans, Joan, ed. *The Flowering of the Middle Ages.* London, 1966.

Farquhar, James Douglas. *Creation and Imitation: the Work of a Fifteenth Century Manuscript Illustrator.* Fort Lauderdale, 1976.

Faulkner, Peter, ed. *William Morris, the Critical Heritage.* London, 1973.

Fenollosa, Ernest F. *Mural Painting in the Boston Public Library.* Boston, 1896.

Ferguson, Arthur B. *The Chivalric Tradition in Renaissance England.* Washington, London and Toronto, 1986.

————. *The Indian Summer of English Chivalry: Studies in the Decline and Transformation of Chivalric Idealism*. Durham, N.C., 1960.

Fitzgerald, Penelope. *Edward Burne-Jones, a Biography*. London, 1975.

Fletcher, R.H. *The Arthurian Material in the Chronicles*. 2nd ed. New York, 1966.

Foçillon, Henri. *The Art of the West in the Middle Ages, II Gothic Art*, trans. Donald King, ed. Jean Bony, London and New York, 1963.

Forrer, Robert. 'Tristan et Yseult sur un coffret inédit du XIIe siècle', *Cahiers d' Archeologie et d'Histoire d'Alsace*. Strasbourg, 1933, 137–179.

Fouquet, Doris. *Wort und Bild in der mittelalterlichen Tristantradition*. Berlin, 1971.

Frankl, Paul. *The Gothic: Literary Sources and Interpretations through Eight Centuries*. Princeton, 1960.

Franklin, Colin. *The Private Presses*. London, 1969.

Frappier, Jean. *Amour Courtois et Table Ronde*. Genève, 1973.

————. *Chretien de Troyes: the Man and his Work*, trans. Raymond J. Cormier. Athens, Ohio, 1982.

————. *Etude sur la Mort le Roi Artu*. Paris, 1961.

————. 'Le Graal et la chevalerie', *Romania* 75 (1954), 165–210.

————. 'The Vulgate Cycle', *Arthurian Literature in the Middle Ages*, ed. R.S. Loomis. London, 1959.

Fraser, John. *America and the Patterns of Chivalry*. Cambridge, Eng., 1982.

Fredeman, William E. *Pre-Raphaelitism: a bibliocritical study*. Cambridge, Mass., 1965.

Fredeman, William E., ed. 'A Pre-Raphaelite Gazette: The Penkill letters of Arthur Hughes to William Bell Scott and Alice Boyd 1886–97', *Bulletin of the John Rylands Library* 49/2 (1967) and 50/1.

Frederick Sandys, 1829–1904. Catalogue of an exhibition at the Brighton Museum and Art Gallery. Brighton, 1974.

Frügmorgen-Voss, Hella and Norbert H. Ott. *Text und Illustration im Mittelalter: Aufsätze zu den Wechselbeziehungen zwischen Literatur und bildender Kunst*. Munich, 1975.

Gaines, Barry. 'The Editions of Malory in the Early Nineteenth Century', *The Papers of the Bibliographical Society of America* 68 (1974), 1–17.

Gardner, Edmund G. *The Arthurian Legend in Italian Literature*. London and New York, 1930.

Gardner, J.S. and Elizabeth Eames. 'A Tile Kiln at Chertsey Abbey', *Journal of the British Archaeological Association* 17 (1954).

Garnier, François. *Le Langage de l'Image au Moyen Age: Signification et Symbolique*. Paris, 1982.

Garrett, Albert. *A History of British Wood Engraving*. Tunbridge Wells, 1978.

Gathercole, Patricia M. 'The Paintings of the Lancelot Manuscripts at the Bibliothèque Nationale', *Romance Notes* 13/2 (1971), 351–57.

Gaunt, William. *Victorian Olympus*. London, 1952.

Gernsheim, Helmet. *Julia Margaret Cameron: Her Life and Photographic Work*. Millerton, N.Y., 1975.

Gerould, G.H. 'Arthurian Romance and the Date of the Relief at Modena', *Speculum* 10 (1935) 355–76.

Gibson, J.S. 'Artistic Houses', *Studio* 1/6 (1893), 215–226.

Gibson, Robin. 'Arthur Hughes: Arthurian and related subjects of the early 1860's', *Burlington Magazine* 112 (1970), 451–56.

Gianfreda, G. *Il mosaico pavimentale della Basilica Cattedrale di Otranto*. 2nd ed. Casamari, 1965.

Giardelli, Arthur. 'Trystan ac Essyllt by David Jones', *Agenda, David Jones Special Issue* 11/4 – 12/1 (1973–4), 50–53.

Gill, Eric. *Foreward to a Treatise upon the Craft of Wood Engraving*. Vancouver, 1967.

Gilson, Etienne. 'La Mystique de la Grâce dans la Queste del Saint Graal', *Romania* 51 (1925), 321–37.

Girouard, Mark. *The Return to Camelot: Chivalry and the English Gentleman.* New Haven and London, 1981.

Goddard, E.R. *Women's Costume in French Texts of the Eleventh and Twelfth Centuries.* Baltimore and Paris, 1927.

Göller, Karl Heinz. 'Arthur: Saint and Sinner', *Avalon to Camelot* 2/1 (1986), 11–12.

———, ed. *The Alliterative Morte Arthure: A Reassessment of the Poem.* Cambridge, Eng., 1981.

Gombrich, E.H. *Symbolic Images: Studies in the Art of the Renaissance.* London, 1972.

Goodman, E.L. 'The Prose Tristan and the Pisanello Murals', *Tristania* 3/2 (1978), 23–35.

Goodman, J.R. 'Malory and Caxton's Chivalric Series, 1481–85', *Studies in Malory*, ed. James W. Spisak. Kalamazoo, 1985.

Gordon, George. 'The Trojans in Britain', *Essays of the English Association* 9 (1924), 9–30.

Gransden, Antonia. 'The Growth of Glastonbury Traditions and Legends in the Twelfth Century', *Journal of Ecclesiastical History* 27 (1976), 37–58.

Graves, Algernon. *The Royal Academy of the Arts.* 8 vols. London, 1905.

Gray, J.M. *Thro' the Vision of the Night: A Study of Source, Evolution and Structure in Tennyson's Idylls of the King.* Edinburgh, 1980.

Green, R.F. 'King Richard II's Books Revisited', *The Library* 31 (1976), 235–39.

Greet, Anne Hyde. *Apollinaire et le livre de peintre.* Paris, 1977.

Grieve, A.I. *The Art of Dante Gabriel Rossetti: The Watercolours and Drawings of 1850–1855.* Norwich, 1978.

———. *D.G. Rossetti's Stylistic Development as a Painter.* Doctoral dissertation, University of London, 1968.

Griffeth, Richard R. 'The Authorship Question Reconsidered', *Aspects of Malory*, ed. Toshiyuki Takamiya and Derek Brewer. Cambridge, Eng. and Totowa, N.J., 1981.

Griffin, Mary E. 'Cadwalader, Arthur, and Brutus in the Wigmore Manuscript', *Speculum* 16 (1941), 109–20.

Grosshaus, Henry. *Hitler and the Artists.* New York and London, 1983.

Grössinger, Christa. 'English Misericords of the Thirteenth and Fourteenth Centuries and their Relationship to Manuscript Illuminations', *Journal of the Warburg and Courtauld Institutes* 38 (1975), 97–108.

Grout, P.B., R.A. Lodge, C.E. Pickford and E.K.C. Varty, eds. *The Legend of Arthur in the Middle Ages.* Cambridge, Eng., 1983.

Grunfeld, Frederic V. 'The Last Holy Grail', *Connoisseur* 211 (1982), 98–99.

Guicheteau, Marcel. *Paul Sérusier.* Paris, 1976.

Hague, René, ed. *Dai Greatcoat: A Self-Portrait of David Jones in his letters.* London, 1980.

Hanning, Robert. *The Vision of History in Early Britain from Gildas to Geoffrey of Monmouth.* New York and London, 1966.

Harker, Margaret F. *Henry Peach Robinson: Master of Photographic Art 1830–1901.* Oxford, 1988.

Harris, Jack T. 'I have never seen a naked Lady of Shalott', *Journal of Pre- Raphaelite Studies* 5/1 (1984), 76–87.

Harrison, Martin and Bill Waters. *Burne-Jones.* London, 1973.

Harten, Jürgen. *Anselm Kiefer.* Catalogue of the exhibition at the Städtische Kunsthalle, Düsseldorf in collaboration with the Musée d' Art Moderne de la ville de Paris. Düsseldorf, 1984.

Haug, Walter. 'Artussage und Heilsgeschichte: zum Programm des Fussbodenmosaiks von Otranto', *Deutsche Vierteljahrsschrift* 49 (1975), 577–606.

———. *Das Mosaik von Otranto: Darstellung, Deutung und Bilddokumentation.* Wiesbaden, 1977.

Haug, W., N.H. Ott, et al. *Runkelstein, Die Wandmalereien des Sommerhauses.* Wiesbaden, 1982.

Hayward, Robert J. 'Sir Arthur Doughty, Shorthand and Alfred, Lord Tennyson', *Archivaria* 21 (1985–6), 103–10.

Henderson, George. *Gothic.* Harmondsworth, 1967.

Henderson, Philip. *William Morris: His Life and Friends*. London, 1967.

Henderson, Philip, ed. *The Letters of William Morris*. London, 1950.

Hermann, H.J. *Franzosische und iberische Handschriften der ersten Halbe des 15. Jahrhunderts*. Leipzig, 1938.

Hibbert, Christopher. *The Search for King Arthur*. London, 1969.

Hills, Paul. *David Jones*. Catalogue of the David Jones exhibition at the Tate Gallery. London, 1981.

———. 'The Romantic Tradition in David Jones', *Malahat Review* 27 (1972–3), 125–37.

Hind, A.M. Introduction to a *History of the Woodcut with a detailed survey of work done in the fifteenth century*. 2 vols. London, 1935.

Hobson, Anthony. *The Art and Life of J.W. Waterhouse R.A. 1849–1917*. London, 1980.

Hodnett, Edward. *English Woodcuts 1480–1535*. Oxford, 1973 [1934].

———. *Image and Text: Studies in the Illustration of English Literature*. London, 1982.

Hoge, James O., ed. *Lady Tennyson's Journal*. Charlottesville, Va., 1981.

———. *The Letters of Emily Lady Tennyson*. University Park, Penn. and London, 1974.

Hollaender, Albert. 'The Pictorial Work in the 'Flores Historiarum' of the so-called Matthew of Westminster (MS. Chetham 6712)', *Bulletin of the John Rylands Library* 28 (1944), 361–81.

Holt, E.S., ed. *A Documentary History of Art, I. The Middle Ages and Renaissance*. Princeton, 1957.

Hopper, V.F. *Medieval Number Symbolism*. New York, 1938.

Hornby, C.H. St. John. *A Descriptive Catalogue of the Books Printed at the Ashendene Press MDCCCXCV–MCMXXXV*. London, 1935.

Horsfall, T.C. 'Painting and Popular Culture', *Fraser's Magazine* 101 (1880), 849–54.

Horvitz, Shelah. 'My Lady of Shalott', *Journal of Pre-Raphaelite Studies* 3/2 (1983), 64–68.

Houghton, Walter E. *The Victorian Frame of Mind 1830–1870*. New Haven and London, 1957.

Hudson, Derek. *Arthur Rackham, His Life and Work*. New York, 1975 [1960].

Hugues, Jean. *50 Ans d' Edition de D.H. Kahnweiler*. Paris, 1959.

Huizinga, J. *The Waning of the Middle Ages: A Study of the Forms of Life, Thought and Art in France and the Netherlands in the XIVth and XVth Centuries*, trans. F. Hopman. New York, 1954.

Hunt, Diana Holman. *My Grandfather, His Wives and Loves*. London, 1969.

Hunt, Tony. 'The Tristan Illustrations in MS London BL Add. 11619', *Rewards and Punishments in the Arthurian Romance and Lyric Poetry of Medieval France*, ed. Peter V. Davies and Angus J. Kennedy. Cambridge, Eng., 1987.

Hunt, W. Holman. *Oxford Union Society: The Story of the Painting of the Pictures on the Walls and the Decorations on the ceiling of the old debating hall (now the library) in the years 1857–8–9*. Oxford and London, 1906.

———. *Pre-Raphaelitism and the Pre-Raphaelite Brotherhood*. 2 vols. London, 1905.

Hutchings, Gweneth. 'Isdernus of the Modena Archivolt', *Medium Aevum* 1 (1932), 204–5.

Ironside, Robin. *David Jones*. London, 1949.

Irwin, David and Francina. *Scottish Painters at Home and Abroad 1700–1900*. London, 1975.

Jackson, Kenneth Hurlstone. 'Arthur in Early Welsh Verse' and 'The Arthur of History', *Arthurian Literature in the Middle Ages*, ed. R.S. Loomis. London, 1959.

James, Henry. *Corporation of London Art Gallery: Descriptive Catalogue of the Loan Collection of Pictures*. London, 1901.

James, M.R. *Catalogue of Manuscripts and Early Printed Books from the libraries of William Morris, Richard Bennett Bertram, fourth Earl of Ashburnham and other sources now in the Morgan Library*. 3 vols. London, 1907.

James, M.R. and C. Jenkins. *A Descriptive Catalogue of the manuscripts in the Library of Lambeth Palace*. Cambridge, Eng., 1930.

———. *Lists of Manuscripts formerly in Peterborough Abbey Library*. Oxford, 1926.

Jerrold, Blanchard. *Life of Gustav Doré*. London, 1891.

Jervis, Simon, introd. *Designs for the Dream King: the Castles and Palaces of Ludwig II of Bavaria*. Catalogue of an exhibition at the Debrett Cooper-Hewitt Museum, New York. London, 1978.

Joachimides, Christos, Norman Rosenthal and Wieland Schmied, eds. *German Art in the 20 Century: Painting and Sculpture 1905–1985*. Catalogue of an exhibition at the Royal Academy of Arts. Munich and London, 1985.

Jones, David. *The Dying Gaul and Other Writings*. London, 1978.

———. *Epoch and Artist*. London, 1959.

Jullian, Philippe. *Dreamers of Decadence: Symbolist Painters of the 1890s*. London, 1971.

———. *The Symbolists*, trans. Mary Anne Stevens. Oxford, 1973.

Kelly, Thomas E. and Thomas H. Ohlgren. 'Paths to Memory: Iconographic Indices to *Roman de la Rose* and *Prose Lancelot* manuscripts in the Bodleian Library', *Visual Resources*, III (1983), 1–13.

Kelvin, Norman, ed. *The Collected Letters of William Morris*. 2 vols. Princeton, 1984–87.

Kendrick, T.D. *British Antiquity*. London, 1970 [1950].

Kennedy, Beverley. *Knighthood in the Morte Darthur*. Cambridge, Eng., 1985.

Ker, N.R. *Medieval Libraries of Great Britain: A List of Surviving Books*. 2nd ed. London, 1964.

Kleinhenz, Christopher. *Medieval Manuscripts and Textual Criticism*. North Carolina Studies in the Romance Language and Literatures 4. Chapel Hill, N.C., 1976.

Klenke, Sister M. Amelia. 'Chrétien's Symbolism and Cathedral Art', *PMLA* 70 (1955), 223–43.

Koechlin, Raymond. *Les Ivoires Gothiques Français*. 2 vols. Paris, 1924.

Kuhn, A. *Die Illustration des Rosenromans*. Freiburg and Breisgau, 1911.

Lacy, Norris J., ed. *The Arthurian Encyclopedia*. New York and London, 1986.

Ladies of Shalott: A Victorian Masterpiece and Its Context. Catalogue of an exhibition by the Department of Art, Brown University, Providence, R.I. Providence, 1985.

Lago, Mary, ed. *Burne-Jones Talking: His Conversations 1895–1898 preserved by his studio assistant Thomas Rooke*. Columbia, Miss., 1981.

Lagorio, Valerie M. 'The Evolving Legend of St. Joseph of Glastonbury', *Speculum* 46 (1971), 209–31.

Lathuillère, Roger. *Guiron Le Courtois: Etude de la Tradition Manuscrite et analyse critique*. Genève, 1966.

Lawson, Paul. 'The Tristan and Isoude Stained Glass Panels', *The Bradford Antiquary*, 3rd ser. 1 (1985), 50–55.

Layard, George Somes. *Tennyson and his Pre-Raphaelite Illustrators*. London, 1894.

Leary, Emmeline. *The Holy Grail Tapestries designed by Edward Burne-Jones for Morris & Co*. Birmingham, 1985.

Lee, J.A. 'The Illuminating Critic: the Illustration of Cotton Nero AX', *Studies in Iconography* 3(1977), 17–46.

Lehmann-Haupt, Hellmut, ed. *The Göttingen Model Book*. Columbia, Miss., 1972.

Lejeune, R. 'La coup de la légende de Tristan dans "L' Escoufle" de Jean Renart', *The Medieval Alexander Legend and Romance Epic: Essays in Honour of David J.A. Ross*, eds. P. Noble, L. Polak and C. Isoz. Millwood, N.Y. and London, 1982.

Lejeune, R. and J. Stiennon. *La Légende de Roland dans l'art du moyen âge*. Brussels, 1966.

Leland, John. *Assertio inclytissimi Arturii Regis Britanniae*, trans Richard Robinson in Christopher Middleton, *The Famous Historie of Chinon of England*, ed. William Edward Mead. EETS OS 65. London, 1925.

Les Miniatures des Chroniques de Hainaut (15ᵉ siècle) with preface by Pierre Cockshaw. Mons, 1979.

Lethaby, W.R. 'The Romance Tiles of Chertsey Abbey', *Walpole Society Annual* 2 (1912–13), 69–80.

Lewis, C.S. *The Allegory of Love: a Study in Medieval Tradition*. New York, 1958 (1936).

Lloyd, John Gilbert. *Stained Glass in America*. Jenkintown, Penn., 1963.

Locke, F.W. *The Quest for the Holy Grail: A Literary Study of a Thirteenth Century French Romance*. Stanford, 1960.

Lods, Jeanne. *Le Roman de Perceforest: origines, composition, caractères, valeur et influence.* Genève, 1951.

Loomis, R.S. 'Arthurian Influence on Sport and Spectacle', *Arthurian Literature in the Middle Ages*, ed. R.S. Loomis. Oxford, 1959.

———. 'Chivalric and Dramatic Imitations of Arthurian Romance', *Medieval Studies in Memory of A. Kingsley Porter.* 2 vols. Cambridge, Mass., 1939.

———. 'Geoffrey of Monmouth and the Modena Archivolt: A Question of Precedence', *Speculum* 13 (1938), 221–231.

———. *Illustrations of Medieval Romance on Tiles of Chertsey Abbey.* University of Illinois Studies in Language and Literature. Urbana, 1916.

———. 'The Tristan and Perceval Caskets', *Romanic Review* 8 (1917), 196–209.

———, ed. *Arthurian Literature in the Middle Ages.* Oxford, 1959.

——— and L.H. Loomis. *Arthurian Legends in Medieval Art.* London, 1938.

Lot, Ferdinand. *Etude sur le Lancelot en Prose.* Paris, 1918.

Lowenthal, David. *The Past is a Foreign Country.* Cambridge, Eng., 1985.

Lucas, E.V. *Edwin Austin Abbey, Royal Academician: the record of his life and work.* 2 vols. London, 1921.

Lukitsh, Joanne. 'Julia Margaret Cameron's Photographic Illustrations to Alfred Tennyson's Idylls of the King', *Arthurian Literature VII*, ed. Richard Barber. Cambridge, Eng., 1987.

Lumiansky, R.M., ed. *Malory's Originality: A Critical Study of Le Morte Darthur.* Baltimore, 1964.

Maas, Henry, J.L. Duncan and W.G. Good, eds. *The Letters of Aubrey Beardsley.* London, 1971.

Mackail, J.W. *The Life of William Morris.* 2 vols. London and New York, 1899.

Mâle, Emile. *L'art religieux du XIIIe siècle en France.* Paris, 1898; trans. Dora Nussey. *The Gothic Image: Religious Art in France of the Thirteenth Century.* New York, Evanston and London, 1958 (1913).

———. *Religious Art in France: the Twelfth Century*, ed. Barry Bober, trans. Marthiel Mathews. Princeton, 1978.

Mancoff, Debra N. *The Arthurian Revival in Victorian Painting.* 2 vols. Doctoral dissertation, Northwestern University, Evanston, Ill., 1982.

Mander, Rosalie. 'Rossetti and the Oxford Murals, 1857', *Pre-Raphaelite Papers*, ed. Leslie Parris. London, 1984.

Marillier, H.C. 'The Nine Worthies', *Burlington Magazine* 61 (1932), 13–19.

Marsland, E.A. *The Nation's Cause: French, English and German Poetry of the First World War.* London, 1990.

Martindale, Andrew. *The Rise of the Artist in the Middle Ages and Early Renaissance.* New York, 1972.

Matthews, John. *The Grail: Quest for the Eternal.* New York, 1981.

Matthews, William. *The Ill-framed Knight: a sceptical inquiry into the identity of Sir Thomas Malory.* Berkeley and Los Angeles, 1966.

McGrath, Robert L. 'A Newly Discovered Illustrated manuscript of Chrétien de Troyes' Yvain and Lancelot in the Princeton University Library', *Speculum* 38 (1963), 583–594.

McKenzie, A. Dean. 'French Medieval Castles in Gothic Manuscript Painting', *The Medieval Castle: Romance and Reality*, ed. Kathryn Reyerson and Faye Powe. Dubuque, Iowa, 1984.

Meale, Carol. 'Manuscripts, Readers and Patrons in Fifteenth-Century England: Sir Thomas Malory and Arthurian Romance', *Arthurian Literature IV*, ed. Richard Barber. Cambridge, Eng., and Totowa, N.J., 1985.

Medieval and Early Renaissance Treasure in the North West. Catalogue of an Exhibition at the Whitworth Art Gallery. Manchester, 1971.

Medieval Miniatures from the Department of Manuscripts (formerly the Library of Burgundy) of the Royal Library of Belgium with commentaries by L.M.J. Delaissé. New York, 1965.

Meiss, Millard. *French Painting in the Time of Jean de Berry: the Late Fourteenth Century and the Patronage of the Duke*. London and New York, 1967.

Meyer, Susan E. *America's Great Illustrators*. New York, 1978.

————. 'N.C. Wyeth', *American Artist* 39 (1975), 35–45, 78–89.

Micha, A. *La Tradition manuscrite des romans de Chrétien de Troyes*. Paris, 1939.

Millar, E.G. 'Les principaux manuscrits à peinture de Lambeth Palace à Londres', *Bulletin de la Société française de reproductions de manuscrits à peintures* 9 (1925), 15–19.

————. *The Parisian Miniaturist Honoré*. London, 1959.

Millard, Charles W. 'Julia Margaret Cameron and Tennyson's "Idylls of the King"', *Harvard University Bulletin* 21/2 (April 1973), 187–201.

Millican, Charles Bowie. *Spenser and the Table Round: A Study in the Contemporaneous Background for Spenser's Use of the Arthurian Legend*. Cambridge, Mass., 1932.

Milner, John. *Symbolists and Decadents*. London, 1971.

Mittler, Elmar and Wilfred Werner. *Die Bibliothek Palatina: Skizzen zu ihrer Geschichte*. Wiesbaden, 1986.

Moore, Susan. 'The Marxist and the Oilman, Morris & Co. at Stanmore Hall', *Country Life*, 14 Nov. (1985), 1494–96.

Moralejo, Serafín. 'Artes figurativas y artes literarias en la España medieval: Romànico, Romance y Roman', *Boletín de la Asociación Europea de Profesores de Español* 17 (1985), 61–68.

Moran, James. *Wynkyn de Worde, Father of Fleet Street*, London, 1960.

Morgan, Nigel. *Early Gothic Manuscripts*. London and New York, 1982.

Morris, May, ed. *William Morris: Artist, Writer and Socialist*. 2 vols. London, 1936.

Morris, Rosemary. *The Character of King Arthur in Medieval Literature*. Cambridge, Eng., 1982.

Morton, W.L. 'Seeing an Unliterary Landscape', *Mosaic* 3/3 (1970), 1–10.

Muccigrosso, Robert. *American Gothic: The Mind and Art of Ralph Adams Cram*. Washington, 1980.

Muthesius, Stefan. *The High Victorian Movement in Architecture 1850–1870*. London, 1972.

Nairne, Sandy and Nicholas Sewta, eds. *British Sculpture in the Twentieth Century*. Catalogue of an exhibition at the Whitechapel Art Gallery. London, 1981.

Nelson, Philip. *Ancient Painted Glass in England 1170–1500*. London, 1913.

Nevinson, John L. 'A Show of the Nine Worthies', *Shakespeare Quarterly* 14 (1963), 103–7.

Newstead, Helaine. 'The Tryst beneath the Tree: An Episode in the Tristan Legend', *Romance Philology* 9 (1956), 269–84.

Newton, Stella Mary. *Fashion in the Age of the Black Prince: a study of the years 1340–1365*. Woodbridge and Totowa, N.J., 1980.

Nickel, Helmet. 'About Arms and Armor in the Age of Arthur', *Avalon to Camelot* I, 1 (1983), 19–21.

————. 'Arthurian Heraldry', *Avalon to Camelot*, I, 3 (1984), 11–12.

————. 'Heraldry', *The Arthurian Encyclopedia*. New York and London, 1986, pp. 278–283.

Ohlgren, Thomas H., ed. *Illuminated manuscripts and Books in the Bodleian Library*. New York and London, 1978.

————, ed. *Illuminated Manuscripts: An Index to Selected Bodleian Color Reproductions*. New York and London, 1977.

Oman, Charles. *Medieval Silver Nefs*. London, 1963.

Ott, Norbert H. 'Geglückte Minne-Aventiure: zur Szenenauswahl literarischer Bildzeugnisse im Mittelalter. Die Beispiele des Rodenecker "Iwein", des Runkelsteiner "Tristan", des Braunschweiger Gawan und des Frankfurter "Wilhelm-von-Orlens"-Teppichs', *Jahrbuch der Oswald von Wolkenstein Gresellschaft* 2 (1983), 1–32.

Ott, Norbert H. and Wolfgang Walliczek. 'Bildprogramm und Textstruktur: Anmerkungen zu den "Iwein"-zyklen auf Rodeneck und in Schmalkalden', *Deutsche Literatur im Mittelalter. Kontakte und Perspectiven*, ed. Christoph Cormeau. Stuttgart, 1979.

Paccagnini, Giovanni. *Pisanello*, trans. Jane Carroll. London, 1973.

Pächt, O. and J.J.G. Alexander. *Illuminated manuscripts in the Bodleian Library*. Oxford, 1966.
Painter, George D. *William Caxton: A Quincentenary Biography of England's First Printer*. London, 1976.
Palmer, Arnold. *More than Shadows: A Biography of W. Russell Flint, R.A., P.R.W.S. with 136 illustrations of his works*. London and New York, 1943.
Palmer, D.J., ed. *Tennyson*. London, 1973.
Panofsky, Erwin. *Early Netherlandish Painting: its Origins and Character*. 2 vols. New York and London, 1971 [1951].
————. ed. and trans. *Abbot Suger on the Abbey Church of St. Denis and its Art Treasures*, 2nd ed. Princeton, 1979 [1946].
Parris, Leslie, ed. *Pre-Raphaelite Papers*. London, 1984.
Parry, Linda L.A. 'The Tapestries of Edward Burne-Jones', *Apollo* 102, 324–28.
Pastoureau, Michel. *Armorial des chevaliers de la Table Ronde*. Paris, 1983.
————. *L'hermine et le sinople: Etudes d' Héraldique Médiévale*. Paris, 1982.
Patmore, Derek. 'The Wall Paintings in the Oxford Union Library', *Studio* III (1936), 324–5.
Paton, L.A. *Studies in the Fairy Mythology of Arthurian Romance*. Boston, 1903; rpt. New York, 1959.
Paulson, Ronald. *Book and Painting: Shakespeare, Milton and the Bible: Literary Texts and the Emergence of English Painting*. Knoxville, Tenn., 1982.
Pauphilet, A. *Etudes sur la Queste del Saint Graal*. Paris, 1921.
Pearsall, Derek and Elizabeth Salter. *Landscapes and Seasons of the Medieval World*. London, 1973.
Pearsall, Derek, ed. *Manuscripts and Readers in Fifteenth-Century England: the Literary Implications of Manuscript Study*. Cambridge, Eng., 1983.
Pellegrin, E. *La Bibliothèque des Visconti et des Sforza ducs de Milan au XVe siècle*. Paris, 1955 and Supplement, Paris, 1969.
Peters, Robert L., ed. *Victorians on Literature and Art*. New York, 1961.
Peterson, William S., ed. *The Ideal Book: Essays and Lectures on the Arts of the Book by William Morris*. Berkeley, Los Angeles and London, 1982.
Pickering, F.P. *Literature and Art in the Middle Ages*. Coral Gables, Florida, 1970.
Pickford, C.E. 'An Arthurian Manuscript in the John Rylands Library', *Bulletin of the John Rylands Library* 31 (1948), 318–344.
————. *L'Evolution du Roman Arthurien en Prose Vers la Fin du Moyen Age d'après le manuscrit 112 du fonds français de la Bibliothèque Nationale*. Paris, 1959.
————. 'The Three Crowns of King Arthur', *Yorkshire Archaeological Journal* 38 (1952–5), 373–82.
Pitz, Henry C. *The Brandywine Tradition*. Boston, 1969.
————. 'The Brandywine Tradition', *American Artist* 30 (1966), 44–49, 74–76.
————. *Howard Pyle: Writer, Illustrator, and Founder of the Brandywine School*. New York, 1975.
'The Place of the Fine Arts in the Natural System of Society', *Douglas Jerrold's Shilling Magazine* 6, 72–81.
Platts, Beryl. 'A brave Victorian venture, the Royal Windsor Tapestry Manufactory', *Country Life*, Nov. 29 (1979), 2003–06.
Plomen, Henry R. *Wynkyn de Worde and His Contemporaries from the death of Caxton to 1535*. London, 1925.
Pointon, Marcia. *William Dyce 1806–1864: A Critical Biography*. Oxford, 1979.
Pollard, Alfred W. *Early Illustrated Books: A History of the Decoration and Illustration of Books in the Fifteenth and Sixteenth Centuries*. London, 1917 [1893].
Porcher, J. *L'enluminure française*. Paris, 1959.
————. *Manuscrits à peintures en France du XIIIe au XVIe siècle*. Paris, 1955.
Powell, Kirsten H. 'Cowboy Knights and Prairie Madonnas: American Illustrations of the Plains and Pre-Raphaelite Art', *Great Plains Quarterly* 5/1 (1985), 39–52.

344   BIBLIOGRAPHY

A Pre-Raphaelite Passion: The Private Collection of L.S. Lowry. Catalogue of an exhibition at the Manchester City Art Gallery with introduction by Sandra Martin. Manchester, 1977.

The Pre-Raphaelites. Catalogue of the exhibition at the Tate Gallery, London. London, 1984.

Praz, Mario. *The Romantic Agony,* trans. Angus Davidson. London, 1933.

Prinsep, Val. C. 'A Chapter from a Painter's Reminiscence. The Oxford Circle: Rossetti, Burne-Jones and William Morris', *The Magazine of Art* 27 (1904), 167–72.

Purvis, J.L. 'The Use of Continental Woodcuts and Prints by the Ripon School of Wood-carvers in the Early Sixteenth Century', *Archaeologia* 85 (1936), 107–28.

Rackham, Bernard. 'The glass-painting of Coventry and its neighbourhood', *Walpole Society* 19 (1930–31), 89–110.

Radford, C.A. Ralegh. 'Glastonbury Abbey' in *The Quest for Arthur's Britain*, ed. Geoffrey Ashe. London, 1968.

Rajna, P. 'Intorno a due antique coperte con figurazioni tratte dalle storie di Tristano', *Romania* 42 (1913), 517–79.

Randall, Lilian, M.C. *Images in the margins of Gothic Manuscripts.* Berkeley and Los Angeles, 1966.

Ranke, F. *Tristan und Isold.* Munich, 1925.

Ransom, Will. *Kelmscott, Doves and Ashendene.* San Francisco, 1952.

Read, Benedict. *Victorian Sculpture.* New Haven and London, 1982.

Reader, Francis W. 'Tudor mural Paintings in the lesser Houses of Bucks', *The Archaeological Journal* 89 (1933), 116–73.

Réau, Louis. *Iconographie de l'Art Chrétien.* 3 vols. Paris, 1956.

Remnant, G.L. *Catalogue of Misericords in Great Britain.* Oxford, 1969.

Renouard, Michel. *Art roman en Bretagne.* Rennes, 1978.

Renton, J.D. *The Oxford Union Murals,* 2nd ed. Privately printed, 1983.

Rickard, P. *Britain in Medieval French Literature.* Cambridge, Eng., 1956.

Ricklef, Jürgen. 'Der Tristanroman der niedersächsichen und mitteldeutschen Tristanteppiche', *Niederdeutsches Jahrbuch* 86 (1963), 33–48.

Ritchie, Anne Thackeray and H.H.H. Cameron. *Lord Tennyson and his Friends with Reminiscences.* London, 1893.

Robinson, Duncan and Stephen Wildman. *Morris & Company in Cambridge.* Catalogue of an exhibition at the Fitzwilliam Museum. Cambridge, Eng., 1980.

Robinson, J.A. *Two Glastonbury Legends.* Cambridge, Eng., 1926.

Robson-Scott, W.D. *The Literary Background of the Gothic Revival in Germany: A Chapter in the History of Taste.* Oxford, 1965.

Rorimer, James J. *The Cloisters, the Building and the Collections of medieval Art in Fort Tryon Park.* New York, 1963.

Rorimer, J.J. and M.B. Freeman. 'The Nine Heroes Tapestries at the Cloisters', *Metropolitan Museum of Art Bulletin,* N.S. 7 (May, 1949), 243–260.

———. *The Nine Heroes Tapestries at the Cloisters, a picture book.* New York, 1960.

Rosenthal, Mark. *Anselm Kiefer.* Catalogue of an exhibition at the Art Institute of Chicago and the Philadelphia Museum of Art. Chicago and Philadelphia, 1987.

Ross, David J. 'Allegory and Romance on a Medieval French Marriage Casket', *Journal of the Warburg and Courtauld Institutes* 11 (1948), 112–142.

Rossetti, William Michael. *Dante Gabriel Rossetti as Designer and Writer.* London, 1889.

———. *Dante Gabriel Rossetti: His Family Letters with a Memoir.* 2 vols. New York, 1970 (London, 1895).

———. *Preraphaelite Diaries and Letters.* London, 1900.

Russell, J.C. *The Field of the Cloth of Gold: Men and Manners in 1520.* London, 1969.

Salaman, Malcolm C. *The Woodcut of Today at Home and Abroad.* London, 1927.

Salet, Francis and Geneviève Souchal. *Chefs-d'oeuvre de la tapisserie du XIVe au XVIe siècle.* Catalogue of an exhibition held at the Grand Palais, Paris and the Metropolitan Museum of Art, New York. Paris, 1973.

Sandler, Lucy Freeman. *A Survey of Manuscripts Illuminated in the British Isles. 2 vols. Gothic Manuscripts [I] 1285–1385*. London and New York, 1986.

Sandoz, Edouard. 'Tourneys in the Arthurian Tradition', *Speculum* 19 (1944), 389–420.

Savage, Ernest A. *Old English Libraries: the Making, Collecting and Use of Books During the Middle Ages*. Detroit, 1968 [1912].

Saxl, F. *The Troy Romance in French and Italian Art*. London, 1951.

Scattergood, V.J. and J.W. Sherbourne, eds. *English Court Culture in the Later Middle Ages*. London, 1983.

Schapiro, Meyer. *Words and Pictures: On the Literal and the Symbolic in the Illustration of a Text*. The Hague and Paris, 1973.

Scheller, R. *A Survey of Medieval Model Books*. Haarlem, 1963.

Scherer, Margaret R. *About the Round Table*. New York, 1945.

———. *The Legends of Troy in Art and Literature*. New York and London, 1964.

Schoepperle, Gertrude. *Tristan and Isolt*. Frankfurt and London, 1913; rpt. New York, 1959.

Scholderer, Victor. *Introduction to Catalogue of Books Printed in the Fifteenth Century now in the British Library*. London, 1949.

Schroeder, Hans. *Der Topos der Nine Worthies in Literatur und bildender Kunst*. Gottingen, 1971.

———. 'The Mural Paintings of the Nine Worthies at Amersham', *The Archaeological Journal* 138 (1981), 241–47.

Schuette, Marie. *Gestickte Bildteppiche und Decken des Mittelalters. 2 vols*. Leipzig, 1927–30.

Schuette, Marie and Sigrid Müller-Christensen. *Das Stickereiwerk*. Tübingen, 1963, trans. Donald King, *The Art of Embroidery*. London, 1964.

Schupp, Volker. 'Die Ywain-Erzählung von Schloss Rodenegg', *Literatur und bildende kunst im Tiroler Mittelalter. Die Iwein-Fresken von Rodenegg und andere Zeugnisse der Wechselwirkung von Literatur und bildender Kunst*. Innsbruck, 1982.

———. 'Kritische Anmerkungen zur rezeption des deutschen Artusromans anhand von Hartmanns *Iwein*: Theorie-Text-Bildmaterial', *Frühmittelalterliche Studien* 9 (1975), 405–42.

Scott, John. *The Early History of Glastonbury*. Woodbridge, 1981.

Scott, Kathleen. 'A Mid-fifteenth-century English Illuminating Shop and its Customers', *Journal of the Warburg and Courtauld Institutes* 31 (1968), 170–196.

Scott, Margaret. *Late Gothic Europe, 1400–1500: The History of Dress series*. London, 1980.

Scott, William Bell. *Autobiographical Notes*, ed. W. Minto. London, 1892.

The Secular Spirit: Life and Art at the End of the Middle Ages. Catalogue of an exhibition at the Cloisters. New York, 1975.

Sewter, Charles. *The Stained Glass of William Morris and his Circle. 2 vols*. New Haven and London, 1974.

Sharrer, Harvey. 'Notas sobre la materia arturica hispanica, 1979–1986', *La Corónica* 15 (1986–87), 328–40.

Shaw, Henry. *Specimens of Tile Pavements drawn from existing authorities*. London, 1858.

———. *Dresses and Decorations of the Middle Ages*. London, 1843.

Shonk, Timothy A. 'A Study of the Auchinleck Manuscript: Bookmen and Bookmaking in the Early Fourteenth Century', *Speculum* 60 (1985), 71–91.

Shurlock, Manwaring. *Tiles from Chertsey Abbey, Surrey representing early romance subjects*. London, 1885.

Sketchley, R.E.D. 'The Art of J.W. Waterhouse, R.A.', *The Art Journal*, Christmas (1909), 1–31.

Smith, Roger. 'Bonnard's *Costume Historique* – a Pre-Raphaelite Source Book', *Costume VII* (1973), 28–37.

Spisak, James W., ed. *Studies in Malory*. Kalamazoo, 1985.

Staines, David. *Tennyson's Camelot: The Idylls of the King and its Medieval Sources*. Waterloo, 1982.

Steer, Francis W. *Misericords at New College, Oxford*. London, 1973.

Stein, Richard L. 'The Pre-Raphaelite Tennyson', *Victorian Studies* 24 (1981), 279–301.

Steinberg, S.H. 'The Nine Worthies and the Christian Kings', *Connoisseur* 104 (1939), 146–49.

Stephens, F.G. 'English Painters of the Present Day, XXXI – William Holman Hunt', *Portfolio* 2 (1871), 38.

———. 'Thomas Woolner', *The Art Journal* (1894), 84.

Stiennon, Jacques and Rita Lejeune. 'La légende arthurienne dans la sculpture de la cathédrale de Modène', *Cahiers de Civilization médiévale* 6 (1963), 281–96.

Stillwell, Richard. *The Chapel of Princeton University*. Princeton, 1971.

Stones, Margaret Alison. 'The Earliest Illustrated Prose Lancelot', *Reading Medieval Studies* 3 (1977).

———. *The Illustration of the French Prose Lancelot in Flanders, Belgium and Paris 1250–1340*. 2 vols. Doctoral dissertation, University of London, 1970.

———. 'Notes on Three Illuminated Alexander Manuscripts', *The Medieval Alexander Legend and Romance Epic: Essays in Honour of David J.A. Ross*, ed. Peter Noble *et al.* London and New York, 1982.

———. 'Sacred and Profane Art: Secular and Liturgical Book Illumination in the Thirteenth Century', *The Epic in Medieval Society: Aesthetic and Moral Values*, ed. Harald Scholler. Tübingen, 1977.

———. 'Secular Manuscript Illumination in France', *Medieval Manuscripts and Textual Criticism*, ed. Christopher Kleinhenz, North Carolina Studies in Language and Literature 4. Chapell Hill, N.C., 1976.

Story, Alfred Thomas. 'The Life and Work of Sir Joseph Noel Patron', *The Art Journal*, Easter (1895), 95–128.

Strachan, W.J. *The Artist and the Book in France: the 20th Century, Livre d'artiste*. London, 1969.

Strong, Roy. *And when did you last see your father?: the Victorian painter and British history*. London, 1978.

———. *The Cult of Elizabeth: Elizabethan Portraiture and Pageantry*. London, 1977.

———. *Splendour at Court: Renaissance Spectacle and Illusion*. London, 1973.

Surtees, Virginia. *The Paintings and Drawings of Dante Gabriel Rossetti (1828–1882): a Catalogue Raisonné*. 2 vols. Oxford, 1971.

———, ed. *The Diary of Ford Madox Brown*. New Haven and London, 1981.

———, ed. *Reflections of a Friendship: John Ruskin's Letters to Pauline Trevelyan 1848–1866*. London, 1979.

———, ed. *Sublime & Instructive: Letters from John Ruskin to Louisa, Marchioness of Waterford, Anna Blunden and Ellen Heaton*. London, 1972.

Sutton, K. 'The original patron of the Lombard manuscript Latin 757 in the Bibliothèque Nationale, Paris', *Burlington Magazine* 124 (1982), 88–92.

Swinburne, Algernon. *Under the Microscope*. London, 1872.

Le Symbolisme en Europe. Catalogue of an exhibition at the Musée Boymans-von Beuningen. Rotterdam, 1975.

Symons, Arthur. 'The Decadent Movement in Literature', *Harper's New Monthly Magazine*, November (1893).

Szklenar, H. 'Iwein-Fresken auf Schloss Rodeneck in Südtirol', *Bibliographical Bulletin of the International Arthurian Society* 27 (1975), 172–80.

Takamiya, Toshiyuki and Derek Brewer, eds. *Aspects of Malory*. Cambridge, Eng. and Totowa, N.J., 1981.

Tatlock, J.S.P. *The Legendary History of Britain*. Berkeley, 1950.

The Tate Gallery. *Illustrated Biennial Report, 1982–84*. London, 1984.

Taylor, Beverly and Elisabeth Brewer. *The Return of King Arthur*. Cambridge, Eng. and Totowa, N.J., 1983.

Temple, A.G. *Guildhall Memories*. London, 1918.

Tennyson, Hallam. *Alfred, Lord Tennyson: a Memoir*. 2 vols. London, 1897.

Thirkell, A.M. *Three Houses*. London, 1931.

Thomas, Marcel. *The Golden Age: Manuscript Painting at the Time of Jean, Duke of Berry*, trans. Ursule Molinaro and Bruce Benderson. New York, 1979.

Thompson, Daniel V. Jr., trans. *The Craftsman's Handbook, 'Il Libro dell' Arte', Cennino d'Andrea Cennini*. New York, 1960 [1933].

Thompson, Raymond H. *The Return from Avalon: A Study of the Arthurian Legend in Modern Fiction*. Westpoint, Conn. and London, 1985.

Thoss, D. 'Ein prosa Tristan aus dem Beistz des Duc de Berry in der Osterreichischen National Bibliothek (Cod. 2537)', *Codes Manuscripti* 3 (1977), 66–72.

———. *Französische Gotik und Renaissance in Meisterwerken der Buchmalerei*. Catalogue of the Exhibition of Manuscripts and Incunabilia of the Austrian National Library. Vienna, 1978.

Toesca, P. *Storia dell' arte italiana II, Il Trecento*. Turin, 1951.

Tolstoy, Nikolai. *The Quest for Merlin*. London, 1985.

Topsfield, L.T. *Chrétien de Troyes: A Study of the Arthurian Romances*. Cambridge, Eng., 1981.

Treharne, R.F. *The Glastonbury Legends*. London, 1967.

Treuherz, Julian. 'The Pre-Raphaelites and Medieval Illuminated Manuscripts', *Pre-Raphaelite Papers*, ed. Leslie Parris. London, 1984.

Tuve, Rosemond. *Allegorical Imagery: Some Medieval Books and Their Posterity*. Princeton, 1966.

Vale, Juliet. *Edward III and Chivalry: Chivalric Society and Its Context 1270–1350*. Woodbridge, 1982.

Valentine, Lucia N. *Ornament in Medieval MSS: A Glossary*. London, 1965.

Vallance, Aymer. 'The Revival of Tapestry-Weaving: An interview with Mr. William Morris', *Studio* 2–3 (1893–4), 98–101.

Van Every, Jane. *With Faith, Ignorance and Delight: Homer Watson*. Aylesbury, 1967.

Van Marle, Raimond. *Iconographie de L'art Profane du Moyen-Age et à la Renaissance*. 2 vols. New York, 1971.

Vaughan, William. *German Romantic Painting*. New Haven and London, 1980.

Verbeke, W., J. Janssens, M. Smeyers, eds. *Arturus Rex, Vol. I., Catalogus, Koning Artur en de Nederlanden*. Leuven, 1987.

Vinaver, Eugène. *The Rise of Romance*. Oxford, 1971.

Wainright, Clive. 'Pre-Raphaelite Furniture', *The Strange Genius of William Burges 'Art-Architect' 1827–81*, ed. J. Mordaunt Crook. London and Cardiff, 1981.

Walker, R.J.B. *A Catalogue of Paintings, Drawings, Sculptures and Engravings in the Palace of Westminster*. 7 vols. London, 1959–67.

Walton, William. 'The Recent Mural Decorations of H. Siddons Mowbray', *Harper's Weekly* 122 (1911), 726–37.

Watkinson, Ray. 'Red House Decorated', *Journal of the William Morris Society* VII/4 (1988), 10–15.

Watts, Mary. *George Frederic Watts: the Annals of an Artist's Life*. 3 vols. London, 1912.

Weaver, Mike. *Julia Margaret Cameron 1815–1879*. Catalogue of an exhibition arranged by the John Hansard Gallery, the University of Southampton and toured by the Arts Council of Great Britain. London, 1984.

Webster, K.G.T. *Guinevere: A Study of her Abductions*. Milton, Mass., 1954.

Wells, Robin Headlam. *Spenser's Faerie Queene and the Cult of Elizabeth*. London, Canberra and Totowa, N.J., 1983.

Whall, Veronica. 'Glass, Lead, and Light', *Stained Glass* XX/1 (1935), 10–14.

Whitaker, Muriel. *Arthur's Kingdom of Adventure: The World of Malory's Morte Darthur*. Cambridge, Eng. and Totowa, N.J., 1984.

———. 'Christian Iconography in the Quest of the Holy Grail', *Liturgy and Literature* (Mosaic 12/2). Winnipeg, 1979.

———. 'Flat Blasphemies: Beardsley's Illustrations for Malory's Morte Darthur', *Mosaic* 8/2 (1975), 67–75.

————. 'Illustrating Caxton's Malory', *Studies in Malory*, ed. James W. Spisak. Kalamazoo, 1985.

White, Gleeson. *English Illustration: The Sixties*. London, 1897.

Whiting, G.W. *The Artist and Tennyson*. Rice University Studies 50 (1964), 1–84.

Wilcockson, Colin, ed. *Letters to William Hayward*. London, 1979.

Willard, C.C. 'The concept of true nobility at the Burgundian Court', *Studies in the Renaissance* 14 (1967).

Williamson, Ian. *Harold Hitchcock: A Romantic Symbol in Surrealism*. New York, 1982.

Withington, Robert. *English Pageantry: An Historical Outline*. 2 vols. Cambridge, Mass., 1918.

Withrington, John. 'The Arthurian Epitaph in Malory's Morte Darthur', *Arthurian Literature* VII, ed. Richard Barber. Cambridge, Eng., 1987.

Wood, Christopher. *The Pre-Raphaelites*. London, 1981.

Woolner, Amy. *Thomas Woolner, R.A. Sculptor and Poet: His Life in Letters*. New York, 1971 [1917].

Wroot, Herbert E. 'Pre-Raphaelite Windows at Bradford', *Studio* 72 (1917), 69–73.

Wyeth, Betsy James, ed. *The Wyeths: the Letters of N.C. Wyeth*. Boston, 1971.

List of Illustrations and Acknowledgements

Black and white

1. Arthur and his Kingdoms. Peter Langtoft's Chronicle of England, BL Royal 20 A II, f. 4. (British Library, London).
2. Alan Lee's Merlin. (Courtesy of *Avalon to Camelot*.)
3. Aubrey Beardsley's Tristram and La Beale Isoud, Malory's *Morte Darthur* (London: Dent, 1893). (J.M. Dent & Sons Ltd.)
4. Lancelot rides in a cart to rescue Guenevere. BL Add. 10293, f. 183 (*Vulgate Prose Lancelot*). (British Library, London).
5. Manuscript page decorated in early Gothic style. Rylands fr. 2, f. 212 (*Vulgate Prose Cycle*). (John Rylands Library, Manchester).
6. King Arthur and the Giant of St Michael's Mount. BL Egerton 3028, f. 49 (*Chronique d'Angleterre*). (British Library, London).
7. Above: Yvain kills Escalados, loses his horse under the portcullis, and encounters Lunete. Below: Laudine and Lunete mourn their dead lord. BN 1433, f. 69^V (Chrétien's *Yvain*). (Bibliothèque Nationale, Paris).
8. Roundels illustrating the Lancelot Cycle. Bodl. Rawlinson Q.b.6, ff. 57, 149^V, 241, 274^V, 311^V, 323^V. (Bodleian Library, Oxford).
    (a). Arthur's feast
    (b). Lancelot in prison
    (c). The queens find Lancelot asleep under an apple tree
    (d). The mystical White Hart with four lions (Christ and the Evangelists)
    (e). Lancelot's madness
    (f). Lancelot arrives at a convent
9. Tourneying knights with distinctive armorials. BL Add. 12228, f. 164^V (*Roman du Roy Meliadus*). (British Library, London).
10. Knights ride into a city. BN nouv. acq. fr. 5243, f. 26^V. (*Guiron le Courtois*). (Bibliothèque Nationale, Paris).
11a. Arthur departs for Avalon. Florence, Cod. Pal. 556, f. 171 (*La Tavola Ritonda*). (Biblioteca Nazionale Centrale, Florence; Foto Sansoni).
11b. Mark slays Tristan. Florence, Cod. Pal. 556, f. 159^V. (Biblioteca Nazionale Centrale, Florence; Foto Sansoni).
12. Sir Gawain decapitates the Green Knight at Arthur's court. BL Cotton Nero Ax. Art. 3, f. 94. (British Library, London).
13. Parzival takes the lady's ring. Heidelberg, Universitätsbibl. Cod. Pal. 339, f. 99^V (*Parzival*). (Universitätsbibliothek, Heidelberg).
14. Wigalois with the Crowned Beast. Leiden Universiteitsbibl. 537, f. 47^V (*Wigalois*). (Universiteitsbibliotheek, Leiden).
15. Modena Cathedral archivolt relief showing the rescue of Guenevere (Winlogee) from Mardoc's tower, ca. 1120–30.
16. Tristram instructs hunters in the etiquette of venery. Chertsey Tile, 1260–80. (British Museum, London).
17. Yvain's horse trapped under the portcullis. Chester Cathedral misericord. (Photograph: author).
18. The Tryst beneath the Tree. Chester Cathedral misericord. (Photograph: author).
19a. North German Tristan wall hanging showing the swallow with Isolde's hair, the dragon adventure and the tryst, *inter alia*, ca. 1370. (Victoria and Albert Museum, London).

19b. Tristan wall hanging from the Cistercian Convent at Wienhausen (Wienhausen III).
20. *Iwein* scenes on linen wall hanging, ca. 1310–20. (Bildverlag Freiburg).
21. Tristainu gives the glove of battle to Amoroldu. Sicilian quilt, 1395. (Victoria and Albert Museum, London).
22. Rhenish casket with Tristan scenes, ca. 1200. (British Museum, London).
23. Parisian casket of ivory, ca. 1300, showing: Gawain attacking the lion; Lancelot on the Sword Bridge; Gawain on the Perilous Bed; maidens awaiting Gawain. (Victoria and Albert Museum, London).
24. Italian maternity tray, 'The Triumph of Venus', ca. 1400. (Louvre Museum, Paris).
25. Burghley Nef (gilded salt cellar) with Tristan and Isolde, 1482–83. (Victoria and Albert Museum, London).
26. Lancelot at the River Marcoise. Pisanello fresco, Palazzo Ducale, Mantua, ca. 1450. (Photograph: author).
27. King Arthur on a camel. Flemish glass of the early sixteenth century. (The Cloisters, Metropolitan Museum, New York).
28. Bronze statue of King Arthur; Maximilian's tomb, Hofkirche, Innsbruck. (BBC Hulton Picture Library).
29. Prince Arthur, son of Henry VII. Stained glass window in Malvern Priory, 1501. (Reproduced in Henry Shaw, *Dresses and Decoration of the Middle Ages*, 1843).
30. Arthur's feast at Camelot. Woodcut from the first printed *Prose Lancelot*, 1488. (Jean Le Bourgeois and Jean Dupré, *Le Livere des Vertueux faix de plusieurs nobles chevaliers*).
31. The Birth of Tristram. Woodcut by the *Arthur*-cutter for Wynkyn de Worde's Malory, 1498. (John Rylands Library, Manchester).
32. Uther, Igraine and the Duke of Cornwall. Woodcut by the *Arthur*-cutter for Wynkyn de Worde's Malory, 1498. (John Rylands Library, Manchester).
33. The Dolorous Lover woodcut used by Copland and East to represent a dead monk. (Courtesy of James Spisak, ed., *Caxton's Malory*, 1983).
34. The Queen's Robing Room, Palace of Westminster. (House of Lords, Crown Copyright).
35. Generosity: Launcelot spares Arthur's life. William Dyce's watercolour version of the Robing Room fresco. (National Galleries of Scotland, Edinburgh).
36. Sir Galahad's Soul Borne to Heaven. H.H. Armstead's Robing Room bas-relief. (BBC Hulton Picture Library).
37. How Arthur attained Excalibur. H.H. Armstead's Robing Room bas-relief. (BBC Hulton Picture Library).
38. Sir Lancelot's vision of the Sanc Grael. Dante Gabriel Rossetti's watercolour study for the Oxford Union mural. (Ashmolean Museum, Oxford).
39. The Wedding Procession of Sir Degrevaunt. Edward Burne-Jones' study for a Red House wall painting. (Fitzwilliam Museum, University of Cambridge).
40. How Lancelot sought the Sangreal. Burne-Jones' stained glass panel for his Rottingdean House. (Victoria and Albert Museum, London).
41. The Lady of Shalott. Dante Gabriel Rossetti's woodcut for Alfred Lord Tennyson, *Poems* (London: E. Moxon, 1857). (Bruce Peel Special Collections Library, University of Alberta, Edmonton, Canada).
42. Shelah Horvitz. 'My Lady of Shalott', 1981. (From the collection of Professor George Landow, Brown University, Providence, Rhode Island).
43. The King's Farewell. Gustave Doré's illustration for Tennyson's *Guinevere* (London: E. Moxon, 1866). (Photograph: author).
44. Gareth and Lynette. Julia Margaret Cameron's photograph. *Illustrations to Tennyson's 'Idylls of the King' and Other Poems*, 1874–75. (George Eastman House, New York).
45. The parting of Sir Lancelot and Queen Guinevere. Julia Margaret Cameron's photograph. *Illustrations to Tennyson's 'Idylls of the King' and Other Poems*, 1874–75. (BBC Hulton Picture Library).
46. Arthur Hughes. The Rift in the Lute, oil painting ca. 1862. (Gordon Bottomley Bequest, Carlisle Museum and Art Gallery).

List of colour plates

1. Arthur Hughes. Sir Galahad, oil painting 1870. (Walker Art Gallery, Liverpool).
2a. Sir Lancelot fights in a tournament as Guenevere watches. Pierpont Morgan Library 805, f. 262 (Lancelot). (Pierpont Morgan Library, New York).
2b. Galeholt watches the lovers' first kiss as the seneschal and ladies converse. Pierpont Morgan Library 805, f. 67.
2c. Lancelot raises the lid of Josephé's tomb. Pierpont Morgan Library 805, f. 161^v.
3. King Arthur and King Ban plan a tournament as Queen Guenevere and courtiers watch. Bibliothèque Nationale fr. 95, f. 291. (Bibliothèque Nationale, Paris).
4. Scenes from Wolfram's *Parzival*. Bayerische Staatsbibl., Munich, cgm 19, f. 50. (Bayerische Staatsbibl., Munich).
5. Tristan kills the dragon which is found and claimed by the false steward. Bayerische Staatsbibl., Munich, cgm 51, f. 67. (Bayerische Staatsbibl., Munich).
6. Tristan arrives at le Chastel dessus la Mer. Bodl. Douce *Guiron*, f. 3. (Bodleian Library, Oxford).
7. The wedding of Arthur and Guenevere in *Chroniques de Hainault*. Brussels, Bibliothèque Royale Albert Ier, f. 39v. (Bibliothèque Royale Albert Ier., Brussels).
8. Galahad draws the sword from the stone. Bibliothèque Nationale fr. 343, f. 4. (Bibliothèque Nationale, Paris).
9. Arthur's coronation. *St Albans Chronicle*, Lambeth Palace Library 6, f. 54^v. (Lambeth Palace Library, London).
10. Frontispiece to a deluxe manuscript of the romance of Lancelot, c. 1400. The scenes show Lancelot's birth, his upbringing by the Lady of the Lake, Lancelot in combat, and his vision of the Grail at the wayside cross. (Paris, Bibliothèque Nationale, MS Arsenal 3479, f. 1. Photo Giraudon).
11. Arthur views paintings revealing Lancelot's love for Guenevere. Bibliothèque Nationale, fr. 112, 193^v. (Bibliothèque Nationale, Paris).
12. Pisanello's fresco of Tristan, Lancelot and Palamedes, Palazzo Ducale, Mantua. (Scala, Milan).
13. Rodenegg Castle, Bolzano, mural showing Iwein at the magical fountain.
14. Rodenegg Castle mural showing the search for Iwein.
15. Perceval, Gawain and Iwain painted on the balcony of Schloss Runkelstein, Bolzano. (Photograph author).
16. Tristan arrives in Ireland and despatches the dragon. Runkelstein mural. (Photograph author).
17. Lohengrin's arrival at Antwerp. Wilhelm Hauschild's fresco in the living room of Neuschwanstein Castle, Bavaria.
18. Tristan's farewell to Isolde and Brangwain. Fresco in King Ludwig's bedroom, Neuschwanstein.
19. King Arthur. Nine Worthies Tapestry, The Cloisters, Metropolitan Museum of Art. (Metropolitan Museum of Art, New York).
20. Arthur's Round Table in Winchester Castle. (Photograph Jeremy Whittaker).
21. & 22.   The Tristan stained glass for Harden Grange executed by Morris & Company, 1862. (Cartwright Hall, City Art Galleries and Museums, Bradford. Photographed by Gerry Waddington).
    (a). Arthur Hughes. The Birth of Tristram.
    (b). Val Prinsep. The departure of Tristram and La Belle Isoude from Ireland.
    (c). Dante Gabriel Rossetti. Tristram and La Belle Isoude drink the love potion.
    (d). Edward Burne-Jones. The marriage of Tristram and Isoude Les Blanches Mains.
    (e). Edward Burne-Jones. The Madness of Tristram.
    (f). William Morris. The recognition of Tristram by La Belle Isoude.
    (g). Edward Burne-Jones. The attempted suicide of La Belle Isoude.
    (h). William Morris. Tristram and Isolde at King Arthur's court.
    (i). Ford Maddox Brown. The death of Tristram.
    (j). Edward Burne-Jones. The tomb of Tristram and Isolde.

23. James Archer. La Mort D'Arthur, oil painting 1860. (Manchester City Art Galleries).
24. W. Holman Hunt. The Lady of Shalott, oil painting 1886–1905. (Manchester City Art Galleries).
25. Edward Burne-Jones. The Attainment of the Holy Grail. Stanmore Hall tapestry executed by William Morris & Co. 1898–9. (City Museums and Art Gallery, Birmingham).
26. J. W. Waterhouse. ' "I am half Sick of shadows" said the Lady of Shalott', oil painting 1860. (Art Gallery of Ontario, Toronto).
27. Frederick Sandys. Vivien, oil painting 1863. (Manchester City Art Galleries).
28. Herbert Bone. The Passing of Arthur. Woven by the Royal Windsor Tapestry Manufactory 1879. (Vigo-Sternberg Galleries, London).
29 Dante Gabriel Rossetti. Arthur's Tomb, watercolour dated 1855, copied 1860. (Tate Gallery, London).
30. William Morris. La Belle Iseult (also called Queen Guinevere), oil painting 1858. (Tate Gallery, London).
31. Arthur Gaskin. Kylwych, the King's Son, tempera painting 1901. (City Museums and Art Gallery, Birmingham).
32. Edward Burne-Jones. The Beguiling of Merlin, oil painting 1874. (Lady Lever Art Gallery, Port Sunlight).
33. Frederick Sandys. Morgan-le-Fay, oil painting 1862–3. (City Museums and Art Gallery, Birmingham).
34. William Russell Flint. Alisander and Alice la Beale Pilgrim in the land of Benoye from Malory's Morte D'Arthur (London: Warner, 1910–11). (Medici Society, Ltd. London).
35. David Jones. Guenever, water colour 1940. (Tate Gallery, London).

I. General Index

II. Art Index